PHILANTHROPY AND THE NONPROFIT SECTOR IN A CHANGING AMERICA

Philanthropy
and the Nonprofit Sector
in a Changing America

edited by
Charles T. Clotfelter and Thomas Ehrlich

published in association with

The American Assembly, Columbia University

Indiana University Press

Bloomington & Indianapolis

This book is a publication of
Indiana University Press
601 North Morton Street
Bloomington, IN 47404-3797 USA

http://iupress.indiana.edu

Telephone orders 800-842-6796
Fax orders 812-855-7931
Orders by e-mail iuorder@indiana.edu

First paperback edition 2001
© 1999 by The American Assembly, Columbia University
All rights reserved

The paper used in this publication meets the minimum requirements of American National Standard for Information Sciences–Permanence of Paper for Printed Library Materials, ANSI Z39.48-1984.

Manufactured in the United States of America

Library of Congress Cataloging-in-Publication Data

Philanthropy and the nonprofit sector in a changing America / edited by
Charles T. Clotfelter and Thomas Ehrlich.
p. cm.
Includes bibliographical references and index.
ISBN 0-253-33521-3 (alk. paper)
1. Charity organization — United States. 2. Charities — United States.
3. Nonprofit organizations — United States. 4. Corporations — Charitable
contributions — United States. 5. Social service — United States. 6. Social
values — United States. I. Clotfelter, Charles T. II. Ehrlich, Thomas,
date.
HV91.P57 1999
361.7'63 — dc21 98-31856

ISBN 0-253-21483-1 (pbk.)

2 3 4 5 6 06 05 04 03 02 01

Contents

Preface / vii
    Eugene R. Tempel & David H. Mortimer

Introduction / ix
    Charles T. Clotfelter & Thomas Ehrlich

1. The Nonprofit Sector in the 1990s / 1
    Elizabeth T. Boris

2. The Evolving Role of American Foundations / 34
    James Allen Smith

3. Foundations and the Government:
   A Tale of Conflict and Consensus / 52
    Barry D. Karl & Alice W. Karl

4. The Economy and Philanthropy / 73
    Edward Wolff

5. Corporate Philanthropy Comes of Age:
   Its Size, Its Import, Its Future / 99
    Reynold Levy

6. Reinventing Philanthropy / 122
    Leslie Lenkowsky

7. Nonprofit Organizations and Public Policies
   in the Delivery of Human Services / 139
    Kirsten A. Grønbjerg & Steven Rathgeb Smith

8. Public Trust in Not-for-Profit Organizations
   and the Need for Regulatory Reform / 172
    Joel L. Fleishman

9. Accountability in a Changing Philanthropic Environment:
   Trustees and Self-Government at the End of the Century / 198
    Warren F. Ilchman & Dwight F. Burlingame

10. Patterns and Purposes of Philanthropic Giving / 212
    Eleanor Brown

11. Communities, Networks, and the Future of Philanthropy / 231
    Julian Wolpert

12. The Roles of Indigenous and Institutional Philanthropy
   in Advancing Social Justice / 248
    Emmett D. Carson

13. Philanthropy and the Case of the Latino
   Communities in America   /   275
      William A. Diaz

14. The Case of Minnesota:
   Institutionalizing Public Spirit   /   293
      Jon Pratt

15. The Case of Kansas City   /   315
      David O. Renz

16. Children in Poverty:
   Reflections on the Roles of Philanthropy and Public Policy   /   347
      Ruby Takanishi

17. The Changing Face of Health Care   /   364
      Bradford H. Gray

18. Lessons for the Future of Philanthropy:
   Local Foundations and Urban School Reform   /   385
      William S. McKersie & Anthony Markward

19. Philanthropy and American Higher Education   /   413
      Michael Rothschild

20. Environmental Philanthropy and Public Policy   /   428
      Richard L. Revesz

21. Philanthropy and Outcomes:
   Dilemmas in the Quest for Accountability   /   449
      Gary Walker & Jean Grossman

22. Philanthropy and Culture: Patterns, Context, and Change   /   461
      Margaret J. Wyszomirski

23. A Tradition in Jeopardy   /   481
      Robert L. Payton

24. The World We Must Build   /   499
      Charles T. Clotfelter & Thomas Ehrlich

Appendix—Trust, Service, and the Common Purpose   /   517

List of Contributors   /   541

Index   /   545

Preface

Philanthropy and the nonprofit sector occupy a position in the American institutional landscape unlike that in any other developed country. Undertaking functions typically assigned to government in other countries, and also accorded unparalleled tax advantages in return for doing so, these American institutions are thought to be central to furthering democracy and the search for social justice. To explore these contributions to our collective lives, to assess changes in the environment in which American philanthropy and the nonprofit sector undertake their work, and to recommend changes in the internal governance and external regulation of foundations and nonprofit organizations, the American Assembly of Columbia University and the Indiana University Center on Philanthropy cosponsored the Ninety-third American Assembly, which was held at the Getty Center in Los Angeles, California, from April 23–26, 1998. Early drafts of these chapters were commissioned as background for that meeting.

The Ninety-third American Assembly is both a benchmark and a guidepost. The report and this volume document where we are in philanthropy and the nonprofit sector at the end of the century. The recommendations will serve as guides not only to individual philanthropists and philanthropic organizations but also to the governments that host them.

The American Assembly and the Indiana University Center on Philanthropy undertook this examination of the future of philanthropy in a changing America under the superb co-directorship of Charles T. Clotfelter, professor of Public Policy Studies, Economics & Law at Duke University, and Thomas Ehrlich, a senior scholar at the Carnegie Foundation for the Advancement of

Teaching and distinguished university scholar at California State University. We also note the essential organizing role of Warren F. Ilchman, past executive director of the Indiana University Center on Philanthropy, whose initiative it was to commence this project, and the project's steering committee whose members gave generously of their time and advice and whose names are listed in the Appendix.

We gratefully acknowledge support from the following organizations that helped to fund this undertaking:

- Carnegie Corporation of New York
- Robert Sterling Clark Foundation
- The Ford Foundation
- The J. Paul Getty Trust
- William Randolph Hearst Foundation
- James Irvine Foundation
- Ewing Marion Kauffman Foundation
- W. K. Kellogg Foundation
- Lilly Endowment, Inc.
- John D. and Catherine T. MacArthur Foundation
- The Andrew W. Mellon Foundation
- The David and Lucile Packard Foundation
- Rockefeller Brothers Fund
- Surdna Foundation, Inc.
- Texaco Foundation
- Robert W. Woodruff Foundation, Inc.

These organizations, as well as The American Assembly and the Indiana University Center on Philanthropy, take no position on subjects presented here in public discussion.

Eugene R. Tempel
Indiana University Center on Philanthropy

David H. Mortimer
The American Assembly

Introduction

Charles T. Clotfelter and Thomas Ehrlich

When we were asked to take on the roles of orchestra leaders for this project, we questioned whether yet one more gathering and one more volume were really needed to explore the future of philanthropy. This introduction explains briefly why we decided to go forward. Based on that judgment, we commissioned 23 papers by the best thinkers we could identify on key dimensions of the philanthropic realm. And we helped organize a three-day conference on "Philanthropy in a Changing America" at the new Getty Center in Los Angeles under the auspices of the American Assembly and the Indiana Center on Philanthropy. Close to one hundred leaders with at least that many perspectives came together at this gathering for three days of intense discussions. Those discussions were enriched by drafts of the papers that follow. The results of their work are reflected in the Assembly report that is included as an Appendix to this volume.

In retrospect, we are deeply convinced that our decision to go forward was right. We hope the case is as compelling to others as it is to us. When we looked back to the last American Assembly on philanthropy, we found "The Future of Foundations," which was held in 1972 (Heimann 1973). The total worth of American foundations was then less than $50 billion. At the gathering we held at the Getty, only a small group of foundation leaders was included along with many others from different fields. Yet the foundations represented at the Getty conference alone hold more than $50 billion in assets. There has been an explosion in philanthropy in the decades since 1972. By 1995, total foundation assets had grown to $227 billion (Renz, Mandler, and Tran 1997, p. 4). Philanthropic giving in 1972 was less than $25 billion. A quarter-century later it is over $150 billion, an increase of more than 50 percent in inflation-adjusted dollars (*Giving USA* 1997, pp. 198–99). More important, the prospect is that an unprecedented transfer of wealth will be made to new foundations over the next decade. At the same time, philanthropy is being urged to take on staggering new burdens in both size and scope as the roles of government are reduced.

At the outset of our initial discussions about the conference and this volume, we concluded that we should not consider foundations in isolation from the nonprofit sector that they support. Our primary emphasis at the conference and in this volume is on the funding organizations—both traditional foundations and new ones established by individuals—that provide support for the nonprofit sector. But we think it is essential to consider the sector as a whole as well as those organizations. First, much philanthropy is organized by entities within the nonprofit sector—such as religious groups and combined appeals—which seek funds directly from individuals, and individual philanthropy is the largest segment of total philanthropy. In 1996, individuals contributed an estimated $120 billion, ten times the amount contributed by foundations (*Giving USA* 1997, p. 198). Second, foundations today face acute pressures to establish priorities, and it is not possible to set those priorities without also considering the institutions in the nonprofit sector that will receive that funding and the "causes" that those institutions support.

With that broad palette in mind, we set about designing a conference and volume to consider four key clusters of issues. First, we asked, what forces will determine the shape and activities of philanthropy and the nonprofit sector in the next decade? How will philanthropy and the nonprofit sector be strengthened or weakened by those forces? How can the challenges of grappling with these forces be transformed into opportunities? In particular, we had in mind a variety of pressures: the devolution of federal programs to the state and local levels; the blurring of lines between nonprofit and for-profit organizations; the changing distributions of income; major new wealth and its concentration; a revived interest in community and civil society; the evolution of religion and religious institutions; globalization; tax and other regulatory reform; and a retreat of government from various policy areas and the rise of privatization and market models. To these nine sets of forces, most conference participants added at least a tenth.

We turned then to considering in what areas philanthropy and the nonprofit sector should concentrate attention in the next decade, and asked whether the institutions of the sector were better equipped to deal with these areas than government or the market, and in what arenas partnerships were needed. We focused particularly on eight areas: poverty and social injustice; educational quality and accessibility; health; vitality of the family; strengthening civil society; contributions of the arts to the quality of life; local, national, and transnational issues of the environment; and access to opportunities afforded by new technologies. Again, almost every conference participant added at least one other area of particular interest.

In light of our tentative thoughts about these tough questions, we turned to whether changes are needed in the management, regulation, or taxation of philanthropy or the nonprofit sector to ensure accountability, efficiency, and innovation. We put special emphasis on these issues: How can philanthropy and the nonprofit sector better assess the impact of their activities? How much of regulation should be left to self-government by autonomous boards of trustees? What revisions in governmental regulation are desirable and feasible—national, state, and local? And in what other ways can efficiency and innovation be encouraged?

Finally, we considered what steps are required to enhance the impact of philanthropy and the nonprofit sector. Together with the need to address serious domestic and global concerns, we wrestled with such issues as strengthening relations with the public and for-profit sectors, educating and engaging the next generation, the dramatic growth in philanthropic resources, the continuing importance of religious institutions, and the special need to stress the basic values of American philanthropy.

In commissioning the papers that follow, we could not hope to cover all facets of philanthropy and the nonprofit sector. We begin with three overview papers that consider the nonprofit sector today and some of its historical background. We then turn to a series of analyses that together give a rich picture of the pressures on philanthropy and the nonprofit sector from all directions. Two papers follow that give in-depth looks at minority populations generally and Latino communities particularly. They provide important insights into the complexities of grappling with some of the most difficult concerns now facing philanthropy and the nonprofit sector. They are followed by six essays focusing on policy areas of special significance in light of the changing forces now swirling around philanthropy and the nonprofit sector: children in poverty; health care; K–12 education; higher education; the environment; and arts and culture. This group of papers concludes with an examination or assessment—how and how much we know about what works in organized philanthropy. Finally, we close with an essay by one of the founders of philanthropy as a discipline, Robert Payton, who reflects on "A Tradition in Jeopardy," and our own thoughts on "The World We Must Build."

Each reader of this volume can decide, of course, whether to concur in our judgment that this is the right time for reevaluating philanthropy and the nonprofit sector, and whether these papers both ask the right questions and together sketch sound answers. Before turning to them, however, we stress one final point, at the same time both obvious and often overlooked.

A premise of this volume and the conference is that the institutions of philanthropy and the nonprofit sector are means to ends, not ends in themselves. As will be evident in reading these papers, people care deeply about the structure and performance of foundations and other nonprofit institutions. It is sometimes tempting to think that what we are doing in this realm is so important that it should somehow be supported for its own sake. But institutions are just instruments, and cannot be better than the purposes they serve.

Those purposes can be separated between ultimate social ends and institutional goals. Ultimate social ends are an expression of the society's fundamental shared beliefs. In American society, freedom of expression, freedom of religion, equality of opportunity, enjoyment of natural beauty, and economic well-being are widely valued as proper social objectives. In pursuit of these ultimate aims, Americans have become accustomed to working within a particular set of institutions, which have been established or have evolved over time through the interaction of social, economic, and legal forces. Among these familiar institutions are those within philanthropy and the nonprofit sector—an incredible range of organizations, including the philanthropic foundations that help support them. Because these institutions are merely means to help pursue ultimate aims, there is little reason to value them for their own sake. Through the complex skein of history, our society finds itself with a certain set of institutions, and a division of duties among them. Institutions themselves are ultimately important, however, only to the extent that they reflect the broader ends of society.

Yet people do express strong attachment to certain of these institutions, as some of the essays in this volume amply illustrate. In fact, much of the current debate about philanthropy and the nonprofit sector exhibits strong normative attachment to the existing institutional landscape. We urge that this debate be minimized in favor of focused attention on the broader issues of social purpose. As Robert Bellah and his colleagues have argued eloquently about our society generally, institutions are crucial in our lives, but "If the central value system is flawed, then it is much more likely that many of its institutional specifications will be problematic as well. Institutional change must then involve changing the value system" (Bellah et al., 1992, p. 288).

The implicit social contract between the nonprofit sector and the rest of society is simply an expression of the institutional division of responsibilities that has become America's way of addressing social problems. That social contract is a good one if it effectively serves the society's ultimate goals. If, for example, the existing configuration of institutional arrangements and responsibilities fosters "social capital," which in turn fosters the pursuit of ultimate goals, then that configuration is praiseworthy. But if social capital is being frittered away by changes in society, and other, more effective means for achieving ultimate goals cannot be found, then it makes sense to consider either alternative institutional arrangements or new policies.

We think that the papers that follow make a powerful collective case that changes are needed along the lines suggested in the Assembly report. We cannot be certain that all observers will agree, but we are confident that what follows is thoughtful, provocative, and challenging reading, worthy of serious consideration.

We close with a few words of special thanks. We are grateful to the conference participants who came to the Getty and made our sessions there so stimulating; to the organizers of that conference and the sponsors of this volume: The American Assembly and the Indiana Center on Philanthropy, and their splendid leaders for this effort, David Mortimer and Warren Ilchman; to Barry Munitz and his colleagues at the Getty Center who did so much to make the conference a success; and, finally, to the writers of these papers. To all of them, we are most indebted.

References

Bellah, Robert et al., *The Good Society* (New York: Vintage, 1992).

Giving USA (New York: AAFRC Trust for Philanthropy, 1997).

Heimann, Fritz, ed., *The Future of Foundations* (Englewood Cliffs: Prentice-Hall, 1973).

Renz, Loren, Crystal Mandler, and Trinh C. Tran, *Foundation Giving* (New York: Foundation Center, 1997).

PHILANTHROPY AND THE NONPROFIT SECTOR IN A CHANGING AMERICA

CHAPTER ONE

The Nonprofit Sector in the 1990s

Elizabeth T. Boris

Policy debates about the role and capacity of nonprofit organizations related to welfare reform and devolution continue to be based on inaccurate conceptions of these organizations, despite recent research. The nonprofit sector consists of mostly small organizations and is characterized by diversity of types, roles, missions, and financial capacity. Most nonprofits do not provide social services, but are important in the civic life of the country. Resources are concentrated in the largest organizations—chiefly hospitals and higher education institutions. Nonprofit organizations are dispersed thinly and unevenly around the country and are not an organized "system." They are individual organizations of civil society, vital parts of the networks of cooperation that permit our democratic society to operate effectively.

The nonprofit sector (also called "civil society") became a beacon of hope in the last decade as political leaders around the globe sought effective and economical solutions to intractable social problems that persisted in the midst of growing democratization and generation of wealth. In many former communist states and newly democratizing states in Asia, Latin America, and Africa, civil society organizations are increasingly recognized as necessary instruments of citizen participation, community building, and economic development. The United States has become the model for a robust civil society, a realm of independent citizen activity outside of both government and business.

The term *civil society* is widely used to refer to the worldwide proliferation of formal and informal associations, organizations, and networks that are separate from, but deeply interactive with, the state and the business sector.

These organizations produce "social capital," the norms of trust and cooperation that permit societies to function (Coleman, 1990, Putnam, 1993).

Civil society in the United States has many names, depending on the emphasized activity: "voluntary," "philanthropic," "charitable," "nonprofit," and many more. The voluntary organizations of civil society are increasingly viewed as central to a successful democracy. Voting and representative government are necessary forms of civic participation, but not always sufficient by themselves to sustain democracy. Citizens participate in democratic governance by joining together to accomplish public purposes, voice their concerns to government, and monitor the impact of business, government, and nonprofit activities on the public.

The presence of voluntary organizations depends on freedom to associate, deliberate, and act together in the public sphere. Associations can help to create social capital and lead to more responsive government and innovative, alternative approaches to solving social problems and improving the quality of life.

America's reputation as a nation of voluntary associations that engage citizens in problem-solving and governance has drawn leaders from many countries to study the U.S. nonprofit sector as they seek to create and strengthen civil society organizations in their own countries. The essential role of nonprofits in the civic sphere, however, is not the one that currently captures the American imagination. U.S. political rhetoric focuses primarily on nonprofits as providers of charity care and the "social safety net" of last resort.

Despite the great variety of nonprofit organizations—schools, churches, hospitals, environmental groups, youth and recreation groups, art museums, research institutions—the welfare services dimension dominates political discussion in the United States. Concerning other organizations that are uniquely nonprofit—civic, social, and fraternal organizations, advocacy groups, community associations, and philanthropic foundations—the political discourse remains uninformed. This largely invisible core of civic participation and civil society is in danger of having its voices silenced through unnecessarily restrictive legislation and having its finances weakened as society focuses on social service provision to the exclusion of almost everything else.

Political and Economic Background

Nonprofit organizations were propelled to U.S. public consciousness during the Reagan administration's wave of budget cutbacks which were designed to dismantle the welfare state in the early 1980s. Government became synonymous with inefficient and ineffective social programs carried out by wasteful bureaucrats. "Charities" were promoted as the nongovernmental saviors of the poor and of those who required assistance—children, aged, and disabled. Nonprofits were viewed as inexpensive substitutes for government programs. They operated closer to the problems, used volunteers and non-unionized labor, collected donations, and were flexible and nonbureaucratic.

The Task Force on Private Sector Initiatives was set up by President Reagan to develop, support, and promote private sector leadership to meet public needs in the face of large reductions in government programs for community development and social services. Instead, according to one of its members, the Task Force became a marketing tool for the idea that the private sector could and should solve society's problems. The Task Force avoided exploration of the role and capacity of nonprofit organizations and of the impact of budget cuts on their ability to serve the public (Lyman, 1989).

Thus, government policies were pursued without concern for the scope or scale of nonprofit operations, much less their financial condition or sources of funding. The prevailing view of a charitable sector sustained exclusively by volunteerism and donations led to exhortations to increase giving and volunteering to compensate for government cutbacks. In the early 1980s, it was not generally known that government grants and contracts provided a significant and rapidly increasing proportion of nonprofit revenues and that philanthropic contributions were a small and decreasing portion, despite pioneering research sponsored in the mid-1970s by the Filer Commission. That research documented the size and scope of the nonprofit sector within the U.S. economy and revealed that government provided almost a third of nonprofit funding (Commission on Private Philanthropy and Public Needs, 1975).[1]

Although much better information now documents the long-standing financial and programmatic relationship between American nonprofits and government in this unique version of the welfare state, the notion of an independent charitable social safety net that can offset decreasing government support for social services has persisted through the 1990s. Nonprofits are expected to become less dependent on a shrinking and devolved government sector and more businesslike: lean, efficient, and effective.

The market replaced the state as the dominant paradigm for progress and development following the rise of conservative politics at home, the retrenchment of welfare states in Europe, and the worldwide collapse of communism. In the United States, federal taxes were cut, reducing the incentive for charitable giving. Market-based strategies were promoted for all nonprofits: increased fees for services, attention to the bottom line, increased marketing and communications, improved fundraising and telemarketing, more joint ventures and mergers, and better overall management (Dees, 1998, Skloot, 1988, Drucker, 1992, Oster, 1995). In collaboration with major universities, some corporate and private foundations supported the creation of management training programs to help nonprofits become more effective and entrepreneurial as they sought to strengthen and diversify their revenue sources.

To a great extent, nonprofits succeeded in maintaining their financial growth through the 1990s, primarily by turning to fees for services and other revenue-generating activities, both commercial and philanthropic. However, Medicare and Medicaid fees (indirect government payments) fueled much of the growth in service revenues. Private contributions continued to grow slowly, but as government and fee revenues grew at a faster pace, private donations became a smaller proportion of nonprofit revenues, declining from 26 percent in 1977 to almost 19 percent of nonprofit revenues in 1996.[2]

As a result of increased fee-based activity, some nonprofit sector leaders began to fear that philanthropic values were being undermined and that nonprofits were becoming "commercialized." Some small businesses complained about competition from nonprofits, while others recognized the potential for profits and expanded competing businesses in fields such as child care and recreation (Hearings, House Committee on Small Business, 1996). Larger corporations purchased health-related nonprofits such as hospitals and nursing homes, which created concern about the buying out of public-serving nonprofits without adequate public oversight or consideration of the consequences. While business (and government) organizations have long been present in fields dominated by nonprofits, and the nonprofit sector's share of the economy has doubtlessly ebbed and flowed over time, the impact of current trends needs to be examined.

As nonprofits began to be perceived as less "charitable," and more like government and business, high-profile scandals involving United Way, Covenant House, and New Era Philanthropy tarnished the myth of pure and effective charity solutions to poverty and social disintegration (Langer, 1990, NY Times, 1995, Walsh, 1995). At about the same time, contributions to the United Way declined, levels of volunteering began to fall, and public trust in nonprofits started to erode.

Religious congregations and religiously affiliated organizations were promoted by some conservative leaders as the most effective and highest form of charitable safety net for the poor because they use values-based methods and faith to "improve" the poor, thereby eliminating welfare dependency (National Commission on Philanthropy and Civic Renewal, 1997). Since most faith-based organizations rely on donations and do not seek government funding—with the notable exception of several of the largest groups, like Catholic Charities and the Council of Jewish Federations—religious organizations are not expected to expand the welfare state or the federal budget. The "charitable choice" provision (section 104) of the 1996 welfare reform bill, The Personal Responsibility and Work Opportunity Reconciliation Act of 1996, was enacted to help religious groups compete for government money, an ironic twist that seems to signal some recognition of the importance of government financing of even faith-based activities to help the poor.

Much is assumed about the activities of faith-based organizations, but little is known about the scope and effectiveness of their services, their beneficiaries, or their capacity and desire to expand their current efforts or take on new responsibilities. Recent evidence suggests that, across the nation, congregations already devote substantial resources to community services, while local studies find that most budgets are meager and directed toward crisis intervention and emergency needs in the neighborhood (Hodgkinson, 1993, Cnaan, 1997, Printz, 1997).

Advocates of an enlarged poverty-alleviation role for nonprofits in the wake of welfare reform and devolution overlook two decades of research on nonprofits' financial constraints and program activities. Nonprofits play a variety of roles in this society, but direct poverty alleviation is not the major role, even for religious organizations. Most nonprofit organizations serve their own local communities through a variety of activities (Wolpert, 1993). Some try to influence the public stance toward the poor through research, advocacy, and public education.

Efforts to promote social justice, equality, and quality of life have suffered a loss of legitimacy as direct charity for the poor is promoted as the only useful form of philanthropy. Activities involving arts, culture, environment, leadership development, research, consumer protection and other types of advocacy, also the province of nonprofits, tend to be devalued by those promoting an increased poverty-alleviation role for nonprofits. Even the sector's name has been changed to refer generically to nonprofits as "service providers" rather than as community organizations, voluntary associations, or social action groups.

Advocates of increased government funding of programs for the poor are dismissed as self-serving proponents of expanded welfare services. This view led Representative Ernest J. Istook (R-OK) and others in Congress to try to restrict legislative advocacy by nonprofits that receive federal grants or contracts, despite the already existing prohibition against using government revenues for advocacy activities. The "Istook Amendment," which Rep. Istook threatened (but failed) to attach to a 1998 appropriations bill,[3] was designed to limit the ability of nonprofits to use their own resources to speak out, educate Congress, and influence policy on any number of issues. No such limitation exists or is contemplated for for-profit government contractors, who already enjoy more expansive access to the political process than do nonprofits.

The impact of such legislation would go well beyond the human service providers and significantly impair the advocacy and civic activities of voluntary organizations. If enacted, it could undermine the most vital rationale for the existence of nonprofit organizations—their role in articulating public needs and preferences. This erosion of support for public advocacy is the most potentially damaging threat to the nonprofit sector. It reveals a fundamental lack of understanding about, or concern for, the complex role of the nonprofit sector in American society.

Scope, Characteristics, and Role of the Nonprofit Sector

We are now better informed than ever before about nonprofit organizations. The path-breaking research begun by the Filer Commission and expanded by others illuminates the history, dimensions, and growth of the nonprofit sector. These critical contributions notwithstanding, information on nonprofits is still fragmentary, focused more on finances than impacts, and biased toward the larger organizations that report to the Internal Revenue Service.[4] With these limitations in mind, what do we know about the evolution and current status of the nonprofit sector that will help us to assess the implications for the changing political and economic landscape?

Scope of the Nonprofit Sector

In the United States a major proportion of key institutions are nonprofit organizations: 51 percent of all hospitals; 58 percent of all social service providers; 46 percent of all colleges and universities; 87 percent of all libraries and information centers; and 86 percent of all museums, and botanical and zoological gardens.

The nonprofit sector in 1996 consisted of approximately 1.5 million organizations, including all tax-exempt organizations registered with the Internal Revenue Service and 341,000 religious congregations that are eligible for tax-deductible contributions but are not required to register with the government. Of the 1.2 million registered nonprofits, 654,000 are recognized by the IRS as public serving or "charitable" organizations, tax-exempt under Section 501(c)(3), and eligible for tax-deductible contributions. The 140,000 "social welfare" organizations tax-exempt under section 501(c)(4) are usually regarded as public serving organizations that are not eligible for tax-deductible contributions; they may elect to do substantial lobbying. These two groups of nonprofits, 501(c)(3)s, including religious congregations, and 501(c)(4) social welfare organizations, are called the "independent sector" in the *Nonprofit Almanac 1996–1997* compiled by Virginia Hodgkinson and Murray Weitzman. While the *Nonprofit Almanac 1996–1997* is the most comprehensive source of data on nonprofit organizations, more refined information is available in the *State Nonprofit Almanac 1997* for the approximately 160,000 operating 501(c)(3) public charities that file IRS Form 990. This group of nonprofits excludes the religious congregations that are not required to file with the IRS, the approximately 50,000 private foundations, and nonprofits with revenues below $25,000 (Stevenson, et al., 1997). (See Table 1.)

The independent sector represents a significant proportion of the economy, with an estimated $621.4 billion in revenues in 1996. Approximately 7 percent of the national income in 1996 was generated in the sector, which employs about 10.2 million workers and another 5.7 million full-time equiva-

Table 1
Number of Nonprofit Entities in the United States, 1989–1996
(Numbers in Thousands)

	1989 Number	Percent	1992 Number	Percent	1996 Number	Percent	1989–96 % change
Total private nonprofit organizations	**1,262**	**100.0**	**1,351**	**100.0**	**1,455**	**100.0**	**15.3**
Tax-exempt orgs. registered with the I.R.S.	993	78.7	1,085	80.3	1,189	81.7	19.7
Total 501(c)(3) charitable organizations[a]	464	36.8	546	40.4	654	44.9	40.9
Total public charities	422	33.4	500	37.0	600	41.2	42.2
Reporting with financial data	138	10.9	165	12.2	200	13.7	44.9
Out of scope organizations	0.5	0.0	0.5	0.0	1	0.1	100.0
Reporting public charities	137	10.9	165	12.2	199	13.7	45.3
Operating	124	9.8	148	11.0	178	12.2	43.5
Supporting	13	1.0	16	1.2	21	1.4	61.5
Mutual benefit	0.5	0.0	0.5	0.0	0.6	0.0	20.0
Non-reporting[b]	284	22.5	335	24.8	400	27.5	40.8
Private foundations	42	3.3	46	3.4	54	3.7	28.6
501(c)(4) social welfare organizations	141	11.2	143	10.6	140	9.6	-0.7
Other reporting tax-exempt organizations	388	30.7	396	29.3	395	27.1	1.8
Religious congregations not reporting[c]	269	21.3	266	19.7	266	18.3	-1.1

Sources: U.S. Internal Revenue Service Return Transaction File, 1997; Stevenson, David, Thomas H. Pollak, Linda M. Lampkin, et al., *State Nonprofit Almanac 1997; Nonprofit Almanac 1996–1997* as updated by Independent Sector, 1998.

(a) All section 501(c)(3) entities are not included because certain organizations, including congregations and conventions or associations of churches, need not apply to the IRS for recognition of exemption unless they desire a ruling.

(b) Includes non-filers and organizations reporting with gross receipts below $25,000.

(c) Estimates of the number of religious congregations in Independent Sector's *Nonprofit Almanac 1996–1997* and 1998 update to the Almanac were 341,000 in 1992 and 1996 and 344,000 in 1989 (number imputed from 1987 and 1992 estimations). The figures above were adjusted to exclude the 75,000 religious congregations that have registered with the IRS and counted under Total 501(c)(3) charitable organizations.

Note: Numbers for 1996 are preliminary.

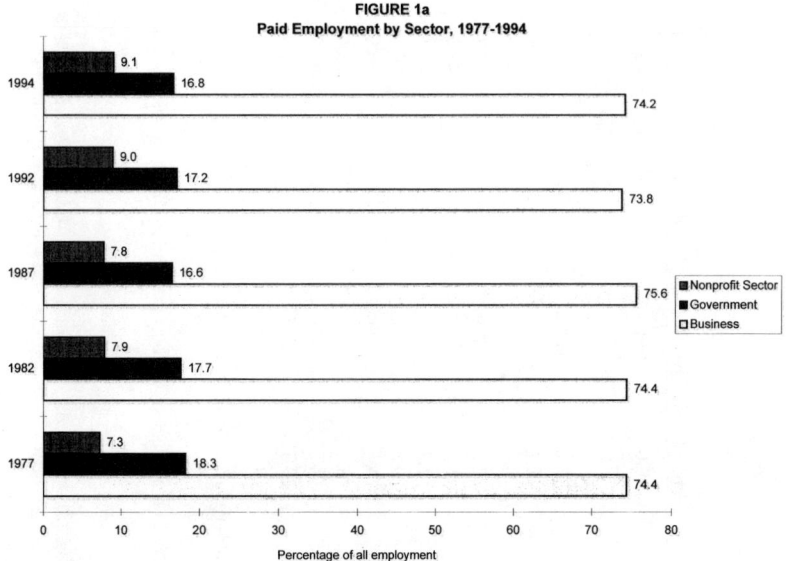

FIGURE 1a
Paid Employment by Sector, 1977-1994

Percentage of all employment

Source: Hodgkinson, Virginia A., Murray S. Weitzman et. al., *Nonprofit Almanac 1996-1997*, p. 140.

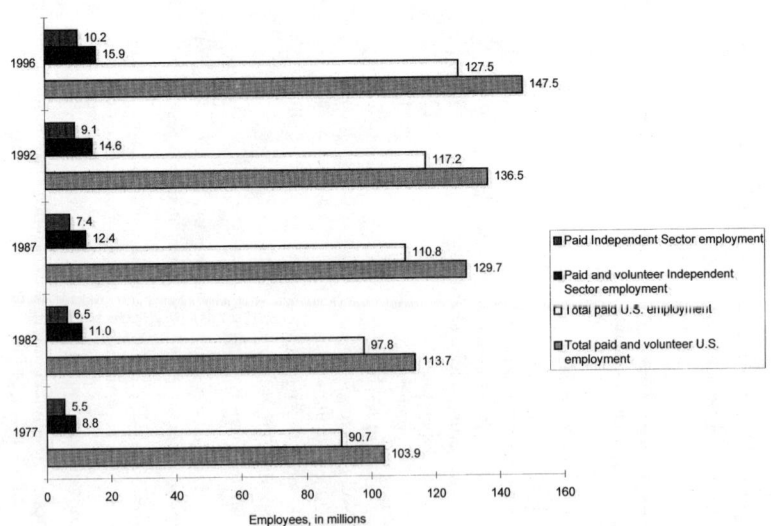

FIGURE 1b
Independent Sector* Employment vs. Total U.S. Employment

Employees, in millions

Source: *Nonprofit Almanac 1996-1997*, as updated by Independent Sector, 1998.
* Includes only public charities (501(c)(3)), social welfare organizations (501(c)(4)), and religious institutions.

Table 2
Growth in Number of Nonprofits,* 1989–1996

Type	1989	1996	Increase	Percent Increase
Arts/culture	13,817	19,509	5,692	41.2
Education	16,939	28,235	11,296	66.7
Environment and animals	3,305	5,799	2,494	75.5
Health	23,039	28,234	5,195	22.5
Human Services	45,156	66,514	21,358	47.3
International	1,196	1,816	620	51.8
Public/societal benefit	8,352	13,615	5,263	63.0
Religion related	5,764	8,846	3,082	53.5
Unknown	6,119	5,036	−1,083	−17.7
Total	123,687	177,604	53,917	43.6

Source: U.S. Internal Revenue Service Exempt Organizations Form 990 Return Transaction Files, 1997, as adjusted by the National Center for Charitable Statistics.

* Includes nonprofit organizations classified as operating public charities that report to the I.R.S. (file Form 990) and are required to do so. Excludes private foundations, foreign organizations, government-associated organizations, and organizations without state identifiers. Organizations not required to report include religious congregations and organizations with less than $25,000 in gross receipts.

Note: Numbers for 1996 are preliminary.

lent volunteers—more than one-tenth of the 147.5 million U.S. workers. (See Figures 1a and 1b.)

The independent sector expanded with the economy over the last two decades. Its percentage of the national income rose from 4.9 percent in 1977 to 6.2 percent in 1996.[5] The independent sector's rate of growth slowed in recent years. Growth averaged 4.2 percent annually between 1987 and 1992 but declined to an average of 2.6 percent annually between 1992 and 1996. In fact, the independent sector's share of the national income decreased between 1992 and 1996, despite continued growth in the number of voluntary organizations. (See Table 2.)

Diversity

The nonprofit sector is characterized primarily by the diversity of its more than one million organizations. The sector has tremendous variation in size, resources, scope, and capacity. There is virtually no limit to the kinds of activities that nonprofit groups undertake. They differ by types of causes—environmental preservation, health education, youth recreation—and by the means they use to reach their goals. They make products like audio tapes for

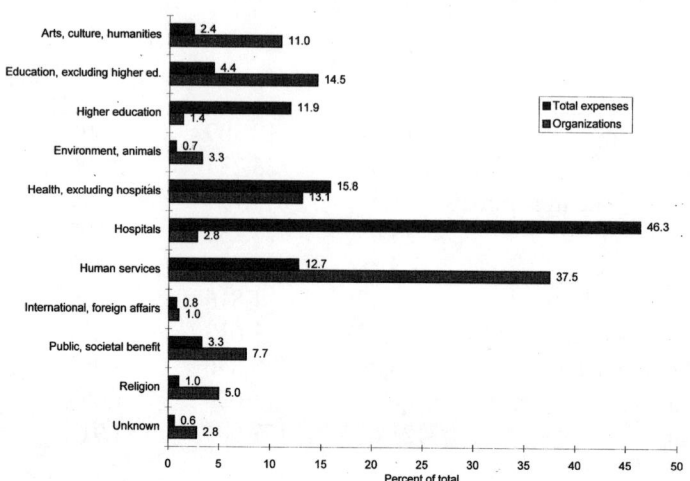

FIGURE 2
Distribution of Nonprofits* and Total Expenses by Activity, 1996

Source: U.S. Internal Revenue Service Return Transaction File, 1997, as adjusted by the National Center for Charitable Statistics.
* Only operating public charities are included. See Table 2 for definition.
Note: Numbers are preliminary.

the blind; create artistic and cultural productions; conduct research; educate and inform; advocate for or protest against political acts and proposals; provide spiritual guidance; and care for the poor, sick, and disabled. They may promote public well-being or benefits for their own members. Some may bring people together; others may be divisive or even destructive.

The diversity of organizations is captured in the National Taxonomy of Exempt Entities (NTEE), a classification system for nonprofit organizations, which divides nonprofits into ten major categories, twenty-six groups, and over 600 subgroups. The major categories are arts, culture and humanities; education; environment and animals; health; human services; international and foreign affairs; public, societal benefit; religion-related; mutual membership benefit; and unknown organizations (Stevenson, et al. 1997). These groups differ significantly in number of organizations and financial resources. (See Figure 2.)

Some observers question whether these diverse nonprofit organizations form a distinctive sector in any meaningful sense, other than their common designation as organizations exempt from taxes and the legal constraint against the distribution of profits (the origin of the term "nonprofit"). These organizations must have a purpose that is broadly public in nature and conduct activities that are "educational, religious, or scientific," among others (Hopkins, 1992). (See Table 3.)

What makes nonprofit organizations a distinctive sector, however, is that they engage people in collective purposes outside of the market and the state,

Table 3
Tax-Exempt Organizations Registered with the IRS, 1996

Section	Description	Number
501(c)(1)	Corporations organized under act of Congress	20
501(c)(2)	Titleholding corporations	7,100
501(c)(3)	Charitable and Religious*	654,186
501(c)(4)	Social Welfare	139,512
501(c)(5)	Labor, agricultural organizations	64,955
501(c)(6)	Business leagues	77,274
501(c)(7)	Social and recreational clubs	60,845
501(c)(8)	Fraternal beneficiary societies	91,972
501(c)(9)	Voluntary employees' beneficiary associations	14,486
501(c)(10)	Domestic fraternal beneficiary societies	20,925
501(c)(11)	Teachers' retirement funds	13
501(c)(12)	Benevolent life insurance associations	6,343
501(c)(13)	Cemetary companies	9,562
501(c)(14)	State chartered credit unions	5,157
501(c)(15)	Mutual insurance companies	1,212
501(c)(16)	Corporations to finance crop operations	23
501(c)(17)	Supplemental unemployment benefit trusts	565
501(c)(18)	Employee funded pension trusts	2
501(c)(19)	War veterans' organizations	31,464
501(c)(20)	Legal service organizations	131
501(c)(21)	Black lung trusts	25
501(c)(22)	Multiemployer pension plans	0
501(c)(23)	Veterans' associations founded prior to 1880	2
501(c)(24)	Trusts described in section 4049 of ERISA	1
501(c)(25)	Holding companies for pensions, etc.	794
501(d)	Religious and apostolic organizations	113
501(e)	Cooperative hospital service organizations	54
501(f)	Cooperative service orgs. of operating educ. orgs.	1
521	Farmers' cooperatives	1,773
Total		1,188,510

* All section 501(c)(3) organizations are not included because certain organizations, such as congregations, integrated auxiliaries, subordinate units, conventions or associations of churches, and organizations with less than $5,000 in gross receipts need not apply for recognition of exemption unless they desire a ruling.

Source: Internal Revenue Service, 1996 Annual Data Book, Publication 55B.

and are independently organized and self-governing. They are perhaps more appropriately identified as civil society organizations: large and small voluntary groups that in the aggregate profoundly affect the quality of life in communities and ultimately in society.

Missions and Origins

The origins, missions, and purposes of nonprofits are also varied. Nonprofit missions are based on religious values, political convictions, personal interests, community consensus, social movements, and more. Individuals, corporations, governments, and religious congregations have all created various nonprofit organizations. Historically, religious congregations figure most prominently in the founding of U.S. nonprofits that served members and the poor at home and abroad (O'Neill, 1989).

Women have established many nonprofits. Before it was widely acceptable for women to work outside the home, many honed their organizational skills in associations they created. Activities ranged from political advocacy (against slavery, for women's rights and the vote, for child labor laws, for peace) and direct social welfare (settlement houses, hospitals, orphanages, birth control clinics), to education (schools, colleges for women) and other health, safety, arts, and cultural activities (McCarthy, 1993, Skocpol, 1995). Women continue to start and participate in nonprofit organizations of all types and constitute over two-thirds of nonprofit employees.[6]

New immigrants and members of racial and ethnic groups have also formed nonprofits to serve their communities and to advocate for their rights and political recognition. The history of these groups and the scope of involvement by African Americans, Latinos, Native Americans, and Asian-Americans are only recently receiving the attention they deserve (Carson, this volume).

While it is difficult to comprehend the nonprofit sector's diversity, we cannot adequately assess the implications of current trends for the field unless we come to grips with the sector's many facets. Lacking uniform information on the myriad of small and informal organizations of civil society, we tend to focus on the public-serving organizations that are eligible to receive tax deductible donations (501(c)(3) organizations), are large enough to file annual reports to the IRS (over $25,000 in revenues), and are required to do so.[7]

Regional Variations

Nonprofit organizations and resources are not uniformly distributed across the country. The numbers generally vary with population levels, so the most populous states—California, Texas, and New York—also have the greatest number of nonprofits. However, there are still marked regional and state differences in the numbers, types, finances, and growth rates of nonprofits. For example, the Northeast has proportionately more arts, culture, and humanities organizations; the Midwest has proportionately more human services groups; and the West has proportionately more environmental groups. About one-third of the nonprofit sector's financial resources are based in the Northeast, where about one-fifth of the population and one-quarter of all organizations are located (Stevenson, et al. 1997). (See Table 4.)

Table 4

Number of Nonprofits and Total Expenses, by Region, 1996
(Dollars in millions)

Region	Organizations	Percent	Expenses	Percent
Northeast[a]	41,766	23.5	164,995	31.1
Midwest[b]	42,801	24.1	130,785	24.6
South[c]	52,982	29.8	140,734	26.5
West[d]	39,900	22.5	93,698	17.6
U.S. Territories	155	0.1	813	0.2
Total	**177,604**	**100.0**	**531,025**	**100.0**

Source: Urban Institute 1998, based on U.S. Internal Revenue Service Exempt Organizations Business Master File and Return Transaction File, 1997.

* Only operating public charities are included. See Table 2 for definition.

(a) Includes: Connecticut, Maine, Massachusetts, New Hampshire, New Jersey, New York, Pennsylvania, Rhode Island, Vermont.

(b) Includes: Illinois, Indiana, Iowa, Kansas, Michigan, Minnesota, Missouri, Nebraska, North Dakota, Ohio, South Dakota, Wisconsin.

(c) Includes: Alabama, Arkansas, Delaware, District of Columbia, Florida, Georgia, Kentucky, Louisiana, Maryland, Mississippi, North Carolina, Oklahoma, South Carolina, Tennessee, Texas, Virginia, West Virginia.

(d) Includes: Alaska, Arizona, California, Colorado, Hawaii, Idaho, Montana, Nevada, New Mexico, Oregon, Utah, Washington, Wyoming.

Note: Numbers are preliminary.

The density of nonprofits also varies by state and region. The states of the Northeast have the highest density of nonprofits (about eight organizations per 10,000 residents), while the southern states have the lowest density with about five organizations per 10,000 residents. For example, Vermont has more than twice the density of nonprofits as Missouri or Ohio. These differences in density may relate to the different histories, cultures, and incomes of the regions. It is also important to note that large cities, particularly the District of Columbia and New York City, serve as national headquarters for numerous organizations, which results in a higher concentration of nonprofits in those areas. (See Figure 3.)

In states with rapidly growing populations, nonprofits tend to grow at faster rates. For example, from 1989 to 1996, Nevada's population grew at a rate of about 5 percent (compared to a national average of just over 1 percent) and its nonprofit sector grew at a rate of approximately 8 percent, compared to the national average of about 6 percent. This high nonprofit growth rate, however, raised the density of Nevada's nonprofit sector to only about four per 10,000 persons, which is still far below the national average of almost seven

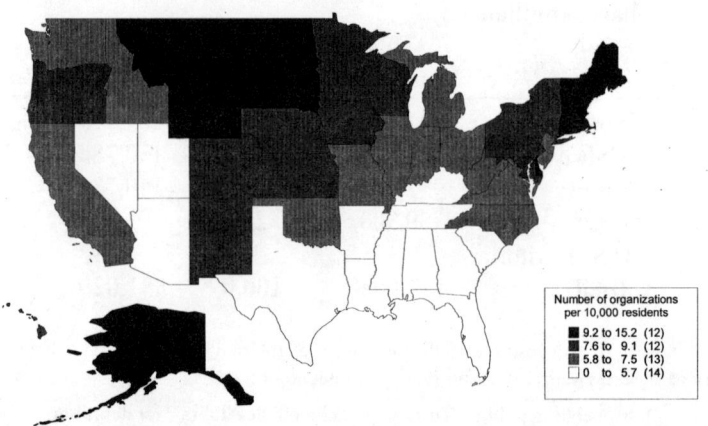

FIGURE 3
Number of Nonprofit Organizations* per 10,000 Residents, 1996

Number of organizations
per 10,000 residents

- 9.2 to 15.2 (12)
- 7.6 to 9.1 (12)
- 5.8 to 7.5 (13)
- 0 to 5.7 (14)

Source: U.S. Internal Revenue Service Exempt Organizations Business Master File and Return Transaction File, 1997, as adjusted by the National Center for Charitable Statistics.
* Only operating public charities are included. See Table 2 for definition.

per 10,000 people in 1996. So despite its high rate of nonprofit creation, Nevada actually lost ground compared to other states, and slipped from 48th to 50th place among the states in number of nonprofits per capita (Stevenson, et al., 1997).

Sources of Revenue

Nonprofit revenues are a complex mix of private and public dollars raised through grants, contracts, fees for services, sales, donations, investment income, special events income, and income from commercial ventures. In the midsize and larger organizations, the complexity of the finances of nonprofit organizations and the multiple levels of reporting and accountability can be mind-numbing and costly (Grønbjerg, 1993).

Sources of revenue vary by subsector and size of organization. In general during the 1990s, the proportion of philanthropic donations decreased, government revenues increased until recently, and program service fees became the largest portion of revenues. Much of the increase in program service revenues is probably related to the growth in Medicare and Medicaid spending. In 1996, government provided about 32 percent of nonprofit revenues, while philanthropy provided 19 percent. For social service organizations, however, the proportion of revenue from government has been closer to half.

These generalizations, however, gloss over the fact that, while the proportion of government revenues increased for health services and educational organizations, they decreased for social and legal services, and arts and

14

Table 5

Finances of Nonprofit Subsectors*: Government Funds, Private Contributions,
and Private Sector Payments as a Percentage of Total Funds, 1977–1992

	1977					1982				
	Government	Private sector payments	Private contributions	Other[a]	Total	Government	Private Sector payments	Private contributions	Other[a]	Total
Subsector										
Health Services	32.4	49.1	7.8	10.7	100.0	34.8	49.1	5.9	10.2	100.0
Education/Research	18.2	52.9	8.8	20.1	100.0	17.0	53.0	8.4	21.6	100.0
Religious Organizations[b]	0.0	0.0	125.0	(25.0)	100.0	0.0	0.0	125.4	(25.4)	100.0
Social & Legal Services	54.4	9.7	32.2	3.9	100.0	54.9	15.2	25.0	4.9	100.0
Civic, Social & Fraternal Orgs.	50.0	11.9	28.6	9.5	100.0	50.0	13.8	29.3	6.9	100.0
Arts and Culture	11.8	29.4	41.2	17.6	100.0	16.7	29.2	39.6	14.5	100.0

	1987					1992				
	Government	Private sector payments	Private contributions	Other[a]	Total	Government	Private Sector payments	Private contributions	Other[a]	Total
Subsector										
Health Services	36.2	51.8	5.4	6.6	100.0	40.7	48.3	3.6	7.4	100.0
Education/Research	18.3	55.3	13.0	13.4	100.0	20.0	57.0	12.7	10.3	100.0
Religious Organizations[b]	0.0	7.4	104.1	(11.5)	100.0	0.0	6.7	94.5	(1.2)	100.0
Social & Legal Services	48.1	18.9	24.8	8.2	100.0	50.1	17.5	20.0	12.4	100.0
Civic, Social & Fraternal Orgs.	48.0	12.8	33.0	6.2	100.0	33.3	20.4	31.3	15.0	100.0
Arts and Culture	15.0	30.0	40.0	15.0	100.0	14.6	24.4	40.2	20.8	100.0

Source: Hodgkinson, Virginia A., Murray Weitzman, et. al., *Nonprofit Almanac 1996–1997*, pp. 193–194.

* Includes only public charities (501(c)(3)), social welfare organizations (501(c)(4)), and religious institutions.

(a) Includes endowment, investment income, and receipts from churches.

(b) Religious organizations both receive contributions and provide them to other organizations within the independent sector. To present net esti-mates for the independent sector and to estimate the sacerdotal activities of religious organizations, adjustments are made in the receipts for the relig-ious organizations that show the estimated amount of money subtracted for use on nonsacerdotal activities. Thus, percentages will not necessarily add up to 100.

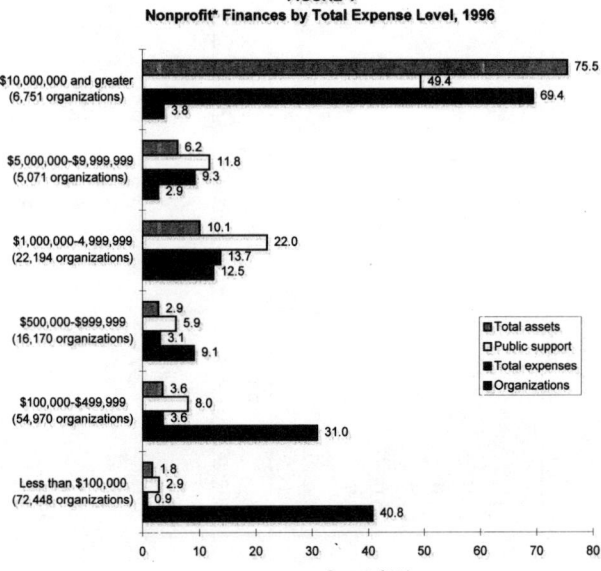

FIGURE 4
Nonprofit* Finances by Total Expense Level, 1996

Source: U.S. Internal Revenue Service Return Transaction File, 1997, as adjusted by the National Center for Charitable Statistics.
* Only operating public charities are included. See Table 2 for definition.
Note: Numbers are preliminary.

culture, but most substantially for civic, social, and fraternal organizations. Unfortunately, this decline occurred among the organizations that are probably least likely to be able to replace government funding. The proportion of government funding clearly varies considerably by type of organization, from less than 15 percent in the arts to over half of social and legal services. (See Table 5.)

Philanthropic contributions received by nonprofits vary from a low of less than 4 percent of revenues for hospitals to 40 percent for arts and culture. Arts and culture organizations managed to increase their proportion of revenues from donations between 1987 and 1996, while social and legal services recorded a significant decline between 1987 and 1992. Recent figures indicate, however, a slightly higher growth rate for contributions between 1992 and 1996 (Kaplan, 1997).

Concentration of Resources

The nonprofit sector is comprised overwhelmingly of small entities with meager resources. Even among those organizations that meet the threshold for reporting to the IRS, most have modest budgets, use only volunteer labor, and operate locally. Resources and employees are highly concentrated in the largest organizations, chiefly among hospitals and universities. A few are huge, with hundreds of millions of dollars in revenues, complex national and international organizational structures, and sophisticated fundraising techniques. Fewer than 4 percent of nonprofits (excluding foundations) that report to the IRS have expenses higher than $10 million, but they are responsible for over two-thirds of the expenditures. (See Figure 4.) A similar size distribution occurs among private foundations (*Foundation Giving*, 1997).

Preliminary analysis of financial data for 1989 to 1995 suggests that the top 1 percent of nonprofit operating charities (excluding foundations) holds almost two-fifths of the entire group's assets (Pollak and Pettit, 1998).

National statistics on the nonprofit sector reflect the dominance of large health care providers and higher education institutions. We learn little about the majority of nonprofits from these figures. Contrary to popular opinion, the social service segment does not dominate the voluntary sector. Even when religious organizations are included and volunteer time is counted, organizations that provide social services employ only about one-third of nonprofit workers. Volunteers provide close to two-fifths of the labor for social services.

Fragmentation

The picture of the nonprofit sector that emerges is one of disparate groups thinly and unevenly spread across the states with great variety in their missions and activities. The majority are community-based, not well known, and probably grossly undercounted. This is not a unified sector; there is no overall structure that unites all the organizations or even those in particular subsectors, with the possible exception of hospitals and higher education.

Coordinating organizations such as national membership and trade associations rarely provide coherence. They may monitor public policy, provide services, and help to spread innovations in management and programs, but few control or oversee the activities of their members. State and local nonprofit associations, like United Ways and Regional Associations of Grantmakers, play a similar role for their members. Oversight and monitoring requirements for government grants and contracts have been a standardizing factor in some subsectors, but the impact is disproportionately felt by the larger agencies that have the institutional capacity to apply for funding.

The nonprofit sector varies by region, by history, and by local political and social culture. People in some regions of the country give and volunteer at much higher levels than in others, reflecting the diverse cultures of philanthropy as well as varying levels of civic effort. These differences profoundly affect the types of organizations, their scale, and financial strength (Wolpert, 1993).

Financial Health of Nonprofit Organizations

From 1989 to 1995, nonprofits enjoyed increases in income and total assets that outpaced inflation. Expenses rose at about the same rate as income. Net income after expenses also rose at a rate higher than inflation. In contrast to this overall portrait, preliminary analysis suggests that approximately two-fifths of nonprofits suffered a decline in revenues in inflation-adjusted dollars. While arts and culture organizations suffered substantial revenue losses, large universities, hospitals, and multi-purpose human service providers were least likely to have a loss in revenues (Pollak and Pettit, 1998).

In another measure of financial health, approximately two out of five nonprofits had net worth that was less than or equal to three months of expenses, while less than one in five had net worth totaling more than two years of expenses. Notably, financially strong organizations had a higher proportion of investment income than those with lower levels of net worth. Indeed, the common denominator of stronger organizations seems to be the existence of investment income—a generalization that applies to arts and culture organizations as well as multipurpose human service providers. Investment assets provide a secure base of income that help larger organizations to maintain their financial health.

These preliminary financial analyses suggest that two-fifths of operating public charities did not fare well in the period from 1989 to 1995 and that a similar number are operating on a very slim margin. The potential vulnerability of such a large proportion of the sector across all program areas is a matter of concern that requires further in-depth analysis, for, while this may be a normal feature of the sector that indicates turnover, innovation, and decline, it also may indicate a far smaller and more fragile sector than the numbers suggest.

Income, Wealth, and Philanthropy

The economic boom of the last two decades brought tremendous growth in personal wealth for those in high-income brackets. The number of billionaires in the United States rose from 13 in 1982 to 170 in 1997, and their net worth reached about $220 billion (Forbes, 1997). Furthermore, the top 1 percent of the population held over one-third of the nation's wealth (Wolff, this volume). Charitable giving, unfortunately, did not rise, but stayed at a relatively low, albeit stable, rate of 2 percent of gross domestic product and 1.8 percent of personal income (Kaplan, 1997). Giving by the country's wealthiest actually declined, as the falling tax rates during the mid-1980s provided less incentive for them to make donations. New foundations have continued to be created, however, and philanthropic giving by foundations and corporations has grown more robustly than individual giving, reflecting strong financial markets. (See Table 6.)

Table 6
Changes in Philanthropic Giving by Source, 1977–1997
(Constant 1997 dollars, in billions)

Type	1977	1982	1989	1992	1996	1997	% Change 1977–1996
Individual	78.3	79.2	102.8	100.3	104.7	109.3	39.6
Foundation	5.3	5.3	8.5	9.9	12.3	13.4	152.8
Corporations	4.1	5.2	7.1	6.8	7.8	8.2	100.0
Bequest	5.6	8.7	9.0	9.3	11.7	12.6	125.0
Total	93.3	98.4	127.4	126.3	136.5	143.5	53.8

Source: AAFRC Trust for Philanthropy, *Giving USA 1998*.

This booming economy has an underside: wealth and income have become more concentrated and economic inequality has grown. Real wages have fallen for middle and lower income families, which has perhaps caused them to curtail both donations and volunteering. Evidence for this interpretation is found in survey data that show giving and volunteering decreased among respondents who reported that they worry a lot about money and that they had less money left over this year than in the previous year (Hodgkinson, 1996).

Private Foundations

More than 16,200 new foundations were formed between 1980 and 1995, which is over 40 percent of the total number of active grantmaking foundations. (Figures in this section are from *Foundation Giving*, 1997, unless noted.) But following a burst of foundation creation in the mid-1980s, the formation rate of new private foundations declined significantly, probably as a result of lower tax rates (and related changes) that effectively increased the cost of donations, and the stock market crash of 1987. (See Table 7.) It remains to be seen whether the new group of billionaires and millionaires will leave their fortunes to foundations, establish trusts for distributing wealth, give directly to institutions, or not give at all. Visible role models like George Soros, Walter Annenberg, and Ted Turner may help to encourage other wealthy individuals to give back to society through private foundations.

With the surge in stock values in the mid-1990s, the assets of private and community foundations also rose to new heights, leading to higher levels of giving by these institutions. In 1996, foundation giving totaled over $12 billion and represented about 9 percent of the approximately $137 billion contributed by individuals, corporations, foundations, and bequests. Founda-

Table 7
Numbers of Foundations,* 1989–1995

Type	1989	1992	1995	% Change 1989–1995
Independent	28,669	31,604	35,602	24.2
Corporate	1,587	1,897	1,946	22.6
Community	282	353	413	46.5
Total	30,538	33,854	37,961	24.3

Source: Renz, Loren, *Foundation Giving* (1997), p. 25.
* As identified by the Foundation Center.

tion giving as a percent of overall contributions increased 1 percent from the year before (Kaplan, 1997). Foundation grants continue to be directed largely to higher education, but include a higher proportion for human services than in the past, rising from 14 percent to almost 17 percent of foundation dollars between 1991 and 1995. Despite pressure to increase the proportion of grants for general operating support, foundations continue to devote most of their grants to specific programs.

In 1995, 44 percent of grant dollars funded special programs; 21 percent funded capital funding; 12 percent went to general support; and 8 percent of grant dollars funded research. For the most part, foundations use their resources for developing new programs rather than sustaining organizations.

Community Foundations

The number of community foundations, created by groups of individuals to pool resources for the benefit of a local area, grew significantly during the 1990s, increasing by 70 percent (from 282 to 413) from 1989 to 1995. The funding patterns of community foundations are strongly local and they are likely to fund initiatives to solve problems of crime, drugs, and the failure of public school systems. Large private foundations like the Lilly Endowment in Indiana, and the Charles Stewart Mott and W. K. Kellogg Foundations in Michigan have helped to seed and strengthen community foundations in their states. Corporations have begun to form partnerships with community foundations. Merrill Lynch & Co. recently formed an alliance with 34 community foundations to help publicize and promote the advantages of making gifts through community foundations (The Conference Board, 1996).

Corporate Giving

Corporate giving also increased significantly in the 1990s. Corporate contributions and grants from corporate foundations reached an estimated

Table 8
Contributions to the United Way, 1989–1996
(Adjusted for Inflation, CPI Index)

Year	Contributions (Billions)	% Change since Previous Year
1989	2.4032	2.3
1990	2.3795	−1.0
1991	2.3275	−2.2
1992	2.1668	−6.9
1993	2.1087	−2.7
1994	2.0769	−1.5
1995	2.0656	−0.5
1996	2.0701	0.2

Source: The United Way of America, 1997.

$8.2 billion in 1997, which represents a 5.1 percent (inflation-adjusted) increase over the previous year and a 20.6 percent increase since 1992 (Kaplan, 1997). A surge in stock values, as well as a sustained record of corporate profits, occurred between 1995 and early 1997. This suggests that many companies have a renewed capacity to rebuild corporate foundation assets that declined over the last decade. However, corporate giving to United Ways, a long-standing favorite of corporations, lost ground as corporations turned toward strategic giving. (See Table 8.) Contributions to federated campaigns have decreased since 1992, when they represented 13.2 percent of total corporate contributions. By 1995, this share had dropped to 10.3 percent (The Conference Board, 1996).

Data suggest that corporate involvement in communities has increased during the 1990s. The amount of corporate contributions (both dollars and non-cash donations) to civic and community groups has increased steadily since a moderate drop in 1992. There has also been a significant percentage increase to health and human services organizations (The Conference Board, 1996).

Foundations are in strong financial condition. Their contributions to the nonprofit sector, while substantial and growing, are only a small proportion of the sector's revenues. These resources, however, can play a pivotal role in strengthening the planning and building the capacity of the nonprofit sector.

Nonprofit Roles Compared to Government and Business

The boundaries of the sector as a whole are imprecisely defined and in constant flux. Businesses and government entities often provide services similar to those provided by nonprofits. As a result, the boundaries of the nonprofit sector are gray areas where there may be few differences among nonprofit, for-profit, and government programs in, for example, substance abuse prevention programs, child care centers, and hospitals.

Historically, nonprofits pioneered public programs that became government responsibilities when the demand grew beyond nonprofits' capacity to respond. These programs include primary education, kindergarten, disease control, and many more.[8] People also created nonprofits because the existing business or government services were not considered sufficient because they were inaccessible, costly, barebones, culturally or religiously inappropriate, ineffective, or not innovative. Nonprofits also pioneered new services, such as fitness centers, that generated demand and the potential for revenue that attracted for-profit providers.

Thus, much of the nonprofit terrain is shared with government entities and businesses. Resistance to these porous boundaries seems to be growing. One example of this resistance is the attempt by businesses to drive out nonprofit competitors, as in the suit brought against the Young Men's Christian Association (YMCA) by health club owners (Gillman, 1987).

Nonprofits sometimes create for-profit subsidiaries when they can make a profit in one program that can be used to subsidize services in another. Nonprofits also use services provided by businesses when it is cost-effective to do so. For example, many colleges and universities contract with commercial food services.

One role of nonprofits may be to identify social service needs and create services to meet those needs—as illustrated by the creation of numerous nonprofits during the spread of AIDS in the 1980s (Chambré, 1994). If the demand for a service grows, depending on the scale and cost, governments and businesses may become involved as a result of nonprofit advocacy. Some of the nonprofit sector can thereby be viewed as the social innovation sector. The innovations pioneered in the nonprofit sector with a mix of philanthropic and other revenues often reach more beneficiaries because of involvement by, and collaboration with, government and business, as nonprofits rarely have sufficient resources to expand and replicate their successful programs. The transition of the American economy from manufacturing to service provision may have accelerated or intensified this transfer of innovative services and budding markets from the nonprofit to the for-profit sector as entrepreneurs sought new services to market. Furthermore, this transfer may be accelerated when government programs provide funding or financial incentives, as in the health arena.

Some Unanswered Questions

An appreciation of the diversity of nonprofits and their varied origins and roles helps to place current political and economic trends into clearer and longer-term perspective. There is not one sector, but a kaleidoscope of many elements that creates a fascinating, changing pattern. An understanding of the diversity of the sector also helps us to raise some important questions, such as: Are there some activities so intrinsically nonprofit in character that government and business should not, as a general rule, undertake them? What should be the criteria for making such decisions?

The diversity of nonprofit providers may give some benefit to society by spurring innovation, cost savings, or community oversight. How can we decide whether society is better served by nonprofit, for-profit, or government programs? Comparative studies are beginning to shed light on the differences, but not much research has been completed. In fact, the answer might be different for each subsector (Gray 1986, Weisbrod 1988, Gelles, 1993).

The combination of a strong economy with growing income disparity, signs of civic disengagement, and devolution of social and welfare program responsibilities to the state level has led a worried nonprofit community to form multiple commissions,[9] and make many attempts to enlarge the philanthropic pie. Projects to promote the formation of new foundations, increase the level of contributions, enhance the visibility of nonprofits, celebrate volunteerism, encourage and require volunteering in high schools, and strengthen service learning in colleges have all been advanced. To date, those efforts do not seem to have increased the sector's resources or impact. How should we assess their consequences?

By 1997, total U.S. employment reached record levels and rising tax revenues eased fiscal constraints at the federal and state levels. Political leaders have begun to talk about increasing government spending. Whether those increases will materialize and be directed toward the issues and activities of concern to nonprofits, particularly those working at the community level, remains to be seen. An analysis of recent federal budget numbers indicates continuing declines in government spending for education, training, employment, social services, and international activities (Abramson, Salamon, and Steuerle, forthcoming).

Summary

The data now available on nonprofit organizations permit us to see how interrelated these nonprofits are with the rest of the economy. Changes in tax incentives seem to affect philanthropic giving and the formation of foundations. Boom markets and recessions affect giving by individuals, foundations, and corporations and appear to affect volunteering, as well. Government retrenchment affects nonprofit revenues as well as the demand for social services. Growth of government payments (Medicare and Medicaid) bolsters revenues in the health sector.

The effect of these forces, however, on the smallest organizations is not well known. Small community-based groups rely much more on voluntary labor. For them, a tremendous amount of effort is expended in raising resources, and a decline in voluntarism might disproportionately handicap their efforts.[10] The vulnerability of most of these organizations, and the negative financial trends for significant numbers of them, is another cause for concern.

Implications of Political, Social, and Financial Trends for the Role of Philanthropy

The portrait of the voluntary sector that emerges is at best a mosaic. The disparate missions create a pattern of activity that meets important social needs, but each organization and each subsector has its own definition of the pubic purposes it serves. This is not simply a service system, nor can it be harnessed for united action, short of natural disaster or war. The sector is better described as the civil society sector, an ebbing and flowing and ever-changing collection of entities engaged in largely uncoordinated, privately generated activities for multiple public purposes.

The political and economic forces of the last decade differentially affected the growth rates, strength, and viability of nonprofit organizations, depending on their areas of activities, sources of revenues, and size. Financial indicators point to healthy growth rates for most types of organizations, but that growth appears not to be keeping pace with overall growth in the economy. Philanthropic giving is steady at 1.8 percent of personal income, despite the creation of vast personal wealth. Contrary to the predictions of those who promoted the benefits of lower tax rates, increased wealth and decreased tax burdens have not resulted in higher levels of philanthropic contributions. In fact, the percentage of households reporting charitable contributions decreased from 73.4 to 68.5 between 1993 and 1996.

Volunteering declined between 1989 and 1993, a trend that may have been related to the declining economic fortunes of middle and lower income people. Between 1993 and 1995, however, this downward slide was reversed as the number of hours volunteered to the nonprofit sector returned to 1989 levels.

The fact that the number of nonprofit entities continues to grow, although at a slower rate after 1992, may also indicate a positive trend. Individuals continue to join together to implement new ideas or to undertake new activities. They recreate nonprofit organizations as they move to the suburbs and to sparsely populated states. This continued growth of voluntary organizations may be a major indicator of the health of civil society; people feel they can make a difference in a common venture.

However, the growth of nonprofits may not be a wholly positive indicator. The creation of so many new groups may also be a sign that people are frustrated with the status quo and the inability of the political system to address their concerns or to provide for needy neighbors. Emergency service providers grew at higher rates between 1992 and 1994 than did core service providers in thirteen states, suggesting that many of the new organizations were created to respond to basic human needs for food, clothes, and shelter (DeVita and Twombly, 1997). The income and expenses of these nonprofits also grew at faster rates than those of core service providers. If this trend is typical, as a recent report by Catholic Charities indicates, and if additional revenues do not meet the growing needs, fewer resources will be available for supporting families before they reach the crisis point—a potentially devastating outcome for families and their communities (Flynn, 1995).

With these trends in mind, we turn to the major forces affecting nonprofit organizations and to some suggestions for the future.

Resources

Despite the continued overall growth of the nonprofit sector, an inescapable conclusion from these data is that many nonprofit organizations are very small and many are financially weak.

Philanthropic foundations, however, are enjoying unprecedented growth in assets. Organized philanthropy could assist nonprofits by learning where resources are most needed and then leveraging additional financial, human, and political resources for those needs. Volunteer labor is very important for human services and community organizations. Philanthropy could help to mobilize additional volunteers, particularly among retired, young, low-income, and minority populations. Research shows the necessity of involving young people in organizations if they are to give and volunteer when they reach adulthood. Structured opportunities for young people to volunteer and receive paid internships in all kinds of organizations would help to pave the way for future participation. Systems that ensure nonprofits can effectively use additional volunteers should also be financed (Hodgkinson, 1996).

Community groups would benefit from greater reserves, income-producing assets, and stable funding streams that would provide a basis of ongoing operating support. A number of options should be explored and tested. The voluntary sector would probably benefit from one or more revolving funds for technical assistance, endowment grants, and bridge loans. Foundations could jointly create a nonprofit banking fund or other type of financial entity to serve nonprofits. A public, private, or combined equivalent of the Small Business Administration might be a boon to nonprofits. The federal government could also take a more active role in strengthening the finances of the voluntary sector by earmarking for nonprofit organizations revenues from the sale of charity stamps or a national lottery, following the examples of the British and Spanish governments.

Devolution and Welfare Reform

Devolution of federal government responsibilities to the state and local level is part of larger global economic and political patterns. Since most nonprofits operate at the local level, devolution itself should not be a problem for many types of organizations, and may bring opportunities for nonprofits to play larger roles in planning and decision-making.

Nonprofit advocacy may become more difficult and expensive as much decision-making is transferred to fifty state capitals. On the one hand, organizations accustomed to influencing policy at the national level may find it necessary to build alliances and funding bases at the state level. On the other hand, new avenues for civic participation may open up for local groups, and the participation gap may be narrowed if community groups carry more weight in decisions that affect their well-being since those decisions are being made locally. Groups unaccustomed to advocacy activities may have to find a public voice. Welfare reform is already generating new community coalitions and involvement of low income people in the policy process (Reid, 1997).

Private foundations have a role to play in welfare reform. They can fund community advocacy and help to create and maintain policy monitoring programs. Foundations can also help to strengthen the organizations that must provide the safety net and the welfare-to-work training and support that will enable poor people to succeed in getting and holding jobs. They can also fund the necessary monitoring and evaluation of the outcomes of welfare reform so that timely corrections can be made when outcomes are negative and replication can be encouraged when workable programs are developed. Finally, there must be better research on the capacity of organizations to handle these new roles.

Foundations can affect social change in areas such as welfare reform, but not by acting alone. The most potent role for philanthropy could be to help change the terms of the debate by, for example, financing activities that give low-income populations a voice in the policy debates.

Social Justice

Prospects for social justice under devolution and welfare reform will be affected by the availability of relevant research and by the effective use of the results to inform and influence the political process. One role for private philanthropy is to see that this research is conducted and to assist in its dissemination by convening stakeholders, calling attention to the problems, and facilitating the role of those who address social justice issues. These groups include, for example, representatives of ethnic and racial minorities and the disabled, as well as children's advocates.

Foundations can also support neighborhood coalitions in low-income communities. Such neighborhoods often face severe resource shortages:

schools are underfunded, neighborhood safety is compromised, jobs and child care are in short supply, job training programs are oversubscribed, family services are scattered and often not accessible, substance abuse programs generally have long waiting lists, and shelters and food banks are often operating at full capacity. Neighborhood coalitions formed to remedy these situations are infrequently funded by organized philanthropy. Nor are such groups likely to raise donations outside of their communities. The problems of poor communities require holistic solutions, not short-term, piecemeal interventions. Helping to build community capacity to plan and to address problems is a long-term strategy that holds promise.

The long-term need is to help low-income people find and keep jobs. Underwriting the full staffing of community agencies may be one strategy to help provide those jobs and to train volunteers in marketable skills, while strengthening communities at the same time. If low-income neighborhoods had the equivalent of a well-staffed, full-services community agency or coordinating mechanism that could provide access to a variety of services and programs for the neighborhood (perhaps with supervised programs for youth, parenting classes, music, art, dance, day care and elder care, a clinic, counseling, a thrift shop, a borrowing service, GED courses, literacy and mentoring services, a housing service, a crisis loan program, and a small business loan program), services would be accessible and jobs would be created. These kinds of programs would ideally be community governed and staffed by both paid workers and volunteers.

The Assessing the New Federalism project, a massive foundation-funded research project at the Urban Institute, is gathering information on policy changes at the state level and the impact on families and children. It will be a major resource for monitoring the impact of devolution and welfare reform on vulnerable populations.

Civic Disengagement

There may be a growing participation gap as income disparity increases and lower-income people are segregated into poor neighborhoods. Outside of religious congregations, their participation in associations and in the political process is more limited than those who are more affluent (Verba et al., 1995). This participation gap poses a major challenge for a democratic society, as studies show that involvement increases with age, education, and income. (Guterbock and Fries, 1997, Hodgkinson, 1996, Pew Research Center for the People & the Press, 1997). The challenge for nonprofits is to involve a broader cross-section of the population in their activities. When asked, minorities give and volunteer at similar rates as the overall population. Myths of disinterest, as well as class and race bias, restrict the involvement of the full spectrum of society in the governance, staffing, and volunteering patterns of many nonprofits. Religious congregations may be the most accessible route to participation by low-income people and African Americans. In these settings, people of varied income and educational levels learn participation skills and are provided with opportunities to develop leadership skills.

Young people may be the most critical population group for sustaining civil society. Youth are almost "traditionally" disengaged but can be involved if they are exposed to positive role models, information, incentives, and tools. Involving them in meaningful activities, mentoring them, and building their skills, leadership capacity and civic understanding is a job for nonprofits, as well as for governments at all levels. To ignore young people, especially children, is to sow the seeds for the eventual decline of civil society and the democratic government on which it depends.

Commercialization

Market forces are ascendant. Nonprofits must take the strengths of the market to heart so that they can do their work more effectively and efficiently. But nonprofits must also be clear about the primacy of their missions and their accountability to their communities and constituencies. Building caring communities through shared efforts—and not the "bottom line"—should drive civil society.

The incursion of business into nonprofit arenas is not new or necessarily negative. There may be areas of nonprofit activity where business scale and capital may be useful, but where business control may be deemed inappropriate. In those cases, we may need to create a new form that uses the community oversight of nonprofits and the business acumen of the for-profit sector. Hospitals and nursing homes may be candidates for such treatment. The question remains, what harm can be done and whose welfare is at stake? If the potential harm is great and the welfare of those who cannot look out for themselves is at stake, there may be an argument for limiting for-profit takeovers.

The Legal Framework

The current legal structure regulating nonprofits may be overly complex, but it is not unworkable. Flexibility should be the watchword of any system that deals with a sector as diverse as this one. Nonprofits on the boundary with government exhibit characteristics of the public sector while nonprofits on the boundary with business exhibit characteristics of businesses. We should not take an absolutist approach to the boundaries that are, and probably always have been, shifting and amoeba-like, and that permit motivated entities to move in new directions. These shifting boundaries are useful to society as a source of innovation and of new opportunities for problem-solving.

The U.S. tax system provides exemptions and incentives for public initiatives—an efficient and socially appropriate mechanism. We may be able to devise some additional incentives in the form of tax credits, a check-off on income tax returns, and others. People trying to form civil societies in other countries recognize our tax incentives as a useful tool.

On the negative side, efforts have been made within the regulatory structure to limit nonprofit advocacy. Attempts, for example, to condition tax exemption or government contracts on such limitation (as does the Istook Amendment, discussed earlier) are disastrous for democracy. Just as associations all over the world are following our lead and opening up democratic discourse, political forces in the United States seek to limit access to the policy process by organizations of those in need. Forces are arrayed so heavily against the poor that their ability to affect legislation is very limited. As mentioned earlier, efforts to limit further the ability of nonprofits to engage in the policy process should be examined carefully in light of the legitimate representational role of nonprofits, especially considering the nearly unlimited access of business corporations to the legislative and executive agencies, regardless of their contracts with government.

Final Note

Nonprofits cannot take the place of governments in terms of accountability, scale of operations, or reach. Nonprofits are not uniformly distributed across the country; neither are philanthropic resources and efforts. Nonprofits are indispensable to their communities but are also primarily accountable to their governing boards rather than to the electorate. They cannot govern or allocate resources to the public equitably. The larger human service providers, usually with direct or indirect government funding, do provide a framework for a significant portion of the country's formal social services. However, congregations and religious bodies, and most of the small entities which do not receive government funds, are important local community emergency and crisis resources.

Creative and realistic solutions to the social problems of the day require a realistic understanding of the role and capacity of nonprofit organizations. Their contributions to the quality of life in this country are varied and occur both independently and in collaboration with government and with business. Both public policy and private efforts to address social needs must acknowledge the strengths and limitations of nonprofits as the demands of devolution and welfare reform grow. Despite these cautions, there are many ways to strengthen nonprofits and their ability to participate in communities and in the political process.

Notes

I would like to acknowledge invaluable research and editorial assistance provided by Rachel Mosher-Williams, research associate at the Center on Non-profits and Philanthropy at the Urban Institute. I am grateful to Charles Clotfelter and Daniel Oran for their close reading of the paper and for their substantive and editorial comments. I would also like to thank Carol DeVita, Tom Pollak, Kathy Pettit, and Eric Twombly for their suggestions and Marie Gantz for her assistance.

1. During the past decade, researchers (Virginia Hodgkinson, Lester Salamon, and others) have made great progress in assessing the dimensions of the nonprofit sector in the United States and in other countries. This has been a difficult job because governments do not collect and maintain data about nonprofit organizations as they do for businesses. In 1981, a group of researchers started the National Center for Charitable Statistics (NCCS) to collect information derived from IRS reporting forms, classify organizations by purpose, and produce periodic statistics. Through the years, NCCS has developed and refined a classification system for nonprofits and issued regular reports. In the past year, NCCS developed the first fiscal year analysis of data from IRS that reveals the growth trends of nonprofits in the 1990s.

2. The *Nonprofit Almanac 1996–1997*, published by Independent Sector, is the most comprehensive source of data on the nonprofit sector in the United States. Figures were updated in *America's Nonprofit Sector, In Brief*, released in May 1998. Data in this paper are from these two sources unless otherwise indicated.

3. FY 1998 Labor, Health and Human Services, Education and Related Agencies Appropriations bill.

4. While data on nonprofits have improved greatly over the past several years, nonprofits are missing from the IRS data sets. The gaps are greatest for smaller social service and advocacy organizations (Grønbjerg, 1994). There are very few data on the smallest nonprofits that are not required to register or file information returns with the IRS. While estimates vary, there may be several million additional formal and informal groups in existence (Smith, 1994). In addition, we are missing most coalitions that are unstaffed, as well as civic and community groups that do not meet the threshold for reporting, those that are unaware of the reporting requirements, and those that chose not to report. This is probably a greater problem that the inclusion of defunct organizations in the file.

5. Includes assigned value of volunteer time.

6. For example, more than 60 women's funds have been established in the past 15 years.

7. Religious congregations are not required to file IRS reports so information on most of them is not available.

8. While it is beyond the scope of this paper, it is instructive to consider that public education was mostly private until the scope became too broad for ad hoc private management and financing.

9. For example: the Penn National Commission on Society, Culture and Community at the University of Pennsylvania; The National Commission on

Civic Renewal, chaired by William J. Bennett and Senator Sam Nunn; and The National Commission on Philanthropy and Civic Renewal, chaired by Lamar Alexander.

10. Ninety-three million people, or 48.8 percent of the U.S. population, volunteered the equivalent hours of 9.2 million full-time employees to nonprofits in 1996. This extraordinary commitment of time is an indication of the importance of these organizations in engaging their communities.

References

"400 Richest People in America." *Forbes* Digital Tool (updated continuously). Online. Internet. 29 September 1997.

Abramson, Alan J., Salamon, Lester M., and Steuerle, C. Eugene. "The Nonprofit Sector and the Federal Budget: Recent History and Future Directions." Forthcoming.

Boris, Elizabeth T. "Civil Society: The Foundation of Democratic Participation." Dissemination Paper #7. InterAmerican Development Bank, Washington, DC, 1997.

Chambré, Susan. "Voluntarism in the HIV Epidemic: Raising Resources for Community-Based Organizations in New York City and Sullivan County." NSRF Working Paper Series. Nonprofit Sector Research Fund, Washington, DC, 1994.

Cnaan, Ram. "Social and Community Involvement of Local Religious Congregations: Findings from a Six-City Study." Paper presented at the 1997 Annual ARNOVA Meeting, Indianapolis, IN, 1997.

Coleman, James S. *Foundations of Social Theory*. Cambridge, MA: The Belknap Press of Harvard University Press, 1990.

Conference Board. *Corporate Contributions in 1996*. New York: The Conference Board, Inc., 1997.

Cortes, Michael. "A Statistical Profile of Latino Nonprofit Organizations in the U.S." Paper presented at the 1997 Annual ARNOVA Meeting, Indianapolis, IN, 1997.

De Vita, Carol and Twombly, Eric. "Nonprofit Organizations in an Era of Welfare Reform." Paper presented at the 1997 Annual ARNOVA Meeting, Indianapolis, IN, 1997.

Dees, J. Gregory. "Enterprising Nonprofits." *Harvard Business Review*, January–February, 1998.

Drucker, Peter F. *Managing the Non-Profit Organization: Practices and Principles*. New York: Harper Collins Publishers, 1992.

Flynn, Patrice. "Responding to Changing Times." Catholic Charities USA 1994 Annual Survey, Washington, DC, 1995.

Gelles, Erna. "Administrative Attitudes and Practices of For-Profit and Nonprofit Day Care Providers: A Social Judgment Analysis." Paper presented at the 1993 Annual ARNOVA Meeting, Toronto, Canada, 1993.

Gillman, Todd J. "Health Clubs Hit YMCAs' Tax Breaks." *Washington Post*, 30 June 1987, E1.

Gray, Bradford H., ed. *For-profit Enterprise in Health Care*. Washington, DC: National Academy Press, 1986.

Grønbjerg, Kirsten A. "Using NTEE to Classify Non-Profit Organizations: An Assessment of Human Service and Regional Applications." *Voluntas*, 5 (3), 1994.

Guterbock, Thomas M., and Fries, John C.. "Maintaining America's Social Fabric: The AARP Survey of Civic Involvement." Report prepared for American Association of Retired Persons, Washington, DC, 1997.

"He Cheated a Charity, Unchallenged," *New York Times*, 5 April 1995, A24.

Hodgkinson, Virginia. *Volunteering and Giving Among Teenagers 12 to 17 Years of Age*. Washington, DC: Independent Sector, 1996.

Hodgkinson, Virginia, Weitzman, Murray, et al. *From Belief to Commitment: The Community Service Activities and Finances of Religious Congregations in the United States*. Washington, DC: Independent Sector, 1993.

Hodgkinson, Virginia, and Weitzman, Murray. *Giving and Volunteering in the United States*. Washington, DC: Independent Sector, 1996.

Hodgkinson, Virginia, Weitzman, Murray, et al. *Nonprofit Almanac 1986–1987*. Washington, DC: Independent Sector, 1986.

Hodgkinson, Virginia A., Weitzman, Murray S., et al. *Nonprofit Almanac 1996–1997*. Washington, DC: Independent Sector, 1996.

Hopkins, Bruce R. *The Law of Tax-Exempt Organizations*. New York: John Wiley & Sons, Inc., 1992.

Kaplan, Ann E. *Giving USA 1997*. New York: AAFRC Trust for Philanthropy, 1997.

Langer, Gary. "Covenant House Reports Evidence on Ritter." Associated Press, 3 Aug. 1990.

Lyman, Richard W. "Reagan Among the Corinthians." *Perspectives* Series, Center for the Study of Philanthropy, City University of New York, 1989.

McCarthy, Kathleen. *Women's Culture: American Philanthropy and Art, 1830–1930*. Chicago: University of Chicago Press, 1993.

National Commission on Philanthropy and Civic Renewal. "Giving Better, Giving Smarter: Renewing Philanthropy in America." National Commission on Philanthropy and Civic Renewal, Washington, DC, 1997.

O'Neill, Michael. *The Third America: The Emergence of the Nonprofit Sector in the United States*. San Francisco: Jossey-Bass Publishers, 1989.

Oster, Sharon M. *Strategic Management for Nonprofit Organizations: Theory and Cases*. New York: Oxford University Press, 1995.

Pew Research Center for the People & the Press. "Trust and Civic Engagement in Metropolitan Philadelphia: A Case Study." Study report, Philadelphia, PA, 1997.

Pollak, Thomas H. and Pettit, Kathryn L. S. "The Finances of Operating Public Charities, 1989–1995." National Center for Charitable Statistics, Washington, DC, forthcoming.

Printz, Tobi J. "Services and Capacity of Faith-Based Organizations in the Washington, DC Metropolitan Area." Paper presented at the 1997 Annual ARNOVA Meeting, Indianapolis, IN, 1997.

Reid, Elizabeth. "Participation of Low-Income People and Organizations in

Welfare-to-Work Coalitions and Networks." Paper presented at the 1997 Annual ARNOVA Meeting, Indianapolis, IN, 1997.

Renz, Loren, et al. *Foundation Giving*. New York: Foundation Center, 1997.

Salamon, Lester M. "The Changing Partnership Between the Voluntary Sector and the Welfare State." *The Future of the Nonprofit Sector*. Ed. Virginia A. Hodgkinson and Richard Lyman. San Francisco: Jossey-Bass Publishers, 1989.

Salamon, Lester M. *America's Nonprofit Sector: A Primer*. New York: Foundation Center, 1992.

Skloot, Edward, ed. *The Nonprofit Entrepreneur: Creating Ventures to Earn Income*. New York: Foundation Center, 1988.

Skocpol, Theda. *Protecting Mothers and Soldiers: The Political Origins of Social Policy in the United States*. Cambridge, MA: Harvard University Press, 1995.

Smith, David H. "The Rest of the Nonprofit Sector I: The Nature of Grassroots Associations in America." Paper presented at the 1994 Annual ARNOVA Meeting, Berkeley, CA, 1994.

Stevenson, David R. *The National Taxonomy of Exempt Entities Manual*. Washington, DC and New York: National Center for Charitable Statistics and Foundation Center, 1997.

Stevenson, David R., et al. *State Nonprofit Almanac 1997*. Washington, DC: The Urban Institute Press, 1997.

Understanding Nonprofit Funding. San Francisco: Jossey-Bass Publishers, 1993.

United States House of Representatives, Committee on Small Business. Hearings on "Government-Supported Unfair Competition with Small Business," July 19, 1996.

Verba, Sidney, Schlozman, Kay Lehman, and Brady, Henry E. *Voice and Equality: Civic Voluntarism in American Politics*. Cambridge, MA: Harvard University Press, 1995.

Walsh, Sharon. "Charity's Troubles Shake Up Nonprofits; New Era's Bankruptcy Filing May Threaten Some Creditors' Survival." *Washington Post*, 17 May 1995, F01.

Weisbrod, Burton A. *The Nonprofit Economy*. Cambridge, MA: Harvard University Press, 1988.

Wolpert, Julian. "Patterns of Generosity in America: Who's Holding the Safety Net?" Twentieth Century Fund Paper. Twentieth Century Fund, New York, 1993.

CHAPTER TWO

The Evolving American Foundation

James Allen Smith

The modern American foundation is an institutional invention that is barely a century old. In the last decade of the nineteenth century, a handful of individuals, schooled in post–Civil War philanthropy and enriched by the postwar industrial expansion, began fundamentally to transform the institutions for holding and distributing charitable resources. While these wealthy donors and their advisers drew on much older charitable traditions and a venerable structure of law, they created a new type of philanthropic foundation, an institutional form that would be copied time and again by other wealthy Americans during the course of the twentieth century. From a scant handful of foundations in existence in the first decades of this century, foundations have vastly increased in number, totaling well over 40,000 as we approach the new millennium. Varying in size, scope and purpose, foundations can be most simply understood as nongovernmental, nonprofit institutions with their own corpus of financial assets privately held and managed by trustees or directors for the pursuit of some public purpose.[1] They are an important part of the larger nonprofit sector even though their numbers and total resources are small compared to the sector as a whole and to overall charitable giving.

If history is indeed a "seamless web," in Maitland's famous phrase, then our search for the first threads that mark the beginnings of foundations must be teased from an old and richly textured historical fabric. Endowments for religious, educational and social purposes had been familiar to Egyptians, Greeks, and Romans and included such notable institutions as Plato's Academy and the vast library in Alexandria. During the Middle Ages endowments were created to sustain monasteries, universities, hospitals, and other charitable institutions throughout western Europe. Indeed, terms from medieval vernacular languages, such as the Old English *foundacioun* and *endowe(n)*, supply a key part of our vocabulary for describing charitable activity.

Although the endowed institutions of the ancient and medieval world with their narrowly defined operations were not like the foundations we have come to know in the twentieth century, these old institutional forms began to shape a body of law and customary practice that made the modern foundation possible. Beginning in antiquity, traditional customs of family inheritance evolved to permit gifts and bequests to charitable institutions. Practices for governing charitable entities also gradually emerged, owing much to medieval Augustinian and Benedictine rules, which gave order to daily life in monasteries, hospitals, almshouses, and other religious bodies; these rules and statutes pointed the way toward our modern structures of trusteeship and corporate governance. Instruments for making gifts and protecting a donor's intent—last wills and testaments, courts of equity, and trust mechanisms—also assumed recognizable legal form during the late Middle Ages. And charitable purposes, which had long been acknowledged by custom, were defined formally in Elizabethan statutes of the early seventeenth century.[2]

On the North American continent many of these historical threads were woven into the fabric of our community and associational life, helping to frame colonial approaches to educating children, aiding the poor, organizing public works projects, and meeting other social needs. Charitable bequests and endowments were not uncommon. Stephen Girard, a Philadelphia merchant and banker, made the single most famous and legally influential bequest in early nineteenth century America when he left the bulk of his $7 million estate to the city in 1831 to establish a school for poor, white orphan boys. His elaborately detailed instructions for the school prohibited ministers and clerics of any denomination from entering the school so as "to keep the tender minds of the orphans . . . free from the excitement which clashing doctrines and sectarian controversy are so apt to produce." His collateral heirs (he had no direct descendants) challenged the will, contending that the city of Philadelphia could not legally accept the bequest. They also maintained that the terms of the trust were too vague to be enforceable and that the exclusion of clergy negated his charitable purposes and violated common law.[3] In unanimously upholding the Girard will in an 1844 decision, the Supreme Court signaled the new directions philanthropy would take in the United States. The city of Philadelphia as a corporate entity had its rights to inherit and manage property affirmed, easing the way for future donors to transfer property to charitable corporations and for those corporations to carry out the donor's wishes.

The Girard decision also expanded upon an 1819 Supreme Court decision in which the trustees of Dartmouth College had sought to protect the private character of their institution from a reorganization scheme engineered by the New Hampshire legislature. The Dartmouth decision had upheld the private

contractual character of the donors' gifts to the college trustees, thus protecting the corporation from the encroachment of public authorities. The subsequent Girard case further clarified conceptions of trusts, charity law, and
equitable jurisdiction. And in permitting Girard to establish his "infidel-
charity school," as John Quincy Adams characterized it, the Supreme Court
acknowledged that charitable purposes were not exclusively rooted in Christian doctrine nor necessarily motivated by a donor's Christian spirit. A legal
route had been opened that would point the way to the modern foundation—
corporate in form, private in character—although the path would not be
direct, linear, and obstacle free.

More immediate antecedents of contemporary foundations can be found
in post–Civil War America. Several well-known nineteenth century endowments, most notably the Peabody Education Fund and the Slater Fund,
undertook important work in the South. The former was established by
George Peabody in 1867 to advance southern education and to foster regional
reconciliation in the years after the Civil War. Peabody's initial gift of $1
million (later increased to $2 million) was expended primarily on public
schools in southern towns and cities and used to improve statewide systems of
education, especially through teacher training. It was dissolved in 1914 and its
assets merged with the Slater Fund, an endowment created in 1882 to aid
black education.[4] These funds served as models for some of the large-scale
philanthropic initiatives of the next, far wealthier generation of philanthropists, especially the efforts to improve southern education and public health
supported by John D. Rockefeller and Julius Rosenwald.

Even more important in setting the stage for the modern foundation was
the concern in the decades after the Civil War with rationalizing, reorganiz-
ing and, in the end, professionalizing charity work. Industrialization, urban
expansion, and immigration gave rise to a host of new charitable institutions
to address the problems of orphans, young working women, public health,
housing, and the numerous ills associated with densely packed, growing
cities. Discussions of "charity organization" and talk of "scientific philanthropy" led to attempts to coordinate the efforts of the benevolent groups that
had burgeoned in the mid-nineteenth century. The charity organization
societies that sprouted in various American cities in the 1870s and 1880s
marked the beginnings of both a more professional approach to charitable
activity and a search for methods of addressing social and economic problems
that would be grounded in science and rationality rather than simple altruistic
sentiment.

The Philanthropic Revolution

It is not altogether an exaggeration to say that the early twentieth century
witnessed a philanthropic revolution. John D. Rockefeller, Sr. and a few other

wealthy donors, most notably Andrew Carnegie and Margaret Olivia Slocum Sage, pioneered in creating a fundamentally different kind of philanthropic institution. In contrast to older endowments, these new foundations would have general and broadly defined purposes. Their governance would be private, relying on self-perpetuating boards of trustees or directors, while their missions would be to serve the public good. And they would use the vast assets they held in trust to create and support other institutions. Since the 1890s these donors and their advisers had conducted a number of institutional experiments in professionally administered philanthropy. They founded new institutions, including the many Carnegie research institutions and specialized funds and the Rockefeller institutes, boards and commissions. The Russell Sage Foundation, whose programs of social investigation and reform began to take shape in 1907, was the model for subsequent operating foundations and served as a prototype for the modern policy think tank. Daniel Coit Gilman, president of Johns Hopkins University, immediately grasped the significance of Margaret Sage's work when she and her advisers announced their ambitious plans for the foundation. He asserted that she and other large donors were creating nothing less than "a new force in civilization."[5] What was new about this "philanthropic revolution"?

Most obviously, the philanthropic revolution was new in scale, with endowments measured in the tens of millions of dollars, that is to say in the hundreds of millions in current dollars (one dollar in 1900 would be worth approximately 15 in the 1990s). Industrial growth and new technologies had produced many substantial fortunes in the half century after the Civil War. According to rough but credible estimates there were fewer than one hundred millionaires in 1880; by 1916 there were more than 40,000 and a handful of those had amassed fortunes in excess of $100 million.[6] Around 1900 Carnegie had assets of about $350 million; Stephen Harkness, whose riches gave birth to the Commonwealth Fund, had more than $100 million; and Russell Sage, who died in 1906, left his widow at least $65 million. By the early 1910s, the richest of all was John D. Rockefeller, who had been worth about $200 million in 1900 but saw his fortune surpass $900 million in 1913, three years after the breakup of the Standard Oil trust.

For the charitably inclined, as Carnegie, Rockefeller, Sage, and Harkness certainly were, fortunes on this scale demanded a more systematic and rational approach to philanthropy. Indeed, Rockefeller's adviser, Frederick T. Gates, often warned him of the crushing weight of the family fortune, declaiming on one occasion, "Your fortune is rolling up, rolling up like an avalanche! You must keep up with it! You must distribute it faster than it grows! If you do not, it will crush you and your children and your children's children!"[7] John D. Rockefeller, Sr. often explained that he had been forced to give up his older habit of retail philanthropy, replacing it with a new practice of wholesale giving. The scale of the new philanthropic trusts brought with it an obsession with organization and structure. Donors and advisers sought to create efficient means for distributing money while working to improve the operations of the institutions to which they gave. Naturally, they looked to the modern business corporation both for its techniques of scientific management and its structures of corporate governance.

The corporate structure allowed the donors to vest in their trustees and their successor trustees the responsibility for defining and redefining the aims of the charitable enterprise as external circumstances changed. Thus, the modern foundation was conceived from the outset as a malleable and evolving instrument capable of responding to new social needs and to changing times. The language of the founding charters is revealing: The Russell Sage Foundation was established in 1907 for "the improvement of social and living conditions in the United States"; the Carnegie Corporation of New York was founded in 1911 "for the advancement and diffusion of knowledge and understanding"; the Rockefeller Foundation was created in 1913 "to promote the well-being of mankind throughout the world"; and most general of all, Harkness's Commonwealth Fund was designed in 1918 "to do something for the welfare of mankind."

The donors and their advisers had come of age as cities and regions were being tied together by rail and telegraph. Their business enterprises had national and international reach as markets for both basic products and consumer goods expanded. It is not at all surprising that the new philanthropic foundations also defined their geographical scope of operations broadly. While some such as the Russell Sage Foundation might devote a fixed portion of their grantmaking to the city where the fortune was made, most of the larger philanthropic foundations sought to play a national or even international role. Several looked to the southern United States as an impoverished and underdeveloped region. A handful looked beyond the United States. Carnegie created diverse funds in his native Scotland and an endowment to explore the conditions for international peace; the Rockefeller health initiatives soon expanded beyond the American South into international terrain.

The new institutions also widened their scope in another way, breaking from strictly sectarian religious concerns. Although the individual donors' lives were often deeply influenced by their religious upbringing, the largest foundations did not work within the framework of a single religious denomination. Even John D. Rockefeller, the most devout of Baptists, was capable of giving to Presbyterian and other Protestant groups and even, on occasion, to Catholic organizations; howls of complaint were sometimes heard from Baptists whose pleas for funding were denied. Looking at the trustees who had been chosen for several of the new philanthropic foundations, Daniel Coit Gilman was impressed by their breadth of perspective. He observed, "They cannot be suspected of personal, sectional, political, or denominational prejudices."

In the final analysis, the most innovative aspect of the new foundations was their conviction that philanthropy could not only be larger in scale, better structured, and broader in perspective but that it should also be more scientific. While the "scientific" philanthropy of the late nineteenth century had been concerned with organization and efficiency, the approaches of the Sage, Rockefeller, Carnegie, and Harkness philanthropies aspired to use scientific methods to comprehend and to remedy social and economic problems. The donors seemed to share a keen fascination with some of the great nineteenth century scientific advances, using those successes, especially in biology and medicine, as examples of what they hoped their philanthropy could accomplish in many other fields of endeavor. The first foundations reflected this bounding optimism and adhered to an almost religious faith in scientifically guided progress. We should not forget, however, that the new philanthropic trusts aroused hostility as well. From the outset the new philanthropic trusts faced a counter-reaction of skepticism and populist suspicion best reflected in the Walsh Commission investigations of industrial relations and the stern congressional opposition to the Rockefeller efforts to win a federal charter for their foundation.

Historical Markers

Notwithstanding Daniel Coit Gilman's early and sympathetic insights into foundations, the study and analysis of American foundations has been slow to develop and often uneven. Over the years official histories, memoirs, and insider accounts have often been countered by contentious journalistic exposés and investigative reports by governmental commissions. Substantial scholarly work did not begin to appear until the late 1950s and it was not until foundation archives began to open, especially the Rockefeller Archive Center in 1974, that the body of scholarly literature grew significantly. There are now more detailed and measured accounts of foundation support for particular fields, including higher education, medicine, museums, international studies, and various public policy issues; there are outstanding histories of individual foundations, especially the Carnegie Corporation and the Carnegie Foundation for the Advancement of Teaching; and there are excellent biographies of some of the leaders of modern philanthropy.[8]

However, the individual books and articles do not yet yield a full narrative story about the modern foundation and its evolution during the course of this century. They do not situate foundations in their changing political, social, and intellectual environments or look at how foundation strategies change from one era to another.[9] Perhaps it is premature for any single scholar to attempt a history of the role played by foundations in American life during the course of the twentieth century. Nevertheless, it seems useful to engage in a preliminary historical exercise, asking how the American foundation has evolved and through what stages it has passed.

Historians inevitably tear into the seamless web of the past. In striving to define history's epochs, eras, or ages, they seek meaningful chronological units to assess change and to think about broad patterns of cause and effect. How would a historian begin to mark the stages of foundation activity in the United States during the past century? What might those eras begin to tell us about the changing role of foundations? Rough chronological markers can be put in place to define five periods in the history of American foundations.

First, we can discern a proto-foundation era, beginning in about 1890 and ending in about 1910. Its start can be dated from the publication of Andrew Carnegie's enduring essay "Wealth" in 1889 and John D. Rockefeller's decision two years later to hire Frederick T. Gates as his full-time philanthropic adviser. This era ended and a new one began with the first efforts to secure a federal charter for the Rockefeller Foundation in 1910 and with the founding of the Carnegie Corporation of New York in 1911.

Second, the period from about 1910 until the early 1930s has the contours of another period in the evolution of foundations. The era began optimisically with the founding of the large general purpose foundations in the early 1910s and continued when several other significant private foundations entered upon the scene, including the Commonwealth Fund and Rosenwald Fund. It also saw the beginnings of the community foundation movement inspired by Frederick Goff's work in Cleveland. It ended not with a crash in 1929 but with the gradual erosion of foundation assets that set in during the early 1930s and the consequent tempering of early enthusiasms about philanthropic accomplishments.

Third, the period from the early 1930s until the mid-1940s was a time when foundations saw their work being shaped by forces well beyond their control, namely the decade-long economic crisis and World War II. In some cases foundation boards curtailed programs of academic research and study and stopped creating new institutions, reverting to simple charitable responses in a time of national economic need. In wartime they sought to apply the knowledge acquired in earlier years and mobilized their staffs to assist government agencies both on the domestic and international front.

Fourth, the period from the late 1940s until about 1970 was defined by a renewed confidence in what foundations might accomplish. Its beginning was best signified by the publication of the 1949 *Report of the Study for the Ford Foundation on Policy and Program* and the dramatic, sometimes stormy entry of that foundation onto the national and international stage.[10] It ended with the passage of the Tax Reform Act of 1969 and the new regulatory regime it imposed on foundations.

The fifth and most recent period began in the early 1970s. Its terminal date, if indeed this era is over, remains debatable. Historians and nonhistorians stand on equal footing when present-day events are being scrutinized for insights into the future. This latest era has been characterized by a number of factors: shrinking resources for foundation programs (a result of both the bear market of 1973–74 and the decade-long period of inflation) and a greater concern for measurable outcomes; the loss of faith in governmental initiatives in the wake of the Great Society; the rise of conservative foundations willing to question public sector activity and to push for policies that will devolve resources and responsibility to states and localities; the increasingly ideological tenor of American public discourse; and most recently, the attempts to delegitimize the public policy advocacy role of foundations and nonprofit organizations. There have been counter-trends of late, including strong financial market performance over the past decade, sharp declines in rates of inflation, and an international environment strongly propelling much of the world toward democratic institutions, market economies, and the construction of civil societies. Whether we can begin to identify a new era, one beginning in the late 1980s or early 1990s, remains to be seen.

Tentative as this outline may be, it can serve as a first rough cut for understanding the changing role of American foundations. While a few chronological markers are in place, what can be said about the space between the markers? What are the fundamental characteristics of foundation activities within each era? What has animated philanthropic strategies and interventions in different periods? Answers to all these questions must be preceded by a strong caveat. A century-long historical perspective inevitably gives greater weight to the works of the largest and oldest of the nation's foundations and consequently to the New York–centered foundations, especially those whose archives have been most accessible and whose officers have been most voluble about their programs. The century-long perspective also tends to give short shrift to regional variations in philanthropy, especially to the newly emerging West Coast foundations, whose histories are shorter and many of whose plans are still unfolding. The focus on the larger foundations also masks the reality that the vast majority of American foundations are small, have little or no staff, and tend to support local institutions (only some 1,500 have grant budgets in excess of $1 million and fewer than 200 of those make grants in excess of $10 million).

The Evolving Role of Foundations

Foundations are simultaneously very strong and very fragile. The wealth they hold, even when financial markets drop, can insulate them from many of the economic winds that buffet other nonprofit institutions as well as commercial enterprises. Their private, self-perpetuating boards of directors are subject to no public ballot, little market discipline, and only minimal government regulation and scrutiny. Yet they are fragile because they must continue to earn and hold institutional legitimacy in a democratic society that is suspicious of concentrated wealth, wary of decisions taken behind closed doors, and sometimes contemptuous of experts and "do-gooders." During the

41

course of this century as the spheres of both the governmental sector and the market economy have changed, foundations have had to redefine their roles. As the size and shape of the nonprofit sector have changed (often as a result of foundation-driven processes), foundations have had to seek new ways of operating. The American foundation has not been a static institutional form in its working methods and strategies; and more profoundly, it has had to find new rationales to maintain its public legitimacy from era to era.[11]

From their different disciplinary perspectives, scholars have supplied a number of theoretical justifications for our society's reliance on the nonprofit sector and, at least implicitly, on foundations. Their explanations range across economic and political theory: the provision of public goods; the enhancement of institutional trust; the increase of institutional efficiency and flexibility; the maintenance of pluralism and diversity; the furtherance of social change and innovation; the provision of social capital, and the construction of civil society among others. With a growing body of scholarship on the nonprofit sector and the increasing professionalism of foundation staffs, these theoretical perspectives resonate in a number of foundation offices when program officers think about their programmatic strategies and the outcomes they seek. But the language and animating perspectives were very different a century ago when donors and advisers first began to think about foundations. What follows is an attempt, necessarily cursory, generalized, and reliant on a scant sampling of archival materials, to trace the broad contours of the ways foundation insiders have thought in each era about the foundation as an institution in our national life.

It is striking to see how often donors, advisers, and foundation officials have been driven to think about their work in terms of scientific metaphors. By the late nineteenth century, when the major new philanthropic initiatives were getting underway, biomedical science offered a compelling concept grounded in germ theory. As metaphor, germ theory did much to inspire the emergence of American philanthropy at the turn of the century and to shape its evolution between the 1890s and the late 1920s. It began to guide inquiry into social phenomena and helped to shape the institutions that supported social investigation and action. The practical applications of Louis Pasteur's germ theory of disease—antiseptic hygiene and vaccines—transformed the practice of medicine and the aims of medical research. Germ theory linked specific diseases to single causal agents. As individual diseases came to be understood and cured, the intellectual appeal of germ theory transcended science, suggesting that there were direct linkages between a problem, the identification of its cause, and ultimately its eradication.

Germ theory gave socially concerned individuals in the late nineteenth century not only the hope of finding the specific sources of the ills they saw around them but also a medical language for thinking about social disorders and how they might be cured. Germ theory offered an insight that held out great hope for philanthropists and social reformers who believed that longstanding problems of society could not only be understood through scientific investigation but that the problems themselves could be permanently eradicated or prevented. There were many people who spoke this new biomedical language; Rockefeller advisor and one-time Baptist minister Frederick T. Gates spoke it more confidently and passionately than most. Gates spent much of the summer of 1897 engrossed in William Osler's textbook, *Principles and Practices of Medicine*. He later described that rather odd choice for vacation reading as a book with a "style that led me on, and having once started, I found a hook in my nose that pulled me from page to page."[12] Gates soon urged Rockefeller to establish an American research institution patterned on the Pasteur Institute in Paris and the Koch Institute in Berlin, a place where medical researchers could devote full time to inquiry into the causes of disease. The stories of the Rockefeller Institute for Medical Research (established in 1901, now Rockefeller University) and the Sanitary Commission for the Eradication of Hookworm (1909) are well known.

Gates spoke often about the link between disease and social misery.[13] He put it best in a speech on the tenth anniversary of the founding of the Institute for Medical Research: "disease is a prolific root of every conceivable ill, physical, economic, mental, moral, social . . . disease with its attendant evils is undoubtedly the main single source of human misery." If germs were the cause of disease, they were also the source of virtually everything else that afflicted human society. And Gates was critical of the nation's charities for not seeking out the fundamental causes of distress. He complained that "the great mass of the charities of the world concern themselves directly or indirectly with relieving or mitigating such evils and miseries of society as are mainly due to disease. But these charities, necessary and beautiful as they are, do not satisfy us, because they do not reach the source of the evil, or decrease its volume. . . . For, unfortunately, disease has not hitherto been intelligently, widely, and scientifically studied, nor with adequate instruments and resources. We yet know little of the causes and processes of disease and almost nothing of its cure."[14] Rockefeller himself echoed Gates in his conviction that philanthropy was an instrument for seeking out the source of social ills. "The best philanthropy," he wrote, "is constantly in search of the finalities—a search for cause, an attempt to cure evils at their source."[15]

The metaphor of the germ had implications for the tasks the new foundations, not merely the Rockefeller philanthropies but other large new foundations, set for themselves. Disease offered Russell Sage Foundation staff members a perspective on their programs whether they were approaching tuberculosis as a source of urban distress, looking at the causes of juvenile delinquency, or examining the status of women, nearly two-thirds of whom lost their husbands to tuberculosis, pneumonia, typhus, or malaria, according to staff member Mary Richmond's research. As a consequence, some foundations tackled specific diseases whose causes had been identified in the preceding decades; some put their money directly into medical research and education; some devoted their resources to making social science as scientific and useful as the biomedical fields had proved to be; and many new research institutions as well as organizations to link researchers were created. The result was to foster specialization and professionalization in a variety of fields, from medicine and public health to economics, sociology, and political science. All of this—the model of large scale institutional research with the aim of direct intervention in preventive programs—had been signaled as early as 1913 when Jerome Greene, Rockefeller's executive secretary, had spoken of the foundation as an organizations that should operate like a "University of Human Need," structured along lines comparable to university departments; he underscored "the importance which scientific research would always have in the prosecution of philanthropic undertakings."[16]

Scientific metaphors are laid down like sediment, one stratigraphic layer upon another. The metaphor of the germ yielded ground to new scientific concerns. World War I, with its successes in chemistry and physics, pushed the Carnegie, Rockefeller, and Sage foundations toward a greater concern with quantification and statistical techniques. Carnegie devoted substantial resources to the creation of the National Bureau of Economic Research, while Sage became the center of the social survey movement. The emphasis on numbers and methods brought with it a realization that progress in the social sciences would be much slower than in the natural sciences. By the late 1920s some foundation executives even began to wonder whether they would ever know enough to undertake preventive action in social and economic fields. As Barry C. Smith, general director of the Commonwealth Fund, put it in 1926 when the foundation reviewed its programs, the foundation was decreasing not only its emphasis on preventing juvenile delinquency, it was placing "decreasing emphasis on the prevention of anything."[17]

The onset of the Great Depression further eroded faith in social science research. By 1934 a committee of the Rockefeller Foundation appointed to review and appraise the Foundation program concluded that "the advance of knowledge, if rigidly defined, is too limited and confining and objective." The Foundation's president, Raymond Fosdick, began to argue for a policy of opportunism, especially where human need was greatest. Indeed, by the early 1930s a new metaphor began to suffuse the language of those working in foundations. There was talk of exploring the reasons for maladjustment and of seeking balance and equilibrium in systems that seemed suddenly out of kilter. The metaphors were drawn, in all likelihood, from physics and the relatively new discipline of psychology. In the early 1930s these metaphors of adjustment and balance began to define a new era for the way foundations would approach their work. The language of balance and adjustment became increasingly evident, especially in the economic stabilization program of Rockefeller's social science division. The ups and downs of the business cycle were, in the words of the Foundation's Edmund E. Day, "the underlying forces in which much of our physical suffering, illness, mental disorder, family disintegration, crime, political upheaval, and social instability have their origins."[18]

A foundation that saw its task as balance and adjustment necessarily had to be flexible and opportunistic in its program. In 1934 Rockefeller's appraisal committee called for "complete adaptability in Foundation matters—both program and organization being subject to constant adjustment to changing conditions.... If our work is to be kept out of ruts, if we are to avoid frustration and stagnation, our programs and our methods must be kept elastic, fresh, alive and open-ended."[19] Balance and adjustment defined the attitude of many foundations during the economic crisis and World War II, especially as they adjusted to their diminishing resources, to a new array of emergency government relief programs, and finally to fundamental changes in the way the federal government defined its role.

The years immediately after World War II marked the beginning of another philanthropic era as the large foundations reassessed their programs in the late 1940s. The older foundations were also soon joined by the Ford Foundation, which had operated as a locally oriented Michigan philanthropy since the 1930s but was on the verge of receiving a huge transfer of Ford Motor Company Stock. Ford began to plan its postwar program when Rowan Gaither was asked in 1948 to explore how Ford might pursue its general mandate to advance human welfare. At Rockefeller the program reviews of 1945 and 1946 had also looked at the effects of the war and the new challenges for philanthropy: "The really significant destruction has been in social and intellectual organization and in the faiths and codes of men. The countless points of self-adjusting equilibrium which existed in all fields prior to the war are now largely blocked off; and the formal and informal codes which regulated the relations of men over wide areas have lost their power as sanctions for conduct."[20] The Rockefeller board and staff concluded that the foundation should begin to focus on questions of human behavior and on ways of making democracy more effective and deepening international understanding.

The Gaither committee report for the Ford Foundation also looked at fundamental values, freedoms, rights, and social responsibilities; it did so with a wide-angled international view and a sweeping reaffirmation of democratic principles. Ford's international program sought to focus on five aims: maintaining world peace through an international system of law and justice; securing a greater allegiance to principles of freedom and democracy; advancing the well-being of people everywhere through economic growth; expanding the commitment to education; and increasing our knowledge of the factors governing human conduct. The Gaither committee concluded that "the evidence points to the fact that today's most critical problems are those which are social rather than physical in character—those which arise in man's relation to man rather than in his relation to nature."[21]

Characterizing the foundation activities that followed from these grand statements of purpose is perilous. In the wake of the victory over fascism and with the contours of the Cold War beginning to emerge, the thinking that shaped the early postwar programs was more explicitly conscious of political values. At the same time foundation interventions were more broadly systemic. If new organizations needed to be created, they were; if long-term professional training and education had to be undertaken, foundations did not shy from those tasks. All of this built upon the half-century of accumulated experience in philanthropy and the growing professionalization of staffs in the preeminent foundations. If one looks for metaphors to characterize the activity in the two decades or so after World War II, it is to be found in engineering, a discipline where application of knowledge is paramount, and arguably in operations research and systems analysis, the two wartime-inspired disciplines that shaped approaches in both policy think tanks and government agencies in the postwar years. Consequently, the role of the foundation was often to design, build, and test the programmatic models which would then be adopted by government.

The end of philanthropy's era of engineering came with the passage of the Tax Reform Act of 1969, the diminishing resources that came with the financial market collapse of 1973–74, and, above all, the waning of faith in large scale governmental interventions. We are too close to this recent era to give it a name or to be able to mark its close. But we can enumerate some of its salient characteristics. First, foundation philanthropy, which at the turn of the century had seemed an instrument for transcending political discord through research and measured policy reform, has become for some foundations a more self-consciously ideological activity. The emergence of sharp ideologically drawn lines has had consequences for our definitions of expertise and for the foundation community's commitment to university-based research. Foundations have pulled back from their older approaches to knowledge building, at least in the social and economic arena, pursuing instead a variety of methods to advance social justice through either rights-based legal and political strategies, political and economic empowerment (from both the right and left), or public policy advocacy in its many forms.

Second, there is far greater self-consciousness of what we in the foundation community and the nonprofit sector more generally are doing. It has taken the form of professional associations such as the Council on Foundations and Independent Sector, a nonprofit research community that has burgeoned over the past decade, and both internal and external pressures for more accountability and for measurable, evaluable results. While the pressures for greater accountability may work to narrow our time horizons and to truncate our imagination and vision, there is simultaneously a broadening force at work. We have become more aware of the role of this sector around the world as nations have liberalized their markets and as political regimes have taken their first steps toward democracy. Whether in Asia or eastern Europe or Latin America, the emergence of civil society—the descriptive term invented in the

The Idea of a Cure Society

eighteenth century has been recovered and refurbished only in the last ten years or so—has given us new perspectives on the role foundations play in different political cultures and social contexts.[22] The history of American foundations has been viewed primarily through two lenses: the relationship between philanthropy and government (or public policymaking) and the relationship between philanthropy and expertise. The concept of civil society widens the perspective on the public sphere in which foundations operate, compelling us to ask about relationships between foundations and the economic marketplace and between foundations and the less formal voluntary sector. Does the growing reliance on the term "civil society" suggest a new stage of development in the history of foundations? Does it succeed the age of germ theory, the period of balance and adjustment, the era of engineering, and the age of ideological philanthropy? Can the concept of civil society help us situate ourselves in the flow of time? Is there an animating conception of philanthropy or another new and persuasive metaphor that can propel our work? With these questions this essay takes an inevitably personal turn. Their answers are not the province of the historian but rather have become the day-to-day obsessions of someone who works in a foundation, has counseled its donor, and seeks to explain to new trustees and staff what a foundation can and cannot hope to do.

Philanthropy in the Age of the Virus

Exactly one hundred years after Frederick Gates was hired to help John D. Rockefeller with his philanthropic obligations, I was asked by a wealthy donor to assist in the planning for his foundation, one which should some day join the ranks of the largest fifty foundations in the United States. Almost a century after Gates had spent his summer reading Osler's medical text, I had been reading about the history of medicine and public health, with the HIV/AIDS epidemic uppermost in mind. Faced with new foundation responsibilities in the summer of 1991, I began to speculate about the optimism of Gates and his contemporaries as they witnessed the extraordinary medical accomplishments of their day and to contrast their hopefulness with the pessimism surrounding the virus that causes AIDS.

Indeed, the emergence of AIDS in the early 1980s had thrust us back into an epoch of concern with infectious diseases, generating fears from which antiobiotics and public health measures had once safely delivered us. Viruses may now represent the principal threat to human survival. As Joshua Lederberg reminds us, "We have no guarantee that the natural evolutionary competition of viruses with the human species will always find ourselves the winner."[23] Viruses pose different problems from those of the parasite causing hookworm and the bacillus causing tuberculosis and the other germs conquered in the first generation of American philanthropy. The HIV assault on

47

the immune system is far more complex than the attack of a germ or parasite and cannot be reduced to a single causal model. Because viruses are genetic fragments living inside the host's cells and exploiting the host's metabolism, they have proved much harder to combat. Moreover, infection with HIV does not progress within a simple step-by-step temporal framework; indeed, there is a long period of latency and the disease proceeds through multiple and overlapping phases. The individual virus does not attack and kill individual cells; rather, the damage is systemic; cells are killed by a variety of phenomena. The long period of clinical latency during which there are no overt clinical symptoms makes the illness more easily transmissible and conceals any pressing need to intervene. Finally, even if there is ultimate success in eliminating the virus one is left with a damaged immune system leaving difficult tasks of enhancing, restoring, or replacing the immune system.

To look at the virus causing AIDS is to see some of the difficulties for both research and for medical intervention. It is also possible to begin to ask how a viral metaphor might apply to the ways in which we conceive contemporary philanthropic strategies. While Gates had seen disease as the root cause of all social ills and the germ as the sole and direct agent, the viral metaphor compels us to think in more complicated ways about cause and effect relationships and the nature of our philanthropic interventions.

At the end of the twentieth century we now understand that many things can alter the balance between man and microbe, even though we cannot always grasp every subtle systemic interaction. It is large scale human action—the clearing of rainforests, the dumping of bilgewater from ships, the expansion of third world urban slums—that brings the first contact with new viruses. And it is global patterns of trade, commerce, and the rapidity of modern transportation that bring the rest of the world into contact with them. Instead of viewing the relationship between man and germ as one in which mankind will prevail by destroying the germ, we must now begin to look for the conditions of equilibrium between host and microbe; we must ask what it is that destroys the equilibrium between the human species and microbes.

The viral metaphor challenges us to think about the role of philanthropy, about the place of scientific inquiry and the organization of knowledge, as well as about specific programmatic actions. First, the viral metaphor reminds us that there is still much scientific research to be done and that foundations should not retreat from knowledge-building. The new intellectual demands are great, in part because they compel us to move from our reductionist scientific habits of mind to larger views. As Stephen Morse of Rockefeller University observes, "Emerging disease is just one more consequence of ecological damage. But addressing the problem could provide common ground for uniting otherwise diverse interests—environmental, agricultural, economic, and health—to simultaneously address a wide range of other concerns as well."[24] Second, the viral metaphor reminds us of the demands of vigilance, what those in public health think when they use the term "surveillance," so that we can be alert to the moments when equilibrium breaks down and respond with appropriate speed. Thus, the age of the virus requires institutional structures that are capable of applying new knowledge quickly, that can respond effectively even in the absence of complete knowledge, and that are less bureaucratic in their operations. Third, the response to HIV/AIDS has already demonstrated the need for new organizational linkages, whether among foundations or across the nongovernmental sector, government, and business. Whether it is foundation affinity groups sharing information about their international initiatives or nonprofit-commercial collaborations for research and drug development, the complexity of responding to the virus requires the invention of new structures and multiple responses, not unlike multiple drug therapies.

Finally, the viral metaphor reminds us that philanthropy must operate in an era when expectations of permanently eradicating the causes of disease or social distress have diminished. This is perhaps the most difficult issue for foundations to face. It contradicts that impatiently optimistic spirit—a yearning for quick and certain results—that has sustained much of the philanthropic enterprise in this century. Knowledge-building, surveillance, adaptiveness, flexibility, and patience are not startling, new insights extracted from our age of the virus. They do remind us, however, that within the process of historical change there are also fundamental continuities of purpose and approach. And if we can look back with respect and sufficient humility to feel that we can learn from those who have preceded us in the philanthropic enterprise then we can begin to transmit a wiser and stronger philanthropic legacy to those who follow in our path.

Notes

1. One of the most succinct definitions of a foundation was offered by F. Emerson Andrews, *Philanthropic Giving* (New York: Russell Sage Foundation, 1950), p. 43. He defined it as "a nongovernmental, nonprofit organization having a principal fund of its own, managed by its own trustees or directors, and established to maintain or aid social, educational, charitable, religious, or other activities serving the common welfare."

2. For a brief historical survey of the legal traditions see Marion R. Fremont-Smith, *Foundations and Government: State and Federal Law and Supervision* (New York: Russell Sage Foundation, 1965), chapter 1. On the earliest beginnings of last wills and testaments in the English legal tradition, Frederick Pollock and Frederic William Maitland, *The History of English Law*, second edition (Cambridge: Cambridge University Press, 1968), vol. II, pp. 314–56. On American legal traditions, Howard S. Miller, *The Legal Foundations of American Philanthropy* (Madison: State Historical Society of Wisconsin, 1961).

3. On the Girard case see Robert A. Ferguson, "The Girard Will Case: Charity and Inheritance in the City of Brotherly Love" in *Philanthropy and American*

Society, edited by Jack Salzman (New York: Center for American Culture Studies at Columbia University, 1987), pp. 1–16.

4. On the Peabody Education Fund and the Slater Fund, John H. Stanfield, "Philanthropic Regional Consciousness and Institution-Building in the American South: The Formative Years, 1867–1920" in Salzman, op. cit., pp. 119–38; Robert H. Bremner, *The Public Good: Philanthropy and Welfare in the Civil War Era* (New York: Alfred A. Knopf, 1980), pp. 185–90.

5. Daniel C. Gilman, "Five Great Gifts," *Outlook Magazine* (August 1907), pp. 648–57.

6. Merle Curti, Judith Green, and Roderick Nash, "Anatomy of Giving: Millionaires in the Late 19th Century," *American Quarterly* 15 (1963), pp. 416–35.

7. Quoted in Raymond B. Fosdick, *The Story of the Rockefeller Foundation* (New York: Harper and Brothers, 1952), p. 3.

8. Two substantial bibliographies are among the most useful introductions to the literature on foundations: Joseph Kiger, *Historiographical Review of Foundation Literature: Motivations and Perceptions* (New York: The Foundation Center, 1987), and more current (and available online) but only for the early period, Thomas Kessner and Ariel Rosenblum, *Philanthropy in American History: The Elite Experience, 1890–1940* (New York: Center for the Study of Philanthropy, CUNY, 1998).

9. Waldemar A. Nielsen sought to remedy that deficiency in his Twentieth Century Fund Study, *The Big Foundations* (New York: Columbia University Press, 1972).

10. *Report of the Study for the Ford Foundation on Policy and Program* (Detroit: Ford Foundation, 1949).

11. In an essay prepared for the Bertelsmann Stiftung, Kenneth Prewitt takes a century-long perspective, exploring how foundation missions are formulated and implemented "Auftrag und Zeisetzung einer Stiftung: Stifterwille, Stiftungspraxis und gesellschaftlicher Wandel," *Handbuch Stiftungen: Ziele-Projekte-Management-Rechtliche Gestaltung* (Weisbaden: Gabler, 1998), pp. 321–58.

12. Frederick T. Gates, *Chapters in My Life* (New York: The Free Press, 1977), p. 181.

13. On Gates and other Rockefeller associates concerned with medical research, see John Ettling, *The Germ of Laziness: Rockefeller Philanthropy and Public Health in the New South* (Cambridge: Harvard University Press, 1981).

14. Gates, *Chapters in My Life*, p. 186.

15. John D. Rockefeller, *Random Reminiscences of Men and Events* (Tarrytown: Sleepy Hollow Press, 1984), p. 112.

16. Jerome D. Greene is quoted in the 1934 report of the committee of "review, appraisal, and program," Rockefeller Archive Center, D. R. 486.

17. The Commonwealth Fund archives are housed at the Rockefeller Archive Center. A brief history of the Fund was published in 1963 and outlines the evolution of the program, *The Commonwealth Fund: Historical Sketch, 1918–62* (New York: Commonwealth Fund, 1963).

18. E. E. Day, "Proposed Social Science Program of the Rockefeller Foundation, March 13, 1933" (a working paper for the special Rockefeller Foundation

meeting, April 1, 1933), Rockefeller Archive Center, Record Group 3, Series 910, Box 2, folder 13.

19. The 1934 report of the three-man committee of "review, appraisal, and program" is in the Rockefeller Archive Center, D.R. 486, p. 39.

20. The documents concerning the 1945–46 policy and program review are in the Rockefeller Archive Center, Record Group 3, S900.

21. Report of the Study for the Ford Foundation on Policy and Program, p. 14.

22. For a history of the term and its recovery, Adam B. Seligman, *The Idea of Civil Society* (Princeton: Princeton University Press, 1992).

23. Joshua Lederberg, "Pandemic as a Natural Evolutionary Phenomenon," *Social Research*, volume 55 (Autumn, 1988), p. 346.

24. Stephen Morse, "Regulating Viral Traffic," *Issues in Science and Technology* (Fall, 1990), p. 84, quoted in Robin Marantz Henig, *A Dancing Matrix: Voyages along the Viral Frontier* (New York: Alfred A. Knopf, 1993), p. 188.

CHAPTER THREE

Foundations and the Government

A Tale of Conflict and Consensus

Barry D. Karl and Alice W. Karl

*An analysis of the impact Rockefeller's
application for a federal charter for his foundation
had on history, political thought + the
3rd sector.*

The relation between foundations and the federal government is probably among the most complex of the historical issues having to do with American philanthropy. From the perspective of American legal history set out by Marion Fremont-Smith there is a clarity to the relationship that has been worked out in efforts to establish a place in American law for what in English law is assigned to charity. In the absence of a law of charity, structures of incorporation have been used in American law to create perpetual corporate bodies that are neither charities nor trusts that would fulfill charitable purposes.[1] These corporate bodies resulted from adjustments made as ad hoc solutions to problems faced by holders of post–Civil War industrial wealth. Such "adjustments" have made it difficult to find methods of distributing that wealth philanthropically without arousing concerns among those assigned the Constitutional responsibility for formulating public policy through Congress, the President, and the federal judiciary. The Constitution's implied emphasis on the authority of states and local communities to control education—the oldest of the policy issues with which philanthropy deals—and social welfare makes the federal role a fragile one.

The philanthropic foundations were neither the flexible civil bodies admired by Tocqueville nor public agencies, yet the rise of the foundation is a virtual tracking of the history of national policy development in the twentieth century. Virtually every area touched by science and technology has been affected. The relations of foundations and policy making could not have changed without disturbing the policy process in American government at all levels. National management participants have thought it necessary to conceal this relationship from public view lest it generate another episode of populist reaction. This essay will show the battles which have led to reformulations of law governing this relationship and the continuing hostility that makes reformulation necessary.

Dependent on public consensus, federal or national attention to problems like education, civil rights, and public health has moved through moments of secure national control that seemed permanent and subsequent rebellions that ended dramatic reform movements as though they were mistakes that violated individual autonomy. One need merely look at the massive issue of slavery, which helped provoke the nation's horrific Civil War, only to be washed away in racism that lasted for another century, to begin again to be resolved. Many such issues require national rather than local management, achieve it for moments that may last through decades, then be rescinded as though it were an error, or even a threat to citizen autonomies. This uncertainty marks the fragility of national management in the United States and the relation philanthropic foundations have had to it: a basic complexity that makes histories of American philanthropy both exciting and difficult to describe.

While regulation and encouragement of charity had been anticipated by the earliest state constitutions, all bodies—initially, informally assembled organizations acting through churches or simply as a responsibility of leading citizens—were viwed as public services whose value to the state was acknowledged by the exemption of the property of donors from taxation. After all, if the service was one citizens needed, the provision of it by private citizens with their own funds had a value the state could afford to reward. Associations did not require chartering by the state until financial responsibility demanded it.

The creation of the foundation as a corporation was a pragmatic step that appeared to solve the problem involved in chartering a corporation that could exist in perpetuity without having to specify what its business would be. The loosening of the requirement that corporations chartered by the state have purposes that could be overseen by the state attorneys general had been a gradual response to the growing number of such corporations and the practical inability to oversee them. Nonetheless, the new freedom to charter a corporation without subjecting it to periodic examinations was still on shaky ground in 1907 when Olivia Sage's lawyers applied to the New York legislature for a charter for her foundation.

Initially the interests of wealthy philanthropists in public policy took the direct form of industrial anti-union protectionism, dramatized nationwide in newspapers by the Ludlow strike of 1911—at a Rockefeller mine in Colorado where troops brought in to protect the interests of the owners accidentally killed women and children. It was difficult to see the predatory senior Rockefeller of Ludlow and his devout young son simultaneously as the brutal managers of their financial interests and benevolent battlers against disease, ignorance, and poverty.[2]

The debates of the presidentially appointed Commission on Industrial Relations (1913) over the philanthropic uses of the Rockefeller, Carnegie, and Sage fortunes were heated by hostilities toward trusts, tariffs, union battles, and "tainted money." While the debates were tied first to the Rockefeller request for a charter from Congress for his new foundation, they established the political character of the relation between foundations and the federal government. It is important to note that what may be the two earliest foundations in the form of "Funds" were the Peabody, created in 1867, and the Slater, created in 1882. Their modern character consisted in the fact that both had trustees selected from among the nation's popular leaders—Civil War generals, ex-Presidents of the United States, distinguished justices from the court system. The purpose was to associate the funds with public distinction rather than wealth. It was a design intended to avoid criticism and it worked, but without relieving public criticism of future efforts. It is likely that its more "modern" step, however, was to put money into the broad field of education rather than founding individual schools with it.

In connection with that transition from schools to education in general, John D. Rockefeller's first big gift was to Spelman College (1884), the name chosen to honor his wife's family. That was followed by his gift recreating the University of Chicago (1890). That in turn was followed by a gift establishing the Rockefeller Medical Institute, now Rockefeller University, in 1901. That led to a change in 1903 with the foundation of the General Education Board, with a much broader mandate for larger issues in the field of education. There was a similar transformation in the selection of trustees. By the opening of the twentieth century one could add university presidents to the list of possible candidates for the presidency of the foundation and for general advisors, although not trustees. They remained significant figures in the business community who had already moved toward philanthropic interests.

Both Andrew Carnegie and John D. Rockefeller had even higher public ambitions. Following at least part of the practice begun with the establishment of the Smithsonian Institution by Congress in 1846, Carnegie wanted his national research body, the Carnegie Institution of 1901, chartered by Congress with ex-officio trustees that included the President of the United States, the Chief Justice of the Supreme Court, and other such dignitaries among the public leaders who would govern it.

Foundations were to be controlled by boards selected by donors who thought of them as trustees rather than as boards of directors who took responsibility for business corporations. When business corporations were subjected to federal taxation and, after that, taxation of all citizens was instituted on the basis of personal income, in 1913 and 1917, it seemed appropriate to offer the same benefit of exemption for good works found in state constitutions. The very language became easily transferred boilerplate for federal tax legislation. If by then there was any debate over the appropriateness of the exemption, we do not have a record of it. When Congress began its first critiques in 1912, the same year the amendment authorizing an income tax became law, tax exemption was not the issue.

When John D. Rockefeller sought a charter for his Foundation in 1908, Congress responded with anger. The fact that Rockefeller's Standard Oil was under attack from the federal government as a trust led President William Howard Taft and his Attorney General to join with the Populist and labor critics of wealth in the rejection of what would have been the gift of the Rockefeller Foundation to the public. Even though Rockefeller was willing to give Congress the power to oversee and reject specific foundations grants and to dissolve the foundation eventually, Congress remained adamant. Since Rockefeller's General Education Board had been chartered by Congress in 1903, neither he nor his lawyers had anticipated the intensity of congressional rage. They had not followed the route of selecting leading public figures in their first moves through Congress, believing it outmoded and, in any case, overridden by the influence they could exercise in Congress. Senator Nelson Aldrich was John D. Jr.'s father-in-law and knew that his influence in the House would be helpful.[3] Foundations and Congress were put on a quasi-collision course that would turn out to be recurrent, unavoidable, and most peculiarly of all, unpredictable.

The subsequent ratification of the 16th Amendment legitimizing the income tax generalized the interests of wealthy philanthropists from the new government concerns about the management of their industries to concerns about the management of their wealth. The new income tax laws of 1913 and 1917 eventuated in the establishment of the Internal Revenue Service as the monitor of all charity and philanthropy, although there, too, one must make careful, basic distinctions. Unpleasant as the whole idea of an income tax seemed to that first generation, it made insignificant inroads on what were really historically unprecedented amounts of individual wealth. The real issue, taxes on estates as well as on property owned by a generation that made much of its wealth on changing real estate values, had older roots in state control of wealth.

Once the fear of great wealth took center stage the critique became universal, whether or not that wealth was being turned to the public good. Thus, while foundations were and have remained a small part of the American commitment to charity and philanthropy, they set the groundwork for federal debate. The battle tapped the roots of the relation between wealth, the ownership of private property, and those seeking opportunity for themselves in a world narrowed by the tides of immigration and the closing of the frontier.

Given the inability of observers to anticipate the hostility that appears from time to time, it would be foolish to predict the future or to look for ways of protecting foundations from the critique, although the temptation seems to be enormous. One must point to habits of institutional relationships between public and private resources for managing the future for American history, but particularly in the last century, to see consequences that are profound.

Much of the governing process in America is invented as it goes along, and, where foundations are concerned, political criticism is stimulated by events that explode on the scene as scandals. The debate is conducted by men and women in Congress who have little experience with foundations. Most policy-makers view foundations as benevolent institutions that control large re-sources left by wealthy men and women whose careers may well have been built on behavior that was not benevolent. Nonetheless, when foundations seek to influence the policy process for purposes they believe good, they can seem indistinguishable in the eyes of their critics from those who try to benefit from legislators and executives.

While foundations grow out of the history of charity their function has moved them to a level of influence and consequence similar to that of the many non-constitutional institutions exercising authority and responsibility over opportunities for advancement and benefits: universities, independent research agencies, hospitals, institutions for dealing with the traditional poor are all part of ancient networks of social support. Before the emergence of unemployment as a fundamental source of poverty, which created poor without a cause, the institutions set up initially by the churches and local communities were designed to support classes of individuals in need.

Industrialization and urbanization changed that direction, one-on-one social concern, and led to a focus on business cycles and the operation of national and world economies with new and different institutions. Our sense of the relation between public and private management is strained as we struggle to improve national systems of education, health care, and other public services. To this add one of the most transforming and unanticipated factors of all, the distinction between widowed or orphaned families that stimulated earlier philanthropic charity and the single-parent families of the age of welfare. The former state of need was clearly understood as accidental, the result of the deaths of parents or the effects of the business cycle on workers. The latter, the welfare family, has come increasingly to be perceived as a consequence of choices made by irresponsible women and men. That distinction breaks what might have been the link between charitable con-cerns for the poor and the public's definition of welfare. The successive critiques of welfare fielded by Charles Murray have given voice to a popular and political concern that may have less to do with the realities of welfare than with the growing inability of those who helped formulate its modern frame-works in the Great Society to reach a consensus regarding the effectiveness of their work.[4]

From the early years of the twentieth century when American governments at all levels were only beginning to examine their responsibilities toward the needy, foundations had taken on that task. They sought to make a distinction between charity and philanthropy that rested on the distinction between outright support of the poor and the search for the causes of their poverty, in order to build institutions that would obviate the need for either charity or welfare by correcting the conditions that brought such needs into focus. To ask whether such institutions provide adequate services and whether they are entitled to tax exemption and the power to influence the political process forces us to examine their relation to our needs without regard to their status as public or private agencies. Large sums of money are involved and the managers of those funds, unlike the self-impoverished managers of the church institutions that controlled such funds for centuries, grow accustomed to lifestyles that may cast an unwelcome light on good deeds.

Generating public criticism makes abuse of trust a public issue. The charters of incorporation foundations receive from the state give them the authority to act in our interests. Whether or not they give us and our government the power to regulate them, even to punish them, moves well beyond the realm where the doing of good protects them from criticism or punishment. As in the case of education and medical care, the distinction between public and private is more complex than when foundations were first created. Whether foundations understand that is worth questioning.

To the extent that we have reexamined our conceptions of democratic government, all the institutions committed to applying new knowledge to the contemporary society are subject to periodic and sometimes frightening looks at the traditions by which we live our lives. The literature of political debate over that century has exhibited strong threads of recurrent argument suggesting that foundations are a benefit that should continue, that they are damaging sources of power that threaten democratic control over policy, or that they represent opportunities that have not been properly utilized or have grown corrupt and must be corrected.[5]

From a general perspective, one can say that foundation support of American universities in particular, and the ideas that have come from the sciences and social sciences that affect national policy-making have influenced the policy process in ways that range from the training of those who go into the various fields of public management to medical research and health care delivery throughout the nation. Programs that in other advanced industrial societies have come into being with the aid of government funding have, in the United States, been affected by funding from foundations and individual philanthropic donors supporting the country's nexus of colleges, hospitals, and research institutions.

Foundations are a central element in the creation and sustaining of the elites who manage both governmental and nongovernmental resources that are crucial to the well-being of generations of ordinary American citizens. As such they are part of a system of informal government that exists within the more familiar frameworks set up by our constitution and our habits of social management, habits that critics of the system are inclined to call "social engineering." The system first came into being in the second half of the nineteenth century, when there were very few governmentally funded programs.

The foundation world that came into being after the turn of the century was based on the assumption that there would be no government programs. While Progressive Era reformers were fighting to establish a federal presence protecting women in the labor force, children's health, and the debate over the unionization of workers, the data on which their public arguments depended and the development of methods for collecting and analyzing it came from privately funded sources. The Russell Sage Foundation, created in 1907, was, virtually until World War II, the major player in such fields of information gathering, along with the establishment of social work as a modern profession. The Rockefeller Foundation and the Rockefeller Medical Institute provided the major funding for medical research and the training of the medical profession. The Carnegie Corporation of New York was the funding behind major thinking in the field of education and race relations in the United States.

Private funding was the way the nation's public leaders kept themselves and the public abreast of problems and issues that the U.S. Congress would not have considered touching with the proverbial ten-foot pole, race relations, birth control, and venereal disease among them. Presidents of the United States and Justices of the Supreme Court depended on the research resources of private institutions for ideas and advice on criminal justice and labor relations, among other problematic areas. It is no accident that the creators of foundations were advised by lawyers and citizen leaders. Elihu Root, for example, served in presidential cabinets, held elected offices when appropriate, and moved easily in the foundation and philanthropic worlds. As a result, the relation between foundations and the federal government has been an abrasive one from the beginning and, deep down, both sides are better off that way.

As relationships go, it is a functional one with a few episodes of genuine respect, periodic moments of very close cooperation both sides are quick to conceal, and a certain amount of bitter hostility, but held together by a utility that may be too profound to be acknowledged by either side.

The distinction between public and private that undergirds so many of today's discussions is a twentieth century idea that would have had little meaning before the First World War. While we often refer to Tocqueville's admiration of American associations, he did not perceive them as private, only as nongovernmental groups with the power to act in the public interest. Translators have sometimes added the term "private" to his discussions of associations in order to make their point, even though it clearly wasn't his. Philanthropic foundations have long been considered private institutions by Americans who know anything about them at all. The distinction between public and private as we understand it today was not part of the vocabulary of the initial donors or of the lawyers who advised them. Donors before them had grown accustomed to dealing with the two major problems that troubled public acceptance of the uses of wealth for public purposes. One was the fear of corporate monopolies that seemed to threaten the rights of other individuals to form groups to engage in similar or even opposing public programs. The other was the belief among many Americans that the purposes of such corporations should be undertaken by the public itself through its legislatures, not by private individuals acting on their personal conceptions of public interest. Both were issues that preceded the anti-trust battles of the late nineteenth century but provided those battles with the historical underpinnings that gave them much of their energy and continued to complicate their meaning.[6]

The first steps in the movement toward privacy for foundations were thus a response to an unexpected critique, not a plan of action. Foundations would remain both private institutions and active influences on public policy. Congress would not charter them, but it would see to their regulation by 1917 by tax laws that did not exist at the time of their invention. It was really not until Congress began to feel threatened by the continuing power of foundations to influence public policy that the subject became part of open debate.

The nature of the attacks and the reasoning behind them have changed over time, although the range tends always to be the same. According to their critics, foundations have tended to promote liberal and radical causes and to reflect Gramscian Marxist control of popular opinion by scholars purchased by the wealth of hegemons.[7]

If one outlines the history of conflict and cooperation in the relation between foundations and the federal government, what one sees is a two-track system of support and hostility that can easily go on simultaneously. The supportive track is based on a view of politics as an elite operation separate from "politics" as self-interest bargaining and devoted to objective commitments to national well-being backed financially by well-off, educated citizens.

It was Wilson as President who appointed the first public committee, the Commission on Industrial Relations of 1913, that attacked the then-new foundations. Wilson saw foundations as many of the first generation of donors and managers saw them—more efficient and effective ways of doing what some among the post–Civil War holders of enormous wealth wanted to do with that wealth. Businessmen who saw the utility of applying standards of industrial efficiency to forms of charity they no longer found acceptable, men like Carnegie and John D. Rockefeller, still saw the money as theirs and accepted the fact that their staffs would look on their responsibilities similarly.

As President of Princeton, Wilson took his appeals for funding directly to donors. Carnegie rejected Wilson's efforts to get funding to upgrade living and social life for undergraduates, but insisted instead on giving Princeton a lake. Carnegie's Hero Fund was his way of working toward leadership, and it did not involve education at all. The fact that foundations were intended to exist in perpetuity and that the large ones would have staffs to manage them meant that there would be a gradual shift away from donor control to control by trustees and independent staffs. The system of self-perpetuating trustees was built on the assumption that a class of civic leaders would maintain itself intact. That was true until after World War II, but afterward one sees the old pattern emerging from time to time. The career path one can trace for McGeorge Bundy was classical: Harvard Society of Fellows (while he worked on the Henry Stimson Memoirs), the Dean of Faculties (although an educational product of Groton and Yale), National Security Advisor for Presidents Kennedy and Johnson, then to the presidency of the Ford Foundation, ending his career supported first by a professorship at NYU and then the Carnegie Corporation in his retirement. Academia, government, and foundation could serve as the three connecting points of an equilateral triangle. Although there was no fixed pattern of motion or direction, all three points were likely to be there in some form.

The historical question one must raise is why the political hostility, and at such an intermittent level from 1908 to the present. Although predicting the future is not a historical function, one can still ask if the hostility is likely to continue. Thus, the historical significance of the Rockefeller battle for a congressional charter is twofold. First, the congressional hostility to foundations began at the beginning. Second, it seems clear that the relation between public and private as both Carnegie and Rockefeller understood it was strikingly different from what we understand it to be today. Just to throw away a good line, had Rockefeller won his charter and had foundations from then on received charters from Congress with similar provisions, there would be no Third Sector today, and no one but a foolish generator of fantasies would talk about an Independent Sector. It's a good example of the way we accept as the logical outgrowth of the historical process practices that were in fact the product of accidental factors no one at the time could have predicted.

Put bluntly, the privacy of foundations is an accident of history, the effect of the anti-trust movement and its political exploiters on an effort by several wealthy Americans to use their wealth to make the federal government more responsive to human need. What happened then would be a pragmatic response to unanticipated criticism rather than evidence of the working out of Tocqueville's early observations about associations. The issue we should be looking at, then, even today, is the public responsibility of foundations in view of an independence forced on them by Congress.

Since the 1880s responsible theorists of social policy had been calling on the managers of the industrial world to pay attention to the needs of workers and the effects of their system of production on modern life. European countries were taking steps to deal with such issues. To be sure, their moral sensibilities were underscored by a fear of revolution by socialist leaders calling for some of the same attention to conditions.

The American situation was complicated by two factors. First, the federal government did not have national labor and industrial policies and was not about to create any. Second, and this is closely related, conditions in the southern states "recently in rebellion" limited what the federal and the state governments were willing or able to do for either poor whites or Negroes. Had federal action been possible, it would have removed traditionally enfranchised citizens' sense of local control. Northern philanthropists centered on education because that was understood as the major deficiency in the treatment of the poor in the South. Foundations were entering areas where a real vacuum in available public services existed and was recognized, but for which there was no possible chance of a national consensus that would enable the federal government to take over or even supplement those services. Southerners remained ambivalent at this invasion, but compromised as long as the actions enabled them to create a new, post-slavery separation of the races. While foundations have been castigated for funding southern racism, they did take an impossible position between a rock and a hard place and stick with it for the next six decades. The compromises that were to affect southern politics for the rest of the century necessitated leaving social policy to the states and local communities of the entire nation.

First, private donors and then, by the Depression, the federal government poured money into the South with the hope that it would help those who needed it but without any certainty that their intentions would be met by local politicians distributing federal resources. And they weren't, at least not in the short run. Modernizing the South meant short-changing African Americans.

Researchers in foundation archives have already discovered that northern philanthropists held many of the same racial views that were traditional in the South. There were differences among the Northerners that we today have little sympathy for; but they were significant in placing a floor under southern unwillingness to improve conditions for Negroes. More important as a generalization about foundation behavior, northern donors found ways of bypassing the absence of consensus by avoiding the trip wires that would detonate opposition. Only those who remember the role foundations played in promoting voter registration drives in the 1960s know how strong those trip wires were and how damaging and destructive the detonations could be.

Even in the 1920s support of birth control, medical services for infants and mothers, and the political power of women were mediated by new and powerful organizations tangled together in a web of opposition that was in need of private support. The League of Women Voters, Planned Parenthood, the increasingly powerful American Medical Association, and an underground movement for sex education in the public schools promoted originally by Mrs. Russell Sage twenty years earlier came together to build little armistices that recognized the tricks of avoiding wars no one could win.

Congress had tried to stop presidents from using outside funding for policy ideas as early as the Taft administration by placing riders in legislation forbidding the solicitation of such funds. Like many of the quasi-constitutional efforts on the part of Congress to stop the growth of presidential power, it never reached the courts for adjudication and presidents simply ignored it, relying correctly on the fact that there weren't that many politicians who were worried about it as long as it didn't affect their immediate interests. Herbert Hoover became a master at fund-raising for such purposes and even celebrated it in press releases. Roosevelt, having decided that businessmen made useful enemies, let others do the solicitation for him and set up carefully hidden drops to conceal his use of foundation funds.

Since 1900 the role of philanthropy has been institutionalized in its relation not only to citizen needs but to the political culture in which we live. What we may need is a way of understanding that relationship and the institutions that have guided it over the last century. It is possible to see some fixed habits in both government and the foundation world that are not as changeable as some of us once thought. American government is perhaps the most volatile in the modern world, given the sensitivity of American political leaders to public will and the public's shifting sense of its own needs. The public, too, is changing as it accommodates new groups, empowers old groups, and acts on the basis of anger produced by specific incidents. Despite the efforts of news media to interpret these events as part of some overall logic, they are only the consequences of a jumble we struggle to put in order.

Congressional concerns before the 1950s had focused on the threat of political influence through contributions to individual campaigns. That concern was reflected first in the Tax Act of 1935, the so-called "soak the rich" bill that actually made the creation of foundations much easier and of much greater use for those protecting their estates from taxation. Congress still did not want to issue charters for foundations, but this bill made it possible to start a foundation during a donor's lifetime and earmark a portion of the estate for inclusion at the time of the death of the donor.

Congressional investigations in the 1950s, Cox in 1952 and Reece two years later, directed attention to two very different criticisms of the foundation world. The first could characterize all American politics: that it was open to corruption by those who were prepared to use the opportunity to sequester wealth to cheat the government of the taxes due it. A tone of populist critique in the Cox investigation was an interesting modernization of the criticism that had been part of the view of the very wealth that had created foundations in the first place. The second criticism, expressed in the Reece hearings, epitomized the McCarthy era; it brought foundations under attack for their supposed support of left-wing causes, and took the stand that foundations reflected ideological positions that ran counter to the traditions of American politics.

Foundation-funded activities began arousing our sense of conspiracy when we got to the Cold War and the foundation funding of CIA programs in eastern Europe and east African educational exchanges involving the Peace Corps. Congress would not have allowed academic travel to eastern Europe, let alone funded it, and it was deemed essential that the United States have a

Filer Commission

presence there. It was only after the fact, when American members of meetings and exchanges discovered their unintended complicity, that some of them got angry. Involvement of foundations with the federal government was a utilitarian practice that worked best behind the scenes, out of the public eye. It was there from the beginning, but it was no one's first choice. What makes the story interesting is that the public furor raised by successive congressional investigations provided the only visible background that made it into the newspapers and that defined the role of foundations for that small portion of the public that even cared to know about it.[8] After foundations began supporting voter registration drives in the South, critics outside of Congress like Alabama governor George Wallace were pressing for both protection and revenge. When it looked as though a forty-year limit on the life of foundations was going to pass Congress, foundations called in their legal forces and began a remarkable lobbying campaign that removed the provision. It was a campaign without precedents. The resulting Tax Act of 1969 could have been a lot worse.

Events surrounding the Tax Act of 1969 made many of the congressional figures in the debate aware of concerns that led even critics of foundations to consider what they considered the unfairness generated by the political heat. The act set requirements for annual spending and reports to the federal government, some of which were ultimately believed to be needlessly punitive and costly for foundations. Some of the requirements necessitated staff enlargement to provide programs for yearly "payout." The authorization of Program Related Investments allowing foundations to lend money for urban redevelopment, which normal banking would not consider, was a useful novelty that has continued to spur urban improvement. In any case, by 1983 Rangle and the Committee on Oversight of the House of Representatives' Committee on Ways and Means led to corrective action.

The Filer Commission's suggestion of an office in the executive branch devoted to the impact of foundations on policy recognized them as quasi-governmental institutions rather than leaving them in the control of the IRS. A post in the executive branch would have acknowledged the utility of foundations to governmental policy-making and given them official governmental standing. No one seemed to know that that was what Rockefeller and Carnegie had wanted in the first place, but never mind. What the powers in the foundation world decided was that it would also void their precious if artificial independence and damage the future possibility of corporate foundations and what was then perceived, inaccurately as it turned out, as the limited number of foundations yet to be born. At that stage the Internal Revenue Service was viewed by foundations as a benign regulator willing to stick with simple statements of fact, even grateful for foundation help in framing regulations of institutions the Service did not yet see as important to their mission.

The Filer Commission's suggestion may be the last effort at a rational approach to foundations as policy institutions rather than as inheritors of the philanthropic traditions of charity in America. It was a major step forward that would, in the aftermath of the Reagan presidency, become a remarkable step backward. The post-1980 approach to philanthropy, encapsulated over the decades since under rubrics like "taking up the slack" and "a thousand points of light," was in effect an effort to return philanthropy to what might even be the pre-foundation era. While any such intention was never explicit, the ultimate inability of the foundation world to acknowledge the impossibility of the assignment—replacing government-supported welfare with private philanthropy—did not become part of a clearly articulated opposition. The absence of a continuing examination of the problem after the initial shock wave has made discussion of the unacceptable alternative impossible.

Since 1994 congressional opposition has been divided into specific issues, in some instances the question of advocacy groups and the Istook Amendment as a somewhat different form of an old political concern over foundation funding of political debates. The placing of advocacy in the same camp as industrial lobbying, in effect, shows either the depth of the opposition or the shallowness of the understanding of what advocacy groups do when they provide those in need with organized support. White House programs extolling volunteerism degenerate into public relations campaigns that separate voluntary charitable acts from the basic involvement in public policy such acts have always reflected. Foundations, meanwhile, move cautiously like post-earthquake occupants returning to buildings that may collapse with a wrong footstep or shift in balance. The paradox inherent in the present state of affairs rests on the inability to reconcile the calls for involvement in voluntary action and charitable support of those in need with the fear that philanthropy holds within it the seeds of a revolution no one seems to understand.

The relation among foundations, the culture of philanthropy in the United States, and the role of congressional politics in the shaping of policies relating to the state of the nation's citizenry at every stage of human development, from the proverbial cradle to the grave, involves a delicate balance. There does seem to be a continuity in the issues, in our methods of dealing with them, and in our seeming inability to create acceptable guidelines that will give those who govern us and those who want to use their wealth for the public good a common ground on which to stand. Several very general points may help us understand the ground that has developed over the last century and suggest the direction we are most likely to take.

It is possible to see some fixed habits in both government and the foundation world that are not as changeable as some of us once thought. American government is perhaps the most volatile in the modern world, given the sensitivity of political leaders to public will and the public's shifting sense of its own needs. The public, too, is a changing body as it accommodates new groups, empowers old groups once restricted from self-control, and acts on the basis of anger produced by specific incidents: the selection of a Justice for the

Supreme Court, a statement by a public official not intended to be heard by the press, or the emergence of a new leader who has nothing to offer but an ability to put their uneasiness into words that sparkle and cut. The proximity of any such event to an election may make all the difference in the world. Despite the efforts of news media to interpret these events as part of some overall logic, they are only that after the fact, the consequences of a jumble we all struggle to put in order.

At its best, the foundation world is a world of plans and programs that are independent of calendars and capable of being much more reflective of long-range needs. Those needs are defined by ideas, particular kinds of ideas — ideas that will produce actions the effectiveness of which can be observed and judged. Despite the long association of foundations with scientific research, the research supported by foundations is confined for the most part to utility. Over the years the utilitarian frameworks have been broadened to include the arts as well as the sciences, and, most important of all, to respond to public needs insofar as they fit into the existing framework set up by the foundation. That response to public interest is not of recent origin; it was proposed by the founders of Russell Sage in 1907 and by the Rockefellers in 1915. It has been used by the Bush Foundation of St. Paul for the last twenty years. The reasons for its introduction were different then than they became in the 1970s. The earlier public interest designs were based on the belief that foundation programs that lacked public support would fail, not on the later idea that foundations had a responsibility to serve the public; but the difference between the two public perspectives is more difficult to define than it might seem at first glance. After all, getting public support is a form of responsibility, and listening to public expressions of need is a highly selective operation that can begin with a plastic cup in an outstretched hand and move toward the calling of a public meeting headed by a self-selecting group. It is still the foundation that selects the needs to be addressed. That freedom to select is its essential distinction from government.

The problem is that selection requires the ability both to distinguish one idea from another and to know when new ones are needed. The generation that created the first foundations had two very remarkable virtues. The first was that they knew that ideas were nothing more than tools they had to find in the heads of other people. They approached ideas with a strong sense of function and no awe whatsoever. They paid for them and expected to use them as they chose. Assembling shifting communities of people who could provide them was easier and cheaper than drilling for oil and making steel. The second was that they had complete faith in their own powers of judgment. The process of doing good was different from the process of making money. It was not a calculable end, and it had an infinite flexibility. It thus was a process, not an end, and it had nothing to do with profits and everything to do with charitable deeds that were consistent with the oldest biblical demands.

One has to take very seriously John D. Rockefeller's belief that giving money away was much harder than making it. It required a very different kind of judgment and a monumental patience his son often found very trying. Ironically, his son is understood as being a far more devout man than his father; yet his father's faith, like Carnegie's in its very different way, was not essentially institutional or routinized. It had that confidence which was committed to being shrewd and solidly simple without being very knowledgeable. All of the first industrial philanthropists were very clear on one central point: philanthropy was not a business engagement and business was not philanthropic. The carryovers from their business practices to their philanthropic ones are far more complex and so are the distinctions. And they understood the distinction far better than any of the rest of us, who occupy only one of their worlds, have been able to understand it.

One has to expand the atmosphere of 1969 to include both the Peterson and Filer Commissions over the previous years of discussion in the foundation world itself. The idea of an office in the executive branch devoted to foundations and nonprofits would have recognized the quasi-governmental policy-making aspect of both rather than leaving them in the control of the IRS and periodic battles with ad hoc congressional committees. To put it as succinctly as possible, John D. Rockefeller 3rd, the main figure in such discussions, believed it possible to build an independent philanthropic world that would use the best of the nation's minds to chart a new course. He did not believe that such a world would be "like" business or charity. There is much to be learned from his sense of the intellectual and organizational structures philanthropy would have to develop.

Today's emphasis on measurement and evaluation and on the growing interest in management control is very different from the philanthropy that donors supported from the beginning. It moves back to the very industrial methodologies that the old donors knew to be necessarily counter to the good works they were working to modernize. It also moves closer to the political interests for which they had come to see themselves as a countervailing power; and if there is any ground for prophecy in our views of the past, one can be sure it will trip wires that have endangered the system before. What may seem worrisome as we look back at the Tax Act of 1969 and the lobbying effort foundations were able to manage is that its cost was high. As is sometimes the case in our volatile political world, part of that cost may well be political leaders who now know more of the ropes than they used to and who can therefore build new alliances that could be even more damaging than they were in 1969.

Ever since 1969, and particularly since the opening of the Reagan administration, the call for philanthropy in general and the foundation world in particular to "take up the slack" has played around the relation between foundations and government like Casper the Friendly Ghost, obviously eager to be loving and sociable, but surprised at the alarm he seems to raise. Only the alarm is remarkably selective and time bound. On October 5, 1981, President Reagan appointed a President's Task Force on Private Sector Initiatives, with William Verity, chairman of the board of Armco, Inc., of Middletown, Ohio, and recently Chairman of the U.S. Chamber of Commerce. In the latter role, Verity had headed a program to stimulate businessmen to press for the election of local representatives and to review federal spending. The issue of *Foundation News* which appeared a month after the announcement of the committee assembled a collection of commentaries so filled with dissent that they scarcely concealed the anger and sense of hopelessness on the part of supporters of social programs of the previous decade. The cautious promises from those who must themselves have realized the impossibility of the President's request seemed hollow. As Nick Kotz, a former reporter for the *Washington Post* and the *Des Moines Register*, put it, "The public is generally unaware that the $40 billion 1981 cutback in federal aid to social services and community development exceeds by 20-fold the total annual foundation spending and corporate giving in this area."[9]

Yet that was fifteen years ago and the election of 1994 was nothing but a date on the calendar. A Republican was President and beginning what we now know to have been a decade and a half of efforts to accomplish what has finally been accomplished, and under a Democratic President: end welfare as we have known it; transform medical care; and, more broadly but less often stated, bring the excesses of the Great Society to an end. Devolution has now become a newly acceptable term and its future an undeniable fact. To be sure, that applies to federal programs, not to philanthropy, but if the line between them is as historically consistent as I have been suggesting, the problem is emerging, or will emerge, or, most likely of all, will be turned into another problem that foundations will have to face. Why? Because foundations, like it or not, have borne the burden of criticism for the efforts of American policymakers to formulate programs of social support. They will get it if they do nothing at all, and they will get it for whatever they do. The only real question is whether what they do contributes to public understanding of the historical changes in which they have been forced to participate.

For a century now it is been possible for leadership in the foundation world to play that role, but it has never been an easy one. For foundations have never been as brave as some of us have wanted them to be or as cowardly as some of us have feared. As this description of their origins has suggested, they are too mired in the mechanisms of our peculiar form of governance to be either one. When their history forces them to choose between self-abnegation and attack, they risk the failure of seeing how utterly impossible that choice really is. It is a strange and unsatisfying role to play, but it may be closer to the realities of our volatile American culture than we will ever be able to understand with anything approaching historical, let alone scientific, clarity. It is for that reason that John D. Rockefeller's failure to get his charter is one of the great moments in foundation history, with the grandest of unintended consequences: it determined the character of the debates over philanthropy and public policy that have driven a century of argument.

When historian Robert Bremner's *American Philanthropy* appeared in 1960 it established what was in effect the model for the way in which American foundations had been operating since their inception at the turn of the century. Foundations and local communities would experiment with social programs that showed promise and watch them for signs of utility and innovation. Those that proved themselves sound would then be adopted by local and state governments and, ultimately, by the federal government. Foundations and philanthropic donors would then move their resources to new projects as local needs directed, and the process would continue. So progressive a model was a logical outgrowth of progressivism, science, and the dreams of scientific replication, and of the optimism built into Progressive reform. The Great Society was in all respects the high point of that cooperative image.[10]

Two questions had been raised all along. Like all of the descendants of America's long flirtation with Progressive reform, the system was, in varying degrees, both apolitical and anti-political. Local political leaders looking for pork-barrel opportunities for their states and communities could find themselves facing a reform opposition that was as old as the job patronage of the Jacksonian era and as continuous as the conservation movement that changed its name generation after generation, perhaps in a half-conscious effort to foil the enemies it made each time around. The second and related opposition came from the careerism of American politics — the money it took to establish a political career and the need to sustain that career from election to election, a need that grew as men and now women saw the conflict between the reform promises that got them elected in the first place and the compromises that sustaining families, educating their young, and assuring protections for retirement and old age required. Reform models that rested on scientific designs and intellectual needs foundered on shoals everyone recognized and no one wanted to change for fear that a new model would exclude them without achieving the ends it promised. Intellect was only part of the body politic. Sustaining the body called for meeting other needs, not all of which looked good in headlines.

The revolution that began in 1981 has continued over the years, and now dominates our understanding of the roles of the three sectors by emphasizing the distinction between public and private and placing up front the assumption that much that was then considered public could be taken over by the private sector. This has become the primary direction of debate. Whether one speaks of "devolution" or "privatizing," one speaks in a language of discourse that is very different from that of two decades ago and vastly different from the entire century of foundation history. While one can certainly argue the possible artificiality of the tripartite distinction in the first place, one cannot avoid the consequences of the proposed dissolutions and reconfigurations that appear when one introduces a level of change that no one seems inclined to admit. It would be hard to deny the incredible effectiveness of the foundation world in providing government with direction, personnel, and methods of examining consequences of change over time. The same is true of what are now known as not-for-profit organizations which foundations have supported. At the same time, private enterprise in the form of corporate contributions to philanthropic needs has always fallen short of what its proponents have hoped for. Also lacking in the corporate world is an intellectual structure that is suitable for philanthropic programs. Profit is not only a standard of measurement in this world; it is a way of life. Carnegie and generations of Rockefellers acknowledged that when they chose to separate their philanthropies from their corporate interests. The seeming ruthlessness that drew them into congressional battles in the first place was a tacit acceptance of the necessity of separating private enterprise from public good.

The entry of ideology has corrupted debates that existed before ideas of conservatism and liberalism joined the fray. It damages a rich dispute by replacing worthy complexity with rigid hostilities, as though a right and a left were somehow realities that had governed the dispute all along. What government can or should do is an American dilemma that is now more than two centuries old. As some historians have repeatedly tried to point out, it has always had less to do with ideas than with practical realities. Those realities rest entirely and exclusively on the availability of opportunities. All three sectors have made their appropriate contribution to those opportunities, taking over from one another and for one another when the need seemed to call for it. Foundations have played a special and continuing role in that process for the last century now. Brought into being by an awareness of lacunae in the openings for new classes of citizens seeking their share, they helped move government into areas where the need was the greatest and the political opposition the weakest. Mistaken readings have generated battles that bring the system into balance for a time, sometimes by threatening its future as a system. American political conflict takes place in a language that is rarely less than life threatening.

Devolution and the Contract with America met needs that bore a strange relation to the Bremner model of philanthropic social reform. If the social sciences had failed to bring about the triumphs in the war against poverty, disease, and mis-education, where else was one to look? In other sciences, most notably medicine, failure signaled the call for more research, new research, studies of failure and success that called on the research community to return to its drawing boards. That did not seem true of social reform and the research on which it was based. As a new model, the Contract with America called for a rejection of the past, a placing of a premium on self-gratification, and an end to reform. The only possible changes seemed to be those that promised to do no harm, that holy vow of the medical profession that was itself under attack by those seeking population control—one of the oldest of the systems of concern supported by philanthropy—and the management of death now that the power to extend life had itself become a major social problem.

The new donors are already suggesting that there will be changes. Unlike the generation a century ago, many are educated in the systems to which they are being asked to contribute, and they will not be innocent of what they perceive as its defects. Like that first generation they will want to control what is done with their wealth; but will they be as confident that future leaders will follow their wishes? Self-perpetuating boards of trustees are no longer an endless hall of mirrors that reflect common beliefs and certify common standards of value and behavior. There was a certain nobility in their acknowl-edgment of the unknowable future that leaders of the future would have to manage; but it is unlikely that they saw the speed and momentum of change that now seems to us a norm. Perpetuity was a different measurement of time for them. The Bible was a common text, however much they may have disagreed with one another on its interpretation.

The new generation of business leaders has already begun to point in directions that bear interesting relations to the Program Related Investments of 1969. Again, the business analogy is being raised to define what is un-derstood as a reshaping of the role of foundations in helping grantees to achieve their ends more effectively. In an article entitled "Virtuous Capital: What Foundations Can Learn from Venture Capitalists," Christine Letts of Harvard's Hauser Center for Nonprofit Organizations and her colleagues propose closer relations between foundations and donees that would parallel the steps followed by venture capitalists in starting new enterprises and leading them to productive independence. Such steps would require partici-pation in management, and service on boards of trustees, along with critical involvement in the ways staff would develop in the process of utilizing funds.[11] While the questions of control and punishment for failure rest benignly at the sidelines of their argument, the very idea was sufficient to generate a critical response from some of the most knowledgeable people in the nonprofit and foundation world. Bruce Sievers, president of one of San Francisco's leading foundations, saw the difficulties involved in what might well have been perceived as a revolution against one of foundation philanthropy's oldest dicta: find good minds and give them the freedom to work without interference. That was the classical position that evolved out of the Rockefeller philanthropies quite explicitly, and implicitly in the ap-proach McGeorge Bundy and his generation had taken at Ford.[12] And Pablo Eisenberg, certainly one of the nation's leaders in the effort of the managers of nonprofits to press on donors the need to look for and encourage imagina-tive independence on the part of donees, saw into the shadows such virtue could cast on the worlds of others like himself.[13]

The historical resonance of the debate may be considerably richer and intellectually more profound than the fears it generates. Letts and her colleagues may be bringing logic and a sense of order to changes which are already taking place and which are likely to be much more important in the future. There have been similar movements in the foundation world itself over the last two decades, although the debate is, like the Letts debate, epicentered in board rooms and lawyers' offices, and at the lunch tables of those who have been overseeing changes in foundations and their management over those years. What critics see as "micromanagement" is already present among foundation officers who see the need to direct what is done with the grants they give. What began in the aftermath of '69 as a need to report foundation activities to the federal government in more detail, or at least the need to be prepared to be questioned about it, has met with an internal need to focus more tightly on what is done with funds for which foundations are responsible. That focus, in turn, has met up with the court cases here and there, particularly in the field of medical research, which hold foundations responsible for experiments carried out after World War II that, over the years, may prove potentially dangerous to subjects. Those were exciting and promising years, years before the age of informed consent, say, when it was unclear where the controls really were. If the doctors and the hospitals are to be held responsible, should the donors be responsible as well?

These are potentially "chilling" questions, as today's pop-legal language has it. They go far deeper into the problems of responsibility than virtuous intent can ever cover. If they point to a new need to make the distinctions John D. Rockefeller 3rd was intent on making, will those frameworks of independence still hold? Can foundations and donors refuse to meddle in such an environment?

The next two decades will be crucial in utilizing and reshaping the system. If the transfer of wealth destined to take place over that period is to join the system or produce a new system of its own, it would be useful to understand both the virtues and the defects of what we have established over the last century. The worlds of public and private are significantly disjoined, at least for the moment, and for the first time in the history of the philanthropic foundation the search for leadership and intelligent management appears to be in a state of crisis. Gerald Freund's *Narcissism and Philanthropy* raises again questions of leadership to which a previous generation of philanthropic managers had sought their era's answers. Freund represented an older generation of philanthropoids who had built the old world of the profession.[14] The two collections of Robert Greenleaf's essays published in 1996 take us down some of the same roads with different landscapes.[15] Greenleaf was a businessman trustee who shared the commitment to faith that one could no longer find at the center of the field. His emphasis on religion and his sense of the necessary parallels between religion and philanthropy seem old-fashioned until one looks at the history from which philanthropy comes.[16] Guides for training leaders have been with us for millennia now, only the older ones recognize the need to understand the character required of all leaders, and much of it has less to do with ethics than it does with power. Many would think that true of politics as well, which may take us back to the most fundamental questions of all.

Notes

1. Marion R. Fremont-Smith, *Foundations and Government: State and Federal Law and Supervision* (New York: Russell Sage Foundation, 1965).

2. Graham Adams, Jr., *Age of Industrial Violence, 1910–1915: The Activities and Findings of the Commission on Industrial Relations* (1966).

3. Raymond B. Fosdick, *The Story of the Rockefeller Foundation* (New Brunswick, NJ: Transaction, 1989).

4. Charles A. Murray, *Losing Ground: American Social Policy 1950–1980* (New York: Basic Books, 1984).

5. Peter Dobkin Hall, "Cultures of Trusteeship in the United States." In *Inventing the Nonprofit Sector* (Baltimore, MD: The Johns Hopkins University Press, 1992), 135–205.

6. Alexis de Tocqueville, "On the Use Which Americans Make of Associations in Civil Life." In *Democracy in America*, ed. J. P. Mayer, trans. George Lawrence (New York: Doubleday Anchor, 1969).

7. Barry D. Karl and Stanley N. Katz, "Foundations and Ruling Class Elites," *Daedalus*, Winter 1987.

8. Christopher Lasch, "The Cultural Cold War." In *The Agony of the American Left*, ed. Christopher Lasch (New York: Alfred A. Knopf, 1968), 63–114.

9. Nick Kotz, *Foundation News*, November–December 1981, p. 13.

10. Robert H. Bremner, *American Philanthropy* (Chicago: University of Chicago Press, 1960).

11. Christine W. Letts, William Ryan, and Allen Grossman, "Virtuous Capital: What Foundations Can Learn from Venture Capitalists." *Harvard Business Review*, March–April 1997, 2–7.

12. Bruce Sievers, "If Pigs Had Wings." *Foundation News and Commentary*, November–December 1997 (1997): 44–46.

13. Pablo Eisenberg, "Venture-Capital Philanthropy: Good and Bad." *The Chronicle of Philanthropy*, August 21, 1997, 35.

14. Gerald Freund, *Narcissism and Philanthropy* (New York: Viking, 1996).

15. Robert K. Greenleaf, *On Becoming a Servant Leader*, ed. Don M. Frick and Larry C. Spears (San Francisco: Jossey-Bass, 1996).

16. Robert K. Greenleaf, *Seeker and Servant, Reflections on Religious Leadership*, ed. Anne T. Fraker and Larry C. Spears (San Francisco: Jossey-Bass, 1996).

CHAPTER FOUR

The Economy and Philanthropy

Edward Wolff

Charitable giving has been growing in the United States in recent years. In 1995 (the last year in my time series), it was at an all-time high, both in total and per person and as a share of income. In this chapter, I explore some of the factors that may be contributing to this upturn in philanthropy.

One can think of three general kinds of factors that affect philanthropy. The first is the level of disposable resources in the hands of the population. This might be thought of as the "supply of charitable contributions." Resources reflect not only the income flows generated in the economy each year but also the wealth of the population. We would therefore expect that as the income and wealth of society increase over time, so will the amount of charitable giving. However, we might expect more than a proportional relation between income or wealth growth and the change in charitable donations. This would be the case if richer families gave not only more money in absolute terms but a higher share of their income or wealth than poorer families.

The second factor is the "cost or price of giving." As is well known, for families that itemize their deductions on the personal income tax return, the net cost of donating a dollar is one minus their marginal tax rate.[1] We might thus expect that as tax rates rise, charitable giving might likewise increase. Support for this argument can be found in a wide range of literature (see Clotfelter, 1985; Joulfaian, 1991; Auten, Cilke, and Randolph, 1992; and Auten, Clotfelter, and Schmalbeck, 1997).

The first two factors are fairly standard in most statistical analyses of giving and are referred to as the "income effect" and "price effect," respectively (see, for example, Clotfelter, 1997). The third factor, which is less standard, may relate to the perceived needs of the populace. This might be thought of as the "demand for charitable donations." As we will see below, much of charitable donations goes to religious organizations, and another large portion goes to educational institutions and to the arts and cultural institutions. This type of giving is not likely to be affected by trends in the economy. Moreover, as Odendahl (1990) suggests, the philanthropic rich are particularly motivated to donate to these types of institutions because they help to service their own needs (such as contributions to an opera company).

However, donations oriented toward human services may indeed be affected by economic trends. In particular, a rising overall poverty rate might induce higher income families to contribute more money for social purposes. Correspondingly, lower support for the poor from government agencies might also induce more philanthropy. We might thus expect that charitable giving will also rise when average welfare (AFDC) benefits or other forms of public assistance fall. This latter effect is also referred to as "crowding out" in the literature, and the evidence to date does suggest that this effect exists but it is relatively small in magnitude (see, for example, Kingma, 1989, and Brown and Lankford, 1992).

The supply and demand effects suggest that philanthropy will be high when there exist a large number of rich families and a large number of poor people as well. This might suggest that charitable giving will increase as the degree of overall economic inequality rises. We will explore the relation between charitable donations and trends in both income and wealth inequality.

Postwar Trends in Income, Wealth, Poverty, and Inequality

Before discussing trends in philanthropic giving, it is helpful to review what has happened to income, poverty, and inequality in the U.S. since the end of World War II. This is, of course, important for its own sake. It is also important both because charitable giving is presumably motivated by a desire to help the poor and because rising income and wealth are a source of charitable donations. As a result, these time trends are germane for assessing the motivation for giving and, perhaps, the moral content of philanthropy.

The last quarter century has witnessed some disturbing changes in the average standard of living, poverty, and inequality in the United States. As shown in Figure 1, median family income (the income of the average family, found in the middle of the distribution when families are ranked from lowest to highest in terms of income) grew by 8.1 percent in real terms between 1973 and 1989 but then declined by 2.3 percent between 1989 and 1996, for a net gain of only 5.6 percent.[2] In contrast, between 1947 and 1973, median family income more than doubled. Personal disposable income (personal income

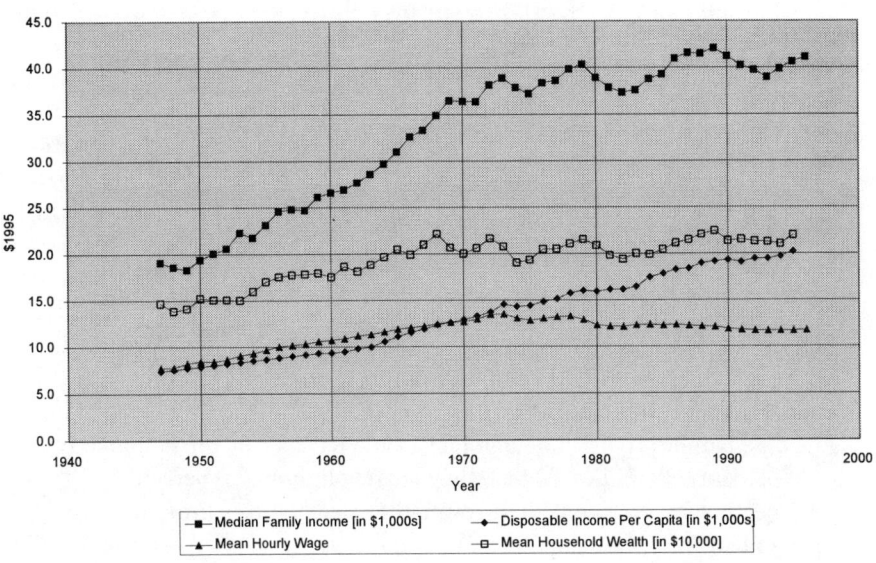

Figure 1. Income, Earnings, and Wealth,
1947-1996

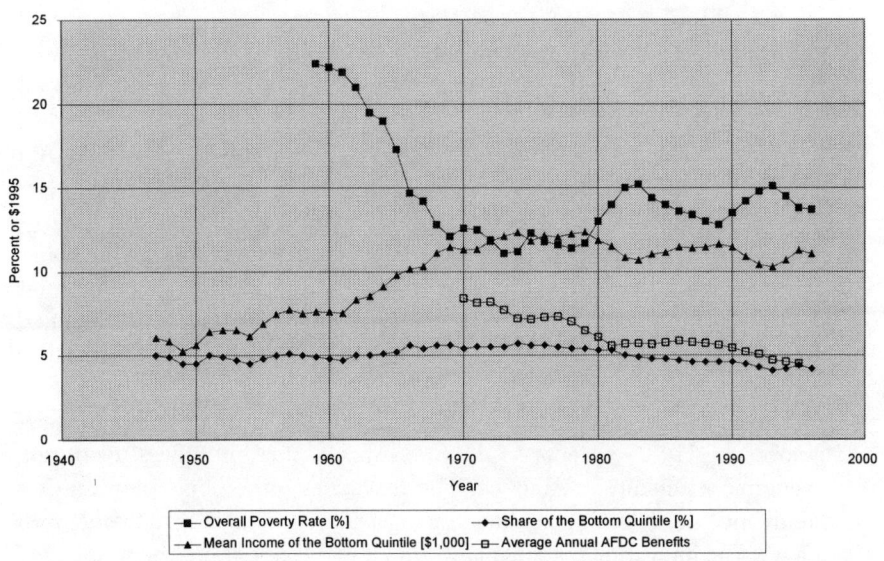

Figure 2. The Poverty Rate, the Share and Mean Income of the Bottom Quintile, and AFDC Benefits,
1947-1996

less tax payments) per capita, after doubling from 1947 to 1973, increased by only 39 percent in the succeeding 23 years. Likewise, average household wealth, after surging by 41 percent over this earlier period, gained only another 5.8 percent in the latter years.

The main reason for this turnaround is that the real wage (average wages and salaries adjusted for inflation) has been falling since 1973. Between 1973 and 1996, the real wage fell by 13 percent. This contrasts with the preceding years, 1947 to 1973, when real wages grew by 75 percent. Indeed, in 1995, the real wage was $11.69 per hour, about the same level as in 1964 (in real terms).

Another troubling change is with regard to poverty. Between 1959 and 1973, there was great success in reducing poverty in America, with the overall poverty rate declining by more than half, from 22.4 to 11.1 percent (see Figure 2). Since then, the poverty rate has generally trended upward, climbing to 15.1 percent in 1993 and then falling slightly, to 13.8 percent in 1995, about the same level as in 1967. Another indicator of the well-being of lower income families is the share of total income received by the bottom quintile (20 percent) of families. At first, their share fell, from 5.0 percent in 1947 to 4.7 percent in 1961, but then rose rather steadily over time, reaching 5.7 percent in 1974, but since then has fallen off rather sharply, reaching 4.4 percent in 1995.

A related statistic is the mean income of the poorest 20 percent of families (in 1995 dollars), which shows the absolute level of well-being of this group (the share of income shows the *relative* level of well-being). Their average income more than doubled between 1947 and 1974, from $6,000 to $12,300, but then fell by 9 percent, to $11,100 in 1996. The difference in post-1974 trends between this series and the share of income of the bottom quintile, which fell much more sharply, is that mean income was rising in the general population after 1974.

Another indicator of deprivation is the average monthly family AFDC (Aid to Families with Dependent Children) benefit received. AFDC or welfare as it is more typically called covers only a small proportion of the poor— historically about 5 percent of the population or about one-third of the poor.[3] However, it is a good indicator of the level of resources available to the most destitute section of the our society Average AFDC benefits have declined drastically over time, from $699 in 1995 dollars a month in 1970 (the first date available for the series) to $376 in 1995.

The United States has also witnessed a disagreeable turnaround in inequality over the last 25 years or so. Figure 3 shows different indices measuring economic inequality in America. The first series is the Gini coefficient for family income. The Gini coefficient ranges from a value of zero to one, with a low value indicating less inequality and a high value more. Between 1947 and 1968, it generally trended downward, reaching its lowest value in 1968, at 0.348. Since then, it has experienced an upward ascent, gradually at first

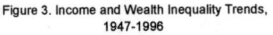

Figure 3. Income and Wealth Inequality Trends, 1947-1996

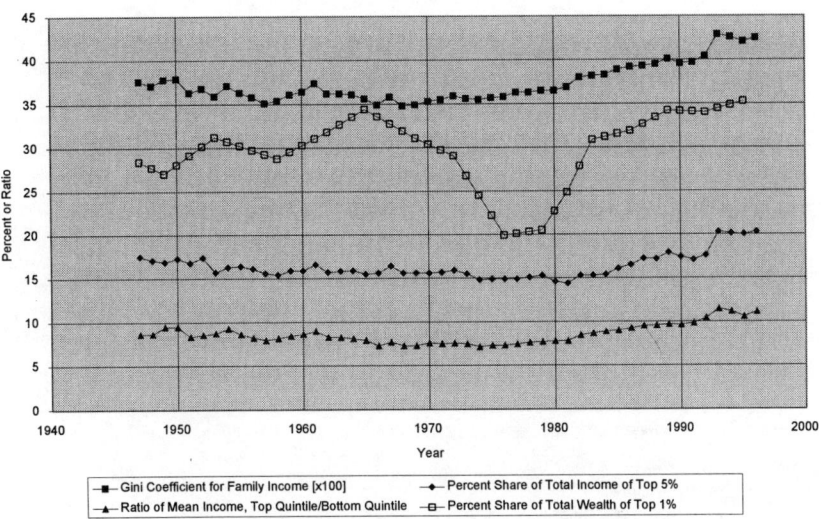

and then more steeply in the 1980s and 1990s, culminating at its peak value of 0.425 in 1996.

The second index, the share of total income received by the top 5 percent of families, has a similar time trend. It fell gradually, from 17.5 percent in 1947 to 14.8 percent in 1974, and then rose after this point, especially in the 1990s, reaching its highest value in 1996, 20.3 percent. The third index is the ratio of the average income of the richest 20 percent of families to that of the poorest 20 percent. It measures the spread in income between these two groups. This index generally falls between 1947 and 1974, from 8.6 to 7.1, and then trends steadily upward, reaching 11.1 in 1996.

The fourth indicator is wealth inequality, as measured by the share of total personal wealth owned by the richest 1 percent of households. It shows a somewhat different pattern, generally trending downward from 28.4 percent in 1947 to 19.9 percent in 1976 and then rising steeply thereafter, reaching 35.3 percent in 1993.

To complete the background information, I also show trends in marginal tax rates, since this affects the price of giving (see Figure 4). The first series is the top marginal tax rate (the marginal tax rate faced by the richest tax filers). Back in 1944, the top marginal tax rate was 94 percent! After the end of World War II, the top rate was reduced to 86.5 percent (in 1946), but during the Korean War it was soon back to 92 percent (in 1953). Even in 1960, it was still at 91 percent. This generally declined over time, as various tax legislation was implemented by Congress. It was first lowered to 70 percent in 1966, then

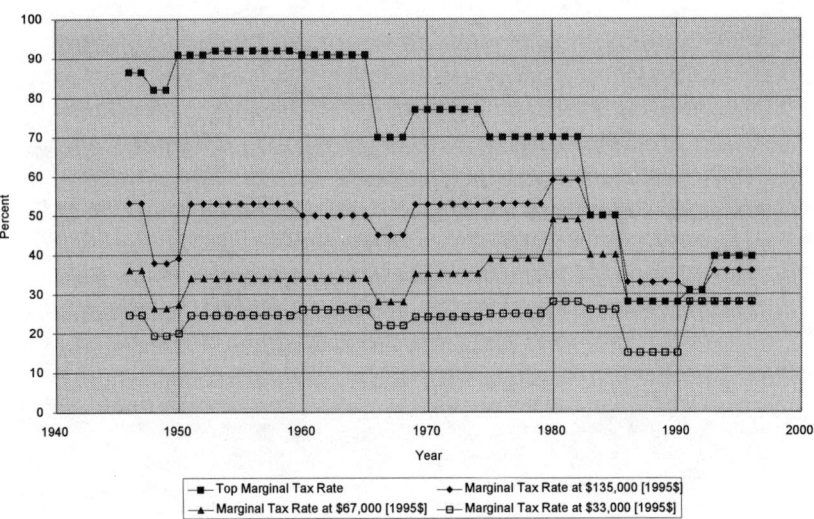

Figure 4. Marginal Tax Rates at Selected Income Levels (in 1995$), 1946-1996

raised to 77 percent in 1969 to finance the Vietnam War, then lowered again to 70 percent in 1975, then to 50 percent in 1983 (Reagan's first major tax act), and then again to 28 percent in 1986 (through the famous Tax Reform Act of 1986). Since then, it has trended upward, to 31 percent in 1991 (under President Bush) and then to 39.6 percent in 1993 (under President Clinton).

The second series shows the marginal tax rate faced by filers with an income of $135,000 in 1995 dollars. This income level typically includes families at the ninety-fifth percentile (the top 5 percent). This series generally has the same trajectory as the first, declining in 1966, rising in 1975, falling in 1983 and 1986, and then increasing in 1991 and again in 1993.

The last two series show the marginal tax rates at $67,000 and $33,000, respectively, both in 1995 dollars. The time patterns are quite a bit different for these than the first two. The marginal tax rate at $67,000 (about the sixtieth percentile) was relatively low in 1946, at 36 percent, generally trended upward, reaching 49 percent in 1980, before declining to 28 percent in 1986, where it has remained ever since. The marginal tax rate at $33,000 (about the thirtieth percentile) was also relatively low in 1946, at 25 percent, but it actually increased somewhat over time, reaching 28 percent in 1991 and since remaining at this level.

All in all, tax cuts over the postwar period have been much more generous for the rich, particularly the super-rich. Since 1946, the top marginal tax rate has fallen by more than half (54 percent), the marginal rate at $135,000 by 32 percent, the marginal rate at $67,000 by 35 percent, and the rate at $33,000 by only 13 percent.

In sum, the last 25 years or so have seen stagnating earnings and income, rising poverty, and rising inequality. In contrast, the early postwar period witnessed rapid gains in both wages and family income, a sharp decline in poverty, and a moderate fall in inequality. Personal tax rates have generally fallen over time but by much more for the rich than the middle class.

Trends in Giving, 1955–1995

I draw my data on philanthropic contributions from the *Statistical Abstract of the United States* for various years. The data span 40 years, from 1955 to 1995, and appear to be reasonably consistent over time. The results here update those reported by Jencks (1987). The major change has been in the classification scheme used to divide donations among various purposes. The number of categories has increased over time, particularly in 1965 and 1970. However, the classification scheme used for the sources of funds has remained unchanged since 1955.[4]

As shown in Table 1, total philanthropic contributions in 1995 dollars approximately doubled between 1955 and 1975 and then just about doubled again between 1975 and 1995. However, the growth was not entirely uniform over time. Between 1955 and 1965, there was a huge surge in charitable giving, with total donations growing at an annual rate of 5.2 percent. Over the next decade, 1965–75, the annual growth rate in total contributions fell dramatically—indeed, by more than half—to 2.5 percent. Since then, the growth rate in philanthropy has steadily increased, to 3.1 percent per year over the 1975–85 period and then to 3.3 percent per year over the 1985–95 period.

One reason for the growth in donations is that the population is rising. A somewhat more revealing statistic is shown in the second column of Table 1, average contributions per capita (again in 1995 dollars). Average contributions per person grew by almost two and a half times between 1955 and 1995, from $213 to $547. Yet, here too, the growth was far from uniform. Indeed, the pattern was almost identical to that for total donations. The annual growth rate fell sharply between the first two decades, from 3.6 percent in 1955–65 to 1.5 percent in 1965–75, and then gradually increased to 2.1 percent in 1975–85 and then to 2.3 percent in 1985–95.

Another reason why total contributions rise over time is that the total output of the economy is growing. This is most appropriately captured by the Gross Domestic Product (GDP), which is the national accounting concept of total output. Total contributions as a share of GDP rose rather steadily, from 1.5 percent in 1955 to 1.9 percent in 1970, fell to 1.6 percent in 1975, and then increased steadily again to 2.0 percent in 1995.

A somewhat better measure to use to compare the growth of charitable contributions is personal disposable income, since, as we shall see below, most charitable giving comes from individuals. Personal disposable income is

Table 1

The Growth of Philanthropic Contributions, 1955-1995 (a)

			Total Contributions as a Percent of:		
Year	Total Contributions [billions 1995$]	Average Contributions [1995$] per Capita (b)	Gross Domestic Product (b)	Personal Disposable Income (b)	Household Worth (c)
1955	35.3	212.5	1.5	2.2	0.4
1960	45.9	254.0	1.7	2.5	0.5
1965	59.1	304.0	1.7	2.5	0.5
1970	75.4	367.8	1.9	2.6	0.6
1975	76.2	352.8	1.6	2.3	0.6
1980	89.9	394.7	1.7	2.5	0.5
1985	103.7	434.8	1.8	2.4	0.6
1990	130.2	521.2	1.9	2.7	0.7
1995	143.9	547.1	2.0	2.7	0.7

Annual Percentage Growth Rates		
1955-65	5.2	3.6
1965-75	2.5	1.5
1975-85	3.1	2.1
1985-95	3.3	2.3
1955-95	3.5	2.4

a. Source for philanthropic contributions: U.S. Bureau of the Census, *Statistical Abstract of the United States*, various years.

b. Source for population, GDP, and personal disposable income data: Council of Economic Advisors, *Economic Report of the President, 1997*.

c. The net worth figures are for the household and nonprofit sector. Pension reserves are excluded from the definition of net worth. Source for the wealth data: Federal Reserve Board of Washington "Flow of Funds," on the Internet.

defined as total personal income (including wages and salaries, self-employment income, interest, dividends, rent, and transfer income) less income and payroll taxes (principally, social security taxes). As the name indicates, this is probably the best indicator of the resources over which the household has direct control. As shown in Table 1, total contributions grew from 2.2 to 2.6 percent of personal disposable income between 1955 and 1970, fell off to 2.3 percent in 1975, and then increased steadily to 2.7 percent in 1995.

Another source of charitable donations is wealth. Wealth is a stock concept and is defined as the current value of all marketable assets less the current

Table 2
Private Philanthropy Funds by Source and Allocation, 1955-1995 (a)

A. Sources of Donations (percent distribution)

Year	Individuals	Foundations	Corporations	Charitable Bequests	Total
1955	82.2	7.3	6.7	3.8	100.0
1960	80.2	8.0	5.4	6.4	100.0
1965	76.0	9.2	6.4	8.4	100.0
1970	75.0	9.9	4.2	10.9	100.0
1975	79.9	7.4	4.5	8.2	100.0
1980	83.7	5.8	4.5	6.0	100.0
1985	80.2	6.7	6.6	6.6	100.0
1990	81.5	6.4	5.3	6.8	100.0
1995	80.8	7.2	5.1	6.9	100.0
Average (d)	79.9	7.5	5.4	7.1	100.0

B. Allocation of Donations (percent distribution)

Year	Religion	Health	Education	Human Services	Arts & Culture	Other(b)	Total
1955	50.0	9.0	11.0	23.0	7.0	[c]	100.0
1960	51.0	12.0	16.0	15.0	6.0	[c]	100.0
1965	49.0	17.0	17.0	7.0	4.0	6.0	100.0
1970	43.2	16.1	16.1	7.3	6.3	10.9	100.0
1975	43.5	14.9	13.4	9.3	10.4	8.6	100.0
1980	45.7	10.9	10.3	10.1	6.6	16.5	100.0
1985	52.2	10.5	11.2	11.6	7.0	7.5	100.0
1990	44.6	8.9	11.1	10.6	7.1	17.8	100.0
1995	44.1	8.8	12.4	8.1	6.9	19.6	100.0
Average (d)	47.0	12.0	13.2	11.3	6.8	9.7	100.0

a. Source: U.S. Bureau of the Census, *Statistical Abstract of the United States,* various years.
b. Includes public and societal benefit, wildlife and the environment, international, and unclassified contributions.
c. Combined with arts and culture in 1955 and 1960.
d. Arithmetic average.

value of debts. Total assets are defined as the sum of: (1) owner-occupied housing; (2) other real estate owned by the household; (3) cash and demand deposits; (4) time and savings deposits, certificates of deposit, and money market accounts; (5) government bonds, corporate bonds, foreign bonds, and other financial securities; (6) the cash surrender value of life insurance plans;

(7) the cash surrender value of pension plans, including IRAs, Keogh, and 401(k) plans; (8) corporate stock and mutual funds; (9) net equity in unincorporated businesses; (10) equity in trust funds; and (11) the value of consumer durables, such as automobiles and televisions. Total liabilities are the sum of: (1) mortgage debt, (2) consumer debt, including auto loans, and (3) other debt.[5] The time trends are quite different for charitable donations as a share of wealth than for donations as a share of GDP or income. Donations rise rather steadily over time as a percent of net worth, from 0.4 in 1955 to 0.7 in 1995.

Table 2 documents both the sources and allocations of philanthropic contributions. On average, over the 1955–95 period, 80 percent of contributions have come from (living) individuals and another 7 percent from charitable bequests, for a total of 87 percent. Foundations have accounted for 8 percent of charitable giving and corporations 5 percent.

Over time, there have been some interesting changes. The share of total philanthropic contributions from individuals fell from 82 percent in 1955 to 75 percent in 1975 but then increased back to 81 percent in 1995. In contrast, the share from charitable bequests jumped from 4 percent in 1955 to 11 percent in 1970 and then fell sharply to 7 percent in 1995. A similar pattern is evident for foundations, whose proportion of total giving increased from 7.3 to 9.9 percent between 1955 and 1970 and then declined to 7.2 percent in 1995, almost exactly the same figure as in 1955. Corporations saw their share of total donations decrease from 6.7 percent in 1995 to 4.2 percent in 1970 and then rise moderately to 5.1 percent in 1995.

Over the last four decades, almost half of all charitable contributions, on average, have been made to religious organizations (see Panel B of Table 2). Another 11 to 13 percent has gone to each of health, education, and human services. Arts and cultural institutions accounted for 7 percent and other venues 10 percent.

Over time, there have been some rather dramatic changes. Religious organizations have fallen rather steadily in importance as a recipient of charitable giving, from 50 percent of total funds in 1955 to 44 percent in 1995. Health organizations saw their share of total giving almost double between 1955 and 1965, from 9 to 17 percent, and then fall off to 9 percent in 1995, almost the same figure as in 1955. Likewise, the proportion of total funds going to education increased from 11 percent in 1955 to 17 percent in 1965 and then retreated to 12 percent by 1995. In similar fashion, the percentage contributed to arts and culture rose from 7 percent in 1955 to 10 percent in 1975 and then fell back to 7 percent in 1995.

The most volatile series is for human services. Its share of total funding fell enormously, from 23 percent in 1955 to 7 percent in 1965, rose to 12 percent in 1985, and then declined to 8 percent in 1995. The biggest gainer over the period as a recipient of charitable giving was the miscellaneous category, including public and societal benefit, wildlife and the environment, international, and unclassified contributions. Its share rose from 6 percent in 1965 to almost 20 percent in 1995.[6]

Who Gave in 1995?

I next investigate patterns of charitable giving in 1995. The results are based on the Federal Reserve Board's 1995 Survey of Consumer Finances. The findings here should shed some light on the factors responsible for changes in the average propensity to give over time.

As shown in Table 3, almost 30 percent of American households reported making a charitable donation of $500 or more in 1995. The average contribution among donees was $2,939. The total amount of charitable giving according to the SCF was $85.8 billion in 1995. This compares to a figure of $116.2 billion for individuals only reported in the *Statistical Abstract of the United States: 1997*, for a 26-percent difference. According to the Survey of Consumer Finances, donations in 1995 amounted to 2.0 percent of personal income and 0.4 percent of personal wealth. This figures are somewhat lower than the corresponding figures in Table 1 of 2.7 percent of personal disposable income and 0.7 percent of net worth. However, all in all, the SCF figures are at least in the same ballpark as those derived from the *Statistical Abstract*.[7] Moreover, the SCF estimates are reasonably comparable to those of Hodgkinson et al. (1996, Appendix D). Hodgkinson et al. find that 68.5 percent of all household made charitable donations in 1996, in comparison to the SCF figure of 29.5 percent. However, this difference is almost certainly attributable to the exclusion of contributions of under $500 in the SCF. Hodgkinson et al., moreover, compute a mean contribution of $696 in 1996. This compares to the SCF figure of $867 in 1995. This discrepancy is not large and is likely due to the oversampling of very rich households in the SCF.

I next consider how charitable giving varies by the age of the householder (household head). As shown in Panel A of Table 3, there is a very striking relation. The percent of households making donations rises with age from 6 percent among the youngest households to 40 percent among those in age group 45–49 and then declines with age, reaching 23 percent among householders of age 80 or more. All told, 32 percent of elderly households (age 65 and over) made contributions in 1995, in comparison to 29 percent of nonelderly households.

A slightly different pattern is evident with respect to the dollar amount of contributions. Among donees only, average donations rise with age, from $1,300 for the youngest households to a peak of $7,500 for householders in age group 65–69 and then tails off with age, falling to $4,500 for householders aged 80 or more. Hodgkinson et al. (1996) report very similar patterns both in terms of the percentage of families who give and their average contributions in 1996. Clotfelter (1985) and Randolph (1995) also find that, after control-

Table 3
Patterns of Charitable Donations, 1995(a)

	Percent of Households making Charitable Donations (b)	Average Donation (Donees only)	Average Donation as a Percent of Income –All Households–	Average Donation as a Percent of Wealth –All Households–
All	29.5	2,939	2.0	0.4
A. Age of Householder				
Under 25	5.5	1,305	0.4	1.2
25–29	15.0	1,206	0.6	0.6
30–34	22.5	1,632	1.0	0.8
35–39	26.2	1,835	1.1	0.6
40–44	36.0	1,883	1.4	0.4
45–49	40.2	1,996	1.3	0.3
50–54	35.6	3,356	1.8	0.3
55–59	37.8	2,740	1.7	0.3
60–64	32.7	3,697	2.8	0.4
65–69	34.9	7,541	6.1	0.7
70–74	38.6	4,722	6.2	0.5
75–79	30.8	2,733	3.2	0.3
80 & Over	22.7	4,488	4.1	0.4
Under 65	28.7	2,255	1.4	0.4
65 & Over	32.4	5,102	5.2	0.5
B. Household Income and Age Class, 1995 Dollars(c)				
Under 10,000	5.5	856	1.0	0.1
10,000–14,999	11.2	860	0.8	0.2
15,000–24,999	19.9	1,316	1.4	0.3
25,000–49,999	32.1	1,496	1.3	0.5
50,000–74,999	42.8	1,877	1.3	0.4
75,000–99,999	61.7	2,491	1.8	0.4
100,000 or over	71.0	10,047	3.3	0.5
(1) Age under 65	28.7	2,255	1.4	0.4
Under 10,000	3.4	816	0.7	0.1
10,000–14,999	6.5	833	0.4	0.2
15,000–24,999	14.8	1,126	0.9	0.3
25,000–49,999	28.6	1,339	1.1	0.5
50,000–74,999	41.2	1,692	1.2	0.4
75,000–99,999	61.9	2,331	1.7	0.5
100,000 or over	70.0	5,590	1.8	0.3

Table 3 Continued

	Percent of Households making Charitable Donations (b)	Average Donation (Donees only)	Average Donation as a Percent of Income –All Households–	Average Donation as a Percent of Wealth –All Households–
(2) Age 65 or Over	32.4	5,102	5.2	0.5
Under 10,000	9.2	881	1.3	0.1
10,000–14,999	18.9	875	1.3	0.2
15,000–24,999	32.2	1,525	2.6	0.4
25,000–49,999	52.0	1,984	3.0	0.4
50,000–74,999	59.0	3,226	3.2	0.3
75,000–99,999	60.0	3,997	2.8	0.2
100,000 or over	77.5	35,195	10.2	0.8
C. Wealth Class (1995 Dollars)				
Under 10,000	9.8	1,305	0.6	1.1
10,000–24,999	18.6	1,313	0.9	1.4
25,000–49,999	30.6	1,324	1.1	1.1
50,000–74,999	28.0	1,076	0.8	0.5
75,000–99,999	30.6	1,647	1.3	0.6
100,000–199,999	38.2	1,815	1.6	0.5
200,000–499,999	55.5	2,223	2.0	0.4
500,000 or Over	74.4	9,113	4.1	0.3
D. Racial/Ethnic Group				
Non-Hispanic Whites	32.0	3,203	2.2	0.4
Non-Hispanic Blacks	19.4	1,451	1.2	0.7
Hispanics	15.7	1,599	0.8	0.5
Others (d)	31.9	1,584	1.1	0.2
E. Marital Status				
Married (e)	36.2	3,243	2.0	0.4
Male, divorced, separated or widowed	24.4	2,241	1.6	0.3
Female, divorced, separated or widowed	21.2	2,423	2.6	0.5
Male, never married	11.9	1,999	0.9	0.2
Female, never married	19.3	1,447	1.5	0.7

Table 3 Continued

	Percent of Households making Charitable Donations (b)	Average Donation (Donees only)	Average Donation as a Percent of Income –All Households–	Average Donation as a Percent of Wealth –All Households–
F. Education of Householder				
0-11 years	12.5	1,425	0.9	0.2
High School	22.3	2,044	1.3	0.4
Some College	30.0	2,167	1.6	0.4
College Graduate	13.2	2,810	2.0	0.4
Some Graduate School	59.8	5,342	3.5	0.6
G. Health of Head of Household				
Excellent	36.2	4,091	2.5	0.5
Good	30.6	2,314	1.7	0.4
Fair	21.1	2,332	1.7	0.3
Poor	14.1	1,658	1.3	0.3
H. Received an Inheritance?				
Yes	43.3	4,529	3.4	0.5
No	25.8	2,226	1.4	0.4

a. Own calculations from the 1995 Survey of Consumer Finances.
b. Includes only contributions of money or property in excess of $500.
c. Age class is determined by the age of the householder.
d. Includes Native Americans, Asians, and all other races.
e. Includes living with a partner.

ling for income and price effects, charitable giving rises with age and the "age elasticity" increases with age, at least up to age 70.

Part of the reason that older households donate more money is that their incomes are greater. However, as shown in the third column of Table 3, even when income is taken into account, the degree of generosity tends to rise with age. Indeed, donations as a fraction of household income rises with age from 0.4 percent for the youngest households to 6.2 percent for those in age group 70–74 and then falls off to 4.1 percent. In 1995, elderly households contributed 5.2 percent of their income while non-elderly ones contributed only 1.4 percent. In contrast,when we look at charitable giving in relation to household wealth, no clear pattern emerges by age group. On average, elderly households were only slightly more generous in relation to their wealth holdings, contributing 0.5 percent of their wealth, than non-elderly ones, who donated 0.4 percent of their net worth.

The pattern of giving is very striking by the income level of the household. Both the percentage of households making contributions and the average dollar amount of those contributions rise sharply with income. Moreover, donations as a proportion of income increases with the income level of the family, particularly between households earning between $75,000 and $100,000 and those making more than $100,000. There is also a tendency for higher income households to donate a higher proportion of their wealth than lower income households, but the differences are not as extreme. The most generous households appear to be elderly ones earning $100,000 or more. Over three-quarters of them made donations in 1995, with an average value of $35,000, which amounted to over 10 percent of their income and almost 1 percent of their wealth. These results are generally in accord with Clotfelter (1997, p. 13), who reports that most previous studies on this subject have found income elasticities for charitable giving in the range of 0.4 to 0.8.

These results differ somewhat from those reported in the *Statistical Abstract of the United States: 1997* (p. 387) and those reported by Clotfelter (1997), which show a U-shaped pattern for donations as a percentage of income, with this share falling sharply between the lowest income class and a broad range of middle income levels before rising again in the highest income categories. I do find the ratio of donations to income rising over the highest income ranges, and I do find a fall-off of this ratio between the lowest and the second lowest income class for households under age 65 but not for households 65 and over. Part of the difference in results is attributable to the exclusion of donations under $500 in the SCF.

A similar pattern is evident when we classify households by the level of their wealth (Panel C). The percentage of households making charitable donations climbs rapidly with household wealth, as does the amount of these contributions. Moreover, the donations as a proportion of their income also increases with the level of household wealth, particularly for the top wealth class of a half million dollars or more of net worth. However, interestingly, donations as a fraction of wealth falls with household wealth. (Ted Turner is very exceptional!)

There are some interesting racial differences (panel D). About one-third of non-Hispanic white households and other racial groups (mainly Asians) made contributions of $500 or more in 1995, compared to 19 percent of non-Hispanic black and 16 percent of Hispanic households. Average contributions by non-Hispanic white households (among donees only) was double that of the other racial/ethnic categories. Non-Hispanic white households also donated the highest proportion of their income—almost double that of the other groups. But, interestingly, non-Hispanic black households and Hispanic households gave a higher percentage of their wealth than non-Hispanic white households.

Married couples are more apt to give than singles (the lowest giving is found among males who had never married). A similar result is also reported by Clotfelter (1997, p. 18). However, relative to their income, the most generous group is women who are divorced, separated, or widowed, and the most generous group relative to their wealth is females who have never married. More educated households also give more (Panel F). The percentage of households making contributions, the dollar amounts of these contributions, the ratio of donations to income, and the ratio of donations to wealth all rise with the level of schooling of the householder and are particularly high among those who attended graduate school. Healthier people also contribute more, both in terms of the proportion who give and the level of the donations as a fraction of their income and wealth.

Households which received an inheritance are much more likely to make a charitable contribution (43 percent among those who inherited versus 26 percent among those who did not). Moreover, the average dollar contribution is higher among inheritors — $4,500 in comparison to $2,200 (among donees only). The total donations of inheritors amounted to 3.4 percent of their income and 0.5 percent of their wealth in 1995, compared to 1.4 percent and 0.4 percent among non-inheritors.

These results do confirm that richer households donate more both in absolute terms and relative to their income. In 1995, households with incomes of $100,000 or more which made up 6 percent of all households accounted for 52 percent of total donations that year, and households with a net worth of $500,000 or more, which were 7 percent of all households, made 53 percent of all contributions. In comparison, Clotfelter (1997, p. 10) reports a somewhat smaller concentration ratio on the basis of 1992 Internal Revenue Service data — namely, that the richest 3.9 percent of all taxpayers made 22.9 percent of all donations.

Philanthropy also rises with the level of education. In 1995, college graduates (including those who attended graduate school) made up 26 percent of all households but contributed 62 percent of all donations. Moreover, those who received appear to be much more likely to give than those who did not. Inheritors as a group comprised 21 percent of all households but accounted for 48 percent of all charitable giving. As a result, we should expect that as income inequality rises and more of total income goes to the richest families, average donations are likewise expected to increase. Moreover, as education levels increase and the fraction of households receiving inheritances rises, the average propensity to give should likewise climb.

Regression Analysis

Before turning to the more formal statistical analysis called multivariate regression, it is helpful to look first at the simple correlations between trends in charitable contributions and the supply, demand, and price factors that might help explain changes in giving over time. It should be recalled that donations as a share of personal disposable income rose between 1960 and 1970 (from 2.46 to 2.64 percent), fell over the next five years and then increased again, reaching a peak value of 2.75 percent in 1989, but then declined to 2.70 percent in 1995. In contrast, charitable giving as a share of total wealth generally trended upward from 1960 to 1995, from 0.50 to 0.66 percent.

The first set shown in Panel A of Table 4 captures the amount of disposable resources in the hands of the population and reflects the available supply of charitable contributions (also see Figure 5). Correlations between median family income, personal disposable income per capita, and mean household wealth on the one hand and contributions as a share of personal income on the other hand are all positive ranging from 0.27 to 0.56. Correlations between this set of factors and donations as a share of personal wealth are also positive and much higher, ranging from 0.61 to 0.89. However, there is very little correlation between charitable donations and average wages.

The next set contains different measures of the well-being of the bottom of the income distribution, which may reflect the perceived needs of the poor (see Panel B). The first of these is the overall poverty rate. Surprisingly, philanthropic activity and the poverty rate are actually negatively correlated (−0.05 between the poverty rate and the ratio of donations to personal disposable income, and −0.47 between the poverty rate and the ratio of donations to personal wealth), suggesting that as poverty goes up, giving declines. On the other hand, the second series, the share of total income received by the bottom 20 percent of families, is strongly negatively correlated with philanthropic activity (correlation coefficients of −0.48 and −0.58, respectively), indicating that as the relative fortunes of the poor get worse, philanthropic contributions increase. Moreover, AFDC benefits are negatively correlated with philanthropic giving (correlation coefficients of −0.33 and −0.62, respectively), indicating that as government largesse to the very poor declines, charitable contributions rise.

As noted in the introduction, if philanthropy is high when there are both a large number of rich families and a large number of poor people, then charitable donations may be related to the degree of overall inequality. As shown in Panel C, the various measures of inequality are all strongly and positively related to philanthropic donations as a share of personal disposable income, with correlation coefficients ranging from 0.46 to 0.64, indicating that as inequality rises, so do contributions. Correlations between inequality and donations as a share of personal wealth are all positive and generally stronger.

A related index is the Standard and Poor 500 stock index, deflated to 1995 dollars, which shows what happened to stock prices in real terms over time. Since the very rich hold a disproportionate share of corporate stocks (in 1995,

Table 4

Correlations between Charitable Donations and Income, Wealth, and Poverty, Trends and Tax Changes, 1960-1995(a)

Poverty, Income, Wealth, or Tax Variable	Total Contributions as a Percent of:	
	Personal Disposable Income (b)	Household Net Worth(c)
A. Resource Availability		
Median Family Income [1995$] (d)	0.27	0.80
Mean Hourly Wage [1995$] (e)	−0.22	0.10
Personal Disposable Income per Capita [1995$] (b)	0.36	0.89
Mean Household Wealth [1995$] (c)	0.56	0.61
B. Poverty		
Overall Poverty Rate (d)	−0.05	−0.47
Income Share of Bottom Quintile of Families (d)	−0.48	−0.58
Mean Income of Bottom Quintile of Families [1995$] (d)	−0.02	0.45
Average Monthly Family AFDC Benefit [1995$] (f)	−0.33	−0.62
C. Inequality		
Gini Coefficient for Family Income (d)	0.46	0.76
Income Share of Top 5% of Families (d)	0.59	0.65
Ratio of Mean Income of Top Quintile to Bottom Quintile (d)	0.51	0.68
Wealth Share of Top 1% of Households (g)	0.64	0.33
Standard and Poor 500 Index Deflated to 1995$ (b)	0.63	0.37

the richest 10 percent of households owned about 90 percent of all stocks), the wealth of the very rich is particularly sensitive to the movement of stock prices. This series is also positively correlated with donations as a share of disposable income (0.63).

The last panel (Panel D) shows correlations between marginal tax rates and donations. As noted in the Introduction, changes in tax rates affect the

Table 4 Continued

Poverty, Income, Wealth, or Tax Variable	Total Contributions as a Percent of	
	Personal Disposable Income (b)	Household Net Worth
D. Personal Tax Rates		
Top Marginal Tax Rate (h)	−0.54	−0.88
Marginal Tax Rate at $135,000 of Income in 1995$ (h)	−0.68	−0.71
Marginal Tax Rate at $67,000 of Income in 1995$ (h)	−0.61	−0.41
Marginal Tax Rate at $33,000 of Income in 1995$ (h)	−0.41	−0.27

a. Source for philanthropic contributions: US Bureau of the Census, *Statistical Abstract of the United States*, various years.

b. Source: Council of Economic Advisers, *Economic Report of the President, 1997*.

c. Source: Federal Reserve Board of Washington, "Flow of Funds," on the Internet.

d. U.S. bureau of the Census, Current Population Surveys, Internet

e. Total, private sector. Source: Council for Economic Advisers, *Economic Report of the President, 1997*.

f. The series is available only from 1970–1995. Sources: U.S. House of Representatives (1994) and Council of Economic Advisers, *Economic Report of the President, 1997*.

g. Source: Wolff (1996). Figures updated to 1995 on the basis of the 1995 Survey of Consumer finances.

h. Sources: 1913–85: Pechman (1983); 1986–95: Federal Income Tax Returns, Form 1040. The rates are shown for married couples filing jointly with two children.

cost of making charitable donations, since for itemizers, the net cost of donating a dollar is one minus their marginal tax rate. However, all four series of marginal tax rates are negatively correlated with charitable giving (correlation coefficients ranging from −0.41 to −0.68 with the ratio of donations to personal disposable income) rather than positively correlated.

Regression Results. We now turn to the final part of the analysis, which is based on multivariate regression. As the name suggests, this is a statistical technique used to sort out the independent contributions of various factors to trends in the variable of interest (the so-called dependent variable). The results as we shall see in a moment are sometimes very different than the correlation coefficients shown in Table 4, since the latter do not control for the effects of other variables on the dependent variable.

I use two different dependent variables. The first is total charitable contributions as a fraction of total personal disposable income and the second is

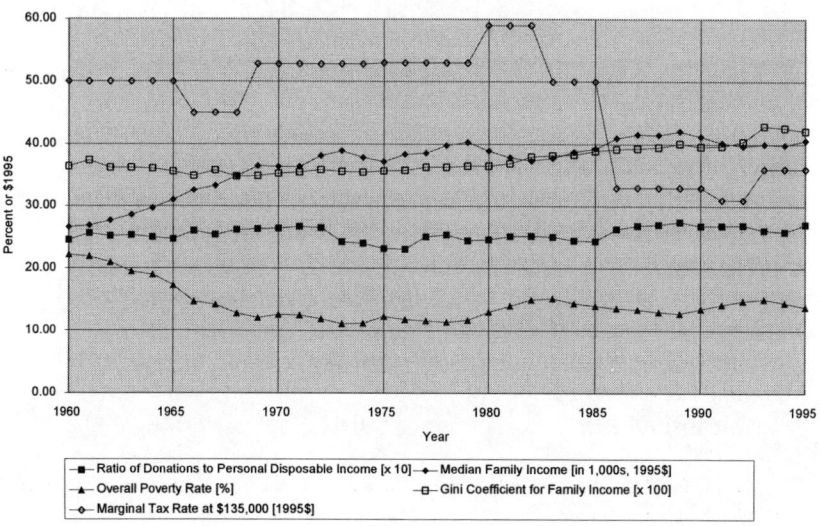

Figure 5. Ratio of Donations to Personal Disposable Income,
Income, Poverty, and Inequality Trends, 1960-1995

total contributions as a ratio to total personal wealth. The explanatory or "independent" variables are those discussed above and shown in Table 4.

Regression results are shown for the first dependent variable in Table 5. Generally, after trying many different combinations of independent variables, I have shown the regressions with the greatest number of significant variables.[8] The results are a bit surprising. Of the four measures of the average level of resources available to the population, the most significant by far is average wealth holdings of households. This variable is generally significant at the 5-percent level. Median family income is occasionally significant but at only the 10-percent level. Personal disposable income per capita and the average real wage are not significant in any specification.

Variables reflecting the extent of poverty in American society and the level of destitution of the poorest families in our country are generally not statistically significant. The overall poverty rate, the income share of the bottom quintile of the income distribution, and average AFDC benefits are not significant in any specification. The mean income of the bottom quintile in 1995 dollars (INCQUINT5) is occasionally significant and with the appropriate negative sign (indicating that as the real income of the poorest 20 percent of families falls, charitable contributions increase) but at the 10-percent level at most (see Specification 1, for example).

Inequality indicators are generally not significant as explanatory variables affecting the level of charitable giving. This is true for the Gini coefficient for family income inequality, the share of total income received by the richest 5

Table 5

Regressions of Donations as a Percent of Personal Disposable Income on Average Well-Being, Poverty, and Inequality Indicators, 1960–1995[a]

Independent Variables	(1)	(2)	(3)	(4)	(5)	(6)
Constant	2.45**	1.69**	2.00**	1.99**	1.36**	1.33**
	(6.83)	(6.22)	(11.45)	(4.65)	(4.34)	(3.81)
MEDFAMINC	0.024#	0.010#				
	(1.93)	(1.74)				
PDIPERCAP			0.008			
			(0.99)			
MEANWLTH				0.045*	0.039*	0.035#
				(2.29)	(2.55)	(1.82)
INCQUINT 5	−0.072#			−0.033		0.007
	(1.75)			(1.23)		(0.26)
WLTHTOP 1		0.016**	0.015**		0.013**	0.014**
		(3.72)	(3.07)		(3.62)	(2.78)
No. of Obs.	35	35	35	35	35	35
R^2	0.575	0.643	0.623	0.583	0.661	0.662
Adj. R^2	0.534	0.609	0.586	0.542	0.629	0.617
Std. Err.	0.076	0.070	0.072	0.076	0.068	0.069
Durb-Watson	1.69	1.65	1.66	1.84	1.77	1.76
Est. Tech.	AR(1)	AR(1)	AR(1)	AR(1)	AR(1)	AR(1)
$\wp_1$	0.63**	0.48**	0.51**	0.56**	0.37*	0.38*

a. t-ratios (absolute values) are shown in parentheses below the coefficient. See footnotes to Table 4 for sources.

Key:
MEDFAMINC: Median family income in 1995$.
PDIPERCAP: Personal disposable income per capita in 1995$.
MEANWLTH: Mean household net worth in 1995$.
INCQUINT5: Mean income of bottom income quintile of families in 1995$.
WLTHTOP1: Wealth share of top 1 percent of households ranked by wealth.
AR(1): First-order autoregressive process: $u_t = ë_t + \wp_1 u_{t-1}$, where u_t is the error term of the original equation and $ë_t$ is a stochastic term assumed to be identically and independently distributed.
\# Significant at the 10 percent level (2-tail test).
* Significant at the 5 percent level (2-tail test).
** Significant at the 1 percent level (2-tail test).

percent of families, the ratio of mean income between the top and bottom quintiles, and the S&P 500 Index, and this is true despite the fact that these variables have a strong positive correlation with donations as a fraction of personal disposable income. The major exception is the share of wealth owned by the richest 1 percent of households (WLTHTOP1), which has a positive and highly significant coefficient (significant at the 1-percent level in almost all specifications). Indeed, this is probably the most significant variable in the model.

The coefficients of the four tax variables, the top marginal tax rate and the marginal tax rate at $135,000, $67,000, and $33,000 of income (in 1995 dollars), are statistically insignificant in almost all specifications but generally do maintain their negative sign. The goodness of fit for a model of this sort is reasonable, with the R^2-statistic varying between 0.58 and 0.66 in most specifications.

Table 6 shows regressions results for the second dependent variable, total contributions as a ratio of total personal wealth. This form yields many more significant coefficients. Both median family income and personal income per capita now appear as highly significant determinants of movements in the ratio of charitable contributions to wealth over time. Both are generally significant at the 1-percent level.[9] Of the various poverty indicators, the only one that is statistically significant is INCQUINT5, the average income of the bottom income quintile (in 1995 dollars). In the first specification shown in Table 6, the variable is significant at the 1-percent level and has the predicted negative coefficient. However, as with the first dependent variable, the overall poverty rate, the income share of the bottom income quintile, and real AFDC benefits are not significant.

Most of the inequality measures are now statistically significant, including the Gini coefficient for income, the share of income received by the top 5 percent of families, the ratio of mean income between the top and bottom quintiles, and the share of wealth owned by the richest 1 percent of households. The most significant of these is the last, the wealth share of the top 1 percent. It is also notable that when this variable is included with INCQUINT5 (the real income of the bottom quintile), the latter becomes statistically insignificant.

The goodness of fit of these regressions as measured by the R^2-statistic varies from 0.81 to 0.85. These figures are much higher than the corresponding ones for the regressions of donations as a share of personal disposable income. These results indicate that charitable giving has a much more stable and predictable relationship to household wealth than to household income.

As indicated in the last two columns of Table 6, I have separated out charitable donations made for human services. The results of these two regressions indicate that this component of charitable giving is very sensitive to the overall poverty rate, rising when poverty increases and conversely. Moreover, these types of contributions seem to depend more on household

Table 6

Regressions of Donations as a Percent of Personal Wealth and Donations to Human Services as a Share of Income and Wealth on Average Well-Being, Poverty, and Inequality Indicators, 1960-1995[a]

	Dependent Variable					
Independent Variables	DON/WLTH	DON/WLTH	DON/WLTH	DON/WLTH	DON/WLTH	DON/WLT H
Constant	0.32**	0.69**	0.15#	0.32**	−0.47#	−0.14*
	(5.53)	(1.17)	(1.94)	(8.40)	(2.03)	(2.70)
MEDFAMINC	0.016**	0.010**	0.013**		0.023*	0.005*
	(6.75)	(7.97)	(5.80)		(2.37)	(2.51)
PPDIPERCAP				0.013**		
				(7.71)		
INCQUINT 5	−0.029**		−0.013			
	(3.62)		(1.43)			
WLTHTOP 1		0.0047**	0.0034*	0.0025*		
		(4.73)	(2.61)	(2.378)		
POVRATE					0.036**	0.007*
					(2.84)	(2.67)
INCGINI					−1.76	−0.30
					(1.57)	(1.23)
No. of Obs.	35	35	35	35	36	36
R^2	0.813	0.838	0.847	0.847	0.284	0.317
Adj. R^2	0.796	0.822	0.827	0.832	0.217	0.252
Std. Err.	0.022	0.020	0.020	0.020	0.058	0.013
Durb–Watson	1.91	1.87	1.88	1.94	1.63	1.74
Est. Tech.	AR(1)	AR(1)	AR(1)	AR(1)	OLS	OLS
$\wp_1$	0.34#	0.29	0.19	0.35#		

a. t–ratios (absolute values) are shown in parentheses below the coefficient. See footnotes to Table 4 for sources and footnotes to Table 5 for key. Also,

DON/WLTH: Charitable donations as a share of total personal wealth. HSERV/PDI: Charitable donations to human services as a share of total personal disposable income. HSERV/WLT: Charitable donations to human services as a share of total personal wealth. INCGINI: Gini coefficient for family income. POVRATE: Overall poverty rate.
\# Significant at the ten percent level (2–tail test).
* Significant at the five percent level (2–tail test).
**Significant at the one percent level (2–tail test).

income than on household wealth (the mean wealth variable is insignificant in these regressions), and do not appear to be sensitive to overall inequality. However, even this form of giving does not appear to respond to changes in AFDC benefit levels (the variable AFDCBEN is insignificant).

The main findings of this chapter are as follows: First, mean wealth is a more powerful predictor of charitable contributions than mean or average income. This suggest that charitable giving responds more closely to changes in household wealth than to changes in income. Second, and rather surprising (if not to say disturbing!) is that total charitable giving does not respond to changes in either the level of poverty or the standard of living of the poorest families in our country. As the fortunes of the poor decline, there is little indication that the rich become more generous and that charitable giving increases. However, the exception is for donations specifically targeted to human services, which are found to be significantly related to the level of overall poverty in the country. Yet, even for this type of giving, no evidence is found for the crowding out hypothesis.

Third, changes in economic inequality do not explain changes in the degree of philanthropic giving relative to personal income, with the sole and notable exception of movements in the share of wealth held by the richest 1 percent of households. They do explain changes in contributions relative to personal wealth, but the strongest effect is from the wealth share of the richest 1 percent. This is consonant with the first finding, since the very rich make about half of all charitable contributions (at least according to the SCF data) and as their resources increase, so does their amount of contributions.

Fourth, at least according to these regression results, there is no new evidence that the level of charitable giving does respond to changes in marginal tax rates, after controlling for other factors. This result seems to fly in the face of previous work on the subject. Clotfelter (1997, p. 13), for example, reports that most studies have found price elasticities for charitable giving in the range of −0.5 to −1.75. However, it should be noted that I am using a very crude indicator of price—namely, correlations between marginal tax rates and charitable giving on the aggregate level. A much better approach is to use microdata or panel data on individual taxpayers to obtain a more accurate measure of the price of giving faced by each person or family. Studies that have used this approach have almost uniformly found a significant price effect, because the biggest variation in price is not over time but among taxpayers at a given time.

In sum, charitable contributions seem largely supply driven rather than demand driven. Moreover, charitable giving seems to depend much more on the wealth of the household than its disposable income. The major exception is charitable giving for human services, which does respond positively to changes in the incidence of poverty in our country.

Notes

I would like to thank Charles Clotfelter for his very helpful comments and suggestions on an earlier draft of this essay.

1. This is not exactly the case for very high income families who face restrictions on their total deductions because of their income level or who may be subject to the alternative minimum tax on their income tax return.

2. All figures are in 1995 dollars unless otherwise indicated. It would actually be preferable to use median household income rather than median family income. Unfortunately, official U.S. Bureau of the Census series on household income begin only in 1967, whereas family income data are available from 1947 onward.

3. The source for these figures is Sources: U.S. House of Representatives (1994).

4. The underlying source for the data in the *Statistical Abstract* is *Giving USA*, which is the more common source for data on philanthropic contributions in the literature.

5. I have used the Federal Reserve Board Flow of Funds data for this wealth series. Technically, the sector includes both households and nonprofit institutions. Moreover, I have excluded pension reserves from the definition of wealth since they are not under the direct control of households (or nonprofit institutions).

6. It should again be noted that part of the apparent change in the allocation of charitable funds over time may be attributable to changes in the classification system for charitable giving.

7. Part of the reason for the lower estimates from the Survey of Consumer Finances is that only donations of $500 or more are reported in the survey. This restriction will exclude a substantial number of households who made smaller donations.

8. Almost all the regressions originally had a severe autocorrelation problem. I have used the standard correction technique, which is to introduce an autoregressive adjustment term.

9. For statistical reasons, the independent variable MEANWLTH (mean household wealth) generally has a negative coefficient. The reason is that the dependent variable is effectively the ratio of average charitable contributions to average wealth, which spuriously induces a negative coefficient on average wealth in the regression.

References

AAFRC Trust for Philanthropy. *Giving USA*. New York: AAFRC Trust for Philanthropy, 1993 and 1995.

Auten, G. E., Cilke, J. M., and Randolph, W. C. "The Effects of Tax Reforms on Charitable Contributions." *National Tax Journal*, September, 1992, 45, 267–290.

Auten, G. E., Clotfelter, C. T., and Schmalbeck, R. L. "Taxes and Philanthropy among the Wealthy." Paper presented at the Conference, "Does Atlas Shrug?

The Economic Consequences of Taxing the Rich," University of Michigan Business School, Ann Arbor, MI, October 24–25, 1997.

Brown, E., and Lankford, H. "Gifts of Money and Gifts of Time." *Journal of Public Economics*, April, 1992, 47, 321–329.

Clotfelter, C. T., *Federal Tax Policy and Charitable Giving*. Chicago: University of Chicago Press, 1985.

——, "The Economics of Giving," Duke University, mimeo, March 1997.

Hodgkinson, V. A., et al. *Giving and Volunteering in the United States*. Washington, DC: Independent Sector, 1996.

Jencks, C., "Who Gives to What?" In W. W. Powell, ed., *The Nonprofit Sector: A Research Handbook*. New Haven, CT: Yale University Press, 1987, 321–339.

Joulfaian, D. "Charitable Bequests and Estate Taxes." *National Tax Journal*, June, 1991, 44, 169–180.

Kingma, B. R.. "An Accurate Measurement of the Crowd-Out Effect, Income Effect, and Price Effect for Charitable Contribution." *Journal of Political Economy*, August, 1991, 97 (5), 460–470.

Odendahl, T. *Charity Begins at Home: Generosity and Self-interest among the Philanthropic Elite*. New York: Basic Books, 1990.

Pechman, J. A. *Federal Tax Policy*, Fourth edition. Washington, DC: Brookings Institution, 1983.

Randolph, W. C. "Dynamic Income, Progressive Taxes, and the Time of Charitable Contributions." *Journal of Political Economy*, August 1995, 103 (5), 709–738.

U.S. House of Representatives, Committee on Ways and Means. *Overview of Entitlement Programs: 1994 Green Book*. Washington, DC: U.S. Government Printing Office, July 15, 1994.

Wolff, E. N. *TOP HEAVY: A Study of Increasing Inequality of Wealth in America*. Updated and expanded edition. New York: Free Press, 1996.

CHAPTER FIVE

Corporate Philanthropy Comes of Age

Its Size, Its Import, Its Future

Reynold Levy

Last year, America's companies gave away $8.5 billion in cash contributions to the nation's nonprofit organizations. That total sum reflects the second successive year, from 1994 to 1995 and from 1995 to 1996, in which corporate donations have increased by roughly $7^1/_2$ percent, more than two and a half times the rate of inflation. Accounting only for cash from philanthropic budgets, the $8.5 billion represents only 30 percent less than the $11.83 billion of contributions attributable to all of the country's private foundations.[1]

When one adds up the dollar value of many other additional sources of corporate support to nonprofits, the nation's businesses may well contribute more in total to the Third Sector than any other single source, except for the time and treasure of individual Americans: cash from sales and marketing budgets; complimentary use of corporate facilities; donations of surplus property; the benefits of executive loans and other forms of employee volunteerism; gifts of products, services, and equipment; advertising and underwriting support. These supplemental sources of assistance have three characteristics in common. Only corporations can supply them. Their impact is significant and growing fast. No one really knows how large is their cash equivalent value and how fast are their rates of growth.

What accounts for this impressive order of magnitude of corporate giving? What substantiates the claim that the corporate share of the nation's charitable contributions will continue to earn the business executive an honored place at the table of philanthropy?

Defining Terms

The strength of corporate philanthropy resides in its location at the intersection of business interest and social need. A company, like a nation or an individual, is driven by its interests. These interests, in turn, are determined by such factors as the content of its business, the nature and scale of its customers and competitors, the degree to which its operations are regulated or monitored by government, and the expressed needs of employees at the principal physical locations of its operation.

The *raison d'être* of companies is to earn a profit, continually increasing the value of the shareowner's stake in them. Theoretically, all of a for-profit's activities should contribute to this end, directly or indirectly, in the short run or over the long term. While a company's philanthropy occasionally marks the difference between a customer gained or lost, such occasions are rare. More often philanthropy offers its contribution to general factors that favorably influence a firm's capabilities and build its assets.

For example, employee pride in the values of the company can be related powerfully to whether and how they are expressed in philanthropic acts. Such pride instills loyalty.

Contributions activity is regarded as an investment in a firm's brand identity, the degree to which it evokes such attributes as trust, caring, reliability, fairness, and diversity.

The reputation of the corporation as a good citizen of the cities, states, and nations in which it operates is in part a function of its philanthropic performance. The body politic gives fuller rein to businesses that demonstrate commitment not just to profit but to employees, customers, and community. Corporate giving is one form of discharging that broader social responsibility.

Cultivating important relationships in the Third Sector can help advance such ends as favorably influencing government officials, recruiting outstanding students and mid-career personnel, and tapping the thinking of the best and brightest talent in the nation's think tanks and universities. All of these and many other connections are facilitated by walking through the doors philanthropists can open.

Exposure to the ideas that percolate in the nation's social action movements — consumer, environmental, civil rights, feminist, labor, free trade — can provide clues about market opportunities worth seizing and hazards to avoid. And the chance for corporate managers to assume important civic roles as nonprofit board members and volunteers and to grapple with nonprofit leadership challenges can be invaluable to the education of future senior executives. In these illustrative ways and through a wide variety of other means commercial firms relate to nonprofit institutions to significant mutual advantage.

Some of those advantages for nonprofits have to do with cash transfers to them in the form of corporate grants. But the relationships between corporations and nonprofit institutions are complex and multifaceted. To characterize them as if they transpired exclusively between a donor and a donee is to engage in caricature. Calling a company a "grantor" trivializes its role in relationship to nonprofits and in society, more generally. Calling a nonprofit a "grantee" reduces its identity to fundraiser and diminishes its status to that of perennial supplicant. Doing so confuses the tail with the dog.

The Corporation and the University

Consider the many connections between the corporation and the university. Many firms look to the university as a primary source of knowledge, nurturing their own research and development capabilities. They view the university as a critical source of employees who are recruited from campus each year. They depend on the university for its important contribution to the quality of life in communities where employees, retirees, and shareowners live and work. They recognize that their employees are graduates who often display a fierce loyalty to their alma maters. And, importantly, they know that the university—its administration, faculty, students, and alumni—houses vital customers for their products and services. All of these manifestations of corporate-university interaction and mutual regard are widely shared across American firms.

To be sure, the university is a special kind of customer. One aspect of its distinctiveness flows from an eligibility to receive tax-deductible gifts. Companies are very aware of that capability, one that universities remind them of on every available occasion.

In 1996, America's corporations contributed about $2.7 billion in cash to higher education. That figure is 31 percent of the total of corporate cash donations of for-profits to charity ($8.5 billion) and 21 percent of the $14.25 billion raised by colleges and universities in that year.[2] No small change. Such gifts are very important to the schools that benefit from them. But they coexist with, and are in no small measure the byproducts of, many other interactions between the university and the company.

Universities enjoy the attendance of tens of thousands of students each year whose tuition and fees are partially to fully subsidized by the companies that employ them. Universities facilitate the placement of their students in part-time and full-time jobs at commercial firms and faculty members benefit from summer internships in, and sabbatical leaves at, the nation's businesses. Companies buy services from the university including research and development and commissioned studies of all kinds. Companies serve the university and its constituencies in their capacity as customers, supplying goods and services, often at discounted rates. And, the university is an outlet for the civic energy of company executives who serve it in a myriad of leadership roles from company volunteer to curriculum development advisor and from member of a distinguished visiting committee to trustee.

The philanthropic relationship between the corporation and the university is animated by all of these other transactions. It does not stand independent of them. Indeed, the nature and magnitude of corporate grant-making to the university cannot be understood in the absence of so many other mutual benefits. Philanthropy is the consequence of these other positive exchanges between the corporation and university at least as much and as often as their cause. Precisely because it rests on a network of business interactions and relationships, precisely because it can be found at the intersection of corporate interest and nonprofit need, corporate philanthropy is relatively secure and stable.

The Corporation as Patron of the Arts

Now consider the arts. Corporate interest in this field is animated by the enormous growth in numbers of institutions, audience size, employment, annual expenditures, economic impact, and burgeoning of tourism. Corporations are drawn to the impressive and impressionable markets forming around the arts. They can be receptive to everything from conveying general brand messages to point of purchase sales. They represent important manifestations of civic pride with which to associate, the better to burnish a reputation for good corporate citizenship. They constitute major outlets for the expenditure of time and treasure by employees and their families. And they offer many opportunities for constructive engagement to the distinct advantage of both the contributing firm and the partner arts organization.

From the company's perspective, arts venues are terrific places to entertain customers and to keep in touch with a community's "movers and shakers." They lend themselves easily to employee involvement and benefit. In the measure that employees and retirees of benefactor companies enjoy the privilege of a matching gift program, or utilize ticket reservation privileges or discounts, or view displays of fine and performing art at the workplace, the connection between what a firm accomplishes in its philanthropy and a direct impact on its key constituencies is thrown into sharp relief.

If the corporation can enjoy so many advantages from a philanthropic and marketing association with the arts, surely the converse is true as well.

No other partner can do so much in so many ways for an arts organization as the committed American company. Beyond its own cash grants, a company can help lead others—sister firms, foundations, suppliers, like-minded partners—to join the cause with support. Inviting colleagues to performances, openings, and meetings to become acquainted with a given arts grantee is a helpful practice. A company can respond affirmatively to invitations to galas, dinners, anniversary celebrations, sports events, theater parties, and other fundraisers. It can provide such in-kind donations as products and services, use of facility space, technical assistance, and executive loan.

It can match the cash contributions of its own employees to an arts organization and communicate news of arts programming to them. It can purchase tickets to arts events and hold corporate meetings in arts spaces. It can advertise on radio and television, in newspapers and magazines, and on billboards and buses about an association with an arts organization or arts event, thereby promoting the bona fides of both the firm and the cultural partner. It can name a given venue as the beneficiary of a marketing campaign, cause-related or otherwise.

From what other single source of assistance can so much be possible?

What's more, a major company's support matters to other donors. It carries an important imprimatur, suggesting that the tests of quality, efficiency, and effectiveness were passed with flying colors. All respected firms are expected to have conducted such due diligence prior to awarding substantial help to any grantee.

Given this mutual attraction, it is hardly surprising that the corporate component of private support for the arts has been growing markedly.

In 1964 it is estimated that only 5 percent or less of the country's corporate contributions were allocated to the arts, for a total of about $16–$21 million. By 1977 corporate contributions to the arts had grown fivefold to $100 million, representing 6.5 percent of corporate giving. In 1995 a Business Committee for the Arts (BCA) study suggested that companies in the prior year had given $875 million in cash to the arts for about 12 percent of their total gifts. It observed that about 35 percent of all U.S. businesses offered cash donations to arts organizations. And it noted that the $875 million was up 32 percent over the $518 million figure of two years earlier in 1993, when it last conducted its survey.

No solid figures exist for the cash value of all of the in-kind support generated by America's companies. BCA conservatively estimates it at 20 percent of the cash total.[3] So add $175 million (or 20 percent of the $875 million) to the grand total of what corporations give to the arts, nationwide. It comes to well over a billion dollars and may already exceed all support from government, a major milestone in the relatively brief history of the American corporation as patron of the arts.

Corporate Self-Interest and Charity: Join the Crowd

The corporation's philanthropic connections to health, social services, the environment, and other fields could be comparably examined. They differ in degree but not in kind. Sustenance and staying power are drawn not so much from grand pronouncements about corporate social responsibility, but from a careful knitting together of corporate purpose and nonprofit need.

None of these observations are intended to deny that part of a company's relationship to the Third Sector is animated by charitable impulse. Employees may leave their valuables behind at home when they go off to work each morning. But they take their values with them to the office. And high among them is helping others and enriching the communities in which they live and work. But eleemosynary intent plays itself out in a real world context.

For companies, nonprofits represent markets, sources of employees, pools of research and expertise, venues for opinion leaders, and expertise from which customers can be won, executives recruited, and intelligence gathered. All are potential sources of community good will.

To ignore the business interests served by interaction with the Third Sector is both conceptually flawed and practically fatal. Acts of pure altruism are rarely encountered. Individual donors may seek to do good for institutions, causes, and people. But why? Does the social status such acts confer, the business opportunities they create, the guilt they relieve, the impulse to immortality they satisfy, or the visibility with which they are often associated have something to do with donor motivation? Of course. And foundation executives and nonprofit board members, or at least those I've been privileged to know, are not themselves devoid of institutional, personal, and professional interests that they wish to advance.

Only infrequently do such motivations diminish the value of the gift. In short, the complexity of motivations that give rise to charitable gifts are not confined to corporations. To assume they are and to pursue some archetype of "pure" philanthropy is to deny reality. Donors are not just idealists. They are pragmatists too. The shareowner would have it no other way.

Some observers are heard to say that there was once a "golden era" of corporate philanthropy, when CEOs like Reg Jones of General Electric, Irving Shapiro of Du Pont, and David Rockefeller of Chase Manhattan Bank articulated an impassioned case for the exercise of corporate social responsibility. Now, it is claimed, something valuable has been lost. Today, philanthropy is viewed as "just another business tool" at least as much the property of a company's sales and marketing division as of its public affairs and public relations departments.

Such contentions are meritless. Roberto Gouizetta, the former Chairman of Coca-Cola, Robert Haas of Levi Strauss, and Louis Gerstner of IBM articulate as moving and as persuasive a brief for corporate philanthropy as did their predecessors. Nor is there evidence to suggest that overall corporate philanthropic performance has deteriorated in quality. To the contrary, many commentators would characterize the last two decades as a period in which corporate philanthropy professionalized and came of age. In fact, a sign of its maturity is the pattern of growth in resources devoted to corporate donations. Cash contributions and related gifts from business to nonprofits have blossomed. The figures simply belie Cassandra-like concerns.

Corporate Philanthropy: Solid Signs of Growth

Indeed, the prospect for growth in the size of corporate philanthropy and other forms of support to nonprofits is very bright. Historically, giving levels have been positively associated with corporate earnings growth, all other things being equal. Well, corporate earnings have been growing on average at double digit rates since the beginning of the first Clinton administration.

Well into its seventh year of economic growth, other vital signs of America's business condition appear exceptionally healthy. Gross Domestic Product (GDP) growth in the 3 to 4 percent range. Low unemployment at $4\frac{1}{2}$ percent. Low inflation at around 2 percent. Low interest rates. High job growth. Between 1992 and 1997 14 million net new U.S. jobs were created. Relatively sharp increases in worker productivity. Federal and state budgets in balance or surplus. Business investment up. Consumer confidence rising to record levels.

Add to all of this the extraordinary appreciation of the value of common stock. Virtually all indices of the U.S. stock market record a rise of more than 20 percent compounded annually over three consecutive years. The Dow Jones Index moved from 3,200 at the beginning of the first Clinton term in office to a high of 8,300 in 1997. Insofar as corporations have established asset-based foundations, grant payouts should rise significantly based purely on the strength of these record breaking returns.

A better external environment for the flourishing of philanthropy in general, and corporate contributions in particular, could hardly be imagined.

Not only are the facts sunny, but perceptions of the very senior businessmen who ultimately approve corporate contributions budgets are also very favorable. As the economic competitiveness of America improves measurably in field after field—from agriculture to pharmaceuticals, aircraft to automobiles, computers to biotechnology, and telecommunications to transportation—the mood of American business is positive and self-confident. Corporate executives have good reason to feel cheerful about their personal financial prospects and the outlook for their firms.

Benefactors and Supplicants

Confidence in the future growth of corporate giving also emanates from the increased professionalism of those directing business donations and those asking for them.

The productivity and creativity of those practicing the craft of corporate philanthropy is indispensable to how the discipline is perceived by insiders. To add value to such company activities as marketing, sales, research and development, recruiting, education and training, customer and employee satisfaction, executive development, and governmental relations while strengthening carefully selected nonprofit institutions and causes is to increase support for philanthropy. Well executed, the art and craft of philanthropy can be found where business interest and social need intersect. The more those points of congruence are identified and exploited, the greater the likelihood that corporate philanthropy will flourish, isolated dissenters notwithstanding.

The second source of optimism resides in the professionals and volunteers who effectively ask for support. The demand side of the equation counts for much in the calculus of decision about how philanthropy and such kindred efforts as cause-related marketing will fare. The greater the frequency, intelligence, and persuasiveness of the solicitations, the more likely senior corporate executives will come to appreciate overall charitable needs. A company has many front doors. The more that well-informed solicitors knock, the more they will be opened to them, with helpful resources at the ready.

For the powers that be in most companies, philanthropy is what philanthropy does, not what it professes. To corporate senior officers, the picture of a benefactor's role is often painted in the concrete examples portrayed by friends, business associates, family members, colleagues, and customers. They present a social need, cast corporate obligation as opportunity, and suggest philanthropy as the avenue to resolution. Multiply those case examples and a collage of activities emerges, impressive in their diversity and energy. Peer influences are powerful.

As the resourcefulness, versatility, and professionalism of those who solicit grow, so too will the net impression that the welfare of nonprofit institutions matters. Out of just such perceptions, corporate contributions to the Third Sector blossom and convictions about the role of philanthropy crystallize.

As one peers into the future from the perspective afforded by the first quarter of 1998, the constellation of forces suggesting a likelihood for record-breaking increases in philanthropy seem terrific. Relatively strong and spirited sources of supply. Highly motivated and resourceful engines of demand. Such a powerful combination, if sustained over time, could well contribute to a general renaissance in American philanthropy. If so, corporations will play a strong supporting role.

Four themes that will characterize the content of business participation in America's philanthropic future are worthy of some explication. The likely emergence of small and midsize firms as engines of corporate giving. The use of philanthropy by American companies conducting business abroad as a tool of international expansion and as a symbol of good corporate citizenship. The salutary impact of technological advances on the aspirations and operations of corporate philanthropy. And, the ascendance of the employee as catalyst and indispensable stakeholder in the exercise of corporate social responsibility.

The Driving Force of Business Philanthropy: Small and Midsize Firms

An accumulating body of evidence suggests that the fastest-growing segment of philanthropy in the for-profit sector is small and midsize business. Until recently, this nascent trend has been hard to detect. The principal sources of data on corporate giving—the Council on Financial Aid to Education, the Conference Board, and the Council on Foundations—have been concentrated exclusively on companies with at least 500 employees and $100 million of revenue. We know much less about the charitable habits of firms with fewer than 500 employees, even though they account for 53 percent of all paid employment in America, than we do about the Fortune 500. But now research has revealed how critical the role of smaller firms has become to business giving. Three studies point to their centrality in the years ahead. Our ignorance is beginning to dissipate.

One new inquiry was devoted to examining small and medium-sized business giving habits in the states of Indiana and Oregon.[4] It found that firms with fewer than 500 employees and $10 million of revenue donate at least as much per employee and as a percent of net income as do larger firms. The importance of that funding is magnified when one considers that small businesses, already dominant in industries like wholesale trade, retail trade, and construction, are currently the fastest-growing segment of commercial firms in America.

We've learned not just about the size of small business philanthropy, but about its composition and character. Smaller firms donate a higher proportion of equipment and service compared to cash than do their larger counterparts. A much larger percentage of employees volunteer their time to charity as well. Only one in five small and midsize companies that give substantial sums away account for the gifts in a formal contributions budget. Most treat donations as operating expenses or as part of the cost of goods sold.

What factors motivate giving by small and midsize businesses? "The strongest factors affecting giving by small companies were the personal values of the owner, the condition of the business. Social responsibility, public relations, and the quality of the organization making the request."[5] In very small firms of 100 employees or fewer it is likely that contribution decisions will be reached by the owner. In midsize firms of 101–500 employees, those decisions are likely to be delegated to a single manager. In firms of over 500 employees, the choices are likely to fall to a group of management employees.

It follows that the more we understand about the owner-managers of smaller firms, the better our grasp on the prognosis for new leading actors in business philanthropy.

Enter *The Millionaire Next Door: The Surprising Secrets of America's*

Wealthy.[6] One of those secrets as revealed by best-selling authors Thomas J. Stanley and William D. Danko is that America now enjoys no fewer than 3.5 million millionaires. They own over 50 percent of the total of $22 trillion of personal wealth that had accumulated in the United States by 1996. While only 20 percent of Americans are self-employed, 80 percent of millionaires can be so described. Most are either professionals like lawyers, physicians, and accountants or small business owners. The vast majority are first-generation millionaires, having inherited little if any funds from parents or other relatives.

It is from the decisions of the burgeoning professional and small business millionaire class and those on the way to joining their ranks that charitable contributions increasingly flow. It is in them that great expectations for future growth are placed. For their amassed wealth is simply staggering and unprecedented. Such affluence renders philanthropic generosity more affordable than ever before in American history. That this already large cohort of millionaire professionals, entrepreneurs, and small business owners is likely to expand from five to seven times faster than the general population is a fundraiser's fantasy come true.

What's more, Stanley and Danko found that one of the ingredients of success for the millionaire next door is fastidious attention to savings and investing. He and she save at rates of 15 to 20 percent of annual income, about four to five times more than the average American. He and she invest from 20 to 40 percent of household wealth in common stock. These are the habits of the affluent and those who aspire to that status. They work. Never with more telling results than from roughly 1991 to 1997.

The third source of evidence pointing to the potency of small business as a community-minded, active, and proud philanthropist comes from the Business Committee for the Arts. Its *BCA Report: 1995 National Survey of Business Support to the Arts*[7] contains some remarkable findings about how robust business support of the arts has been of late, with small firms leading the way:

> Businesses with annual revenues of $1 million and more gave $875 million, a record high, to the arts, in 1994. Nearly half the businesses surveyed supported the arts, and allocated an average 19 percent of their philanthropic budget to the arts. *Nearly three-quarters of the total dollars contributed to the arts in 1994 came from companies with $1 million to less than $50 million in annual revenues.* [Emphasis added.]

> Businesses with annual revenues of $1 million and more gave $518 million to the arts in 1991. In 1991, 38 percent of businesses surveyed supported the arts and allocated an average 11 percent of their philanthropic budget to the arts.

> The median dollar amount contributed to the arts in 1994 was $2,000, compared to $1,000 in 1991.[8]

These figures are larger than those reported by the Contributions Council of the Conference Board and by *Giving USA*. The reason is clear. These sources asked only large companies about their charitable support of the arts and generalize from that sample. They therefore miss the high-growth philanthropic story. America's fast-growing small business sector is its leading indicator.

There is a lot more to know about the small businesses of America in terms of both their existing philanthropy and their potential. What we've recently discovered, however, is enough to encourage nonprofits to solicit this part of the business community more efficiently, effectively, and energetically. Its members are sure to write new acts in the unfolding drama of business as benefactor.

Much of small business giving is obligation-based. Many small business owners locate their operations in or near their own home towns. As members in good standing of the community, they are alert to the needs and aspirations of their customers, who are also often friends, suppliers, and colleagues.

The appeals of the local Boy and Girl Scout troop, baseball and soccer teams, community center, and arts ensemble are difficult to turn away. When loyal customers solicit support for heartfelt causes and concerns, their requests can hardly be ignored or greeted with indifference. Campaigns for United Way, the town social service organization, and the neighborhood Meals-on-Wheels operation gain momentum from peer solicitation, modeling, and pressure. Over time, contributions to charity come to be seen as something expected of small business owners.

Real excitement is generated, however, when small and midsize firms move from thinking of charitable contributions as societal dues to viewing them as business opportunities. Creativity and generosity blossom as philanthropy is viewed as a form of enlightened self-interest as well as an expression of altruistic impulse. The ability to shape support of nonprofit institutions and causes so as to motivate employees, enhance brand image, involve customers, and garner good will needn't be confined to large corporations.

International Philanthropy: Prime Time for an American Export

Among the fastest growing components of corporate philanthropy is international giving. Starting at a very low funding base compared with such traditional categories of support as education, health, social services, and the arts in the United States, in total American companies increased overseas giving at rates of roughly 15 percent for each of the last seven years. The Conference Board reported that in 1988 the offshore donations of large firms totaled just $197 million. By 1995 that figure had roughly doubled to $400 million.[9] Considering that in these years overall corporate cash gifts to charity were essentially flat, this boomlet is impressive, particularly so because it excludes financial support of overseas nonprofits from corporate expense budgets like advertising, marketing, sales and public relations, and in-kind donations of equipment and personnel. Available data in those areas are fragmentary and unreliable, the more so because many companies direct international donations to U.S.-based nonprofits where they are credited to American domestic giving.

Something significant is under way. As they might ask in show business, does overseas giving have legs? Will it strengthen and endure? What business dynamics propel international philanthropy? What government policies and accomplishments undergird the commercial growth that will support it? And what has changed abroad to render philanthropy better understood and welcome almost everywhere?

One of the most dramatic transformations of American business in recent decades is its so-called globalization. Since the 1960s the overseas international transactions of American companies have roughly tripled as a percentage of Gross Domestic Product, rising from 6 percent in 1964 to 17 percent in 1996. Another sign of the intensification of American commerce overseas is the expansion of U.S. investment. American-owned foreign assets grew threefold from less than a trillion dollars in 1982 to about three trillion by year-end 1993.[10] Such explosive growth is evidence that more and more American companies are traveling along an international commercial continuum with such destinations as a mature domestic business; a U.S.-centric business with some overseas operations and investment, a multinational business, and a truly global business.

Both a cause and consequence of this phenomenon have been major reductions in the cost of transportation and communication and the virtual elimination of tariffs and other barriers to international merchandise trade. Accelerating these trends of market openness and export expansion is a major theme of President Clinton's foreign policy. It reflects a priority high on the agenda of American business. Indeed, recent achievements of U.S. policy are important indications of even more American overseas commercial activity in the years ahead.

In Mr. Clinton's first term in office what has been termed an international trade triple play was sharply executed.[11] The U.S. negotiated and the Senate approved a global treaty embodying a major new round of tariff reductions on goods, the creation of a World Trade Organization equipped with dispute resolution authority, and a commitment to begin in earnest unprecedented negotiations about reducing barriers to trade in services. This worldwide agreement was complemented by the formation of two major regional trade alliances of which America is a leading member—the North American Free Trade Agreement (NAFTA), a formal treaty receiving Senate approval, and the Asia Pacific Economic Cooperation (APEC) accord. Both NAFTA and APEC members are committed to widening and deepening trade among its members.

All of this activity closely corresponds to the cardinal importance placed by American businesses on enlarging their overseas markets and improving their global competitive position. It is no accident that many of America's most successful firms derive substantial portions of their revenues from outside the United States. Of the twenty companies at the top of *Fortune* Magazine's most admired list for 1997, sixteen either already receive more than 40 percent of their total revenue from outside America or are well on their way to achieving that objective: Coca-Cola, Merck, Microsoft, Johnson & Johnson, Intel, Pfizer, Procter & Gamble, 3M, Hewlett-Packard, Corning, Levi Strauss, Walt Disney, McDonald's, General Electric, and Boeing.

Since corporate philanthropy is closely aligned to business interests, one would expect to see a growing involvement of corporate contributions in advancing international business. In fact, that very dynamic is fully at work. It will gain significant momentum and become a mainstay of American corporate philanthropy over the next decade.

Typically, the involvement of philanthropy in foreign affairs begins with a corporate connection to American nonprofits that employ experts on international politics and economics and on the specific countries in which a company wishes to conduct business. The growth in number and influence of American nonprofit think tanks devoted to better understanding of foreign nations owes much to corporate participation and financial support. With such terms as export quotas, foreign exchange rates, unilateral economic sanctions, GATT, WTO, NAFTA, and APEC entering the working vocabularies of more and more business executives, it is no surprise to find them gathering where they are intelligently discussed.

Outfits like the Berkeley Economic Roundtable, the Council on Foreign Relations, the American Enterprise Institute, the Center for Strategic and International Studies, the Brookings Institution, the Institute for International Economics, the Japan Society, and the Asia Society house and attract experts on the facilitators and inhibitors of global trade. In addition to these and many other freestanding public policy organizations, corporations find it useful to associate with university-based institutes devoted to the study of industries, countries, and issues of international interest. These nonprofits not only provide a sanctuary for learning from resident subject matter authorities, but also a place to network with both American movers and shakers and their foreign counterparts. Besides, the task forces they convene, studies they commission, and policy recommendations they advance do much to shape the opinion climate in Washington and in overseas capitals.

A second area of expression of early interest in nonprofits by companies exploring foreign market entry is foreign-based public policy organizations and the overseas affiliates of U.S. nonprofits. Aspen Berlin, Aspen Tokyo, and Aspen Italia, the World Economic Forum with its now famous annual global conference in Davos, the Trilateral Commission, the Royal Institute of International Affairs, and Bildersberg are among those that attract senior executive involvement. As in America, corporate philanthropy helps open the doors to such institutions and provides them a share of the wherewithal to conduct their business generally or to undertake specific programs and projects of mutual interest.

The third area of early philanthropic involvement for American companies in international matters is responding favorably to calls for humanitarian assistance wherever in the world they are intent on building a business. Offering cash, food, medical supplies, drugs, and equipment to help the victims of natural disasters like earthquakes, tornadoes, famines, and cyclones, or to assist the casualties of man-made calamities like civil wars, ethnic rivalries, and social disorder is not uncommon for American companies. Kobe, Japan, Bosnia, and Rwanda were major sites of worldwide humanitarian assistance in 1995 and 1996.

Those firms with operations or aspirations in particular countries might choose to assist U.S.-based nonprofits that provide emergency relief services. Often referred to as NGOs (nongovernmental organizations), outfits like CARE, the International Red Cross, the International Rescue Committee, the U.S. Committee for UNICEF, and Catholic Relief Services are the beneficiaries. Other companies choose to direct support to NGOs organized inside the afflicted country. Still others steer their funds to multilateral institutions like UNICEF or the United Nations Development Program.

It is a sign of increased voluntary philanthropic interest that American NGOs are becoming far less reliant on federal government funding than was the case only a short time ago. In late 1995, the General Accounting Office reported that whereas international humanitarian NGOs had received 42 percent of their budgets from the U.S. government in 1982, a decade later only 13 percent of their funding came from federal sources.[12] These NGOs have successfully appealed to foreign governments and to private philanthropy, including corporations, broadening and diversifying their support.

These threshold manifestations of corporate contributions activity frequently broaden out as firms expand their business overseas. As their employment grows, as office space is leased and factories built, and as foreign firms are retained to supply goods and services, corporate operations cast burdens on public facilities. Companies find themselves being asked to contribute to building expansion or curriculum enrichment of schools in which the children of their employees are enrolled. They are approached to assist the health care organizations located close to where employees live and work. They are solicited to help celebrate local holidays and support leading cultural events. Rare is the American company unwilling to discharge such minimal community obligations.

As in the case of small business, the most enduring impact of philanthropic engagement comes as firms recognize the opportunities and not just the duties of being a good corporate citizen. Companies with a substantial overseas presence need to source not just their goods and services but their human talent. Savvy firms ask what contribution philanthropy can provide to connecting them to foreign universities and therefore to the best and brightest of their graduates and the research products of their laboratories and institutes. Companies wishing to become or remain important and recognized players in overseas markets need to cultivate relations with key influentials in business, government, and the media. How can philanthropic support of home-grown nonprofit institutions facilitate coming to know them and help command their attention? Companies seeking acceptance as indigenous economic forces rather than as branches of a U.S.-centric operation find advantages in being viewed as citizens in good standing of the countries in which they do business. Being alert to societal needs and joining others in helping to satisfy them through culturally appropriate ways and means offers a competitive edge.

A handful of American firms have appreciated these obligations and benefits for decades. The reputation of Chase Bank in Latin America for the promotion of its gifted visual artists is widespread. IBM, celebrating its eightieth birthday of continuous operations in countries like Japan and Germany, enjoys a well-earned high regard for its many societal contributions as well as its business leadership. Citibank's underwriting of the European, Asian, and Latin American tours of the New York Philharmonic demonstrates the potency of using the arts to entertain customers and influentials overseas. The major $5 million commitment of American Express to a "Save the Monuments Campaign" intended to help catalyze the restoration and repair of a hundred long-neglected landmarks located on seven continents is an impressive piece of philanthropy.

So, what's new? And, what's different now?

The vigorous pursuit of business interests abroad continues to render international philanthropy desirable for U.S. companies. But the extraordinarily rapid growth of the Third Sector around the world makes such giving possible and increasingly sought after. The leading scholar of the size and scope of nonprofits overseas, Lester Salamon, has characterized their recent rise as nothing short of revolutionary:

> From the developed countries of North America, Europe, and Asia to the developing societies of Africa, Latin America, and the former Soviet bloc, people are forming associations, foundations, and similar institutions to deliver human services, promote grass-roots economic development, prevent environmental degradation, protect civil rights, and pursue a thousand other objectives formerly unattended to or left to the state.
>
> The scope and scale of this phenomenon are immense. Indeed, we are in the midst of a global "assocational revolution" that may prove to be as significant to the latter twentieth century as the rise of the nation-state was to the latter nineteenth. The upshot is a global third sector: a massive array of self-governing private organizations, not dedicated to distributing profits to shareholders or directors, pursuing public purposes outside the formal apparatus of the state.[13]

While new nonprofits are being spawned weekly throughout the developing and developed world, it is important to recognize that they supplement an embedded base of existing institutions. Many Americans are surprised to learn of their number. Take Western Europe, for example. While in the United States Third Sector employment as a percentage of the national total is 6.8 percent, comparable figures for France (4.2%), the United Kingdom (4%), Germany (3.7%), and Italy (1.8%) are hardly insignificant. Another indicator of the economic role of nonprofits is to weigh their expenditures as a proportion of the GDP. Here, too, the U.S. leads at 6.3 percent. But to the surprise of many, the United Kingdom at 4.8 percent, Germany at 3.6 percent, France at 3.3 percent, and Italy at 2 percent register Third Sector organizations as a substantial part of their respective economies.[14] All of these figures exclude organized religions and the charities associated with them. Their inclusion would lift Third Sector impact noticeably.

My optimism about the future growth and maturation of international philanthropy is rooted in a recognition of the order of magnitude of existing nonprofit organizations combined with the new cohort exploding on the scene. Their collective clout is being felt as recognition spreads that the problem-solving capacities of government acting alone are severely circumscribed. Public resources are finite. Taxpayer resistance to new taxes is high. Voluntary associations are forming or strengthening as vehicles for self-improvement, self-expression, and self-help. They have tapped new societal sources of energy and initiative, complementary to the indispensable exercise of state power.

Corporations will pay attention to such a major social transformation. The most savvy among them will figure out how to position themselves with what some call "nonstate actors." It hardly goes unappreciated that today's NGOs deliver more development assistance to Third World countries than does the entire UN system. When the time comes to renew China's Most Favored Nation trade status, corporations cannot help but observe that outfits like Human Rights Watch and Amnesty International receive a respectful hearing of their views. When the NAFTA treaty was being negotiated the Bush administration found itself compelled to respond to a broad coalition of NGOs concerned about pollution, health and safety, immigration, and child labor. Ultimately, the agreement incorporated labor and environmental issues.

The ascension of nonprofits abroad in sheer number makes their presence dramatically different in degree. Their collective influence on the delivery of services and on public policy decisions makes their impact different in kind. Jessica Matthews sets forth the case:

> At a time of accelerating change, NGOs are quicker than governments to respond to new demands and opportunities. Internationally, in both the poorest and richest countries, NGOs, when adequately funded, can outperform gov-

ernment in the delivery of many public services. Their growth, along with that of the other elements of civil society, can strengthen the fabric of the many still-fragile democracies. And they are better than governments at dealing with problems that grow slowly and affect society through their cumulative effect on individuals—the "soft" threats of environmental degradation, denial of human rights, population growth, poverty and task of development that may already be causing more deaths in conflict than are traditional acts of aggression.[15]

This combination of quantitative impact and qualitative clout, of service delivery potency and government influence, is the kind of development that changes minds and moves resources. Bullishness about the common stock of overseas business philanthropy is fully merited. Watch, therefore, for continued growth in the corporate share of the $2 billion of American philanthropy directed to international affairs in 1995. More and more companies will join the early pioneers of overseas giving. To do otherwise isn't just uncharitable. To do otherwise would deprive them of an important business asset.

Technology Ascendant, Philanthropy Transformed

A momentous chunk of uncharted territory awaits nonprofit adventurers and explorers, philanthropists not least among them. What do technological advances portend for soliciting gifts, for grantmaking and, most importantly, for the aspirations and operations of nonprofits? Surely this consequential and tantalizing question is high on the agenda of every forward-looking Third Sector organization.

What will be the collective impact of such technological innovations as e-mail, voice mail, fax, compact (digital) disc, cellular phone, beeper, VCR, cable (and interactive) television and computer software on philanthropy, generally, and on corporate philanthropy, particularly? How will ease of access to the Internet, to surfing the Web, to accessing information from multiple data bases and to encountering ideas and people in cyberspace affect the Third Sector's constituent institutions? How will using multimedia devices facilitate learning and the processing of work? How will easy access to interactive modes of communication to express views and respond to prompts help condition the new environment of philanthropy?

From a commercial perspective, it is not yet at all clear whether the World Wide Web will become an advertising medium, a subscription medium, a transaction medium, or comprise some blend of these business arrangements. If the electronic relationship of buyers and sellers is fuzzy, equally obscure is how grantors and grantees and nonprofits and their clients will be affected by the awesome capabilities of emerging technology. Hardly a sizable educational, health, social service, or arts institution and scarcely a substantial foundation is not right now in the throes of considering this very question.

Already we can sense that significant change has crept upon us. The ubiquity of voice mail in business. The extraordinary levels of market penetration of telephone answering machines, cable television, the computer, the fax machine, the VCR, the pager and the wireless phone at home and at work. The number of us who telecommute at least several days each week, if not full time. The exponential growth of Internet access subscribers and of calls to toll-free number databases. The speedy proliferation of corporate, private foundation, and nonprofit Web pages. Something is going on when Third Sector professionals ask one another over drinks how many "hits" their Web page enjoyed last week.

But we also surmise that these are merely illustrations of early adaptation to the possibilities afforded by technology. Compared with what is shortly to come, they are elementary and rudimentary. The unprecedented speed and comprehensiveness of technological change carries profound consequences for nonprofits. Some are imaginable. Most are simply unknown.

Pilot experiments in interactive media with American family subjects conducted by companies like Time-Warner, Disney, and Microsoft are revealing. They suggest that Americans are eager to use these powerful new means of communication to learn about what's going on in their own towns and neighborhoods and to stay in touch with the movers and shakers of their own immediate environment. If it is true that access to the Internet and to other multimedia channels of communication will be used at least as much to discover the news from the local school, church, community center, Boy Scout troop, or theater as to learn about a national event or an international development, then the salutary contribution of nonprofits to social cohesion could be even more far-reaching in the future than at present.

In what ways these new digitized packets of voice, video, and data will influence how we govern nonprofits, deliver services through their good offices, reach to those with a need or an interest and spur involvement, even stimulate generosity, comprises an almost virgin field ready for cultivation. Bold pioneers, venturesome cartographers and thoughtful gardeners will be in high demand.

Questions, all replete with possibility, tumble one over the other.

Will the Internet help even the playing field among competing grant applicants by allowing all comers equal and timely access to donor information, far more accessible and up-to-date and far less costly than is now the case with predominantly printed materials?

Will the Internet significantly increase the interaction among grantors, among grantees and between donors and donees, offering a convenient channel of on-line communication that operates at all hours, across any physical distance?

Will the Internet encourage conversational learning between philanthropic staff and nonprofit executives? For example, might a donor release draft guidelines to a target audience of nonprofits seeking comments and criticisms before releasing them in final form? For example, might donors create "chat rooms" for subsets of their donees to explore a problem or exploit an opportunity? Since turnaround is fair play, might a group of nonprofits address an issue of shared philanthropic concern in a collective voice using the Internet to project messages to an audience of one or more donors?

To what extent will the Internet's multimedia capabilities be exploited to complement e-mail and voice communications with two- (or more) way audio and video, allowing for electronic meetings where live, face-to-face encounters are not logistically possible or are simply too expensive?

How conducive will the Internet be to improving the efficiency and effectiveness of processing foundation business? How much will it reduce travel? To what degree will it allow questions and concerns common to many to be handled by electronic broadcast bulletins rather than by one-on-one correspondence, phone calls, or meetings? In what other myriad ways can the labor- and paper-intensive processes of philanthropy be re-engineered, using technology to cut expenses, add value, and speed decision time?

Each passing month records startling advances in the capabilities of software and communications technology. The feature functions of the television, telephone, and computer are expanding. Applications are multiplying rapidly. Hardware, transmission, and transaction costs are plummeting. Evidence is beginning to accumulate that the use of high technology has increased by orders of magnitude America's productivity at the manufacturing plant, in wholesale and retail distribution, and in such industries as insurance, travel, brokerage, and banking. And we are just beginning to see significant changes emerge in how some hospitals deliver health care and colleges and universities educate their students.

But for the vast preponderance of foundations and nonprofit organizations, the revolution in technology has not yet begun to transform the way business is conducted, let alone alter how it is conceived. That time fast approaches.

It would be well for the very corporations whose inventiveness and innovations gave rise to these capabilities to turn some of their philanthropic attention to possible Third Sector use of them. A few do. They need a lot more company. Helping to realize the vast potential of nonprofits for using technology well is a mission worthy of many enlightened corporations. Increasing the organizational effectiveness of nonprofits. Reaching their own employees, clients, customers, and volunteers faster, more reliably and at lower cost. Highlighting their social agendas before targeted audiences. By such supportive undertakings business has within its power the capacity to prove beyond a shadow of a doubt that its giving works.

Employee-Centered Philanthropy

Conventional wisdom has it that the diffusion of modern technology to American workplace and home has empowered employees, enabling authority to be spread widely throughout the corporation. Access to information has never been easier and quicker. Managers much closer to the customer or to a production process can reach informed and timely decisions on the spot. The delays and distortions associated with orders emerging from the upper reaches of a distant hierarchy to the workers below are now regarded as anathema. Modern corporations are oriented more horizontally, less vertically. Action is taken more in deference to who knows what, rather than who knows whom, or where someone happens to be situated on a table of organization.

The very same hardware and software capabilities that are helping to convert the workplace more to a meritocracy hold promise as well of transforming the relationship of employees to corporate philanthropy. Testing the sentiments of a segment of employees about the value of potential philanthropic initiatives is easy, fast and inexpensive. E-mail and teleconferencing simplify the process of eliciting employee views on possible community relations projects.

Convening employee focus groups to discuss the implications of a projected change in matching gift rules is as simple as setting up a "chat room" on the subject or combining fax transmissions with telephone conference calls. To reverse field, reaching employees with news about opportunities for voluntary service or with requests for assistance to help meet sudden community needs is no more than an audio broadcast or Internet message bulletin away.

The abundance of communication options available to corporate philanthropists will alter not just how and how often employees are informed and engaged. It will transform existing policy in many firms. One example should help enliven this prediction.

At most companies in 1997, the United Way continues to monopolize the charitable payroll deduction program. This remarkable invention encourages employees to reach a decision only once each year about their level of charitable contribution. After they do, portions of every paycheck are automatically deducted and electronically transmitted to the United Way. In no small measure, the powerful advantages of reaching captive audiences of employees with a charitable appeal and offering them a convenient way to give explains how United Way became a $3.5 billion annual fundraising juggernaut.

The next decade will see the end of United Way's privileged insider use of payroll deduction and dominance of highly visible employee workplace solicitation. Irresistible pressures will arise to allow other selective groups of charities, such as united arts drives, environmental coalitions, and disease-specific appeals, to enjoy their own opportunities to reach employees and to invite use of the charitable payroll deduction in their name. Just as matching gift eligibility rules have been significantly liberalized to allow not just colleges and universities but many kinds of charitable organizations to participate, so too will openness and choice come to characterize the diversity of nonprofits having access both to employees and to payroll deduction plans.

The employee who on any given day can with a single phone call change how his or her 401(k) savings plan is invested or opt several times a year to change features of health insurance by clicking on a computer mouse will find charitable paternalism inexplicable and intolerable. Its days are numbered. Choice beckons.

Technology enables employees of any income class to be better informed about available options when they decide how to donate funds and to volunteer their time. It permits those in charge of the philanthropic function to determine employee preferences and increase employee awareness and knowledge as never before. Concurrently, the American economy has produced hundreds of thousands of executives and small business owners who are themselves able to be important individual philanthropists. So record-breaking have been corporate earnings, so buoyant and long-lasting has been the rise in the American stock market, and so conducive to private wealth creation are deferred compensation schemes and stock option set-asides that trillions of dollars will transfer between generations over the next decade.

The corporation as benefactor may become less important to nonprofits than the corporation as identifiable network through which wealthy, and, hopefully charitably generous, business people are reached. The nonprofit that sees a business as a medium through which to access a significant and growing number of affluent individuals as well as a purely institutional source of support will enjoy a sustainable fundraising advantage. The corporate philanthropist, eager to maximize the favorable impact of the firm on the commonweal, will view senior executives not just as institutional allies and partners but as potential large-scale benefactors able to give generously on the strength of their own daunting resources.

To put matters starkly, the charitable contributions record of Microsoft, Berkshire-Hathaway, Time-Warner, and Nike may well matter less to Third Sector organizations than the generosity of their respective chairmen and senior officers, Bill Gates, Warren Buffett, Ted Turner, and Phil Knight. They number among the about 75 members of a relatively new but fast-growing "club" in America, one composed exclusively of billionaires. That growing cadre and the some 250,000 American deca-millionaires collectively wield far more philanthropic clout than the companies that spawned their wealth. Corporate insiders who are in a position to influence the size and direction of the giving of such Americans will perform an extraordinarily valuable service.

The staggering, wholly unprecedented accumulation of private affluence over the last decade and a half promises to open a new era in the annals of American philanthropy. The current generation's equivalent of Andrew Carnegie, John D. Rockefeller, and Julius Rosenwald are barely identified. Who will join George Soros and Walter Annenberg as the new giants of generosity? The number of Americans with the capacity to give away $10 million or more each year is simply awesome.

Corporate philanthropy has never constituted *more* than 7 percent of total cash charitable contributions in any given year. Individual donations have never been *less* than 84 percent. One way to articulate a major challenge both to the corporate philanthropist and to the fundseeking nonprofit is to ask this question: How can we leverage the resources of the modestly growing 7 percent to expand significantly the sums contributed by individuals? Casting the issue this way offers another powerful reason to place employees generally, and wealthy executives, in particular, at the very center of the corporate philanthropic enterprise. For it is they who will determine more than any other force whether giving grows at rates consistent with America's economic good fortune or drifts into an era of complacent self-indulgence.

In the future, corporate philanthropists will be judged not only by the charitable performance of their business, but also by how well employee contributions in time and treasure were encouraged, catalyzed, recognized, and rewarded. In the future, nonprofits will assess their corporate fundraising not only by what a target business opted to donate, but also by how many of its employees give substantially. The burgeoning affluence and economic comfort of millions of Americans remind us that insofar as philanthropy is concerned individuals are the dog, companies the tail.

Creating a corporate culture of caring will redound to the benefit of generosity all around. Employees will take pride in the fact that the business that absorbs so much of their time and attention stands for something beyond the undiluted pursuit of self-interest. Companies will reflect in their giving the public spirited inclinations of their employees.

Whether from their perspective as donors, volunteers, or customers, employees are emerging as leading forces in recasting the role of corporate philanthropy for the new millennium.

The four nascent trends just depicted are animated by corporate philanthropy as a dynamic and growing enterprise. It is an endeavor hardly confined to large business or circumscribed by America's borders. It is a craft soon to be transformed by the deployment of affordable innovations in communication and information processing technology. And it is an undertaking that stands on the shoulders of employees. They bring their values about giving and volunteering to the workplace. They are bound and determined to demonstrate that business success is not at all incompatible with the exercise of social responsibility. Quite the contrary.

The unbounded potential of corporate philanthropy and related activity is woven into the American creed that a free people can organize themselves to solve problems collectively. One indispensable expression of that solidarity is democratic self-government. Another critical and pre-existing form of social compact is manifested in voluntary efforts to organize for public benefit. Employees arrive at work each morning believing that there is no reason why the companies that retain them cannot help to advance American democracy and enrich its pluralistic Third Sector. At the end of the day, a healthy polity and a thriving social order set the context for personal fulfillment and business success. Contributing to these outcomes is both benevolent and self-interested. It is the product of an optimistic, can-do attitude. It is also the result of minding one's business.

Notes

1. Ann E. Kaplan, *Giving USA: The Annual Report on Philanthropy for the Year 1996*. New York: AAFRC Trust for Philanthropy, 1997, pp. 16–20 and 38–40.

2. Ibid., pp. 44–46 and 113–122.

3. Business Committee for the Arts Report, "The 1995 National Survey of Business Support for the Arts," New York: BCA, 1995.

4. Dwight F. Burlingame and Patricia A. Frishkoff, "How Does Firm Size Affect Corporate Philanthropy?" In Dwight F. Burlingame and Dennis R. Young, *Corporate Philanthropy At The Crossroads*. Bloomington and Indianapolis: Indiana University Press, 1996, pp. 86–101.

5. Ibid., p. 93.

6. Thomas J. Stanley and William D. Danko, *The Millionaire Next Door: The Surprising Secrets of America's Wealthy*. Atlanta, GA: Longstreet Press, 1996.

7. BCA Report, "The 1995 National Survey of Business Support for the Arts." New York: BCA, 1996, p. 2.

8. Ibid., p. 3.

9. Linda B. Gornitsky, "Benchmarking Corporate International Contributions: A Research Report." New York: The Conference Board, Report Number 1103–96-RR, 1996.

10. C. Fred Bergsten, *Whither APEC? The Progress to Date and Agenda for the Future*. Washington, DC: The Institute for International Economics, 1997.

11. C. Fred Bergsten, *America in the World Economy: A Strategy for the 1990s*. Washington, DC: The Institute for International Economics, 1988.

12. Shepard Forman, "Paying for Essentials; Resources for Humanitarian Assistance." Background paper presented at a conference held on September 11 and 12, 1997, in Pocantico, New York by the Center on International Cooperation, New York University.

13. Lester M. Salamon, "The Global Associational Revolution: The Rise of the Third Sector on the World Scene," *Occasional Paper*. No. 15. Baltimore: Johns Hopkins University Institute for Policy Studies, April 1993.

14. Lester M. Salamon and Helmut K. Anheier, *The Emerging Nonprofit Sector: An Overview*. Manchester and New York: Manchester University Press, 1996.

15. Jessica T. Matthews, "Powershift," *Foreign Affairs*, January–February 1997, Volume 76, Number 1, p. 63.

CHAPTER SIX

Reinventing Philanthropy

Leslie Lenkowsky

By most measures, the American philanthropic world seems to be doing well and getting better.[1] Nonetheless, almost regardless of point of view, its leaders declare it to be at least greatly challenged, if not in serious distress. The source of this paradox is chiefly that government (and, though not the focus of this paper, business) are in the midst of reinventing their roles and purposes as the twentieth century comes to an end. Yet, that quintessential creation of this century—the large, nationally oriented philanthropic institution—is still unsure about its place in American life.

Judging by the outward signs, the health of the nation's philanthropic sector seems robust. Individual charitable giving continues to rise, keeping pace with the nation's economic growth. Foundations are more numerous and wealthier than ever before; some have so much to spend that they are hard-pressed to do so thoughtfully. New ways of making donations, such as through funds managed by investment companies, are appearing and flourishing. Although, measured against pre-tax net income, corporate contributions budgets are not as generous as they used to be, American business is relying more extensively on other avenues for helping favored causes, including allowing employees to take time off with pay to "volunteer."

The number of charities in the United States keeps increasing. In 1996, the Internal Revenue Service recognized over 625,000 organizations as "501(c)(3)" groups, entitled to exemption from taxation and to receive tax-deductible gifts. Another 500,000 or so fell into other tax-exempt categories and perhaps an even greater number—consisting of religious organizations, local affiliates of national charities, self-help groups, informal associations, and the like—do not even show up in the count. While most of these are small, the larger ones have become quite large indeed, whether measured in terms of members, income, or assets.

Looming on the horizon is an intergenerational transfer of wealth—to "baby boomers" from their parents—that some analysts value in the trillions of dollars. Together with the enormous new fortunes being created around high technology companies such as Microsoft and Hewlett-Packard, it is likely to fuel an outpouring of philanthropic ambitions well into the next century. The media's growing attention to the giving habits of the rich and famous will undoubtedly help sustain it.

Yet, one need not spend too much time reading or listening to seemingly knowledgeable experts to get a much different picture of the condition of the philanthropic world. While allowing that opinions might differ over whether or not a "true 'crisis'" exists, wrote one scholar recently, "it seems clear that a challenge of potentially historic proportions is at hand" (Salamon, 1997, p. 4). From a different standpoint, a commission of prominent citizens, chaired by former Tennessee Governor Lamar Alexander, concluded that "American charity is sorely in need of reform and renewal if it is going to lead the way to a new era of rebuilding broken neighborhoods and aiding the people who live in them" (National Commission on Philanthropy and Civic Renewal, 1997, p. 5). Several other study groups and projects (including the American Assembly's) have also come into being recently to address the problems supposedly besetting philanthropy.

Three years ago, in an article that leaped from the pages of a relatively obscure academic journal to the "Style" section of *The Washington Post*, Harvard political scientist Robert Putnam contended that Americans were participating less often in civic organizations and social clubs (Putnam, 1995). Notwithstanding contrary evidence (Ladd, 1996), the thesis has caught on, helping to spark a well-publicized "summit" of national leaders in Philadelphia last April that promoted increased volunteering and corporate giving. Through AmeriCorps and other programs, the Clinton administration has made energizing civic spirit, especially among young people, a distinguishing feature of its agenda. Not to be outdone, leading Congressional Republicans have offered their own proposals for encouraging greater use of charitable institutions, including religious ones, to address the nation's social problems (Coats and Kasich, n.d.).

It is, of course, conceivable that the philanthropic world could be flourishing, yet also in need of help. Like blind men examining an elephant, those who look at the vast domain of American philanthropy can readily draw inferences from one portion of it that are incomplete or misleading with respect to the whole. While charitable contributions overall may be rising, donor generosity (measured, for example, by the percentage of income given away) has not much varied for over twenty years.[2] If many hospitals and educational institutions look well-heeled these days, human service agencies or arts companies still often struggle to make ends meet. Although nearly half the population (and a larger proportion of young people than adults) claim to volunteer a significant amount of time each year to help their communities, so much seems to remain undone that the level of civic engagement hardly looks munificent.

Indeed, at least in part, the current anxiety about the state of the philanthropic world reflects a heightening of expectations for it. Historically and comparatively, of course, as Alexis de Tocqueville recognized in proclaiming the American habit of forming "associations" the "mother of all other forms of knowledge" (de Tocqueville, 1988, p. 518), the United States has always given its voluntary and charitable organizations an unusually large role in serving the public. But increasingly in the 1930s and with accelerating speed during the 1960s, government—and especially the federal government—became more concerned about and involved with the kinds of issues—helping the poor, caring for the sick, feeding the hungry, and the like—that had traditionally been major preoccupations of philanthropic groups. So extensively did the public sector expand its efforts, in fact, that when leaders of the philanthropic world contemplated its health a quarter-century ago, they focused principally on whether or not, if then-current trends continued, there would be much left for them to do.[3]

Today, the situation seems to have changed dramatically. Even traditionally liberal politicians now claim to want to reduce the size of the public sector, or reform it to "steer" but not "row" (Osborne and Gaebler, 1993, pp. 25–48). Likewise, since the election of Ronald Reagan, conservatives have not only sought to reduce public spending, but also called upon the nation's voluntary groups to take on more responsibilities in American life. Far from fearing marginalization, what now worries the philanthropic world's leaders is that they may be expected to do too much.

At the same time, a new challenge is arising from a different direction: the business world. Especially in health care and education, for-profit companies are increasingly—and successfully—undertaking activities that once were the nearly exclusive domain of nonprofit groups. Moreover, in seeking new sources of revenue, many traditional charities have resorted to charging higher fees and generating other kinds of market-driven income. As a result, the line between business and philanthropy has become blurrier, and sometimes vanished altogether, as when nonprofits "convert" into for-profit corporations. What this growing convergence might mean for the special status charities have long enjoyed and more importantly, for how they actually operate, remains unsettled—and, to many, unsettling (Lenkowsky, 1997).

Thus, the crisis the philanthropic world faces is more one of identity than size and scope.[4] If the United States is embarked on a course that leads away from the kind of active, national government that has characterized it for much of the twentieth century, what should nonprofit groups, many of which have grown dependent upon the public sector, do? If American industry is discovering new ways of doing well by doing good, how should American charities respond? And if the values of neither politics nor commerce are to dominate the activities of the philanthropic world, which ones should?

Answering these questions is no simple matter for a sector of society that is most often identified by what it is not, or what it is between. Nonetheless, if the philanthropic world is to make better use of the resources it has (and is likely to obtain), a clearer understanding of what it is, and where it can best fit in American life, might help.

Philanthropy and Nation

In 1909, an editor named Herbert Croly, the most distinguished man of letters of his day, published a book called *The Promise of American Life*. In it, he observed that "the American dream" remained alive and well in the hearts of his countrymen, including those newly arrived on the nation's shores. What was diminishing, however, was the capacity to achieve it. The United States was now continental in size, industrial in its economy, and heterogeneous and urbanized in its population. Yet, its public philosophy—its ideas about how to achieve the "Promise"—was mostly still that of the coastal, small-craftsman-and-farmer society of its birth. (So too, for the most part, were its charitable organizations.) Croly called on the nation to adopt a new philosophy, one which accepted a more active national government and strived to build a national community in order to pursue "the American Promise" in the vastly different world of the twentieth century (Croly, 1965).

It is surely not coincidental that *The Promise of American Life* appeared at the same time the first modern philanthropic foundations were coming into existence. Indeed, as Karl and Katz have written, the efforts of these early grantmakers can be seen as ways of trying to address problems of national scope during a period in which the powers of the national government were weak (Karl and Katz, 1981, p. 238). Moreover, what came to be their preferred tools—the mobilization of expert knowledge—was entirely consistent with the thinking of Croly and other "progressives," who mistrusted the political class of their day.

Not long after, however, the size and scope of American government at all levels began to grow, affording both opportunities and challenges to the philanthropic world. Foundations and charities gained potentially rich and powerful allies for their efforts to deal with the issues of concern to them. But at the same time, they acquired potentially far-reaching and domineering rivals for identifying and serving the public interest.

Through the 1970s, the philanthropic world largely managed to accommodate itself to the greatly expanded role of government. Working in partnership with the resource-rich, but supposedly idea-poor, public sector, it found itself able to undertake programs of social reform its own resources could not hope to sustain. Indeed, for awhile, one of the measures of an effective foundation or charity was whether or not the demonstration project it had funded and carefully nurtured could become the model for a new federal initiative. More than a few did.

A new way of thinking about the role of the nation's voluntary and charitable groups also began to emerge. By helping not only to create, but also to implement, government programs, the nonprofit sector could make them more flexible and effective. As the Commission on Private Philanthropy and Public Needs—the Filer Commission—put it:

> The sector ideally should not compete with government so much as complement it and help humanize it. . . . Nor because of instititutional inertia or self-protectiveness should it or parts of it stand in the way of proper extensions of government into areas where, because of the demands of scale or equity, the private sector simply cannot fill a collective want. The sector should not be at odds with government, in other words, so much as outside of it and in addition to it. (Commission on Philanthropy and Public Needs, p. 48)

Political scientist Lester M. Salamon would later term these arrangements "third-party government."[5]

Whatever they might be called, they were enormously rewarding to the parties involved. The participation of so many well-respected nonprofit groups broadened the base of support for public programs and made their expansion more palatable in a country that was still ambivalent about the proper role of the national government. Professionals in the philanthropic world became interchangeable with their counterparts in government, giving rise to a new job description—"the in-and-outer." Public grants and contracts swelled the coffers of the nation's charities. Indeed, some of them owed their very existence to the need to find operating partners for new government programs.

To be sure, populist suspicions about the influence of organizations built on private wealth remained. And from within the philanthropic world itself occasionally arose concerns about loss of autonomy or opportunities to innovate. The bulk of the nation's charities had little if any role in "third-party government," chiefly because of their religious commitments. Likewise, most small foundations—and even a few large ones—focused their efforts on modest undertakings, relatively close to home, rather than put their resources behind campaigns for social reform on a national (or international) scale.

Still, as Robert H. Bremner has observed, the interplay of philanthropy and government became greater in the 1960s than it had been since the New Deal (Bremner, 1988). Although such partnerships had occurred many times before in American history, they had never reached the scope or degree of self-consciousness as those which developed out of the Great Society. For large and powerful portions of the philanthropic world, promoting bold initiatives for reshaping the nation's social, political or economic structure—invariably on behalf of the "public" (or at least particular segments, such as the poor and minorities)—became central to their missions. Encouraging citizen activism and advocacy as tools to support them grew in popularity.

The New Public Philosophy

Then along came Ronald Reagan. Starting in the 1980s, government itself, and especially the federal government, seemed to reverse course. Frustrated by the apparent lack of progress in addressing issues such as school reform and welfare dependency and spurred by an electorate less willing to pay for new experiments in social policy, public officials began to question the nature of the partnership that had developed with the philanthropic world. Instead of seeing government as resource-rich but idea-poor, they began to imagine just the opposite. Rather than looking at the philanthropic world as an important place for developing and implementing new ideas for social progress, they viewed it as a potential source of money and volunteers to carry out plans devised inside public bureaucracies.[6]

Private philanthropy should take more "responsibility for solving public needs," White House officials suggested.[7] And why not? If government and philanthropy could be partners when taxpayers were willing to pay the bills, why not when they weren't? Virtually the entire philanthropic world resisted this suggestion vigorously, arguing that their resources were not nearly sufficient to replace cutbacks in government spending. But this argument (and the considerable research used to buttress it)[8] implicitly conceded the principle that philanthropic dollars were interchangeable with public ones, just not as plentiful.

In addition, the Reagan administration proposed to curtail political advocacy by nonprofit organizations. This too grew out of the complex relationship between government and philanthropy that had developed during the previous decades. Going back nearly to Croly's time, the use of federal funds to lobby the public sector had been forbidden. With the widespread expansion of government support for philanthropic groups, including a growing number that viewed advocacy as crucial for their missions, enforcement became more difficult. By trying to promulgate new rules to ensure that only the funds a charity obtained from private sources would be used for political activities, the Reagan administration ignited a furious protest that simply underscored how important influencing the actions of government had become to the philanthropic world (Salamon, 1984).

Exactly where this turnabout in public philosophy has left the nation's nonprofit groups is a complex question. Salamon and various colleagues have argued that reductions in the federal budget have had a significant impact on nonprofit revenues. Nonetheless, through the end of the Bush administration, nonprofit income had grown more rapidly than the U.S. economy as a whole, with government support (including state and local) responsible for 40 percent of the increase (Salamon, 1997). Federal funding priorities have undeniably changed, adversely affecting some parts of the philanthropic world (such as groups engaged in the arts, community development, or international aid) and helping others (notably, higher education and health care). But whether these shifts reflected defensible programmatic considerations or indiscriminate budget tightening is open to argument.[9]

Narrowing eligibility for government assistance in areas "of interest" to nonprofits (as Salamon puts it) has potentially increased the need for greater philanthropic support, although the claims of middle- or upper-income people whose federal benefits have been reduced are not necessarily ones for which charities might feel responsible.[10] In any event, notwithstanding President Clinton's declaration that "the era of big government" was over and the election of three Republican Congresses, the 1990s may be shaping up to be a better period for federal support of nonprofits than the previous decade (Abramson and Salamon, 1997).

Likewise, despite efforts by conservative legislators, no significant new restrictions on advocacy by philanthropic groups have been enacted. In response to concerns about violations of campaign finance rules, the Internal Revenue Service is reportedly paying closer attention to the activities of nonprofit groups, but the likelihood of new legislation is doubtful. Ironically, the most conspicuous casualty of the debate over political involvement by charities has so far been the Speaker of the House of Representatives, Newt Gingrich, who paid a sizable fine for failing to consult his lawyers before using 501(c)(3) groups for ostensibly partisan purposes.[11]

Notwithstanding oft-expressed concerns that public support distorts and harms charities, conservatives in Congress and elsewhere have not been reluctant to make proposals that would increase the amount of government entanglement with nonprofits and their supporters. One favorite idea, publicly financed "vouchers" for education, would, if enacted, substantially enlarge federal, state, and local government payments to nonprofit elementary and secondary schools. Another seeks to create new income tax incentives to induce donors to increase their contributions to charities officially designated as benefiting the poor. Aided by the enactment of welfare reform in 1996, which included a "charitable choice" provision, Republican governors, such as Wisconsin's Tommy Thompson and Michigan's John Engler, and mayors, such as Indianapolis' Stephen Goldsmith, have sought to enlist nonprofit groups (including religious ones) in helping to reduce the number of public assistance recipients. If not enthusiastic supporters, Republicans have also acquiesced in the Clinton administration's major initiative for the philanthropic world: a series of programs to recruit and pay "volunteers" to work full-time with charities in communities throughout the United States.[12]

Philanthropy and Devolution

Although it is today more likely to be called "privatization" than "third-party government," the relationship between philanthropy and the public sector thus remains extensive. However, as a result of federal budget concerns as well as lowered public confidence in Washington, the national government no longer looks like the preeminent partner it once was. Even where national involvement continues to be significant, growing support for "devolution" is shifting much of the initiative for policy innovations to state and local arenas.[13] If, following Croly's lead, Americans have spent most of the twentieth century seeking national solutions to the country's problems, they now seem more intent on looking for answers rooted in local communities and institutions.

For the pace-setters in the philanthropic world, this could present a major challenge. Having blazed the path toward an active national government even before political support existed for one, many foundations and other nonprofit groups may now find themselves dealing with a much different environment. Among the reasons that the partnership with Washington developed so readily is that most of the participants on both sides were likely to have been educated in similar schools, pay attention to similar newspapers and journals, react similarly to perceived problems, and share much else as well. In short, they were part of a national community which may have disagreed from time to time over priorities and methods, but generally possessed similar outlooks.

That may not be the case in statehouses or city halls. Devolution is not just a financial or administrative change, which can be smoothed over through training programs and similar efforts to create a common operating framework. It is potentially a political shift as well, where local goals and values may bear on policies in ways that will seem wrongheaded, catastrophic, distasteful, or worse to those with a more cosmopolitan perspective. Ideas about what to do with welfare recipients, how to educate children, or how to punish criminals are apt to be different in state capitals, city halls, or community centers from those discussed in conference rooms in New York, hotels in Washington, or museums in Los Angeles. To succeed in the future, large parts of the philanthropic world will need to figure out what to do in these less charted waters.

Some groups have already tripped on the minefields. In trying to promote "state initiatives" in health policy, for example, the Robert Wood Johnson Foundation encountered a "backlash" against its efforts in several states that ultimately threatened their downfall. Notwithstanding the approval of some key officeholders, other officials, along with parents and interested groups, protested that foundation projects aimed at improving health care for adolescents or controlling medical costs were offensive to local values. Wrote two observers of these confrontations:

> Foundations and those who evaluate their work should recognize that discussion, better staffing, technical aid and diffusion of knowledge can tidy up the messiness of health politics only so far. Some conflicts are, so to speak, "hardwired" into complex policy problems by the very nature of decision making in a democratic society. (Stevens and Brown, 1997, p. 93)

This is not a new problem for the philanthropic world.[14] But it may well become a more frequent one.

In its report, *Giving Better, Giving Smarter*, the National Commission on Philanthropy and Civic Renewal offered advice to grantmakers to help them avoid these pitfalls. They will need to devote more of their resources to addressing "tangible problems" and less to testing "the grand theory" of social change, the Commission maintained. They will have to spend more time getting to know the recipients of their support and less to study and "talking to one another." They will need to become more accustomed to working with faith-based charities and other groups embodying strong moral convictions, which are likely to be more prevalent and influential away from Washington. And, if they really wish to open "paths of self-reliance for the poor," grantmakers will have to look harder for partners who are more "entrepreneurial" than governmental in their outlook, as well as be more willing to use "hard-nosed evaluation" to gauge the effectiveness of their work (National Commission on Philanthropy and Civic Renewal, pp. 19–20, 113–18).

These recommendations undoubtedly mix the Commission's preferences with its assessment of the requirements for successful philanthropy at the grassroots. Even so, they invoke an old and honorable tradition in American philanthropy, exemplified by the contrast between Stephen Girard's charitable work and Benjamin Rush's during the Federalist period in Philadelphia. As Bremner has noted:

> Girard responded to specific needs rather than to general causes. Unlike Rush and other humanitarian reformers who came before and after him, Girard felt under no obligation to try to cure or prevent social disorders or to try to remold society by any means other than economic self-interest. Yet, within the limits of a somewhat misanthropic philosophy, Girard, in times of emergency, was capable of acts of public usefulness and private kindness. (Bremner, p. 39)[15]

The key question facing the philanthropic world today is whether or not, in the wake of the centralizing forces of twentieth century American life, it can—and should—go back to this earlier vision of its role and purposes.

Dilemmas of Devolution

Indeed, many organizations—including that relatively modern invention, the community foundation—would argue that they have been operating in this mode all along. Even in philanthropy's formative years, some of its most celebrated activity, such as establishing libraries, improving education for southern blacks, and eradicating parasitic diseases, was undertaken by donors in places far from Washington (not to mention, one might add, far from where they themselves lived). While seeking to influence federal priorities, national charities and voluntary groups often maintained an energetic local presence as well. In fact, one of the attractions of "third-party government" for national policy-makers is that it seemed to give them well-established local conduits for implementing and adapting their designs for social change.

Yet, thinking nationally but acting locally is not necessarily the same as being responsive to pressing community concerns. Instead of trying to promote the latest theories for reforming education, the latter might entail undertaking programs to create more good schools, or enable more disadvantaged children to attend the ones that exist. Instead of experimenting with new models of health care, it might involve devoting resources to care for the sick or help those at risk to avoid becoming ill. Instead of devising ingenious strategies to alter the social or economic factors supposedly producing poverty, it could mean focusing efforts on aiding the poor to find and keep jobs, shelter or family support. The view from the ground floor is always different—and invariably less panoramic—than the one from the top. To be effective in an devolutionary era, the philanthropic world may have to rely more on a microscope than a telescope to see what needs to be done.[16]

To many, such lowering of sights reeks of timidity, if not wastefulness of scarce philanthropic resources. It suggests that local problems can be separated from national ones, and that local solutions can succeed apart from more systemic changes. It also counts critically on the willingness and capacity of communities to address their own needs. Much of the philanthropic energy that gravitated toward national outlets did so precisely because grassroots initiatives seemed—at least to those trying to promote them—inadequate to the task, or bogged down in local inertia or opposition. Even today, areas in need of help may be poorly endowed with philanthropic resources, while those in which they are plentiful may put them to use in ways that seem self-serving or remote from more urgent concerns not far away.[17] According to Salamon and others, "third-party government" developed precisely to cope with these kinds of "voluntary failure" (Salamon, 1995, pp. 44–48).

However, responding to persistent and deep-seated local concerns is not inherently a less challenging (or reasonable) use of resources by the philanthropic world than trying to deal with them from afar. In each case, the test should be what is accomplished, not what is attempted. Nor is a concentration on community-based solutions incompatible with acknowledging the potential contribution of broader factors (such as, for example, the nation's economic growth rate); it merely accepts the limitation that charitable and voluntary groups may be better able to influence one rather than the other. And while they are inevitably dependent upon the willingness of people to help voluntarily, philanthropic concerns can—and do—change. Apart from any new incentives public policy might provide (such as tax credits for gifts to groups that aid the poor), attaching greater importance to—and placing greater burdens on—locally oriented charities may call forth different kinds of philanthropic responses as well.

To be sure, some areas have more charitable resources than others. Moreover, as Salamon's research in the 1980s showed, government aid was especially useful in making up for shortages in communities where the nonprofit sector was not well established or well supported. Nonetheless, since public social welfare funding was also greater in cities that relied extensively on charitable efforts, the redistributive impact of government spending between philanthropically wealthy and poorer areas could not have been substantial (Salamon, 1995, pp. 76–79). In any event, devolution does not necessarily mean that federal financial help will no longer be available, but only that Washington may send it with fewer strings attached.

For example, because of the baseline chosen for calculating its block grant, the 1996 welfare reform, the Personal Responsibility and Work Opportunity Reconciliation Act, has initially provided more federal money to most states than they would have had under the public assistance and social services programs it replaced. Whether or not these funds will be applied to areas where philanthropic support is in short supply, though, will now more closely reflect state and local political considerations than national ones.

Private donors can also direct their gifts to areas that might lack other charitable resources. This was precisely what early philanthropists, such as Andrew Carnegie and Julius Rosenwald, did, taking care to ensure that local support existed for their efforts.[18] Today, perhaps the best-known example of this sort of "revenue-sharing" is the Lilly Endowment's "community foundations initiative," through which the nation's wealthiest foundation contributes a sizable amount of funds to locally oriented grantmakers throughout Indiana. Although Lilly has occasionally been criticized for focusing too much of its attention on its home state, its program may turn out to be a model that is particularly suited for a period in which attempting to leverage national developments may be less fruitful than enhancing community capacity.[19]

Still, many of the issues the philanthropic world tries to address have consequences that go beyond state or local boundaries. Education is the quintessential example: a predominantly community concern (and responsibility) that has profound implications for the nation's economy, governability, and culture. Likewise, though perhaps to a lesser degree, so do social welfare and health services. How effectively communities address these issues will be important not just for themselves, but for neighbors near and far as well. If support for a more active national government partly reflected an awareness of these "spillover" effects, a growing preference for devolution will not make them disappear.

Even so, philanthropic efforts directed at the grassroots are by no means incompatible with achieving nationally beneficial results. Much depends on what they try to accomplish. If local school reform groups, for instance, sought to ensure that students could perform at "world-class" levels of proficiency, the nation's productivity would increase and illiteracy diminish. If community-based clinics tried to reduce the number of children who were not immunized or were born prematurely, the health of the nation's population would improve and the burdens that might otherwise fall on health-care systems throughout the country decrease. If grassroots groups tried to place welfare recipients in sustainable jobs, the national poverty rate would go down and expenditures for public assistance diminish. In short, achieving national goals does not necessarily require using national means.[20]

Can Philanthropy Reinvent Itself?

It does, however, require an appropriate and effective vision of what to do. In this respect, charitable and voluntary groups are often said to have advantages over government-sponsored programs, since they can be more flexible, embody values that might not be broadly shared, incorporate religious instruction and other methods that the public sector must eschew, and are more likely to be held to account, if not by those they aim to serve, then by their supporters. However, these same advantages can be liabilities if they cause philanthropic organizations to be too accommodating, pursue causes of marginal importance (or worse), adopt methods that are limiting and unproductive, and induce excessive concern about offending important patrons. Moreover, whether or not the nonprofit sector has more know-how for addressing difficult community problems than government does remains an open question.[21] As a result, if more will be expected of the philanthropic world in the future, one might wonder how well it can really respond.

Among the reasons for concern is the increased dependency of the nation's charitable and voluntary groups on fees for service and other commercial income, as well as the growing influence of for-profit ventures (including many that began as nonprofit ones) in areas once principally of interest to the philanthropic world.[22] This has led some to worry that "market" values may supersede charitable ones, causing organizations to judge their activities by what they are worth, rather then whether they are worthwhile. Government officials have also begun more actively questioning the propriety of tax-exemption and other kinds of official favoritism for groups that look and operate more like businesses than charities.[23] In contrast, others believe that a healthy dose of "entrepreneurialism" could be useful for many nonprofits and enable them to accomplish their charitable missions more effectively (Emerson and Twersky, 1996). Some have even encouraged grant-makers not just to think of themselves as "venture capitalists," but also to behave like them (Letts, Ryan and Grossman, 1997).

Much work remains to be done to assess the consequences of the commercial revolution in the philanthropic world. But in the meantime, remembering Adam Smith's famous dictum—"It is not from the benevolence of the butcher, the brewer, or the baker that we expect our dinner, but from their regard for their own interest"—might not be a bad idea (Smith, 1937, p. 14). If not as noble as altruism, the profit-motive is by no means inconsistent with doing good for others.

A more troubling source of concern is the legacy of "third-party government." The impetus for the current enthusiasm for devolution is partly the belief that government priorities would be different (and better) if they were more closely connected to grassroots realities. Whether or not this really is true remains to be seen, and not just in the public sector. After so many years of viewing themselves as partners with the federal government, it would not be surprising if large segments of the philanthropic world have come to identify more with its purposes than with community ones (insofar as the two may differ). Nor are the political, professional, and cultural values and outlooks that have facilitated relationships with federal agencies (and within national charities) apt to vanish, just because the initiative for social change is becoming more localized.

For some, this is the silver lining in the dark cloud of devolution. It suggests that not much will be different if the philanthropic world shifts its attention to the grassroots, except for the scope of operations. But for others, it implies a new form of "voluntary failure": the inability of the nation's charities to pursue innovative or diverse courses of action because they have come to think alike. While, as advocates of this strategy suggest (Olasky, 1996; Woodson, Sr., 1998), new—and more effective—charities or voluntary groups may emerge once the edifice of "third-party government" is torn down, much of the philanthropic world may still pursue visions that, for better or worse, are similar in the future to what they have been in the recent past.

In a devolutionary era, however, they may at least have to bear greater responsibility for such choices. For among the more unfortunate consequences of its burgeoning alliance with the public sector is that the philanthropic world grew more heavily dependent on government. Its activities became subject to increased regulation, its revenues and expenditures impacted by the terms and availability of public funds, its choices of missions and methods constrained by legal and political requirements. "Voluntary failure" became a rationale for government intervention, not for correcting and improving the work of the nation's philanthropic groups, or encouraging more active forms of citizen involvement.

If it merely replaces the federal government with dependency on state and local ones, devolution will not much alter this pattern. But if it refocuses interest and attention on what community organizations and citizen groups actually accomplish (or fail to achieve), it will create the conditions for doing so. Whether or not this will prove welcome to a philanthropic world that has grown accustomed to sharing—and diffusing—responsibility with various levels of government is another matter.

This much is clear. After nearly a century of pursuing national purposes through national means, the philanthropic world, like public policy, faces the challenge of reinventing itself to be more relevant to the values and problems of local communities. The change will undoubtedly not be smooth. However, the real measure of its consequences will be found in its impact not on the finances and relationships of "third-party government," but on how success-fully the nation's charitable and voluntary groups determine what they ought to do and how they ought to do it.

Notes

1. Throughout this paper, I will be using "philanthropy" or "philanthropic world" broadly to refer to both donors (such as foundations) and organizations that undertake charitable activities. When it is necessary to distinguish between the two groups, I will do so.

2. According to the annual editions of *Giving USA*, Americans gave 1.86% of their incomes to charities in 1995, the same proportion they gave in 1973. In between, the figure went as high as 2.00% and as low as 1.74% (AAFRC Trust for Philanthropy, 1996).

3. "Decreasing levels of private giving, increasing costs of nonprofit activity and broadening expectations for health, education, and welfare services as basic entitlements of citizenship have led to the government's becoming a principal provider of programs and revenues in many areas once dominated by private philanthropy. And government's growing role in these areas poses fundamental questions about the autonomy and basic functioning of private nonprofit organizations and institutions" (Commission on Private Philanthropy and Public Needs, 1975, p. 16).

4. For earlier examples, see Hall, 1992, pp. 13–83; Karl and Katz, 1981, pp. 236–70.

5. The concept was first presented in his article "Rethinking Public Management: Third Party Government and the Changing Forms of Government Action," which appeared in the Summer 1981 issue of *Public Policy*. It was republished as chapter 1 in Salamon, 1995.

6. To be sure, a number of conservative philanthropic organizations, including several private foundations and think tanks, played key roles in developing and promoting the Reagan administration's agenda. But in general, their domestic policy recommendations called for reducing federal funding and increasing reliance on state and local government, as well as local nonprofit groups, families, and individual effort. See, for example, Meyer, 1982.

7. This was the charge given to the Task Force on Private Sector Initiatives, appointed by the Reagan administration in 1981.

8. Under the direction of Lester Salamon, the Urban Institute sponsored "The Nonprofit Sector Project," which issued a series of reports on the changing nature of the financial relationship between nonprofit organizations and government, both nationally and in selected sites throughout the country.

9. One of the largest changes, for example, involved the replacement of the Comprehensive Employment and Training Act (CETA) with the Job Training Partnership Act (JTPA) in 1982. Although this meant a significant cutback in federal funds for nonprofit groups, CETA was widely regarded as an ineffective program.

10. For further discussion of this and other issues in interpreting the impact of changes in federal spending on nonprofits, see Lenkowsky, 1996.

11. Similarly, a group created by Republican political leader Jack Kemp in 1995 to examine the feasibility of a "flat tax" was denied tax-exemption by the Internal Revenue Service. See "Jack Kemp's Tax-Study Group Loses Court Decision Over Tax-Free Status," *The Wall Street Journal*, February 13, 1998, p. B7.

12. A major component of this effort, the Points of Light Foundation, was actually a creation of the Bush administration.

13. The 1996 welfare reform is the most conspicuous example of this. Although Washington will continue to pay a large share of the costs, state governments now have much greater control over their public assistance programs than they previously had.

14. An often-cited example of a philanthropy's role in generating controversy is the Ford Foundation's effort, in the late 1960s, to promote "community control" of schools in New York City. Black nationalists soon clashed with teachers, triggering a dispute that attracted nationwide attention. Even though, for the Ford Foundation, this was a local project, critics charged it was an attempt to impose a theory of social change without sufficient regard for the ethnic dynamics of the community in which it was to be tried.

15. See also the exchange from *McGuffey's Reader* (1844) between Mr. Fantom and Mr. Goodman on "true" and "false" philanthropy, reprinted in O'Connell, pp. 59–61.

16. "Telescopic philanthropy" is how Charles Dickens in *Bleak House* (and George Eliot in *Middlemarch*) characterized certain Victorian donors, "whose charity increases directly as the square of the distance."

17. The mismatch need not just be geographic. Wealthy donors may give little if any help to charities serving low-income people. See Odendahl, 1990.

18. Before providing the funds to build libraries, Carnegie required communities to agree to maintain them. Rosenwald insisted on local support for the schools he helped to build, even in the poverty-stricken, rural South, where it was more likely to be given in "kind" or by volunteers than in cash. Especially in thinking about low-income areas, philanthropic resources should not be equated only with money.

19. The Lilly Endowment also supports projects of national scope, both within and outside Indiana. However, its concentration on underwriting community initiatives distinguishes it from most other grant-makers its size. Milwaukee's Lynde and Harry Bradley Foundation, which sponsored the National Commission on Philanthropy and Civic Renewal, has likewise added to its portfolio of national grants a program of unrestricted gifts to selected grassroots organizations throughout the United States.

20. Standard-setting has traditionally been an important activity for national voluntary groups. In a devolutionary era, it is likely to become even more so,

though the potential for controversy may also grow, insofar as the views of national groups about what is desirable differ from those of local counterparts.

21. By "know-how," I simply mean an understanding of what might be necessary, for example, to reduce teenage pregnancy or increase reading scores among children from disadvantaged backgrounds. While the philanthropic world may have no surer sense of this than government agencies do, its supposedly greater ability to experiment and evaluate ought to enable it to find out (though pursuing effectiveness may not be the only—or even most important—motive for many charities and voluntary groups).

22. According to the *Nonprofit Almanac 1996–97* (Hodgkinson and Weitzman, 1996), "private-sector payments" accounted for 39.1 percent of nonprofit revenues in 1992, more than twice as much as "private contributions." In *Holding the Center*, Salamon (1997, p. 28) estimates that over 50 percent of the growth in nonprofit revenues between 1982 and 1992 stemmed from increased fees and charges, particularly for education and health care. These figures do not, of course, include the incomes of for-profit hospitals, schools, child care agencies, and other companies doing business in areas normally associated with philanthropic activities.

23. See, e.g., *City of Washington v. Board of Assessment Appeals and Washington and Jefferson College*, Opinion of the Supreme Court of Western Pennsylvania, November 20, 1997, upholding the tax-exemption of a college.

References

AAFRC Trust for Philanthropy. *Giving USA 1996*. New York, 1997.

Abramson, Alan J., and Salamon, Lester M. "The Nonprofit Sector and the Federal Budget: Update as of September, 1997." Report for Independent Sector, Washington, DC, 1997.

Bremner, Robert H. *American Philanthropy*. 2nd edition. Chicago: University of Chicago Press, 1988.

Coats, U.S. Senator Dan, and Kasich, U.S. Congressman John. "The Project for American Renewal." Unpublished paper, Washington, DC, n.d.

Commission on Private Philanthropy and Public Needs. *Giving in America: Toward a Stronger Voluntary Sector*. Washington, DC: 1975.

Croly, Herbert. *The Promise of American Life*. Belknap Press Ed. Cambridge, MA: Harvard University Press, 1965.

Emerson, Jed, and Twersky, Fay, eds. *The New Social Entrepreneurs: The Success, Challenge and Lessons of Non-Profit Enterprise Creation*. San Francisco: The Roberts Foundation, 1996.

Hall, Peter Dobkin. *Inventing the Nonprofit Sector and Other Essays on Philanthropy, Voluntarism and Nonprofit Organizations*. Baltimore, MD: Johns Hopkins University Press, 1992.

Hodgkinson, Virginia A., and Weitzman, Murray. *Nonprofit Almanac: Dimensions of the Independent Sector 1996–97*. Washington, DC: Independent Sector, 1996.

"Jack Kemp's Tax-Study Group Loses Court Decision Over Tax-Free Status." *The Wall Street Journal*, February 13, 1998, p. B7.

Karl, Barry D., and Katz, Stanley N. "The American Private Philanthropic Foundation and the Public Sphere, 1890–1930." *Minerva*, 1981, 19 (2), 236–70.

Ladd, Everett C. "The Data Just Don't Show Erosion of America's 'Social Capital,'" *The Public Perspective: A Roper Center Review of Public Opinion and Polling*, 1996, 7 (4), 1–6.

Lenkowsky, Leslie. *The "Contract with America": An Opportunity for Philanthropy*. Essays on Philanthropy No. 22. Indianapolis: Indiana University Center on Philanthropy, 1996.

Lenkowsky, Leslie. "Big Charities Must Help Fill City Coffers." *Chronicle of Philanthropy*, December 11, 1997, p. 51.

Letts, Christine W., Ryan, William, and Grossman, Allen. "Virtuous Capital: What Foundations Can Learn from Venture Capitalists." *Harvard Business Review*, 1997 (March–April), Reprint 97207.

Meyer, Jack A., ed. *Meeting Human Needs: Toward a New Public Philosophy*. Washington, DC: American Enterprise Institute, 1982.

National Commission on Philanthropy and Civic Renewal. *Giving Better, Giving Smarter: Renewing Philanthropy in America*. Washington, DC: 1997.

O'Connell, Brian, ed. *America's Voluntary Sector*. New York: The Foundation Center, 1983.

Odendahl, Teresa. *Charity Begins at Home: Generosity and Self-Interest among the Philanthropic Elite*. New York: Basic Books, 1990.

Olasky, Marvin. *Renewing American Compassion*. New York: The Free Press, 1996.

Osborne, David, and Gaebler, Ted. *Reinventing Government: How the Entrepreneurial Spirit is Transforming the Public Sector*. New York: Plume (New American Library), 1993.

Putnam, Robert D. "Bowling Alone: America's Declining Social Capital," *Journal of Democracy*, 1995, 6 (1), 65–78.

Salamon, Lester M. "Nonprofit Organizations: The Lost Opportunity." In John L. Palmer and Isabel V. Sawhill, eds., *The Reagan Record*. Cambridge, MA: Ballinger, 1984.

Salamon, Lester M. *Partners in Public Service: Government-Nonprofit Relations in the Modern Welfare State*. Baltimore, MD and London: Johns Hopkins University Press, 1995.

Salamon, Lester M. *Holding the Center: America's Nonprofit Sector at a Crossroads*. New York: Nathan Cummings Foundation, 1997.

Smith, Adam. *The Wealth of Nations*. Modern Library ed. New York: Random House, 1937.

Stevens, Beth A., and Brown, Lawrence D. "Expertise Meets Politics: Efforts to Work with States." In Stephen L. Isaacs and James R. Knickman, eds., *To Improve Health and Health Care 1997: The Robert Wood Johnson Foundation Anthology*. San Francisco: Jossey-Bass, 1997.

Tocqueville, Alexis de. *Democracy in America*. J. P. Mayer, ed. George Lawrence, trans. New York: Harper Perennial, 1988.

Woodson Sr., Robert L. *The Triumphs of Joseph*. New York: The Free Press, 1998.

CHAPTER SEVEN

Nonprofit Organizations and Public Policies in the Delivery of Human Services

Kirsten A. Grønbjerg and Steven Rathgeb Smith

Periodically in American history, a series of events and developments combine to focus attention squarely on our institutional capacity to address human service needs and the role that the nonprofit and public sectors, individually and jointly, can and should play in meeting these needs. This is such a time. In this essay, we examine a series of major public policy developments and structural changes in the nonprofit sector itself which we believe are in the process of fundamentally altering the public policy role of nonprofit human service agencies. We are far from sanguine that the result will be a more coherent and effective human service system.

To be sure, nonprofit human service agencies have faced major public policy challenges and undergone significant restructuring throughout American history. However, the current policy issues facing nonprofit human service agencies seem to be of a substantially broader scope and greater magnitude than in the past. As we show, welfare reform, the extension of the managed care model, privatization of government services, the push for performance evaluation, restrictions on nonprofit advocacy, challenges to nonprofit tax-exempt status, and the changing relationship between church and state highlight ongoing debates about the role of nonprofit agencies in the delivery of human services.

As we also show, the emergence of these policy challenges for nonprofit human service agencies are occurring against a backdrop of restructuring in institutional philanthropy and in the nonprofit sector itself. The United Way, long a mainstay of private donations for many local community agencies, is undergoing a substantial shift in orientation and implementation of its mission. Corporate giving programs are becoming more strategically focused and competition for foundation founding has increased. In addition, nonprofit human service agencies face new questions about how to position themselves in the market. Not only are for-profit firms entering service areas previously dominated by nonprofits, but nonprofit agencies are themselves becoming more entrepreneurial or profit-oriented as evidenced by their forming alliances with business, participating in cause-related marketing, and creating for-profit subsidiaries.

The outcome of this restructuring of nonprofit human services has profound consequences not only for the agencies but for American social policy in general. The proper place of nonprofit human service agencies within the public policy arena is at the center of the current debate on the direction of federal social policy. Conservatives argue that the federal government should reduce its support of social programs and nonprofit human service agencies should rely upon community support and private donations rather than public funding.[1] Liberals, including many nonprofit human service agencies, such as Catholic Charities, U.S.A., counter that government support is essential if adequate social services are to be provided to people in need. More generally, this debate reflects controversy on whether or not it is possible to make a clear distinction between the public and private sectors and the capacity of the voluntary sector to address social problems without the support of government (Smith, 1997).

This essay examines arguments about the appropriate boundaries of the state and nonprofit sectors in depth. To do so, we first provide an abbreviated portrait of the nonprofit human service sector itself to highlight the difficulty of generalizing about these agencies. We then present a theoretical framework for understanding the mechanisms and structures under which public policies interact with nonprofit human service agencies, that is, direct government grants and contracts, government financed fees, tax credits and deductions, tax-exempt bonds, and government regulations. Along the way, we describe recent public policy changes in these structures.

We then turn our attention squarely to a broad set of issues that affect the role and capacity of the nonprofit human service sector, e.g., devolution and the rise of managed care, new directions in philanthropy, nonprofit entrepreneurship, political advocacy, and new roles for religious agencies. We conclude with a discussion of nonprofit human service agencies within civil society and our recommendations on how we should approach the evolving and changing place of nonprofit human service agencies in public policy.

Mapping the Nonprofit Human Services Sector

Given the important role of the nonprofit human service sector in the policy debate and its extensive interactions with government in the delivery of human services, it is surprisingly difficult to present an adequate description of the sector's scope and structure. There is no clear definition of the activities that should be included, nor are there comprehensive and up-to-date data on the organizations involved in such activities to adequately classify them by auspices.

Defining the scope of activities to include involves decisions as to whether to focus only on traditional social services (e.g., counseling, child welfare, custodial care) or also those involving closely related fields. Given the complexities of social problems—for example, the interaction of health, social well-being, and job opportunities available in local communities, we have opted for a fairly broad definition. We include traditional social services, crime and legal related services, employment and job related services, food and agriculture, housing and shelter, public safety, recreation and sports, and youth development. We also pay attention to civil rights and community improvement, as well as some health-related activities, especially mental health and substance abuse.

However, existing classification systems make it difficult to document the scope of activities involved. Both the Standard Industrial Classification (SIC) system and its replacement, the North American Industrial Classification System (NAICS), designed to categorize economic activities, lump together broad ranges of nonprofit-dominated services. Systems developed specifically for the nonprofit sector, while more inclusive and elaborate, do not correspond well to SIC or NAICS, are out-of-date (Activity Codes used by the Internal Revenue Service), or are overly complex and not applied to the majority of tax-exempt organizations (National Taxonomy of Exempt Entities).[2]

There are also fundamental problems in identifying organizations engaged in providing relevant services and the auspices under which they operate, e.g., for-profit, government, or nonprofit. Without such information, it is next to impossible to determine the financial scope of the nonprofit human service sector, or the share of services that it provides. The available data come from two sources: the IRS list of tax-exempt organizations and the Census of Service Industries (conducted every five years with annual updates from a sample of organizations). Both are problematic.

The IRS list of tax-exempt organizations is inadequate because churches (roughly 350,000 nationwide) and very small organizations are exempt from registering with the IRS. Although some do register, many (perhaps most) church-affiliated organizations, volunteer-driven entities, and self-help groups do not (Smith, D. H., 1997; Grønbjerg, 1991). The absence of financial information for roughly two-thirds of charitable organizations registered with the IRS[3] makes it even more hazardous to estimate the size of the sector from this database.

The Census of Service Industries excludes religious organizations and those without employees. It examines tax-exempt organizations only in fields with a substantial number of such organizations and defines some fields, e.g., higher education, as "out of scope." As a result, the 1992 Economic Census identifies only 208,911 tax-exempt establishments, while the IRS lists over one million tax-exempt entities for the same period. Moreover, the Census uses the SIC classification system, and thus tracks only traditional social services, not the broader array we focus on.

The exclusion (de facto or explicit) of religious organizations, smaller nonprofits, and volunteer-based organizations from both of these major databases is important. While the formal economic contributions of these organizations to the nonprofit human service sector may be small, they make up a significant proportion of the organizations involved. And, to the extent that they rely on and actively engage volunteers more than larger organizations, their social impact may well exceed their economic share. Finally, many churches provide a broad range of human services (Hodgkinson and Weitzman, 1993).

In short, national estimates of the scope and dimensions of the nonprofit human service sector are fraught with uncertainty. Even so, it appears that the nonprofit sector has grown significantly in recent years and that the human service component has done better than the sector overall. The most recent (1996–97) edition of *The Nonprofit Almanac* estimates that total nonprofit employment increased from 5.5 million employees in 1977 to 9.7 million in 1992, or by a factor of 1.8 (Independent Sector, 1996: 145). However, nonprofit employment in "social and legal services," the closest fit to our definition of human services, increased by a factor of 2.2 from 715,000 in 1977 to 1,585,000 employees in 1992, or from 13 percent of total nonprofit employment to 16.3 percent.

The employment growth has been particularly noteworthy among agencies providing residential care (up by a factor of 2.5), individual and family services or other social services not elsewhere classified (up by a factor of 2.4), and job training and related services (up by a factor of 2.3). In contrast, nonprofit employment in legal services increased by a factor of only 1.7 and in child day care services by a factor of just 1.5. The relatively low growth rate in legal services is perhaps expected, given major cuts in federal spending for these types of programs. The trend for child day care is more surprising given strong demand for these services. However, for-profit day care services, including many franchise operations, have proliferated in recent years, undoubtedly absorbing a significant, and perhaps growing, share of the demand.

Similar developments may explain why employment in nonprofit health services has grown at a more modest rate than social and legal services, up from 2.5 million employees to 4.4 million over the 1977–92 period, or by a factor of 1.8. The health service field, of course, remains the single largest nonprofit employment sector, accounting for more than 45 percent of total employment in the sector.

These employment trends are broadly consistent with Independent Sector

(1996: 190–91) estimates of total funds available to nonprofit organizations, up by a factor of two from $255 billion in 1977 to $508 billion in 1992 (in constant 1992 dollars). Combined funds for social and legal services grew at a somewhat higher rate, up from $23 billion in 1977 to $56 billion in 1992, or by a factor of 2.4.

We want to emphasize two additional points about these data. First, local communities may deviate significantly from these aggregate national patterns, although differences in timing and sampling criteria make comparisons across communities or trend analysis for any one community next to impossible. We are aware of only two studies (Salamon, 1987: 106–7; Stevenson, Pollak, and Lampkin, 1997: 11) that systematically examine the scope and financial structure of nonprofit organizations across communities. Both find notable regional variations, but published findings do not separate out human services. Indeed, the Chicago metropolitan region has about half of the state's nonprofit human service organizations, but two-thirds of the state's population (65 percent).

Second, aggregate trends are likely to obscure a great deal of variation among individual organizations. The trends reflect mainly the experience of very large agencies that account for the bulk of revenues and expenditures, not the more typical experience of smaller human service agencies. In fact, we know little about what is happening at the organizational level—how many human service agencies are doing well, how many are deteriorating, or how serious or promising the conditions are. Indeed, longitudinal analysis for individual agencies reveals significant shifts from year to year in individual revenue sources and major changes in total revenues (Grønbjerg, 1993; Smith and Lipsky, 1993).

Similarly, cross-sectional analyses show great diversity in organizational strategies and resources (Grønbjerg and Nagle, 1994). Most human service organizations provide a range of services, mainly targeted on the basis of age or residence, rather than income or race and ethnicity. A substantial minority belongs to funding federations, while smaller numbers have religious affiliations. Most are fairly young, especially day care agencies, while residential agencies are older. Average revenues are quite high, but most agencies are small and there are major differences in size among various types of organizations. Government funding accounts for more than half of the combined revenues, followed by donations, then fees, dues, and service charges. About equal proportions of organizations rely primarily on government funding, on donations, or on fees and service charges, but organizations vary in the extent to which they rely on these major funding sources. Government funding is especially important to larger organizations.

We have no directly comparable information on how these patterns have changed over time. However, some trends are evident for member agencies of United Way of Chicago.[4] While not representative of the general human service sector, because the agencies tend to be larger and more organizationally sophisticated than the average human service agencies, the trends are revealing.

Over the 1989–94 period, combined revenues of the 140 United Way member agencies grew by a robust 72 percent to $890 million. Government funding more than doubled (up by 120 percent) and by 1994 accounted for 58 percent of total revenues, up from 45 percent in 1989. Fee revenues grew by 67 percent, maintaining their overall share of revenues (15 percent). During the same period, contributions (exclusive of United Way support) grew by a respectable 41 percent, but because that was less than the overall growth rate, these sources dropped from 17 to 14 percent of total revenues. Investment and other income grew by an anemic 12 percent over the 5-year period and dropped from 14 to 9 percent of total revenues. United Way funding declined overall by 8 percent and by 1994 constituted only 5 percent of total revenues, down from almost 10 percent just five years previously.

If true of other human service agencies, these findings suggest that nonprofits were successful in obtaining new government funds during the 1980s and 1990s. Of course, individual agencies may have experienced hardship, closed down, or curtailed individual programs, and some clients may have more difficulty obtaining service than before. But many nonprofits have increased their budgets substantially, especially the larger, more politically influential and savvy agencies with good relationships with government funders. By the same token, United Way provides a declining share of funds for human service agencies.

Overall, the nonprofit human services sector is a major economic force at both the national and local level. However, the sector is not easy to pigeonhole and the diversity among organizations and local communities makes it difficult to go much beyond aggregate data at the national level. Unfortunately, even these data have gaps and inconsistencies.

A Theoretical Framework for Understanding Nonprofit Human Service Agencies and Their Relationship to Public Policy

To a large extent, scholars of the nonprofit sector, social policy, and nonprofit human service agencies can be divided into two basic camps: a *demand side* explanation rooted in the preferences or demand of the citizens for certain public services provided through the nonprofit form; and a *supply side* explanation emphasizing the importance of public policies—i.e., the supply of public resources and the corresponding incentives among the citizenry created by the public policies.

Demand-side explanations are represented by Weisbrod (1975; 1989) who suggests that nonprofit agencies are created in response to inadequacies in government services that leave a minority segment of the population with unmet needs. The focus of many nonprofit human service agencies on issues affecting a small segment of the population appears to fit with this explanation. Hansmann (1980) argues that nonprofits arise in response to contract failure: donors unable to judge the quality of the agency receiving their donations are likely to prefer a nonprofit organization because it gives them assurance that their donation will not be used for private gain. More recently, Hansmann (1996) has expanded this argument to emphasize how the nonprofit form solves problems associated with both contracting and ownership under those conditions. Salamon (1987) indicates that nonprofits are often unable to adequately respond to social needs so that government ends up providing funding to overcome the *philanthropic failure*. All of these explanations tend to view nonprofit agencies as driven by the outcome of private demand and public policy as reflecting particular private interests held by large (or influential) groups.

In this chapter, we present an alternative perspective which is more reliant on a supply-side explanation—that is, public policy has had important, and sometimes unexpected, effects on the preference of individuals to choose the nonprofit organizational form to provide human services. Policy has also influenced the incentive of nonprofits to undertake different privately oriented initiatives as well. Since policy is constantly changing and evolving, the form, role, and character of nonprofit human service agencies will also vary over time (see Dobbin and Boychuk, 1996; Smith, 1997; Smith and Lipsky, 1993; James, 1987).

Understanding the Government-Nonprofit Relationship

Government funding of nonprofit activity is a source of substantial discussion among policymakers and scholars. Indeed, this subject is often part of larger policy debates affecting the nonprofit sector including welfare reform, devolution, and government policy toward advocacy and lobbying by nonprofits. For the most part, the focus of these discussions is on direct government funding of nonprofit agencies. However, government contributes to the resources of nonprofit agencies in many different ways in addition to direct grants and contracts: e.g., fees and third party payments, tax credits and deductions, tax-exempt bonds, and regulations encouraging nonprofit service delivery. Moreover, the contribution of these other forms of government funding (and private sources of funds from for-profit ventures) to nonprofit revenues is growing in importance to many nonprofit agencies as direct funding and contracts become scarcer and more competitive. Put another way, organizational forms are becoming much more complex among nonprofit human service agencies, even as policymakers talk about an idealized version of nonprofit agencies which is reliant upon community donations and goodwill.

The following sections provide a detailed overview of these different revenue streams important to nonprofit human service agencies: direct grants and contracts, fees and third party payments, tax credits and deductions, tax-exempt bonds, and regulations. In these sections, emphasis is on the changing revenue mix of nonprofit human service agencies and the impact of these changes on nonprofit agencies and their role in service delivery.

Direct Grants and Contracts

As noted, government funding of nonprofit social and health agencies dates back to the colonial era. In the postwar period, an important evolution in the structure of direct public funding of nonprofit agencies has occurred. In the 1950s, many different types of agencies received public subsidies and grants. Typically, these subsidies were provided with relatively minimal accountability requirements; nonprofit agencies were assumed to use the money wisely and in the best interests of their clients. State and local government — the primary funder of social services in this period — was also quite small and underfunded with little capacity to monitor nonprofit grantees.

Beginning in the 1960s, public funding increased, spurred by large rises in federal funding. Over time, federal, state and local governments found themselves with increasingly sizable proportions of their service activities provided by nonprofit agencies. In some states, such as Massachusetts and Illinois, entire state departments contracted out their services to nonprofit agencies. Initially, many of the new federal and state grants lacked stringent guidelines and regulations. Over time, though, various federal, state and local agencies discovered that they now were in charge of a very large service system, albeit one provided by nonprofit agencies. In order to rationalize this system (Brown, 1983) and ensure that government agencies were maintaining accountability for the expenditure of public funds, the regulation of government contracts became much more stringent, even to the point of sometimes specifying the names of the clients to be served by the agency (Smith and Lipsky, 1993; Grønbjerg, 1993).

The big jump in federal funding of nonprofit agencies during the 1960s and 1970s is apparent in the numbers. Federal spending for a variety of social welfare services such as vocational rehabilitation, child welfare, counseling, and child care rose from $416 million in 1960 to $8.7 billion in 1980 (in nominal dollars) (Bixby, 1996, 70). Much of this money was channeled to nonprofit agencies either directly through federal grants or via state and local governments which received federal grants. As a result of the growth in federal support for these types of social welfare activities, federal spending as a percentage of total government expenditures on these social welfare services increased from 36.6 percent in 1960 to 64.6 percent in 1980 (Bixby, 1996, 74). State spending on social services also rose significantly (albeit less dramatically than federal spending), spurred in part by matching requirements for the receipt of federal dollars. Between 1960 and 1980, state and local spending on social welfare services increased from $722 million to $4.8 billion (Bixby, 1996, 71).

In short, nonprofit human service agencies became increasingly reliant on federal revenue supplemented with state and local government support. Nonprofit human services greatly expanded in scope, with the growth financed primarily by the federal government. As a result, the relative cost of services was shifted from individual clients and consumers and private donors to the federal government. Private philanthropy, such as the United Way, dropped sharply as a percentage of the total budget of nonprofit human service agencies.

In contrast to the 1960s and 1970s, federal spending in the 1980s and 1990s is more difficult to characterize. Federal spending on some social service programs has dropped. For example, federal spending on the same array of social welfare services referenced above only increased from $8.7 billion in 1980 to $10.8 billion in 1993, a drop in per capita expenditures from $99.92 to $87.04 in constant (1993) dollars (Bixby, 1996, 73). This drop is also evident in selected programs. Federal spending on job training for the disadvantaged—a service provided substantially by nonprofit human service agencies under contract—has dropped from $3.1 billion in 1975 to $862 million in 1996 in constant 1990 dollars (House Ways and Means Committee, 1996, 932). The Title XX Social Services Block Grant (SSBG), a significant source of funding for a wide variety of nonprofit human service agencies, has dropped in value from $6.8 billion in 1977 to $2.8 billion in 1996 in 1996 dollars (House Ways and Means Committee, 1996, 680).

But many other federal programs have risen since 1980 despite the changes in federal policy undertaken by the Reagan and Bush administration in the 1980s. While SSBG has dropped, federal child welfare spending has risen through other programs. Federal spending for foster care, adoption, and child welfare under Titles IV-B and IV-E of the Social Security Act rose from $788 million in 1985 to an estimated $4.3 billion in 1996 in nominal dollars (House Ways and Means Committee, 1996, 695). These federal funds are not entirely spent by nonprofit agencies. But many states use this money under Titles IV-B and IV-E to support the foster care and child welfare activities of their contract agencies. Headstart, the preschool program for the poor, is delivered primarily by nonprofit human service agencies. Federal funding for this program increased from $818 million in 1980 to $3.5 billion in 1995. Enrollment reached an all-time high of 750,696 children in 1995 (House Ways and Means Committee, 1996, 935).[5] Federal drug control funding for drug and alcohol services has risen since the beginning of the Bush administration. In the Department of Education alone, funding for the Safe and Drug Free Schools Act, a significant source of revenue for local nonprofit service providers and community partnerships, is slated to rise from $466 million in FY 1996 to a proposed $620 million in FY 1998 (Executive Office of the President, 1997b, 331).

Federal health care programs rose sharply in this period, in part because the structure of several key programs encouraged states to refinance programs with declining federal budgets (e.g., SSBG) to funding available under federal health programs. For example, total government expenditures for Medicaid, the federal/state health care program for the disabled and the poor, rose from $25 billion in 1980 to $156 billion in 1995 (House Ways and Means Committee, 1996, 896). States had an incentive to shift costs for eligible programs such as mental health and some child welfare programs from capped state or federal grants to Medicaid, an open-ended program with a 50-percent federal match. This allowed many nonprofit human service agencies to avoid cutbacks, although it often meant expensive compliance costs due to Medicaid regulations. Many service agencies providing residential care for the mentally ill and developmentally disabled also took advantage of this refinancing option, often at the behest of state and local government officials.

This shift is also consequential for nonprofits because this refinancing through Medicaid usually means that the revenue stream for nonprofit agencies becomes more uncertain. For example, contracts in the human service field usually provide agencies with good estimates of their income from a given source over a given period of time, usually a year. In contrast, fee income depends much more on unpredictable decisions by individual clients and/or individual professionals as to the amount and quality of services that should be provided (Grønbjerg, 1993).

Expenditures for Medicare, the federal health care program for the elderly, also rose sharply since 1980, from $34 billion to $148 billion in 1993 (Bixby, 1996, 70). Most of this money goes to health care institutions such as hospitals. A few specific programs of the larger Medicare programs on the boundary between a health care service and a social service have risen even more sharply. Medicare reimbursement for hospice care did not exist in 1980; in 1994 expenditures reached $1.3 billion with a substantial portion devoted to nonprofit hospice programs, mostly free-standing (House Ways and Means Committee, 1996, 181). Medicare-funded home health care, initially a relatively small program, rose from $1.6 billion in 1980 to $16 billion in 1995 (House Ways and Means Committee, 1996, 177). While many home health care providers are subsidiaries of hospitals, many nonprofit human service agencies have also developed home health care programs, especially AIDS service providers and large multi-program human service agencies.

The scope of government contracting with nonprofit service agencies varies greatly across the country, reflecting a variety of political and historical circumstances. States in the Midwest and Northeast tend to do more contracting in part because they had many nonprofit agencies in existence when federal funding arrived in the 1960s and 1970s. Also, many of these states had administrators and elected officials eager to take advantage of federal funding which was earmarked for local nonprofit programs. The Midwest and Northeast also tend to have longer traditions of local philanthropic support of community organizations, so many nonprofit agencies were able to combine public and private funds to expand services through the contracting (especially since some federal programs required matching funds). States in the South and West have tended to do more selective contracting and have relied more heavily upon public sector service delivery until relatively recently. In these states, the enthusiasm for privatization and reinventing government among elected officials is producing greatly expanded contracting even for services long considered the province of the public sector such as child protection.

Fees

While direct contracting and grants are the most extensive form of government financing of nonprofit agencies, fees and other less direct methods of financing are a growing portion of nonprofit revenues. "Fees" is really an umbrella term for an assortment of revenue sources collected from individuals and organizations: rent payments from residents at a homeless shelter; reimbursement from Medicaid and private health insurance plans; payments from individuals for a counseling session; money from the sale of items made by program clients; and income from technical assistance programs.

On nonprofit agency financial statements and tax returns (Form 990), fees are usually on a separate line from direct government grants and contracts, with the implication that fees are not government revenue. In reality, though, fee income for many nonprofit agencies is heavily reliant upon government funds. Some fees are direct government payments such as Medicaid reimbursement for mental health or health care services, Supplemental Security Income (SSI) for the disabled poor, or Section 8 housing subsidies to low-income housing organizations. These three examples are also noteworthy since they are programs that have continued to rise during the 1980s and 1990s. The sharp increase in Medicaid has already been noted. Less well known to the public is the continuing growth of SSI, an important source of income to many nonprofit residential programs. The number of SSI recipients increased from 4.1 million in 1980 to 6.5 million in 1995 with total annual payments rising from $15.2 billion in 1980 (in 1995 dollars) to $27 billion in 1995 (House Ways and Means Committee, 1996, 260–261).[6] Many nonprofit residential programs for the mentally ill and developmentally disabled rely upon SSI payments to pay the client's rent and other expenses.

Other fees are subsidized by government. For example, day care programs serving low-income clients are eligible for special voucher programs which allow these clients to afford the child care. Many of these day care programs also receive direct grants which allow them to lower the cost of service to eligible clients, thus allowing greater program access. These subsidies not only increase nonprofit revenues from fees but stimulate demand for nonprofit programs and services to higher levels than they would otherwise be. Government agencies may also agree to use the services of a nonprofit training program; the nonprofit agency collects the revenues as fees but in reality it is another way of government financing of a valued public service provided by a nonprofit agency. Of course, part of the fee income for many nonprofit organizations is also private in the sense that it is a direct payment from an individual or private organization.[7]

While fee income is an increasing source of income for many nonprofit agencies, it is also an increasingly uncertain, sometimes fragile revenue source, especially given competition for government funds, the diminishing government funds in some areas, the expansion of managed care, and the redesigning of government programs under the new welfare reform laws. For example, mental health care agencies may have relied upon Medicaid payments from the state for a substantial portion of their income. However, new managed care arrangements are likely to reduce this amount and make the remaining Medicaid funds more unpredictable.

Tax Credits and Deductions

Tax credits and deductions as a form of government financing of nonprofit activity, like fees, tend to receive less attention from policymakers and scholars than direct funding. And like fees, tax credits and deductions are growing as a valuable source of nonprofit revenues either directly or indirectly. Two noteworthy examples of tax credit financing of nonprofits are the child care and dependent credits and the low-income housing tax credit. The child care credits help offset the cost of child care and dependent care (such as home health services), making nonprofit (and for-profit) services more affordable. It also underscores the complicated public/private character of fee income for nonprofit human service agencies. If a parent pays tuition to a nonprofit human service agency and then claims a child care tax credit, is the tuition really private?

The tax credit for low income housing demonstrates the equally complicated situation regarding devolution and the role of the federal government in supporting nonprofit human service agencies. Support from the federal Housing and Urban Development (HUD) agency for the new construction of low-income housing units has dropped sharply in the last 20 years.[8] Yet, this drop in direct HUD funding has occurred at the same time as the growth of the Low-Income Housing Tax Credit (LIHTC), a creation of the 1986 Tax Reform Act. LIHTC budget authority rose from $313 million in 1987 (the first year of the LIHTC) (House Ways and Means Committee, 1996, 821) to $2.6 billion in 1996 (Budget of U.S. Government, FY 1998, 1997a, 294).

These tax credits allow private investors to reduce their tax liability by purchasing tax credits to build low-income housing. This tax credit program has spurred the creation of nonprofit community development and housing organizations to build low-income and affordable housing. Many nonprofit housing development organizations also provide an array of social services. In addition, many of these organizations are involved in the HUD-financed Enterprise Zone (EZ) program, offering a mix of direct grants, loans, and tax credits to revitalize distressed urban areas.

Tax deductions also help finance nonprofit activity by reducing the cost of private donations (Clotfelter, 1985). Their value to the individual may be less than twenty years ago due to tax reform which has reduced marginal tax rates. Pending tax proposals such as the flat tax could further diminish the value of the charitable tax deduction and potentially reduce the propensity of people to give with serious effects on the nonprofit sector (Clotfelter and Schmalbeck, 1996).

Tax-Exempt Bonds

Large nonprofit institutions such as hospitals and universities have taken advantage of tax-exempt bonds for decades. These bonds help nonprofit organizations finance the cost of capital improvements such as a new building or the renovation of an older structure. What's new is the growing use of tax-exempt bonds by smaller nonprofit organizations such as housing development organizations, child welfare agencies, and mental health centers.

In part, this new involvement is a ripple effect of changes in federal policy. The reduction of federal spending in many areas of social policy—and the concomitant increased competition for remaining public (and private) funds —has encouraged nonprofit agencies to seek new sources of revenue to finance their operations. In this environment, tax-exempt bonds are an attractive option especially given that nonprofit agencies can obtain large amounts of financing that are very difficult to find from private donors. Additionally, the debt payments on the bonds can be financed over a period of many years. Many nonprofit housing organizations also combine tax credits and bond financing to create a comprehensive package to build and operate low income housing units (Affordable Housing Finance, 1997, 6–9; Thompson, 1996).

The movement of smaller nonprofits into the tax-exempt bond market has been facilitated by the establishment of special nonprofit institutions to serve these needs. For example, the Illinois Facilities Fund, itself a charitable, tax-exempt institution, has provided technical advice to many nonprofits about a broad range of facility related issues, including the issuance of tax-exempt bonds. The Fund has also explored the creation of pooled tax-exempt bonds that would be available to groups of nonprofit human service agencies.

Regulations

The ability of nonprofit agencies to tap government revenue is affected by prevailing regulations. Many government agencies give preference to nonprofit agencies in their contracting for public services. For instance, the state of Massachusetts created an elaborate network of private social service agencies in the 1970s and 1980s through government contracting; state officials were very reluctant to contract with private, for-profit agencies, so they were essentially excluded from the market for contracts. Similarly, the Illinois Department of Children and Family Services routinely renewed contracts for child welfare services with its pool of providers (all nonprofit agencies) without any efforts to open the contracts for rebidding.

Many government programs also contain set-asides for nonprofit and for-profit agencies. The tax-credit program for low-income housing, for instance, has a set-aside for nonprofit housing developers in the IRS regulations. Many states have their own set-asides for nonprofits as well. In a related vein, the state of Rhode Island recently passed legislation that created high barriers to the acquisition of nonprofit hospitals by for-profit firms.

These regulations are obviously different from direct financing, but they nonetheless are quite important to the overall government financing picture. They carve out a role for nonprofit organizations in service delivery and guarantee that nonprofit agencies in specific categories will be assured of government financing.

A More Complicated Relationship

Since 1945, nonprofit agencies have undergone a series of transformations. In the 1950s, nonprofit human service agencies were a residual part of the total human service system, providing service delivery in a few niches such as emergency assistance, child welfare, and counseling, primarily financed through private donations. This changed in the 1960s and 1970s with the advent of the Great Society and War on Poverty. The result was a greatly expanded network of nonprofit human service agencies and substantial dependence on government funds. The relative contribution of private donations, including the United Way, to nonprofit agency revenues declined dramatically, even though the actual dollars involved increased on an absolute basis.

The 1980s and 1990s are a period of important, sometimes subtle changes in nonprofit revenues and the relationship of nonprofit human service agencies to public policy. While some nonprofit agencies have suffered financially, many nonprofit agencies have grown substantially as they tapped new sources of government revenues including fees from programs such as Medicaid, new government contracts, tax credits, and tax-exempt bond money. Obtaining these revenues can be a very competitive process, so nonprofit agencies have also stepped up their fundraising programs with many, even relatively me-dium-sized, agencies undertaking capital campaigns. Further, fee income from for-profit and entrepreneurial ventures rose, albeit to varying extents depending upon the agency and the service category. Nonprofit human service agencies have a more diversified funding base, although government funds through a variety of sources remain an essential component of nonprofit revenues. Many human service agencies continue to be primarily reliant upon government funds.[9]

Public policy itself remains a key determinant of nonprofit revenues and service mix. In one of the most notable examples, the Low-Income Housing Tax Credit program created an entire industry of nonprofit housing developers and enlisted a broad array of investment bankers and major corporations in supporting the continued existence and growth of this program, even in the face of major congressional opposition (Shashaty, 1997, 4).

The Restructuring of the Nonprofit Human Service Sector

The changes in government revenue support of nonprofit organizations including its increasing complexity have spurred important shifts in the form and character of nonprofit human service agencies and their role in public service delivery. This in turn is having ripple effects on the private philanthropic community. As this section details, the result is a more diverse, but less distinctly nonprofit, human service sector.

Devolution and the Rise of Managed Care

As noted, the devolutionary policies of the 1980s had a decidedly mixed impact on nonprofit agencies given rising federal health care expenditures and the creation of new grant and tax-credit programs. Nonetheless, the coming years may be a different story given the recent changes in federal policy and legislation pending in Congress. In addition, managed care has moved beyond health care to social services with potentially profound effects on nonprofit human service agencies.

Welfare reform, passed in August 1996, devolved responsibility for managing and developing welfare programs to the states. Now, states have substantial flexibility in use of their federal welfare funds; states can even use money previously earmarked for income maintenance programs for social services such as child care and job training. Pending legislation in Congress would devolve responsibility for federal housing programs and the Medicaid program to the states as well, although the fate of this legislation is unclear.

While the states have more flexibility in program design and funding allocation, they are also subject to very specific program targets established by Congress, underscoring once again that devolution—on closer inspection—may not be as devolutionary as people assume. These federal regulations are especially important to nonprofit agencies because states will rely upon nonprofit agencies to provide services that will meet these targets. In some areas, such as welfare-to-work and time limits, the new welfare reform legislation represents greater federal control over welfare services than before.

Despite the complexity of welfare reform, a few observations can be offered based upon the initial implementation experience of the legislation. Larger, multi-service agencies are likely to adapt their services to fit the new criteria used by states in allocating welfare-related funding. These agencies often have considerable flexibility and discretion in how they allocate their large variety of funding sources among a long list of program activities, as well as powerful board members and strong connections to political actors. Indeed, many have direct access to political lobbyists. The agencies at considerable risk are smaller, more focused agencies who tend to be undercapitalized and politically weak. They could be in serious financial crisis if government decides to reallocate their funds since they do not have the resources or the capability to alter their service mix. The loss of these smaller agencies could have a negative impact on local services because these smaller agencies often provide niche services targeted toward a specific neighborhood or client group; thus these services might be transformed considerably if they were absorbed into the operations of a larger human services agency.

Agencies will also need to be more outcome-oriented since states will strive to meet federal targets by requiring nonprofit agencies providing welfare-related services to meet performance standards or lose their funding (or not get paid at all). The imposition of performance standards will tend to financially squeeze agencies because outcome-based funding (rather than annual contracts) tends to limit the ability of nonprofits to cross-subsidize their operations (James, 1983). With annual contracts, nonprofits can build into the budget support for various expenses, such as administration, that are much more difficult to adequately fund in a performance-based contract since these contracts are structured to pay agencies only for the costs of certain activities such as job training and placement.[10]

Further squeezing nonprofits is the advent of managed care arrangements for social services. Until recently, government directly contracted with a nonprofit human service agency to provide an identified service such as mental health counseling or foster care. In the early years of widespread contracting in the 1960s and 1970s, most contracts entailed a direct relationship between government and the nonprofit agency. For example, the federal government would directly contract with a local community mental health center to provide mental health services to the local population. Likewise, a state Department of Social Services would directly contract with a local nonprofit child welfare agency.

This government–nonprofit agency relationship tended to be the norm until the late 1980s, when a wave of managed care rolled through state and local government human services. The model of managed care human services was consciously borrowed from health care where health maintenance organizations and other forms of managed care have captured an increasing portion of America's health insurance business. Despite variations, the basic principle of managed care is to provide incentives for service providers such as doctors and hospitals to economize by paying them on a capitated basis. Thus, a HMO will be paid by an employer to take care of a certain number of individuals; the HMO has an incentive to keep costs under the reimbursement level since if costs exceed revenues they will not receive additional funds. This managed care arrangement contrasts with the previous cost-reimbursement form of payment where providers were paid retrospectively for their incurred costs; any reasonable costs were reimbursed according to an agreed-upon schedule.

Nonprofit human service agencies were until recently also paid on a cost reimbursement basis. The attractiveness of managed care is that it places a limit on reimbursement by state government and shifts the risk of managing nonprofit contract agencies to a third party contractor. Thus, managed care makes the relationship between government and nonprofit agencies more complicated and indirect. For instance, in states such as New Jersey and Massachusetts, the state department responsible for child welfare services has replaced its direct contracts for foster care and related services with private agencies with a large contract with a third party agency which is paid on a capitated basis to manage the foster care services for the state. This third party agency then subcontracts with private agencies for the provision of services. Managed care is also quite prevalent in mental health services and various health care programs including state Medicaid programs.

From the perspective of nonprofit agencies, managed care increases uncertainty on clients and revenues since the agency does not have a guaranteed annual number of clients, as was often the case under the traditional direct government-nonprofit contracts. It also blurs the lines of accountability since the new third party agency can create confusion and obfuscation regarding the appropriate agency responsible for ensuring the provision of quality service and the judicious use of public funds. Managed care also shifts the risk of service delivery outcomes from the state agency (and to an extent the private agency) to the third party managed care organization. But usually these managed care organizations are not very open to outside scrutiny, especially by clients and consumers.

New Directions in Philanthropy[11]

The increased competition for and uncertainty about public funding prompted by welfare reform, devolution, and managed care is further intensified by changes underway within private philanthropy.

As this section details, important funders of nonprofit human service agencies, including the United Way and private foundations, are changing their funding practices with profound effects on nonprofit human service agencies.

Multiple factors account for these changes in private philanthropy. Demographic, social, and economic trends have severely aggravated community conditions in many locations, especially the inner cities of major metropolitan areas. Significant, enduring changes in political power structures have added to the complexity. There have also been important developments in institutional philanthropy, such as United Way organizations, foundations, or corporate giving programs. With the possible exception of the Aramony scandal at United Way of America, however, none of these developments have generated the level of visibility and attention that public policies have received. We review some of the more important of these trends that are relevant to the human service sector.

United Way Developments

United Way funding in many communities has stagnated and failed to keep up with growth in other sources of funding for human service agencies. This reflects only in part the impact of the Aramony scandal in the early 1990s, since the national trends precede this event by several years (Bothwell, 1993). More important have been structural changes in the resource base of UW systems.

The Combined Federal Campaign law of 1987 and growing acceptance of donor designation have diverted UW-raised funds to agencies or activities that are not part of the UW allocation system. Even where such designations remain fairly small, the decision by many UW organizations to consider designated dollars separate from and in addition to membership allocations, e.g., the "last" rather than the "first" dollars counted toward UW allocations, changes the relationship between UW and its member agencies.

Changes in corporate and economic structures are also important. Economic restructuring away from manufacturing and toward service industries has meant a decline in firms with well-established UW campaigns and well-paid workers and a growth in those with little tradition of UW involvement and large numbers of non-unionized, low-wage workers. Corporate downsizing means smaller payrolls from which to solicit donations and fewer executives available to make the appeals. The growth in smaller firms and in self-employment compounds the problem, since UW is ill equipped to solicit such firms or self-employed or retired workers. Corporate takeovers and dominance of multinational corporations with less commitment to local regions have further reduced the ability of UW organizations to maintain corporate support (Kanter, 1995). In addition, corporate tendencies to view philanthropy as marketing opportunities do not easily reconcile themselves to the community fund model in which UW volunteers set priorities and allocate funds accordingly.

These factors help explain why many UW campaigns have stagnated or even declined. In the Chicago region, campaign revenues are down 13 percent, from a high of $105 million in 1992 to $91.5 million in 1996. In Cleveland, overall pledges declined by 19 percent over the 1990–97 period. Regional conflicts have aggravated these trends for some UW systems as the growth in suburban populations and economic power relative to that of central cities has surfaced within the UW system, at times facilitated by an organizational split between the city and suburban allocation systems.

Although many UW campaigns appear to be recovering some of the lost ground, these structural trends have important implications for the ability of the UW to maintain its role as the largest and most institutionalized source of philanthropic support for the human service sector. It is less clear how these trends impact the ability of UW play a leadership role in identifying and addressing community needs (Grønbjerg, et al., 1996). Interviews with philanthropic funders suggest that everyone knows of United Way as an organization. Indeed, United Way was one of the top three (but never the top) philanthropic funders mentioned when foundation and public agency officials were asked a series of network questions about a long list of local philanthropic funders. However, few philanthropic and even fewer public funders have any in-depth understanding of the issues and transformations that United Way is facing.

Developments in Corporate Philanthropy

The same factors that threaten the workplace success of UW campaigns affect direct corporate donations to nonprofit human service agencies. As noted above, growing international competition and corporate takeovers have encouraged corporations to view their philanthropic activities as closely linked to marketing, promotions, or public relations. That means careful targeting of corporate philanthropy to business activities. Frequently, it also means a tendency to seek out prestigious and well-known grantee organizations, such as major arts and cultural organizations or institutions of higher education.

Nationally, corporate donations doubled on a per capita basis (in constant dollars) between 1975 and the early 1980s (Grønbjerg, 1993: 76–77), but since then have stabilized. However, corporate support for health and human services has remained level throughout the period, reflecting a relative shift in corporate support away from these service areas.

Developments among Private Foundations

Both family and independent foundations are closely tied to corporations. Most have corporate or business representatives as members of their boards of directors, foundation assets and earnings that stem from corporate earnings, and were founded by individuals whose wealth derives from business activities. The rapid run-up in stock prices in recent years has significantly expanded the assets of many foundations. Because foundations must pay out at least 5 percent of their assets each year, foundation grant levels have increased correspondingly.

The growth in corporate executive compensation along with corporate mergers and acquisitions has increased the number of individuals with significant levels of assets, contributing to the more than $10 trillion in assets that are estimated to await generational transfer within the next 20 years or so (Avery, 1994). Indeed, charitable gifts in the tens of millions of dollars by major corporate executives are becoming frequent—witness recent enormous gifts by George Soros and Ted Turner.

Developments in Community and Public Foundations

The number of community foundations has expanded in recent years (Foundation Center, 1997). A major factor in this growth is likely to be the increase in personal wealth described above. As net assets reach a sufficiently high level to exceed inheritance tax exemptions, the establishment of charitable trusts becomes an attractive tax alternative. By providing professional management for many small trusts, community foundations accommodate asset holdings that are not sufficiently large to warrant the establishment of separate foundations. They also solve the problem of how to manage charitable trusts for those with wealth but no heirs or with unreliable heirs. In addition, several major foundations (e.g., the W. K. Kellogg Foundation, the Ford Foundation, and the Lilly Endowment) have stimulated the development of community foundations in smaller communities. Others have sought to encourage community foundations to expand their focus on particular activities, e.g., cultural participation in the case of the Lila Wallace–Reader's Digest Fund.

While these patterns suggest that corporate funding and foundation support may have expanded in recent years, this is not true across the board. Philanthropic funding for human services, especially from corporate giving programs, appears threatened by the greater efforts of corporations to closely link their charitable donations to marketing and profits. These developments may push nonprofit human service agencies toward entrepreneurial activities.

As for philanthropic funders themselves, interviews with a stratified sample of 50 such funders in the Chicago region suggest that very few take a clearly planned approach in dealing with the impact of the changing human service environment. Rather, we are left with the impression that a substantial proportion of philanthropic funders are somewhat isolated and considerably constrained by their mission and other factors that control their primary source of funding. Rarely do they have the time or take the opportunity to go beyond those boundaries. They react to what agencies tell them are community needs, are aware of broad policy issues highlighted in the mass media, and know about a small number of large philanthropic funders in the local community. These traits seem to be concentrated among smaller funders, especially family and corporate foundations.

There are, of course, examples of the opposite as well, philanthropic funders who make sustained and systematic efforts to scan the environment and who pay a great deal of attention to public policy developments and community needs. Prominent examples include the Ford Foundation, Annie E. Casey Foundation, Robert Wood Johnson Foundation, and MacArthur Foundation. These, and others with a more local focus, are actively involved in various external planning efforts related to their primary focal area and collaborate with both public agencies and other philanthropic funders in these areas. But they are few in number and found primarily (although not exclusively) among those awarding large volumes of grants.

In between these two extremes are a sizable number of philanthropic funders who make more or less aggressive efforts to keep informed about important developments, especially in public policy, and to network with other philanthropic funders. They rely heavily on regional associations of grantmakers, in this case the Donors Forum of Chicago, to provide these informational resources. Some are also involved in United Way needs assessment or priority grant activities. However, there is little direct evidence that these funders are involved in networks beyond the philanthropic sector, or that they use the networks to actively shape their environment or restructure their activities in view of public policy developments or other environmental trends. Rather, they make adjustments at the margin.

These approaches and developments are occurring against a backdrop of major reforms in the social safety net, curtailment in public spending for human services, and more intensively negative attitudes toward those who rely on human services. While there is growing, although far from universal, recognition that philanthropy does not have the financial capacity to compensate for the large scale changes in public policies, the financial limitations may not be the most significant. The philanthropic community does not appear to have the institutional capacity to address these issues. The United Way—under pressure to take a more leading role in priority-setting at the local level—could conceivably assume this role, but is constrained by a lack of resources and political will; this responsibility would inevitably generate controversy and conflict at least among some community groups and service providers. A United Way chapter is not an organization that easily confronts political conflict, as is evident in the well-publicized controversies about United Way funding of Planned Parenthood and the Boy Scouts in some communities.

Entrepreneurship and Ventures

The increased competition for public funds and private philanthropy is spurring nonprofit agencies to tap for-profit ventures and entrepreneurial activities for income. This trend in turn is transforming the nonprofit organizational form, blurring the boundaries between nonprofit and for-profit organizations.

These new ventures can include an almost dizzying array of initiatives and programs, including: cause-related marketing; affinity credit cards; contracts between nonprofit agencies and for-profit companies; the creation of for-profit subsidiaries, or even separate for-profit companies to tap new markets.

The examples are almost as varied as nonprofit human service agencies themselves. An AIDS service agency in the Pacific Northwest has entered into a cause-related marketing arrangement with a large national company whereupon the proceeds of a particular product are given to the agency. The agency has created a for-profit subsidiary to handle the considerable sums of money expected by this new agreement. In another example, a human services agency in Seattle eschews government funding and relies upon contracts with big local employers such as Boeing and Starbucks for training services for agency clients. A nonprofit architectural firm serving local nonprofit agencies merges with a for-profit firm and creates a for-profit subsidiary. A nonprofit housing developer in Durham, North Carolina, has a formal partnership with a for-profit developer whereupon the two firms share the income earned from a low-income housing project.

These are only few of the many instances of the rapidly growing importance of for-profit ventures and partnerships to nonprofit human service agencies. While this new-found role is indicative of changes in public funding and private philanthropy, it is also evidence of the philosophical shift underway in social policy. Nonprofit human service agencies expanded and even prospered during the 1960s and 1970s based upon certain assumptions about the welfare state and social policy: (1) government should ensure that people in need received appropriate service; (2) quality services meant professional services delivered by qualified staff; and (3) nonprofit agencies funded by government represented the best strategy to expand services to people in need. Many people associated with these programs in both the government and nonprofit sectors felt nonprofit human service agencies should be entirely reliant upon government funds; that private charity was demeaning and represented a retreat from government's obligation to serve people in need. For-profit or entrepreneurial ventures were regarded with skepticism or derision by many social welfare advocates and since government was providing adequate funding, they were deemed unnecessary. It was a philosophy closer to prevailing notions in Europe where government provided directly or through voluntary service agencies extensive and diverse personal social services (Smith and Lipsky, 1993; Kahn, 1972).

In the 1980s and 1990s, these assumptions fell into disfavor. Many nonprofits did not like the government regulations that accompanied government funding, especially the regulations dictating client eligibility and appropriate service models. For instance, a widely heralded drug treatment program, Delancey Street, based in San Francisco, refuses to accept government funds because they want to retain control over their operations. Their rehabilitation program involves direct client involvement in the management of the program and raising money for the program through the sale of services such as landscaping, furniture-moving, and a restaurant. They almost completely eschew the professionals characteristic of more mainstream human service programs. More recently, many welfare-to-work programs with a self-help philosophy have adopted similar service models. The proliferation of these arrangements represents an implicit repudiation of the professional, entitlement service model of the 1970s: rather than seeing a professional social worker, clients in drug rehabilitation are working at a local business.

Another factor contributing to the increased involvement of nonprofit human service agencies in entrepreneurial ventures is rising competition from for-profit service agencies and growing interest of for-profit companies in human services. For-profit agencies have existed for many decades in selected niches of human services such as residential treatment for emotionally disturbed children and counseling programs. Often these programs would take clients that nonprofit programs could not adequately accommodate. Part of the reason for a lack of a more extensive presence of for-profits appears related to the cost of service. For-profits could not take advantage of private donors to subsidize the service; thus nonprofits had a considerable edge in pricing. Many donors and clients no doubt preferred nonprofits as well due to the problems of trust and contract failure with for-profits (Hansmann, 1980).

The rise of government funding encouraged the entry of for-profit firms into service categories traditionally dominated by nonprofits (Schlesinger, Marmor, and Smithey, 1987). The absence of private donations was not a major impediment to expanding service, since for-profits could now charge the government for the cost of service. However, even after the growth of government funding of nonprofit agencies, for-profit service delivery was slow to take off because of the reluctance of government officials to contract with for-profit firms.

In recent years, government officials—encouraged by the push for privatization, efficiency, and reinventing government—are more receptive to contracting with for-profit service agencies, producing more competition between nonprofit and for-profit organizations, especially in service categories such as job training, mental health programs, and residential care. In another noteworthy development, for-profit businesses with a social commitment are actually supporting or even providing social services traditionally delivered by nonprofit agencies. Perhaps the best example is Ben and Jerry's, the well-known ice cream company. They are not only donating money to a variety of social services but are providing job training to welfare recipients in some of their stores and have even received public funds for these efforts. This entrepreneurship encourages other for-profit businesses and offers a model for nonprofits to undertake for-profit ventures as well.

In short, the growing involvement of nonprofit human service agencies in for-profit ventures means that the traditional focus on nonprofit agencies as key providers of human services is becoming less and less useful. It is increasingly difficult to discern simply by looking at a nonprofit organization how much of its service mix is nonprofit and for-profit activity. The sector distinctions between for-profit and nonprofit are no longer as relevant as they once were. One implication is that private philanthropy, despite the attention given to its role in supporting human services, may actually decline further in terms of its contribution to overall nonprofit human service agency revenues. It is also likely to mean that more and more human services will be subject to some type of market test; those programs without adequate revenues are likely to be dropped or curtailed much more quickly than in the past.

Political Advocacy

Changes in public policy and the political climate in general make this an uncertain time for nonprofit human service agencies as political actors. It is part of American culture that nonprofit organizations play a critical role in advocacy and representing citizen grievances and viewpoints to the government (de Tocqueville, 1955 ed.). In social policy, this has certainly been true at various points in American history, particularly during reform periods such as the Progressive era (Skocpol, 1992; Sklar, 1992). However, in the early post–World War period, advocacy by voluntary associations for human services was relatively limited, especially at the state and local level.

This relative non-involvement changed markedly in the 1960s and 1970s. Federal funding fueled the expansion of the nonprofit human service agencies. Many voluntary associations supported the expansion of public social service funding but this new money and the accompanying policies and regulations created keen interest on the part of nonprofit service agencies in the shaping and influencing of public policy. Due to extensive government funding, nonprofit agencies now had direct and ongoing relationships with government officials. Over time, nonprofit agencies became more involved in political advocacy and formed new statewide or regional associations to advocate for their collective interests. In some cases, the creation of these new associations was abetted by government officials who saw statewide associations as potential allies (Smith and Lipsky, 1993).

The effectiveness of the advocacy of nonprofit human service agencies is difficult to assay as well as controversial. Many individuals opposed to an expansive public sector role in funding social services regard the nonprofit advocacy as a key reason for the growth of federal social spending. Many nonprofit agencies also like to portray themselves as politically influential. But a closer examination of many policy issues reveals a more complicated story. For example, many of the nation's nonprofit human service agencies were vehemently opposed to welfare reform but it was passed nonetheless.

At the state and local level, funding cutbacks are instituted despite aggressive lobbying by nonprofits. This is not to suggest nonprofit associations and their allies are without political influence but it is to suggest that their influence may be overstated; other groups and political forces may be much more important on a particular social service concern. Further, nonprofit service providers often choose to focus their advocacy and lobbying on the more arcane arena of regulations that can involve direct negotiations with government administrators. Nonprofit human service agencies may be weak in affecting funding levels but very powerful in shaping regulatory policy pertaining to service delivery.

Despite this uncertain political impact, many policymakers at the federal level have targeted the advocacy role of nonprofit agencies as a major problem and a potential abuse of their tax-exempt status. Rep. Ernest Istook (R-OK) introduced the so-called Istook Amendment in 1995 (Let America Speak Coalition, 1995). This legislative proposal would have effectively barred most nonprofit agencies receiving federal funds from engaging in most forms of political advocacy and lobbying; even educational campaigns by nonprofit agencies on issues such as welfare reform or child care would have been considered inappropriate activity.[12] This Amendment failed to garner much support but Rep. Istook and his allies have continued to introduce variations of the Amendment. It is unlikely that the issue will fade away anytime soon.

Due to the Istook Amendment controversy, many nonprofits are much more conscious of any activity that is even remotely related to political advocacy. Some self-censorship may be occurring with nonprofits reluctant to speak out on issues for fear of being accused of illegal political activity (even though the chances are probably remote). However, a more profound problem is that the controversy on Istook—which consumed the time and energy of many national nonprofits including the Independent Sector—distracted attention from the more fundamental issue of nonprofit advocacy: the inequities in representation and resources. Many nonprofit human service agencies, especially the smaller community-based service organizations, do relatively little direct advocacy. They lack resources and many are afraid that if they aggressively advocate, government officials will be angered and retaliate against them in lower contract awards, onerous regulations, or even the denial of contracts. The problems in representation are not unique to nonprofit human service agencies; growing inequities in political participation and representation are a national phenomenon (Verba, Schlozman and Brady, 1995; 1997). Nonetheless, nonprofit human service agencies have a special advocacy burden given that they represent vulnerable, politically powerless populations. Nonprofit human service agencies will be challenged in the coming years to devise successful advocacy strategies that meet with the expectations of policymakers and the public about the proper place of nonprofit agencies within the political process.

New Roles for Religious Agencies

Many of the nonprofit human service developments discussed above promise to become even more complex as a result of the growing prominence of religion on the American political agenda. There are several closely related issues. First, although not necessarily a direct consequence of the new politics of religion, there is greater attention to linkages between religion and human services. We now know with some confidence that a substantial majority of religious congregations, perhaps 90 percent, engage in human service activities, especially youth programs. A similar proportion have programs or activities related to health, especially visitation and support for sick and shut-ins.

Of congregations engaged in human service activities, nearly three-quarters participate in, support, or are affiliated with programs in other organizations and nearly half both run programs in their own congregations and in affiliation with other organizations (Hodgkinson and Weitzman, 1993: 2). These numbers suggest a truly impressive involvement by religious congregations in the delivery and support of human services, although the involvement of congregations in human services tends to be clustered in a subset of human services where religion is perceived to have a special advantage, notably child welfare and material assistance (Smith and Sosin, 1998).

We also have some beginning knowledge of the extent to which separately incorporated nonprofit human service organizations have strong religious connections. A survey of Illinois nonprofit human service organizations shows that about one-fifth of the surveyed organizations had some formal religious affiliation (Grønbjerg and Nelson, 1998)—they received funding from a religious affiliation, were affiliated with a religious body, order, or denomination, or were operated or governed by such. Because of the limited sources available from which to generate survey mailing lists, this is most likely an underestimate of the extent to which human service organizations have formal religious affiliations.

Small[13] religious nonprofits, in particular, appear more financially vulnerable, as reflected in low levels of annual surplus and assets relative to expenditures, compared to both larger religious agencies and other smaller agencies without religious affiliations (Grønbjerg and Nelson, 1998). The specter of financial vulnerability appears to extend to the congregations themselves and has served as the impetus for a major initiative by the Lilly Endowment to examine the financing of American religion. The result of these efforts suggests that while there is a perception of a crisis in congregational finances, there are good reasons to think that it is a crisis mainly in comparison to an unusually flush period in American religion during the recent past.

Developments on the political front have increased the saliency of observations about the extensive involvement of congregations in human services. The religious right, especially the Christian Coalition and the so-called Moral Majority, working in collaboration with important segments of the

Republican Party, has engaged in direct and tenacious efforts to expand the role of religion and of religious organizations in American society.

In the human service field, this is an extension of long-standing heated arguments about the legitimacy of services related to reproductive behavior (e.g., birth control, abortion). However, over the last several years, these efforts have moved into arenas more directly relevant to a broader range of human services. There is now an ongoing agenda to make government subsidies, grants, and contracts in the human service and educational fields available to proselytizing religious congregations. This latter represents a notable departure from past practices of maintaining a clear separation of church and state.

Some of these efforts have been successful. The so-called Charitable Choice provision of the welfare reform legislation, passed in 1996, allows organizations that function pervasively as congregations to receive federal funding to administer social services and public health benefits. Senator John Ashcroft (R-MO) and others have already introduced similar provisions into the American Community Renewal Act, the Substance Abuse and Mental Health Reauthorization Act, and the Older Americans Act. Reportedly, Senator Ashcroft plans to include the proposal in every public health and social service bill in Congress.

If sustained, these political developments are likely to have major implications for the human service delivery system. They promise to raise difficult questions about conditions of employment in the sector, access to services, and accountability and monitoring. Specifically, as currently formulated, the Charitable Choice provision permits religious institutions that receive government funding as service providers to discriminate in their employment on the basis of religion. In terms of service access, there does not appear to be any requirement that program beneficiaries be notified that they can seek services from another provider, should that be their preference, although the state must make alternative providers available if beneficiaries object to a religious provider. There is also some debate as to how extensively government monitoring agents can audit program expenditures if religious organizations choose not to segregate government funds from their own.

Most likely, the expansion in the definition of service providers eligible for public funding will bring increased competition for nonprofit human service providers, especially for the large segment of secular agencies that already receive such funds. In addition, the blurring of the state-religion boundary is likely to affect philanthropic funders in the human service field, especially United Way and corporate funders. They either depend on broad public support for their activities (in the case of United Way) or seek to use their philanthropic activities to generate public goodwill (in the case of corporate philanthropy).

United Way is already facing difficult issues in some communities (mainly large metropolitan areas) because of its support of Boy Scout organizations and other religiously oriented organizations that do not wish to employ gays and lesbians. Traditionally, most United Way organizations have sought to avoid having to choose among religious factions (and antagonize one or another segment of donors) by emphasizing the funding of human services and distancing themselves from the appearance of funding religious activities. Indeed, many have modeled their actions on those of the public sector, arguing that public policies reflect community consensus. The contradictory and divisive religious values that now permeate the political landscape in Washington therefore promise to become equally problematic for United Way. By the same token, corporate philanthropy is likely to be affected as well.

Clearly, major changes are sweeping through nonprofit human service agencies due to privatization and devolution, increased competition for philanthropic funding, new societal expectations for the roles of churches and human service agencies, and the entry of churches and for-profit businesses and service agencies into service markets previously dominated by nonprofit agencies. What is unclear is the overall direction these changes will be taking American social policy and nonprofit human service agencies in particular.

Historically, scholars of American social policy regarded the United States as a "laggard" compared to European countries (Wilensky, 1957; Flora and Heidenheimer, 1982) due to the more limited character of American social services and the important role of private charity compared to state funding and service entitlement. Esping-Anderson (1990: 26–29), in rejecting this bipolar model, suggested that advanced industrial countries could be divided into three basic categories depending upon the extent to and the manner in which the state buffered the effect of money and position in the economy. In his scheme, the United States represents the "liberal" welfare state, dominated by work-ethic norms infused into means-tested assistance and modest social insurance plans. In this model, the state encourages the market in various ways—by guaranteeing only a minimum and by subsidizing private welfare systems. The result is a society that provides only limited protection for individuals from such risks of modern life as unemployment and old age.

The development of nonprofit human services and their connection to public policy in the last 25 years indicates that the picture for the United States is indeed more complicated than standard comparisons of the U.S. and European welfare states would suggest. Government support of nonprofit agencies expanded in the 1960s and 1970s due in part to the vision of European social democracy supported by many policymakers and scholars in the United States. At first glance, the 1980s would appear to be a retreat from this vision; and to some extent it was, given the decline in federal funding for some programs. Yet the expansion of many federal programs, the refinancing of human services to take advantage of health care financing, and the growing role of the private sector in supporting human services demonstrates that the United States should be distinguished from other advanced industrial countries by the manner in which it provides human services (Rein, 1995; Esping-Anderson, 1990). This is not to suggest that other countries do not provide more generous programs through public funding. Sweden, France, and many other countries have, for example, much more extensive direct public funding of child care, preschool, and other programs.

In the United States, the state subsidizes private welfare systems, and nonprofit human service agencies provide an array of services in close cooperation with the public sector. Despite attempts by policy makers to cut back on programs, the number of agencies continues to grow, albeit slowly. These organizations depend upon a variety of direct public grants and contracts but increasingly they also rely on an array of indirect public subsidies, non–human service grants, and earned income from for-profit and entrepreneurial ventures. As a result, the more conventional method of comparing countries based upon direct public expenditures has become less and less relevant. Nonprofit human service agencies are becoming more complex with less distinct organizational boundaries: although the delivery vehicle may be nonprofit, the funding is increasingly from a variety of sources. Indeed, the delivery vehicle may no longer be nonprofit even if a nonprofit is involved, given the proliferation of for-profit subsidiaries and partnerships with for-profit entities. Close connections between the public sector and nonprofit agencies make the relationship even more blurred and difficult to characterize. For example, some nonprofits have both 501(c)(3) status and classification as a public development authority.

Today, nonprofit human service agencies are at the intersection of America's social policy. Our skepticism and aversion to government lead us to turn to nonprofits, yet America's political system does allow policymakers to embrace public efforts to support people in need—the financing is public, but the delivery mechanism is nonprofit. We try to curtail public support of nonprofits through privatization, devolution, and legislation of a regulatory sort, but new programs are created even as some programs are curtailed. If the recent past is any guide, current efforts to drastically limit public support of nonprofits are likely to be unsuccessful. The American political system appears to offer too many opportunities at the federal, state, and local level for new methods of public and private support. In this sense, nonprofit human service agencies both embody and exemplify the many contradictions and puzzles of our social policy.

Notes

1. This argument was recently raised in the Bradley Commission report (National Commission on Philanthropy and Civic Renewal, 1997).

2. So far, the NTEE classification system has been applied only to the 36 percent of those registered as public charities under IRS section 501(c)(3) that file tax returns. This leaves out non-filing charities and tax-exempt organizations registered under other sections of the IRS code, or more than 80 percent of all IRS-registered tax-exempt organizations.

3. Ostensibly, "non-filers" either have too few revenues (e.g., below $25,000) to meet filing requirements or file as part of a parent organization. However, this may not hold for all non-filers (Grønbjerg, 1994).

4. This summary is based on Grønbjerg et al., 1996.

5. Headstart enrollment reached an early peak in the late 1960s and then went into a long decline before enrollment and funding rose again in the 1980s.

6. Supplemental Security Income is indexed for inflation, an important contributing factor to the rise in benefits. SSI serves the blind, aged poor ineligible for Social Security, and the disabled. Almost all of the growth in recipients has been with the disabled.

7. Even so-called private funds are frequently intermingled with government support, so it is sometimes impossible to separate the mix of public and private funds either for individuals or private organizations.

8. For example, the number of HUD financed housing units fell from 247,667 units in 1977 to an estimated 17,731 units in 1996 (House Ways and Means Committee, 1996, 919). New budget authority of HUD has fallen from $28 billion in 1977 to $14 billion in 1996 in current dollars (or a drop from $71.3 billion to $14 billion in 1996 dollars) (House Ways and Means Committee, 1996, 921). Many nonprofit agencies, especially agencies for the mentally ill and developmentally disabled, took advantage of some of this HUD new construction money.

9. Aggregate data on revenue trends are consistent with this perspective. The available data suggest that the government funding from grants and contracts has more or less kept up with overall revenue growth for the social and legal service field. The share attributable to these sources has declined slightly from 54 percent in 1977 to 50 percent in 1992 (Independent Sector, 1996: 193–94). The relative importance of contributions and fees has changed, however, with fees increasing from 10 percent to 18 percent of revenues and donations declining from 32 to 20 percent. As we noted, some fees reflect government payments, rather than private sources, thus the figures on income from grants and contracts understates the continued dependence of social and legal service agencies on government funds. The trend in donation revenues is consistent with data reported by the American Association of Fund-Raising Counsel (1996). *Giving USA 1996* shows that the share of private contributions going to human services declined from 14 percent during the 1960s to 9 percent in the early 1990s. More refined breakdown by subsectors is not available.

10. To be sure, agencies can try to bill for administrative-related expenses under performance contracts but it is more difficult.

11. This section is based on Grønbjerg et al., 1996, and Grønbjerg and Jones, 1997.

12. Most nonprofit human service agencies are 501(c)(3) organizations. As such, they are limited to spending 25 percent of their overall budget on political advocacy which is defined as the more direct forms of lobbying such as hiring a

lobbyist rather than letters to legislators on an urgent public issue such as welfare reform.

13. Defined here as organizations with less than $500,000 in annual expenditures or less than 20 FTE staff members.

References

Affordable Housing Finance. 1997: "Many State Agencies Prepare to Wrap Up Tax Credit, Tax-Exempt Bond Rounds," *Affordable Housing Finance*, 5, 3 (May–June): 6–9.

American Association of Fund-Raising Counsel. 1996: *Giving USA 1996*. New York: American Association of Fund-Raising Counsel.

Avery, R. B. 1994: "The Pending Intergenerational Transfer." *Philanthropy* (Winter).

Bixby, A. K. 1996: "Public Social Welfare Expenditures, Fiscal Year 1993," *Social Security Bulletin*, 59, 3 (Fall): 67–75.

Bothwell, R. 1993: "Federated Giving: Recent History, Current Issues". National Committee for Responsive Philanthropy: Washington, DC.

Brown, L. D. 1983: *New Policies, New Politics*. Washington, DC: Brookings.

Clotfelter, C. T. 1985: *Federal Tax Policy and Charitable Giving*. Chicago: University of Chicago Press.

Clotfelter, C. T. and R. L. Schmalbeck. 1996: "The Impact of Fundamental Tax Reform on Nonprofit Organizations," in *Economic Effects of Fundamental Tax Reform*, ed. H. J. Aaron and W. G. Gale. Washington, DC: Brookings. pp. 211–246.

Dobbin, F. and T. Boychuk. 1996: "Public Policy and the Rise of Private Pensions: The US Experience since 1930," in *The Privatization of Social Policy?* ed. Michael Shalev. London: Macmillan. pp. 104–135.

Esping-Anderson, G. 1990: *Three Worlds of Welfare Capitalism*. Princeton, NJ: Princeton University Press.

Executive Office of the President. 1997a: *Budget of U.S. Government, FY 1998*. Washington, DC: Government Printing Office.

Executive Office of the President. 1997b: *Budget of U.S. Government, FY 1998: Analytical Perspectives*. Washington, DC: Government Printing Office.

Flora, P. and A. J. Heidenheimer. eds. 1981: *The Development of Welfare States in Europe and America*. New Brunswick, NJ: Transaction Books.

Foundation Center. 1997: *Foundation Giving, 1997 Edition*. New York: The Foundation Center.

Grønbjerg, K. A. 1993: *Understanding Nonprofit Funding: Managing Revenues in Social Service and Community Development Organizations*. San Francisco: Jossey-Bass.

Grønbjerg, K. A. and E. Jones. 1997: "Philanthropic Human Service Funders in a Changing Environment," Paper presented at the ARNOVA meetings, Indianapolis. (December).

Grønbjerg, K. A. and A. Nagle. 1994: "Structure and Adequacy of Human Service Facilities: Challenges for Nonprofit Managers," *Nonprofit Management and Leadership*, 5 (No. 2): 117–40.

Grønbjerg, K. A. and S. Nelson. 1998: Mapping Small Religious Nonprofit Organizations: An Illinois Profile," *Nonprofit and Voluntary Sector Quarterly*, 27, 1 (March): 13–31.

Hansmann, H. 1980: "The Role of the Nonprofit Enterprise," *Yale Law Review*, 89 (April): 835–899.

Hansmann, H. 1996: *The Ownership of Enterprise*. Cambridge, MA: Harvard University Press.

Hodgkinson, V. and M. Weitzman. eds. 1993: *From Belief to Commitment: The Community Service Activities and Finances of Religious Congregations in the United States. Findings from a National Survey, 1993 Edition*. Washington, DC: Independent Sector.

House of Representatives, Ways and Means Committee. 1996: *The Green Book*. Washington, DC: Government Printing Office.

Independent Sector. 1996: *The Nonprofit Almanac*. Washington, DC: Independent Sector.

James, E. 1983: "How Nonprofits Grow: A Model," *Journal of Policy Analysis and Management*, 2, 3 (Fall): 350–366.

James, E. 1987: "The Nonprofit Sector in Comparative Perspective," in *The Nonprofit Sector: A Research Handbook*, ed. W. W. Powell. New Haven: Yale University Press. pp. 397–415.

Kahn, A. J. 1972: "Public Social Services: The Next Phase—Policy and Delivery Strategies," *Public Welfare* (Winter): 15–24.

Kanter, R. M. 1995: "World Class Companies and World Class Communities: A Contradiction, Tension, or a Partnership?" Paper presented at the American Sociological Association, Annual Meeting, Washington, DC.

Lipsky, M. and S. R. Smith. 1989–90: "Government, Nonprofit Agencies and the Welfare State," *Political Science Quarterly*, 104, 4 (Winter): 625–648.

National Commission on Philanthropy and Civic Renewal. 1997: *Giving Better, Giving Smarter: Renewing Philanthropy in America*. Washington, DC: The National Commission on Philanthropy and Civic Renewal.

Rein, M. 1996: "Is America Exceptional? The Role of Occupational Welfare in the United States and the European Community," in *Privatization of Social Policy?* ed. M. Shalev. London: Macmillan. pp. 28–43.

Salamon, L. M. and A. J. Abramson. 1984: "The Nonprofit Sector," *The Reagan Experiment*, ed. J. L. Palmer and I. V. Sawhill. Washington, DC: The Urban Institute. pp. 219–243.

——. 1987: "Partners in Public Service: The Scope and Theory of Government-Nonprofit Relations," *The Nonprofit Sector: A Research Handbook*, ed. W. W. Powell. New Haven: Yale University Press. pp. 99–117.

Schlesinger, M., T. R. Marmor, and R. Smithey. 1987: "Nonprofit and For-Profit Medical Care: Shifting Roles and Implications for Health Policy," *Journal of Health Politics, Policy and Law*, 12, 3 (Fall): 427–457.

Shashaty, A. R. 1997: "Archer vs. Clinton: The Rematch," *Affordable Housing Finance*, 5, 3 (May/June): 4.

Sklar, K. K. 1992: "Explaining the Power of Women's Political Culture in the Creation of the American Welfare State, 1890–1930," in *Gender and the Origins of Welfare States in Western Europe and North America*, ed. Seth Koven and S. Michel. New York: Routledge.

Skocpol, T. 1992: *Protecting Soldiers and Mothers: The Political Origins of Social Policy in the United States*. Cambridge, MA: Harvard University Press.

Smith, D. H. 1997: "The Rest of the Nonprofit Sector: Grassroots Associations as the Dark Matter Ignored in Prevailing "Flat Earth" Maps of the Sector," *Nonprofit and Voluntary Sector Quarterly*, 26, 2 (June): 114–131.

Smith, S. R. 1997: "Civic Infrastructure in America: The Interrelationship Between Government and Voluntary Associations," paper commissioned for the National Commission on Civic Renewal. College Park, MD: University of Maryland.

Smith, S. R. and M. Lipsky. 1993: *Nonprofits for Hire: The Welfare State in the Age of Contracting*. Cambridge, MA: Harvard University Press.

Smith, S. R. and M. R. Sosin. 1998: "Are Faith-Based Agencies Really Different?" unpublished paper.

Stevenson, D., et al., 1997: *The State Nonprofit Almanac*. Washington, DC: The Urban Institute Press.

Thompson, A. 1997: "Developers Enjoy Strong Markets, As Agency Targets Rehab, Unserved Areas," *Affordable Housing Finance*, 5, 3 (May/June): 50–53.

de Tocqueville, A. 1955 ed.: *Democracy in America*. New York: New American Library.

Verba, S., K. L. Schlozman, and H. E. Brady. 1995: *Voice and Equality: Civic Voluntarism in American Politics*. Cambridge, MA: Harvard University Press.

Weisbrod, B. A. 1989: *The Nonprofit Economy*. Cambridge, MA: Harvard University Press.

Weisbrod, B. A. 1975: "Toward a Theory of the Voluntary Non-Profit Sector in a Three-Sector Economy," in *Altruism, Morality and Economic Theory*, ed. E. Phelps. New York: Russell Sage Foundation.

Wilensky, H. L. and C. N. Lebeaux. 1957: *Industrial Society and Social Welfare*. New York: The Free Press.

CHAPTER EIGHT

Public Trust in Not-for-Profit Organizations and the Need for Regulatory Reform[1]

Joel L. Fleishman

The myriad of large and small, formal and informal, rich and poor, old and new not-for-profit organizations share one characteristic—their dedication to an interest larger than—indeed other than—themselves. It is that interest which defines them as a sector. All of the organizations in the sector depend to a greater or lesser degree on the support of the public, through donations, patronage or tax benefits enacted by government. Continued public support depends on continued public trust in the bona fides of the not-for-profit sector. That trust can be gradually undermined by instances of fiscal irresponsibility, mismanagement, wastefulness, and fraud within the sector, as well as by the huge recent increase in assets held by not-for-profit organizations. The present accountability-enforcing arrangements of the state and federal governments are entirely inadequate, as they currently function, to detect, deter, and punish illegal actions by a tiny number of organizations, which, if not appropriately dealt with, could poison the well of public good will toward not-for-profit organizations. This paper proposes three complementary and sequential strategies for policing and defending the legitimate not-for-profit sector—(1) an internal not-for-profit sector strategy, (2) a joint not-for-profit sector/governmental strategy, and (3) the establishment of a new federal agency.

The Many Threads of Not-for-Profit Organizations Are One Fabric

All who wish to understand the strength and vibrancy of democratic institutions at home in America or abroad in the rest of the world would do well to keep constantly in mind that the great variety of not-for-profit organizations—religion, social welfare, private education higher and lower, private health organizations, the rich variety of advocacy in behalf of every area of public policy and then some, the arts, think tanks, the many kinds of foundations—constitute, despite all of their differences, one *sector* distinct from both government and the for-profit sector. What all such organizations share is an explicit commitment to serve the public interest as seen through the many-faceted prism of free minds deliberating and associating together. Their commitment to exclusively public-benefiting ends distinguishes them from their for-profit fellow private sector compatriots, while their exclusive reliance on voluntariness stamps them as fundamentally different from the public sector, which alone has the power to coerce cooperation and obedience. The fact that many of them receive significant amounts of support from several levels of government does not miraculously transform them into public sector organizations, nor does the fact that many of them increasingly rely on revenues generated from earned income metamorphose them into for-profit entities. That they frequently engage in joint ventures or partnerships with both government and for-profit enterprise compromises neither their private nor their public-serving character. That some of them exist primarily for the community of those who create and sustain them does not make them any the less public-serving; the free association of Americans in together building countless smaller voluntary communities to fulfill their needs and serve their interests within the larger nation is exactly what a "republic of republics," as some of the founding fathers termed it, is all about. Their privateness remains inviolate, and indeed it is that public-serving privateness that constitutes their distinctiveness, that makes them frequently attractive and often necessary for the accomplishment of ends that neither government nor for-profit enterprise alone or together could serve as well or at all. Despite the amazing variety of threads, colors, textures, and tensile strengths that both altruistic and mutual-benefit not-for-profit enterprises come in, their privateness weaves them into a single fabric.

Yet few of us who are engaged in, or who have interests or affiliations in, the rainbow of particular realms of the not-for-profit universe remember always to think of ourselves not only as environmental, social welfare, educational, health, arts, public policy or other kinds of subsector participants, but also as citizens of the not-for-profit universe. We fail to recall that the right we all share—the right of working privately on public and mutual-interest problems—and the privilege we all share in common—the privilege of acting privately while being sustained by public subventions—can quickly be called into question as a consequence of real or perceived misbehavior by those in any single subsector of the not-for-profit sector. It is no exaggeration to say that we had all better hang together or we will surely hang separately.

More than ever before, it is absolutely essential for each of us to define our loyalties broadly, not confining them only to those particularities that especially interest us but to expand them to include the not-for-profit universe as a whole, the universe that embraces all not-for-profit organizations whatever their mission. It is, after all, the conception of that larger universe that legitimates the variegated sector as protected, valued and tax-favored expressions of individual and group loyalties and interests in our democratic society. While the sector surely does not depend for its survival on its tax-favored status, it would seem to be unarguable that the tax privileges accorded the sector contribute substantially to its financial health and vigor. Let us not forget, therefore, that it is the conception of not-for-profit enterprise as a whole, and the belief that such enterprise is socially beneficial, that make possible the continued rich flowering of not-for-profit organizations that constitute the sector. Political or governmental threats to any single subsector, therefore, are threats to the entire sector. Governmental efforts to circumscribe tax exemption or the tax deductibility of contributions to any single subsector will, whatever assurances or promises may be made, sooner or later affect all other subsectors. If the tax system is overhauled radically, the changes are likely to affect all forms of not-for-profit institutions equally.

The virtues of the organizations and subsectors to which each of us commits ourselves go without saying. Our involvement in them speaks for itself. Rarely, however, do we also feel a larger loyalty to the not-for-profit universe as a whole. I believe that we all need to make a habit of keeping constantly in mind both the part and the whole, and do our best to nudge our fellow members and sympathizers into the same recognition that their individual charitable acts strengthen not only our particular organizations but also the not-for-profit sector as a whole. What seems to me to be at stake is the continued dynamism of the whole sector which facilitates free expression of interests in American society; as the sector thrives, so will the parts about which we especially care. We should make it a point to help our fellows understand that we are raising money not only for the institution or cause that embodies the particular interest about which we ourselves care passionately, but that, by doing so, we thereby become part of something much larger, that our doing so strengthens a vital component of a comprehensive sector that defines the very distinctiveness, indeed the uniqueness, of American society.

Taking pride in being part of the not-for-profit sector as a whole should not be difficult. Its size alone is surprising to anyone who has not thought about the sector as a sector. According to the latest estimates, the not-for-profit sector contributes at least 7 percent of America's GDP, probably more, and constitutes 10 percent of our work force. Moreover, for most of the last twenty years, it has been the fastest-growing of the three sectors.[2] Other than religious institutions, 60 percent of the NFP sector organizations currently in existence were established since 1971, according to Independent Sector's excellent *A Portrait of the Independent Sector*.[3] Moreover, from 1980–1990, the NFP sector's contribution to employment growth was 12.7 percent, about 25 percent higher than its current share of the work force.[4]

During the last thirty years, Americans' charitable giving, which of course provides only part of the revenues of the sector—now about 19 percent for the sector as a whole—has ranged from a low of 1.7 percent of GDP in 1977 to a high of 2.3 percent of GDP in 1965, and it has remained stable at 2 percent over the past 8 years.[5] That is roughly three times larger than the next nearest country's percentage of GDP devoted to charitable giving—the U.K. Of course, all Americans can afford to contribute more, and should, but that in no way gainsays the fact that, as a nation, Americans are at present the most generous people in the world. There is no justification for deprecating the present level of generosity of Americans, as some have done recently, in order to exhort them to be even more generous. One of the great challenges facing us is to persuade our fellow Americans of the greater sense of fulfillment that would arise from giving more than we now do.

Overall, the entire NFP sector budget is now around $700 billion. And this does *not* include the value of volunteered time, which is about 4 hours every week for about 100 million Americans, or 20 billion hours a year. Valuing that time at what is thought to be an appropriate level brings the NFP Sector budget to more than $900 billion.[6] Compare these figures to the entire federal budget which, excluding defense, entitlements and interest on the national debt, comes to only $277 billion.[7] ONLY!

The Other-Serving and Public Goods Nature of the Not-for-Profit Sector

But there is a characteristic more persuasive than sheer size for feeling pride in being part of the NFP sector. Ours is a sector that, at its core, is dedicated not to serving itself but to satisfying the needs of others and to creating public goods. If profit is the bottom line of our sister for-profit sector, "not-for-profits" are almost what their name insists. Any profit that they make cannot inure to the personal financial benefit of those who run them. Nobody "owns" them; those who run them are trustees for the benefit of others. In Western legal tradition, trustees have long been held to the highest, most exacting standards of stewardship both in substance and in appearance, and even if today's standard of not-for-profit directors' duty of care is not called "the trust standard," there remains a great deal of that standard's content in the prevailing standard of "business judgment."[8] Therein lies the answer to the compulsive classifiers who puzzle over the essence of our sector. This sector is not just "not-for-profit," but *for* the most praiseworthy character of human behavior—voluntary giving to others for their, not the giver's, benefit.

In *Measure for Measure,* Shakespeare has Duke Vincentio say it better than anyone else:

> Heaven doth with us
>   as we with torches do,
> Not light them for themselves,
>   for if our virtues
> Did not go forth of us,
>   'Twere all alike
> As if we had them not.[9]

As an aside, one cannot help but be amused by the fact that the U.S. Department of Commerce, in its national economic accounting, regards the not-for-profit sector as constituting "consumption" and not "production."[10] In that perverse idea, it is apparently following a view attributed, erroneously I think, to Adam Smith in *The Wealth of Nations.* The more accurate view, I am certain, is that of Tocqueville, who insisted that "The wealth of a democratic society may well be measured by the quality of functions performed by private citizens." Tocqueville's wealth shows up dramatically in American society not only in the avowedly charitable social service subsector, but just as prominently in the private education and health institutions which constitute about 80 percent of the NFP sector's revenues.

The American idea of the not-for-profit sector as an organizational model is an exceedingly powerful one. It promises the public great freedom to associate ourselves voluntarily to achieve socially worthwhile ends of our own choosing. Our freedom to do so is much greater and our record in so using it is much longer than in many societies where achieving most social ends requires the formal—and rigid—mechanisms of the state itself.

The Need for Government Regulation of the NFP Sector

The not-for-profit sector produces public and quasi-public goods and services; it is the social equivalent of the for-profit sector which produces private and quasi-private goods and services. For both not-for-profit and for-profit sectors, the distinctive hallmarks are voluntary action, individual and group initiative, flexibility, autonomy, and freedom from bureaucratic strictures, all to be exercised subject to the ground rules established by government. The public sector, as viewed from the for-profit and not-for-profit sectors, is best seen as umpire and police officer. Its hallmark is the power to coerce, a power which, if used sparingly, can enhance rather than restrict freedom, but which, when power-drunk or corrupted by what Shakespeare called "the insolence of office," tends to ride roughshod and indiscriminately over liberty. Contrary to some of today's prevailing wisdom, government is *not* an evil, even a necessary evil. Its ground rules are absolutely essential boundaries for ordering liberty. Even Nobelist Milton Friedman concedes that government has an indispensable role as umpire.[11] Without them, the liberties we all enjoy would be undermined by the license of the few who respect no constraint other than their own self-will. There is, as National Center for Law and Philanthropy director Harvey Dale observes, a Gresham's Law of Regulation, which predicts that, without governmental monitoring and enforcement of laws proscribing fraud and self-dealing, among other objectionable behavior that damages us all, the good guys will observe the rules, the bad guys will flout them with impunity, and, if enough bad guys get away with it, the arena of private action will be vitally undermined. The for-profit and not-for-profit sectors therefore *need* governmental regulation and enforcement at some level simply to assure everyone's maximum freedom to compete and cooperate in achieving their view of the public good to the fullest possible degree, protected from the actions of those who know no public good but their own self-aggrandizement. Marion Fremont-Smith puts the purpose of regulation succinctly: "[I]t is to assure the public that there is a mechanism by which government can compel compliance with an accepted set of standards that we as a society are agreed should be observed by the entities which are the subject of regulation. The set of standards we have imposed on the managers of charities have been designed to assure that those managers will be faithful to the purposes of the organizations they administer; that they will not use charitable funds to benefit themselves . . . ."[12]

At best, then, when government exercises its power with a light hand, it increases the not-for-profit sector's freedom to fulfill its voluntariness through private citizens' actions in partnership with others. At worst, government can appear as an alternative that can potentially supplant private initiatives, a source of coercive power that can, if it wishes, undermine the attractiveness of private initiatives by, among other ways, diminishing tax incentives, and which continuously threatens to stifle free association by regulating it from a tiny bit all the way to a state of utter nonexistence. Such harm to the not-for-profit sector will not occur without some cause, and nothing, I might add, seems so likely to increase public sector intrusions upon the freedom of the not-for-profit and for-profit sectors as will a public outcry triggered by alleged law violations, fraud, or financial chicanery, or the appearance or reality of personal or organizational misdeeds.

NFP Misbehavior as a Threat to the Entire Sector

So the greatest threat to the not-for-profit sector is the betrayal of public trust, the disappointment of public confidence. Virtually all knowledgeable observers of the not-for-profit scene believe that an overwhelming proportion of not-for-profits are honorably run, even if not most efficiently and effectively. That admirable context, however, does not provide much protection to the sector when a sequence of highly publicized disgraceful not-for-profit misdeeds occur. Moreover one can be certain that any such occurrences are bound to be highly publicized, because to do so is the duty—and the glory—of a free press, whose primary function in democratic society is to keep the institutions of society honest by providing the public with information needed to make necessary corrections in existing arrangements.

At the same time, I must say, however, that if that is the glory of the press, as it surely is, its constantly recurring shame is that the press almost always neglects its equally vital duty to put the "bad" news it reports into the context of the "good" news that forms the backdrop. It is almost always the case, too, that there is far more "good" news to report than "bad," and that it takes much more effort to gather it than does the "bad" news that comes in over the transom, as it were. The consequence is that, almost invariably, the press presents a picture badly out of focus, one that is unnecessarily alarming to the public, and, even worse, that frequently undermines the public's confidence in the possibility of effective action. The result of that imbalance is to create an atmosphere of hysteria which can sometimes lead to throwing out the baby with the bath.

That is the single greatest threat to the NFP sector today. A potentially huge problem for the sector can be created by the tiny fraction of not-for-profit sector organizations which have been found to be wilfully dishonest or which engage in illegal practices, and by the unethical individuals acting within otherwise reputable organizations. It should pain all of us merely to recite the litany of recent miscreancy, but it is important to do so here if only to be reminded of how large and visible a group they amount to, even if they constitute the tiniest of fractions of the sector as a whole: the conviction of Jim and Tammy Bakker;[13] the conviction of William Aramony of the venerable United Way of America;[14] the conviction of John Bennett of the Foundation for New Era Philanthropy;[15] the forced resignation of Bruce Ritter of Covenant House;[16] the forced resignation of Peter Diamandopoulos as president of Adelphi University;[17] the allegations concerning improper dealings among the Trustees of the Bishop's Estate;[18] the allegations concerning improper behavior by the officers of the Freedom Forum Foundation;[19] the allegations concerning the questionable use of not-for-profit organizations by politicians for partisan political purposes;[20] the accumulating evidence of escalating percentages of funds raised in the name of charities retained by for-profit fundraising firms;[21] the Common Fund investment loss caused allegedly by inadequate Board supervision of its investments;[22] the Stanford University indirect costs controversy;[23] and the debate over lobbying by not-for profits,[24] and the allegations concerning questionable compensation to officers of Minnesota Public Radio and an affiliated for-profit organization.[25]

These and other disreputable occurrences challenge each of us to take vigorous preventive action to defend the sector as a whole from being tarred by their brush. But remember that they were, with the exception of New Era, the result of failures of the boards of directors charged with governing each of them. A directly related and much more extensive problem is posed by the far larger number of organizations which are sloppily and inattentively run but which have not, at least as yet, manifested public instances of gross improprieties of the character just noted. There are far too many not-for-profit boards made up of directors who do not direct, to quote William Bowen in his recent book.[26] For some time, too, there has been a strong undercurrent of criticism about excessive salaries and perks for not-for-profit executives, which surfaced in the wake of the Aramony affair but focused on the heads of local United Ways, as well as in the Adelphi University events cited above. Such irresponsibility by not-for-profits has the potential of doing far more damage to the sector than the likely few instances of wrongdoing by the willfully dishonest. It is the incipient "United Way" problems that should give us most cause for worry.

An equally explosive potential problem for that part of the sector which has endowments has come to the fore only recently because of the continuing rocketing of the stock market. The astronomical growth of foundation, university, and other endowments seems likely to exacerbate public mistrust of the not-for-profit sector, especially that of foundations which experience year-to-year asset growth four or five times higher than the mandatory 5-percent payout rate. At some point, a growing chorus of critics will begin demanding some higher payout rate or some cap on the size of endowments. Such disparity between asset growth and payout is certainly not mismanagement of any kind, but the failure to recognize the time bomb that it constitutes, and develop a reasonable strategy for dealing with it, would be.

The vibrancy of the not-for-profit sector depends on its freedom, which in part depends on continued facilitation and friendly policing by the public sector—the political and governmental apparatus. That vibrancy would be quickly undermined—as it was in 1969—by public sector action triggered by political hostility, opposition, vindictiveness, and intrusiveness.

Moreover, public sector support of the not-for-profit sector depends to a large degree on the reputation of the not-for-profit sector among the public. By and large, the NFP sector has happily enjoyed strong public support over the years,[27] and has been spared all but occasional significant harassment by public authorities. When the public or government has intervened, it has done so because politicians have sensed a disenchantment among the public with the not-for-profit sector, disenchantment triggered by alleged notorious incidents of not-for-profit sector default. The most important recent example was the series of House hearings orchestrated by Congressman Wright Patman during the 1960s which culminated in the stringent but not wholly unwelcome 1969 Tax Reform Act, levying the first tax ever imposed on foundation assets. Within the past year, there have been frequent reported intentions to convene new congressional hearings on the NFP sector, but thus far they have been headed off by prompt, concerted action led by Independent Sector, the Council on Foundations, and other institutions of the sector. Moreover the umbrella organizations of the sector have taken the lead in calling for regulation which they regard as necessary. They were instrumental in drafting and achieving the 1996 enactment of the intermediate sanctions legislation, which gives the IRS badly needed enforcement provisions in addition to the preexisting power to revoke tax exemption. If, however, NFP sector misconduct continues to occur, it is not likely that even the determined efforts of the NFP sector's leadership will be able to derail congressional or other hearings on the apparent lack of NFP sector accountability.

NFP Misbehavior as a Betrayal of the Public's Trust

Such incidents grate against public sensibility because the public rightfully regards the not-for-profit sector as inherently partaking of a kind of sacredness. The sector's guiding philosophy is supposed to be altruism, the voluntary, charitable doing for others. The public expects, and has a right to expect, the not-for-profit sector to behave properly, to forego personal inurement, to abide by the rules, to do the right thing. The not-for-profit sector is different in that respect from the political and for-profit sectors. The public cynically believes, with Mark Twain, that there is no distinctively American criminal class but politicians. (Twain actually said "Congress" but I think he would approve the expansion of the class.) Mencken went Twain one better when he cautioned that "If experience teaches us anything at all, it teaches us this: that a good politician, under democracy, is quite as unthinkable as an honest burglar." The public has long, perhaps always, suspected those who seek office as being much more frequently self-seeking than public-serving. So it is not surprised by the peccadillos of politicians.

Americans are not surprised either by for-profit sector executives caught with their fingers in the till; they know that greed is legitimately the driving motive behind profit. As Adam Smith put it, "it is not from the benevolence of the butcher, the brewer, or the baker that we expect our dinners but from their regard to their own interest."[28] The public understands and accepts that, among the for-profits, greed and self-seeking promotion will at times inevitably burst through the boundaries of legality. But the public is more than surprised and shocked when self-serving greed intrudes in the domain of other-benefiting altruism—the not-for-profit sector. It feels profoundly betrayed. If the public could be educated to distinguish between bona fide legitimate not-for-profit organizations and greed-motivated bad actors determined to use the not-for-profit form and banner for self-inurement, much of the danger—but not all of it—could be dissipated.

Given today's widespread public disillusionment with virtually all kinds of social institutions and elites, it would be surprising if the NFP sector could escape the public's cynical eye. Indeed, in the wake of recent opinion research evidencing the erosion of public support and a desire for more governmental regulation, there has predictably followed a rising swell of political and journalistic criticism, especially of universities, hospitals, and religious institutions. But the notorious debacles are not alone. Indeed, recently published books have criticized—incorrectly and unjustifiably, I think—the administration of such widely admired and broadly supported organizations as the Girl Scouts, the American Cancer Society, and the American Red Cross.[29] Surely mom, apple pie, and the American flag will be next.

The Pervasive Problems of NFP Noncompliance with Legal and Financial Requirements and the Inadequacy of Government Supervision

Behind the iceberg tip of those all-too-public defaults, however, there is other evidence that no one is minding the NFP store. According to a 1988 GAO study, 48 percent of all 990s filed were lacking at least one of the required schedules. Other studies suggest that, even when all of the schedules are filed, enough called-for data are not provided to warrant requesting more. Perhaps there has been some improvement in recent years. According to an IRS response to my inquiry in 1996, of the 380,094 organizations required to file the 990 in 1994, 368,633 filed them, and the IRS requested additional information on only 23,824 990s, or about 8 percent.

That said, the 990 form itself is hardly a model of clarity in specifying the precise information sought, so it should be little surprise that the IRS has to request more information from 8 percent of the filing organizations. More-over, most of the information provided on the 990s is not especially useful to those, whether accountability-enforcers or grant-seekers, who need more detail. Regardless, the governmental policing agencies—the attorneys gen- . eral of the states and the IRS at the federal level—are woefully understaffed and can't begin to provide adequate oversight. For example, the IRS' limited staff can audit only 1 percent of the 990s annually filed. The reason that is so is that IRS Division of Employee Plans and Exempt Organizations (EP/EO) staffing has remained virtually static during the past two decades, despite its assumption of major increased responsibilities during that period.[30] Accord-ing to a recent article by James J. McGovern, formerly Assistant IRS Commis-sioner for EP and EO, and Phil Brand, long-time senior IRS official in the EO area, EP/EO staffing has risen only from 2075 in 1975 to 2100 in 1997, a 22-year span in which the number of IRS-certified tax-exempt organizations increased from 700,000 to 1.1 million, almost doubling, according to Inde-pendent Sector figures. In 1994, that article reports that the House Ways and

Means Subcommittee on Oversight "found that the IRS had insufficient resources to adequately regulate [sic] public charities, and recommended that the staffing and funding levels allocated for the IRS's exempt organizations examination and compliance activities be increased."[31] The authors go on to note that "EP/EO is the only technical function at the Internal Revenue Service that has been subjected to downsizing and whose employees have received RIF notification."[32]

Even more devastating are the cumulative consequences reported by McGovern and Brand:

> Another area of risk is guidance for the nation's tax-exempt organizations. There has been massive federal tax legislation since the enactment of ERISA. During the past 23 years, the Internal Revenue Code has been amended by 205 Public Laws. This flood of major tax legislation nearly brought the tax administration system to its knees. . . . A corresponding guidance crisis has developed with respect to the nation's tax-exempt organizations. During the past 23 years, 433 exempt organizations revenue rulings were published. Four hundred and six of those rulings (94 percent) were published between 1974 and 1983. The remaining 27 rulings (6 percent) were published in the past 14 years. Two revenue rulings have been published in the past five years. Only seven exempt organization items were listed on the 1997 Treasury/IRS Business Plan. Three of those projects were carried over as incomplete from the 1996 Business Plan.[33]

The situation was regarded as so critical that the ABA Tax Section Committee on Exempt Organizations called it to the attention of the House Ways and Means Oversight Committee in 1994 as follows:

> There has been very little published advice on which taxpayers can rely (e.g., regulations, revenue rulings) in more than a decade. There are numerous key issues as to which there is no advice or conflicting advice, such as how much unrelated income is "insubstantial" for purposes of maintaining exemption or how allocations are to be made in the case of assets used for both exempt and taxable purposes. In other areas there are dozens, sometimes hundreds, of private rulings involving an issue as to which the Service and Treasury have issued no precedential advice, such as hospital reorganizations and joint ventures.[34]

The capacity of the states to enforce accountability is not much better, if indeed as good. According to the National Association of Attorneys General, there are, in the entire United States, only about 80 state-employed attorneys with regular responsibility for charitable entities, a third of whom are divided between New York and California.[35,36] According to Fishman and Schwarz, "Most state offices of the attorney general lack even one full-time lawyer charged with oversight of charitable organizations."[37] It must be noted, however, that the figure of 80 does not include employees—some of whom are attorneys—on the staffs of agencies in about 17 states in which regulatory authority resides with officials other than the attorney general. No one believes that the current number of NFP accountability-enforcing personnel at both the state and federal levels can begin to do the job that needs to be done if NFP accountability is to be strong enough to deter misconduct and convincing enough to reassure the public about the probity of the NFP sector.

Even if governmental authorities had adequate staff to police not-for-profit organizations, the sector itself is an arena of individual and social activity greatly permeated by constitutionally guaranteed freedoms of speech, association, and religion. While some governmental policing is essential to define the bounds of legality, and while it seems clear that such boundary-setting, if narrowly defined, in fact expands freedom for the overwhelming number rather than constricting it, we should not automatically and instinctively turn to government to do the necessary policing of not-for-profit activity, unless it is absolutely necessary. Beyond the point of necessity, the more governmental policing of voluntary activity, the more likely the exercise of First Amendment rights will be chilled. Moreover, it says something telling about our sector's sense of personal insecurity when our first impulse on being faced by NFP sector real or imputed transgressions is to turn to government to clean house for us.

I have reluctantly concluded that, while the not-for-profit sector does need to redouble its efforts to police itself, a restructuring of the governmental accountability-enforcing mechanisms is required, too. But first let's consider the nongovernmental accountability-enforcers.

Nongovernmental Organizations with Accountability-Enforcing Missions

There are voluntary watchdog organizations, both the institutional ones focusing explicitly on accountability, such as the National Charities Information Bureau, the Philanthropic Advisory Service of the Council of Better Business Bureaus, the American Institute of Philanthropy, the National Committee for Responsive Philanthropy, and also subject matter–specific ones, such as breast cancer and lung cancer activists, children's advocates, and social service critics.

Other organizations also focus on accountability by seeking to strengthen the functioning of the boards and staffs of not-for-profit organizations, such as the National Center for Nonprofit Boards, the Association of Governing Boards, the Independent Sector, and the Council on Foundations. In addition, the burgeoning centers for nonprofits in cities and states across the country play an increasingly effective role in assisting not-for-profits in compliance with legal and financial requirements and in the strengthening of management and boards.

In addition to the watchdog organizations, which have been in existence for some years, new entities have been created with the purpose of significantly increasing the amount of information about not-for-profit organizations available to the public. Philanthropic Research, Inc.'s GuideStar web page[38] and CD-ROM promise to be increasingly useful devices to inform both the public and the press about the functioning of not-for-profit organizations in ways that are much more user-friendly than the 990 returns filed with the IRS. Based both on 990 information and on additional information solicited by PRI from individual organizations, GuideStar reports are much more comprehensive, presenting detailed information that answer the questions most prospective donors have about the organizations they are considering supporting.

There are still other sources of policing help. Another mechanism for policing accountability is the press which, in its time-honored muckraking tradition, has usually been the primary ferret of most of the chicanery that has been uncovered in the NFP sector. As the court of first resort for alleged wrongdoing, and, with its particular zeal for showcasing hypocrisy in any setting, the press may well be the most effective "policeperson" around. Unfortunately, the zealousness of the press in pursuing "scandals" in the NFP sector has sometimes led journalists to wrong blameless individuals and institutions, thereby doing a serious injustice to the sector itself. Many of the charges leveled at the NFP sector by Gaul and Borowski in their series of articles for the *Philadelphia Inquirer*[39] and subsequent book[40] were ill founded,[41] triggering much hostile governmental action against not-for-profits in Pennsylvania, which only now, four years after the fact, seems at last to be diminishing.

It is not simply the singleminded zealousness of the press that is the problem; it is the fact that, when the press zeroes in on what it perceives to be a default of the not-for-profit sector, it does so, as I noted above, almost always without placing the discovered problem in the larger context in which it belongs, thereby creating a serious, potentially harmful imbalance in the public mind. A recent example was the *New York Times*'s page-one article entitled "Charities Use For-Profit Units to Avoid Disclosing Finances."[42] Leave aside the fact that the headline was utterly misleading; the reasons charities use for-profit subsidiaries are to generate income for the tax-exempt entities and to make it easier to comply with the Unrelated Business Income Tax. The fact that some charities do not disclose the salaries paid to their chief executives or other senior officers who hold positions in both the not-for-profit and for-profit organizations is incidental, and, I think, inexcusable. At present the law is not entirely clear about the requirement of disclosure and should be amended so to require.[43] The article, however, failed to point out that many—perhaps most—charities do routinely disclose the salaries involved in such arrangements, creating the inference that it is the arrangement that is at fault rather than the failure to disclose. The truth is that the spread of such not-for-profit operation of for-profit subsidiaries is one of the most promising recent developments in the not-for-profit sector, and should be applauded rather than implicitly condemned, as well as continuously monitored to avoid improprieties.

And of course, while we don't usually think of it this way, an irresponsible journalist's zeal can be just as effective in chilling the exercise of First Amendment rights as can government itself. Besides, to rely primarily on the press for our housecleaning is to wait until the horse is out of the barn.

All of the nongovernmental accountability-enforcing organizations serve an important and useful purpose and should be applauded for keeping a fire lit under the sector. They are no substitute, however, for energetic efforts within organizations, and especially in boards of directors, to keep their own houses clean. Every organization—every board of directors—has to be for itself a robust source of continuous scrutiny.

The Urgent Need for New Accountability-Enforcing Strategies with National Scope and Adequate Policing Powers

The primary problem affecting the NFP sector in the U.S. is that no one is in charge; no entity or group of entities has the capacity and the power to monitor, police, and, where necessary, defend the sector. Some say that that's a good thing, too, because if some agency were in fact in charge, it would be likely to do a great deal of harm. That is the argument against any strong form of governmental regulation, and I am basically sympathetic with it. I also subscribe to the belief that if it ain't broke, don't fix it.

Alas, however, I now believe that the NFP accountability-enforcing mechanism is in fact broken. For the long-run good of the sector, we cannot continue to rely on an inadequately staffed and insufficiently powerful IRS, the vagaries of inadequately staffed and usually not-very-interested offices of state attorneys general which, in any event, have difficulty in policing a sector which routinely crosses state and national boundaries many times a day, the limited scope and vision of voluntary watchdog agencies, the new information-providing organizations, and the investigatory, inflammatory press.

When exempt organizations cannot get timely advice from the IRS, no one can be said to be in charge. When rumors circulate for months about alleged wrongdoing by tax-exempt organizations, and no entity or entities with adequate authority take the initiative in investigating, no one may be said to be in charge. When criticism of the NFP sector begins to generate threats of legislative action, and there is no official or quasi-official organization with the responsibility of coming to the defense of the sector, if appropriate, no one may be said to be in charge. Moreover, when existing governmental agencies with the responsibility for collecting and making publicly available data on the functioning of the sector, and charged with submitting reports to Congress along with recommendations for legislative action to improve the functioning of the sector fail to do so for lack of time, personnel, and funding, no one may be said to be in charge.

The truth is that there is no entity at present—public, private, or joint— which has the authority to establish and police standards of compliance on a national scale, yet the existence of such standards and both actual and perceived compliance with them are essential if the public is to continue to feel justifiably comfortable in trusting not-for-profit organizations. That trust by the public is the indispensable foundation for the tax-favored treatment with which the public now benefits the NFP sector so mightily. If government is to permit the NFP sector to continue to play the central role it now has, the foundation of trust must be shored up with adequate accountability-enforcing mechanisms.

Three Complementary, Sequential Strategies for Policing and Defending the Not-for-Profit Sector

In considering the task of accountability-enforcement, it is important to keep in mind that there are two distinct, quite different problems. One is that posed by unscrupulous individuals or groups whose intention is to defraud the public under cover of a fake not-for-profit mask, and the other is that posed by the unwise, injudicious, or careless—but not illegal—patterns of action by bona fide not-for-profit organizations. The former cannot possibly be dealt with adequately by the not-for-profit sector alone, although, as the following strategies suggest, energetic not-for-profit sector initiatives could significantly enhance the public sector's capacity to do the job with which it is charged. The latter task appropriately belongs to the not-for-profit sector alone, be- cause any governmental intrusion into the functioning of bona fide not-for- profit organizations beyond the requirements of law would be likely to chill the free functioning of the sector.

A Not-for-Profit Sector Strategy

If the not-for-profit sector umbrella organizations were willing to create a joint nongovernmental accountability-enforcing organization with coura- geous, energetic, skilled leadership determined to root out and publicize malfeasors, that would be everyone's strongly preferred strategy. Perhaps The Independent Sector, the Council on Foundations, the National Charities Information Bureau, the National Center for Nonprofit Boards, and other similar organizations could be persuaded to create an adequately staffed, foundation-supported consortium to take on the mission of policing both the bad actors and the bona fide not-for-profit organizations. Surely there are skilled personnel with IRS or state attorney-general experience who would jump at the chance to defend the uprightness of the not-for-profit sector from the base of an adequately financed organization operating under the aegis of the sector's authoritative, distinguished organizations. An alternative, or supplement, to foundation-funding of such an accountability-enforcing organization could be, as Brian McConnell suggested some years ago, an organization financed by the contributions of not-for-profit sector organizations based on their assets or size of their budgets, self-levied in return for some "official" seal of bona fideness by the consortium. Were initial foundation support made available for the founding of such a not-for-profit sector accountability-enforcing entity to begin with, perhaps widespread voluntary contributions by organizations in the field would enable the entity eventually to become self-supporting.

Such an organization would be charged with taking the initiative to investigate rumors of fraud or malfeasance, and, if found to warrant official governmental action, would urge such action by state or federal authorities, depending on the nature of the malfeasance. It might also choose to make public the charges, once they had been investigated fully. In performing these functions, the entity would act in the same spirit as that in which professional ethics enforcement bodies, such as those of the state bars, function.

In addition to investigating instances of malfeasance, such an entity should also take the initiative in establishing standards of functioning appropriate to various kinds of not-for-profit organizations that go beyond the requirements of law. Indeed, it should also take responsibility for recommending desirable changes in state and federal law when necessary.

A Joint Not-for-Profit Sector/Governmental Strategy

As an alternative to, or in conjunction with, a not-for-profit sector strategy alone, a joint sector/governmental strategy should be pursued. The organization of state charities enforcement official, the National Association of State Charities Officials, does excellent work but has focused on improving the current mechanisms for enforcement, such as the harmonization of state and federal reporting requirements, and not on the investigation of reported instances of alleged malfeasance. Perhaps foundations should make funds available to NAAG/NASCO for a national clearinghouse of information on abuses by tax-exempt organizations, investigate instances of such abuse, and work jointly with appropriate state and federal authorities to activate legal proceedings by those authorities when necessary.

A New Federal Agency for Policing and Defending
the Not-for-Profit Sector

The third strategy—a new federal agency—is a strategy of last resort, which should be pursued only after it has become clear that, for whatever reason, the two prior strategies cannot be made to work. If the third strategy were to be pursued, great pains should be taken to ensure that its powers are narrowly focused, that its charter is restricted to "the rules of the game" whereby not-for-profits function, that it be prohibited from dealing with the substance or content of the programs of not-for-profits, and that all of its actions be subject to court review by the standards of strict scrutiny required when First Amendment interests are at stake.

Obviously, one would give careful thought first to strengthening the IRS Exempt Organization Office, and that should certainly be done whatever else may be contemplated. The IRS, which has primary responsibility for certifying tax exemption at present, does not have and almost certainly never has had adequate personnel to police compliance with the regulations it promulgates. Indeed, as noted above, it cannot even ensure that the primary reporting forms it requires—990s and 990PFs—be accurately completed and filed, and can manage to audit only a tiny fraction—1 percent—of the 990s that are filed.[44] Even with the new intermediate sanctions which Congress legislated in 1996, the woefully understaffed IRS can do little but respond to egregious violations that come to its attention through the press or otherwise. Several attempts have recently been made in Congress to appropriate additional funds to the IRS EO Office but all proved unsuccessful when the Treasury Department deemed it improper to target an appropriation to a particular division within the IRS.

While the Internal Revenue Code underscores the independent integrity of the Exempt Organizations Office, it is likely to be always the case that the Office will remain a Cinderella in the kitchen so far as adequate staffing is concerned. The primary function of the IRS is to maximize the revenues from the taxes owed by individuals and corporations to the government, and it is not surprising that the IRS would find it expedient to pay less attention to the tax-exempt organizations, which, by definition, do not pay taxes, than to those entities from which taxes are collected. That doesn't necessarily mean that there has to be something grudging about the way the IRS looks at organizations that do not have to pay taxes. I have great admiration for Alan Pifer, formerly President of the Carnegie Corporation, but I'm inclined to disagree with his observation more than twenty years ago that IRS regulation "is characterized by a negative rather than positive attitude toward charity. . . ."[45] Considering the degree of understaffing, the IRS has done an excellent job over the years. It has proved again and again to be able to maintain its independence and objectivity in the face of frequently great political pressure.

The U.S. Charities Regulatory Commission

From time to time, it has been suggested that a new federal entity be created for the purpose of overseeing the NFP sector. Two of the primary research papers presented to the Filer Commission urged the creation of such an entity, although they differed as to its proposed scope and its location within the government.[46] I believe that the time has come to consider seriously the establishment of such an entity.

If we were starting from scratch, I would favor the creation of an independent agency—perhaps called the U.S. Charities Regulatory Commission —with commissioners appointed by the President subject to Senate confirmation, and would empower that agency with all aspects of the regulation of not-for-profit organizations, including the granting of tax-exemption in the first place. The primary responsibility of the agency would be to keep tabs on the procedural—not substantive—functioning of not-for-profit organizations so as to assure the public that tax exemption is not used as a shield for fraudulent or illegal purposes. It would be empowered to investigate instances of alleged wrongdoing, it would have the power of subpoena, and it could institute civil or criminal proceedings as appropriate on its own motion. It would be charged with supervising interstate charitable solicitation, and creating the guidelines and disclosure requirements necessary to ensure that charitable solicitation is not used for fraudulent purposes.[47] It would be responsible for monitoring the functioning of the NFP sector as a whole, gathering data and creating databases about the sector, commissioning studies on various aspects of the sector, reporting periodically to Congress on the operation of the sector, issuing regulations to guide the sector in conforming with applicable laws, and making recommendations for legislative changes that may be thought desirable. It would, in other words, function very much like the SEC and the FTC, the most analogous federal agencies, do today.

We are not, alas, starting from scratch. I conclude, therefore, that the best solution would be to leave with the IRS the authority to certify tax exemption initially and to be the primary recipient of the 990s and 990PFs. I reach that conclusion for several reasons. First, the IRS Exempt Organization Office is inherently and inextricably tax-collection-related because the "E" is exemption from taxes. Secondly, determining tax deductibility of contributions also cannot be separated from the IRS because such decisions are inevitably related to tax return processing. Third, decisions concerning unrelated business income tax liabilities cannot be separated either, for the same reason. Finally, it would not be good policy to lose the ninety years of IRS track record of legal determinations regarding various exempt organization tax matters.

Those factors lead me to believe that a new U.S. Charities Regulatory Commission should have the power to do everything else enumerated above, obviously working closely with the IRS Exempt Organization Office and with the Federal Trade Commission. It would be best if it were established as a fully independent agency, because having its sole focus on the NFP sector would increase the likelihood that it would in fact succeed in paying the attention to the sector that it deserves. Being independent, however, means being small in comparison with other government agencies, and that means being vulnerable. I would favor taking the risk of such vulnerability, but one can reasonably argue that independence is less important than having an entity endowed with the requisite powers, even if that entity were lodged within another larger entity.

It has been suggested in the past that the Department of the Treasury would make sense as a home for such an entity, because that would facilitate closer cooperation with the IRS.[48] I believe, however, that a better arrangement would be to lodge the new Commission elsewhere. It would also seem reasonable to consider the Securities and Exchange Commission as a home, because that Commission already performs, with regard to the activities of the securities industry, many of the same information-gathering and publicizing tasks, as well as the investigatory and judicial proceeding–initiating functions, that seem called for with regard to the NFP sector, and has enjoyed widespread admiration over a long period of time for the professional, objective, and nonpartisan way in which it has operated. The SEC has done the best job of any governmental agency in effecting public disclosure of the information it is charged with eliciting from the entities under its regulatory jurisdiction and the demonstrated experience in doing so would be most useful in performing the same task for not-for-profit organizations.[49] The Federal Trade Commission would also be a possibility, because it has already taken initiatives with regard to allegedly fraudulent charitable solicitations.

I am less concerned with where such an entity is located than I am with the importance that consideration be given to establishing it as part of a strategy of last resort. If it were created with sufficient power of independent action and either fully independent or nested in a sympathetic environment which reinforced its autonomy, it would add immensely and complementarily to the supervisory and regulatory functions now performed by the IRS EO Office. It would constitute a staff source for a possible Annual President's Report on the Not-for-Profit Sector, analogous to the President's Economic Report. It would give significant leadership to satisfying the urgent need for better databases of reliable information on the NFP sector, preferably by nongovernmental researchers and organizations. It would take the initiative in doing reports on particular problem areas in the NFP sector, either at the request of Congress, such as the Treasury Report of 1965 did with respect to the issues then of most concern, or on its own motion. It would target resources on fraud detection and prevention. It would have power to investigate and initiate civil and criminal proceedings and impose penalties. It would accumulate experience and skill in scam identification and prevention. It would monitor charitable solicitation practices nationally and investigate patterns of improper practices. To be effective, its nonpartisanship and objectivity would have to be guaranteed, and it would have to have assured funding adequate to its mission.

It would also be important to provide that any new regulatory agency, as a matter of policy, have the power to defer to state accountability-enforcing authorities who have earned the reputation for effective action with respect to NFP compliance with laws and regulations.

The not-for-profit sector is far too essential to the healthy functioning of American society for it to remain vulnerable to attack and without official defenders when unscrupulous individuals, by subverting the not-for-profit form to their personal inurement, bring disrepute to the sector as a whole. The American NFP sector is the envy of the world and deserves the same official attention to its proper functioning as we give to other sectors of the economy. It is every bit as important that the NFP sector be, and be perceived as being, honest and trustworthy, just as it is that the securities and marketing industries be. In view of the sacredness of charity in all its dimensions, perhaps it is even more important.

Notes

1. I acknowledge with profound thanks the willingness of Harvey Dale, Bob Boisture, Zoe Baird, Richard Blumenthal, and Tom Troyer to read and comment on various drafts of this chapter. Each of them has been most helpful. Any errors or insufficiency of judgment that remain are solely attributable to the carelessness or stubbornness of the author. Let me also acknowledge the many constructive comments made to me by participants in the American Assembly on "The Future of Philanthropy," which will be evident to them in the differences between the original version and the published chapter. Finally, let me thank my research assistant David James, my assistant Susan Kaminsky, and my editor and colleague Charles Clotfelter for their continuing help in bringing these ideas to a state of presentability.

Readers should note that my use of the term "not-for-profit" organization or sector is intended to convey the same meaning as the word "nonprofit," which is used by other writers in this volume. Moreover, the particular focus of this chapter is the charitable not-for-profit organizations and sector, but to save space and for reasons of economy of style, I have chosen to omit the word "charitable" rather than repeat it endlessly.

2. According to Hodgkinson, Weitzman, et al. (1996), pp. 140–141, in 1994 (preliminary figures), total U.S. paid nonagricultural employment was 114 million, of which 10.3 million, or 9.1%, was in the nonprofit sector. The annualized rate of job growth from 1977 to 1994 was 1.9% in all sectors, 3.0% in business (service component only), and 3.3% in the not-for-profit sector. From 1992 to 1996, it appears that business sector job growth increased slightly faster than that of the not-for-profit sector. According to "The State of the Independent Sector: Overview and Highlights," Interim Update of *The Nonprofit Almanac* (Independent Sector, 1998), "The annual rates of change in the national income account for the business sector was 3.5% including volunteer time and 3.6% excluding volunteer time. For the independent sector, its national income account grew at an average annual rate of 2.6% when volunteer time was included and 3.2% when volunteer time was excluded. In comparison, between 1987 and 1992, the

independent sector component of material income increased at an average annual rate of 4.2%, including volunteer time, and at 6%, excluding volunteer time."

3. Hodgkinson, Weitzman, et al. (1993), p. 14.

4. Salamon and Anheier (1994), p. 37.

5. Caplan, ed. (1997), p. 28.

6. According to Hodgkinson and Weitzman (1996), p. 30, there are 93 million Americans who volunteer, contributing over 20 billion hours a year. Valuing that time at $12.84/hr (the average hourly nonagricultural wage, inflated 12% to estimate fringe benefits) yields an estimated contribution in time of $200 billion; even at minimum wage (currently $5.15/hr), volunteered time would still be worth over $103 billion.

7. See Office of Management and Budget (1998), table 2–2, p. 12, for federal budget figures. In fiscal year 1997, non-defense discretionary spending accounted for $277 billion, which is 17% of the total $1.6 trillion budget.

8. See Fishman and Schwarz, pp. 160–200.

9. Act I, Scene I.

10. According to Rudney (1987), p. 63:

A serious constraint in government that inhibits data collection is that nonprofit organizations as productive enterprises go unrecognized in the official U.S. National Accounts. The National Accounts are intended to provide a realistic economic model of the economy. Yet nonprofits are included as consumers, like households, of the nation's output and not as contributors to the nation's output. The unrealistic treatment tends to constrain data collection on nonprofit organizations by government agencies.

11. Friedman (1962), p. 25: "These then are the basic roles of government in a free society: to provide a means whereby we can modify the rules, to mediate differences among us on the meaning of the rules, and to enforce compliance with the rules on the part of those few who would otherwise not play the game."

12. Fremont-Smith (1995).

13. James (1991); Harris (1989); Klott (1987).

14. *United States v. Aramony* (1996); Hall (1995); Arenson (1995); Glaser (1994).

15. Carnes (1997); Stecklow (1996); Stecklow (1995).

16. Farber (1990); *Washington Post* (1990); Blumenthal (1990).

17. Lambert (1997); Lambert (1996a); Lambert (1996b).

18. Cannon (1997); Purdum (1997).

19. Bailey (1995); *Washington Post* (1993); Farhi (1993).

20. Abramson and Wayne (1997); Wayne (1997); Babcock (1997).

21. Weiss (1997); *United Cancer Council* (1997); Carton (1987).

22. Mathews (1995b); Mathews (1995a).

23. Wagner (1992); Workman (1992).

24. Seelye (1997); Marcus (1996); Murawski and Stehle (1995); Gaul and Borowski (1993b).

25. Abelson (1998b,c).

26. Bowen (1994).

27. According to Hodgkinson and Weitzman (1996), pp. 71–85, 57% of Americans have a "great deal" or "quite a lot" of confidence in institutions of

higher education and 55% in religious organizations, compared to 56% in small business, 54% in the military, 24% in major corporations, 23% in federal government, and 16% in Congress. "Nearly eight out of ten respondents . . . stat[ed] that they 'strongly agreed' or 'agreed' that the need for charities is greater now than five years ago. Over seven out of ten respondents agreed with the statement that charitable organizations play a major role in making our communities better places to live. . . . six out of ten respondents agreed that charities play an important role in speaking out on important issues." Id., p. 76.

28. Smith, 1776.

29. Bennett and DiLorenzo (1994); Hawks (1997).

30. McGovern and Brand (1997). See also American Society of Association Executives (1993), which reports that

Between 1980 and 1992, the IRS approved more than 353,000 new nonprofit organizations, an average of 29,000 a year. While those numbers were growing, the staff of the IRS Exempt Organizations Division was cut from 509 to 495 employees. The ratio is now one IRS employee for every 2,240 nonprofit organizations. In 1988, the IRS examined less than 12,000 tax-exempt organizations, a 50% drop from eight years prior. Today, the IRS examines about 1% of the roughly 450,000 nonprofits that file Form 990 tax forms annually.

31. McGovern and Brand (1997), point 20.

32. Id., point 21.

33. Id., points 22 and 23.

34. Id., point 24.

35. Billitteri (1998), p. 34.

36. *Chronicle of Philanthropy* article listing the state by state figures.

37. Fishman and Schwarz (1995), p. 247.

38. Found at http://www.guidestar.org/

39. Gaul and Borowski (1993a).

40. Gaul and Borowski (1993b).

41. Independent Sector (1993).

42. Abelson (1998a).

43. It appears to have been the intention of lawmakers to require not-for-profits to report on the 990 any instances of compensation where the "officer, director, trustee or key employee of the organization received more than $10,000 in compensation from related organizations. . . . AND such compensation provided to that individual by the filing organization totaled more than $100,000." See IRS "Specific Instructions for Form 990," line 75—Compensation from related organizations.

44. American Society of Association Executives (1993).

45. Asher (1977), p. 76.

46. See Ginsburg, et al. (1975), Yarmolinsky and Fremont-Smith (1976a), and the related paper by the same authors, Yarmolinsky and Fremont-Smith (1976b).

47. I recognize that there is a line of cases, including Schaumburg v. Citizens for a Better Environment, 444 U.S. 620, 100 S.Ct. 826 (1980), Secretary of State of Maryland V. Joseph H. Munson Co., 467 U.S. 947; 104 S.Ct. 2839 (1984), and Riley v. National Federation of the Blind, 487 US. 781, 108 S.Ct. 2667 (1988), which make it constitutionally difficult to regulate charitable solicitation.

48. Ginsburg, et al.

49. I am indebted to Professor Harvey Goldschmidt of Columbia University Law School for suggesting that the SEC might well be the best home for the entity. It should be noted that at least one of the research reports to the Filer Commission advocated a new agency modeled on the SEC. See Ginsburg et al. (1975), p. 2641. In addition, readers should see an excellent article by Professor Regina E. Herzlinger, entitled "Can Public Trust in Nonprofits and Governments Be Restored?," in the March/April 1996 issue of the *Harvard Business Review*. In that article Professor Herzlinger proposes a solution to the accountability enforcement problem which she calls DADS, which initials stand for Disclosure, Analysis, Dissemination and Sanctions. She suggests that the SEC's ability to perform such functions with regard to the for-profit sector could well be a model for some appropriate agency or agencies to use in increasing the accountability of the not-for-profit sector.

References

Abelson, Reed. 1998c. "Issues of Self-Interest; Suddenly, Nonprofit Work Gets Profitable," *New York Times*, March 29, 1998, sec 4, p. 3.

Abelson, Reed. 1998b. "At Minnesota Public Radio, a Deal Way Above Average," *New York Times*, March 27, 1998, , D3.

Abelson, Reed. 1998a. "Charities Use For-Profit Units to Avoid Disclosing Finances," *New York Times*, February 9, 1998, A1, A12.

Abramson, Jill, and Leslie Wayne. 1997. "Both Parties Were Assisted by Nonprofit Groups in 1996," *New York Times*, October 24, 1997, A1, A28.

American Society of Association Executives. 1993. "Hire More Employees, Association Executives Tell IRS." *Tax Notes Today*, Doc 93–12163, November 26, 1993; available in LEXIS, FEDTAX;TNT library.

Arenson, Karen W. 1995. "Former United Way Chief Guilty in Theft of More Than $600,000," *New York Times*, April 4, 1995, A1.

Asher, Thomas R., et. al. 1977. "Private Philanthropy: Vital and Innovative or Passive and Irrelevant: The Donee Group Report and Recommendations" (Donee Group Report). *Research Papers Sponsored By The Commission on Private Philanthropy and Public Needs* (Filer Commission), Volume 1: History, Trends, and Current Magnitudes. Washington: Department of the Treasury, 1977, pp. 49–85.

Babcock, Charles R. 1997. "Gingrich Courts Support: Use of Tax-Exempt Groups Integral to Political Strategy." *Washington Post*, January 7, 1997, A1, A6.

Bailey, Anne Lowrey. 1995. "Settlement at the Freedom Forum." *Chronicle of Philanthropy*, January 12, 1995.

Bennett, James T., and Thomas J. DiLorenzo. 1994. *Unhealthy Charities: Hazardous to Your Health and Wealth*. New York: Basic Books, 269 pp.

Billitteri, Thomas J. 1998. "Rethinking Who Can Sue a Charity: Hospital Conversions Spur Push to Expand Rights to General Public." *Chronicle of Philanthropy*, March 12, 1998, pp. 1, 34.

Blasko, Mary Grace, Curt S. Crossley, and David Lloyd. 1993. "Standing to Sue in the Charitable Sector." *University of San Francisco Law Review* 28 (Fall 1993), pp. 37–84.

Blumenthal, Ralph. 1990. "Ritter Inquiry Cites Reports From the 70's." *New York Times*, August 4, 1990, sec. 1, p. 25.

Bograd, Harriet. 1994. *The Role of State Attorneys General in Relation to Troubled Nonprofits*. Yale University Program on Non-Profit Organizations, Working Paper No. 206. New Haven: Yale University, 51 pp.

Bowen, William G. 1994. *Inside the Boardroom: Governance by Directors and Trustees*. New York: John Wiley & Sons, Inc., 184 pp.

Bureau of Economic Analysis. 1997. "Updated Summary NIPA Methodologies." *Survey of Current Business*, September 1997, pp. 12–33.

Cannon, Lou. 1997. "Corruption Charges Catch Beloved Hawaii Charity in Furious Undertow." *Washington Post*, December 23, 1997, at A3.

Caplan, Ann E., ed. 1997. *Giving USA 1997: The Annual Report on Philanthropy for the Year 1996*. New York: American Association for Fund-Raising Counsel Trust for Philanthropy, 219 pp.

Carton, Barbara. 1987. "Low Charity Return Is Alleged; Alexandria Fund Raiser Cites Campaign 'Start-Up' Expenses." *Washington Post*, April 18, 1987, A4.

Chisolm, Laura B. 1996. "Accountability of Nonprofit Organizations and Those Who Control Them: The Legal Framework." *Nonprofit Management and Leadership* 7, no. 2 (Winter 1996).

Edie, John A. 1987. "Congress and Private Foundations: An Historical Analysis." Washington: Council on Foundations, Occasional Paper No. 4, September 1987. 35 pp.

Farber, M. A. 1990. "Founder of Covenant House Steps Aside in Church Inquiry." *New York Times*, February 7, 1990, A1.

Farhi, Paul. 1993. "New York Probes Neuharth-Led Foundation; Freedom Forum of Arlington Investigated for Financial Irregularities." *Washington Post*, March 18, 1993, A1.

Fishman, James J., and Stephen Schwarz. 1995. *Nonprofit Organizations. Cases and Materials*. Westbury, New York: The Foundation Press. 1042 pp.

Fishman, James J. 1985. "The Development of Nonprofit Corporation Law and an Agenda for Reform." *Emory Law Journal* 34, pp. 617–683.

Fremont-Smith, Marion. 1995. "Government Regulation of Philanthropy." Discussion draft in author's possession. 30 pp.

Fremont-Smith, Marion. 1989. "Trends in Accountability and Regulation of Nonprofits." In *The Future of the Nonprofit Sector*, Virginia A. Hodgkinson, et al., eds. San Francisco: Jossey-Bass, pp. 75–78.

Friedman, Milton. 1962. *Capitalism & Freedom*. Chicago: Univ. of Chicago Press, 202 pp.

Gaul, Gilbert M., and Neill A. Borowski. 1993b. *Free Ride: The Tax-exempt Economy*. Kansas City: Andrews and McMeel, 197 pp.

Gaul, Gilbert M., and Neill A. Borowski. 1993a. "Warehouses of Wealth: The Tax-free Economy" (seven-part series). *Philadelphia Inquirer*, April 18–24, 1993.

Ginsburg, David, Lee R. Marks and Ronald Wertheim, "Federal Oversight of Private Philanthropy" (1975), *Research Papers Sponsored By The Commission on Private Philanthropy and Public Needs* (Filer Commission), Volume V: Regulation. Washington: Department of the Treasury, 1977, pp. 2575–2696.

Glaser, John S. 1994. *The United Way Scandal: An Insider's Account of What Went Wrong and Why.* New York: John Wiley & Sons Inc., 1274 pp.

Hall, Charles W. 1995. "Ex-United Way Chief Sentenced to 7 Years; Prosecutors Praise 'Tough' Penalty in Aramony's Looting of Charity." *Washington Post,* June 23, 1995, A1.

Hansmann, Henry B. 1981. "Reforming Nonprofit Corporation Law." *University of Pennsylvania Law Review* 129, no. 3 (January 1981), pp. 497–623.

Harris, Art. 1989. "Jim Bakker Gets 45-Year Sentence; Televangelist Fined $500,000; Eligible for Parole in 10 Years." *Washington Post,* October 25, 1989, p. A1.

Hawks, John. 1997. *For a Good Cause?: How Charitable Institutions Become Powerful Economic Bullies.* Birch Lane Press, 240 pp.

Hodgkinson, Virginia A., Murray S. Weitzman, et al. 1996. *Nonprofit Almanac 1996–1997: Dimensions of the Independent Sector.* San Francisco: Jossey-Bass Publishers, 326 pp.

Hodgkinson, Virginia A., Murray S. Weitzman, et al. 1993. *A Portrait of the Independent Sector: The Activities and Finances of Charitable Organizations.* Washington: Independent Sector, 97 pp.

Hodgkinson, Virginia A., and Murray S. Weitzman. 1996. *Giving and Volunteering in the United States: Findings from a National Survey.* Washington: Independent Sector, 212 pp.

Independent Sector. 1993. *Responding to Recent Media Criticism—A Brief Guide.* Washington: Independent Sector, 4 pp.

James, George. 1991. "Bakker's 45-Year Prison Term Set Aside." *New York Times,* February 13, 1991, B6.

Karst, Kenneth L. 1960. "The Efficiency of the Charitable Dollar: An Unfulfilled State Responsibility." *Harvard Law Review* 73, no. 3 (January 1960), pp. 433–483.

Klott, Gary. 1987. "PTL's Ledgers: Missing Records and Rising Debt." *New York Times,* June 6, 1987, Sec. 1, p. 8.

Lambert, Bruce. 1997. "New York Regents Oust 18 Trustees from Adelphi U." *New York Times,* February 11, 1997, A1.

Lambert, Bruce. 1996b. "Adelphi President Describes Buying Art on Expense-Paid Trips," *New York Times,* August 1, 1996, B4.

Lambert, Bruce. 1996a. "Head of Adelphi Testifies About Escalating Income." *New York Times,* July 31, 1996, B4.

Marcus, Ruth. 1996. "FEC Details Case Against Christian Coalition." *Washington Post,* August 1, 1996, A10.

Mathews, Jay. 1995b. "Investment Firm for Universities to Close; $138 Million in Losses by Rogue Trader Cited; Common Fund Still Seeking Damages." *Washington Post,* September 8, 1995, B1.

Mathews, Jay. 1995a. "Trader Hid His Mistake From Supervisors for Three Years: Common Fund Says Failure to Hedge Investments Turned Small Embarrassment Into $128 Million Loss." *Washington Post,* July 4, 1995, E1.

McGovern, James J., and Phil Brand. 1997. "EP/EO—'One of the Most Innovative and Efficient Functions Within the IRS.'" *Tax Notes Today*, August 25, 1997, Vol. 97, pp. 164–197. Available in LEXIS, FEDTAX;TNT library.

Murawski, John, and Vince Stehle. 1995. "House Panel Approves Bill to Tighten Limits on Lobbying and Litigation by Charities." *Chronicle of Philanthropy*, August 10, 1995, pp. 35–36.

Office of Management and Budget. 1998. *Citizen's Guide to the Federal Budget: Budget of the United States Government Fiscal Year 1999.* Washington DC. 41 pp.

Purdum, Todd. 1997. "Hawaiians Angrily Turn on a Fabled Empire." *New York Times*, October 14, 1997, A1.

Rudney, Gabriel. 1987. "The Scope and Dimensions of Nonprofit Activity," pp. 55–64 in Walter W. Powell, ed., *The Nonprofit Sector: A Research Handbook.* New Haven: Yale University Press, 464 pp.

Salamon, Lester M., And Helmut K. Anheier. 1994. *The Emerging Sector: An Overview.* Baltimore: The Johns Hopkins University Institute for Policy Studies. 140 pp.

Seelye, Katharine Q. 1997. "House Rules May Rein In Liberal Advocacy Groups." *New York Times*, January 16, 1997, B8.

Smith, Adam. 1776. *The Wealth of Nations.*

United Cancer Council, Inc. v. Commissioner of Internal Revenue. 1997. U.S. Tax Court, December 2, 1997. 109 T.C. No. 17.

Wagner, John. 1992. "Stanford Chief Leaves Mixed Legacy After Research Funds Dispute." *Washington Post*, September 4, 1992, A23.

Washington Post (staff). 1990. "Nun Is Named Successor to Ritter As President of Covenant House." July 12, 1990, A4.

Washington Post (staff). 1993. "3 Trustees Quit Freedom Forum Board." April 29, 1993, B14.

Wayne, Leslie. 1997. Wayne, "Watchdog Group Is Under Scrutiny for Role in Teamster Race." *New York Times*, September 22, A18.

Weiss, Rick. 1997. "Questions on Expenses Dog AIDS Bike-Trip Organizer," *Washington Post*, June 9, 1997, A6.

Workman, Bill. 1992. "GAO Spreads Overcharge Blame: It Says Auditors Missed $400 Million in Universities' Padded Research." *San Francisco Chronicle*, August 28, 1992, A7.

Yarmolinsky, Adam, and Marion R. Fremont-Smith. 1977b. "Judicial Remedies and Related Topics." *Research Papers Sponsored By The Commission on Private Philanthropy and Public Needs* (Filer Commission), Volume V: Regulation. Washington: Department of the Treasury, 1977, pp. 2697–2704.

Yarmolinsky, Adam, and Marion R. Fremont-Smith. 1977a. "Preserving the Private Voluntary Sector: A Proposal for a Public Advisory Commission on Philanthropy" (1976). *Research Papers Sponsored By The Commission on Private Philanthropy and Public Needs* (Filer Commission), Volume V: Regulation. Washington: Department of the Treasury, 1977, pp. 2857–2868.

CHAPTER NINE

Accountability in a Changing Philanthropic Environment

Trustees and Self-Government at the End of the Century

Warren F. Ilchman and Dwight F. Burlingame

Discussions of governance of nonprofit organizations are frequently given to sentimentality and piety. The piety comes from the presumption that philanthropic organizations are doing "the work of the Lord," that in their programs they embody the trust that donors and recipients alike have placed in them, and that in their management are individuals dedicated to mission and unresponsive to this-worldly gain. The sentimentality arises from the widely held belief, usually citing Tocqueville, that the strength of American democracy derives from the tradition of self-governance through voluntary associations presided over by neighbors. While there is some truth in both the piety and the sentimentality, there is also much in practice that varies from these ideals and many trends are afoot that make achieving these ideals more difficult.

The subject of this essay is accountability. "Accountability" normally means fulfilling the expectations of those who have authority for the work to be undertaken. As such, accountability or governance is a subject of profound importance in political theory. By whose authority may one act? By whose authority is an act deemed fulfilling of mission? Who decides? Who governs? As such, accountability is not about pieties and sentimentalities. It is a subject about limits and who sets them.

It is our contention that nonprofit organizations are little regulated by external governmental bodies.[1] Once the mission is established for tax purposes and broad understandings as to governance and the use of financial resources are accepted, nonprofit organizations are then regulated by their boards and the wider nonprofit community of opinion. While it is true that nonprofit organizations within certain areas of activity such as health and education are subject to similar public regulations as are those in the for-profit and state sectors engaged in those same areas and while it is true as organized entities that they must observe certain safety and employment practices that are required of all organizations, they are otherwise free to pursue their missions as their staff and boards please. There is no Federal Trade Commission, no Securities Exchange Commission, no anti-trust scrutiny, for the work of the nonprofit sector to be reviewed. No agency questions mergers—other than for self-dealing—or conversions into for-profit status. Whether to issue affinity charge cards or endorse commercial products may be the concern of the media, but no public agency—local, state, or national—considers it within their authority to question, other than to determine whether the income is taxable.

And unlike government and the for-profit sectors, there are no voters or stockholders. Although there are members and donors who might play a similar role, as certain nonprofit organizations come to depend more on earned income, large donors recede as independent judges, and "customers" are distant and unempowered. As the federal government is replaced by states and municipalities as sources of funds for some nonprofit organizations, oversight by the contracting government agency becomes attenuated. Boards of directors—voluntary, part-time, largely self-selecting—are the major mechanism in the nonprofit world in America to ensure faithfulness to mission and performance. The community of citizens committed to philanthropy as one way to address national problems remains the only court of appeal.

The subject of limits for nonprofit organizations should be of considerable importance. These organizations are given privileges of tax-exemption and, for many of them, tax deductibility for their donors—a special treatment not enjoyed by others. In 1996, $151 billion were privately donated to further the work of nonprofit organizations. These organizations also command considerable resources—in 1996 they had $450 billion in revenues and $650 billion in assets (Hodgkinson, 1996). The work of nonprofit organizations affects the health, education, and well being of whole communities. Their advocacy helps shape the political agenda and monitors the performance of our politically constituted governors. Finally, their calling to "do good" reminds citizens of their mutual obligations and the fact that communities exist for cooperation as well as for competition.

While governments do little to ensure accountability of nonprofit organizations, there is the "system" of board governance and it is very extensive. The most obvious aspect of accountability is the long-standing expectation that the actions of the nonprofit organization would be authorized and reviewed by a largely self-selecting board of governors. Indeed, so extensive is this system today that an estimated ten million Americans serve in capacities where they determine the leadership, monitor the performance, and are expected to secure the necessary resources to achieve an organization's mission. More individuals serve in such capacities than serve in similar governance capacities at the local, state, and federal governmental levels — providing, thus, more experience in aspects of civil society than politics offers citizens in the state.[2]

Developing the Trustee System of Governance

The prevailing system of governance by autonomous largely self-selecting boards of trustees, however, was not foreordained. It is true that its roots go back to England and the Common Law, and, apart from the vestries of religious communities, Harvard had the first board of trustees on this continent. It is also true that the practice of governance through largely self-selecting trustees was ubiquitous, ancient, and worldwide. Virtually every Great Tradition has examples of charitable trusts governed in this manner.

But its existence in the early United States was contested. Although the vestry system made the practice common for religious bodies and their educational institutions also had "trustees," there was considerable opposition to voluntary associations and to charitable trusts undertaking what we now call philanthropy. The ideas swirling around the Revolutions of 1776 and 1789 held that this activity could exist only if it secured its agency from the state and operated at its pleasure. Thomas Jefferson and the Jeffersonians in general were particularly loath to see philanthropic organizations separate from the political process and aspire to exist in perpetuity (Hall, 1997).

Ultimately the opposite viewpoint won. The Dartmouth College case in 1819 prevented the state of New Hampshire, then controlled by the followers of Jefferson, from altering the board of trustees of Dartmouth College, establishing the principle that boards were autonomous and determined by their charter of organization and, without cause, could not be interfered with. The McLean case in 1828 established the "prudent man" standard for trustees, thus ending the ambiguity of the liability of trustees for the resources in their charge. Finally, the McGill and Girard cases (1833 and 1854) settled the question of whether eleemosynary organizations could hold and receive property.

Settled legally did not, of course, mean accepted politically. By the end of the nineteenth century, however, in what one scholar calls an aggressive effort to promote New England–style civil privatism, the present structure of our nonprofit sector was in place. It emerged out of an amalgam of trust law, the emerging rules of incorporation of businesses, and practice (Hall, 1997). The individual "right to assemble" under the First Amendment had been transformed into the collective "right to associate." Nonprofit organizations — whether charitable or membership in constitution — could possess property, were to be overseen by boards drawn from the community or their member-ship, usually by appointment and occasionally by election, and these boards were to avoid self-dealing. Boards had the policy-making and approving responsibility; they ensured that the organization was meeting its mission and doing it legally. What was charitable was settled in practice and eventu-ally institutionalized in the tax code. Individual philanthropy was the chief source of income. Fees could be charged, but the direct sale of products was to be avoided, as well as the appearance of "commerce." State assistance to nonprofit organizations was acceptable, but not dominant. With some changes, such as the composition of boards becoming more reflective of society as a whole and the responsibilities of trustees made more uniform through model codes, what was forged in this period is what most people believe still exists today.

What Is Expected of Trustees

In this dispensation, what has come to be expected of trustees or directors?[3] Nonprofit boards are charged with several obligations under the general concept of fiduciary. This concept or notion is a fundamental principle that argues that board members are to act unselfishly and in the best interests of their institutions to the best of their ability. Under the fiduciary concept directors are held to three duties: the duty of care, the duty of loyalty, and the duty of obedience.

The duty of care is a standard of conduct applied to discharging a director's responsibilities. Nonprofit board members must carry out their duties in good faith with a degree of "care" and skill. One carries out the duty of care by being interested in the organization and acting in good faith when decisions come before the director. The duty of care does not speak to the question of the correctness of a decision, but rather to the manner in which the board member carried out the decision.

The duty of loyalty speaks to the responsibility of the director to act in a manner that will not harm the organization served. It also prohibits directors from obtaining personal benefit or gain that should rightly belong to the nonprofit organization. This duty presupposes approaching decisions objec-tively and avoiding any conflicts of interest that might impair that objectivity.

The duty of obedience is a less recognized duty of nonprofit board mem-bers. It mandates that directors carry out the purposes of the organization as spelled out in its articles of incorporation and other legal documents. A director would be acting contrary to this duty if, for instance, she or he joined in authorizing the expenditure of funds for lobbying and political activity that exceeded the limits of the tax code (Fishman, 1995; Axelrod, 1994; Oleck, 1994; and Middleton, 1987).

Regulation of the Nonprofit Sector by Governments

This, then, is what the present model expects to be the behavior of members of boards of trustees. It may well be inquired how these behaviors are enforced. The state is ostensibly the focal point of regulation, with the attorney general in all but one state the responsible agent and the state court systems the point of resolution (Fremont-Smith, 1994). Although there are cases that have interpreted these duties and some action taken against boards through removing directors and even the organization's tax-exempt status, these cases are few and far between. More recently, issues of conversions of nonprofits into for-profits have engaged attention as has the case of Minnesota Public Radio (Stehle, 1998), but most attention in the handful of states where attorneys general are active are high-profile cases dealing with televangelists or dead heiresses and artists. Successful prosecutions have been limited. Those on record, such as the Sibley Hospital and the Adelphi University cases and the out-of-court settlement with Boston University, may set some precedents, but they are so case-specific as to give little guidance as to how well the state regulation system works, when and if it does work.[4]

Other activities by cities and states have tried to define what is "nonprofit" as a prelude to changing the tax status of an organization or enforcing a community standard on the practices of nonprofit organizations. The future of these efforts is problematic. Municipalities have also been largely unsuccessful in using their police powers in curtailing activities of nonprofit organizations that are not in local favor. And while not directed to the stewardship of trustees directly, municipalities and states have tried to regulate fundraising by specifying place, method, and levels of expenditure on fundraising. These have all fallen afoul of the Supreme Court as contrary to the First Amendment, and the present melange of requirements for fundraiser registration and disclosure often exempt religious, health, and educational institutions, and many organizations simply refuse to comply. In other words, states and municipalities do very little in holding nonprofit organizations accountable for their missions.

If the states and municipalities do little publicly to regulate, can the same be said about the federal level? Here the focus is on the Internal Revenue Service. Although it is often incomprehensible to students of philanthropy outside of the United States that the tax code is the chief vehicle for regulation of nonprofit organizations in this country, such is the case. Since 1917 and the beginning of tax deductibility, the federal tax system has been the chief definer of what is in and out of the nonprofit sector. It has defined how far and at what cost in taxes a nonprofit organization can undertake commercial activity. The code has shaped what can be done by nonprofit organizations in politics. In the 1969 tax act it limited control by parent companies of foundations and established minimal payout rates. It has also defined what corporations may do philanthropically. By the recent Taxpayers Bill of Rights, it has determined the appropriate means by which compensation for nonprofit officers can be set and what constitutes self-dealing. The recent act also requires accessibility by the public to the financial statements of the organizations. By allowing penalties to be levied against persons and not the organizations alone, it could affect self-dealing. Moreover the intermediate sanctions it authorizes allow enforcement to occur without going to the ultimate sanction of revoking an organization's nonprofit status (Peregrine, 1996).

While the tax code and revenue legislation have doubtless helped shape the behavior of the nonprofit sector, it has not been the Internal Revenue Service's active enforcement that has made the difference. Indeed, audits have been relatively few and are expected to be fewer in the future. Implementing the new legislation is almost interminable. Coupled with the politically uncertain status of the present system of taxation and of the IRS altogether, the prospects of seeing "public regulation" at the federal level grow are unlikely.

In brief, while the law exists for public accountability and for sanctions, it is not applied at any level with any intensity. While various efforts at curtailing advocacy and other activities are being discussed, the court record suggests that most efforts in this area will not succeed.

Why So Little Regulation

The comparison with regulation of government and the for-profit sector is instructive. For governments at all levels in the United States, there is highly institutionalized distrust. Through constitutions and practice, individuals in the legislative and executive policy-making levels are limited by terms and forced to stand for periodic elections or approvals by other branches of government. There is public debate and even attempts at constitutional amendments to limit the number of terms. When the state is prosecuting individuals, governments are so distrusted that unanimity is required on the part of juries and great effort is spent to find disinterested members of juries. For all of this public resources through taxation are legitimately spent. Moreover, so great is the demand for monitoring those in government that citizens pay as individuals considerable amounts of money for newspapers and newsmagazines, the preparation of reporters to provide that intelligence, and indirectly through advertising to assure news reporting on television. The public is also willing to support at universities the study of government and the improvement of public management.

A similar situation is the case for the for-profit sector. So distrustful is the public of business that governments are authorized to spend large sums from public revenues to ensure product safety, investment protection, competition, truth in advertising, etc., etc. Membership on boards of publicly held firms is specified and prospecti and annual reports are required. Moreover, so interested are various publics in monitoring the activities of business that there is a flourishing private sector industry providing information, from general and evaluative data like that provided by a Bests, Bloomberg, or Standard and Poors to more interpretative news provided by the many business journals. Through donations and other means, universities are further encouraged to offer economics and programs in business administration to ensure a prepared next generation.

In contrast, there is no move afoot to use public resources to monitor the nonprofit sector. What is available for the Internal Revenue Service to undertake audits of nonprofit organizations comes from a dedicated excise tax on private foundations. It has been the experience of the authors that those state offices charged with regulating the nonprofit sector are among the least well staffed and housed and the most under-computerized of all state activities. Few journalists are dedicated to the subject, the number of national journals on the subject are few and the nonprofit equivalents of Standard and Poors— i.e., the National Charities Information Bureau, the Philanthropic Advisory Service of the Better Business Bureau, and the American Institute of Philanthropy—exist primarily on grants and gifts. Finally, it has been only until recently that institutions provided instruction on philanthropy or prepared individuals for service in the nonprofit sector.

Why is this the case, especially given the size and importance of the nonprofit sector? There are many explanations. First, the nonprofit sector represents the "trust" sector and is thus thought less in need of attention. Indeed the paucity of cases over the last decade—Covenant House, the televanagelists, New Era Foundation, Adelphi and Boston universities, and the United Way of America—suggest that the trust may be warranted.[5] And it is the "trust" status of the nonprofit sector that may be chiefly in jeopardy by the changing environment of philanthropy. Second, it can be argued that the nonprofit sector is not often seen as a sector and hence "regulating it" is difficult to comprehend by the public and legislators alike. Third, the nonprofit sector is so dispersed and many of its constituents so small that it is hard to regulate and the returns to regulation are relatively meager. Finally, in a cynical vein, it might be argued that the nonprofit sector represents the interests of the rich and the religious and many of its activities serve the poor and disadvantaged. It is bad politics to regulate the interests of the rich and the religious, and the poor and disadvantaged do not count politically.

Whatever the explanation, philanthropy receives little regulatory attention to accountability at any level from governments. For one analyst, this disregard is a source of the sector's creativity and innovation (Gaul, 1993). For another, it is the prologue for major legislative attention—attention that should be paid by those within philanthropy before others determine from outside what should be the case (Dale, 1994).

The Scope of Self-Governance

The present system of self-regulation by board members, by their expectations about what is expected of them, is reinforced by a variety of nonprofit organizations purporting to serve the sector as a whole. The evaluative community is diverse and hardly of one mind. It may well be argued that the chief regulators of the nonprofit world in America are those standard setters for lawyers and accountants that shape what nonprofit leaders hear about as correct behavior and what they must produce on their financial statements. The American Bar Association's Business Law Section model codes may not have persuaded governments so much as they have persuaded lawyers about what to say to their nonprofit clients. Likewise with the Financial Accounting Standards Board and the American Institute of Certified Public Accountants. What their members determine as acceptable for financial statements shape what nonprofit boards expect to take to their publics annually.

In addition to these, there are the direct monitors of standards that were identified earlier: the National Charities Information Bureau, the Philanthropic Advisory Service, and the American Institute of Philanthropy. They may depend on non-market support, and they are duplicative and limited in range and readership, but their judgment about conforming to standards becomes part of the public perception. Likewise with the more ideological judgments of the Capital Research Center and the National Committee for Responsive Philanthropy. Third, there are explicit standard setters for the sector: the Council on Foundations, the Foundation Center, the INDE-PENDENT SECTOR, the National Council of Nonprofit Boards, the Association of Governing Boards, the National Committee on Nonprofit Associations, and the Philanthropy Roundtable, all dedicated to gathering the like-minded and encouraging improvement. Finally, there are those organizations that try to improve the performance of those who serve philanthropy: the American Association of Fund Raising Counsel, the National Society for Fund Raising Executives, the Association of Healthcare Philanthropy, the Council for the Advancement and Support of Education, and the National Committee for Planned Giving. These and other organizations— most arising in the last twenty years—exist to inform and improve the understanding of those serving in and responsible for individual nonprofit organizations. Armed with codes of ethics, but little inclination to enforce them, these organizations seek to influence how individual nonprofit organizations behave so as to sustain the sector.[6] Coupled with a rising national press interest in the subject and a sector-specific press—some 70-plus publications at last count—it can be argued that accountability of non-profit organizations does not lack for spokespeople, analysts, critics, or champions.

Contemporary Challenges to the System

Self-governing nonprofit organizations held in place by the gravity produced by the community of concerned individuals in organizations committed to standards and the improvement of performance of the nonprofit sector may seem attractive as a vision or even as a modus operandi. But there are key forces accumulating that will affect that vision. For these forces, the system as it emerged from the nineteenth century and modified little in the interim is not well prepared. Are boards of trustees able to handle these challenges without national perspectives on their implications for philanthropy? We think not.

These forces are not simply those involved with scale and complexity of decisions that these voluntary boards now make or are made under their authority. Some boards—voluntary, self-selecting, part-time—oversee the activities of organizations with annual budgets in the millions and billions and make decisions about expenditures and access that rival what governments make in cost and scope. It would be hubris to think that their board members were prepared to the degree that would be desired to take such decisions.

But it is to other challenges that we turn, where the rebuttable presumption of the competence of boards is present. The first challenge is economic in character. It has many facets and can best be summarized by the phrase "blurring the lines between the for-profit and nonprofit sectors." Among the facets is the palpable fact that for-profit firms have entered areas that, for the last century, have been the province of the nonprofit sector and are proving that they are profitable. Healthcare, foster and eldercare, job training—for-profit firms in innumerable fields have demonstrated that profit is possible and have encouraged conversions of nonprofit organizations to for-profit status or for creating of for-profit subsidiaries. More will follow.[7]

A second facet of this blurring the lines stems from the intense competition for funds that now exists among nonprofits and the rise of cause-related marketing in corporate philanthropy. This competition has lowered the standards of fundraising by sanctioning such efforts as product endorsements and charitable gaming. When respectable colleges issue affinity charge cards, educational radio features "premiums," and national charities launch lotteries, it should be seen that the nonprofit sector has gone a long way towards accepting the values of the marketplace. In this process, management gurus goad nonprofit leaders to behave like business people and to look at the market model as the mirror for good behavior. Customers, not donors or beneficiaries; products, not services!

It can be argued that responsiveness to customers might be the best way to improve performance of nonprofit organizations. On the other hand, what is at jeopardy when a nonprofit hospital converts to for-profit status, when a nonprofit organization creates a for-profit subsidiary, when a nonprofit organization endorses products or conducts a lottery, it is the lodestone of trust that is eroded. If the motivation shifts from "because it is right and necessary" to "because it affects the bottom line," then the chief asset and *raison d'être* of the nonprofit sector—trust in objectivity—is lost. Donors and beneficiaries alike can no longer be sure, can trust. The trustee who says whatever earns money to pursue our mission is acceptable may be speaking the epitaph of the nonprofit sector.

This is a classic dilemma. What is advantageous for the individual is damaging to the whole. The freedom from ambiguity on this issue of "disinterested interest" has been a chief source of philanthropic motivation; it has given confidence in the decisions of physicians, the rectitude of those who receive donations, and the mission of those who serve the needy. To put this at jeopardy for the whole sector while it serves the immediate short-term interest of the particular organization is the temptation that this shift in the economic environment for nonprofit organizations has presented.

The second great force is political. By a succession of policies and acts over the last seventy-five years, the nonprofit sector was isolated from politics. We are on the verge of a reversal of that policy. First, governments have retreated from areas that once were their prerogative. Who will fill the vacuum? In the absence of a willing political process, who will help shape the public debate? Second, nonprofit organizations of varying persuasions have already entered the political process as advocates, critics, and participants in public policy-making. What once were clear limits are now lines in the sand. Like the issue of "profit," the issue of political preference is one where the interests of the few may jeopardize the operating space for the many.

The third force that has begun to affect the nonprofit sector is the likely shakeout in the number of nonprofit organizations. There are too many to be supported, too much infrastructure that takes away from service, and too little stress on performance. Accountability to law, yes; accountability to donors' wishes, yes; even accountability to beneficiaries' expectations. But there is nothing in the nonprofit environment that induces boards to seek better performance in the accomplishment of mission, no trade benchmarks, only the exhortations of individuals enamored of the marketplace to look like the private sector. There is no ethic of the desirable merger or of the benign assisted organizational suicide. The notion of "permanently failing organizations" is apt—and tolerable—for many organizations in the nonprofit sector, lurching from crisis to crisis and never performing at their very best.

What We Know and What Might Be Done

Boards of directors have been studied by various researchers for over 40 years. However, most of the research has been dominated by an interest in the service and control functions of the board. Much of the literature has been expressions of what worked best in a particular instance or what should be done. Key variables associated with board composition include board size, gender, and occupation. Pfeffer (1973) and Provan (1980) found that increased board size and the composition of the board were related to the amount of funds raised. Siliciano (1990, 1993) found that boards which were involved in strategic planning activities had higher performance in funds raised and productivity measures. Board size had no significant effect. The gender findings support earlier arguments and findings by Middleton (1987) and Zald (1969) that women have less access to economic resources. Increased numbers of women on the board, however, increased the social performance effectiveness.

In a study of nonprofits in Canada, Bradshaw, Murray, and Wolpin (1992) found that a high emphasis on strategic planning was the single most important process characteristic in perceived board effectiveness. Other significant variables included good meeting management, common vision, involvement in day-to-day operations, and avoidance of board-staff conflict. The size of the board and number of committees were not significant variables. In a study reported by Gray (1996) the researchers found that effective boards regularly evaluate their own performance. Green (1995) found that boards that have involvement with staff other than the executive director are more effective than those who do not. He also found that board evaluation increased effectiveness as well as periodic review of key financial control mechanisms.

Herman and Heimovics (1990) found that successful executives facilitated interaction in board relationships. Judgements by chief executives of their board effectiveness is somewhat related to following recommended board practices (Herman, et al., 1997). Much is to be done empirically in the study of board effectiveness. Herman (1990) argues for such measures as constituent and client satisfaction, outcome indicators, and reputational measures. None of these elements speak directly to a role for external (governmental) oversight.

In all three instances mentioned earlier—simulating profit, redefining political responsibility, and establishing benchmarks for performance and viability—what might seem to be issues that individual boards should wrestle with turn out to be ones where general guidance is necessary. In each, there should be a national commission drawn from leadership in the field prepared to explore the options for boards and their organizations and specify consequences for the whole of the field if certain options are accepted. Among other issues, these three challenges should be part of the agendas of the associations that serve the nonprofit sector—their annual meetings, special seminars, and newsletters. They should be explored systematically in the media concerned with philanthropy. The conclusions of the commissions should be supported by foundations in their grantmaking and by the organizations dedicated to strengthening boards and their decision-making capacity.

What emerged at the end of the nineteenth century as a mode of governance for philanthropy will be stretched to address the challenges that the end of the twentieth century brings. There is, however, no alternative to this system. It would be fruitless to look to governments for guidance and enforcement. It is only by means of strengthened informed boards, supported by a community of opinion from the nonprofit sector, and assisted by foundations that the America's sphere of trust will be preserved.

Notes

1. Our claim is made even in recognition of the considerable laws that affect nonprofits. See for example Bruce R. Hopkins, *The Law of Tax-exempt Organizations*, 7th ed. Wiley, 1998; and Howard L. Oleck and Martha E. Stewart, *Nonprofit Corporations, Organizations, & Associations*, 6th ed. Prentice Hall, 1994.

2. We estimate that there are 1,300,000 individuals in a "trustee" capacity in government and 9.6 million in the nonprofit sector. Estimates based on the *U.S. Statistical Abstract*, 1997 and *The Nonprofit Almanac, 1992–93*, 1992.

3. There are different legal standards for trustees of trusts and directors of nonprofit corporations even though the terms "director" and "trustee" are often used interchangeably (Fishman, 1995). For purposes of this article, the authors are concerned with directors of nonprofit organizations. The primary distinction from the business corporation being the nondistribution constraint (Hansmann, 1981). Directors of nonprofit corporations are held to a lower standard of care than charitable trustees. States have adopted different approaches to the treatment of nonprofits but an increasing number follow the Revised Model Nonprofit Corporation Act (RMNCA), which was approved by the American Bar Association in 1987 (Fishman, p. 66).

4. For an alternative view, see H. Bogard, "The Role of State Attorneys General in Relation to Troubled Nonprofits." PONPO Working Paper #206, New Haven: Program on Non-Profit Organizations, Yale University, 1994.

5. For an alternative judgment, see G. M. Gaul and N. A. Borowski, *Free Ride: The Tax-Exempt Economy*. Kansas City: Andrews and McMeel, 1993.

6. INDEPENDENT SECTOR, *Ethics and the Nation's Voluntary and Philanthropic Community: Obedience to the Unenforceable*, Washington, 1991.

7. For an early effort to reformulate the sector in preparation for this growing commercialization, see H. Hansmann, "Reforming Nonprofit Corporation Law." *University of Pennsylvania Law Review*, 1981, 129: 497–623. For a current perspective, see E. Brody, "Agents without Principals: The Economic Convergence of the Nonprofit and For-Profit Organizational Forms." *New York Law School Law Review*, 1996, 40, 457–536.

References

Axelrod, N. R., "Board Leadership and Board Development." In R. D. Herman and Associates, *The Jossey-Bass Handbook of Nonprofit Leadership and Management*. San Francisco: Jossey-Bass Publishers, 1994.

Bradshaw, P., Murray, V., and Wolpin, J., "Do nonprofit boards make a difference? An exploration of the relationships among board structure, process, and effectiveness." *Nonprofit and Voluntary Sector Quarterly*. Fall 1992, 21 (3): 227–249.

Bradshaw, P., Murray, V., and Wolpin, J., "Women on boards of nonprofits: what difference do they make?" *Nonprofit Managnement and Leadership*. Spring 1996, 6 (3): 241–254.

Dale, Harvey. Norman A. Sugarman Memorial Lecture, Mandel Center for Nonprofit Organizations, Case Western Reserve University, 1994.

Fishman, J. J., and Schwartz, S., *Nonprofit Organizations: Cases and Materials*. Westbury: The Foundation Press, 1995.

Fremont-Smith, M. R., "Government Regulation of the Independent Sector." Working Paper, Research Symposium Honoring Brian O'Connell, Washington, 1994.

Gray, S. T., "Board self-assessment," *Association Management*, January 1996, 48 (1): 156–157.

Green, J. C., "The effectiveness of boards of directors of nonprofit organizations serving developmentally disabled adults." Doctoral dissertation, The Clarement Graduate School, 1995.

Hall, P. D., "Remedying the Incompleteness of Democracy: An Overview of Board Governance in America." Unpublished manuscript, Yale University, 1997.

Herman, R. D., and Tulipana, F. P., "Board staff relations and perceived effectiveness in nonprofit organizations," *Journal of Voluntary Action Research*, October–December 1985, 14 (4): 48–59.

Herman, R. D., Renz, D. O., and Heimovics, R. D., "Board practices and board effectiveness in local nonprofit organizations," *Nonprofit Management and Leadership*, Summer, 1997, 7 (4), 373–385.

Herman, R. D., "Methodological issues in studying the effectiveness of nongovernmental and nonprofit organizations," *Nonprofit and Voluntary Sector Quarterly*, Fall 1990, 19 (3): 293–306.

Herman, R. D., and Heimovics, R. D., "The effective nonprofit executive: Leader of the board," *Nonprofit Management and Leadership*, Winter 1990, 1 (2): 167–180.

Hodgkinson, Virginia, et al., *Nonprofit Almanac: Dimensions of the Independent Sector. 1996–1997*, San Francisco: Jossey-Bass, 1996.

Middleton, M., "Nonprofit Boards of Directors: Beyond the Governance Function." In W. W. Powell, ed., *The Nonprofit Sector: A Research Handbook*. New Haven: Yale University Press, 1987, 141–153.

Oleck, H. L, *Nonprofit Corporations, Organizations, and Associations*. 6th ed. Englewood Cliffs: Prentice Hall, 1994.

Peregrine, M. W., Nilles, K. M., and Palmer, M. V., "Complying with the New

Intermediate Sanctions Law," *The Exempt Organization Tax Review*, 14 (August), 1996, 245–253.

Pfeffer, J., "Size, composition and function of hospital boards of directors: A study of organization environment linkage," *Administrative Science Quarterly*, 1973, 18: 349–363.

Provan, K. G., "Board power and organizational effectiveness among human service agencies," *Academy of Management Journal*, 1980, 23 (2): 221–236.

Siliciano, J., "The board's role in the strategic management of nonprofit organizations: A survey of eastern U.S. and Canadian YMCA organizations." Doctoral dissertation, University of Massachusetts, 1990.

Siliciano, J., and Floyd, S., *Nonprofit boards, strategic management and organizational performance: An empirical study of YMCA organizations*, PONPO Working Paper no. 182. Yale University, February 1993.

Siliciano, J. I., "The relationship between formal planning and performance in nonprofit organizations," *Nonprofit Management and Leadership*. Summer 1997, 7 (4): 387–403.

Stehle, V., "Sale of Catalogue Business Nets Profits for Minnesota Public Radio—and Top Officials," *The Chronicle of Philanthropy*, April 9, 1998, p. 38.

Zald, M. N., "The power and function of boards of directors: A theoretical synthesis," *American Journal of Sociology*, 1969, 75: 97.

CHAPTER TEN

Patterns and Purposes of Philanthropic Giving

Eleanor Brown

An eminent commission on philanthropy in America recently concluded that "[i]ndividual giving is haphazard, misdirected, and misspent" (National Commission on Philanthropy and Civic Renewal, 1997, p. 6). Earlier times found us no more self-satisfied and secure in our habits of charity. In the 1790s the threat to sensible philanthropy came in the form of widespread disenchantment with both education and religion, two institutions widely seen as effectively promoting charitable behavior, with perhaps as few as one-third of the population attending church regularly (Hall, 1995). And even in colonial times, so eminent a spokesperson as Cotton Mather feared unwise benevolence, urging the people of Boston in 1698, "Instead of urging you to augment your charity, I will rather utter an exhortation . . . that you may not *abuse* your charity by misapplying it" (Bremner, 1988).

At the close of the twentieth century, there is a certain urgency to the question of whether American generosity can be channeled and in what volume it will flow to meet our changing social, economic, and political landscapes. Government safety nets for the poor are being dismantled. Government support for sometimes-decadent artistic production and sometimes-arcane scientific "pure research" is being scrutinized with an eye toward containing the federal budget. Our Toquevillean fantasy of small close-knit American towns confronts a reality of big cities and suburbs where trust is down and "mainstream" churches see their memberships in decline. Will individual philanthropy rescue us from this century's fin-de-siecle apocalyptic vision?

In this essay, I review the patterns and purposes of American philanthropy in the 1990s. The goal is to get a sense of where philanthropy may be headed, as we move into an era of diminished expectations for the scope of federal funding. The paper considers individual philanthropy in the forms of charitable contributions, volunteer labor, and bequests. For each of these, we first examine the questions of who gives, how much is given, and who the beneficiaries are. We then address some of the important determinants of giving, and what they augur for individual philanthropy in the coming decades.

Charitable Donations, Volunteer Labor, and Bequests in the 1990s

In 1996, it is estimated that living individuals gave $119.9 billion to nonprofit causes, and another $10.5 billion went to nonprofit groups in the form of bequests (*Giving USA*, 1997). At prevailing compensation rates, the value of volunteer time donated to not-for-profit or other organizations is estimated to be $201.6 billion, with another $59 billion worth of time spent directly in service of others, without mediation by any organization (Hodgkinson and Weitzman, 1996). To give a comparative sense of how much money these sums represent, we note that in 1996 their sum was more than enough to finance Social Security and far more than the $226 billion the federal government spent on income security programs (*Economic Report of the President*, 1997).

There is no perfect data set for measuring any of the three components of individual philanthropy. One of the best sources of information on individual contributions is the biennial survey conducted by the Gallup Organization for Independent Sector (IS). Because of the limited size of the survey, which includes fewer than 3,000 households, the IS data are not likely to capture the large but infrequent gifts of the very wealthy. Because the wealthy are especially likely to donate appreciated assets to institutions conducting endowment and capital campaigns, certain gift categories (health, education, and the arts) may be underrepresented in surveys not focused on the very rich. The IS data also yield lower total estimates of individual giving than emerge from the *Giving USA* data and other sources (Schervish and Havens, 1997a). They are perhaps best viewed as giving a good look at the patterns of contributions for low- to upper-middle-income households, i.e., those with incomes below $100,000.

The IS data on volunteers remain the best nationwide survey of volunteering. Bequest data are drawn principally from Internal Revenue Service data, which principally represent gross estates big enough, before deductions, to be subject to bequest taxation.

Estimates of the average amount contributed to charity by American households in 1995 range from just under $700 to more than $1,100. The results of the Independent Sector's 1996 survey suggest that households gave an average of $696 to charity in 1995. Schervish and Havens (1997a) refine this estimate and compare it to values obtained from other surveys. Restricting attention to data collected from respondents who identified themselves as heads of household, who might reasonably be expected to be more knowledgeable about the family's contributions, raises the estimate of average household contributions to $749. This is still below the estimates they obtain from two surveys conducted by the University of Chicago's National Opinion Research Corporation. The 1995 Survey of Consumer Finances, which codes as zeroes the contributions of households giving less than $500 annually, nonetheless gives a much higher estimate of average giving, $972. The 1996 General Social Survey, when attention is restricted to heads of households, yields an estimate of average giving of $1,099, almost as big as the per-household average of $1,167 implied by the *Giving USA* data (Schervish and Havens, 1997a).

The *Giving USA* estimate of individual giving implies that households gave 1.9 percent of personal income in 1995 (*Giving USA*, p. 64). The ratio of estimated giving to personal income has been fairly stable over the past quarter century, ranging from 1.8 to 2.0 percent. This stability is likely to represent offsetting forces rather than an immutable relationship between giving and income. While changes in the tax code in the 1980s made it substantially more costly to give, for example, the decade also showed dramatic increases in stock market wealth and educational attainment (see for example Clotfelter, 1990 and Brown, 1997b).

In the IS data on individual giving, the lion's share, 59.9 percent, went to religious organizations. The second largest share went to human services (9.8 percent), followed closely by education (9.3 percent) and health (8.3 percent). These four categories together account for seven-eighths of personal giving. The other categories considered in the survey are youth development (4.2 percent of giving), arts, culture and humanities (2.9 percent), international (2.4 percent), public/societal benefit (1.9 percent), environment (1.7 percent), private and community foundations (1.6 percent), adult recreation (1.6 percent), and other (0.4 percent) (Hodgkinson and Weitzman, 1996).

Levels of charitable giving vary widely across households. In 1995, almost a third of the IS sample (31.5 percent) reported no contribution. Another 15 percent gave less than $100. At the other end of the spectrum, 15 percent of the households made contributions of $1,000 or more. Households with higher incomes were more likely to make donations, and gave more on average. About half of the households with incomes under $20,000 made no contribution, while almost nine out of ten households with incomes of at least $100,000 gave. Among this highest-income group, the average level of giving was $3,379 (op. cit., p. 1–49).

Auten, Clotfelter and Schmalbeck (1997) show that the trend toward more nearly universal giving continues through the upper income brackets. Using tax data for 1995, they find that the percent of itemized returns with charitable contributions rises steadily with income. Starting from a low of 87 percent reporting donations in the income range $25,000 to $50,000, the percentage with charitable deductions rises to 95 percent of households in the $100,000-$200,000 range. For households reporting incomes of at least $2.5 million, the percentage is 97.8.

One way to look at the average generosity of various income groups is to examine the percentage of household income given away. As noted above, Americans overall give about 1.9 percent of personal income to charity. Income groups are roughly equally generous, in terms of the fraction of their income they give away, across the income spectrum, with households in the highest income brackets giving modestly larger fractions than others (Schervish and Havens, 1995; Auten et al., 1997).

Volunteering, while not as widespread a phenomenon as charitable giving, is a prevalent form of philanthropy in America. IS estimates that 93 million adult Americans, or 49 percent of the adult population, did some volunteer work in the 12 months preceding their May 1996 survey. Among those who volunteered, the average number of hours volunteered was 4.2 hours per week, yielding an economy-wide annual estimate of 20.3 billion hours volunteered.

One way to get a sense of how much time 20 billion hours is would be to translate it into full-time-worker equivalents. Working 40 hours a week, 50 weeks a year, a full-time worker puts in 2,000 hours annually; therefore, 20 billion hours is equivalent to the labor power of ten million full-time workers. Another way to bring into focus what 20 billion hours represent is to translate hours into a dollar measure. IS applies average wage rates, with an adjustment to include fringe benefits, to value volunteer labor at $201.5 billion. This number can be thought of as an estimate of what nonprofit organizations and others utilizing volunteers would have had to pay in order to get the labor that was donated to them. Alternative methodologies take into account the likely productivity of volunteer labor in the sectors of the economy where it is most often employed, and of the value of volunteer-assisted services to clients. From this perspective, 20.3 billion hours of volunteering yields benefits to clients in the range $113 billion to $161 billion. Based on the value of time they give, the volunteers themselves enjoy similar amounts of benefit from their involvement in volunteering (Brown, 1997a).

The prevalence of volunteering increases with income and education, and peaks in the age group 35–54. Women, people who work part-time, who are married, or who have a religious affiliation are more likely than their counterparts to volunteer (Hodgkinson and Weitzman, 1996).

In the 1996 IS data and in the 1996 General Social Survey, about a quarter of the adult population report at least one volunteer activity related to religion. The two surveys also agree that about 17 percent of adults volunteer for education, and about 15 percent for youth development. The IS data show 13 percent of respondents volunteering in the area of human services; in the GSS data, about 10 percent volunteer in human services. The same is true for health; 13 percent of the IS respondents volunteer and 10 percent of the GSS respondents volunteer. The largest discrepancy across the surveys is found in the category of informal volunteering. The IS data include in this category not only volunteering that is not mediated by any organization but also volunteering done for organizations on an *ad hoc* basis rather than as part of an ongoing commitment. This may explain why 20 percent of IS respondents report informal volunteering, in contrast to the much lower 7 percent found in the GSS. The final category of giving to involve at least 10 percent of respondents in either survey is the category of work-related volunteering, which in the GSS involves 12 percent of respondents, in contrast to 8 percent in the IS data.

The third form of individual philanthropy, after charitable giving and volunteering, is bequeathing. Compared to charitable giving by living individuals, the amount of money conferred through charitable bequests is small. In 1996, charitable bequests are estimated to total about $10.5 billion, ranking between corporations ($8.5 billion) and foundations ($11.8 billion). The biggest of these three is one-tenth as much as charitable donations by living individuals.

A principal source of data on bequests is estate tax returns. Estate tax returns are filed for estates worth at least $600,000. In 1995, of an estimated 2,286,000 deaths in the U.S., only 69,766 estate tax returns were filed, representing 3 percent of the decedent population (Auten et al., 1997). This 3 percent of the decedent population accounts for more than 93 percent of the $9.8 trillion in estimated bequest giving for 1995. These data reflect the bequest behavior of only a small part of the population, but they capture a very large share of the dollars bequeathed.

Besides wealth, the other important demographic variable that predicts charitable bequest behavior is marital status. Single women, followed by single men, are the most likely to make charitable bequests. Among married persons, charitable bequests are much more likely to be observed after the second half of the couple dies. Only 8.9 percent of the estate tax returns of married men indicated a charitable bequest, in contrast to 27.1 percent of widowed and otherwise unmarried men's. Among women decedents for whom estate tax returns were filed, 7.6 percent of married women's returns had charitable bequests, far less than the 28.4 percent of unmarried women's returns.

Gender differences in the propensity to bequeath are due almost entirely to differences in the propensity to be married at the time of death. Among estate tax filers for 1995, 64 percent of male decedents were married at the time of death, compared to only 25 percent of female decedents married at the time of death.

In 1995, 19 percent of estate tax returns reported charitable bequests. The Internal Revenue Service, in its Estate Study, classifies each gift according to donee type, using six categories: religion; social welfare; private foundations; education, science, and medicine; arts and humanities; and other (Eller, 1997). Among estates with net worth of up to $10 million, the donee category receiving the biggest share of charitable bequests was education, medical and science purposes. At levels of net worth above $10 million, private foundations received more money from bequests than any other category. Overall, of the $9.2 billion in charitable bequests identified in estate tax returns, 36.4 percent went to private foundations, followed by 26.9 percent bequeathed to education, science, and medical causes. Religion was the category receiving the most bequests but it accounted for only 10 percent of dollars bequeathed. Only 3 percent of charitable bequests went to the arts and humanities, and not even half that much, only 1.4 percent, went to social welfare. The category "other" accounted for 21.4 percent of charitable bequeathing in 1995 (Auten et al., 1997).

Looking across the three avenues for personal philanthropy, can we identify a "unified theory" of who gives how much to whom? There are some regularities. First, there is substantial variation in generosity within all income levels. Second, religion involves more people than any other category of beneficiary. This is true for charitable giving, volunteering, and charitable bequests. Because religion's share of giving tends to shrink as income increases, it captures a bigger share of volunteer hours than it does charitable donations and a bigger share of charitable donations than it does charitable bequests.

Although there are some unifying themes that underlie individual philanthropy, most of the research on the determinants of philanthropy is specific to charitable contributions, to volunteering, or to bequests. The next three sections of this paper review, in turn, research on the determinants of these three forms of individual philanthropy.

Determinants of Charitable Contributions

The economic determinants of charitable giving have been on the research agenda of economists for at least two decades. The data used in economic research on charitable giving comprise both household survey data and federal income tax return data. Prominent among the limitations of survey data is their reliance on recall for accurate information. Important economic variables, such as wage rates, may be omitted from surveys, while other variables, such as income, may be reported only as falling within given intervals. The advantage of survey data over tax data is their potential wealth of demographic data, such as age and educational attainment.

Tax data contain some demographic information, such as marital status, the number of dependents a taxpayer has, and whether the taxpayer or spouse is over age 65. Tax data allow economists to distinguish between earnings and other sources of income, but they do not contain wage rates. The biggest drawback to the use of tax data for studying charitable giving is that only itemizers report charitable gifts. Because the bulk of charitable giving is done by itemizers, tax data may tell us a fair amount about giving; they cannot tell us much about the behavior of typical low-income households, since these households would not generally be filing itemized tax returns.

Before turning to economists' favorite explanatory variables, income and the after-tax cost of giving, it is worth noting that education consistently emerges as an important determinant of charitable giving. Quite apart from the effects of education on a household's income, education has an independent, positive effect on how much a person gives to charitable causes. Over the 1980s, the proportion of the population having finished at least high school rose from 66.5 percent to 77.6 percent, and the proportion having finished college rose from 16.2 percent to 21.3 percent (Brown, 1997b). As we look at variables that are likely to affect giving over the next decades, upward trends in the levels of educational attainment of U.S. citizens give us one clear, positive reason to expect giving to continue to increase.

We know that charitable giving increases with income. Given that the fraction of income given away shows such consistency across time, and at any time across income groups, there is a temptation to suppose that giving is roughly proportional to income. Perhaps Americans will always give 2 percent of their income, no matter what. This view of giving as proportional to income has been tested empirically and rejected in favor of more sophisticated models (Clotfelter 1990) that include information on the tax treatment of giving.

The Tax Reform Act of 1986 gave us a dramatic example of how sensitive the timing of deductible giving may be to changes in tax brackets. It was well known in advance that TRA86 would cut marginal tax rates in 1987, reducing the tax advantage of giving for most itemizers. In 1986, itemized deductions totaled $54.5 billion. In 1987, they were $49.3 billion (Clotfelter, 1990). Although the stock market decline in 1987 may also have affected giving in that year, much of the 10-percent difference between the two years' giving is likely to be due to the tax advantage of accelerating giving into 1986.

One of the biggest challenges facing economists as they try to quantify the responsiveness of giving levels to income levels is that economic theory tells us to look at "permanent" income, a smoothed version of actual income, to predict expenditures. This is because economists have observed that people save and dissave (or borrow) to smooth their consumption from year to year. Temporarily high income won't lead to much extra giving, and temporary shortfalls in income won't cause people to cut back much. This implies that relying on annual data, in which some rich and poor people are only temporarily so, will lead economists to under-predict the responsiveness of giving to long-term changes in income.

Recently, panel data have become available that allow researchers to track specific individuals through time. This allows a calculation of permanent income, and the effects of temporary movements in income and tax rates can be separated from long-term effects. Focusing on long-term effects, there is now reason to believe that giving responds perhaps proportionately to changes in income. Taxpayers respond to long-term shifts in their tax prices of giving, too, but the effect is much less than proportionate; recent research suggests that a 10-percent change in the tax price of giving may elicit as little as a 5-percent change in the level of giving (Randolph 1995; Barrett, McGuirk, and Steinberg, 1995).

The sensitivity of donors' contributions to their tax rates is clearest among upper-income households. This may be due to their being more likely to consult with tax advisors, or, because their levels of giving and taxpaying are higher, they are more aware of their tax brackets. Clotfelter (1990) shows that the dramatic reductions in marginal tax rates ushered in with the Tax Reform Act of 1986 led to a redistribution of giving within the top income quintile, with those whose rates came down the most accounting for a smaller share of giving after the tax cuts were in effect. Because the highest-income Americans contribute so large a share of charitable donations—the 1 percent with the highest incomes made 16 percent of all donations in 1994—measures of the tax-sensitivity of giving that are based on the entire income spectrum are likely to understate the tax sensitivity in the strata from which most dollars come.

Social scientists outside economics have looked at other social trends that may affect giving, including people's notions of civic engagement and concern for others. Political scientist Robert Putnam has sparked widespread debate with his articles chronicling the decline in Americans' propensity to join groups such as bowling leagues and book clubs (Putnam 1995a, 1995b). His thesis is that membership in non-hierarchical groups leads citizens to trust one another, which in turn leads them to be civic-minded. Although his focus is on political behaviors supporting democratic institutions, such as voting, the links between social engagement and civic engagement suggest that positive engagement with others beyond the personal sphere is likely to lead to additional forms of engagement, including charitable giving. In the 1996 IS data, 76 percent of group members made charitable contributions, in contrast to just 37 percent of those reporting no group affiliation. Respondents who reported belonging to both a religious organization and at least one nonreligious organization were especially likely to make donations: a full 90 percent of these respondents reported having made charitable gifts in the past year (Hodgkinson and Weitzman, 1996).

Determinants of Volunteering

Much of what we know about the determinants of volunteering is derived from the biennial surveys conducted for Independent Sector. As with charitable giving, people who are actively involved in their communities do the most volunteering. People who report belonging to a church or other organization volunteer an average of 2.3 hours per week. Among people who report no group affiliation, average hours volunteered per week total only 0.6. There is an interesting difference between religious belonging and membership in groups other than congregations. Among respondents who did not attend church but who belonged to some other group, 65 percent volunteered. Among respondents belonging to a congregation but to no other group, 38 percent were volunteers. While much lower than the proportion volunteering among members of secular groups only, the congregants-only level of volunteering is still twice that of respondents who belong to no group at all, among whom the rate of volunteering is 19 percent.

Generally speaking, propensities to volunteer increase with social status. Higher proportions volunteering are found among college graduates, among married persons, persons living in higher-income households, persons who are employed, and people who own their own homes. One explanation for the link between social position and volunteering is that position brings with it networks of acquaintances, and networks bring a greater likelihood of being asked to volunteer. One consistent pattern found in the IS data is that people who are asked to volunteer are more likely to volunteer than others, and being part of groups almost certainly makes one more likely to be asked. In the 1996 data, of the 43 percent who were asked to volunteer, 85 percent did so. Of the 54 percent who reported that they were not asked, only 21 percent volunteered.

This pattern may suggest that people in search of volunteers know pretty much whom to ask; only 9 percent of nonvolunteers report that they didn't volunteer because no one asked them. A second hypothesis about the link between social position and volunteering is that the sense of empowerment that may correlate with social position is an ingredient in making people feel that their volunteering is worthwhile. Hodgkinson (1995), using data from Independent Sector surveys, reports that among the 13 percent of adults agreeing strongly with a statement that it was within their power to improve the welfare of others, eight out of ten volunteered. Among the 21 percent who disagreed with the statement, three out of ten volunteered. Although less pronounced, this pattern was clear among teenagers as well. Among the 15 percent who strongly agreed, three-fourths volunteered, in contrast to four-tenths of the 18 percent who disagreed with the statement. A sense of efficacy seems an important ingredient in getting people to volunteer.

Of particular policy interest is the impact of community service requirements. Research shows that people who volunteer as youths are more likely than others to volunteer as adults. Some of this correlation is due to self-selection, of course, as people with a tendency to volunteer simply begin to do so at an early age. But some of it probably reflects the formative impact of the early volunteer experience. In a survey of teen-aged volunteers, respondents were asked how important several potential benefits of volunteering had been in their own case. Of the eighteen options, the three most frequently cited as important were "I learned to respect others," "I gained satisfaction from helping others," and "I learned to be helpful and kind." These were rated as "very important benefits" by almost half the sample (48.3, 46.0, and 44.5 percent, respectively). Gaining satisfaction reveals nothing about whether the volunteer experience was a source of personal change that might lead to future volunteering, since it may have been the case that these young volunteers knew that they would enjoy volunteering. But the other two top benefits involve learning, and the lessons learned are almost certainly ones that foster future volunteering.

Schools are an important institution in getting young people to volunteer. In the survey cited above, 78 percent of youthful volunteers found at least one of their volunteer assignments through their school. As more and more schools implement community service requirements, the level of teenage volunteering will automatically increase; it is reasonable to expect that cohorts who experience community service in their youth will be more inclined to volunteer as adults.

Economists have explored whether the tax treatment of charitable deductions might affect the supply of volunteer labor. If people see donating time and donating money as somewhat interchangeable ways of accomplishing similar goals, then tax policy that affects charitable donations could affect volunteering as well. If, for example, marginal tax rates rise, increasing the tax advantage associated with giving money, people might choose to spend a little more money and a little less time in the pursuit of their philanthropic goals. To date, studies seem to show that giving time and money go together (Menchik and Weisbrod, 1987; Brown and Lankford 1992; Andreoni, Gale, and Scholz, 1995). Rather than acting as substitutes, the two forms of involvement in philanthropy are gross complements, with volunteering as well as charitable giving increasing when the tax breaks associated with giving go up. There is not much agreement on the magnitude of this relationship, but just knowing that efforts to stimulate donations through the tax code will not necessarily hurt volunteering is a useful lesson for policy-makers.

Determinants of Bequest Behavior

We know from estate tax data that the likelihood of observing a charitable bequest is diminished if the person is survived by a spouse. Because they are not deductible, bequests to children are not reported in estate tax data, but one can safely assume that the presence of living children creates a likely choice for the disposition of a decedent's estate. In the Health and Retirement Survey, covering individuals born in the 1930s, 38 percent of the sample reported that they were "probably" or "definitely" going to leave "a sizeable inheritance" to their heirs (Health and Retirement Survey, 1995). Nonprofits compete with both spouses and children in the dispensation of bequeathed wealth.

Just as income is an important factor in annual charitable giving, so wealth at time of death is another important determinant of the likelihood and magnitude of charitable bequests. In considering a typical household with bequeathable wealth, it is useful to think of the level of wealth at time of death as depending on, first, how much wealth has been accumulated by the time a person reaches retirement, and how much spending of wealth there is during retirement.

Surveys have found that the most important motive behind household saving is a desire for precautionary liquidity (Reynolds 1997). Among the elderly, precautionary holdings of wealth guard against the uncertain expenses of unusually long life or of expensive medical conditions. Recent years have witnessed an increased range of financial options for persons wishing to insure against such risks. There are increased opportunities to annuitize wealth, thereby hedging against the expense of long life, and there are many "Medi-Gap" insurance programs to pick up shares of medical costs not covered by Medicare. Instead of having to save large sums to protect against catastrophic health costs, for example, people need only to save enough to pay insurance premiums and copayments. The size of "accidental bequests," saved for contingencies that never arose, falls as financial markets grow more sophisticated.

The effect on bequests of reduced levels of precautionary wealth holding can be substantial. From 1960 to 1990, the fraction of assets held in annuitized form doubled for older men and quadrupled for older women. Looking at these increased opportunities for annuitization since 1960, Auerbach (1995) estimates that aggregate bequests are 40 percent lower today than they would have been without the observed shift into annuitized wealth. (There is also evidence that wealth holdings insure against neglect from would-be heirs [Bernheim, Shliefer, and Summers, 1985]. Insurance markets have made few inroads in this area, and to the extent that wealth holdings do double duty as hedges against both expense and inattention, estates are unlikely to be annuitized entirely.)

There is evidence that estate tax rates affect both the size of charitable bequests and the variety of causes toward which they are directed. Joulfaian (1991) finds that higher estate tax rates, by reducing the after-tax cost of leaving a deductible charitable bequest, significantly increase the size of bequests. He also finds that higher marginal tax rates lead donors to leave bequests to organizations in a wider set of activities, rather than just leaving more money to a core set of charitable beneficiaries.

It has been estimated that an unusually large amount of money, on the order of $10.4 trillion, will be passed on via bequests during the fifty-year period 1990–2040 (Avery and Rendall, 1993). Using gross estates on which tax returns have been filed as a point for comparison, the projections imply that, relative to recent years, the amount of income passing through estates will be about twice as large in the first decade of the next century, and about three times as big in the second decade. Researchers have naturally asked whether such large wealth transfers will mean a windfall for charitable organizations.

Any exploration of the implications of large bequests on the horizon will be speculative. Still, there is a good deal of money at stake, and it is worth considering systematically how the estimate of $10.4 trillion is reached, and what we know about the prospective decedents that may shed light on their propensity to make charitable bequests.

The estimate of $10.4 trillion covers the half century 1990–2040. There is little reason to consider that part of this time horizon that lies behind us, so I focus on future bequests. Because projections grow less reliable the farther they stretch into the future, I consider bequests up to the year 2020. Two major sources of uncertainty are inflation and the performance of financial markets. The reliability of projected rates of return in the form of capital gains has been questioned (Reynolds 1997), and even small errors in projected rates of return compound into large errors in projected wealth over long horizons. Uncertainty over inflation rates and real rates of return makes projections more than a quarter century forward highly speculative.

Limiting our attention to the period from now to the year 2020 cuts the $10.4 trillion estimate to roughly $6 trillion (Avery 1994). This, however, understates the size of the resource transfer of interest to nonprofits. Avery and Rendall ignore entirely a group of prospective decedents most likely to leave large sums to charitable causes. Their research focus is on the behavior of the prospective inheritors of wealth, not on how much the older generation might bequeath to charity. Because they are interested in the fortunes of the baby boomers who stand to inherit a great deal from their parents, Avery and Rendall *exclude from their sample all childless couples and individuals*. The $6 trillion is only the share of future estates that pit nonprofits against potential heirs. The projected bequests of childless couples and individuals need to be added to this number to arrive at the size of the resource transfer we can expect to see over the next two decades.

Avery and Rendall do not report the fraction of their sample dropped because it consisted of childless individuals and couples. Another major study of the bequest behavior of the elderly, however, reports the proportion of childless in its sample. Hurd (1987) uses data from the Longitudinal Retirement History Survey, and, ideal for our purposes, excludes from his sample individuals and couples who do not have positive levels of bequeathable wealth. In his remaining sample, individuals with living children constitute 70 percent of all individuals, and couples with living children constitute 85 percent of all couples. Overall, couples and singles with living children are 76 percent of the sample. If childless households and the households of parents have similar levels of wealth, ignoring the bequests of the childless could understate the amount bequeathed by almost one-third.

It is important to note that the heads of household in Hurd's data were born between 1906 and 1911; because of low fertility rates during the depression, the 24-percent childlessness rate in this cohort may overestimate childlessness among subsequent generations, especially those that gave birth to the baby boom. Still, it may be that the $6 trillion excludes something on the order of 15 to 20 percent of the population with bequeathable wealth, and these are the people who, in weighing their bequest options, are not considering bequests to their children. One might worry that, having no children, these households might squander their wealth, but Hurd finds otherwise, stating that parents "choose consumption rates that are indistinguishable from the rates of people of similar wealth levels but who have no children" (Hurd, 1987, p. 307). Accounting for the wealth of childless households adds perhaps another $1 trillion to the estimated transfer.

Where does this leave us? Based on the projections made by Avery and Rendall, limiting our attention to the time period from now to the year 2020, and adjusting for households eliminated from Avery and Rendall's sample, $7 trillion seems a reasonable ballpark estimate for the volume of resources passing through estates in the next two decades. On average, this represents roughly a tripling of the level of total gross estates reported in recent years on estate tax returns. In thinking about how much of this wealth might flow to nonprofit organizations, several considerations weigh in:

Current levels of giving from bequests. In 1992, deductions for charitable contributions amounted to 8 percent of the gross estates for which estate tax returns were filed. If this proportionality were to be maintained as the flow of gross estates triples, then tripling the current level of charitable bequeathing will bring something on the order of an extra $21 billion (in today's dollars) in charitable bequests annually.

Current levels of bequeathing as a proportion of charitable donations. Because the amount of money passed to nonprofits through bequests constitutes about 7 percent of contributions to nonprofit organizations, a tripling of bequest giving would increase overall giving by about 14 percent.

Closely held businesses. Murphy and Schervish (1995) report that 42 percent of the wealthiest 1 percent of Americans are owners of small businesses. For estate tax returns filed in 1995, about 10 percent of gross assets were in the categories of farm assets, closely held stock, limited partnerships, and other noncorporate businesses (Eller, 1997). Businesses are likely to be bequeathed whole, or as whole as tax liabilities allow. Individuals who have most of their asset portfolios tied up in a farm or a business are not likely to make charitable bequests as generously as the wealthy who hold their wealth in more liquid forms. In dollar terms, something like 10 percent of the $7 trillion transfer may not be up for grabs.

Competing bequest options. Among the generations who will contribute to the $7 trillion transfer are the generations that gave birth to the baby boom. The high levels of marriage and parenthood represented in this cohort suggest that many estates will be left to spouses and to children. These competing claims on the bequests of the parents of the baby boom suggest, other things equal, that a smaller proportion of the $7 trillion may find its way into the coffers of charitable organizations.

On average, the rich live longer than the poor, and generations before the parents of the baby boom will still figure prominently in the wealth transfers of the next two decades. In estate tax data for returns filed in 1995, almost half (48 percent) of gross estate value accrued to the estates of decedents aged 80 or older (Eller, 1997). In the year 2000, the population aged 80 years and older will comprise the generations born before 1920. This group includes the parents of the small generations born during the Depression of the 1930s. This is good news for the advocates of nonprofits who have their eye on the $7 trillion transfer: in the early part of the period 2000–2020, a larger-than-average fraction of bequeathable wealth is likely to be in the hands of generations with fewer children to whom they may pass it along.

Communities of participation and "the long civic generation." One determinant of giving that has emerged in survey data is that people who are asked to give are most likely to give. Closer examination shows that not all forms of asking are equally persuasive. Schervish and Havens (1997) find that phone and door-to-door solicitations are associated with lower fractions of income given away. In contrast, being asked by a friend, a business associate, or a member of the clergy is related to larger proportions of income given. These results suggest that the larger people's networks of social and civic engagement, the greater the number of contacts who might elicit donations.

Putnam (1995) documents the unusually high levels of civic participation among generations of Americans born before 1930. The cohort born between 1925 and 1930 is more trusting, more likely to join groups, more likely to vote, and more likely to read newspapers than other cohorts. Cohorts that came before them also had high levels of civic engagement; beginning in 1930, there has been a steady decline in engagement for cohorts born during at least the succeeding 40 years. Because generations born before 1930 are most likely to be involved in groups and in civic life generally, the positive "civic engagement effect" on the proportions of their estates bequeathed to philanthropic causes will be higher than for them than for later generations.

Again, this is good news for the early years of the $7 trillion transfer period. Even as far into the future as 2010, the group aged 80 years and older is born before 1930. In the first half of the twenty-year transfer period, most of the wealth is likely to be in the hands of members of the "civic generations," people who are more likely than others to be engaged with and to care about the facets of life addressed by nonprofit organizations.

Levels of educational attainment. Because information on charitable bequests comes from tax data that do not contain information on the level of educational attainment of the decedent, little is known about the relationship between education and bequest behavior. However, it is clear that annual giving is positively related to education, independent of the effect education has on raising income. If this positive relationship between giving and education applies to bequests, then the steady climb in educational attainment from one generation to the next suggests that bequests over the next decades should include larger proportions of bequeathed wealth designated for charitable causes.

Philanthropy in an Era of Devolution

American philanthropy is not centered on the needs of the poor. Charitable donations and volunteer time have religion as their principal focal point, and only 1 percent of bequests goes directly to human services. Can we expect philanthropy to provide additional resources in support of the poor as government retreats from the notion of entitlement?

Support for human services is broader than the data classification scheme suggests. About 10 percent of religious giving supports human services; adding this to the human services category in the Giving and Volunteering data yields an estimate of roughly 16 percent of charitable donations devoted to human services.[1] If half of the volunteer work classified as "informal" can also be classified as human service–related, then about 16 percent of volunteer time is also devoted to human services. Although only 1 percent of charitable bequests goes to social welfare, 19 percent goes to private foundations, which in turn will devote 15 percent of their spending to human services, yielding an effective rate of support through bequests of about 4 percent. Additionally, it is probable that some donations and volunteering classified as health-related are also serving low-income populations. So, while the human-services category does not dominate any of the three branches of individual philanthropy, it attracts something like one-sixth of the support given through charitable donations and volunteer time. This is a substantial base of support.

Religious congregations are an obvious set of institutions that can play a part in mobilizing increased resources for human services, should conditions deteriorate for low-income households. Foundations are also well positioned to respond to moments of increased need. If the volume of wealth transferred via bequests swells in the coming decades, foundations will have the option of devoting their share of these bequests to social welfare without cutting back in other areas of commitment.

In the absence of extraordinary institutional initiative, it is unlikely that private philanthropy will come close to replacing the dollars withdrawn from federal income-support programs. Economic studies of the rates at which individual philanthropy steps in to offset cuts in public funding often find only a few cents' increase in donations for every dollar of reduced funding, with high-end estimates in the neighborhood of a 30-percent replacement rate (see for example Steinberg, 1995).

From Tocqueville's reflections on England's poor laws through the National Commission on Philanthropy and Civic Renewal's commentary on America in the 1990s, it has been observed that private philanthropy establishes a distinctly different relationship to the needy from that of government. For better and for worse, private charity can discriminate among worthy and unworthy cases, and can mix religion and other moral stances into the aid package. And as low-income groups continue to grow in political sophistication and power, there is likely to evolve to serve them a cadre of low-dollar-cost, volunteer-intensive grassroots agendas that are far less dependent on cash than were the government programs that used to address their communities' needs. This means that we should not expect philanthropy to fill government's shoes, replacing the safety net when government withdraws it. Philanthropy has its own shoes, and they are likely to be powered by a different mix of cash and local initiative, with less interest in seamless safety nets, than were the federal programs now in retreat.

Most Americans are actively philanthropic, volunteering their time and/or giving their money to charitable organizations. Religion is the area of giving that is central to the philanthropy of most people, but it does not dominate the giving of the rich, who favor medical and education-centered opportunities for giving. Charity toward the poor is part of the mix but it is not the principal focus of the rich or of the non-rich, of charitable donations or of time volunteered or bequests.

Today's elderly Americans are as a group accumulating more wealth, possibly on the order of several trillion dollars more, than they are likely to consume. The next two decades will be a time in which many of the elderly and their beneficiaries will have the resources to respond to philanthropic opportunities.

Whether or not individual philanthropy will respond dramatically to changes in government spending patterns is likely to depend on the behavior of institutions that lie outside the scope of this study. A large number of studies by economists have found that individuals, when left to their own devices, respond only modestly to offset changes in levels of government spending. Given the current patterns and purposes of individual giving, it seems reasonable to speculate that substantial increases in the volume of philanthropy aimed at human services and social welfare are most likely if there is an institutional response to demonstrated need. Institutions that are well positioned to call forth increased individual philanthropy and to translate it into charity toward the poor include religious organizations, which can mobilize their congregations, and foundations, many of which can exercise some fungibility of funding across areas of need.

The federal government is also an institution whose policies affect individual philanthropy. Most financial philanthropy comes from high-income households whose giving is especially sensitive to tax policies. Charitable donations and bequests have been found to respond, respectively, to income tax rates and to rates of estate taxation. Higher tax rates at the margin shift to the government more of the cost of deductible gifts, and donors respond to these incentives. While few would seriously suggest raising tax rates simply to lower the price of giving, the tax code provides opportunities for influencing the giving behavior of the wealthy. For example, one tax change aimed at stimulating the giving of the wealthy to nonprofit organizations would be loosening the restrictions on the proportion of annual income that can be given away and claimed as a deduction on the income tax. Similarly, changes in the tax rules governing the establishment of private foundations could make it relatively attractive simply to bequeath money to existing nonprofits.

Regardless of how institutions appeal to the generosity of individuals, there is no reason to think the nonprofit sector will pick up where government left off. Locally designed programs will be tailored to local needs and local resources, including volunteers. If history is a guide, many of the aid packages supported by individual philanthropy will contain sizeable doses of morality and expectations for the behavior of their beneficiaries.

Note

1. Data from *Giving USA*, which are less dominated by low- and middle-income households who are proportionately more interested in human services and religion than are the rich, generate a smaller estimate of about 13 percent.

References

Andreoni, J., Gale, W., and Scholz, "Charitable Contributions of Time and Money," manuscript, 1995.

Auerbach, A. "The Annuitization of Americans' Resources: A Cohort Analysis," National Bureau of Economic Research, Working paper no. 5089, 1995.

Auten, G., Clotfelter, C., and Schmalbeck, R. "Taxes and Philanthropy among the Wealthy," manuscript, 1997.

Auten, G., Rudney, G. "The Variability of Individual Charitable Giving in the US," *Voluntas* 1990, 1 (2), 80–97.

Avery, R. "The Pending Intergenerational Transfer," *Philanthropy*, Winter 1994, pp. 5, 28, 29.

Avery, R., and Rendall, M. "Estimating the Size and Distribution of Baby Boomers' Prospective Inheritances," *Proceedings of the Social Statistics Section*, American Statistical Association, 1993, pp. 11–19.

Barrett, K., McGuirk, A., and Steinberg, R. "Further Evidence on the Dynamic Impact of Taxes on Charitable Giving," manuscript, 1995.

Bernheim, B. D., Shleifer, A., and Summers, L. "The Strategic Bequest Motive," *Journal of Political Economy*, December 1985, 1045–1076.

Bremner, R. *American Philanthropy*, 2nd edition. Chicago: University of Chicago Press, 1988.

Brown, E. "Assessing the Value of Volunteer Activity," manuscript, 1997a.

———. "Taxes and Charitable Giving: Is There a New Conventional Wisdom?" *1996 Proceedings of the 89th Annual Conference of the National Tax Association*, 1997b, 153–159.

———, and Lankford, H. "Gifts of Money and Gifts of Time: Estimating the Effect of Tax Prices and Available Time," *Journal of Public Economics*, April 1992, 321–341.

Clotfelter, C. "The Impact of Tax Reform on Charitable Giving: A 1989 Perspective," in Joel Slemrod, ed., *Do Taxes Matter? The Impact of the Tax Reform Act of 1986*. Cambridge: MIT Press, 1990, 203–235.

Eller, M. "Federal Taxation of Wealth Transfers, 1992–1995," *Statistics of Income Bulletin*, Winter 1996–97, pp. 8–23.

General Social Surveys, 1972–1996: Cumulative Codebook. Chicago: National Opinion Research Center, 1996.

Giving USA 1997. New York: AAFRC Trust for Philanthropy, 1997.

Hall, P. D. "A History of Leadership Education in the United States," P. Schervish, V. Hodgkinson, M. Gates, and Associates, eds., *Care and Community in Modern Society*. San Francisco: Jossey-Bass, 1995, 193–225.

Health and Retirement Survey, wave I, 1995. Website www.umich.edu/~hrswww.

Hodgkinson, V. "Key Factors Influencing Caring, Involvement, and Community," in P. Schervish, V. Hodgkinson, M. Gates, and Associates, eds., *Care and Community in Modern Society*. San Francisco: Jossey-Bass, 1995, 21–50.

Hodgkinson, V., and Weitzman, M. *Giving and Volunteering in the United States* Washington, DC: Independent Sector, 1996.

Hurd, M. "Savings of the Elderly and Desired Bequests," *American Economic Review*, June 1987, 298–312.

Joulfaian, D. 1991. "Charitable Bequests and Estate Taxes," *National Tax Journal*, June 1991, 169–180.

Menchik, P., and Weisbrod, B. "Volunteer Labor Supply," *Journal of Public Economics*, 1987, 32, 159–183.

Murphy, T., and Schervish, P. "The Dynamics of Wealth Transfer: Behavioral Implications of Tax Policy for the $10 Trillion Transfer," manuscript, 1995.

Randolph, W. "Dynamic Income, Progressive Taxes, and the Timing on Charitable Contributions," *Journal of Political Economy*, August 1995, 709–738.

Reynolds, A. "Will Future Bequests Ensure Ample Funds for Private Charities?" in J. Barry and B. Manno, eds., *Giving Better, Giving Smarter: Working Papers of the National Commission on Philanthropy and Civic Renewal*. Washington: National Commission on Philanthropy and Civic Renewal, 1997, 73–83.

Schervish, P., and Havens, J. "Embarking on a Republic of Benevolence," manuscript dated October 24, 1997a.

——. "Social Participation and Charitable Giving: a Multivariate Analysis," forthcoming in *Voluntas*, September 1997b.

Steinberg, R. "What the Numbers Say," *Advancing Philanthropy*, Summer 1995, 26–31.

CHAPTER ELEVEN

Communities, Networks, and the Future of Philanthropy

Julian Wolpert

Why analyze communities, networks, and the future of philanthropy? Communities no doubt need strengthening. Philanthropy plus charity and volunteerism, with their annual contributions of $150 billion and millions of hours of volunteer labor, certainly do contribute to communities and their networks and can probably do an even better job in the future. Why then do these apparent truisms carry so much baggage and lie at the tip of a highly controversial debate that has been filling academic journals, the organs of think tanks, as well as the popular press?

The issues, their implications, and the arguments of advocates can only be sifted in general terms in this essay, but many questions remain. The diagnoses of community deficiencies touch upon deeply felt ideologies and values and the proposed remedies have strong distributional consequences, partisans, and advocates. My concern here is focused on the issue of how well American communities, aided by philanthropy, can and will take care of their own. Fortunately, much of the discussion can be organized under a few themes: the societal concerns that are amenable to solution at the community level; the capacity of current community resources of social capital and infrastructure to sustain safety nets and to enrich variety and quality of life; the extent of disparities in these resources between and within communities; the ability to mobilize resources and the consensus for targeting them to high priority purposes; and the additional responsibility for local communities attributable to federal cutbacks and devolution.

The Community and Philanthropy Contexts

Let's look at the terms and their current baggage. The "community" context refers here to the social structures and social networks of local places but can refer to tiers in a continuum from neighborhood to a metropolitan region. Community suggests localism, neighborhood of residence, affiliation group, partisanship, ethnicity, and the "village that it takes to raise a child." In the language of Becker, Coleman, and Putnam, viable communities have social capital, social infrastructure, deeply interlocked social networks, and civic engagement.[1] They yield the side benefit of social income to their residents through their own well-being and that of others in their social environment. Deficiencies in social capital and network structure below some threshold level are presumably accompanied by negative spillover effects for individuals and households including cultures of dependency, delinquency, and other forms of social pathology.

The Community as a Resource

The community context is significant because of America's tradition of home-rule and the recent antigovernment national shift favoring local control. Localism implies targeting the community as the unit in our national civil society expected to take on the burden of fostering engagement and solving social issues. Extreme advocates of localism prefer a locally based society of distinct supportive communities and a nation comprised of many such communities, rather than a national community.[2]

Before seizing upon the community (or the neighborhood) as the unit which is broken and the panacea for fixing what ails society, a number of thorny questions arise for which we have no adequate answers or even good data. Is community decline irreversible, i.e., are community resources of social capital irreplaceable once lost? What does it mean to strengthen a community? Should the assessment of strong and weak communities be based solely on levels of social pathology or do some positive indicators provide clues about ideal communities? How do those in strong communities assist their weaker members and those in other communities? How do we evaluate networks, levels of engagement, and civic participation for their impacts on community life and their residents? What is the role then of individual self-reliance, families, and government and what is philanthropy's niche in enhancing individual and community well-being?

Philanthropic Investment in Community Social Capital

The phraseology and metrics of philanthropy are equally imprecise. Philanthropy generally refers to efforts to help mankind through investments in social infrastructure (i.e., support of educational, cultural, health, and human service institutions and their programs.) On the other hand, charity is more explicitly redistributory, referring to gifts or volunteer labor targeted directly (or through agency intermediaries) to the needy. Generosity is a more general and inclusive term that refers to efforts directed at improving the quality and variety of life for all members of society, including oneself.

Presumably, philanthropy, charity, and volunteerism can help provide, as partners to government and the private sector, the infusion of social capital, infrastructure, and donated labor to help sustain viable communities or compensate for the deficits (Salamon, 1995). Philanthropic assistance can help reduce "transaction costs" in communities by building trust and a spirit of reciprocity and cooperative effort. These expectations seem reasonable and may even be effective for many types of communities and neighborhoods. But, why should philanthropy give higher priority to communities, rather than pervasive national problems? Why should communities be viewed as curative for deficiencies that often are more general and national in scope? Do nations get strengthened one community at a time? Is a bottom-up approach better than one which is top-down? Doesn't it also take a nation to raise a child? Then, do individuals and families enhance communities through their generosity, or the reverse, or does the mechanism work in both directions?

Local or National Communities

Consider if generosity were more directed at a national rather than the local level, could it strengthen the nation as well as its communities and families? Would it be better to have an integrated country with shared responsibility for needs wherever they occur? Conservatives say this has already been tried and found wanting (National Commission, 1997). They point to the destructive effect of federal entitlements that do not build self-sufficiency or self-reliance.

Can an agenda for social justice be pursued effectively through voluntary associations, the private sector, and government solely at local levels? If soup kitchens in Boise, Los Angeles, or New York run out of food with hundreds still hungry, who is responsible—the nation or the local community? If Omaha lacks an elite amenity, like a ballet company of its own, how should it be provided, if at all? Should generosity focus on structural issues in our national society and defer to government the responsibility for safety nets and essential services? Alternatively, should philanthropy confine its attention to local charitable efforts and civic amenities and remove itself from issues of broad social change? Is philanthropy merely a "nice to have" supplement that enhances the well-being of only certain kinds of communities or is a larger role to be encouraged?

Philanthropy as Enlightened Self-Interest

Therein lies the controversy. Generosity has traditionally had a highly localized structure dedicated largely to churches and other nonprofit service organizations used by contributors, their families, and neighbors. The preferred targets of philanthropic donations become de facto subsidized channels of public sector support through tax deductions. Can philanthropy, charity, and volunteerism transcend purely local efforts? Some small portion already does, but the overwhelming share of grants, contributions, and volunteer efforts takes place in the community of residence where donors and their families can benefit directly or indirectly from the services and still get a tax deduction (Wolpert, 1993).

If donors absorb the benefits of their generosity in their own immediate area, why then do our communities still need strengthening? Is generosity insufficient, badly targeted, or crowded out by government? How can donations and volunteer time be increased and better allocated? Should they be increased and at what cost to tax payments? Could as much money be raised if the targets and impacts were more distant and less visible, if the beneficiaries were less like us, and if the funds were spent in a manner that might displease us? Would a tax deduction for donations even exist if the contributions had to be dedicated solely for truly charitable purposes?

These questions are the iceberg that underlies the simple truisms about the potential contribution of generosity to our communities. These questions have long been debated in academic journals because they touch upon fundamental theoretical concerns. But prompted by the renewed emphasis on self-reliance, family values, and localism, the debates have also prominently entered Congress, think tanks, and the popular press over the past several years with simplifications, wishful thinking, and distortions that have not been illuminating.

Preferences, Flaws, and Remedies

Underlying the debates about community and philanthropy are some fundamental notions of personal welfare that reflect Americans' preferences for community life and the means of expressing civic responsibility through philanthropy as well as government at national or local levels (Wolpert, 1996). When examined collectively for a nation of communities, these personal welfare preferences have certain fundamental flaws that ignore other societal imperatives. The proposed remedies for these flaws differ along the political continuum from conservative to progressive, but virtually all lack rigorous demonstration and evaluation. The evidence to be presented suggests little prospect of substantial change in philanthropy's community role.

Community Preferences

Americans' personal vision of community includes preferences such as:

• residence in communities with similar kinds of people and tastes for amenities and with people who are self-reliant but occasionally need help to cope with crises;

• donor control and targeting over charitable contributions;

• autonomy of the philanthropic sector from government control but minimal meddling by philanthropists with public policy issues; and

• a home-rule perspective on government that equates taxes paid with services demanded and received.

Flaws

These principles of ideal communities have a number of flaws, including:

• residence in socially homogeneous communities separates the affluent from the needy, those able to provide help from those requiring aid;

• reliance on local social capital does not allow for remedies that require assistance from outside one's community;

• donor targeting of contributions and volunteer labor that is ultimately self-serving and leaves inadequate provision for truly charitable assistance;

• contributions that may be adequate to support services and amenities that users demand, but does not assist the needy;

• poorer communities that are more affected by federal cutbacks and devolution than affluent communities;

• donor fatigue that arises when need for assistance is prolonged;

• the widening of community social and economic disparities; and

• philanthropy leaders who tend to be overly "gun shy" about advocacy efforts and lobbying for social change.

Conservative Remedies

The conservative remedies tend to favor:

• strengthening of communities to help them take care of their own;

• charities that are more charitable and less concerned with social change;

• a "tough love" and often faith-based approach by community volunteers targeting assistance to truly needy to promote self-reliance;

• elimination or cutbacks in government and charitable efforts that encourage dependency;

• other efforts based on the view that locals have a better sense of what's needed than the federal government; that virtually all societal problems are best addressed at the community level; that local resources are sufficient to provide the aid and services that are needed; and that local civic pride and market mechanisms are reliable forces that ensure a decent community quality of life.

Progressive Remedies

The progressive remedies tend to favor:

- greater social integration of communities;
- reliance on higher tiers of government to ensure safety nets and essential services supported by progressive taxation of income;
- a professional and secular approach to provision of services;
- an independent but junior partner role for philanthropy that fosters progressive social change through advocacy and funding of demonstration programs; a supplementary role for philanthropy relegated to maintaining an independent voice for social change and helping to enrich quality of life.

This highly abstracted listing of preferences, flaws, and advocates' remedies illustrates the challenges and limitations that constrain philanthropy's current niche and future role. Philanthropy can neither fulfill the agenda of conservatives by becoming the principal agent of social renewal nor satisfy progressives who want courageous advocacy by philanthropy's leaders on behalf of structural reforms in private and public sectors. Philanthropy will most likely continue doing precisely what it does now, i.e., a variety of good works that improve community well-being, but do not solve fundamental problems.

Philanthropy's Contribution to Community Life

Some specific facets of philanthropy's potential contributions justify its prominent community role and privileged tax status:

- the prospect that donated funds can make a greater contribution to community life than if collected through income and estate taxes by state and federal government and allocated according to a public sector agenda;
- the autonomy and financial resources of the philanthropic sector that enable it to have an independent and influential voice on civic issues that can be contrary to the agenda of private and government sectors;
- the contributions are targeted to institutions such as churches, universities, and museums which can help make us better people, more compassionate, more educated, and more cultured;
- the donations are investments which can have multiplier effects in creating better communities and a better society; and
- targeting of contributions by knowledgeable and independent donors can be preventative, i.e., social insurance against community breakdown that is harmful if neglected in early stages.

The Community Complement of Nonprofit Services

As might be expected, more is likely to be accomplished when and where philanthropy, charity, and volunteerism are plentiful than where they are scarce. The tangible evidence of engagement is apparent in the better equipped museums, private schools, more active churches, public radio stations, family service centers, hospitals, clinics, and other nonprofit organizations supported at least partially by donations and volunteers. The less visible artifacts are the strong networks of volunteers and the positive spillovers of this engagement on these communities. A more complete complement of nonprofit services usually equates to greater community well-being.

Nonprofit organizations are pervasive in virtually every type of American community. Their local presence implies access and availability for community residents and entitlement to the services they provide. Nonprofits can reduce the financial burdens of local governments. They recruit and mobilize residents for collective efforts, train and empower local leaders, contribute to the local economy, pay rent, wages, and wage taxes, employ women and minority members, and their facilities often enhance surrounding property values and tourism. On the other hand, nonprofits could consume their donated revenues largely for administrative costs and salaries, capture government funding better used for direct transfers, and neglect client satisfaction in their provision of service. Board involvement and community vigilance are needed to ensure that funds are well spent, programs are well targeted, and services are effective.

The Evidence about Communities and Generosity

Are generosity and a dense complement of nonprofit organizations causes or symptoms of strong communities and their networks? If they are mutually reinforcing, then which is the best lever for intervening when communities are not functioning adequately? Is it better to employ donations and volunteers to help build community networks and organizations or to use the community's current social capital, however deficient, to encourage greater mutual assistance and volunteerism? The answer depends on the community's resources, capacity, and willingness to give and volunteer and what government provides in transfers and services to local residents. If the community shows evidence of strong networks and engagement but lacks the resources to do more, the needed remedies are likely to be quite different from contexts where needs are profound and community cohesion is largely absent.

Advocates for a more prominent local role for philanthropy and volunteerism argue that critical assistance to fragile communities can salvage and perhaps even enhance the efforts of local churches and other self-help organizations that are the major remaining elements of neighborhood social structure (National Commission, 1997; Schambra, 1997). Support of programs that provide day care, mentoring of young people, tutoring, job placement, employment training, drug counseling, and recreational services can presumably enhance local well-being and simultaneously help to build local networks that can sustain these programs with the community's own resources. This has been a traditional role for philanthropy—why has it not succeeded better?

Community Disparities

The most severe challenge for both liberals and conservatives about philanthropy's role arises from the unequal distribution of needs among America's communities. The evidence shows increasing residential segregation of Americans by income and a significant decline in the number of mixed income neighborhoods and their populations, at least since 1970.[3] The neediest communities are becoming increasingly needy. The separation is also generally reinforced by municipal boundaries which help to delimit external impacts of concentrated poverty on more affluent neighboring communities. However, even those large cities with mixtures of low, moderate, and upper income residents tend to have de facto segregation in parallel communities.

Patterns of Generosity

Can American generosity address the challenge of social and economic disparities between communities? The evidence from a 1990 study of giving rates in America's largest eighty-five metropolitan areas (Wolpert, 1993) showed that, other things being equal, contribution are greater in communities that:

- are more affluent;
- have less local need or social pathology;
- have lower minority representation among the local needy;
- have less income inequality;
- target a larger share of donations to churches and civic amenities; and
- have higher levels of state and local government safety net support.

Distributional Effects of Philanthropy

The relevance of these findings imply that if the benefits from both our donations as well as our public sector services are largely absorbed locally, then:

* little provision is left for truly charitable behavior by either local government or philanthropy;
* donation levels cannot be raised except through additional incentives and concessions to donors;
* local sources of social capital and infrastructure in needier communities are generally insufficient for churches, private schools, social services, hospitals, and arts and cultural facilities;
* the major revenue sources for nonprofits that provide social services, counseling, job training, and community development must come (as they currently do) from federal and state government sources;
* donations are most needed in those communities which lack the resources and where local government hasn't the capacity to assist—and most plentiful where local government and the market can and often does provide substitutes for many of the services now enhanced through donor contributions (i.e., the spatial mismatch problem);
* the potential beneficiaries for truly charitable efforts are remote and can be invisible;
* charitable donors in "surplus" communities would need to "export" their gifts outside their own communities and volunteers would have to commute to the deficit places; but
* tax deductions for charitable giving would probably not exist at all if the privilege were reserved only for truly charitable purposes (i.e., some leakage is an essential part of transfer policies).

The Freedom to Give

The right to give also implies "freedom to give" and the opportunity for selective targeting. The converse implies the right "not to give" despite indications of need or to withdraw support when donors disapprove of the way funds are spent. The choices available to benefactors make philanthropy and volunteerism a very leaky redistributive mechanism. Becker's extension by analogy from family benevolence to community generosity has limited applicability in such contexts (Becker, 1974). Potential donors tend to be members of different families and communities than those needing assistance. Unlike the family unit whose contractual obligations are specified by law, relations within communities and obligations to other communities have no regulations but only good will to bind their members. It is difficult to build a case that philanthropy and volunteerism are more efficient and equitable agents of redistribution than progressive taxation. In fact, the insufficiency and "misallocations" of philanthropy in the nineteenth century provided the stimulus for liberals' support of coercive public provision of collective goods (Katz, 1989).

The Asymmetry of Philanthropy and Volunteerism

Donors and volunteers like to feel they are not just contributors but the instrumental *cause* of benefits. The evidence from numerous studies of inner cities and rural communities shows, however, that needs are frequently so profound that donors or volunteers cannot by themselves bring about solutions. Sustained assistance is needed rather than token gifts and good deeds. Furthermore, the asymmetry of the relation between donors and recipients tends to validate the superior status, moral stance, and rectitude of contributors and volunteers. The hazard here is the prospect of using philanthropy and volunteerism in a paternal fashion to enforce conformity to the social values and moral norms of donors. Donors are unlikely to permit recipients to specify the magnitude and form of the assistance they need. This is the traditional mediating role for professional caregivers who help determine which forms of interventions are most helpful.

The motivation for generosity in affluent and middle-income communities is pursuit of "enlightened self-interest." The community is more likely to feel like an extension of the family in socially homogeneous communities. In Becker's terms, donors exchange personal income and volunteer time for social income. If Americans increasingly segregate themselves by community and jurisdiction, then the need for local charity becomes obviated, but there is still ample scope for enhancing the quality and variety of life. Since donations depend more on income and wealth than need, opportunities can readily be found to absorb the contributions and volunteer labor. Affluent communities can probably benefit from community strengthening and can easily absorb additional amenities provided through donations. The same tax deduction applies whether one contributes to an already well endowed local arts and cultural center or to the Salvation Army or Catholic Charities which sponsor homeless shelters and food kitchens in a neighboring community.

Presumably, most of the attention recently devoted by conservatives to community building is targeted not to gaps in affluent communities or even middle and working class suburban communities but to problematic inner city neighborhoods of concentrated poverty that are especially vulnerable to safety net cuts. Here, the debates by conservatives and liberals are most strident and likely to become even more so in the next year or two when the time limits on welfare eligibility and the further withdrawal of food stamp aid have had their full effects.

Contribution levels and their targeting necessarily make philanthropy only a minor partner in alleviating immediate needs for food and shelter (Ostrander, 1989). The financial and technical support needed to rebuild substandard housing, create jobs, and provide job referral and day care services in all the communities requiring such efforts exceeds what can be expected from national or local philanthropy and volunteers. In communities where philanthropy is more active, donations and volunteers can support a few demonstration programs, requiring substantial public sector funding to follow through on promising services that prove to be effective. Barring a sudden miracle in Colin Powell's America's Promise and similar campaigns to attract mentors and other volunteers to assist needy communities, their residents must rely primarily on their own inadequate social capital or public sector programs to effect change.

Faith-based Efforts

What is the potential of voluntary action that is rooted in faith-based and other forms of social commitment? A great deal, according to some advocates, who note the continuing strength of strong church affiliation in many low income communities. In addition to America's Promise, we now have: Partners for Sacred Places; the Christian Community Development Association; the National Committee on Philanthropy and Civic Renewal; the National Center for Neighborhood Enterprise; the Civil Society Project; Faith and Families; and the Center for Effective Compassion. However, many of these groups are funded largely by conservative foundations who also support fiscal policies that would widen income disparities and reduce federal government expenditures for poverty programs.

Faith-based groups have provided in their pronouncements only anecdotal and undocumented descriptions of success stories in a few communities. The report of the National Commission on Philanthropy and Civic Renewal, for example, cites several community-based programs that are "unconventional (when compared to government programs) and effective." The descriptions contain no admissions of failures, no commitments for substantial financial support, and no designs for operating programs sufficient to address the most serious effects of concentrated poverty, i.e., the need for more and better jobs; more realistic safety net support; and more investment in community development. Faith in Families, for example, was launched by Governor Fordice of Mississippi in early 1995 to enlist religious congregations in helping to move people from welfare to work. Congregations are expected to select eligible families and provide them with counseling, child care, transportation, and help with job interviewing skills. In the program's first two years 82 women were reported to have found jobs and 77 have left the welfare rolls, but Mississippi has 38,000 families on welfare (Castelli, 1997). It is difficult to ignore criticisms from nonprofit leaders that programs like Faith in Families are not fostered by humanitarian concerns; the real motivation is to reduce welfare rolls; even well-intentioned efforts can have modest success at best; and the program efforts are more likely to be diversions from the true agenda of fiscal conservatives, which is to undermine the vision of a national community (see Harvey, 1997; Kaminer, 1997; and Castelli, 1997). Nonprofit spokesmen argue that prudence and concern for the most vulnerable segment of our society would imply that safety nets not be dismantled purely on the basis of vague promises from advocates who assume no responsibility to help restore federal entitlements if their efforts fail.

In contrast to the hyperactivity of conservative groups, liberals have no apparent national or local agenda except to try to counter some of the most severe steps in the dismantling of the national welfare state. Liberal communities, having decades ago surrendered reponsibility for safety nets to federal and state government, use philanthropy primarily to augment variety and quality of life in their own communities. Neither is there anything equivalent to the armies of volunteers enlisted in the civil rights and anti-poverty campaigns of the 1960s.

Nonprofits in Philadelphia's Center City and Suburbs: A Vignette

Philadelphia, the sixth largest metropolitan area, has benefited little from the recent national upsurge in jobs. Its center city has lost 100,000 jobs in the past decade and the welfare load is the fourth largest in the nation. More than 25,000 welfare recipients are likely still to be jobless when the welfare reform deadline is reached. Many of its center city neighborhoods score badly on all the social and economic indicators of distress and continue to experience economic disinvestment. Cutbacks in transfer payments and food stamps will have a further multiplier effect on the economy in their communities.

What can philanthropy do to meet these challenges? The Philadelphia metropolitan area includes more than five thousand nonprofit organizations (not including churches) in the arts, education, health and human service categories, of which more than 75 percent are headquartered in the center city. Those nonprofits in low income center city residential neighborhoods are primarily providers of social, health, and employment training services that receive almost all their revenues from government grants and pass-throughs and very little from charitable gifts or grants, even when providers are church related. The revenues from the federal government are targeted for substantial cuts, which may or may not be made up by state and municipal grants. The nonprofit organizations in Philadelphia's affluent suburban neighborhoods receive some donations but are primarily supported by volunteers and user fees. Few Philadelphia suburbanites commute to center city to volunteer.

The Three Faces of Generosity and Parsimony

Philanthropy, mediating organizations, and volunteerism do not alone sustain civil society. The more instrumental impacts arise from private sector and governmental activities. Furthermore, the values, preferences, and networks of potential charitable donors and volunteers are not segmented differently depending on the sector in which they participate. They are the same people who reside in communities and participate in the private market and in government. The range of motivations from pure altruism to entirely self-serving behavior are present in all these arenas and trends in one sector are mirrored by shifts in the others. Philanthropy in America's communities largely parallels the agenda of the national society, the private sector, and local government.

The Corporate Philanthropy Role

Philanthropy cannot undo the harm or compensate for the effects on communities of corporate downsizing or plant closures or for overly generous property tax incentives offered to corporations to forestall their threat to abandon communities with vulnerable labor markets. Corporate philanthropy is generally not sufficient in magnitude nor targeted to the harm to communities caused by disinvestment and relocation decisions.

What can the private market do to strengthen community well-being? Businesses can hire and train community residents who are handicapped or have minimal job skills, pay livable wages and provide adequate employee benefits, assist the retraining of workers affected by plant and office closings, pay local taxes that are at least commensurate with services received, become active advocates for improvements in public schools and community colleges, and apply corporate philanthropy to priorities that communities target.

The Role of Local Government

A community's generosity is also reflected through its local government and the taxes residents are willing to pay for enhanced and redistributive public services. What is the difference in this expression of public-mindedness versus the charitable alternative? The evidence shows that it matters little, because in either case residents are paying for the services and amenities that are demanded and used whether through government or nonprofit providers. The charitable form implies cross-subsidies to enable the less fortunate to consume beneficial services. However, the same is true of local property taxes, i.e., those who pay the same tax rates do not necessarily receive equal use of public schools, libraries, and garbage disposal. The main difference then is the opportunity to be a free-rider on many types of nonprofit services by not contributing or by opting out of cross-subsidies in one's residential community by choosing to live in a place where taxes equate to one's preferences for services.

What can local governments do to express their generosity? They can be more inclusive, make provision for affordable and mixed income housing, encourage state equalization in the financing of public education, etc. These efforts are likely to have much greater long-term impact on strengthening households, families, and communities than charitable donations. Philanthropy cannot undo the harm or compensate for the effects of income and racial segregation. Disinvestment by the private sector and government in low income communities and outmigration of the upwardly mobile tends to erode neighborhood networks, reduce the resources of local donors, and swamp local nonprofit providers with needy clients (Wilson, 1996).

The Challenge for Philanthropy

The long-term evidence on giving patterns would appear to indicate that no dramatic changes are likely to occur in the numbers of volunteers and the level of donations or their targeting, barring major new federal tax legislation affecting charitable deductions. The philanthropic community for the most part is not inclined to alter its current priorities and fulfill a residual role dictated by government's withdrawal from key safety net support. Many leaders in the community have been outspoken about the limited potential of philanthropy to assume greater responsibility for maintaining safety nets and the need to reject the notion that charitable giving and volunteers can or should substitute for publicly supported programs.

What more can philanthropy do to enhance its contribution to community life? Some philanthropies already practice various forms of equal opportunity and affirmative action policies through greater inclusiveness in their allocation committees and funding programs. Many charitable organizations are active advocates and lobbyists for federal protection of the most vulnerable in our society.

The large national foundations can continue to monitor national impacts of devolution and the allocations of block grants by states and localities and help to identify communities that are most adversely affected by cutbacks. They can augment their seed support of innovative programs in: public education; employment training; outreach to medically underserved populations; protection of air and water quality; and community mobilization. They can step up their advocacy and lobbying roles when the evidence points to shortcomings in the federal decentralization and devolution experiment.

The more conservative foundations merit an opportunity to pursue efforts that mobilize faith-based, local organizations to provide compassionate direct services within and across racial and ethnic communities; recruit volunteers and mentors to assist receptive families, households, children, and teenagers; rigorously evaluate the impacts of their programs on communities; and attempt to separate their service agenda of assistance to the needy from their fiscal agenda of tax relief. The experience of sincere donors and volunteers in providing direct service to severely distressed families can provide better clues about what they can and cannot accomplish.

Locally based and community foundations, in addition to the efforts carried on the large national foundations, can learn more about local community needs, listen to local civic leaders about ways to strengthen community well-being, and target larger shares of their grants to needy communities in their midst. Some local philanthropies are already responding to immediate needs for food and shelter in their communities and have reallocated their grant programs. Informed and influential local leaders of philanthropies and nonprofit organizations may be able to broker partnerships with public officials and business groups to augment their own limited efforts and to lobby for greater assistance from state and federal government when local solutions are clearly insufficient.

Philanthropy's future role in communities is almost certain to change little from its current pattern. The ceiling has probably been reached for contributions and volunteerism that cross communities, that are true "gifts" and ask nothing in return in the form of tax incentives or benefits donors themselves can use. Philanthropy's role in middle and upper income communities is assured and need cause little concern. The enormous needs of the lowest income urban and rural communities exceed the capacity of donors and volunteers to address. The current community development demonstration programs funded by national and local foundations have little chance for self-sustainability, attracting government funding, or replication on a nationwide basis. Valuable time is also being lost in encouraging faith-based groups to experiment with piecemeal efforts that have little prospect of offering comprehensive solutions.

The focus on strengthening communities and their networks may be the only game in town now that prospects are dim for federal efforts to create a more equitable national society. In the interim, prominent future roles for philanthropy and charity consist primarily of continuing to perform their traditional roles in enhancing the variety and quality of community life, exercising independent voices on issues requiring public attention, and helping to alleviate the most pressing problems in vulnerable communities.

Notes

1. See Becker (1974), Coleman (1990), and Putnam (1993) for an extended discussion of these concepts.

2. See Schambra (1997) and National Commission on Philanthropy and Civic Renewal (1997).

3. See Abramson (1995), Frey (1995), Frey and Fielding (1995), Jarkowsky (1997) and Case and Katz (1991) for analysis of these trends and their impacts.

References

Abramson, Alan, et al. "The Changing Geography of Metropolitan Opportunity: The Segregation of the Poor in U.S. Metropolitan Areas, 1970 to 1990." *Housing Policy Debate*, 1995, 6 (1), pp. 45–72.

Becker, Gary. S. "A Theory of Social Interactions." *Journal of Political Economy*, 1974, Vol. 82, No. 6, pp. 1063–1083.

Case, Anne C. and Lawrence F. Katz. "The Company You Keep: The Effects of Family and Neighborhood on Disadvantaged Youths." Cambridge, MA: National Bureau of Economic Research, 1991.

Castelli, Jim. "Faith-Based Social Services: A Blessing, Not a Miracle." Progressive Policy Institute, Policy Report No. 27, Washington, DC, 1997.

Coleman, James S. *Foundations of Social Theory*. Cambridge: Harvard University Press, 1990.

Frey, William H. "The New Geography of Population Shifts: Trends Toward Balkanization." In Reynolds Farley, ed. *State of the Union—America in the 1990s*. New York: Russell Sage, 1995.

Frey, William H. and Elaine L. Fielding. "Changing Urban Populations: Regional Restructuring, Racial Polarization, and Poverty Concentration." *Cityscape* 1995, 1(2), pp. 1–66.

Harvey, Thomas J. "Government Promotion of Faith-Based Solutions to Social Problems: Partisan or Prophetic?" The Aspen Institute Nonprofit Research Fund, Washington, DC, 1997.

Hochman, H. M. and J. D. Rodgers. "Utility Interdependence and Income Transfers through Charity." In Kenneth E. Boulding et al., eds., *Transfers in an Urbanized Economy*. Belmont, CA: Wadsworth, 1973.

Jarkowsky, Paul A. *Poverty and Place: Ghettos, Barrios, and the American City*. New York: Russell Sage, 1997.

Kaminer, Wendy. "Unholy Alliance" *American Prospect*. Nov.–Dec., 1997.

Kasarda, John D. "Inner-City Concentrated Poverty and Neighborhood Distress: 1970 to 1990." *Housing Policy Debate*, 1993, 4(3), pp. 253–302.

Katz, Michael. *The Undeserving Poor: From the War on Poverty to the War on Welfare*. New York: Pantheon Books, 1989.

Kramnick, Isaac and R. Laurence Moore. "Can the Churches Save the Cities?" *The American Prospect*, Nov.–Dec., 1997.

Massey, D. S. and N. A. Denton. *American Apartheid: Segregation and the Making of the Underclass*. Cambridge: Harvard University Press, 1993.

National Commission on Philanthropy and Civic Renewal. *Giving Better, Giving Smarter*. Washington, DC, 1997.

Ostrander, Susan. "The Problem of Poverty and Why Philanthropy Neglects It." In Virginia A. Hodgkinson and Richard W. Lyman, eds. *The Future of the Nonprofit Sector*. San Francisco: Jossey-Bass, 1989.

Putnam, Robert D. "The Prosperous Community: Social Capital and Public Life." *The American Prospect*, 1993, no. 31.

Salamon, Lester M. *Partners in Public Service: Government-Nonprofit Relations in the Modern Welfare State*. Baltimore: Johns Hopkins University Press, 1995.

Schambra, William A. "Local Groups Are the Key to America's Civic Renewal." *The Brookings Review*, 1997, Fall 1997, pp. 20–22.

Smith, Steven Rathgeb and Michael Lipsky. *Nonprofits for Hire: The Welfare State in the Age of Contracting.* Cambridge, MA: Harvard University Press, 1993.

Wilson, Julius. *The Truly Disadvantaged.* Chicago: University of Chicago Press, 1987.

Wilson, Julius. *When Work Disappears: The World of the New Urban Poor.* Cambridge: Harvard University Press, 1996.

Wolpert, Julian. "Social Income and the Voluntary Sector," *Papers*, 1977. Regional Science Association, Vol. 39, pp. 217–229.

Wolpert, Julian. *Patterns of Generosity in America: Who's Holding The Safety Net?* New York: Twentieth Century Fund, 1993.

Wolpert, Julian. *What Charity Can and Cannot Do.* New York: Twentieth Century Fund, 1996.

CHAPTER TWELVE

The Roles of Indigenous and Institutional Philanthropy in Advancing Social Justice

Emmett D. Carson

Creating a nation in which all citizens are treated equitably and have uniform access to opportunities based on their skills and talents continues to be America's unrealized dream. Despite the Constitution's strong references to equality and the addition of several amendments that explicitly guarantee equal access and participation to all citizens, significant disparities based on race and gender continue to exist in the areas of employment, housing, and wages. It is an unfortunate reality that it has often fallen to those groups who have borne the burden of societal indifference and legalized injustice, and who often have the least resources to provide for their basic human needs, to also be the catalysts for social justice. Philanthropy has played a complex role in promoting social justice issues. As our society and its institutions confront both old and new forms of social injustice, it is imperative to develop a better understanding of the relationship between the indigenous philanthropy of culture-specific groups and the institutional philanthropy of foundations in promoting social justice. Social justice is used here to include both the provision of basic human services and social justice advocacy efforts to promote human equality.

There is a widespread belief that foundations are a major source for venture capital to test new and often controversial ideas. If these ideas are proven to be successful, they are adopted by the government, business, or nonprofit sector to replace or augment existing practices. As Robert Bremner observes in his classic work, *American Philanthropy*:

> We are all indebted to philanthropic reformers who have called attention to and agitated for abatement of the barbarities inflicted by society on its weaker

members. We are all, in some degree, beneficiaries of philanthropy whenever we attend church, go to college, visit museums or concert halls, draw books from libraries, obtain treatment in hospitals, or spend leisure hours in parks. . . . We continue to rely on philanthropy for support of scientific research, for experimentation in the field of social relations, and for diffusion of knowledge in all branches of learning.[1]

While there are numerous examples of the innovative leadership provided by foundations to support the development of hospitals, libraries, education, arts and culture, and scientific research, foundations have not shown the same level of risk-tolerance in the area of social justice advocacy.[2] This is not to suggest that foundations have been indifferent to issues of social equality but rather that they are more sensitive to prevailing public opinion before deciding to provide support for a given social justice effort, especially when it involves social advocacy. One measure of foundations' support of social justice causes is the amount of money that is directed to assist the specific needs of racial and ethnic groups or for social justice advocacy.

Foundations have focused only a small amount of their total grant monies on programs directed at helping people of color or on advocacy-related social justice activities. It is an important caveat that the statistics below do not account for foundation support of programs focused on disadvantaged people that may disproportionately help a particular racial or ethnic group. Based on data from the Foundation Center, in 1995 foundations collectively awarded $12.3 billion in grants. An examination of the grantmaking by the larger foundations in 1996 indicates that all non-white racial/ethnic minority groups received $674.4 million (9.3 percent); immigrants and refugees received $48.7 million (0.7 percent); women and girls received $417 million (5.7 percent); and civil rights and social action causes received $81.6 million (1.1 percent).[3] While these statistics likely understate the total level of foundation support for the aforementioned groups and causes, they do reveal that the interests of racial and ethnic groups are not high priority areas for most foundations. Notwithstanding the total contributions of foundations, they pale in comparison to the contributions made by individuals. *Giving USA* estimates that of the $143.8 billion contributed in 1995, 88 percent ($126 billion) came directly from individuals. By contrast, foundations were estimated to have contributed 7 percent ($10 billion).[4]

The purpose of this chapter is to examine the interplay between the indigenous philanthropy of selected culture-specific groups and the institutional philanthropy of foundations to advance and sustain social justice activities. The term culture-specific group is used to refer to groups of people who have in common immutable characteristics such as race, ethnicity, language, and gender, and a shared history due to these characteristics. Indigenous philanthropy describes the collective efforts of culture-specific groups to pool their financial and volunteer resources to address group concerns. Institutional philanthropy refers to foundations created by wealthy philanthropists. As individual members of various culture-specific groups become wealthy, they have also established foundations. However, unlike their counterparts, the foundations created by individuals whose culture-specific group has experienced social injustice appear more willing to support social justice issues.

The thesis that emerges from this analysis is that in the area of social justice, the indigenous philanthropy of culture-specific groups and institutional philanthropy engage in a tug of war to influence each other's grant-making priorities as well as the attitudes of the broader public. It appears that progress on social justice is most likely to occur when foundations support the social justice efforts initiated by culture-specific groups after they have gained sufficient public support. Stated differently, it is only when culture-specific groups pursue their social justice agendas long enough and publicly enough to have them become acceptable to the broader public that foundations appear to become willing to support their activities.

This essay is divided into seven sections which describe how culture-specific groups—Native Americans, early immigrants, African Americans, Asian Americans, Latino Americans, and women—have utilized their indigenous philanthropy to support social justice activities in conjunction with and, at times, in opposition to the institutional philanthropy of foundations. The last section concludes with several observations about the implications of this analysis for supporting current and future social justice efforts. The consistent picture that emerges is that each culture-specific group has relied on its indigenous philanthropy to provide, first, basic human services—food, clothing, and shelter—and later, to challenge the larger systemic social injustices confronted by their communities that have, in part, created the need to provide group members with basic necessities. In conditions of severe social inequity, the mere act of survival through the provision of basic needs, especially in earlier times, can be seen as an act of social justice advocacy. Remarkably, nearly every group's earliest efforts began by relying on some form of mutual aid or revolving credit organization to support these dual social justice activities.

Several of the groups have moved through complete cycles of evolving social justice priorities in which they achieved their initial objectives by influencing public opinion and gaining foundation support. This allows the group to redirect part of its indigenous philanthropy to support the next level of social justice activities. For example, American society and the African American community shifted from a belief in separate but equal public accommodations to a belief that separate could never be equal. Such societal shifts in thinking affect the priorities of both indigenous and institutional philanthropy. Some culture-specific groups, despite having a substantial history in the United States, have yet to see elements of their social justice agenda accepted by the broader society or foundations. It also seems clear that the indigenous philanthropy of African Americans has, at times, served as an important model for the indigenous philanthropy of other culture-specific groups.

It is important to note that there are several significant limitations to this analysis. Each group profiled has had a long and unique history in the United States that is integral to understanding the character and focus of their indigenous philanthropy. Another issue is that within each broad culture-specific category, e.g., Asian Americans, there are major subgroups with different views and beliefs, e.g., Japanese, Chinese, Vietnamese, etc., as well as multiple viewpoints and ideas within each subgroup. Unfortunately, these histories cannot be adequately examined within this document. Another concern is that there are over 38,000 foundations in the United States. The priorities of each of these institutions are different, and it is probable that important examples of foundation action and inaction on social justice issues have been overlooked. Therefore, all of the generalizations that are made about a shared view within a particular culture-specific group or among foundations are subject to challenge. Yet another concern is the overall lack of research on the philanthropic traditions of various cultural groups or case study research on how and why foundations selected specific priorities related to a particular cultural community or social justice issue. These limitations should be kept in mind in reviewing how the indigenous philanthropy of culture-specific groups and institutional philanthropy have helped to shape social justice issues over time.

Native American Philanthropy

Philanthropy by Native Americans began long before there was a United States. Helping and generously assisting others has been an important feature of Native American culture and has been embedded into American tradition through the national Thanksgiving holiday. Perhaps one of the most unfortunate misinterpretations of indigenous philanthropy in the Native American community is that the term "Indian giver" has been distorted from its original purpose — to epitomize an individual willing to give all his or her belongings away (known as *potlatch* to many tribes), so much so that people returned items — to represent someone who gave things away only to ask for them back.[5] After Europeans arrived in the New World, the lives of Native Americans were inalterably changed and there was considerable concern among various Native American nations and tribes for the fate of their people. Early treaties between Native Americans and various European countries, and later states, included provisions for funds for Native Americans. Early benefactors of schools such as Dartmouth, Harvard, and Yale gave their charitable contributions on the condition that part of it would be used to provide education to Native Americans.[6] Nothing ever came of these promises. Such has been the pattern of broken promises encountered by Native

Americans in their relationships with the U.S. government as well as business and nonprofit institutions.

An early aim of the U.S. government and individual philanthropists was to "civilize" Native Americans through Christian education during what has been termed the "Missionary Era" by scholars of Indian philanthropy. The Civilization Fund was established by Congress in 1819 to support church groups' efforts to make Native Americans "good Christians." By the late 1800s, American philanthropists who were interested in Native Americans were engaged in selecting young men to leave their reservations to be educated in the East. Often, the young men selected were those with whom the philanthropists felt most comfortable and who they believed were the least inclined to retain their traditional customs. However horrible and misguided the practice of taking young men from their tribes and sending them east to boarding schools such as the Carlisle Indian School may seem today, in the context of that time period it was viewed as a legitimate way to transition Native Americans into the dominant Euro-American culture.[7] It is worth noting that the Canadian government, which had similar practices of separating children from their families to attend residential schools, recently offered a formal apology to its indigenous peoples and established a "healing fund" of $245 million.[8]

Clearly the first "pan-Indian" movement in the country, the Society of American Indians, founded in 1911, involved many of the young men who earlier had been removed from their reservations to be educated in boarding schools. The Society was active in attempting to implement many of the recommendations of the Meriam Report, issued in 1928 by the Bureau of Indian Affairs, which called for radical reform of Native American schools and hospitals. The Society's focus, consistent with the beliefs of the benefactors who had befriended many of the members as youth, was on helping other Native Americans to assimilate into and gain larger acceptance by the larger society.[9]

In the 1940s two groups were formed to address concerns over Native American land allotment. The National Congress of Native Americans was founded primarily by Native Americans to try to advocate for a fair apportioning of Native American lands and to determine the effect that the Eisenhower policy of termination was having on Native American tribes. The termination policy refers to Congressional legislation that "terminated" the legal existence of several tribes, mainly in the Northwest. The tribes' land was sold—mostly to the timber industry—at very low prices. The profits were divided among the tribe members and the tribe was then considered "terminated."[10] The Association of American Indian Affairs, which was founded by mostly non-Indian benefactors, also focused its efforts on land allotment and U.S. policy toward Native Americans.[11]

The 1960s and the Civil Rights movement helped to inspire a new wave of social justice efforts supported by the indigenous philanthropy of Native

Americans. In 1961, the Fund for the Republic sponsored a meeting of over 500 Native Americans at the University of Chicago to produce a "Declaration of Indian Purpose." From this meeting, the National Indian Youth Council was formed. The Council would develop into one of the most radical voices of the Native American rights movement. In 1968, the American Indian Movement (AIM) was formed to serve as a civil rights organization and to respond to police brutality against Native Americans. These groups began a general call for Native American rights that evolved into calls for greater public recognition of tribal rights and sovereignty.[12]

By 1965, the Ford Foundation, among others, was actively supporting demonstration projects on reservations by funding the Indian-controlled school movement. Some foundations began to accept Native American requests for programs that had as key aspects community involvement, tribal responsibility, and respect for Native American languages and cultures.[13] Recall that 150 years earlier, the accepted societal perspective had been to assimilate and eliminate Native American culture. The advocacy efforts of Native American organizations supported by their indigenous philanthropy contributed significantly to altering perspectives about the importance and value of Native American culture.

By the 1970s, several institutional philanthropies such as the Ford Foundation and the Robert Wood Johnson Foundation were regularly supporting Native American causes—for example, the Native American Rights Fund (NARF), supported by the Ford Foundation, and the Council for Energy Resource Tribes, supported by the Atlantic-Richfield Company (ARCO). During this time, it appears that foundations shifted away from support of community-specific demonstration projects on reservations. By the 1980s, foundations began to reduce funding for Native American–controlled institutions, perhaps due to concerns about the growing militancy of groups such as AIM as well as changing grantmaking priorities.[14]

In 1988, the American Indian College Fund was established by tribal college presidents (similar to the United Negro College Fund, started in 1944) to help tribal colleges present a united front in their fundraising and to foster public education about tribal colleges.[15] Community supported groups like the Eagle Staff Fund Collaborative, the Brown Beacon Project, the Michigan Native American Foundation, and the Cook Inlet Region Inc. were all created in the 1990s and are working to meet tribal needs, promote education, career development, and awareness of tribal heritage, and to bridge gaps in understanding between tribes and their neighboring non-Indian communities. The Eagle Staff Fund Collaborative is also working on improving relations between the foundation world and Native Americans. Another effort is a project by the Native American Rights Fund to create an endowment to support American Indian causes around the country.

Revenues generated from casino gambling represent another promising development in Native American philanthropy. The Mashantucket Pequot

Tribe of Massachusetts, for example, contributed $10 million to the National Museum of the American Indian in 1993.[16] It should also be noted that Indian-run casinos that often have sovereignty status have no legal or moral mandate to contribute any of their revenues for charitable purposes.[17] Notwithstanding the future potential of these efforts, foundation support for Native American projects and organizations remains limited. Support for Native American projects by the largest foundations in the United States in 1996 accounted for just 0.9 percent ($65 million) of all grants awarded.[18]

Early European Immigrant Philanthropy

During the nineteenth century and beginning of the twentieth, European immigrants poured into the United States. Between 1830 and 1850, there was a huge influx of Irish immigrants, and between 1890 and 1930, immigrants from southern and eastern Europe streamed through such famous gateways to America as Ellis Island. A majority of these immigrants did not speak English, and a large number were practicing Catholics and Jews. These two distinguishing characteristics made their transition into life in America, an English speaking and, until then, predominately Protestant nation, extremely difficult. New immigrants formed a wide variety of mutual aid associations, fraternal organizations, and rotating credit groups to provide not only financial and legal security, but protection and nourishment for their distinct cultures and religions.

In 1836, the Ancient Order of Hibernians of America was founded by Irish Americans to provide both a culturally supportive fraternal organization and to give death benefits to members' families. The organization thrived and still exists today, providing scholarships and conducting other philanthropic work.[19] In 1843, Jews living in New York founded the first lodge of B'nai B'rith, an organization that initially sought to help new Jewish immigrants find work, and began to combat the growing discrimination against Jewish people. The organization, now known as the B'nai B'rith Anti-Defamation League, is one of the largest Jewish organizations operating in the United States today.[20]

During the next wave of immigration, immigrants from Poland, Slovakia, Czech, Romania, Hungary, Italy, and Sicily all formed mutual aid and benevolent societies to help ensure each group's socioeconomic survival and advancement in America. Between 1870 and 1890, more than 49 Czech mutual aid societies were founded in Chicago, and more than 35 Italian mutual aid societies, called *societa di mutuo soccorso*, were founded in Cleveland.[21] There were also several organizations that focused on helping immigrants regardless of country of origin. For example, the Illinois Immigrants Protective League was founded in 1908 to guard against unscrupulous treatment of immigrants by American employers.[22]

Organizations representing immigrant interests continued to spring up throughout the country. The Alliance of Poles in America (1895), the Alliance of Transylvanian Saxons (1902), the Banker's Mutual Life (1892, originally the Scandinavian American Fraternity), the Catholic Women's Fraternal of Texas (1894, originally the Union of Czech Catholic Women of Texas), the Danish Brotherhood of America (1881), the Portuguese Union of California (1880), the Serb National Federation (1901), the Sons of Norway (1895), and L'Ordine Figli D'Italia in America (1905, the Order of Sons of Italy in America) all still exist today. While these organizations had rather humble beginnings, today they are major philanthropic contributors to their communities and some rank among the largest insurance providers in the country.[23]

African American Philanthropy

Organized black philanthropy began in the first black churches, mutual aid societies, and fraternal organizations of the early eighteenth century. Black churches were especially important in collecting and dispersing funds to provide for human services and to support social advocacy.[24] In time, national organizations, charities, and foundations would emerge that focused on such social justice causes as abolition of slavery, civil rights, and education, among other areas. The history of black philanthropy is important because there is strong evidence that the successful indigenous philanthropy of this group has been adopted and adapted by other groups in pursuit of their own social justice causes.

The first black self-help organizations were founded to address the basic needs of free African Americans in northern cities who had no access to social welfare assistance from either the state or mainstream nonprofit organizations. An important concern to African Americans at this time was to prove that they warranted equal treatment from the larger society. As a result, they supported programs that minimized the possibility that "unacceptable" behavior by other African Americans could be used as a reason to further diminish their rights and status in the society.

The first known African American mutual aid organization was the African Union Society of Newport, Rhode Island, founded in 1780. The society focused its efforts on the moral rectitude of free blacks and recorded births, deaths, and marriages, as well as arranging apprenticeships for young blacks in various trades.[25] Another early mutual aid organization, the African Lodge No. 459 (later the Prince Hall Grand Masons), was founded in Boston in 1787 and was the first black society of freemasons. The lodge gave members protection against reenslavement due to delinquent debt and also helped the poor. Also in 1787, the Free African Society of Philadelphia was created to aid free blacks and support religious institutions. This society even provided aid to the larger community, as did several other African American organizations. In

1793, during an outbreak of plague, the Free African Society provided the entire city of Philadelphia with extensive nursing and burial services.

The unifying issue that most concerned African Americans in the first half of the nineteenth century was the legalized practice of slavery. Mutual aid organizations and churches focused much of their fundraising and volunteering efforts toward assisting escaping slaves through the Underground Railroad. From 1800 until the Civil War, African Americans created large numbers of mutual aid and fraternal organizations that relied on indigenous philanthropy to support anti-slavery efforts and provide the social services that African Americans could not get from either the U.S. government or existing white charitable organizations. One example of an effort that was supported by institutional philanthropy at this time was the Tappan family's support of the American Colonization Society, founded in 1817, which sought to send African Americans to Africa.[26] This activity, which was advocated by a minority of African Americans, led in part to a significant number of African Americans immigrating to Liberia in the 1840s.

Fraternal organizations like the International Order of Twelve Knights, the Daughters of Tabor, the New York Society (1810), the Union Society of Brooklyn (1920), and the African American Female Intelligence Society (1832) were vital to the health of various African American communities in the North.[27] In the South, where after 1835 southern states began to outlaw black fraternal and mutual aid organizations, black charitable organizations managed to carry on and maintain both their benevolent work and their work to free slaves.[28] The Resolution Beneficial Society of Washington, D.C. (1818), the Christian Benevolent Society (1939), and the Unity and Friendship Society of Charleston, South Carolina, defied the ban on their existence in support of their communities.[29] While the work of mutual aid societies and fraternal organizations was not generally viewed as threatening to the social order in the North, southern whites saw these groups as powerful support networks for the Underground Railroad and adamantly opposed to their "peculiar institution" of slavery.

There was enormous activity on the part of African Americans in nearly every community to use their indigenous philanthropy to support the social justice activities of their organizations. In 1835, there were forty black mutual aid organizations in Baltimore and eighty in Philadelphia. By 1848, in Philadelphia, almost half of the adult African American population was affiliated with some form of mutual aid society.[30] After the Civil War, the U.S. government established programs to assist the newly freed slaves. In 1865, the Bureau of Freedmen, Refugees, and Abandoned Lands (the Freedmen's Bureau) was created. The Freedmen's Bureau, aided by close to one hundred independent volunteer freedmen's aid societies, worked to give assistance to both former slaves and impoverished whites. During its seven years of existence, the Freedmen's Bureau established four thousand schools and forty hospitals, as well as distributing free food. In essence, what had formerly been the province of small African American–run societies was now seen by the public as an appropriate job for the American government.

Coinciding with emancipation was the growing wealth of many white American men who had made, and were still adding to, fortunes built on the incredible opportunities of the industrial revolution. While African American fraternal groups continued to spring up, such as the Eastern Stars, Foresters, Household of Ruth, Daughters of Isis, and Protective Order of Elks of the World (a fraternity that provided scholarships to African Americans), newly wealthy institutional philanthropists and their foundations began to take an interest consistent with public opinion in the basic and vocational education of African Americans, particularly in the South. In 1867, the Peabody Fund was established to push for universal education as a way to integrate ex-slaves and poor whites in the southern states. The fund continued these efforts until it merged into the Slater Fund in 1910. The mission of the Slater Fund, founded in 1882, was to provide for universal education. The black colleges it supported included Booker T. Washington's Tuskegee Institute and the Hampton Institute in Virginia. In 1937, the Slater Fund merged with the Jeanes Fund and Virginia Randolph Fund to form the Southern Education Fund, which still exists today.

In 1902, John D. Rockefeller created the General Education Board which was involved in all aspects of black education during the early to mid 1900s.[31] In fact, between 1902 and 1960 the board distributed $62.5 million in support of black education. In 1911, the Phelps-Stokes Fund was established to administer a bequest from Caroline Phelps Stokes to increase educational opportunities for African Americans, Native Americans, and poor whites. The fund shifted its emphasis in the 1940s to supporting historically black colleges through the Cooperative College Development Program. The program dispensed more than $6 million to black colleges and helped establish the United Negro College Fund in 1944.[32]

In 1917, Julius Rosenwald started the Rosenwald Fund which was exceptional in its willingness to support social justice causes, especially as they related to African Americans.[33] The fund established 5,357 public schools in fifteen southern states. The schools were built with both money from the fund and the indigenous philanthropy and manual labor from the local African American community in which the school was being built. The Rosenwald Fund supported fellowships for African American school teachers, black hospitals, and efforts to improve black-white relations. Unlike most foundations, though, the Rosenwald Fund did not focus its funding simply on training African Americans in farming and trade skills. Rosenwald scholarships were given for higher education in the liberal arts and sciences. Most foundations were unwilling to challenge southern beliefs that the academic education of African Americans was either pointless or dangerous to the status quo. A trustee of the General Education Board was quoted in 1899 as saying, "The Negro should not be educated out of his environment. Industrial work is his salvation. . . . Except in the rarest of instances, I am bitterly opposed to the so-called higher education of Negroes."[34]

One barrier that even the Rosenwald Fund was not prepared to challenge was that of separate education for blacks and whites. Most foundations essentially accepted the Jim Crow laws of the South and sought only to strengthen black educational institutions as opposed to encouraging integrated education. By the 1930s, foundations began to shift their focus toward academic education and also funded several comprehensive studies of the adverse socioeconomic conditions and legal barriers confronting African Americans. Among the most famous, *An American Dilemma*, written by Gunnar Myrdal in 1944, was supported by the Carnegie Corporation of New York.[35] The report concluded that the American dilemma was the inconsistency between the stated belief in equality and social justice for all and the legal barriers that prevented African Americans from fully participating in American society.[36]

Foundations continued to support efforts at ensuring that African Americans be moral and upstanding citizens. Money flowed into the Negro Boy Scouts, the National Negro Business League, and the National Urban League. Fear that the lack of progress in race relations might encourage African Americans to embrace communism led to greater support of efforts to improve race relations. For example, the Rosenwald Fund created the Commission on Interracial Cooperation in 1919 and also supported the American Council on Race Relations.[37]

The 1950s and 1960s brought a new wave of African American activism. The new call among African Americans was for civil rights and for the end of separate but equal—a policy that remained unaddressed by institutional philanthropists. Nonprofit civil rights groups like the NAACP, as well as the NAACP Legal Defense and Education Fund, the Congress of Racial Equality (CORE), and the Southern Christian Leadership Conference (SCLC), surged into prominence and, relying largely on indigenous philanthropy, challenged Jim Crow laws in the South and de facto segregation in the North. The success of legal groups by African Americans led to the creation of similar groups by the Latino and Asian communities, e.g., the Mexican American Legal Defense Fund and the Asian American Legal Defense and Education Fund. More importantly, the success of these social justice advocacy efforts against Jim Crow provided a greater measure of equal access and treatment under the law for all racial and ethnic groups and women.[38]

Some foundations did support these efforts. Primary among them were the Rockefeller and Ford Foundations, which launched equal opportunity programs focused on supporting integrated education. The Ford Foundation also heeded the call of civil rights groups for work to improve the socioeconomic and political conditions of the urban poor, a group in which African Americans were disproportionately represented.[39] Between 1960 and 1970, the Ford

Foundation awarded more than $25 million for its Great Cities School Improvement project and the Gray Areas project, both of which focused on aiding poor children and residents of urban areas in education, health, housing, and welfare.[40]

In the 1970s, new forms of charitable organizations were developed. African Americans continued to have a wide array of strong social service organizations, but the large role of the government and foundations led some to wonder how independent those organizations could be on behalf of African American interests. In 1972, the National Black United Fund (NBUF) was formed with crucial support from the Cummins Engine Foundation.[41] NBUF's mission was to develop a fundraising mechanism that would allow it to raise money primarily from African Americans and distribute that money to black organizations. In a series of court battles that ultimately involved the U.S. Supreme Court, NBUF won the right to access the federal government's work-site charitable payroll deduction campaigns and later gained access to the campaigns of many private employers.[42] NBUF's efforts would ultimately serve as a model for a wide range of groups to develop alternative funds to support their causes including women, Latinos, environmental and arts groups, among others.

As their socioeconomic status has improved, individual African Americans have begun to support causes that reflect their interests. The Jackie Robinson Foundation[43] and the major contributions made by Reginald Lewis to Howard and Harvard universities and by Bill Cosby to Spelman College are the first signs of what is certain to be a growing number of black philanthropists distributing the wealth they accumulated in technology, entertainment, and other industries.[44] While African American indigenous philanthropy continues to evolve, with a handful of significant exceptions, foundations provided only modest support to African American programs, 2.4 percent ($177.5 million) in 1996.[45]

Latino American Philanthropy

To understand the indigenous philanthropy of the American Latino community, there must be a recognition of many different people and traditions that are encompassed under this term. In the United States, Latinos or Hispanics are people who are likely to speak Spanish and come from Mexico, Puerto Rico, Cuba, and Central and South America. In addition, there are distinct Latino subgroups that exist only in the United States, such as the Tejano communities in Texas and the Manito communities in New Mexico.[46] Adding to the complexity, Latinos can be of either European or African descent. Over time, Latinos in America have maintained at least three strong philanthropic traditions: support for extended family networks, involvement with the Catholic church, and use of *mutualistas,* or mutual assistance associations, to provide for basic social services and social justice activities.[47]

One of the largest migrations of Latinos to the U.S. occurred after the Mexican American War in 1848. Approximately one million Mexicans, one-tenth of Mexico, found that land formerly owned by Mexico was now part of the United States.[48] Dispossessed Mexican Americans created the first *mutualistas* throughout the Southwest such as La Sociedad Hispano Americano De Benfecio Mutua, which was founded in Los Angeles in 1875, and La Alianza Hispano-Americana, founded in Tucson in 1894. While La Sociedad Hispano concentrated mainly on organizing commemoration of Mexican national holidays, La Alianza Hispano-Americana provided sickness and death benefits to 10,000 members throughout the Southwest and fought political battles with whites in Arizona who were trying to usurp political power from Mexican Americans.[49]

From 1900 to 1939, there was a significant expansion of Mexican American organizations, mostly made up of new *mutualistas* which provided both sickness and death benefits and served to help preserve and recreate social networks. La Sociedad Benito Juarez and La Union Patriotica Benefica Mexicano Independiente were founded at this time and established dozens of chapters throughout the Southwest and later the Midwest.[50] *Mutualistas* also aided in the development of the Mexican American labor unions. Since major U.S. unions would not admit Mexicans, or any Latinos, a federation of mutual aid societies throughout southern California gathered in Los Angeles in 1927 and formed the first Mexican American labor union, La Confederacio de Uniones Obreras Mexicanas. Mexican labor unions did not last long and were disturbed by the Communist Party's attempts to unionize the canning, packing, and various other industries in California. Mexicans would remain active participants in the formation of nearly every future labor union founded in the Southwest.[51]

In 1917, a federal law was passed making all residents of Puerto Rico citizens of the United States.[52] While Puerto Rican Americans joined many of the growing Latino organizations in the United States, they have not utilized their charitable organizations to the same degree as either Mexican or Cuban Americans.[53]

The first formal Mexican-led civil rights organizations were started in the early twentieth century. Primary among them was El Primer Congreso Mexicanista, which was founded in 1911.[54] The Congreso was formed to unite Mexican Americans in action against discrimination and segregation in schools and to address civil rights violations. La Liga Protectora Latina was formed in Phoenix in 1914 for the express purpose of combating a proposed city council ceiling of 20 percent on the number of Mexican Americans Phoenix companies and factories would be allowed to hire.

In 1939, the Congreso de Pueblos de Habla Espanola, an amalgamation of *mutualistas*, labor, and civil rights advocacy groups, was formed. The groups included not only Mexican Americans but other Latino groups, especially Puerto Ricans. The group's efforts at civil rights reform and general Latino advocacy ended by 1945 when many of its key leaders were deported. The FBI investigated the group for Communist influence, and many of its members were drafted for World War II. The League of United Latin American Citizens (LULAC), founded in 1929, refused to join the Congreso, and instead sought to promote good citizenship in an effort to change the public image of Mexican Americans. Beginning in the 1940s, however, LULAC was an important advocate as it pressed for Latino legal and educational rights.

After World War II, returning GIs formed organizations like the Community Service Organization (CSO) and the Unity League to advocate for political power in Los Angeles. The two groups merged shortly after forming and the CSO became less political over time, serving more as a *mutualista* to southern Californian Latinos. In the late 1950s, two other important groups were founded: the Mexican American Political Association (MAPA) in California, and the Political Association of Spanish-Speaking Organizations (PASSO) in Texas. MAPA, PASSO, and the CSO became identified with the "Chicano Movement" in the late 1960s.

By the 1970s, other groups, inspired by the Chicano Movement, took the lead in addressing civil rights concerns, organizing Vietnam anti-war protests and championing the formation of migrant farm labor unions such as the United Farm Workers Union in California. There were also calls for "Chicano Power" (adopted from the "Black Power" slogan) and for study of the "spiritual and geographic origins of Chicanos."[55]

Starting in the late 1960s, institutional philanthropy, primary among them the Ford Foundation, began to provide resources to Latino organizations. Federal governmental agencies also began to make economic resources more available to Mexican American communities. In the 1970s and 1980s a new type of organizational model developed. The Council of Mexican American Affairs (CMAA), a group of professionals, created an umbrella association to facilitate leadership and aid for the Mexican American community in Los Angeles. In general, a new emphasis was placed on aiding Latinos to achieve business and corporate success.

Today, Latino advocacy and support groups like the National Council of La Raza, the Mexican American Legal Defense and Education Fund, and the Cuban American National Foundation (CANF) continue to push for many of the same causes championed by the first *mutualistas* in the 1870s.[56] They also have championed new concerns such as Latino voter registration and cultural preservation. Latino organizations continue to have difficulty in securing funding from institutional philanthropy. In 1996, foundations contributed 1.2 percent ($88.9 million) of all grantmaking to Latino groups or causes.[57]

Asian American Philanthropy

The concepts of philanthropy and charity are deeply embedded in the diverse languages and cultures of Asian Americans. There are, of course, many Asian nations represented in America today, among them, China, Japan, Korea, the Philippines, Vietnam, Cambodia, Laos, and Thailand.[58] Unfortunately, there has been scant research on the indigenous philanthropy of Asian Americans. Asian Americans, more so perhaps than any other group, have yet to attract significant support for their causes from institutional philanthropy. At least part of the difficulty is that the interests of various Asian groups are so different, and yet intertwined, that it has been difficult for them to coalesce around a single issue. Another difficulty is the false public perception that Asian Americans represent a "model" minority community with few social justice concerns.[59] These difficulties likely contribute to small amounts that the larger foundations contribute to Asian American programs, 0.3 percent ($25 million) in 1996.[60] As a result, indigenous philanthropy remains a crucial element of most Asian American communities. The philanthropic practices of the Asian Americans whose families have immigrated to the United States in the largest numbers—the Chinese, Japanese, Koreans, and Filipinos—are examined below. Regrettably, the philanthropic research on each of these groups is extremely limited.

Chinese immigration began in the 1770s, and by the Gold Rush of the 1840s, the number of Chinese immigrants increased significantly. After nearly three decades of anti-Chinese legislation by the state of California, the U.S. passed the 1882 Exclusion Act, which was the first immigration law to bar the entry of a specific ethnic or cultural group to America. As designed, the law resulted in a dramatic decrease in Chinese immigration for the next sixty years. In 1943 the Magnuson Act effectively repealed the 1882 Exclusion Act, and the McCarran-Walter Act of 1952 made Chinese immigrants eligible for citizenship.[61]

Chinese immigrants relied heavily on mutual aid organizations. By 1854, Chinese mutual aid and revolving credit societies were so well established that the Chinese Six Companies (CSC) was founded. CSC was composed of a group of *sign tohng* or family associations that eventually became the Chinese Consolidated Benevolent Association (CCBA).[62] The primary purpose of the *sign tohng*, beyond community survival, was the management of burials, which were free to members. During the Great Depression, some *sign tohngs* even provided daily meals for members. Today, these family associations remain very active, and many, which have grown considerably in wealth, set aside a significant portion of their dues to support charitable activities.

The CSC functions much as a credit union for its members and also provides money in cases of emergency. Today, the San Francisco CSC, the largest in the country, works in three areas: the education of Chinese children, management of the Chinese Hospital and its charitable work, and management of various projects benefiting the community. It was the San Francisco CSC, in collaboration with the Chinatown Salvation Army, that in 1985 raised $160,000 for victims of the Mexico City earthquake, and in 1988 raised $333,787 for victims of the Yunnan, China, earthquake.[63] Rotating credit associations, or *wui*, continue to be heavily used by many in Chinese American communities, and family associations remain the largest recipients of Chinese philanthropy outside of immediate family.

As early as 1883, Japanese immigrants were replacing Chinese immigrants as a major source of cheap labor in the United States. Unlike Chinese immigrants, Japanese immigrants were, from the start, allowed to bring their entire families into the country, something that greatly aided in their community building. From the 1880s until World War II there was a steady stream of Japanese immigration.[64] Early Japanese immigrants formed prefecture associations called *kenjinkai*. Like *nihonjin* or Japanese people associations, *kenjinkai* are voluntary associations. The *kenjinkai* helped newly arrived immigrants with food, shelter, and other needs. They also sponsored fundraising activities to help new immigrants get established. In addition, these organizations helped with marriages and funerals as well as with obtaining legal residency.[65]

In 1900, the Nippon Jikei Kai (Japanese Charitable Association) was established to assist the needy and was supported by successful Japanese Americans. The group later established the Japanese Cemetery in northern California, which it maintains to this day. Japanese Americans also formed the Japanese Association of America to keep communications open with the Consulate of Japan. After the San Francisco earthquake of 1906, citizens of Japan rushed money and aid to San Francisco and, more recently, after the quake of 1989, Japan gave more aid to San Francisco than all other countries combined — $10 million.[66]

The American Loyalty Club, founded in 1918, helped members to secure their rights as American citizens in San Francisco. In 1930, in an effort to combat the hostilities toward Japanese Americans, the Japanese American Citizens League (JACL) was founded. After World War II, the JACL worked to gain citizenship for new immigrants, to establish a nondiscriminatory immigration law, and to get repayment for the material losses suffered by all Japanese Americans residing on the West Coast who had been "relocated" and "evacuated" by the American government during World War II.[67]

Other groups were established to unite the Japanese American community by providing activities for women and children. By 1941, women had formed the San Francisco Mothers' Society, Kinomon Gakuen Mothers' Society, a YMCA Mothers' Club, a *Sojoji Funkai* (a women's home), and a Sister's Home. These groups provided care for new Japanese immigrants and sought to teach them about American skills and society.[68] No doubt these groups were strongly influenced by a need to present the most loyal, all-American appearance they possibly could to help combat the hostilities and poor treatment that all Japanese Americans were receiving before and during World War II. Japanese indigenous philanthropy also supported the building of a YMCA, a YWCA, and a Salvation Army, all in "Japantown." All of these organizations went out of business as Japanese Americans were interned during World War II.

Kenjinkai still operate today. A study done in the early 1990s suggests that Japanese Americans still prefer to give to persons or groups within their immediate circle or closer in social distance. It appears that Japanese American philanthropy remains largely focused on mutual benefit to support basic social services and has not identified social justice advocacy as a priority area at this time.[69]

Korean immigration to the United States began in 1885 as a means of escaping political turmoil in Korea. A second wave started in 1903 when Hawaii began to look for a source of cheap labor for its sugar plantations. Korean immigration fell drastically between 1928 and 1948 but resumed after World War II.[70]

Korean American philanthropy revolves around *kye*, traditional rotating credit groups. *Kye* are used to acquire enough money to start businesses and often grow out of social or business groups called *chin-mok-hoe* (social clubs), *dong-chang-hoe* (school alumni associations), or greengrocer, fish market, or laundry associations. These associations are used as a means of networking as well as a means of fostering social cooperation.[71] High school associations are particularly strong groups with many Korean Americans giving *chee-won* or *cheewonkum* (donations) to educational institutions through alumni associations. In this way, college alumni associations fill the role of professional associations within the Korean American community.

Korean language media—TV, newspapers, and radio—are used as coordinating centers for fundraising and crisis control. Korean American business associations also serve as political and social clubs with members regularly sponsoring parties as well as political activities.[72] The other strong focus of Korean American philanthropy is the church. More than 70 percent of Korean Americans are Protestant, and many use their churches as a center of social activity and community information. Korean Americans give the most money to causes associated with their churches, like the YMCA.[73]

Filipino immigration began slightly after the initial Korean immigration in 1910. The United States had gained control over the Philippines and arranged for Filipino students to be sent to the U.S. to study. These students were required to return to the Philippines, and once they returned, many became public advocates for the "American Way." Again, this is similar to what other groups experienced. Between 1910 and 1938, many of the Filipino students who came to the U.S. did not finish their schooling and decided to remain in the continental U.S., working in agriculture or domestic service. A second wave of Filipino immigration, consisting primarily of "war brides," began during World War II and lasted well into the 1950s.[74]

In Tagalog, a Malaysian dialect, *tulong* means providing help or aid to those in need. *Tulong* is a central feature of Filipino American life and includes providing money, shelter, and food. It is practiced most often within the family and the community and tends to only occur when someone is in immediate need of assistance.[75] Filipino Americans have also established more structured forms of *tulong*. For example, the Filipino American Council of San Francisco helps Filipinos address issues in the areas of employment, health, and English language proficiency, among other programs.[76]

Filipino Americans also have a tradition of establishing mutual benefit groups, or *barangay*, within their neighborhood communities. Usually, these groups are composed almost exclusively of people from the same region of the Philippines. These groups serve as the central fundraisers for their community as well as for organizing the sending of money back to the Philippines to their extended families and churches. Filipino American philanthropy, like Korean American philanthropy, remains largely focused on their immediate family and community.

Women and Philanthropy

The history of organized women's groups that have sought to improve the status and treatment of women is well documented. Unlike the other culture-specific groups examined, women have confronted social justice challenges resulting from their gender as well as added difficulties that can arise from being a woman of color. The goals and causes fought for by American women have grown and evolved over the last 250 years to include not only such generally "domestic" causes as care for widows and children and relief for soldiers, but abolition, temperance, suffrage, education, as well as equal and reproductive rights. Some of the earliest known philanthropic efforts by women in America were to aid poor women and children. The image of charity as women's work has been strengthened over the years as both religious authorities and moral pundits agreed that care for society's less fortunate and disabled members was a proper responsibility for Christian women.

The Society for the Relief of Poor Widows and Small Children was started in 1797. It was staffed solely by women who worked to provide relief to those they deemed worthy recipients.[77] Similarly, the Benevolent Society of St. Thomas was founded in 1793 by free African American women to help each other, as well as the less fortunate of any sex and race in Philadelphia. In the 1800s, new roles for women's philanthropic and charitable organizations began to emerge. The Female Moral Reform Society, among other groups, was founded in New York City with the idea that care for the poor was important but that systematic change in the morals of all New Yorkers would be necessary to improve conditions for all in the city. Some women's groups were also actively supporting the abolition movement. In 1836, of the more than 500 anti-slavery societies in the United States, fifty or more were all female.[78] The irony of supporting freedom and equality for slaves while women were prohibited from voting, owning land, or taking legal recourse against a physically abusive husband was not lost on women who would later advocate equality for women.

By 1843 organizations such as the New York Association for Improving the Conditions of the Poor had been created, and in 1853, the New York Children's Aid Society was established. Both of these groups were founded long after many smaller, and lesser known, women's reform groups had begun to canvass through New York City in an effort to reveal the appalling conditions under which the city's poor were living. The Civil War marked a period of strong collaboration between women-led charities and institutional philanthropies as both bound together to tend to a nation of wounded, sick, and displaced people. The United States Sanitary Commission, founded in 1861, was actually made up of many smaller, often female-led groups, such as the Women's Central Relief Association and the Northwestern Sanitary Commission.

The suffrage movement was, in part, born out of the frustration of many women who, while allowed to be members of many male-dominated antislavery societies, were not allowed to speak or be recognized at meetings. There was also a belief that allowing white women to vote would offset the votes of African Americans. Rejecting the accepted women's role that male-run societies had forced onto them, controversy grew and several women broke away from the abolition movement to focus on women's rights. In 1848, the landmark Seneca Falls Convention called for women to have true equality with men in all legal matters, including the right to vote. While support for traditional charitable activity continued through women-run mutual aid groups, a growing number of women's groups began to champion less socially acceptable causes, including temperance, education, workers' rights, and suffrage.

The Women's Christian Temperance Union was founded in 1874, while the Woman Suffrage Association and the American Woman Suffrage Association were founded earlier in 1869. Women had begun to promote temperance as early as the 1830s when temperance had been the work of "elite men." But from the 1840s onward, many of the societies promoting legal prohibition were all female and were considered the norm. During this period, institutional philanthropy found it far easier to support the temperance movement than the suffrage movement. Suffrage campaigners would have to wait nearly forty years before suffrage would be viewed as an appropriate cause for financial support by traditional institutional philanthropies.

During the later half of the nineteenth century, groups like the Young Women's Christian Association, the New England Women's Club, the Colored Women's League, the Women's Era Club, the General Federation of Women's Clubs, and the National Association of Colored Women were formed to provide not only inspirational support, but training, financial aid, and improved education, often incorporating calls for temperance, suffrage, and equality. It should be noted that, consistent with the larger society, racism and discrimination were prominent features of the many mainstream women's organizations which led to conflict and distance from the Black Women Club Movement of hundreds of African American women's groups. These African American women's groups were created to combat the negative perceptions of African American women that resulted in their being largely denied participation in the suffrage organizations.[79]

Denied access to the new worker's unions, women started their own, such as the Women's Trade Union League, the Women's Educational and Industrial Unions, and the Women's Loyal Union.[80] In 1893, in an amazing sign of recognition for the multitude of women's charities, societies, and clubs flourishing across the nation, the World's Fair Colombian Exposition featured not only a Women's Building but a Congress of Representative Women.

The industrial revolution contributed to the acquisition of wealth and social power by a number of women. Whether their money was inherited or the result of their own empire building, these women, starting in the late 1800s, used their philanthropic resources to shape major organizations, often to be more inclusive of women in their operations. For example, in 1899, Mary Elizabeth Garrett negotiated an agreement with Johns Hopkins University to contribute a large sum toward the founding of its medical school, provided the school would admit and train women as doctors on an equal footing with its male students.[81]

In 1905, Elizabeth Milbank Anderson founded the Milbank Memorial to fund research in epidemiology and nutrition as well as help orphans and new immigrants. In 1907, Margaret Sage founded one of the major philanthropic institutions in the United States today, the Russell Sage Foundation. Madame C. J. Walker, an African American millionaire through the sale of black cosmetics, founded an academy for girls in West Africa and was very supportive of African American education generally. Women continued to move into the area of institutional philanthropy in the 1930s with groups like the Macy Foundation, founded to do medical research by Kate Macy Ladd, the Institute for Advanced Studies, founded by the Carrie Bamberger Fund, and the Hogg Foundation for Mental Health, founded by Ima Hogg.[82]

Also in the early 1900s, several schools and associations were founded by African American women to provide education and training to young black women. The National Training School for Women and Girls, founded in

Washington, D.C., in 1909 by Nannie H. Burroughs, and the Phillis Wheatley Association, a boarding house and training school, also for black women, was founded in Cleveland, Ohio, in 1912.[83] As Darlene Clark Hine has written, "by 1920 determined black women had established in [most northern] communit[ies], homes for the aged, hospitals and sanitariums, nursing schools and colleges, orphanages, libraries, gymnasiums, and shelters for young [black women]."[84] The suffrage movement also began to move to the forefront of the American political agenda at this time.

In 1916, the National Women's Party (NWP) was started, a breakaway group from the National American Women's Suffrage Association (NAWSA), to advocate more aggressively for suffrage. And, through the continued work of both the NWP and the NAWSA, as well as eventual support of the Democratic party, the 19th Amendment was passed by Congress in 1919 and ratified by the states in 1920. However, as soon as one battle was won, women moved onto others: in 1921, the first version of what is now known as the ERA or Equal Rights Amendment was drafted.

In the 1950s, American society was inhospitable to women's social activism. Prominent figures like Adlai Stevenson reminded women that when they finished college they would have to put away such "preoccupations" and focus on being good housewives and mothers.[85] By the 1960s, social justice activism in the United States reached new heights. Women founded two major new women's groups to push for equal and reproductive rights. Many women, trained through their grassroots work in the civil rights and student movements, realized that those organizations were run almost solely by men with agendas that rarely included issues of concern to women. This was reminiscent of how the abolition movement had been a training ground for women who would lead the suffrage movement. No longer satisfied with a subservient role in society, the National Organization for Women (NOW) was founded in 1956 to lobby for equal rights and fair treatment for women.[86] NOW members included many former members of the Student Non-Violent Coordinating Committee (SNCC), the Southern Christian Leadership Conference (SCLC), and the Students for a Democratic Society (SDS).

The Planned Parent Federation of America was founded in 1916. However, at the time, many women felt that their efforts were better concentrated on the issue of suffrage. By 1969, five years before the historic decision in *Roe v. Wade*, the National Abortion Rights Action League (NARAL), later renamed the National Abortion and Reproductive Rights Action League, was founded to call for safe and legal abortion services. It was just one of many abortion and reproductive rights groups that, along with groups like NOW, worked for the legalization of abortion and contraception devices.

In 1985, the National Network of Women's Funds was created, and by 1989 had 50 member organizations.[87] These organizations are largely focused on addressing women's and children's issues. Women's organizations have successfully moved through several cycles of using their indigenous philanthropy to support a social justice agenda and attracting the support of institutional philanthropy.

The relationship between the indigenous philanthropy of culture-specific groups and institutional philanthropy in advancing social justice issues is intricate and complex. The examination of the histories of Native, African, Latino, Asian, and European immigrant Americans and women suggests that their indigenous philanthropy has been essential in providing basic human services and, to varying degrees, in supporting social justice advocacy. There are at least two remaining issues that warrant discussion. First, why have some culture-specific groups been very active in social justice advocacy and others not? Equally interesting, why has institutional philanthropy, widely believed to be the primary source for venture capital for new and controversial ideals, apparently not fulfilled this role in the area of social justice advocacy? Both of these questions are important in understanding how current and future social justice activities will be supported by the indigenous philanthropy of culture-specific groups and institutional philanthropy.

In assessing why some culture-specific groups have been active in social justice advocacy and others have not, several observations emerge. African Americans and women have had the most success in this area, which is likely due, in part, to the nature of their social protest and numerical size. The issues of abolition of slavery, legalized segregation, and suffrage confronted widespread practices that were condoned by American society that involved large numbers of the culture-specific, group. This is not to say that the issues of tribal sovereignty, Puerto Rican independence, or reparations for Japanese internment, among others, are not equally important. Rather, these groups have been hampered in gaining greater support from the larger society due to their smaller population size, the diversity of opinion by other subgroups within the same culture-specific group, and the lesser magnitude of their indigenous philanthropy that results from having a smaller population size. The large size of these two groups—African Americans and women—is an important factor because it provided each group with enough people, allowing for diverse opinions, to organize, generate, and direct a significant portion of their indigenous philanthropy to social justice advocacy.

It is also probable that the large population of African Americans and women affected by social injustice made it more likely that the broader society would be more aware and somewhat more sensitive to their concerns. Another important consideration is that the success of African Americans and women in pursuing their social justice advocacy efforts has had positive benefits for all racial and ethnic groups and reduced the need for those groups to mount their own efforts in those areas. The possibility also exists that the cultural predisposition of some groups may contribute to an unwillingness or discomfort on the part of some groups with pursuing social justice advocacy. As the Latino and Asian populations experience significant population growth in the years ahead, they are likely to experience greater success in advocating their social justice interests.

Given the prevailing nonprofit literature, it may appear somewhat surprising that institutional philanthropy has not played a more prominent role in supporting the social justice advocacy of culture-specific groups. However, upon reflection, the reticence of foundations in this area is understandable. In general, foundations are created by wealthy people who have benefited from the status quo and who, in social matters, are likely to be more conservative than progressive. The indigenous philanthropy of wealthy women as well as the philanthropy of individuals like Julius Rosenwald suggests that as members of various culture-specific groups achieve greater economic success and establish their own foundations, it is likely that their institutions will be more supportive of social justice advocacy efforts than foundations established in earlier generations.

Another explanation for the reactive rather than proactive involvement of institutional philanthropy in social justice issues has to do with the racial and ethnic composition of the boards and staffs of foundations. The Council on Foundations has found that there are few members of racial and ethnic groups that serve on their boards or staffs. A total of 90 percent of foundation governing boards and 84 percent of foundation professional staffs consist of white Americans.[88] There is strong anecdotal evidence that suggests that foundations are more likely to develop grantmaking priorities that support a wide range of culture-specific groups when they have a diverse board and staff than when they do not.[89] If this is true, foundations are not likely to become more proactive in supporting social justice issues in the foreseeable future unless they diversify their boards and staffs.

Finally, it is important to note that foundations have good reason to be concerned that support of social justice advocacy might inadvertently lead to greater scrutiny from Congress. It is widely believed that the Ford Foundation's support of voter registration efforts in the 1960s led Congress to develop stricter rules for governing foundation activities in this area, specifically, the Tax Reform Act of 1969. This incident is often cited as the reason why foundations are generally reluctant to support social justice advocacy, although they are not legally prohibited from funding these activities. While there are some efforts underway to encourage foundations to become more active in supporting public policy advocacy, to date these efforts have had only modest success.

In closing, the indigenous philanthropy of culture-specific groups will continue to have to play a leadership role in addressing social justice issues. As these efforts show promise, they will influence the beliefs of the larger public and attract the support of institutional philanthropy. In this way, the indigenous philanthropy of culture-specific groups is an essential element of efforts to address old and new problems of social inequality.

Notes

1. R. H. Bremner, *American Philanthropy*. Chicago: University of Chicago Press, 1960, p. 3.

2. S. A. Ostrander, "Charitable Foundations, Social Movements, and Social Justice Funding." *Research in Social Policy*, vol. 5, 1997, pp. 172–173.

3. R. MacLean and D. McLeod, eds., *The Foundation Grants Index 1998*, 26th edition. New York: Foundation Center, 1997, pp. xv and xxv.

4. *Giving USA*. New York: AAFRC Trust for Philanthropy, 1996, p. 12.

5. C. S. Kidwell, "The Indian Giving." *Foundation News*, vol. 31, no. 3, May–June 1990, p. 27.

6. R. Adamson, "Money with a Mission: A History of Indian Philanthropy." *Tribal College: Journal of American Indian Higher Education*, vol. VI, no. 3, p. 26.

7. Ibid.

8. A. Depalma, "Indigenous tribes in Canada receive formal apology." *New York Times*, January 8, 1998, p. A1.

9. Adamson, p. 26.

10. Ibid., p. 28.

11. Ibid.

12. Ibid.

13. Ibid.

14. Ibid., p. 29.

15. M. Ambler, "Indians Giving: New Philanthropy in Indian Country." *Tribal College: Journal of American Indian Higher Education*, vol. VI, no. 3, Winter 1994, p. 14.

16. J. A. Joseph, "Options for Giving and the Native American Tradition: A Discussion Paper." p. 16.

17. "A Summary Report of the December 9, 1994 Forum." *American Indians in Philanthropy*, American Indian Research & Policy Institute, p. 3.

18. *The Foundation Grants Index 1998*, p. xxv.

19. *Records of the Ethnic Fraternal Benefit Associations in the United States: Essays and Inventories*. University of Minnesota, Immigration History Research Center, 1981, p. 54.

20. G. Osofsky, "The Hebrew Emigrant Aid Society in the United States (1881–1883)." In G. E. Puzzetta, ed., *American Immigration and Ethnicity*. Volume 5, Immigrant Institutions. New York: Garland Publishing, Inc., 1991, p. 262.

21. R. F. Harney, "Boarding and Belonging." In G. E. Puzzetta, ed., *American Immigration and Ethnicity*. Volume 5, Immigrant Institutions. New York: Garland Publishing, Inc., 1991, p. 33.

22. R. F. Harney, "From Voluntary Association to Welfare State: The Illinois

Immigrants' Protective League." In G. E. Puzzetta, ed., *American Immigration and Ethnicity*. Volume 14, Americanization, Social Control and Philanthropy. New York: Garland Publishing, Inc., 1991, pp. 44–46.

23. *Records of the Ethnic Fraternal Benefit Associations in the United States: Essays and Inventories*, passim.

24. E. D. Carson, "Patterns of Giving in Black Churches." In R. Wuthnow and V. Hodgkinson, eds., *Faith and Philanthropy in America*. San Francisco, CA: Jossey-Bass Publishers, 1990.

25. E. D. Carson, "Philanthropy and Foundations." In J. Salzman, D. L. Smith, and C. West, eds., *Encyclopedia of African-American Culture and History*. New York: Simon & Schuster Macmillan, 1996, Volume 1, p. 2137.

26. Bremner, p. 48.

27. Carson, "Philanthropy and Foundations," p. 2137.

28. E. D. Carson, "The Evolution of Black Philanthropy: Patterns of Giving and Voluntarism." In R. Magat, ed., *Philanthropic Giving: Studies in Varieties and Goals*. Oxford University Press, 1989, p. 95.

29. Carson, "Philanthropy and Foundations," pp. 2137–2139.

30. Ibid., p. 2137.

31. C. P. Henry, "Big Philanthropy and the Funding of Black Organizations." *The Review of Black Political Economy*, vol. 9, no. 2, Winter 1979, p. 176.

32. Carson, "Philanthropy and Foundations," p. 2138.

33. E. R. Embree, and J. Waxman, *Investment in People: The Story of the Julius Rosenwald Fund*. New York: Harper & Brothers Publishers, 1949, p. 39.

34. Carson, "Philanthropy and Foundations," p. 2138.

35. Henry, p. 177.

36. Ibid.

37. Carson, "Philanthropy and Foundations," p. 2139.

38. Ibid.

39. Henry, pp. 179–180.

40. Carson, "Philanthropy and Foundations," pp. 2139–2140.

41. E. D. Carson, "The National Black United Fund: From Movement to Social Change to Social Change Organization." *New Directions for Philanthropic Fundraising*, No. 1, Fall 1993, pp. 53–71.

42. Ibid., pp. 65–67.

43. *Jackie Robinson Foundation Scholar's Handbook*. New York, NY: Jackie Robinson Foundation, 1989.

44. J. E. Fairfax, "Black Philanthropy: Its Heritage and its Future." In C. H. Hamilton and W. F. Ilchman, eds., *New Directions for Philanthropic Fundraising*. San Francisco, CA: Jossey-Bass Publishers, 1995, no. 8, Summer 1995, pp. 9–21.

45. *The Foundation Grants Index 1998*, p. xxv.

46. M. Cortés, "Three Strategic Questions about Latino Philanthropy." In C. H. Hamilton and W. F. Ilchman, eds., *New Directions for Philanthropic Fundraising*. San Francisco, CA: Jossey-Bass Publishers, 1995, no. 8, Summer 1995, p. 28.

47. Ibid., p. 28.

48. A. Camarillo, "Mexican Americans and Nonprofit Organizations: An Historical Overview." In H. E. Gallegos and M. O'Neill, eds., *Hispanics and the Nonprofit Sector*. New York: The Foundation Center, 1991, pp. 16–17.

49. Ibid.

50. Ibid., pp. 19–20.

51. Ibid., p. 21.

52. Ibid., pp. 3–4.

53. C. Rodriguez-Fraticelli, C. Sanabria, and A. Tirado, "Puerto Rican Nonprofit Organizations in New York City." In H. E. Gallegos and M. O'Neill, eds., *Hispanics and the Nonprofit Sector*. New York: The Foundation Center, 1991, p. 48.

54. Ibid., pp. 21–24.

55. Ibid., pp. 27–29.

56. *Pluralism in Philanthropy*. The Researcher's Roundtable. Washington, DC: Council on Foundations, 1989.

57. *The Foundation Grants Index 1998*, p. xxv.

58. S. Shao, "Asian American Giving: Issues and Challenges (A Practitioner's Perspective)." In C. H. Hamilton and W. F. Ilchman, eds., *New Directions for Philanthropic Fundraising*. San Francisco, CA: Jossey-Bass Publishers, 1995, no. 8, Summer 1995, p. 54.

59. *Invisible and in Need: Philanthropic Giving to Asian Americans and Pacific Islanders*. A Report of Asian Americans and Pacific Islanders in Philanthropy. December 1992, p. 1.

60. *The Foundation Grants Index 1998*, p. xxv.

61. B. Smith, S. Shue, J. L. Vest, and J. Villarreal, *Ethnic Philanthropy: Sharing the Giving: Money, Goods and Services in the African American, Mexican, Chinese, Japanese, Filipino, Korean, Guatemalan and Salvadoran Communities of the San Francisco Bay Area*. San Francisco: University of San Francisco, 1994, p. 161. Revised ed., *Philanthropy in Communities of Color*. Bloomington: Indiana University Press, 1999.

62. Ibid., pp. 178–179.

63. R. Lee, *Guide to Chinese American Philanthropy and Charitable Giving Patterns*. Pathway Press, 1990, p. 25.

64. Smith, et al., p. 186.

65. Ibid., p. 201.

66. Ibid., p. 179.

67. Ibid., p. 201.

68. Ibid., p. 203.

69. Ibid., p. 205.

70. Ibid., p. 208.

71. Ibid., p. 222.

72. Ibid., p. 223.

73. Ibid., p. 221.

74. Ibid., p. 136.

75. Ibid., p. 149.

76. Ibid., p. 158.

77. A. F. Scott, "Women's Voluntary Associations: From Charity to Reform." In K. D. McCarthy, ed., *Lady Bountiful Revisited: Woman, Philanthropy, Power*. New Brunswick, NJ: Rutgers University Press, 1990, pp. 39–43.

78. Ibid.

79. E. D. Carson, *A Hand Up: Black Philanthropy and Self-Help in America*.

Washington, DC: Joint Center for Political and Economic Studies, 1993, pp. 18–19.

80. Scott, p. 43.

81. W. A. Nielsen, *Inside American Philanthropy: The Dramas of Donorship*. Norman, OK: University of Oklahoma Press, 1996, pp. 90–91.

82. Ibid., pp. 90–97.

83. D. C. Hine, "We Specialize in the Wholly Impossible: The Philanthropic Work of Black Women." In Kathleen D. McCarthy, ed., *Lady Bountiful Revisited: Women, Philanthropy, Power*. New Brunswick, NJ: Rutgers University Press, 1990, pp. 79–90.

84. Ibid., p. 71.

85. B. Friedan, *The Feminist Mystique*. New York: Dell Publishing Co., 1963, p. 15.

86. S. Evans, *Personal Politics: The Roots of Women's Liberation in the Civil Rights Movement and the New Left*. New York: Vintage Books, 1979, pp. 38–45.

87. Ostrander, p. 183.

88. Council on Foundations, *Foundation Management Report, Eighth Edition*. Washington, DC: Council on Foundations, 1996, pp. 73 and 160.

89. E. D. Carson, "Diversity and Equity among Foundation Grantmakers." *Nonprofit Management Leadership*, vol. 4, no. 3, Spring 1994, pp. 331–344; L. C. Burbridge, *Status of African Americans in Grantmaking Institutions*. Indiana University Center on Philanthropy, 1995, pp. 58–59; W. A. Diaz, "The Behavior of Foundations in an Organizational Frame: A Case Study." *Nonprofit and Voluntary Sector Quarterly*, vol. 25, no. 4, December 1996, pp. 453–469.

CHAPTER THIRTEEN

Philanthropy and the Case of the Latino Communities in America

William A. Diaz

The story of Latinos and philanthropy is a story, in the words of the late Paul Ylvisaker, of "dreamers" and visionaries. It is also one of a community which emerged on the philanthropic scene as a new disadvantaged American "minority" that will soon come to represent one in four Americans. The essay below traces the history of Latinos in philanthropy from their emergence as a new target population for grantmakers, through their incorporation into the programs of the major national foundations, and into the boards and staffs of organized philanthropic foundations. Its third section discusses recent developments whereby Latinos are developing their own vehicles for grantmaking. Finally, the essay looks to the future in a section on trends and forces that is optimistic about the prospects of Latinos becoming a dominant force in American philanthropy drawing, in part, on the growing wealth *within* the Latino community.

Emergence: The Pioneers

Two small foundations, Rosenberg in San Francisco and the John Hay Whitney in New York, sowed the seeds in the 1940s and 1950s for what would later blossom into major grantmaking programs for Hispanics by the larger national foundations. The Rosenberg Foundation was endowed by Max Rosenberg, one of three brothers who had made their fortunes with Rosenberg Brothers and Company, a major national and international dried fruit producer. In the 1940s, the foundation's trustees decided to focus, among other things, on problems in the "fertile valleys" of California which produced the fruits that made possible the original endowment (Rosenberg Director's Manual, 1997). Among the subsequent issues that the foundation attacked was the plight of farm workers. As the population of farm workers became more heavily Mexican American, "the problems of Mexican Americans in California came to the foundation's attention early" (Chance, 1991, p. 82).

Between 1947 and 1959, the Rosenberg Foundation made 23 grants to Mexican American–related projects of one sort or another. However, these grants were mostly to non–Mexican American organizations to serve the Mexican American population. Included, for example, is a grant to the American Friends Service Committee to start an outdoor education project for the children of Mexican American farm workers.

Arguably the single most significant Mexican American grant by Rosenberg, however, was the support it provided for a symposium on Mexican Americans in honor of Charles De Young Elkus, a deceased trustee. Elkus had been Max Rosenberg's lawyer and confidant and had drafted the foundation's trust instrument. He also had a deep interest in Mexican Americans and American Indians. The board chose to honor him with this symposium, an unusual activity for the foundation, because they realized he was the most important person they had known in relation to Max Rosenberg and the foundation (Chance, 1991, p. 88). Ruth Chance, the foundation's executive director at the time, also had been struck by the lack of research on Mexican Americans in the Southwest. In her own words, [this] "stirred my interest because California's largest minority apparently wasn't receiving much attention and very few resources were going into their problems" (Chance, 1991, p. 90).

Chance consulted Herman Gallegos, a young Chicano community organizer and activist, in the shaping of the symposium. Papers were commissioned in such areas as educational achievement, employment, migratory labor, census data, and leadership development. Experts were invited to attend from all over the country, making it a national event.

Chance invited Paul Ylvisaker, director of the Ford Foundation's Public Affairs Programs, to attend. "I had worked with Paul at Ford and had the warmest admiration for him" (Chance, 1991, p. 89).

Ylvisaker had already contracted with the University of California at Los Angeles "to produce a study of the status of Mexican Americans that would be widely accepted by mainstream policy makers and funders and would raise their consciousness about the existence of serious problems in the Mexican American community" (Oppenheimer-Nicolau, 1990, p. 10). The study was being conducted by Leo Grebler, an immigration expert. Partly because the Grebler research team initially did not include a Mexican American, it got off on the wrong foot. Moreover, the study was academic and intended to be long range.

Ylvisaker realized that work directed toward immediate problem solving would be needed. He was impressed with the Rosenberg symposium, and, in particular, the ability of Mexican American experts and scholars to reach consensus. The symposium, which occurred in late 1965, eventually led to a Rosenberg-supported book: *La Raza: Forgotten Americans* (Samora, ed., 1966).

Based on its success, Ylvisaker asked three of the authors most involved, Ernesto Galarza, a labor organizer and writer, Julian Samora, a Notre Dame professor of sociology, and Gallegos to look at what the Ford Foundation might do to help Mexican Americans (Gallegos, 1989, p. 36). In a series of conversations with Gallegos, Ylvisaker was at once expansive and cautionary about the purpose of this exploration.

Gallegos asked if Ylvisaker wanted to know if Mexican Americans needed their own version of the Urban League. "No," replied Ylvisaker, "I want you to go out and dream your dreams. Then you come back and tell me what you see out there." At the same time, Ylvisaker told Gallegos: "I don't want to jump into a pool and not find any water there. We made a lot of mistakes with blacks and I don't want to see us repeat the same problems [with Mexican Americans]" (Gallegos, 1989, p. 37).

The consultants' report to Ylvisaker, later published as *Mexican Americans in the Southwest* (Galarza, et al.), led to a major Ford commitment to create the Southwest Council of La Raza to support local community development and political organizing activities in the Southwest. It also began a long and deep history of Ford Foundation involvement with Latinos.

In the sixties, Ford's support enabled a set of large-scale organizations to develop, which survive today and have provided a permanent and firm base for expanding the social, economic, and political influence of Latinos on a national scale. Among these are the Mexican Legal Defense and Education Fund, Aspira, the Puerto Rican Legal Defense and Education Fund, the Southwest Voter Registration and Education Project, and eight locally based Community Development Corporations (Oppenheimer-Nicolau, 1990).

Herman Gallegos was central both to Rosenberg's symposium and the Ford consultancy. He was known to Rosenberg through a 1958 grant for farm labor organizing in San Bernadino county in which he was involved, and he was known to Ford's Ylvisaker prior to the Rosenberg symposium while working as a youth worker for the Ford-funded Bayview Hunter's Point Youth Opportunity Center (Gallegos, 1989, p. 37).

Gallegos was positioned to provide this key role partly as the result of a Whitney Foundation minority opportunity fellowship grant which had supported his graduate studies at the University of California at Berkeley's School of Social Work. The Whitney Fellowship program promoted many young Latinos into leadership positions by assisting them in earning advanced degrees, and thus providing leadership to their communities.

The story is told that John H. (Jock) Whitney, a child of privilege and an officer in the Army Air Corps, was captured during World War II by the

Germans and thrown together with other POWs, many of color and much less advantaged than he. He learned that many of these POWs did not fully share his values and love of the American creed because they were excluded from its benefits. On his return, therefore, Whitney supported the creation of the fellowship program to find and assist those minorities who could provide leadership to their communities and the nation, and help all people to share in its benefits and values. The Whitney Foundation recognized early on that Latinos needed to be included, and Gallegos was one of the beneficiaries of that recognition.

It is worth noting here that Ford's programming with respect to Mexican Americans faced severe political problems in the late 1960s and, as a consequence, shifted significantly from any voter registration and advocacy that the Southwest Council supported through subgrantees to "hard" programming (meaning education, housing, and economic development). The story is detailed by Siobhan Oppenheimer-Nicolau in her monograph, "In the Eye of the Storm" (Oppenheimer-Nicolau, 1990). In essence, a subgrantee of the Southwest Council of La Raza, the Mexican American Unity Council (MAUC), subgranted funds to an organization of young Chicano activists, MAYO, who, in turn, supported a slate of candidates in local elections in Texas. Unfortunately this angered Congressman Henry B. Gonzalez, just as Congress was looking into foundation grantmaking and debating new regulations for private foundations. This debate would lead to the 1969 Tax Act which among other things regulates the political activities of private foundations. MAYO's rhetoric also was especially militant, distressing the local Anglo establishment greatly (Oppenheimer-Nicolau, 1990).

In retrospect, the tragedy of this episode is that it led Ford away from supporting Hispanic participation in the political process at a point when Hispanics could have had an early and important impact on public policy. The same can be said of the overall chilling effect of the 1969 Tax Act, and the Congressional hearings leading up to it, on private foundation support for public policy related activities in the Latino and other minority communities.

Incorporation: A New National Population

In this early stage, however, the relationship of Latinos to philanthropy was driven largely by the grantor, whether Ruth Chance or Paul Ylvisaker. However farsighted and responsive to such leaders as Gallegos, they, as the initiators of the relationship, set its terms.

Prior to 1980, Latinos were generally viewed as distinct country of origin groups with regional settlement patterns in the U.S.: Mexican Americans in the Southwest, Puerto Ricans in the Northeast, and Cuban Americans in the Southeast, particularly Florida. In 1980 an important change in the U.S. Census's enumeration of population was instituted that created a new national category encompassing them all: "Hispanic." Prior to 1970, the Census Bureau used various items to identify people of Spanish origin: respondent's place of birth; parents' place of birth; mother tongue; Spanish surname; and, on occasion, race (Bean, Tienda, 1987, p. 39). Each of these raised conceptual and methodological problems. For example, the Spanish surname item did not differentiate between those who acquired or lost their Spanish surnames through intermarriage with non-Hispanics and those who acquired their names through birth (Bean, Tienda, 1989, p. 46).

For both political and statistical reasons, efforts to improve the coverage of the Hispanic population at a national level resulted in several items designating Hispanic national origin or descent in the 1980 census. The most significant was the self-identification item, which required all persons to indicate whether they were of Spanish/Hispanic origin or descent. The Spanish/Hispanic origin item is subjective; individuals indicate whether they perceive themselves to be Hispanic. "This identifier is the closest approximation to the sociological concept of ethic group identity" (Bean, Tienda, 1989, p. 48). Another important difference between the 1970s and 1980s Spanish origin items—the percentage of the populations sampled had direct implications for the success of the 1980 census in reducing undercounting. Consequently, the 1980 enumeration of the Hispanic origin population was the most complete in the history of the U.S. census to that time (Bean, Tienda, 1989, p. 49). The 1980 census counted 14.6 million Hispanics, an increase of 61 percent from 9.1 million in 1970. This increase also represented very real population increases from migration and high fertility rates. By comparison, the total U.S. population grew by 11 percent in the same period. Hispanic population growth brought added visibility to the Hispanic population in the media and signaled the emergence of a "new American minority," facing serious problems of poverty as well as language barriers and discrimination. *Time* magazine proclaimed the 1980s "The Decade of the Hispanic" (Russell, 1978).

The philanthropic "charge" into the Hispanic population during the 1980s, sparked by dramatic population growth, led to a corresponding increase in grants to benefit Hispanic populations. However, reporting on grants intended to serve special populations, such as Latinos, is impaired by the limitations of available data from the Foundation Center. Grants that do not specifically name a minority group or groups, but may benefit them, are not included in the total. For instance, a grant targeting low birth weight babies in urban centers would not be counted in this category unless the grant description specifically mentioned a racial or ethnic minority. In addition, the Foundation Center only collects data for grants over $10,000. Therefore, these numbers cannot be considered comprehensive and may undercount grants serving Latinos.

As shown in Figure 1, grants which specifically target Hispanic populations in their descriptions rose from $7.5 million in 1980 to $85 million in

Grants to the Hispanic Population 1960-1994
(in constant dollars)

Figure 1[1]

1993. The most dramatic growth was from 1984 to 1985, when giving to benefit Hispanic populations more than doubled. Although grantmaking in this area leveled off in the late 1980s, the totals grew again from 1990 to 1993 by 56 percent.

In this same time period, grants to benefit special populations in general also increased dramatically, from $57 million in 1980 to $558 million in 1993. However, grants to benefit Hispanics did not increase by a statistically significant rate greater than the growth in grants to benefit all special populations. Thus, in 1980, grants to benefit Hispanics were 13.3 percent of the total grants in the minority category, while in 1993, grants to Hispanics were 15.23 percent of the total to minority populations.

Latino grantmaking through the 1980s was led by three national foundations: the Carnegie Corporation and the Ford and Rockefeller Foundations. The total amounts expended by these foundations for domestic Hispanic-related grants between 1980 and 1989 were $30 million (rounded) at Carnegie, $61 million at Ford, and $24 million at Rockefeller, a total of about $115 million (Diaz, 1997). This amount represents about 15 percent of their total grant expenditures during this period. Considering the array of programming options and opportunities available to these three large, broadly chartered foundations it is impressive that Latino-related grants obtained 15 percent of their grantmaking resources in the decade spanning the 1980s.

According to the Foundation Center, grants from larger donors, such as these three foundations, have typically represented a large percentage of total grantmaking to benefit special populations. The total grant allocations from all sources to benefit the Hispanic population during the 1980s was $253.9 million. Therefore, giving from Ford, Carnegie, and Rockefeller represents approximately 45.5 percent, or almost half, of all dollars for Hispanic initiatives during the 1980s.

The three foundations took different approaches toward Hispanic grantmaking which represented two different grantmaking philosophies about incorporating "new" populations into grantmaking programs. Carnegie and Rockefeller integrated Latinos into their ongoing programs while giving them greater emphasis. Ford, on the other hand, created a separate population-specific initiative, although Latino grantmaking continued in other programs as it had all along. An analysis of the results of these two different approaches suggests that both could be effective in increasing grantmaking to Latino-related issues and organizations provided there was strong commitment from the foundations' leadership to Latino grantmaking (Diaz, 1997).

The 1980s also brought a shift in emphasis in grantmaking to Latinos with a new attention to public policy research on this "new" emergent population that would inform policymakers about its needs. As an example, the Carnegie Corporation made a grant of $21,600 to the Claremont Colleges for the creation of the Tomas Rivera Policy Institute, a Mexican American policy research "think tank." The Rockefeller Foundation made significant grants to the National Council of La Raza (formerly the Southwest Council of La Raza) for a major new policy research program. A major component of the Ford Foundation's new Hispanic initiative was devoted to policy research and the production of reliable and objective information on Hispanics and their condition.

This shift signaled an attempt by both Hispanic activists and their foundation supporters to be more "strategic" and to "leverage" federal and state policy in more favorable directions to meet Hispanic needs. However, it is likely that policymakers are more responsive to election returns than to rationality. In that regard Carnegie and Ford broke new ground in support for programs to encourage more foreign-born Latinos to naturalize and take the first step toward participation in the political process. While the hasty naturalization of many Latinos in time for the 1996 presidential election recently became politically controversial, the legal Americanization of foreign-born Hispanics remains a fruitful area for foundation work. It both empowers Hispanic immigrants politically by giving them the vote, and benefits American democracy by making these Latinos part of a common civil society.

In parallel to the trend of increased dollar amounts in Hispanic giving, there has been an increase in Hispanic participation in philanthropic foundations as board and staff members. According to the Council on Foundations' Foundation Management Report and the Foundation Salary Report, which rely on biennial surveys sent to Council members and nonmembers

Growth in Hispanic Board and Staff Members
1984-1996

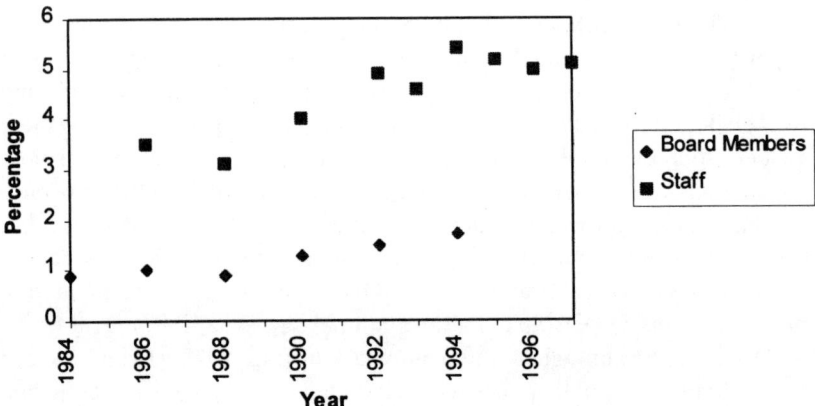

Figure 2[2]

across the foundation community, from 1984 to 1994, the number of Hispanic board members tripled, representing an approximate 1-percent increase in total foundation trustees. Full-time Hispanic staff increased from 140 in 1996 to 206 in 1997, representing a 47-percent increase, or a 1.5-percent increase of total full-time staff members across all foundations.

Figure 2 illustrates this trend, showing the strong rise in the percentage of Hispanic board and staff members between 1984 and 1997. Hispanic board members and full time, paid staff are represented as a percent of the total across foundations.

Another major development in the 1980s was the creation in 1985 of the Puerto Rican Community Foundation (PRCF) with the support of the Carnegie Corporation and the Ford and Rockefeller Foundations. The first community foundation on the island, the PRCF also created a precedent for later efforts to develop self-help funds on the mainland devoted exclusively to Latino grantmaking.

This second state of *incorporation* of Latinos into philanthropy differed from the first in that Latinos brought greater power to their relationship with philanthropy. A power born, yes, of sheer demographic might and presence, but a power nonetheless. Finally, Latinos went from being grantseekers exclusively to grantmakers, albeit within foundations still largely controlled by non-Latinos.

In recent years, Latinos have moved to another level in relation to philanthropy: the creation of their own philanthropic organizations and programs.

Independence: Self-Help Initiatives

Latinos' interest in finding new ways to increase their voice in the future of philanthropy is coinciding with the interest of philanthropic institutions in increasing the diversity of their programs and governance. A result of this convergence has been the emergence of special Hispanic funds, some affiliated with community foundations. These funds represent a trend toward community-based, self-help institution building. This section will address this new development in philanthropy, as well as a potential Funders Collaborative to support Latino nonprofit organizations.

The development of the Latino community funds may be the culmination of all the efforts to involve Latinos in philanthropy. In this new context, Latinos are not just grant recipients or foundation staff members or trustees, but organizers, planners, and creators of their own philanthropies. With many leaders within the Hispanic community expressing the view that philanthropy has not fully or sufficiently reached them, these funds give Latinos the ability to take control of the situation and do it for themselves.

Three Organizational Models

Hispanic community funds can be broken down into three organizational models: The Workplace Giving Model, the Community Foundation Field of Interest Model, and the Independent Model. Nevertheless, the funds share common strategies to generate contributions. These strategies include benefits, charitable drives, and soliciting funds from individuals, corporations, and foundation donors.

Latino funds that fall under the Workplace Giving Model generate money from their community through worksite fundraising drives that channel monies raised back into community-based nonprofits. These funds are alternatives to the similar campaigns run by the United Way of America, which, according to the National Committee for Responsive Philanthropy (NCRP), has not been supporting new and small agencies. The characteristics of these unsupported agencies frequently coincide with the those of the nonprofit sector for minority communities.

Hispanic Community Foundation Field of Interest Funds have typically begun as a specific, targeted fund affiliated with a community foundation. The idea has been to build endowments that generate a return for grant-making exclusively to Latino issues and needs. The functions of these funds are commonly managed and controlled by an advisory board of Latino community leaders that are supported by the initial granting foundation's staff. Thus, the functions are potentially biased toward the granting institution's agenda. While, in general, many minority leaders in philanthropic organizations encourage this type of community funding, there is some concern that if the community funds were unrepresentative of Hispanics originally, then the community foundations may be able to benefit from increased funding without being pushed to expand in areas of minority involvement.

The Independent Hispanic Fund Model consists of community-driven efforts to develop free-standing, private grantmaking institutions that are neither dependent upon workplace giving campaigns nor affiliated with a local or regional community foundation. These funds, however, also must protect themselves from the potential problem of having the agendas of their original donors imposed upon them. It is important to note, however, that in the case of Latino community funds, the donors' agendas are deeply rooted in the group-specific grantmaking and community interests of the minority community—the interests, in other words, that are commonly underrepresented in mainstream philanthropy.

Self-Help Initiatives

Latino community funds that have developed over the last decade across the nation include the Hispanic Community Foundation of the Bay Area (HCF), the Hispanic Federation of New York City (HFNYC), the United Latino Fund (ULF), the Greater Kansas City Hispanic Development Fund (HDF), the Hispanic Fund of Lorain County, and El Fondo de Nuestra Comunidad of St. Paul. HDF in Kansas City is the oldest of these funds, originated by the Kansas City Community Foundation in 1984. Its catalyst was a $1 million grant from the Hall Family Foundation following their discussions about creating more effective ways to reach Hispanic nonprofit organizations in Kansas City. An initial needs assessment followed this discussion and identified four major funding priorities. The fund is overseen by a seven-member advisory committee of local Hispanic community leaders. These individuals are responsible for recommending grant awards to the community foundation's distribution committee, which generally follows their advice. The four priorities are cultural awareness, community leadership development, human services, and civic participation. HDF has also worked to increase communication between the community foundation and the local Hispanic community.

HFNYC was formed when studies conducted by the Tri-State United Way, which were supported by the Ford Foundation, showed the need for strengthening and supporting Latino community-based organizations in the New York City area. In 1989 it was founded as an umbrella organization to raise money for 60 Latino health and human services agencies in New York. It is governed by a 16-member board that includes reputable trustees, based on their previous foundation experience.

The Hispanic Community Foundation of the Bay Area (HCF) was originally the Hispanic Community Fund. It was created to 1989 to respond to the perceived lack of philanthropic involvement in the Latino communities in the San Francisco Bay Area. In 1991 HCF started a three-year community survey that was sponsored by the Ford Foundation. Education, employment, and health were identified as the three most critical issues facing Latinos in the area. The results emphasized that Latinos should receive services from other Latino agencies because of cultural and linguistic factors. HCF has a 13-member board of trustees that are primarily Latino in ethnicity.

The United Latino Fund (ULF) originated with a 1989 ARCO and Ford Foundation–sponsored study. Conducted by the Tomas Rivera Center, a Latino think tank, the study concluded that Latinos should be more broadly engaged in setting the agenda and priorities for funding efforts within their own communities. The ULF was created to help achieve this goal in 1990 with a grant from the Ford Foundation. The focus was to develop a program that would provide support for the needs of grassroots Latino nonprofit organizations through voluntary giving. ULF raises and distributes its funds through a 40-member Community Planning Council, which is 50 percent Latino. This Council is charged with the responsibility of developing funding priorities and making allocation recommendations. A nine-member board of local Latino community leaders makes the final decisions.

The Hispanic Fund of Lorain County was started in 1986 in memory of a local Latino leader. It was not active until 1990 and since then has convened area Hispanic leaders to develop an endowment to support local Latino community needs. The fund is governed by a board of 13 trustees, all of whom are Latino.

El Fondo de Nuestra Comunidad recognizes the impact of rapid demographic change in the St. Paul area. It originates from the St. Paul Foundation's creation of Diversity Endowment Funds in 1994 for various ethnic communities modeled on the Kansas City Hispanic Development Fund. The St. Paul Foundation invited 13 local Latino leaders to establish an organizing committee for El Fondo. The first year of grantmaking for El Fondo was 1996. Its grantmaking focuses on supporting community self-help capacity building initiatives in volunteerism, leadership development, and nonprofit management, and promoting projects that facilitate dialogue and access between ethnic groups in the St. Paul area.

Assessing Strengths and Weaknesses of Existing Initiatives

An assessment of the Hispanic community funds reveals both positive and negative characteristics. The Latino funds appear to be attracting new contributors and money to the field. The support provided by these funds tends to be delivered with greater flexibility and responsiveness to grassroots community groups than traditional funders are able to provide, since these funds are in closer proximity to the community. Another advantage of the Hispanic funds' proximity is that it creates a unique environment for experimentation with alternative techniques of support.

Latino community funds are also serving as a mechanism by which Latinos can learn about and support the independent sector in their community. Until this time, Latinos have been active in supporting each other on a one-to-one basis or through religious institutions. The introduction of secular philanthropic institutions gives the Latino community a new notion of giving. From an educational standpoint, local philanthropic institutions are learning as well. The community funds are highlighting the needs of the Latino community and its nonprofits. The Latino funds also serve as a training ground for Latino philanthropic practitioners, creating a new generation of Hispanic individuals that can provide their expertise as members of boards of trustees, consultants, and advisors.

On the negative side, the funds may be too broad in their focus. They are criticized for not paying enough attention to program development and evaluation issues in their grantmaking. Likewise, they may not be paying significant attention to the strategic grantmaking that larger foundations are often drawn to, in the form of targeted initiatives.

The Latino funds are also criticized for their lack of community support. Many observers point out that there are relatively low levels of community donations and marginal assistance from established Latino leaders and groups in support of these funds. Another area of criticism is the leadership of these funds. The CEOs and trustees are not considered to have the community credibility, management expertise, and/or experience in private grantmaking necessary to effectively lead the funds. As a result, many practitioners and advisors question the long term viability of the funds.

Two final criticisms include the excessive overhead costs incurred by these funds and the issues of separatism and diversity. In regard to overhead costs, it has been noted that the operating budgets of these funds commonly exceed the monies they grant to community organizations. This imbalance has been observed to be as large as three or four to one. On a positive note, in 1997 the Kellogg Foundation provided a grant of $100,000 to address many of these issues through a planning and networking self-help project involving all the Hispanic funds.

The question of separatism poses a special problem for the Latino funds in terms of fundraising viability with other organizations. A common argument is that Latino funds encourage Latino communities to segregate themselves from mainstream philanthropy and society as a whole. This represents a movement away from the notion of many funders that new philanthropic institutions should be working to bring people together around a common civic culture.

Yet, by supporting Hispanic nonprofits and the participation of Hispanics more generally in nonprofit and philanthropy activities, the Latino funds may actually be assisting the political integration of Hispanics into American civil society. Recent research by the author confirms for Latinos what Verba and Nie found for the general population in their classic study, *Participation in America: Political Democracy and Social Equality* (Verba and Nie, 1972). There is a very strong positive correlation between Latino membership in nonprofit organizations and political participation as measured by voting in national elections and voter registrations. This suggests that general support from foundations for Latino and other nonprofits that encourage Latino participation in their membership and activities has a positive "integrating" impact on Latino political and civic participation.

Equally important, the Latino community funds have evolved to support the needs of the Latino community which studies have shown are not being met by mainstream philanthropic institutions. With the introduction of community funds, it is not surprising that some observers would begin to criticize their organization and implementation. The positive aspects of these funds include: (1) they increase the quantity, responsiveness, and lessons of philanthropy to Latino nonprofits; (2) they orient U.S. Latinos toward the culture of organized philanthropy; (3) they expand philanthropic understanding of Latino community needs; (4) they involve Latinos in philanthropy; and (5) they facilitate coordination among Latino nonprofits. In general, the main criticism of Latino funds is their need to demonstrate greater viability, professionalism, community support, and impact. If they cannot demonstrate these qualities their support will diminish.

A second major new development is plans for a Funder's Collaborative for Strong Latino Communities being undertaken by Hispanics in Philanthropy (HIP), the national affinity group of Hispanic grantmakers. The collaborative would provide a new vehicle to involve funders, especially those wishing to increase their investments in Latino communities, but with little track record or resources in this area. It would offer new linkages among funders, individual donors, and other potential partners that would result in greater coordination and focus.

HIP hopes to raise about $15 million over five years for the Collaborative which would focus its grantmaking on initiatives that:

- build new nonprofit leadership among younger Latinos
- expand the resource base of Latino nonprofits and multiply partnerships with other groups
- forge new forms of partnership among U.S. and Latin American nonprofits and foundations

♦ create new strategies to access and apply new technologies to expand organizational capacity

Trends and Forces

Demographic

The U.S. Latino population continues to grow rapidly. On June 1, 1997, there were 29.2 million Latinos in the U.S., comprising about 11 percent of the total population. This represented a 29-percent increase since July 1, 1990. In comparison, the non-Hispanic white population had only grown 3 percent between 1990 and 1997. By the middle of the twenty-first century, the Latino population is expected to reach 95.6 million or 24.5 percent of the total U.S. population. By 2025, Latinos will be the nation's largest race or ethnic group, at close to half of the total population (45 percent) (Census Bureau, 1992). Latinos continue to be heavily concentrated in California, Texas, New York, Florida, and Illinois, which together account for 74 percent of the nation's Latino population. Moreover, as the population grows it also continues to disperse, creating new significant minorities in such "non-Latino" places as small midwestern towns and the Washington, D.C. suburbs of Arlington, Virginia, creating both fear and apprehension among those already settled in these communities.

In addition, the Hispanic population is young; about half are under 26.5 years old as of June 1, 1997. In comparison, non-Hispanic whites were more than a decade older, with a median age of 37.3 years. The obvious challenge for Latinos and the U.S. economy will be preparing and incorporating young Latinos into the workforce as older Americans retire. Put more starkly, the social security benefits of the current workforce will depend heavily on the success of this transition.

Economic

Ours is a world of tightening resources and continuing, if not increasing, disparities both within and among nations. Global competition and markets, as recent events suggest, make it more likely that a cold in one nation's economy can cause pneumonia in others'. The social strife that might accompany any economic problems in Latin America, could, in turn, lead to increased migration from there. At the same time the spectacular growth of the U.S. stock market has swelled the endowments of private foundations, creating new large pools for strategic grantmaking that could be directed toward Latinos' needs.

A third factor is the growth of the Latino business and professional class, representing a new pool of wealth for philanthropic self-help initiatives. It is noteworthy that in 1993, over 170,000 Latino households had incomes of more than $100,000, according to the U.S. Census Bureau. Hispanic households, moreover, are relatively frequent contributors to charitable organizations when asked. Sixty-five percent of Hispanic households reported charitable contributions in the Independent Sector's 1994 survey of giving in the United States (Independent Sector, 1994).

Social and Political

The U.S. response to migration from Latin America, especially Mexico, has been schizophrenic, warring over itself welcoming, tolerating, screening, or excluding. Currently, the popular attitude, driven by xenophobia, racial, and ethnic prejudice, as well as fear of linguistic diversity, political differences, and economic competition, is one of discouragement. In this climate, philanthropy, as exemplified by the creation of the Emma Lazarus Fund within George Soros's Open Society Institute, can be a voice of tolerance and reason. The fund believes that the increasing hostility to newcomers in the U.S. is antithetical to the values of an open society and attempts to combat this hostility through its programs. Therefore, the fund seeks to help legal immigrants become active participants in American society. It provides grants to nonprofit organizations to help legal immigrants to naturalize, including civics education and English as a Second Language programs, and to advocate for immigrants' rights.

On the fiscal policy front, the political consensus on the balanced federal budget makes federal funding for new social programs to address Hispanic needs much less likely.

Hispanic need for nonprofits is almost certain to increase. A range of socioeconomic challenges confronts Latino communities. The Latino poverty rate is nearly three times that of non-Latinos and more than 40 percent of Latino children grow up in poverty.

Latinos, like other groups before them, have taken recourse in voluntary action as a means to address the problems they face as a community. Yet the nonprofit organizations that result, like others, face the double bind of seeing public funding for social and other services decline while demands for their services increase. Because they serve as sympathetic and language-friendly service providers, Latino nonprofits remain the social safety net for their growing population. At the moment, however, philanthropy has not responded. According to one estimate, although Latinos constitute about 11 percent of the population, less than 2 percent of the $12 billion granted by private foundations in 1995 went to Hispanic nonprofits (Ramos, 1996).

Moreover, about three-quarters of this amount comes from only 7 foundations. These data suggest that there is the clear potential for expanding the grantmaking base for Latino giving.

Latinos will become more creative and effective in the competition for resources. Both the Hispanic funds and the potential Funders' Collaborative demonstrate new approaches for gathering resources for the Latino community. The Hispanic funds have already drawn the support of local, regional, and national funders. The affinity group Hispanics in Philanthropy has grown to 350 members and its various programs demonstrate another opportunity for Latino grantmakers to be effective advocates within philanthropy for their communities.

In addition, efforts are currently underway to develop new strategies for tapping into the growing wealth within the Latino community to increase self-help philanthropy, much like what has occurred within the Jewish population of the United States.

The growing size of the Latino population will be another favorable influence on both private and public funding. Latinos voting in the 1996 presidential election totaled 4.9 million, a 16-percent increase over the number voting in 1992. This compares with an 8-percent decrease in voting for the total population. Funders, as it was once said of the Supreme Court, do follow the election returns. The increasingly competitive potential of Latinos and their nonprofits may assure a larger share of a growing philanthropic pie. Certainly the growing presence of Latinos at the regional and local level will put added pressure on community and regional foundations to respond.

The Direction Ahead

Recognizing the tension between funding to Hispanics as a separate population and the desire to integrate them more fully into American society (a desire most Latinos themselves share), there are a number of funding strategies and programs that can serve both purposes.

As suggested earlier, citizenship is to Hispanics as voting rights were to African Americans. It is the first step toward civic participation and incorporation; it carries both rights and responsibilities. Yet, the process of naturalization remains daunting for most foreign-born Latinos. Programs to assist Hispanics with this process have now appeared and received support from such foundations as the Carnegie Corporation and most recently from the Emma Lazarus Fund within George Soros's Open Society Institute.

Related to citizenship are English language training programs. Most, if not all, foreign born Latinos understand that the key to economic success in the U.S. is the ability to speak English. Moreover, the ability to speak English is another key to the acceptance of Latino newcomers by established residents. Unfortunately, English language programs are currently swamped and badly in need of support and, perhaps, technological enhancement to reach more "customers."

K–12 education programs for Hispanic youths are a third important area where foundation support could be helpful. Latino youths have the highest dropout rates of all school-age children. Without an educated cohort of young people the economic and political future of the Latino population of America will remain bleak.

Latino culture and art are rich and constitute a major contribution to the arts and culture in America. One need only tick off the names of artists Frieda Kahlo and Diego Rivera, ballerina Alicia Alonso, actresses Chita Rivera and Rita Moreno, and actors such as Jose Ferrer and Raul Julia. The Rockefeller Foundation has played an important role in recent decades in supporting Latino arts. West Coast foundations also provide support to local artists. Others should follow.

Finally, the Latino infrastructure of nonprofit organizations, like the population itself, is young. Partly as a result, it suffers from inexperienced leadership which remains fragile. General or targeted support to strengthen these organizations would lead not only to better services for the population they serve, but to more opportunities for leadership training, and through the involvement of the Latino community in their activities to higher voter registration and participation rates as discussed above (Diaz, 1996). The new Funders' Collaborative now being considered by Hispanics in Philanthropy may provide the vehicle to support this infrastructure more generously.

Notes

The author wishes to acknowledge the contribution of Jodie Kaden, Christie Routel, and Jennifer Ringold in the preparation of this paper.

1. The data used in Figure 1 are from the Foundation Center's *Foundation Giving*, 1982–1995.

2. The data for Figure 2 are from the Council on Foundations, *Foundation Management and Foundation Salary Report*, various years.

References

Bean, F. D. and Tienda, M. *The Hispanic Population of the United States.* New York: Russell Sage Foundation, 1987.

Chance, Ruth Clouse. "At the Heart of Grants for Youth," an oral history conducted in 1990 by Gabrielle Morris, The Regional Oral History Office, The Bancroft Library. University of California, Berkeley, 1991.

CPS 1992 population estimates and projections, Census Bureau Public Information Office, 1992.

Diaz, W. A. "Latino Participation in America: Associational and Political Roles," *Hispanic Journal of Behavioral Sciences*, 1996, 18 (2). 154–174.

Diaz, W. A. "The Behavior of Foundations in an Organizational Frame: A Case Study." *Nonprofit and Voluntary Sector Quarterly*, 1996 25 (4), 453–469.

Diaz, W. A. "Foundations and "New" Populations: Three Cases of Latino Grant-making in the 1980s." Research report for Aspen Institute's Nonprofit Sector Research Fund, 1997.

Galarza, E., Gallegos, H., and Samora, J. *Mexican Americans in the Southwest.* Santa Barbara: McNally and Loftin, 1969.

Gallegos, E. "Equity and Diversity: Hispanics in the Nonprofit World," an oral history conducted in 1988 by Gabrielle Morris, The Regional Oral History Office, The Bancroft Library. University of California, Berkeley, 1989.

Giving and Volunteering in 1994. Washington DC: Independent Sector, 1994.

Oppenheimer-Nicolau, S. *From the Eye of the Storm.* New York and Washington: Hispanic Policy Development Project, 1990.

Ramos, H. A. J. and Kasper, G. "Latinos and Community Funds: A Comparative Overview and Assessment of Latino Philanthropic Self-Help Initiatives" (working draft). Berkeley, CA: Hispanics in Philanthropy, 1996.

Rosenberg Foundation. Directors' Manual, 9 (revised June 1997).

Russell, G. "It's Your Turn in the Sun." *Time Magazine*, 112 (16), 42–48, 1978.

Samora, J., ed. *La Raza: Forgotten Americans.* Notre Dame, IN: University of Notre Dame Press, 1966.

Verba, S. and Nie, N. *Participation in America: Political Democracy and Social Equality.* Chicago: University of Chicago Press, 1972.

CHAPTER FOURTEEN

The Case of Minnesota

Institutionalizing Public Spirit

Jon Pratt

Casual explanations for the contemporary Minnesota ethos give credit to native generosity as perhaps adopted values from Anishinabe tribes, a little bit of Norway and Sweden in the most Scandinavian of states, or even the weather.[1] However, Minnesota could not be considered to be a hospitable environment for honest government, economic success, racial tolerance, or philanthropy until after World War II. Earlier in its history Minnesota was more likely to be recognized for political corruption, civil discord, prejudice, and economic inequality.

A key ingredient in realigning the state's orientation was a shift in business leadership, ultimately represented by a public commitment to give away 5 percent of corporate profits for community projects.

The new business values were made clear in the August 13, 1973, issue of *Time* Magazine, which hailed Minnesota in a cover story titled "Minnesota: A State That Works," with a photo of Governor Wendell Anderson catching a fish.[2] Central to *Time's* descriptions of what made Minnesota tick were descriptions of fundraising drives and community organizations, mentioning the Urban Coalition, Orchestra Hall, the Institute of the Arts, the Citizens League, the Urban League, the Mayo Foundation, and the Guthrie Theatre.

The idea for the story came from Gregory Wierzynski, *Time's* Chicago Bureau Chief, while covering Minnesota politics for the 1972 election. Wierzynski sat in on precinct caucus meetings, which he found surprisingly civil and fair, and noticed that local news broadcasts in Minneapolis covered snowmobile accidents, city council resolutions, and a pronouncement by the governor—not the crime, scandal, and corruption of other cities. As the story developed, Wierzynski looked for defining characteristics of the Minnesota way of life:

> Part of Minnesota's secret lies in people's extraordinary civic interest. . . . Even more important than corporate giving is personal fund raising. Fund drives underway or about to begin in the Twin Cities amount to a staggering $300 million, of which $136 million has already been raised. The business effort is twofold—one for cultural activities and one for social and civic affairs.

Time went on to highlight the lakes, buildings, tax reform, and clean politics of the state. Accompanying photos of Honeywell CEO Stephen Keating, Cowles Media chair John Cowles, Jr., and five Dayton brothers, stockholders in the Dayton Hudson Corporation, were descriptions of their commitment to community fundraising:

> The Daytons are best known as patrons of the arts. Kenneth Dayton, 51, is deeply involved in fundraising for a new $18.5 million music center complex, which he hopes will rival Washington's Kennedy Center in architecture and acoustics. Bruce B. Dayton, 55, is raising $26 million for the Minneapolis Institute of Arts, with a new wing designed by Yamasaki. The Guthrie Theatre is primarily the contribution of John Cowles, Jr., head of the Minneapolis Star and Tribune Co. But the list of big business contributors and fundraisers is much longer.

While the Dayton Hudson Corporation and other companies were respected as business successes, this set of CEOs preferred to be recognized for their accomplishments on behalf of the community. The heady feeling that the growing corporations could simultaneously tackle urban problems and museum expansions was tempered by a fear that the new business ethic, and the accompanying corporate philanthropy, would disappear when the postwar business leadership retired.

To spread their practice of philanthropy, the Minneapolis Chamber of Commerce created the Five Percent Club in 1976 (since renamed the Keystone Awards). This system sought to perpetuate and formalize philanthropic commitment by setting a fixed percentage, 5 percent of their pretax profits.[3]

In 1976 the Five Percent Club was unique, and received both praise and criticism depending on one's view of the proper uses of corporate funds. The Five Percent Club drew John D. Rockefeller III to speak to the Minneapolis Chamber of Commerce in 1977: "I heard so much about the City of Minneapolis, about its Chamber of Commerce, about the public spirit of its business community, about your remarkable Five Percent Club—that I feel a bit like Dorothy in the Land of Oz. I had to come to the Emerald City myself to see if it really exists."[4]

While not quite the Emerald City, the Minneapolis-based Five Percent Club added participating companies and expanded its geography to include businesses throughout the state. In 1994 the *Chronicle of Philanthropy*[5] rated Minneapolis as having the highest level of charitable giving overall among fifty U.S. cities it studied, and the highest per capita level of corporate contributions. The *Chronicle* compared cities based on per capita contributions to national organizations, the United Way, community foundations, and per capita contributions by corporate foundations, independent foundations, and community foundations. By 1996 Minnesota had 4,187 financially active charities, with 189,794 employees and annual expenditures of $10.4 billion. Nonprofit employees now make up 8 percent of Minnesota's employed workforce, up from 6.8 percent in 1987.[6]

The last ten years have seen Minnesota's nonprofit sector grow faster than the state's economy as a whole, with total wages paid in the sector rising an average 6 percent per year (in constant dollars), and the number of firms and the number of employees both growing by 5 percent per year. This growth underscores the fact that nonprofits are a larger factor in Minnesota's economy than for the nation as a whole. Minnesota's 8 percent nonprofit share of the state's paid workforce is substantially higher than the national average of 6.8 percent.[7]

IRS business filings verify that Minnesota's nonprofit sector is proportionally larger than the national average, as shown in a new Urban Institute[8] analysis. While Minnesota ranks as the 20th state by population, it ranks 18th for total expenses by nonprofit organizations, 17th for total assets of nonprofit organizations, 16th for the amount of charitable contributions to these organizations, and 13th for the number of active organizations.

In addition to high levels of charitable giving and nonprofit activity, Minnesota ranks at or near the top for common quality of life measures in comparison with other states:

- 1st for longevity in women, and 2nd for longevity in men
- 1st for workforce participation by adult women, and 2nd for workforce participation by adult men
- 1st for voter turnout
- 1st for high school graduation rate
- Top five ranking for SAT and ACT scores for the last 20 years

Does the system of philanthropy in Minnesota deserve credit for creating this high quality of life, or is charitable activity simply the byproduct of an otherwise successful economy and society? An important critical shift, simultaneous with the growing public spirit among leading corporations, was an increase in state and local government expenditures—often in partnership with philanthropy. The state's history makes clear that Minnesota's charitable impulse is less the result of longstanding social attitudes and cultural habits than it is a strategic intervention by leaders able to refocus attention from private conflicts to public benefit projects. A redefinition of the "Minnesota way of doing things" led to the creation of a strong base of charitable institutions and support organizations, backed by a widespread generosity and a conviction that "it's probably always been this way."

Historical Roots: Nonprofits, Politics and Social Mores, 1858–1945

As a mostly rural, agriculture-based economy from statehood in 1858 until about 1945, Minnesota had mostly conservative business and political leaders and a small set of philanthropic and nonprofit institutions.

An influential corps of New England Yankees was recruited to form an industrial and financial class in the Minnesota Territory in the 1850s, many of whom brought their working capital with them. This group included George Draper Dayton (dry goods), Cadwallader Washburn (grain milling), Amherst Wilder (overland and river transport), Alexander Wilkin (riverboat and property insurance), Charles A. Pillsbury (grain milling), and Thomas Barlow Walker (logging). James J. Hill, builder and owner of the Great Northern Railroad, emigrated from Canada.

The picture of philanthropy in Minnesota before 1945 shows a broad mix of purposes and several generous families (Dayton, Washburn, Wilder, Pillsbury, Walker, and Hill). The successful entrepreneurs of the nineteenth century believed in philanthropy as a responsibility of their private wealth, not of their businesses.

Before statehood the Catholic and Episcopal churches had a central role in evangelizing to Native Americans and early settlers, and the local priest, Lucien Galtier, successfully changed the name of the settlement outside Fort Snelling from Pig's Eye to St. Paul in 1841. The first nonprofit chartered in the territory was the Minnesota Historical Society (1849), to record and preserve the story from the beginning. (One item to record could have been the many name changes of nonprofit organizations—this chapter describes organizations with their present names only.)

Many of Minnesota's early organizations were formed to help young people, including the YMCAs of St. Paul (1856), Minneapolis (1866), Red Wing (1869), and Winona (1886); and the YWCAs of Minneapolis (1891), Austin (1906), St. Paul (1907), and Duluth (1909). The Sheltering Arms Foundation (1882), Washburn Child Guidance Center in Minneapolis (1883), and the Children's Home Society in St. Paul (1889) began as orphanages and evolved into broader agencies focused on children. The Boy Scouts were organized in Minneapolis (1910) and St. Cloud (1919), and the Girl Scouts in Minneapolis (1912), St. Paul (1912), and Duluth (1920).

Lutheran Social Services (1865), the Women's Christian Association (1866), Catholic Charities (1869), and Jewish Family Service (1911) began offering religiously sponsored human services, especially to the poor. The Salvation Army also set up operations to help the poor in Minneapolis (1886),

Austin (1895), and Virginia (1896). A "poor farm" was set up in northern Ramsey County (site of the current State Fair grounds), where the destitute could contribute to their own survival.

The relief of the poor and the sick in St. Paul was largely vested in the YMCA in 1875. Daniel R. Noyes, the organization's president, appealed in the St. Paul *Pioneer Press* for "Systematic Charity," and recommended creation of a new organization similar to the New York Society for the Prevention of Pauperism.[9] Noyes hoped that the new organization would reduce indiscriminate giving which, he claimed, only encouraged idleness and deceit. He also called for detecting and exposing "unworthy" applicants for aid in addition to improving the conditions of the poor. The St. Paul Society for Improving the Condition of the Poor was formed in 1876 to provide direct relief, but discussions continued about how to register and investigate applicants for relief. This led to the formation of Associated Charities (1892), which kept a Central Registration Bureau of the names of people applying for aid. By 1895 James Jackson, its general secretary, reported to the board that over 7,700 names were listed. "We feel warranted in saying," Jackson wrote, "there are few cities in the country where the individual condition of the unfortunate, the shiftless or the fraudulent is so well known as in St. Paul."[10] As the new charities sought to weed out the unworthy from the worthy, social workers sought to promote professionalism in their field by forming the Minnesota Social Service Association in 1893.

During the late eighteenth century the tide of immigrants into the state swelled, especially from Germany, Sweden, Norway, Denmark, and Finland, and to a lesser extent from southern and eastern Europe. Pillsbury Neighborhood Services (1879) was formed with support from the grain milling family to provide assistance to immigrants, including widows and orphans. It sent home visitors to help them adjust and give them advice about homemaking and child rearing.

Thomas Barlow Walker began publicly displaying his art collection in 1879, which later became the Walker Art Center. Other organizations formed to sponsor performances and make the arts available to the public included the Schubert Club (1882), Thursday Musical (1892), Minneapolis College of Art and Design (1895), the Duluth Art Institute (1896), the Minnesota Orchestra (1903), and the Minneapolis Institute of the Arts (1915).

By the turn of the century the state's mostly agricultural and logging economy had developed the Twin Cities into a railroad and flour-milling center for the upper Midwest, with increasing revenue from iron ore mining and light manufacturing. Political development and civic leadership were comparable to other states of that era, with graft and corruption commonplace. Lincoln Steffens published "The Shame of Minneapolis" in the January 1903 issue of *McClure's Magazine*, documenting the system of payoffs to the mayor and police chief from organized prostitution, gambling and burglary rings:

The mayor was the head of the graft organization; Dr. A. A. Ames had made his brother, Col. Fred W. Ames, chief of police. The boss-mayor organized and tried, through his brother, to direct the police graft. But this police graft was, like New York's, a deliberate, detailed management of the police force, not to prevent, detect or arrest crime, but to protect, share with, and detect the criminals. The so-called moral element of the people played into the hands of the police criminals, as in New York, by requiring strict laws against vice and crime.[11]

"Doc" Ames was removed from office and sent to prison, along with his brother, yet succeeding Minneapolis administrations were also forced to make accommodations with vice. Community consensus was elusive on a broad spectrum of issues, including the role of public parks. The American Federation of Labor opposed the city purchase of shoreline surrounding 13 Minneapolis lakes as simply creating "playgrounds for the rich."

One of the state's largest charities got its start when St. Paul businessman Amherst Wilder died on November 11, 1894, and left the bulk of his estate to "best operate in a permanent manner to relieve, aid and assist the poor, sick and needy people of the City of St. Paul." After his wife and daughter died, and litigation had upheld the will, the Amherst H. Wilder Foundation (1910) began operation as a social service organization endowed with $2.6 million. One of the first services of the new charity was to open public baths to counter disease and poor living conditions for residents of the riverflat shantytown and Swede Hollow, next to downtown St. Paul.

Immigrant groups also formed associations to help new entrants adjust to American life and to preserve their culture, including the Danebod Folk School in Tyler (1886), Sons of Norway in Minneapolis (1895), Alliance Française (1920), and the American Swedish Institute (1929). Scientific research and public education, including display of preserved animals, were the goal of the Bell Museum of Natural History (1872) and the Science Museum of Minnesota (1907). The Animal Humane Society was formed in Hennepin County in 1891.

In addition to a large number of religious sponsored hospitals, nonprofits formed to promote public health included the Laura Baker School in Northfield (1897), the Lung Association in Hennepin County (1903), American Red Cross in St. Paul (1918), Courage Center (1928). The Mayo Foundation (1918) converted the Mayo Brothers' successful local private practice into a medical research, education, and diagnostic center, working in tandem with St. Mary's Hospital in Rochester.

The Minneapolis Foundation was formed in 1915; the year after, Cleveland formed the first Community Foundation in the country (though it did not have staff until 1970). Junior Leagues were formed in St. Paul (1917), Duluth (1920) and Minneapolis (1923) to raise funds for community service projects and develop leadership opportunities for women.

Establishment of the St. Paul Urban League (1923), the Minneapolis Urban League (1925), the Hallie Q. Brown Community Center in St. Paul (1929), and the Phyllis Wheatley Community Center in Minneapolis (1932) created community organizations controlled by African Americans with some financial and board participation by whites.

Minnesota had an almost unbroken record of Republican governors and legislatures from 1858 to 1930, but the Depression triggered major political and economic shifts. The farm economy sank to its lowest point, and farmers organized to halt foreclosures through the Farm Holiday movement.

From 1931, the year Floyd B. Olson was sworn in as the first Farmer-Labor Party governor, to 1944, when the Farmer-Labor Party merged with the Democratic Party, Minnesota's political and social environment was in turmoil. Farmers were battling banks and grain companies over prices and financing; labor was organizing for higher wages, and business leaders were united in opposition to both causes. In Minneapolis, business leadership was focused on opposition to labor unions and "agitators" through their organization, the Citizens Alliance:

> In the primary matter of maintaining the open shop in Minneapolis, the Citizens Alliance had a record of almost unbroken success. With a permanent and well-paid staff, a corps of undercover informers, and a membership of eight hundred businessmen, it had for nearly a generation successfully fought and broken every major strike in Minneapolis.[12]

On New Year's Day in 1934, 65 of Minneapolis' 67 coal yards were hit by strikes and quickly won wage increases. A massive trucking strike followed, pitting 3,000 truckers seeking union recognition against thousands of businessmen-deputies recruited by the Citizens Alliance to back up the police. In a pitched battle witnessed by at least 20,000 participants and onlookers, the Citizens Alliance was routed and their attorney killed by a blow to the back of the head with a sawed-off baseball bat.

The conflict was thrown in the lap of Gov. Floyd B. Olson, who had made a name for himself as an ambitious Hennepin County Attorney. Olson had solid standing with his party's left wing for convicting both the righthand man of the Citizens Alliance and the Exalted Cyclops of the North Star chapter of the Knights of the Ku Klux Klan. Olson called out the National Guard and declared martial law, arresting leaders and raiding the headquarters of both sides in the strike. Eventually the union was recognized and the strike was settled, but not until after six months of strife, several more deaths, and 46 union pickets shot in the back.[13]

Olson's biggest legislative battle in 1934 was with the Republican controlled Senate, which was blocking relief legislation, and with the state's largest banks, Northwest Bancorporation of Minneapolis and First Bank Stock Corporation of St. Paul. After bringing thousands of angry farmers into the capital, Olson finally got the senators to pass his program of a farm mortgage moratorium, appropriation of relief funds, an old-age pension, and an emergency banking act.

It was in this atmosphere that the platform of the Farmer-Labor Party called for the abolition of private enterprise and the establishment of virtually total Socialism:

> We therefore declare that capitalism has failed and that immediate steps must be taken by the people to abolish capitalism in a peaceful and lawful manner and that a new, sane and just society must be established; a system in which all the natural resources, machinery of production, transportation and communication shall be owned by the government and operated democratically for the benefit of all the people and not for the benefit of the few.
>
> To protect citizens from exploitation through industrial profits, we demand public ownership of all mines, waterpower, transportation and communications, banks, packing plants, factories and all public utilities. Provided that this shall not apply to bona fide cooperatively owned and operated enterprises.

A Grand Canyon divided the political party ruling Minnesota and the leadership setting the business agenda. Both sides had successfully developed disciplined institutional networks and mobilized substantial resources, but were on an unsustainable course. Many business leaders were disgusted by the tactics of the Citizens Alliance, and many Farmer-Laborites were taken aback by the extreme language of the 1934 platform. Unions broadened their gains after the truckers' strike, and employers gradually accommodated their demands. Floyd B. Olson's death from cancer in 1936 left the Farmer-Labor Party without its key political strategist, and after diminished success at the polls it merged with the Democratic Party in 1944.

Institutionalizing the Public Spirit: 1946 to the Present

The postwar era was ripe for a new generation of leaders. New faces on the political scene included Hubert Humphrey, elected DFL mayor of Minneapolis in 1944 and U.S. Senator in 1948, and Orville Freeman, elected first DFL governor in 1954.

Minnesota's economy tipped from being primarily agricultural in 1952, when manufacturing displaced farming as the major source of income. At the same time that a new political liberalism took hold, a second generation of business leaders took office at Dayton Hudson, Cowles Newspapers, and the Piper Jaffrey Companies. In 1946 each of the companies began donating 5 percent of their pretax profits to charitable causes, including arts, human services, and sometimes their family churches.

The Charities Review Council was formed in Minneapolis in 1946 as a response to the multiplicity of war reconstruction charities, some of them bogus. The CRC would review the finances of organizations and give donors, including businesses, advice on their worthiness. Minnesota was also coming to grips with its social intolerance and racial injustice. The denial of hospital privileges to Jewish doctors by Minneapolis hospitals led to a major fund drive in 1945 to build the 200-bed Mt. Sinai hospital in Minneapolis, led by Jay Phillips.[14] The Minneapolis Branch of the American Automobile Association began admitting Jewish members in 1947, and major employers slowly began to integrate their workforces.

Honesty and competence of charities was an ongoing concern for community leaders, which came to a head in the Sister Kenny scandal. The Sister Kenny Institute (1942) was formed in Minneapolis to support the work of Sister Kenny, an Australian nurse who pioneered a successful treatment for the atrophied limbs of polio victims, and received considerable national attention and contributions. Marvin Kline, the Institute's executive director and a former mayor of Minneapolis, successfully raised over $20 million for polio treatment. Unfortunately, $11 million of this was eaten up in fees by a Chicago mail order firm hired by Kline, including illegal kickbacks to Kline. Kline became the second Minneapolis mayor to go to prison, spending three years in Stillwater State Prison on both federal and state convictions, for mail fraud and illegally boosting his 1958 salary as executive director (from $25,000 to $48,000).

Prosecution of the Sister Kenny case helped increase the visibility of the state's young attorney general, Walter Mondale, and led to the creation of the Charities Division of the Attorney General's Office. The Sister Kenny Institute, which had been a source of community pride and then embarrassment, was reconstructed with a new board made up of prominent business leaders.

During the 1960s the number of nonprofit organizations increased, as a result of broadened knowledge of how to form and finance organizations, and because of an increase in government contracting and grantmaking to organizations. As state institutions for the mentally ill and retarded were scaled back in the 1950s and 1960s, nonprofits became the preferred vehicle to provide community based services with government funds.

The state preference for nonprofit health providers was written into state law, requiring that all health maintenance organizations be nonprofit corporations. Despite a national wave of hospital conversions from nonprofit to for-profit auspices, Minnesota has only nonprofit– or local government–owned hospitals. By 1996 health care accounted for 56.8 percent of Minnesota nonprofit employment.[15]

A confrontation with Minneapolis police in the black community in 1967 grew into a small-scale insurrection that left buildings burned and nerves shattered. Leaders in the business community quickly made financial commitments to organizations serving the community and that triggered a major philanthropic response and led to the creation of the Urban Coalition. The founding Board of Directors of the Urban Coalition included three CEOs, Minneapolis Mayor Arthur Naftalin, a variety of community organization representatives, and the chair of the school board. The Urban Coalition quickly became both a major public voice and an initiator of reforms in housing, civil rights, police-community relations, and education.

New immigrants and growing populations increased the diversity of organizations, with the startup of Sabathani Community Center (1967), Project for Pride in Living (1972), KMOJ Radio (1976), African American Family Services (1977), MIGIZI Communications (1977), Accessible Space (1978), Hmong American Partnership (1990).

Board members and fundraisers for organizations that served low-income populations formed a coalition in 1983 to redirect corporate and foundation grants to their communities. Organizers felt that they were at a disadvantage in fundraising, and did not receive the quantity or size of grants that were going to larger institutions, including colleges and the University of Minnesota. The Philanthropy Project was a three-year effort with 130 organizational members, including the Urban Coalition, the Project for Pride in Living, the American Indian Center, and the Community Clinic Consortium. The project sponsored tours and presentations for trustees and foundation staff, and published three research studies documenting the extent to which foundation and corporate grants went to organizations that served low income people, women, communities of color, and rural populations. The project's final report[16] concluded that between 1981 and 1985, the share of Minnesota grant dollars going to disadvantaged constituencies increased from 28 to 38 percent of total grants. After the Philanthropy Project ended in 1986, the project's staff and board formed the Minnesota Council of Nonprofits to address a broader range of issues, including the relationship between nonprofits and government.

The fund drives described in *Time* magazine, and the Five Percent Club cited by John D. Rockefeller III, were the most visible evidence of Minnesota's institutional support base for philanthropy. A larger network of support organizations reinforced these efforts, some initiated by business leaders and others formed by philanthropic and nonprofit leaders. The support organizations grew over an eighty-year period into a broad infrastructure with four main functions:

a. Increase charitable contributions
b. Increase volunteer labor
c. Enhance the management capacity, earned income, and coordination of organizations
d. Facilitate successful relations between nonprofit organizations and state and local government and the media

Minnesota Philanthropic Support Organizations

Four major support organizations were formed before the war: the Minneapolis Foundation (1915), United Way of Minneapolis (1919), United Way of the Saint Paul Area (1920), and the Saint Paul Foundation (1940).

Twenty more support organizations were formed over the next fifty years: the Volunteer Center (1945), Charities Review Council of Minnesota (1946), Minnesota Private College Council (1948), United Arts Fund (1954), Minnesota Council on Foundations (1969), Minnesota Citizens for the Arts (1975), Keystone Awards Program (1976), Cooperating Fund Drive (1978), Minnesota Planned Giving Council (1978), Management Assistance Program for Nonprofits (1979), Minnesota Nonprofit Assistance Fund (1980), Virginia McKnight Binger Human Services Awards (1985), National Center for Social Entrepreneurs (1985), Minnesota Initiative Funds (1986), HealthFund of Minnesota (1986), Minnesota Council of Nonprofits (1987), Center for Nonprofit Management, University of St. Thomas (1991), Institute for Renewing Community Leadership (1992), Minnesota Futures Fund (1996), and the One Percent Club (1997).

Individually each of these support organizations has a specific task in supporting one or more aspects of nonprofit activity. Collectively, these institutions share in inculcating the population, especially leaders, in the belief that philanthropy and voluntary activity is not only a social good, but also an essential element of social legitimacy. They also promote positive public opinion toward charitable activity and the fundraising efforts behind them.

While comparable organizations in these categories exist in other states, the scope and magnitude of Minnesota activity is clearly on the high end. The next four sections describe the major roles performed by these support organizations.

Increase Charitable Contributions

The Minnesota Keystone Program (formerly the Five Percent Club) codified the new business leadership thinking of the 1950s and 1960s into a recognition program designed to spread the practice of business tithing:

> The Minnesota Keystone Program symbolizes the strong bridge between community needs and business resources. Successful businesses are essential to the survival of Minnesota's communities. Healthy, safe communities help businesses thrive. Through the Keystone Program, organizations are encouraged to make and maintain corporate investments in the community and are publicly recognized for those significant and generous actions. [17]

The Minneapolis Chamber of Commerce launched the Five Percent Club in 1976 with 23 participating companies, including Cowles Media

Company, Dayton Hudson Corporation, Medtronic, Norwest Bank, and Piper Jaffrey Companies. The program inspired business leaders in several U.S. cities and one other country, Costa Rica, to establish tithing clubs, which have been found to have a positive impact on giving.[18]

The Keystone Program provides support to companies interested in beginning a contributions program. Program materials instruct companies how their giving can evolve: (1) growth in dollar value contributed, (2) increased formality of budget and structure, (3) narrower subject focus and larger, longer commitments, and (4) more employee involvement in decision making.

Have the formalized expectations of the Keystone Program given Minnesota corporate philanthropy staying power? Two examinations of Twin Cities corporate grantmaking by Joseph Galaskiewicz (1979–81 and 1987–89) sought to identify the factors that explain changes in corporate giving. Galaskiewicz' first study had suggested that "the Twin Cities were witnessing the end of an era. Intensely personal networks of social influence orchestrated by an economically powerful and socially prominent elite were going to be replaced by community institutions that would motivate, reward and legitimate corporate community service."[19]

Part of the rationale for institutionalizing corporate contribution levels was the impending retirement of the business leadership, and a fear that new CEOs from outside the community would scrap donations to increase profits. Galaskiewicz found that while the CEOs turned over between the studies, the contributions did not drop. However, Galaskiewicz' analysis of interviews, CEO country club memberships, CEO friendship patterns, CEO birth locations, and corporate charitable commitments convinced him that the credit didn't belong to the Keystone Program so much as to informal social structures: "The informal social structures were more durable than the more organized efforts and that much giving in 1987–89 was still driven by the CEOs' personal ties to local philanthropic leaders. The new old-boy network proved to be just as effective as the old old-boy network in soliciting funds and communicating expectations."

Galaskiewicz credited executive involvement in local business organizations, educational organizations, social service agencies, and task forces as being an important factor, and recognized one strategy in particular:

> Clearly, networks were critical in sustaining the Twin Cities grants economy, but without the civic and voluntary associations to help build and nurture these ties, the networks would have atrophied and had a difficult time surviving.
>
> In interviews in both periods, I heard over and over again how important it was to recruit new CEOs onto the boards of nonprofit organizations and into business and social clubs. Stories were told about a new CEO in town who at first would slash the contributions budget but then suddenly increase contributions the next year, having served on a prominent cultural board. It was in these arenas that executives were solicited for contributions, socialized into

the local culture, and where trust, mutual respect, and norms of reciprocity are created.[20]

Over half of the Twin Cities CEOs have turned over since Galaskiewicz' second round of data collection, and rates of contribution have held steady. By 1996 the program, renamed the Keystone Program, had added a new level, 2 percent givers, and reported 147 participants at the 5 percent level and 90 organizations at the 2 percent level.[21] In addition to maintaining participation, enforcement of historic charitable obligations has played an important role in several corporate takeover battles and corporate buyouts.

In response to attempted hostile takeovers of Dayton Hudson Corporation and the Saint Paul Companies, the Minnesota legislature held hearings and passed legislation favorable to maintaining local ownership. In both cases the companies' charitable contributions, and the relatively uncharitable track records of their pursuers, were major topics of discussion and dread. In the buyouts of Pillsbury, Cowles Media, and Piper Jaffrey, the new owners felt obliged to pledge publicly that they would continue the philanthropic commitments. Local norms, whether because of informal social networks or formal institutions, held sway.

With increases in the stock market, higher asset values increasing private foundation payout requirements, and increased profits tied to Keystone Program commitments, Minnesota is experiencing a boom in its grants economy:

Foundation	Year Formed	1997 grants (\$ millions)[22]
McKnight Foundation	(1953)	76.2
Bush Foundation	(1953)	21.2
Northwest Area Foundation	(1934)	16
Andersen Foundation	(1957)	16.7 (est.)
Blandin	(1945)	13.7
Otto Bremer	(1940)	12.5
Corporation		1997 grants (\$ millions)
Dayton Hudson		45.8
Norwest Bank Corporation		21.0
US Bancorp		18.2
General Mills		16.8
3M		16.1
Cargill		11.3
Honeywell		10.3
St. Paul Companies		10.9
Community Foundations		1997 grants (\$ millions)
Saint Paul Foundation	(1940)	27.0
Minneapolis Foundation	(1915)	13.8

Institutionalizing philanthropy involves getting other people to be philanthropic. While virtually every nonprofit organization undertakes its own search for donations, one of the most common strategies is to organize community wide drives in which peers perform the solicitation. The community foundations (Minneapolis and Saint Paul Foundations), the United Way organizations, United Arts Fund, Cooperating Fund Drive, Health Fund of Minnesota, and the Minnesota Initiative Funds perform this function. The two largest community foundations have sponsored several of the most innovative philanthropic initiatives, including the AIDS Funding Consortium (1988–94), the St. Paul Foundation's Diversity Endowment Fund, and the Bigelow Foundation's Children, Families and Community Initiative.

Six Minnesota regional Initiative Funds were established in areas outside the Twin Cities in 1986 by the McKnight Foundation to make local decisions on developing grants programs for their areas. Over the next ten years the foundation made $114 million in grants to the six funds, and helped them develop independent community boards, raise local funds, build endowments, and operate grants and business loan programs. By 1996 the Initiative Funds (in Duluth, Bemidji, Owatonna, Hutchinson, Fergus Falls, and Little Falls), had made more than 5,000 grants, 1,560 business loans, and developed net assets of $108 million.[23]

Minnesota's foundations grew to make the state third highest in the U.S. for per capita foundation assets (after Michigan and New York), with 180 foundations listed in the 1997 *Foundation Directory*, published by the Foundation Center. Minnesota's two largest private foundations, Bush and McKnight, were established in the 1950s with gifts of 3M stock, which increased in value over 100 times by 1998. Two Minnesota founders of food product companies put more than $200 million of their assets into charitable foundations: the Hormel Foundation (1946) and the Schwann Foundation (1997).

Two new Minnesota campaigns are seeking to increase charitable contributions. In 1998 the Minnesota Planned Giving Council launched a "Leave a Legacy" campaign encouraging people to leave funds to charities in their will or estate plans. Research on charitable bequests by the Minnesota Council of Nonprofits revealed that this type of giving is the least likely to benefit organizations that serve communities of color (.6% of funds) or women (1.4% of funds).[24] Equity in the beneficiaries of philanthropy is especially challenging for planned giving, where the connection between the donor and the recipient institutions is generally the strongest.

The One Percent Club is the most recent addition, modeled after the earlier Five Percent Club, and inspired by the advocacy of donating a portion of net worth in *Wealthy and Wise* by Claude Rosenberg Jr.[25] The One Percent Club was organized in 1997 by Joe Selvaggio, former director of the Project for Pride in Living (an inner city social service organization) and Ken Dayton (one of the original founders of the Five Percent Club). After three months, seventy-five people, mostly wealthy people with substantial assets, signed the pledge: "I/We agree to contribute 1 percent or more of my/our net worth annually to the tax-deductible cause(s) of my/our choice. I/We understand this entitles me/us to membership in an association of 1 percent givers who believe strongly in the wisdom of philanthropy."[26]

Sixty-five of the signers agreed to let their names be known, risking increased solicitations, and ten asked to remain anonymous. The One Percent Club actively recruits additional signers onto its pledge, maintain a speakers' bureau, and seeks to lead by example. At least part of the appeal being made by the One Percent Club advocates for philanthropy with a critique of government:

> We have a unique opportunity. For the first time in this country's history, we have both the wealth and the means, in the form of dedicated nonprofit organizations, to heal our nation's social and cultural ills. 1 percent can make a difference. Nonprofits have literally moved in next door to the problems in our communities. Like small businesses, they are more flexible, innovative and cost effective than big government programs. When you invest in them, you are putting your dollars directly to work in the most efficient ways available today.[27]

Increase Volunteer Labor

People who volunteer and attend church services are more likely to make charitable contributions, though the behaviors are more concomitant than causal. Minnesotans have a high rate of volunteering, and the state is the second highest per capita as a source for Peace Corps volunteers.

Over fifty organizations and projects are organized along the lines of the Volunteer Center in St. Paul, which matches individuals to volunteer assignments. The Minnesota Office of Citizenship and Volunteer Services, a state agency in the Department of Administration, helps promote volunteers to state agencies, and provides training and information for other volunteer programs. The Management Assistance Program (MAP) for Nonprofits recruits corporate volunteers to assist nonprofit organizations improve their management.

Virginia McKnight Binger Human Services Awards were begun by the McKnight Foundation to recognize the importance of individual volunteers, especially people who have proven their commitment through years of service. In addition to being part of a gracious event and publicity, the ten award recipients receive $7,500 each.

Enhance Management Capacity and Ability to Generate Income

While promotion of a philanthropic and volunteer ethic has been important in Minnesota, the full strategy involves both a push and a pull. One former Minnesota governor observed that it wasn't just that Minnesotans were so generous, but that the organizations making requests had become more effective at making requests.

Efforts to improve the capacity, and the accountability, of the demand side have received less attention but have also been a focus of activity. Active donors wanted to make sure that their donations were going to organizations that were spending the money effectively, and formed the Charities Review Council of Minnesota in 1946.

The Minneapolis Foundation and other local funders formed the Minnesota Nonprofit Assistance Fund in 1980 to provide cash flow loans and financial advice to struggling nonprofits. A former Control Data executive formed the National Center for Social Entrepreneurs in 1985 to become more successful at generating income from fees and sales, at the same time meeting community needs. The University of St. Thomas serves as home to the Center for Nonprofit Management, the Institute for Renewing Community Leadership, and the Partners Internship Program, each furthering a different aspect of nonprofit leadership development.

Conspicuous among the failures of Minnesota philanthropy has been the demise of low income, constituency-controlled organizations in the 1980s and 1990s. Negative audit reports, deficits, and dissolution followed years of foundation grants and government contracts to The Way, the St. Paul American Indian Center, the Minnesota Clients Council, the Whittier Alliance, the Phoenix Group, People of Phillips, and others. The abundance of management support available in the state was not able to help these organizations keep basic books and maintain cash flow.

In 1996 the Minnesota Council of Nonprofits, the Minnesota Council on Foundations, and the Minnesota Council of Churches joined to cosponsor a fund to assist nonprofits in restructuring in response to welfare reform. The Minnesota Futures Fund received $1.3 million in contributions from Minnesota foundations and corporations, and $750,000 from the State of Minnesota.

Several Minnesota nonprofits have used the reliable philanthropic support to build substantial enterprises of earned income. The classic example is Minnesota Public Radio (MPR), which began merchandising Prairie Home Companion memorabilia and turned it into a multimillion–dollar catalog and music business, run by a for-profit subsidiary. Hazelden was an early pioneer in residential chemical dependency counseling, and launched a publishing business with books, tapes, and calendars supplying half its income. The economic success and entrepreneurialism by many organizations was welcomed by the press and the public, but the use of for-profit subsidiaries has raised some hackles (especially concerning compensation for MPR executives paid both by the charity and its for-profit subsidiary).[28]

Facilitate Successful Relations with State and Local Government

The many foundation grants and corporate contributions have operated alongside the growing state and county investment in nonprofit services. At the same time, the growing nonprofit sector has sometimes looked like a tempting source of new tax revenue. Several of the support organizations established ongoing relationships with legislators, county commissioners, and state agency heads to inform them of the workings of the sector.

The Minnesota Council of Nonprofits was formed as a state association of nonprofits in 1987, and immediately organized opposition to the governor's proposal to eliminate the charitable exemption from paying the state's 6.5 percent sales tax. In succeeding years MCN, the Minnesota Council on Foundations, the Private College Council, Minnesota Citizens for the Arts, and United Way organizations have repeatedly made the case that maintaining the sales and property tax exemptions preserves the contributions of charitable donors. As with some other issues, major Minnesota corporations participate in business leagues that want to expand the tax base to include nonprofits, and simultaneously support organizations that make the opposite case.

Assessing the Public Spirit: Minnesota Public Attitudes and Generosity

Regrettably, tracking poll and prior research are unavailable for Minnesota attitudes toward philanthropy before the 1990s. Some people assume that Minnesotans had an inbred philanthropic gene going back decades. A clear goal of the Five Percent Club and now the One Percent Club has been to promote and reinforce social norms of charitable giving.

In a 1995 public opinion poll commissioned by the Minneapolis *Star Tribune* and WCCO, Minnesotans reported that they were far more likely to give to nonreligious causes than the nation as a whole.[29]

	% Minnesota	% United States
Religious	61	49
Health Organizations	57	26
(such as heart or cancer research or your local hospital)		
Human Services	45	27
Education	39	17
Environmental Causes	27	12
Arts, Culture, and Humanities	18	8

An ongoing concern for philanthropic leaders has been that as the economic base of the nonprofit sector grows, including increased employment, revenues and real property ownership, the public will reduce its contributions and its toleration for exemptions from taxes. Beginning in 1989 the Minnesota Council of Nonprofits began polling on public support for tax exemptions. The poll was conducted by the Minnesota Center for Survey Research of the University of Minnesota, administering the same wording to 800 adults in Minnesota:

> Nonprofit organizations provide social service, health services, education and arts to the public. Under Minnesota law, nonprofit organizations have been free from paying sales or property taxes because their services benefit the public. Do you agree or disagree that nonprofit organizations should CONTINUE to be free from paying taxes . . . strongly agree, somewhat agree, somewhat disagree, or strongly disagree?

	% 1989	% 1993	% 1997
Strongly Agree	41	48	60
Somewhat Agree	38	36	28
Somewhat Disagree	12	10	9
Strongly Disagree	9	6	4
Total	100	100	100

Overall this poll shows increased public support for nonprofit tax exemptions over the period 1989–97, from 79 percent agreeing in 1989 to 88 percent in 1997.[30] Young people (18- to 34-year-olds, 93.2%) and people with a college education (91.2%) were most like to support tax exemptions. Although all demographic groups showed agreement over 75 percent, people 75 and older (78.9%) and people with less than a high school education (75.1%) were somewhat less likely to express support.

Several other factors did not prove to be statistically significant: income, political party affiliation, geographic location, household status, or household composition. The lack of a split along income or political party lines is encouraging, since these would create the most problems for legislators.

Increasing public support is a positive development, especially given the increased visibility and financial activity by nonprofits in the state during the same period. The time period covered coincided with two national charity scandals (United Way of America and New Era Philanthropy), and increased publicity about nonprofit executive compensation. Some people within the nonprofit sector have felt that erosion of trust or support was taking place during the same time period. While the questions did not specifically address attitudes regarding accountability, the willingness to abide tax freedom for nonprofits is a proxy for general support for the value of philanthropy to the community.

Lessons for the Public Spirit and Philanthropy

The growth of Minnesota's nonprofit sector, and the increasing role of philanthropy, have come at a time of increasing population and a generally healthy economy. While the philanthropic commitments by business leaders are sometimes written off as Minnesota exeptionalism, they have established a firm grip on new executives and influenced public expectations.

The overall reason for the growth of Minnesota's commitment to philanthropy is not the economy, since the state ranks 15th in median national disposable income and 16th in per capita personal income.[31] Several conclusions are possible, however:

• The best customer of philanthropy is an educated person, and a young person, as indicated by the poll results. Not only does Minnesota have a high rate of charitable giving, but more information is publicly available on charities in Minnesota than any other state, including libraries stocked with the *Minnesota Nonprofit Directory*, toll-free 800 number access to the Charities Review Council, and the Attorney General's Office Charities Division website.

• Business leadership influences the larger community. The location of 14 Fortune 500 companies in the state is important, as are the visible, persistent leadership and formal structures of commitment—especially the Keystone Program.

• Receptivity to social messages has been self-reinforcing, resulting from the repetition of the value of charitable giving and volunteering message from multiple channels of workplace, support organizations, and community leaders.

• Creating the public spirit of philanthropy developed a new self-image of state pride and accomplishment, and overcame the old divisions. Within the state, the former history of factionalism, poverty, and graft is long forgotten, and most Minnesotans assume that things have always been this way.

• Fairness in distribution of grants is an ongoing challenge. While major educational and cultural institutions have thrived, including the Carlson School of Management and the Ordway Music Theatre, they operate in an understated competition with health clinics, human services, environmental groups, neighborhood associations, and small nonprofits. Successful capital campaigns for the Minneapolis American Indian Center, Turning Point, and the Seed Academy showed that organizations serving communities of color can get some large contributions. A $20 million campaign by Penumbra Theatre and Walker-West Music Academy, announced in 1998, raised the ante significantly.

• An important unexplored area is the link between the public's decision to make charitable contributions and its willingness to pay taxes. Minnesota is considered a high tax state, ranking 5th among the states in personal tax load.[32] While Minnesota's corporations, including the Keystone Program organizations, have long sought to lower the state's personal income tax and commercial/industrial taxes rates, they have never pulled out all the stops in this campaign. The state's high tax rates are matched by high rates of charitable giving, both individual and business, while states with lower tax rates generally report lower levels of charitable giving.

Minnesota isn't the Cooperative Commonwealth that the Farmer-Laborites envisioned, or the open shop of the Citizens Alliance. Minnesota still has its share of persistent poverty, urban sprawl, and violence. However, the state has made sufficient peace in its politics and employment relations to achieve high workforce participation and a healthy diverse economy.

A defining feature of Minnesota that shows no signs of dissipating is the public spirit: a now institutionalized expectation of ongoing involvement and contributions from businesses and individuals. A highly visible and networked Third Sector has emerged that influences how much Minnesota allocates, through philanthropy and public funds, to tackle social problems and improve the quality of life.

The Future of Philanthropy

The future appears to be bright for philanthropy in Minnesota, with increased participation in the Keystone Program, a jump in private foundation grants, growing support for tax exemptions, and improved management and board capacity in most organizations. The balanced growth of nonprofit revenue — including strong charitable, government and earned income — means that most community organizations are on a path of sustainable development.

Perhaps Minnesota's greatest challenge is to come to grips with the potential of philanthropic and nonprofit activity in the state, since it is a larger factor in the state's economy and public life than in any other state. As a significant economic and political influence, can philanthropy and nonprofits reposition themselves in the public eye from being beneficial but disconnected, resource-short, gap-fillers? Nonprofits in the years ahead need to be seen as a successful and essential element of a healthy society, but can only do so if accurately and consistently understood.

The next progression seems to include increased linkages between institutional philanthropy and public officials, and greater coordination between support organizations emphasizing charitable giving and their counterparts focused on government relations.

Just as early in the state's history, when business leadership moved from economic warfare to the common ground of charitable institutions, there is a growing appreciation of the possibilities of collective action involving the Minnesota business community, government, and nonprofits together. Welfare to work programs, urban schools, and environmental mediation are bringing together all three sectors as players in a mixed economy and democratic, pluralistic society. The results are often messy, but there is a growing experience base and comfort level with these multisector collaborations, and an expansion that gets included in private expressions of the public spirit.

Notes

1. "Minnesota: It's colder than you think," Minneapolis *Star Tribune*, July 4, 1996, p. A12. Winters in Minnesota are colder than those experienced by 97% of the people who live in the U.S., with a mean temperature of 14 degrees in January and February. Only Alaska and North Dakota are colder, though most Alaskans live in the Anchorage area or the panhandle, areas warmer than southern Minnesota.

2. "Minnesota: A State That Works," *Time*, August 13, 1973, pp. 24–35.

3. In 1976 5% was the highest amount deductible from the corporate income tax as a charitable contribution, later raised to 10%.

4. Joseph Galaskiewicz, "An Urban Grants Economy Revisited: Corporate Charitable Contributions in the Twin Cities, 1979–81, 1987–89," *Administrative Science Quarterly*, September 1997, Vol. 42, p. 445.

5. "The Midwest's Charitable Advantage," *Chronicle of Philanthropy*, February 22, 1994, p. 22–23.

6. Jon Pratt and Chris Sullivan, *Minnesota's Nonprofit Economy* (St. Paul: Minnesota Council of Nonprofits, 1997), p. 5 [based on Minnesota Department of Economic Security, 1987–1996 ES–202 Employment Data].

7. *The Nonprofit Almanac 1995–96*, Independent Sector, Washington, DC (1996).

8. Carol J. De Vita, "Viewing Nonprofits across the States," *Charting Civil Society* (Urban Institute, Center on Nonprofits and Philanthropy, August 1997), p. 3. The report's table of the 50-state "Distribution of Public Charities in States by Activity, 1992," was based on 1993 U.S. Internal Revenue Service Exempt Organizations/Business Master File and Return Transaction File.

9. Mark Haidet, A *Legacy of Leadership and Service* (Family Service of Greater Saint Paul, 1984), p. 2.

10. Haidet, p. 3.

11. *Autobiography of Lincoln Steffans*, New York: Literary Guild (1931), p. 376.

12. Charles Rumford Walker, *American City* (New York: Farrar & Rinehart, Inc., 1937), p. 240.

13. John Beecher, *Tomorrow Is a Day* (Chicago: Vanguard Books, 1980), p. 272.

14. Walter Parker, "Sinai founding helped to heal a civic illness," St. Paul *Pioneer Press*, July 1987, p. A1.

15. Pratt, p. 7.

16. *Minnesota Philanthropy and Disadvantaged People* (Minneapolis: Philanthropy Project, 1986).

17. *Minnesota Keystone Program*, 1996 Participants, Greater Minneapolis Chamber of Commerce (1996), p. 2.

18. Peter Navarro, "Why do corporations give to charity?" *Journal of Business*, 61 (1988): pp. 65–93.

19. Galaskiewicz, p. 467.

20. Galaskiewicz, p. 468.

21. *Minnesota Keystone Program*, 1996 Participants, Greater Minneapolis Chamber of Commerce (1996), p. 2.

22. Robert Franklin, "For charities, when getting's good, giving is, too," Minneapolis *Star Tribune*, January 26, 1998, p. B3.

23. *McKnight Foundation Annual Report 1996*, p. 9.

24. Catherine Eberhart and Jon Pratt, *Minnesota Charitable Bequest Study* (Minnesota Council of Nonprofits, 1992).

25. Claude Rosenberg, Jr., *Wealthy and Wise* (Boston: Little Brown and Company, 1994).

26. Brochure, *The One Percent Club*, Minneapolis, 1998.

27. *The One Percent Club.*

28. Reed Abelson, "Charities Use For-Profit Units to Avoid Disclosing Finances," *New York Times*, February 9, 1998, p. A1.

29. Robert Franklin, "8 of 10 in the state donate to a wide variety of charities," Minneapolis *Star Tribune*, December 17, 1995, pp. 1A, 19A.

30. *Minnesota State Survey* (Minneapolis: Minnesota Center for Survey Research, January 1998), p. 36.

31. *Compare Minnesota, An Economic and Statistical Fact Book*, Minnesota Department of Trade and Economic Development (1996), pp. 17, 23, 36.

32. *Compare Minnesota*, p. 56, state and local tax revenue per $1,000 of personal income, Fiscal year 1992.

CHAPTER FIFTEEN

The Case of Kansas City

David O. Renz

> In Kansas City, Missouri, there is occurring a quiet but startling
> revolution in the administration of human services funded by the
> state and federal government.
>
> — *John W. Gardner*

In the fall of 1997, 20 Greater Kansas City foundations, nonprofit organizations, higher education centers, government agencies, corporations, and civic associations gathered to celebrate their first year of work in partnership to strengthen the quality of early childhood care and education services in their region. These organizations had come together fifteen months earlier to ratify and sign a compact in which they each promised to do their part in a collaborative effort to strengthen and enhance the quality of these services and build a much stronger system by which future services would be provided, managed, and monitored. Each organization of this group, known as the Partners in Quality for Early Childhood Care and Education (PIQ), brought its own unique perspective and knowledge base to this initiative, and each committed to action within its own sphere of influence. And by the end of the first year, they had indeed begun to have an impact through the work of this unusual cross-sector, multi-organization partnership.

Earlier that same year, another quite different cross-sector collaborative initiative also gained recognition for its significant accomplishments on behalf of the metropolitan region. This collaboration, the Block Grant Response Initiative, developed in a more reactive mode to help the Kansas City community address the potential issues and impacts of federal devolution and the block grant approach to human services funding. Driven by legislative decisions at the federal level, the Kansas City initiative brought together and catalyzed action among leaders of units of state and local government, the business community, the philanthropic community, and schools and universities. The Kansas City response was among the earliest of these initiatives to spring forth in metropolitan communities in the United States, and was quite successful as a vehicle to bring the sectors together to plan and facilitate a productive and systematic community approach.

These stories illustrate two of more than thirty cross-sector initiatives and collaboratives now underway in the Greater Kansas City metropolitan community. Their stories are among the most successful, yet they also may be prototypical of an increasingly common phenomenon in both Kansas City and many other metropolitan regions of the United States. These cases illustrate the growth of partnerships, alliances, and collaboratives that are emerging to cross the boundaries of the public, private, and philanthropic sectors to address in new and innovative ways the challenges that confront our communities.

Representatives of other communities come to Kansas City to examine these new kinds of initiatives, yet many leave telling their hosts, "That's great for you, but we're not Kansas City. This could only work here!" Kansas Citians themselves do consider their situation unique in some respects. It is their own stated judgment that Kansas City is the "partnership capital of the world." And they understand that no other place is identical to Kansas City. But is it true that these strategic innovations are so unique to Kansas City that they have limited applicability to other communities? What has enabled some of these exciting and unusual initiatives to emerge, and what should we learn from them? What has worked well as these innovations have developed, and what could or should have been handled better? And how might these cases evolve, given the realities of a changing philanthropic climate, devolution in government, and trends in the nature and activities of nonprofit organizations?

We suggest that the case of Kansas City illustrates the early stages of development of a range of innovative strategies by which philanthropy, business, and government are collaborating to address the changing demands of a dynamic urban community. Nonprofit and philanthropic organizations and their leaders are playing key leveraging roles that are enabling Kansas City to explore and adapt a range of innovative strategies and opportunities. This case helps us begin to understand how a strong and entrepreneurial philanthropic sector is building community by engaging and facilitating new patterns of leadership and governance, community social capital, a shared community vision and theory of change, a vital network of mediating organizations, a network of civic and social entrepreneurs, and capacity to creatively employ a diverse array of indigenous resources. The Kansas City experience provides useful illustrations of distinct ways, some new and some not so new, that the philanthropic sector[1] in Kansas City is moving beyond "playing at the margins" to revitalize and sustain a healthy metropolitan community.

The Context of Kansas City

Located near the heart of the nation, Kansas City is a moderate-sized metropolitan community by urban United States standards. Its demographics and urban issues are relatively comparable to many other urban metropolitan communities. In 1990, metropolitan Kansas City was home to nearly 1.6 million people (Mid-America Regional Council, 1993), and the region had more than 582,000 households. Fewer than one quarter, however, are located in the urban core, whereas thirty years earlier the proportion was about 50 percent. And this urban core is especially likely to be home to a particular segment of the population. Of the region's households earning less than $10,000 per year, 48 percent were located in the core. Relocation of jobs and households to the suburbs, coupled with urban core deterioration and disinvestment, have resulted in a critical cycle of decline that has affected Kansas City in ways similar to many other metropolitan regions. Unlike most other major metropolitan areas, however, Kansas City, Missouri, recently has begun to experience an increase in the urban core population—considered by many to be a bellwether for positive change.

Kansas City also is a community that is divided by a state line; the region is nearly equally split between the states of Missouri and Kansas. As would be expected in matters where state policy and politics make a difference, such as education, social welfare, and human services policy, there are unique state-based differences that separate otherwise similar organizations and communities. As urban communities in states in which the majority of legislators live outside urban and suburban communities, the Kansas City communities often find themselves with little political sympathy or legislative support in their efforts to address many of their most difficult urban and suburban issues. At times, their problems and needs are met with outright hostility.

Similar to most modern metropolitan regions, Kansas City is fragmented by many governmental boundaries. Cities, counties, school districts, water districts, and a myriad of special service and tax districts all add complexity to the challenges of regional coordination. In total, 114 municipalities, eight counties, and numerous other special districts serve and segment metropolitan Kansas City. The federal government also has a significant presence, both as the region's largest employer and as a major property holder.

History and politics add to the fragmentation and bifurcation of the metropolitan region. The state line remains an ongoing reminder of some of the differences that stem from the Civil War era when Missouri and Kansas were the final states to take (opposite) sides on the question of slavery. Such history sometimes appears to have relevance to both the politics of interstate relationships and the state of racial relations within the region. The forces encouraging regional fragmentation continue to be significant.

Kansas City's philanthropic sector is vital and significant in the life of the community. In 1997, well over 6,000 nonprofit organizations served the community.[2] Philanthropic giving in Kansas City is substantially greater than would be expected for a community its size. In 1994, *The Chronicle of Philanthropy* ranked Kansas City as eleventh in philanthropic giving among all United States metropolitan regions, whereas its rank in per capita income was 25th. In 1996, 490 private foundations and philanthropic trusts served the community and, collectively, their assets amounted to over $3 billion (Clearinghouse for Midcontinent Foundations, 1997). These philanthropic institutions paid out over $150 million in grants that year.

It is in this context that metropolitan Kansas City is working to build and redevelop a healthy and self-sufficient community. It is in this context that leaders from government, the business community, and the philanthropic sector have been collaborating to create new and innovative ways to create and sustain the city's future.

Coming Together to Build Kansas City

The organizations described in the introduction are but two illustrations of more than thirty current cases of organizations and people coming together across sector boundaries to address community needs and issues. They are somewhat unique in that they are initiatives with a focus on system change, although there are a dozen more that also have such change as a primary focus. At least sixteen other initiatives have developed in response to emerging community issues and, while they began in a more reactive mode, most have evolved into broader efforts to build community capacity and systems. Table 1 presents a summary of these initiatives.

We describe these two cases of cross-sector community initiatives, the Partners in Quality for Early Childhood Care and Education and the Block Grant Response Initiative, to illustrate the nature of these increasingly typical collaborations, how they emerge, and how they develop.

Building a System for Quality Early Care and Education

The Partners in Quality for Early Childhood Care and Education (PIQ) is an instructive case of an initiative to cross sector, agency, and programmatic boundaries to accomplish system change. PIQ has brought together Kansas City foundations, nonprofits, college and university centers, corporations, civic associations, and many leaders of other community organizations to improve the quality of early childhood care and education (ECE).

PIQ is, in fact, the latest and most encompassing of several collaborative community studies and initiatives designed to strengthen the provision of ECE services. One of its predecessor initiatives was the Metropolitan Council

Table 1
Key Instances of Collaboration

Primary Illustrations (meta-collaborations, each a somewhat different model or approach)

1. Block Grant Response Initiative (collaboration among organizations of all sectors in community)
2. Local Investment Commission, especially including its Comprehensive Neighborhood Services/Caring Communities program (hybrid government-nonprofit organization, coordinating networks of service delivery and activity among numerous government, education, and nonprofit organizations and programs)
3. Early Childhood Care and Education Initiatives, including:
   - Metropolitan Council on Child Care (MCCC, a coordinating intermediary organization)
   - Partners in Quality for Early Care and Education (PIQ, a multi-sector organizational membership collaborative)
4. Neighborhood Redevelopment Initiatives, including multiple intersecting initiatives:
   - KC Building Blocks (KC Local Initiatives Support Corporation—LISC)
   - Kansas City Neighborhood Alliance and associated neighborhood associations and community development corporations ("CDCs")
   - Kansas City's Community Policing initiative (also other city government projects)
   - Numerous initiatives of individual Community Development Corporations (CDCs)
5. Community Information Systems Development Initiatives, including collaborations to link data bases of various community networks and units of government (including connections among United Way, Community Resource Network, Mid-American Assistance Coalition, Kansas City Neighborhood Alliance, and the community data bases of Kansas City Missouri city government [e.g., crime statistics, code enforcement, property ownership]).

Additional Inter-Sector Initiatives and Collaborations:

1. Partnership for Children
2. Bi-State Cultural District/Union Station Development
3. Brush Creek Partners
4. Maternal and Child Health Coalition
5. COMBAT Anti-Drug Tax initiative
6. Empowerment Zone/Enterprise Communities program
7. Community Outreach Partnerships Center (COPC) program
8. The Child Abuse Network
9. Coalition for Positive Family Relationships
10. C-squared Collaborative (a collaboration of four of these collaboratives)
11. The Heart of America United Way's Performance Outcomes Measurement initiative
12. Vital Signs Initiative

Table 1 Continued

Related Smaller Scale Alliances and Collaboratives:

There are a myriad of significant yet smaller-scale alliances and collaboratives that also exhibit (and demand) many of these same characteristics but which do not substantially cross discipline, sector, or service area boundaries. Many are linked with those listed above, as well.

1. GOS: Alliance of Gillis, Ozanam, and Spofford Homes
2. The Children's Campus
3. Kansas City Church Community Organization (KCCCO)
4. 18th and Vine District
5. Mid-American Assistance Coalition (MAAC)
6. YouthNet
7. KC Metrolink
8. Interdistrict Education Alliance
9. The Promise Project
10. Youth Opportunities Unlimited
11. Association of United Way Agencies (AUWA)
12. SeniorLink
13. Mid-America Health Alliance

on Child Care (MCCC), itself a multisector collaboration created to plan and coordinate the development and delivery of quality child care in Kansas City. MCCC had its genesis in a 1988 future issues study process conducted by Kansas City Consensus, the local citizens' league. The conclusion of this process was that meeting the child care needs of its children would be critical to Kansas City's future, and that the limited and fragmented set of services then available were inadequate to meet these needs. This sentiment reflected an emerging community consensus, as well, because several other community and nonprofit task forces of the time also had determined that availability and quality of care were critical issues. One strategy to address these issues was to create the Metropolitan Council on Child Care (MCCC). A subsequent Consensus planning process, known as COMPASS, reaffirmed the community's focus on these issues by declaring that Kansas City should aspire to become the "Child Opportunity Capital of the World."

From the beginning, the vision for the MCCC was to develop and sustain a community-wide system by which quality care and education would be available to all in Kansas City who needed or desired it. MCCC was to draw representatives of all key stakeholders to the table, and its role was to be limited to that of catalyst and convener. It would provide no direct services.

The regional council of governments, the Mid-America Regional Council (MARC), became the home for this new entity. This was largely because MCCC needed an interested but neutral host organization with no other role in child care and, partly, because MARC had helped with initial organizing and had expressed the willingness to play this role and provide certain in-kind support. Then and now, MARC views quality ECE as a regional issue.

Representatives of all stakeholders were asked to work together via the MCCC. School districts, government agencies, local nonprofits, universities, foundations, and other community leaders convened at MCCC's table. Many already knew each other from previous work on community task forces and plans focused on children's issues. A major initial grant from the new and fast-growing Ewing Marion Kauffman Foundation, coupled with Junior League funds and in-kind support from MARC and the University of Missouri–Kansas City, provided initial operating support to help turn this idea into a reality. Community interest and involvement was very high — over 200 interested citizens and community leaders participated on the various MCCC committees and task forces of the time.

About this same time, the United Way and the Greater Kansas City Community Foundation and Affiliated Trusts together created and funded an additional intermediary to promote and develop additional programs to serve children. This organization, the Partnership for Children, was to develop Kansas City's version of a nationally prominent program, Success by Six, and it became another actor in the early care and education domain (although its focus would be broader). The Partnership also became another forum for community leaders to meet to discuss issues affecting children.

Another major philanthropic initiative also helped to strengthen the growing interest in early childhood. A moderately large family foundation, the Francis Families Foundation, decided that ECE issues would be its primary domain. Francis, with the help of the community foundation and nonprofit ECE agency leaders, developed a partnership with a local community college and began the process of granting what eventually would amount to over $10 million for the development of a major ECE teacher education and child development center, the Francis Child Development Institute. The Francis family members already were viewed as important civic leaders, and their actions drew additional attention and interest to the ECE cause.

Work by the Partnership for Children also strengthened community concern about quality of care. A widely publicized annual "community report card" on conditions for Kansas City children, prepared by the Partnership, documented how few young children were educated and cared for by trained practitioners. MCCC, foundation, and nonprofit leaders used such information to catalyze interest in quality care as they continued to build a broader constituency for community-wide action.

The Ewing Marion Kauffman Foundation, a major original funder of the MCCC, determined that ECE would be a key element of its programming, and its ECE program officer, Stacie Goffin, began encouraging additional discussions about strategies to increase the quality and effectiveness of the early care and education community. Goffin was the University of Missouri–Kansas City professor who helped create and staff the MCCC during its initial period of operation, and she left the university to direct the Kauffman Foundation's activities and grantmaking in ECE. Well-networked and linked to the MCCC and other ECE community leaders, and willing to assertively raise the issue with others in all sectors who could be interested, Goffin began to nurture a new initiative that would weave together the work of the various actors. Her ideal, shared by many others associated with MCCC, was to accelerate the development of a *system* to strengthen the long-term viability and capacity of the ECE community. Their ultimate goal for this system was to increase the quality of care and education provided to young children.

In typical Kansas City fashion, Goffin and her colleagues held multiple conversations with various leaders from foundations, nonprofit organizations, government agencies, and colleges and universities, plus those advisors among the community's business and civic elite who were most active in ECE issues. She raised a provocative question: If we had a million dollars to strengthen ECE quality, how would we spend it?

Kansas City ECE leaders again came to the table—this time at the Kauffman Foundation—to explore strategies to strengthen quality. A key element under discussion was education for ECE practitioners. The Partnership for Children, through its leadership committees (many overlapping membership with MCCC's governing council), had set as a community goal to have, by the year 2000, 90 percent of the Kansas City children who were in early care and education programs in a setting with at least one care provider with a degree in early care and education. Multiple task force discussions developed around the question of how to achieve this goal. The result was the creation of a three-year $1 million scholarship initiative, funded by the Kauffman Foundation and to be administered by the MCCC. This initiative had four thrusts: (1) to provide degree-program scholarships to individual early childhood educators, (2) to deliver basic leadership training to center directors, (3) to facilitate institutional connections among the early childhood programs of local higher education institutions, and (4) advocacy of a subsidy for programs with credentialed staff. In parallel, Kauffman made a number of other grants for programs to develop and strengthen the ECE community through leadership and management development, accreditation support programs, and advocacy and policy development.

Concurrent and interwoven with the discussions about ways to develop what became the "scholarship initiative," Goffin and others encouraged discussion of ways to improve quality through stronger collaboration among ECE leaders and institutions. The idea resonated in this environment of growing leader interest. These discussions were given additional impetus by the passage of federal welfare reform legislation, with the expectation that it would pressure numerous single parents into full-time employment and many more young children into early care and education centers.

Many in these strategic discussions were interested in creating an overarching vehicle to focus on building a system for ensuring quality. These discussions involved many parties—other funders, service providers, center leaders, university professors, and certain leaders among the civic elite. They broadened to incorporate business leaders, government leaders, consumers, regulators, and teachers. Given the relatively great coherence in the perspective shared by most of these stakeholders, it was possible in a relatively short period of time to articulate a vision and set of principles to which the ECE leadership community could subscribe. The result was an aligned group of organizations and leaders that came together in August of 1996 to sign a joint statement of commitment to do their part to increase quality in early care and education—the Partners in Quality for Early Childhood Care and Education. Appendix A presents the principles to which the partners subscribed by their signatures.

When asked why PIQ was successful, partners reported that it was bringing essentially all of the necessary people and parties to the table. Said one, "The composition of the partners in Partners in Quality makes it (ECE) a commu- nity issue—an agency, funder, community, education, and business issue." People saw the potential to leverage the interests of the groups in the broader community, as well. "The coming together of disparate groups of people, each with a different piece of the issue, has achieved a certain mutual reinforcing" (Clay, 1997).

PIQ represents a diverse set of organizations and institutions, coming together across all sectors and from multiple levels of government, too. Many of the signatories represent civic elite leadership in Kansas City, and all play some form of leadership role in the broader community. Table 2 describes the roles and institutional affiliations of those who came together to sign the joint statement. PIQ continues to develop, and additional foundations and employ- ers have joined. And with heightened levels of political and governmental interest developing through the fall of 1997—both President Clinton and Missouri Governor Carnahan announced major initiatives to strengthen quality of care for young children—it is very possible that Partners in Quality will gain additional political (and, perhaps, financial) capital with which to achieve their vision.

The Block Grant Response Initiative

Another substantive example of Kansas City sectors coming together to address a critical emerging issue is that of the Block Grant Response Initiative, begun in March of 1995. Unlike the early care and education initiatives and true to its name, this initiative began as a reaction rather than a proactive strategy for system change. It grew to become a multifaceted community strategy to ensure that Kansas City was as well prepared as possible to address the federal government's transition to block grants as a part of federal devolu- tion and welfare reform.

The Block Grant Response Initiative began with a conversation between two philanthropic community leaders, the top executives of the United Way and the Greater Kansas City Community Foundation. They agreed that the issue was potentially critical to Kansas City's future and that the community should prepare to address it. The director of the Missouri Department of

Table 2
Originating Organizations and Roles
Partners in Quality in Early Care and Education

Administration for Children and Families, U.S. Department of Health and Human Services	Federal agency responsible for developing programs that serve young children
The Civic Council of Kansas City	Membership organization of business civic elite
The Early Childhood Higher Education Consortium	Network of higher education institutions that provide education for EDE providers
Ewing Marion Kauffman Foundation	Large Kansas City independent foundation
Francis Child Development Institute and The Francis Families Foundation	Combination of community college ECE teacher education center and major family foundation
Greater Kansas City Association for the Education of Young Children	Professional membership association of teachers, managers, and leaders in ECE domain
The Greater Kansas City Chamber of Commerce	Broad membership organization of businesses
The Greater Kansas City Community Foundation and Affiliated Trusts	Largest community foundation in Kansas City, and collection of trusts it administers
Heart of America Family Services	Major nonprofit human services agency
Heart of America United Way	Local affiliate of the United Way
KCMC Child Development Corporation	Major multi-site nonprofit early care and education agency (including Head Start)
Metropolitan Council on Child Care	Regional ECE planning and coordination agency
Metropolitan Kansas City Child Care Resource and Referral Network	Network of nonprofit resource and referral agencies in ECE arena
Mid-America Regional Council	Kansas City region's council of government
Midwest Center for Nonprofit Leadership, University of Missouri – Kansas City	University-based leadership and management development center (with special ECE program)
The Partnership for Children	Kansas City nonprofit encouraging programs to improve the quality of life for children; local affiliate of Success by Six

Additional organizations have joined the Partners in Quality since its initiation, including Hallmark Cards, Citicorp Credit Services, Kansas City Public Television, and HOMEFRONT.

Table 3
Organizations and Roles Block Grant Response Community Leaders

Corporate CEO	Church Network Leader
Civic Elite/Community	Volunteer Corporate CEO
Chief of Police	Representative of City Manager
Representative of Mayor	Organized Labor Leader
County United Way CEO	CEO, Suburban Community Foundation
Corporate Utility CEO	Civic Elite/Community Volunteer
President, Largest K.C. Family Foundation	CEO, County Mental Health Board
President, Chamber of Commerce	County Prosecutor
Partner, Law Firm	Corporate CEO, Regional Bank
Board Vice Chair, Major Nonprofit Health Care Conglomerate	Senior Utility Executive
CEO, Largest Independent Foundation	Corporate CEO
President, Regional United Way	Executive Director, Civic Council
County Executive	Civic Elite/Senior Corporate Executive
Civic Elite/Community Volunteer	CEO, Metro Council of Governments
U.S. District Attorney	President, Kansas City Community Foundation

Senior Executive, Regional Nonprofit Research Corporation

Social Services (DSS) agreed with their assessment, agreed that Kansas City might demonstrate an innovative community response, and offered to help in whatever ways were appropriate. The two philanthropy executives then invited fourteen key community leaders to join them in a meeting with the DSS director to learn about the issue and discuss ways that Kansas City might proceed. (Table 3 describes the range of roles gathered at this meeting.) This group, to be known as the "Block Grant Community Leaders Group," became the senior leadership for this effort.

The group agreed that the issue demanded attention. In the dialogue with the DSS agency head, the group decided it would be important to develop a three-element coordinated response to block grants: (1) propose a decision-making "blueprint" that could guide legislative action; (2) identify key capacity issues in Kansas City; and (3) develop and implement an advocacy plan to encourage state legislators to adopt the "blueprint" and act in ways that would support Kansas City's strategies for managing the block grants and its capacity issues.

Each expressed willingness to bring their organization "to the table" and to do what they could to help address it. In practical terms, this meant the foundation leaders were committing some (unspecified) amount of money and staff support, government was using its official linkages and what staff support it could legitimately offer, business leaders were involving others in the business community and spreading the word, and nonprofit leaders were sharing information and staff support. All were committing to sharing whatever they could afford in terms of in-kind staff time and resources, information and knowledge, their explicit political support, and an ongoing commitment to work together on this issue. Some had existing projects whose focus could be revised to help address the issue, and they committed to find ways to do so. The group met on about a quarterly basis.

United Way staff took the lead in moving the process forward, with the consent of the others at the table. With such high level sanction, they were able to quickly convene two additional cross-sector groups—additional tiers of community leadership—to collaborate on strategies and tactics. Both were comprised primarily of executive directors and other very senior executives of nonprofit organizations.

One of these tiers of leadership and activity was the "Block Grant Response Team," essentially an operating group of executives representing the leaders who participated in the initial meeting. The breadth of institutional involvement was equally great, as Table 4 illustrates. This group met regularly—sometimes as often as every couple of weeks—to begin the planning and coordinate work on the initiative, parts of which were implemented by affiliated organizations and parts of which were contracted to consultants and experts who would work under the leadership of individual team members. No central initiative budget was created. Rather, each organization brought what it could to the effort by using resources it had or to which it could gain access. When a new resource was needed, one or two of the team's members would offer to locate or engage it, usually covering the cost from their own coffers.

Concurrently, a third tier or network of leaders was being convened. This group was known as the "Block Grant Service Area Representatives." Meeting almost as a council, and comprised of executive directors whose nonprofits likely would be affected by the block grant policy, this group had representatives from each of the key service areas deemed to be at risk during the transition. One person each represented (unofficially—there was no formal designation process within the community) program interests such as domestic violence, emergency assistance, early childhood care and education, and

Table 4: Organizations and Roles
Block Grant Response Team

Senior Executive, Nonprofit Agency	Manager, Community Foundation
Staff Leader, Regional United Way	Community Volunteer/Civic Elite
Deputy Director, State Agency	Government Affairs Manager, Chamber of Commerce
Vice President, Community Foundation	Political Consultant
Executive Director, LINC	Senior Executive, United Way
Senior Executive, United Way	Director, University Nonprofit Center
Director, Organized Labor	Manager, United Way
Senior Executive, Independent Foundation	Director, Nonprofit Research Institute
Director, County Office	CEO, Regional Council of Governments
Program Officer, Community Foundation	CEO, United Way Planning Agency

Senior Program Officer, Major Independent Foundation

health. Each person at the table brought the perspective of their segment of the nonprofit service community. And each worked to link that segment with the process, and to do whatever it would take to keep board and executive leaders in their service area connected to the process. As Table 5 reports, 21 program areas were represented in the process.

The United Way staff served as the linkers and facilitators for this three-tiered process, working under the general direction of the community leaders group and its two lead conveners (the heads of the United Way and community foundation). They provided administrative support, coordinated meetings, and maintained a communication process to link the various elements of the process.

Working as a set of teams, these groups proceeded to tackle the block grant issue. Their work over the initial two years of the initiative is illustrated by these strategies and activities:

• A bi-state forum was convened to inform nonprofit leaders about the impending changes due to block grants, and about what might happen in Missouri and Kansas.

Table 5: Organizations and Roles
Block Grant Response Initiative
Service Area Representatives

Division Director, State Human Service Agency	Director, City Housing and Development Dept.
CEO, Large Nonprofit Early Care and Education Agency	CEO, Nonprofit Cerebral Palsy Agency
Director, United Way Child Welfare Programs	Social Services Director, Children's Hospital
CEO, Community Health Center and Community Development Corporation	CEO, Nonprofit Children's Center
	CEO, Emergency Assistance Agency Network
Staff, Assistive Technology Program	CEO, Nonprofit Jobs & Training Agency
CEO, Network of Youth Development Agencies	
CEO, Legal Aid Agency	Director (Aging), Regional Council
	Director, State Jobs Program
CEO, Neighborhood Alliance and Community Development Corporation	CEO, Nonprofit Children's Agency
	CEO, Food Shelf Network
CEO, Local Initiatives Support Corporation	CEO, Sexual/Domestic Abuse Agency
CEO, AIDS Council	

• The service providers team developed a set of "potential impact statements."

• The Block Grant Response Team developed recommendations for state-level decision making around block grant issues, planned an advocacy strategy, and developed a vision statement and set of principles to guide the redesign of services and flows of funds under block grants.

• Meetings involving all levels were arranged with various federal administrators to learn more about implications for particular children's programs and funding areas.

• Forums were held to encourage foundation and nonprofit leaders to begin contingency planning to effectively deal with this likely new environment. National policy experts suggested options for the community to deal with impending changes.

• Regular state and federal legislative updates were organized and published by the United Way, and distributed to all community agencies and initiative leaders.

• A local foundation contracted with the RAND Corporation to develop a Block Grant simulation game that could be used by planners and policy makers.

• An experienced lobbyist was hired by the initiative, funded by several of the affiliated organizations and based at the offices of the Greater Kansas City Chamber of Commerce, to plan and implement the advocacy activities in Missouri.

• The Response Team worked with Missouri advocacy organizations to shape policy and strategy and share information.

Significantly, much of the work of this initiative focused on Missouri. Although one of the initial activities in April of 1995 was a forum that presented speakers and information from both states, the actual work activity began with a focus almost exclusively on Missouri. The Response Team did find this emphasis a concern and began to involve a couple of representatives from Kansas United Way organizations, but the involvement was primarily focused on information sharing, not equal engagement in planning and action. This kept the process more manageable, but it also skewed the focus toward Missouri.

Community leaders consider the Block Grant Response initiative relatively successful. It raised legislator and leader awareness of its agenda and the principles it advocated for state decision making, it increased the preparedness of local officials and agencies to address the block grant system, and it set in place expectations and guidance for future legislative action. It also increased inter-agency and cross-sector connectedness and relationships across Kansas City.

Additional Instances

Three additional cases help us illustrate some particularly unusual variation in the breadth and depth of such collaborative initiatives in Kansas City.

LINC: The Local Investment Commission. The Local Investment Commission, or LINC, also recently recognized its substantial progress during its five years as a cross-sector, multi-organization alliance designed to improve the quality of social and economic life for the citizens on the Missouri side of the Greater Kansas City metropolitan region. LINC is an initiative that grew from the roots of a systemic reform initiative for the Jackson County office of the Missouri Department of Social Services (DSS). LINC is an especially intriguing case of collaboration and alliance building across sectors because, although LINC's image is of one organization, it actually is two: the Jackson County office of Missouri's Department of Social Services plus a sister nonprofit corporation. The work of the two is integrated through shared executive and governance structures.

LINC describes itself as a citizen-driven community collaborative involving efforts by the State of Missouri to work with citizens and neighborhood, business, civic, and labor leaders to improve the lives of children and families in Kansas City and Jackson County. The actual Commission is comprised of 36 people, including senior corporate executives, civic and neighborhood leaders, parents, and foundation officials. It oversees a range of programs. The delivery of these programs occurs primarily through nonprofit agencies and school-based community programs and alliances. Funding for LINC comes from traditional state social services streams plus state funding through an innovative, multi-department collaborative known as the Family Investment Trust. Substantial direct and in-kind support and funding also derive from local and national Kansas City foundations.

This is truly an inter-sector collaboration, with operational alliances with local and state governments, school districts, nonprofit agencies and foundations, neighborhood groups, private sector corporations, community health groups, and higher education leaders. Many government delegations and research teams from across America and other parts of the world have visited LINC to learn more about this unique approach to bridging sectors to build community and provide for the welfare of children and families.

Neighborhood Redevelopment Initiatives. There are numerous cross-sector collaborations underway in Kansas City that are focused on rebuilding and strengthening neighborhoods. One of the largest and most inclusive is KC Building Blocks, developed by Kansas City's office of the Local Initiatives Support Corporation (LISC) in collaboration with the Kansas City Neighborhood Alliance and associated nonprofit community development corporations, the city of Kansas City, Missouri, and its Community Policing initiative, and various nonprofit agencies. But there are several other initiatives also underway. Many are loosely interconnected, as they overlap and intersect with each other. These are less fully integrated with each other, yet there is a relatively clear, emerging community vision and agenda around neighborhood development and vitality issues.

Community Information Systems Development Initiatives. Another increasingly significant set of collaborations has been developing around the use of the various data bases and information networks that exist to support and inform the planning and delivery of many governmental and nonprofit services. These initiatives, several of which have now begun to come together to seek financial support from the federal government, are underway to link these data bases and make them available to neighborhood and nonprofit agencies through on-line inquiry and mapping programs. One leading initiative will link the information systems of the United Ways, the Mid-American Assistance Coalition (emergency assistance agency network), Kansas City Neighborhood Alliance (network of certain neighborhood organizations and community development corporations), and the data bases of Kansas City, Missouri, city government (including locally referenced data bases that provide neighborhood crime statistics, and code enforcement and property ownership information). Various information utilities also are becoming available through this network (e.g., e-mail, Internet access).

Key Leverage and Success Factors

Kansas City clearly has demonstrated a strong propensity to create cross-sector, increasingly comprehensive initiatives for building and rebuilding its community. Perhaps it is "ahead of the curve." To the extent that the case of Kansas City represents success—or, at least, the early stages of what may well be a longer-term success—what should we be learning from it? What has been making a significant difference in this community's capacity to bring together its philanthropic, public, and private sectors to address significant issues and opportunities?

The Kansas City experience affirms much current writing and research about communities and community building. For example, we find the lessons of Kansas City consistent with the Wilder Foundation's recent work on community building and collaboration (Mattessich and Monsey, 1997) and recent literature on the implications of social capital (Potapchuk, 1997).

Seven key leverage and success factors stand out for their contributions to the emergence and performance of Kansas City cross-sector collaborations:

1. New patterns of leadership and governance, grounded in and emerging from historically prevalent patterns.
2. Effective strategies for strengthening and tapping the community's substantial social capital.
3. A relatively widely shared community vision and ethic, including an emerging and increasingly widely shared "community theory of change."
4. A vital and evolving infrastructural network of mediating organizations and processes.
5. A pool of talented social and civic entrepreneurs.
6. The availability of a diverse array of resources and the willingness and capacity to mobilize them, sometimes in unconventional ways.
7. A strong and entrepreneurial philanthropic sector.

All of these factors interact, but the seventh factor is especially important because it is woven as an integrative thread through all of the rest. Nonprofit and philanthropic organizations and their leaders are playing key leveraging roles that are enabling Kansas City to explore and adapt a range of innovative strategies and opportunities.

New Patterns of Leadership and Governance

There is a powerful but almost paradoxical pattern of community leadership emerging in Kansas City, an increasingly diverse multilevel "system" that often remains driven by the action and commitment of a relatively small civic elite. This evolving system links new levels of grassroots decision making with a strong tradition of civic elite leadership. At its best, this new pattern represents a unique interactive approach to linking people of various institutional, sector, and community roles. It bridges multiple levels of community leadership and action, from grassroots neighborhood leaders to councils of civic elite leaders.

Yet there remains a civic leadership hierarchy in Kansas City that is exceptionally influential, particularly outside of the halls of representative government. These leaders, to a large degree, are the family owners and chief executives of the city's major corporations. Many have become major philanthropists, as well. They work together, they play together, they serve together on multiple boards—business and philanthropic. This core of leadership has facilitated the startup of many of Kansas City's cross-sector collaborations and, in difficult times, kept them going. When the Block Grant Response initiative needed its fast and decisive start, these leaders were at the table. A key factor in LINC's influence and staying power has been the high level of involvement of some of the city's most influential executives. To get a cross-sector initiative moving, one still needs to bring some of these key power brokers to the table. And, although in transition, Kansas City has not and cannot soon afford to do away with this more concentrated and centralized elite leadership power.

But the community, including many of these civic leaders, has recognized that its future depends upon moving beyond this overly narrow mode of leadership. Even while engaging this concentrated source of legitimacy and power, these new collaborations are building multiple new levels of leadership from the broader community and working to develop the skills of people who can make them work. Already, we see that a delicate balance has emerged among the various levels and settings in which decisions must be made and accepted. Decision processes within these new collaborations are being shaped consistent with this new orientation as they support the multiple loci of community decision making that Kansas Citians believe will be essential to success. The best illustration of this is the Local Investment Commission, which clearly demonstrates through its neighborhood school-based governance structures that it is committed to building multiple levels of community leadership.

Strengthening and Tapping Social Capital

Kansas City has the good fortune of having a reasonably substantial amount of social capital, and it has been quite effective in recognizing and tapping this capital to empower its cross-sector community collaborations. As much of the recent literature describes (e.g., Putnam, 1995; de Souza Briggs, 1997;

Potapchuk, 1997), social capital is comprised of the resources embedded in and empowered by the community's social relationships; the norms, values, trust, and reciprocity that make it easier for the people of a community to work together. Social capital is rather a "chicken and egg" phenomenon—you need it to build it, and Kansas City has been fortunate that it has had adequate social capital to support many of these collaborations. And as these collaborations are effective in crossing sector and hierarchical boundaries, they enhance the social capital needed to power future initiatives. Kansas City culture and traditions have played a powerful role in enabling these collaborations, as well.

Because Kansas City is a relatively small metropolitan community, the density of these webs of social connection, especially among those interested in working to address community issues and specific problems, is particularly great. Those in leadership roles come together often, even though the specific forums and issues differ from day to day. Social cohesion is quite substantial in this environment, and communication structures already exist to enable many of the necessary relationship-building connections. They include, for example, the numerous committees and task forces found in LINC, in PIQ, and in essentially all of the other collaboratives. Some cohesion exists because it is sustained along family lines among the civic elite, but also is strengthened through participants' multiple overlapping community roles. And with the broadening of the community's leadership, this process is becoming more extensive and inclusive while still drawing energy from the coherence at the core. Those who take on leadership roles quite quickly become embedded in these webs. Further, given the size of the community, many people end up playing these multiple roles that overlap, thus enhancing both the basis and likelihood of cross-sector linkages.

This capital extends, for better and worse, to the modes of conduct. People are expected to work together in the community's interest. A major expectation of a senior Kansas City corporate executive is that he or she will play some active community leadership role. Although such expectations have diminished in many cities around the nation, given the changing corporate environment, it remains relatively strong in Kansas City. Community service also remains an expectation of those who have the personal means to allow it.

Further, as one local leader notes, "civility is highly regarded here," and people do try to work together. However, it does not necessarily make the real work easier or the outcomes more likely to be achieved. While politeness sometimes interferes with honest and clear communication, it certainly advances the ability (and, perhaps, willingness) of people to talk together about common needs and issues. Turf can be an issue, of course, but it is not allowed to be an absolute barrier.

This dynamic has been amply illustrated in the several future issues and planning initiatives that have led to many of Kansas City's current cross-sector collaborations. To a degree that frustrates some, many Kansas Citians regularly come together to study issues and problems and articulate shared visions of what to do about them. At least seven major "community-wide" assessment and planning initiatives have been undertaken over the past decade. Although none were truly community wide, all developed broader strategic perspectives and visions for major segments of the metropolitan region. All have sought (and to a moderate degree, achieved) wide community involvement—each adding to the store of social capital and creating new local level leadership opportunities as they create the bases for future action.

Most of the new Kansas City collaboratives have come together around "banks" of pre-existing social capital, supporting hypotheses that social capital makes a difference. The Partners in Quality initiative grew from at least two prior cycles of relationships and ECE-related collaborative-building activities. The Block Grant Response initiative drew upon both current civic relationships and those built through earlier and concurrent initiatives that involved many of the same people and institutions. Among the collaborative initiatives that are starting more slowly or doing less well, a significant gap that they must address is that of relationship building. They suffer from inadequate social capital and must find ways to develop it.

Of course, one of the implications of working with existing social capital is that it resides in the webs of existing relationships. Therefore, its effective use predisposes that the new collaboratives will emerge and develop within these existing social networks. This also makes it more difficult for new leaders and participants to become readily and fully engaged. Some Kansas Citians have been working to move beyond these constraints by regularly involving a few new people at a time in these new collaboratives. Further, the numerous civic leadership development programs (e.g., Kansas City Tomorrow, Kansas City Centurions) contribute to the development of social capital by creating forums for emerging leaders to interact. These programs continue to be very active and successful, and their alumni appear to maintain many of the connections they developed while active members.

Kansas City is working to build social capital at multiple levels, including at neighborhood and local levels, in civic and faith-based institutions and organizations, and among the members of various service communities and professions. It is increasingly accepted (although not articulated) that the development of social capital in all segments and levels of the community is integral to creating Kansas City's desired future.

Shared Community Vision, Ethic, and "Theory of Change"

There is emerging in Kansas City a relatively widely accepted vision of a desired future for the city. The community's successful collaboratives have grown from and contributed to the development of this vision. As noted earlier, there have been several recent initiatives by which many Kansas City citizens and community leaders have come together to discuss and plan their community's future. Although none of these "comprehensive" processes has had the authority or constituency necessary to cover the entire geographic area of greater metropolitan Kansas City, each brought together diverse segments of the regional community to examine issues and challenges, identify assets and opportunities, articulate core values and a unifying vision, and propose community goals and strategies to act on them. Several have built on the essence of the Kansas City Consensus vision that Kansas City become the "Child Opportunity Capital of the World," particularly by linking this vision with themes of building healthy families.

In spite of the diversity of these plans, emerging through these processes are a de facto set of shared values and key elements of a vision for the future. All reflect the essence of a shared culture and embody an ethos of hope. In fact, in some respects, we observe that there also is emerging from these processes an integrating community-wide "theory of change" to which a majority of community leaders subscribes. This theory includes such tenets as the need to systematically integrate the delivery of a comprehensive set of services at the local level, that this system of delivery be responsive to and governed by the people of the community, that the system be assets-based and build on community strengths (versus a focus on gaps and needs), and that there is a focus on prevention and outcomes that the people of the community will value. Particularly significant is that this theory of change, itself, embodies a community systems perspective that demands collaboration across sectors and service boundaries.

The approved set of principles that guide the work of the Local Investment Commission and its various committees and task forces illustrates this community theory of change (presented in Appendix B). And although its official service territory includes only Jackson County in Missouri, its approved mission, vision, and principles are highly consistent with the visions and values that guide and are articulated in the work of many of the region's other cross-sector collaborations.

Kansas City culture and traditions have played a powerful role in enabling these cross-sector, inter-institutional collaborations. This community and those who take lead roles in these collaboratives tend to have a clear bias for action. They also have a bias for working together, although they want to do more than meet and collaborate for collaboration's sake. True to the clichés, the community does demonstrate a Midwest populist ethic, rooted in agrarian traditions such as community barnraising. This ethic of coming together and pooling resources for common causes is illustrated by the community's willingness to pool and tap public dollars to address community needs. Kansas Citians have been willing to tax themselves to pool resources, for example, to provide mental and public health services. Jackson County passed the nation's first anti-drug tax—a sales tax to fund programs to eradicate drug and substance abuse. And when these resources have been raised, the community has entrusted a good share of them to the nonprofit sector to provide the services.

Kansas City's culture, of course, shapes its approach to community development and change. In recent years, the community has rejected certain approaches used in other cities. For example, although there certainly are small-scale examples of each, Kansas City has eschewed the use of confrontive organizing techniques such as characterized the early work of Saul Alinsky; it has rejected strategies of highly concentrated control by a few highly placed corporate chief executive officers; and it has tended to ignore the demands of relatively isolated strident community activists. None of these approaches is consistent with Kansas City's emerging ethic and theory of community building initiative and change.

Mediating Organizations and Processes

Part of what has made a difference in Kansas City is the presence of a vital and growing set of organizations and structures—some permanent and others temporary—that link and facilitate action by key community actors and organizations to work across existing sector, professional, geographic, and functional boundaries. This exceptional array of mediating entities facilitates communication, dialogue, information sharing and learning, and planning and action. Most are nonprofits, and some are focused on particular segments of the community. Examples include the Mid-America Regional Council (the region's association of governments), Kansas City Consensus, the Kansas City Neighborhood Alliance, and the Kansas City Church Community Organization. Membership organizations also have been linkers, particularly within their segments of the community. The Greater Kansas City Council on Philanthropy, the Chamber of Commerce of Greater Kansas City, and the Coalition for Positive Family Relationships are examples.

Organizations in the philanthropic sector are often particularly well suited to play these roles, and they have been useful in settings where other organizations are limited by the formal constraints of operational or political boundaries or structures (such as state lines). This is especially true for situations in which certain types of advocacy are needed. The Greater Kansas City Community Foundation and Affiliated Trusts, the Ewing Marion Kauffman Foundation, and the Heart of America United Way, to name a few, regularly use their community positions to convene and facilitate. Often, they use their positions and resources to facilitate communication and prod collaboration.

An additional and critical intermediary function in periods of major change is to support and advance community learning processes—the community equivalent of research and development. The Kansas City community has been fortunate to have foundations and nonprofits that demonstrate a commitment to such development and capacity building, drawing upon a

individuals, holding that system accountable, and changing public attitudes toward the system.

LINC Guiding Principles:

1. *COMPREHENSIVENESS:* Provide ready access to a full array of effective services.

2. *PREVENTION:* Emphasize "front-end" services that enhance development and prevent problems, rather than "back-end" crisis intervention.

3. *OUTCOMES:* Measure system performance by improved outcomes for children and families, not simply by the number and kind of services delivered.

4. *INTENSITY:* Offering services to the needed degree and in the appropriate time.

5. *PARTICIPANT INVOLVEMENT:* Use the needs, concerns, and opinions of individuals who use the service delivery system to drive improvements in the operation of the system.

6. *NEIGHBORHOODS:* Decentralize services to the places where people live, wherever appropriate, and utilize services to strengthen neighborhood capacity.

7. *FLEXIBILITY & RESPONSIVENESS:* Create a delivery system, including programs and reimbursement mechanisms, that are sufficiently flexible and adaptable to respond to the full spectrum of child, family, and individual needs.

8. *COLLABORATION:* Connect public, private and community resources to create an integrated service delivery system.

9. *STRONG FAMILIES:* Work to strengthen families, especially the capacity of parents to support and nurture the development of their children.

10. *RESPECT & DIGNITY:* Treat families, and the staff who work with them, in a respectful and dignified manner.

11. *INTERDEPENDENCE/MUTUAL RESPONSIBILITY:* Balance the need for individuals to be accountable and responsible with the obligation of the community to enhance the welfare of all citizens.

12. *CULTURAL COMPETENCY:* Demonstrate the belief that diversity in the historical, cultural, religious, and spiritual values of different groups is a source of great strength.

13. *CREATIVITY:* Encourage and allow participants and staff to think and act innovatively, to take risks, and to learn from their experiences and mistakes.

14. *COMPASSION:* Display an unconditional regard and a caring, nonjudgmental attitude toward participants that recognizes their strengths and empowers them to meet their own needs.

15. *HONESTY:* Encourage and allow honesty among all people in the system.

Notes

1. Throughout this paper, the term "philanthropy" is intended to include the work of foundations, nonprofit agencies, and other private voluntary and not-for-profit entities.

2. Based on data of IRS Master Data Files. This number does not include most religious congregations and those nonprofits with budgets of less than $25,000 per year.

References

Clay, P. L. "Partners in Quality for Early Care and Education: Implementation Evaluation. Interim Report of Initial Interviews." Unpublished evaluation report for the Partners in Quality in Early Care and Education and the Ewing Marion Kauffman Foundation, July 29, 1997.

Clearinghouse for Midcontinent Foundations. *The Directory of Greater Kansas City Foundations. Eighth Edition.* Kansas City, MO: Clearinghouse for Midcontinent Foundations, 1997.

de Souza Briggs, X. "Social Capital and the Cities: Advice to Change Agents." *National Civic Review.* 1997, 86 (2), 111–118.

Greene, E., Millar, B., and Moore, J. "The Midwest's Charitable Advantage." *The Chronicle of Philanthropy.* February 22, 1994, p. 1, 22–25.

Mattessich, P. W., and Monsey, B. R. *Community Building: What Makes It Work? A Review of Factors Influencing Successful Community Building.* St. Paul, MN: Amherst H. Wilder Foundation, 1997.

Mid-America Regional Council. *Metropolitan Kansas City's Urban Core: What's Occurring, Why It's Important and What We Can Do.* Kansas City, MO: Mid-America Regional Council, 1993.

The National Commission on Philanthropy and Civic Renewal. *Giving Better, Giving Smarter: The Report of The National Commission on Philanthropy and Civic Renewal.* Washington, DC: The National Commission on Philanthropy and Civic Renewal, 1997.

Potapchuk, W. R., ed. *National Civic Review. Special Issue on Community Building and Social Capital.* 1997, 86 (2).

Putnam, R. "Bowling Alone: America's Declining Social Capital." *Journal of Democracy.* January 1995.

CHAPTER SIXTEEN

Children in Poverty

Reflections on the Roles of Philanthropy and Public Policy

Ruby Takanishi

The United States has the dubious distinction of having the highest child poverty rate among the industrialized nations—about four times the rate of our peer nations in the Western world. Disproportionately large numbers of African Americans, American Indians, and specific groups within the Latino and Asian American populations grow up in poverty. Overall, children in poverty are white. With these stunning facts in mind, one would expect to find the public and private sectors focused on the reduction, if not the elimination, of child poverty in America. Sadly, such is not the case.

On the public policy agenda, the reduction of child poverty has been eclipsed by welfare restructuring, specifically the time limits and work requirements of the Personal Responsibility and Work Opportunity Reconciliation Act (PRWORA) of 1996. Some predict that those who successfully make the transition from welfare to work will find themselves in a low-wage labor market, and remaining below or near the poverty line with less access to child care, food, and housing subsidies as well as difficulties in obtaining health care. Thus, low-income families will continue to be challenged in meeting the basic requirements for their children's optimal development.

A Primer on Child Poverty

A brief overview of the nature and "facts" of child poverty in the United States will provide a context for a discussion of the roles of public policies and private philanthropy in this area. There is strong consensus that the official poverty threshold, developed in the 1960s for the War on Poverty, is not an accurate measure of the economic resources needed by families to survive today (Citro and Michael, 1995). Alternative measures of poverty, such as relative poverty (50 percent of the median family income), are being used. The U.S. Census Bureau is currently developing alternative scenarios for recalibrating the official or governmental poverty line. This process, which must be approved by the U.S. Office of Management and Budget, will be a lengthy and politically charged process. For the purposes of this discussion, unless otherwise indicated, the official poverty measure is used.

The United States has the highest child poverty rate of all industrialized nations. In 1996, 21 percent (14.6 million) of all American children under age 18 lived under the poverty line. Among certain ethnic groups, child poverty is unacceptably high: in 1995, 41.9 percent of African American children and 40.0 percent of Latino children under the age of 18 lived in official poverty. American children are worse off than they were three decades ago. In 1969, 14 percent of children lived in poverty, and by the late 1990s, that rate was above 20 percent. Children below the age of six are more likely to be living in poverty than older children, because their parents are younger and more likely to be earning lower wages. Research indicates that this younger age is just the time when poverty is most likely to adversely affect later school achievement and impair cognitive development (McLoyd, 1998). Because the United States has not instituted protections similar to the European social welfare states, American children with parents working full-time, year-round at low-wage jobs are more likely to be living in poverty (National Center for Children in Poverty, 1998).

Poverty, Despite Work: Impoverished Discussions about Child Poverty

There is a curious absence from the research, policy analysis, and advocacy about child poverty in America. What is too often overlooked is that many millions of American families—as many as 14 million—have at least one full-time, year-round worker, but remain in or near poverty because of low wages (Swartz and Weigert, 1995). Others desire full-time work, but involuntarily are employed part-time or in the contingent labor force. While the term "working poor" is being used more in policy discussions and media coverage than in the past, partially because of growing recognition that the 1996 welfare restructuring will increase their numbers (see below), there is no standard definition of the group. Some estimates of working poor Americans are as high as 30 million. These families have not until recently been eligible for health insurance and child care subsidies, or early childhood programs such as Head Start. Ongoing research will provide better understanding of the numbers, characteristics, and living conditions of these families both at the national and local levels and of how their children are faring before and after PRWORA.

As the 1996 welfare legislation is implemented, the numbers of working poor families are likely to increase as individuals move off public assistance—many with low skills and limited work experience—and enter the low-wage labor market. There they will encounter the current working poor, and competition for jobs will ensue. The resentment of the existing working poor toward those moving off welfare is beginning to be documented. As one example, reports of competition between the working poor and former welfare recipients for extremely limited child care subsidies, which are critical for stable work among low-income parents, are surfacing and will intensify.

Current discussions about poverty, including child poverty, have an air of unreality about them, because they do not, for the most part, acknowledge that millions of people remain mired in poverty, even though they are working forty hours a week or more. Welfare restructuring may provide the impetus for public policy and philanthropy to finally address this economic reality. Americans believe that "work should pay" and, as the public begins to see that the current generation of the "deserving poor" are individuals who work hard, "play by the rules," and are still unable to provide for themselves and their children, pressure for change can build. Americans may be more likely to accept governmental assistance for families.

Ideas about the Causes of Child Poverty

How people understand the causes of child poverty is crucial to the formation of public and private policies. Americans have long believed that poverty is caused by individual actions, not by structural or class factors (Hanson, 1997). In European countries, by contrast, people are more likely to attribute lower economic circumstances to the existence of a "class structure." In America with its traditions of individualism and self-reliance, it is not surprising that poverty is often seen as a condition brought about by inadequate motivation or effort, and lack of self-control (Kelso, 1994).

In the case of child poverty, the well-being of American children is closely connected with their parents, that is, children are poor because of the bad actions and decisions of their parents. Typical American behavioral attributions include beliefs that parents of children in poverty are irresponsible; that they have children out of marriage; that they have too many children; that they are lazy and do not work hard or long enough to pull themselves out of poverty. In the United States, the "race factor" intersects with poverty, so that there is a misconception that poverty is predominantly a condition of African American families. An analysis of public images of poverty in weekly news magazines and major television networks reinforces these beliefs by the portrayal of the poor as more African American than is the case, and by the underrepresentation of the elderly and working poor in media coverage (Gilens, 1995). Despite evidence that challenges or disproves these beliefs (Bok, 1996), the Personal Responsibility and Work Opportunity Reconciliation Act (PRWORA) of 1996, as its title suggests, clearly reflects these values in its provisions with respect to work requirements and the importance it attaches to individual effort.

In more benevolent times, Americans supported educational interventions such as Head Start, which they believed provided more equal opportunity for poor children to begin a competitive educational experience in schools. Americans supported two-generational programs that aimed to assist both the parent/mother and the child by combining job training with parental education and early childhood programs. Thus, mothers would be better prepared to exercise individual initiative in the job market and in providing a home environment supportive of their child's learning. The evaluations of these programs indicate that the outcomes for mothers' employment and for children's well-being are modest (McLoyd, 1998). Americans still believe in supporting families, but now less so with respect to poor families. There is a pervasive sense that "we tried it and it failed. There is not much more government programs can do."

In fact, those centrally involved in the design and implementation of early education interventions agree that these programs have modest effects on children and families. Gregory Duncan, an economist concerned about the impact of poverty on children, has called for cost-benefit analyses in which spending on income-transfer programs and service delivery programs are compared and "judged by the benefits they produce relative to their costs" (McLoyd, 1998, p. 199). Vonnie McLoyd, a distinguished psychologist who has studied the influence of socioeconomic disadvantage on children's development for many years, notes: "Setting aside the issue of comparative benefits, it is clear that the prevalence of poverty in American has not been substantially reduced by antipoverty policies whose core strategy involves educating or ministering to the acute needs of poor children and families in the absence of job creation and the presence of massive numbers of jobs that do not pay parents living wages. At best, service delivery programs have only blunted the force of poverty and rendered modest improvements in children's environmental circumstances and developmental outcomes. The stressors and the resource deficits of chronic poverty are simply too multifarious and contagious" (McLoyd, 1998, p. 199).

This is not the place to discuss adequately a complex set of circumstances regarding the efficacy of different approaches to addressing child poverty in America (for an excellent collection of articles on children and poverty, I recommend the Summer/Fall 1997 issue of *The Future of Children*). But it is worth pointing out that such a discussion is critical at this time in the history of American public and private policies toward children in poverty. Undoubtedly, both Duncan's and McLoyd's views will be grist for further debates.

McLoyd's conclusions are particularly relevant as foundations and government consider current and future strategies for addressing child poverty.

Responses of Private Philanthropy: Diverse and Scattered

How does private philanthropy address child poverty? Two current strategies include, first, targeting problems that are closely associated with poverty, such as poor schools, youth violence, adolescent pregnancy, and the need for child welfare services, and second, by developing and funding major initiatives in low-income neighborhoods, sometimes called place-based strategies. American philanthropy is a diverse sector. Even within the foundations that have an interest in children and families and focus on poverty, grantmaking responses vary.

The founding mothers and fathers of mainstream American philanthropic organizations strongly believed in the individual and her or his power to make a difference in the course of his or her life. The donors, in many cases, were self-made captains of industry and their philanthropic impulses matched their values and experiences. This may explain, in part, why much of mainstream philanthropic efforts to combat child poverty reflect an underlying belief in the empowerment of individuals as a strategy to reduce poverty, rather than focusing on structural factors such as a low-wage labor market or underemployment. These grantmakers are likely to support educational and service programs, including those of a preventive nature aimed to provide children and sometimes their families with an equal starting point in the race for individual achievement. The mantra of "empowerment" of parents and citizens is often evoked.

To be fair, some foundations recognize that a human capital development approach must be combined with a social capital development one. Thus preventive, education, and health services are combined with economic and community-building efforts in neighborhoods. These efforts are often called comprehensive community initiatives (CCIs) for children, and represent partnerships among foundations, nonprofit organizations, and local government (for a description of alternative approaches, see Stagner and Duran, 1997). CCIs, which vary in their design elements, typically seek to address child and family poverty through coordination of health, education and social services.

Despite significant investments, largely by foundations, Matthew Stagner and Angela Duran, in their review of evaluations of CCIs, report that information about the effectiveness of CCIs is scarce. The evidence that is available indicates that many past efforts have achieved only modest successes, and data on child outcomes are particularly limited. Members of the Aspen Institute Roundtable on Comprehensive Community Initiatives for Children and Families argue that traditional methods of evaluating CCIs are not appropriate to comprehensive, community-based efforts, and have developed alternative approaches (Fulbright-Anderson, Kubisch, and Connell, 1997). Thus, private foundations continue to support comprehensive community initiatives; some of these initiatives are combined with public initiatives such as the Enterprise and Empowerment Zone efforts of the federal government. Most of the grants are made to programs and community organizations, with smaller amounts for research, evaluation, and policy analysis and advocacy work.

In the wake of PRWORA, foundations have been largely reactive to current policies such as devolution of responsibilities for child and family services to the states. Philanthropy, for the most part, is doing little to challenge or provide a counterforce to historic changes in public assistance to children and families who find themselves in poverty. Philanthropic funds are focused on tracking welfare reform at the state and local levels, and supporting community economic development and community building strategies. Foundations are also supporting efforts for national and, to a lesser extent, state organizations to provide technical assistance to the states in implementing the new welfare provisions. Foundations are supporting the startup operations for information exchange and technical assistance to shape policies on child-related issues through new organizations such as the Welfare Information Network (WIN). Sustaining these efforts, including garnering governmental funds for what has traditionally been seen as a federal role—information gathering, technical assistance, and dissemination—will be addressed in the coming years as the roles of government at different levels are renegotiated.

There is a widespread acceptance of an age of incremental change, especially in the area of access to child health insurance and child care programs, and apparent satisfaction with approximating systemic or large-scale change. While this current stage of devolution has created opportunities for state innovation, it has also resulted in a perverse situation in which it is by the luck of the draw that a child with a low-income parent finds him or herself in a state with more or less supports for sound development. Existing income inequalities are further exacerbated by devolution in which some states are more supportive of families and their children than are others (Douglas and Flores, 1998). A first-year report card on PRWORA, issued by the Tufts University Center on Hunger and Poverty (1998), indicates that only a few states are taking advantage of devolution to come up with innovative approaches to support children and their families in poverty.

In summary, philanthropy today is not leading on the child poverty issue. Its activities have essentially followed public policy, and for the most part, not attempted to counter it and identify alternative directions, at least not yet. Several of the large national foundations with interests in child poverty are engaged in reprogramming activities, partially because of leadership changes.

The philanthropic agendas to address the immorally high rates of child poverty remain to be shaped.

My assessment of public policy and philanthropy in relation to child poverty acknowledges the role that philanthropy has played in advancing our understanding of child poverty, and efforts to address it. What is most troubling is that philanthropy today and its leaders have not asserted the sector's unique role in providing alternatives to the current public strategies to address child poverty. This policy paralysis is especially true among the so-called progressive foundations. A report of the National Committee for Responsive Philanthropy concludes that a small group of conservative foundations did much to create the conditions for devolution and the reversal of public attention and interest in addressing poverty. While some may disagree with this attribution of pervasive influence to conservative funders, it is still the case that progressive foundations could do much more to provide balance in current policy discourse about child poverty than they have so far.

A Universal Approach to Reducing Child Poverty: An Antidote to Incrementalism

Child poverty is not intractable; it can be reduced by governments that choose to pursue certain public policies. This fact is one which needs to be highlighted in the current social climate in which certain statements are accepted without question, e.g.,"We lost the War on Poverty," or "Government cannot reduce poverty, only people can." Economists studying child poverty in advanced economies observe that even though most Western nations have experienced similar changes in family structure (divorce and the rise in single parenthood) and in the structure of their labor markets (lower wages, fewer jobs for unskilled workers) in the 1980s and 1990s, child poverty rates in these economies vary widely from less than 3 percent in Scandinavia to over 20 percent in the United States. Timothy Smeedling, Lee Rainwater, and Sheldon Danziger (1997) conclude that the differences in these poverty rates "reflect differing values and choices, not technical economic constraints." They propose an approach to poverty reduction that puts together a package that includes family allowances, refundable tax credits, income supplements for those in low-wage labor markets, child support assurance, and universal access to health insurance and child care for children and their parents.

The United States stands alone as the only advanced economy that has no family allowance, no universal health insurance for children and adults, and relatively limited support for early childhood programs, especially before the age of compulsory schooling (elementary and secondary education). It is one of a handful of countries that has no paid parental leave, especially during the first few years of a child's life. Smeedling, Rainwater, and Danziger argue that if these generic elements of a family support policy were in place in the United States, the child poverty rate would be greatly reduced, possibly to the single digits as in European nations.

If one accepts this basic needs approach to family support for the reduction of child poverty (see, for example, Barbara Bergmann's [1996] *Saving our Children from Poverty*), it is noteworthy that no major foundation concerned with children now uses this basic needs approach as a template for grantmaking. Some foundations focus on access to child health insurance (e.g., Robert Wood Johnson) or early childhood programs (e.g., Carnegie Corporation of New York). Others (Ford Foundation) support organizations such as the Center for Budget and Policy Priorities which focus on income security and tax policy issues affecting low-income families and IDAs, while the Rockefeller Foundation focuses on job creation and urban school reform. Annie E. Casey Foundation, which focuses its grantmaking totally on economically disadvantaged youth, is currently funding neighborhood-based change. None of the foundations has a coherent vision of poverty reduction around which to organize its grantmaking activities strategically.

Opportunities for Philanthropic Leadership

Child poverty must be placed within the broader context of what is happening economically, socially, and culturally in the United States. Taking this perspective provides cause for worry. The inroads made on the budget deficit and the end of the Cold War, combined with economic prosperity for some, have created optimal conditions for investing more resources in the development of human and social capital, especially among children and youth. This is just the time to support universal health care, broad-based, affordable, quality child care for working parents, excellent and equitably funded schools, job creation, and needed improvements in the infrastructure of our urban and rural areas. Yet this is just the time when investments in human and social capital are declining, and are severely constrained by the joint pressures to hold the deficit down and to increase entitlements for older persons. Income inequality, which is the widest in the Western world, remains a disturbing fact of life in the world's oldest democracy. The fallout from current economic and social inequalities, especially when entangled with race and ethnicity, should be of much greater concern than they now are. The consequences are threats to the economic, political, and civic vitality of our nation.

Private foundations can play an influential and strategic role in addressing child poverty in the United States. In so doing, private philanthropy must reaffirm one of its fundamental principles: ideas matter. The following ideas, for example, have had a profound influence on policymakers and the public's perception about the effectiveness of governmental programs: "We lost the War on Poverty. Government programs do not reduce poverty; they encourage dependency and the intergenerational transmission of poverty." These notions are often promulgated through selective and distorted use of examples. We need to think carefully about how these ideas can be challenged, especially for a public that apparently believes them.

Foundations, therefore, must come to terms with a rapidly changing communications environment in which they have been thrust. At one time, releasing reports and coverage in national and local newspapers would be considered a successful dissemination effort. But today, when "mass communications" no longer exists, and the ways in which citizens obtain information are highly segmented and highly competitive, there is an enormous challenge in figuring out how to reach key constituents or audiences, not to mention the crafting of credible, appealing messages that we would find accurate and ethical. Messages are the starting points, but sustained discourse across the sectoral lines with committed people with a resulting social strategy is also essential. The role of civil society in this discourse is obvious, but not easy. These are hard tasks that foundations must take on if we are to have any chance to reduce child poverty in the United States.

In the following sections, I describe what philanthropy can do to contribute to the reduction of child poverty in the United States. I suggest a mix of long-term activities with uncertain outcomes as well as near-term, specific activities which can contribute to the longer-term goals.

Crafting a Social Compact to Address Poverty

Within most of our lifetimes, we have witnessed changes in the social compact between individuals and public and private institutions and organizations in meeting the basic human needs of children. What the papers prepared for this American Assembly meeting point to is the changing relationships among individuals and organizations on a wide range of social issues. The United States is unlikely, under any circumstances, to adopt the social welfare strategies of its Western European allies. Those strategies themselves are under considerable pressure for change. With the voluminous research, analyses, and experience related to addressing child poverty, this is just the time to rethink the social compact related to hardworking American families who are unable to meet the basic needs of their children and themselves.

At the moment, the policy discourse on poverty in the PRWORA era seems to be proceeding on two tracks. One group tends to emphasize the importance of income, income security, and benefits such as health insurance. Another group tends to emphasize the work ethic and the importance of personal discipline and responsibility, marriage, and caring relationships among family members. It is more than likely that both economic resources and the behavior and attitudes of parents and family members toward their children matter, and that both should be addressed by American public and private policies. Bringing together these polarized positions or partial solutions to child and family poverty is exactly the kind of activity that philanthropy was founded to do: addressing the big, difficult-to-solve issues; convening individuals and groups with different experiences and positions; and going beyond the PRWORA approach to ending "welfare as we know it."

For those of us who believe that PRWORA is a disaster, our responsibility is to be offering carefully considered alternatives to it, even as welfare changes are being implemented at this early stage. Put more bluntly: If and when things "get really bad"—say, an economic recession—what coherent set of ideas, strategies, and solutions will we have to offer? How will these be communicated to various audiences? How can we win the hearts of Americans so that they will find unacceptable the suffering of so many of their fellow citizens? How can we lay the foundations for a post-PRWORA era?

At present, most of the necessary ideas, analyses, and policy options exist, but they are in limbo or exile, outside the arena of policy debate and public awareness (as examples, see Garfinkel, Hochschild, and McLanahan, 1996, and Handler and Hasenfeld, 1997). These conceptual building blocks must be brought together around the banner of a new social compact among civil society, government, business, and American families, many of whom are the families of children in poverty. Trying to understand and specify roles for these sectors in a time of change will be difficult. But these are precisely the hard issues that philanthropy should be addressing. No other sector in American society is uniquely charged or responsible for such a task. No other sector is likely to take on such a task.

I envision the broad outlines of a fundamental social compact as follows: If adult family members work hard in jobs where their minimum wage earnings do not enable them to provide adequately for their children's needs, it is the responsibility of extrafamilial institutions, both private and public, to assist parents and families. (There will always be adults who, for reasons of disability, will find it difficult or impossible to fulfill this part of a social compact; advanced societies, such as ours, must find ways to support them in dignity through genuine safety net provisions. This population, sometimes referred to as the "difficult to reach," is itself a neglected group in social welfare policy.) The elements of a combined public (e.g., income supplementation) and private support (e.g., flexible working hours) are known, but must be brought together in a package that both supports families and serves the common good.

Another key task is developing a social and political strategy for making these proposals happen through the broad involvement of all Americans. The role of faith communities or the religious sector in this discourse, differentiated from their role as service providers (Printz, 1998), will be essential to restore or reinforce a moral meaning to poverty as part of a set of values involving social and economic justice (see, as one example, the pastoral letter of the National Conference of Catholic Bishops, 1997).

Crafting this new social compact is a "big" item for a philanthropic agenda regarding children and poverty. There are also smaller, more specific agenda items that could contribute to this larger enterprise in the near term.

Stimulate Public Discourse about Poverty

While there is strong consensus within the academic community that the poverty threshold must be changed to reflect current family circumstances, any resolution will be a political one and will affect the allocation of currently limited resources for human services. When the National Research Council report, *Measuring Poverty* (Citro and Michael, 1995), which urged a revision of the poverty definition, was released, politicians declared it "dead on arrival."

If, as Allan Hanson (1997) has suggested, "the meaning of poverty has been lost," there is an immediate opportunity to reengage Americans about poverty in our midst. The work of governmental agencies such as the U.S. Census Bureau and the U.S. Office of Management and Budget should ideally take place in the context of an informed public and broad discussion about poverty in the United States. Foundations can support national briefings for key agency staff and legislators; stimulate media coverage of the issues involved in redefining poverty and what the practical effects might be on children and families. The moral and ethical dimensions of poverty should be an essential part of the public discourse. Faith communities at the national, state, and local levels should be key participants in discussions involving issues of personal responsibility, social and corporate responsibilities, moral principles, and human rights. Given the importance of employment and job issues, the roles of labor unions cannot be overlooked.

I have previously emphasized the values that underlie current public policy related to child poverty (for a historical analysis of how Americans have struggled with social policy regarding poverty, see Katz, 1996). These values are related to how people think about the causes of poverty in America. Foundations can support efforts that examine and clarify competing conceptions of poverty and its causes through research, polls, media portrayals, and civic engagement. Foundations can support individuals and organizations that are engaged in the creation of ideas, upon which responsible messages can rest, that go beyond the current parameters of welfare debate. Going beyond will mean aiming for a synthesis or accommodation between cultural and economic approaches to understanding poverty in America. The identification of leadership for this discussion is not entirely clear; however, here again, the role of foundations as leaders in convening across sectors and the identification of powerful new voices is critical.

Articulate a Unified Approach to Reducing Child Poverty

The United States currently has a dual system of public assistance. For poor people, it categorizes people and makes governmental assistance contingent on certain conditions. For the more affluent, there is a system of social assistance that many may not recognize as such, e.g., Dependent Child Care Tax Credit or the Mortgage Interest Tax Deduction. What the United States lacks is unified approach to social assistance. Through its targeted programs and tax policy approaches, lower income families are more likely to be left out or disadvantaged in relation to middle-income and more affluent families. These are the very families that will be most affected by state and local responsibilities for social services. For example, child care, an essential family support service in an era when all able-bodied adults, including mothers of young children, are expected to work outside the home, uses the tax system as a financing mechanism. Middle class families receive rebates through the Dependent Child Care Tax Credit system, while low income families who owe little or no tax do not benefit. In the current devolution process, lower income families eligible for limited child care subsidies (currently one out of ten eligible children receive such subsidies) are subject to the vagaries of state plans, while middle class families are not. This is one of the areas in which foundations can support work to create a genuinely equitable system of access and affordability for families who need good child care, a basic need for working families.

Foundations can support national, state, and community leaders and other credible messengers who put forward a unified approach to reducing child poverty. These approaches cut across race and ethnic lines and can garner broad public support. Americans do care about helping those less fortunate (Bok, 1996), but are not sympathetic to those they perceive are not carrying their weight. The crafting of social insurance approaches that Americans across a broad economic spectrum perceive as fair should be on the agenda of foundations.

Question Devolution: Is America a Nation?

Devolution has the potential for beneficial innovation to reduce child poverty, but also can result in dissipating energies that could be used in other, possibly more productive ways. If "fifty flowers" are encouraged to bloom, the logistics of and resources needed to track the consequences in 50 states (not to mention devolution to the counties) might be a windfall for the communications and information technology industry as well as research organizations, but is proving difficult for several reasons. The collection of relevant and comparable data on child outcomes, for example, must involve the cooperation of participating states. More often than not, states and localities do not have the capacity to collect timely, reliable information about key child outcomes. In some cases, the data that are collected vary across states. Certain features of managed health care may make it difficult to track client-provider contacts, as one example. The costs of well-designed studies are considerable, and with the massive scale of welfare restructuring, comparison groups are not often available. The complexity and continuing change in the implementation of devolution in each state also make it difficult to sort out what factors make a difference in what outcomes. Therefore, from a purely research perspective, studies of devolution are entering unknown territory. This is not to argue that large, national foundations should not support these efforts, but that research investments are not sufficient. The work of foundations regarding devolution must be further diversified.

A fundamental issue that requires attention is one of fairness. The resources, supports, and life chances of individual children will continue to be affected by where they happen to live. This has always been the case in the United States, but efforts of the New Deal and the War on Poverty were aimed at increasing equality of opportunity for children, especially in states and localities where access to basic resources was thwarted by discriminatory practices. Devolution in its current form is likely to reverse that situation. Early reports of how states are implementing PRWORA support the fear that devolution of child and family services to the 50 states is further unleveling the playing field for millions of American children (Center for Hunger and Poverty, 1998). This situation is clearly not supportive of longstanding American traditions of fair play.

Strategic philanthropy must raise questions about national guidelines or even standards in the provision of basic human services such as child health care and child care. The 1997 Balanced Budget Act includes relatively large provisions to increase access by children of working poor families to health insurance. However, each state has wide discretion in implementing the State Child Health Insurance Program, known as SCHIP, including benefit packages. Foundations, by supporting organizations, need to raise some of the following questions: Should all American children receive a certain set of health benefits? Should all American children receive a certain level of quality health care? The discussion of national standards, even the most minimal, is absent from the current discussions of increasing funds for child care. The result is that tax dollars will continue to be used to pay for child care that is inadequate or even harmful.

While Americans do not value equality of condition, they do support equality of opportunity. We have tended to overlook why we have had national policies in the first place. Such policies were aimed at addressing unequal access to resources such as education and social services by individuals who were receiving unequal treatment (discrimination) at the local and state levels. But national policies are important in a more fundamental sense: they are important to assure that all American children, regardless of their circumstances and the state in which they live, will be guaranteed a certain level of safety, support, and opportunity. We seemed to have, hopefully temporarily, turned our backs on this basic guarantee.

Philanthropic dollars can support efforts to think about what constitutes an appropriate national role in addressing child poverty. What can private philanthropy and nonprofit organizations do to strengthen a national infrastructure for social assistance that is universally based, including child care and child health insurance, and assures a basic or minimum level of support? The strengthening of national organizations in this phase of devolution is necessary to address these issues from a national level. We can no longer avoid the longstanding issue of appropriate roles for the national government regarding child poverty in an age of devolution. One troubling circumstance is that national organizations, responding to the increased roles for states, are turning their attention to providing technical assistance and other services to states. The impact of this trend on the capacity of these organizations to monitor and influence national policy is not yet clear.

In the current era of devolution, the connections among community-based organizations, city and state governments, and national organizations working on poverty issues are important, but not adequately addressed. Foundations are supporting community- or neighborhood-based organizations that are not connected with state groups working on similar issues. Foundations support capacity-building at the state level, but these efforts are often not connected with kindred national organizations. Community-based organizations complain that national organizations are not relevant to their interests. In the child and family policy area, the ten largest foundations funding in this area tend to support community organizations and programs with smaller support for national organizations. Few are now supporting state-level organizations. It is an odd state of affairs. If this scenario is accurate, foundations need to address how their current grantmaking reflects directly or indirectly their ideas about points of leverage with respect to child poverty, and the need to link national, state, and local policies as part of their grantmaking strategies. On the one hand, local and state innovation should inform other states and communities and national policies, and certain standards for the nation should be in place.

Examine the Privatization of Child and Family Services

The role of the private, nonprofit sector in delivering a range of services to children in poverty is not particularly new. In cities such as New York, there is

Figure 2. Number of For-Profit and Nonprofit HMOs, 1985-1996

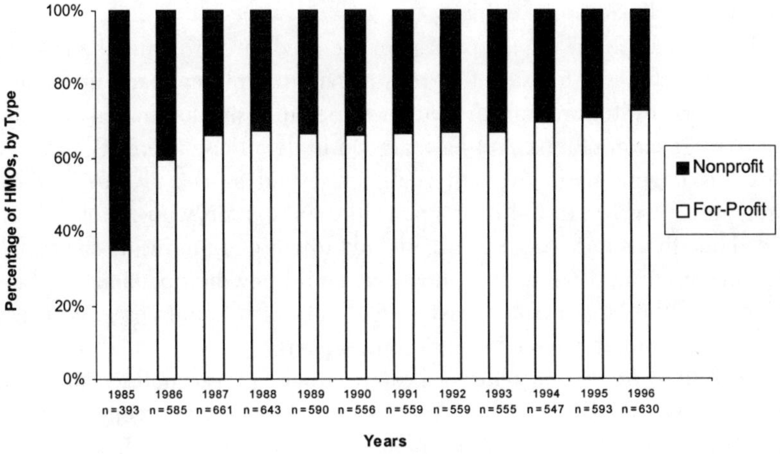

Source: InterStudy, Part II: Industry Report, 1985-1996

underwent a for-profit transformation during the 1980s (Figure 2) and the most recent figures show 73 percent of plans (with 61% of enrollees) are for-profit.

The Hospital-HMO Contrast: The Role of Public Policy

Why is the ownership history of hospitals and HMOs so different? Specific historical and policy factors can be identified that affected the ownership makeup of both fields.

The earliest nonprofit hospitals developed in the eighteenth and nineteenth century, before legal concepts and structures clearly distinguished nonprofit and public institutions. Hospital censuses early in the twentieth century reported that about half were for-profit. These were mostly small physician-owned facilities that were operated as extensions of their practices and bore little resemblance to the corporate-owned institutions of the current era. The for-profits' share declined continuously through the century, until the Medicare law was passed. The nonprofits' share was bolstered by policy decisions regarding exemption under 501(c)(3) of the Tax Code as charitable organizations, and access to federal matching funds for capital projects under the Hill-Burton program begun in the late 1940s. The Hill-Burton program was phased out in the 1970s, and different provisions were made for helping hospitals meet their capital needs. Reimbursement for capital costs was built into the payment structure of the Medicare program, and nonprofit hospitals

369

were able to gain access to tax-exempt debt. Debt and retained earnings became the major sources of capital for nonprofit hospitals. Thus, they had to operate in a businesslike fashion.

In the years following the passage of the Medicare program, the for-profit hospital sector was transformed from a marginal player made up of small proprietary institutions into an investor-owned industry dominated by a handful of huge corporations. As I have argued in detail elsewhere (Gray, 1991), this was largely an inadvertent result of several aspects of the Medicare program. First, because this program, in combination with Medicaid, provided health insurance for the largest and most difficult-to-insure share of the nation's uninsured population, hospitals could now be operated profitably. Medicare (the largest payer) covered its share of hospital costs and private insurance based its payments on hospitals' charges.

Second, it proved possible for hospitals that were so inclined to "game" Medicare's cost-based reimbursement in countless ways to generate profits out of a so-called cost-based payment system (Gray, 1991, chapter 6). For example, Medicare could be asked to reimburse hospitals for the "cost" of goods and services that they had bought at a considerable markup from suppliers owned by related organizations.

Third, Medicare payments included a generous profit margin (called "return-on-equity" payments) for for-profit hospitals. The inclusion of return-on-equity payments for-profit facilities provided specific stimulus to the growth of the investor-owned industry. This is, I believe, the only specific legislative action intended specifically to benefit the for-profit hospital industry. This effect on hospitals was unintentional in a sense, however, since the return-on-equity provision had resulted from the lobbying efforts of the largely for-profit *nursing home* industry. (Ironically, Medicare provided only very limited nursing home benefits.)

Fourth, Medicare capital reimbursement policies not only reimbursed providers for interest and other capital costs incurred in building or purchasing facilities, but also paid depreciation costs. Because the cash flow from a facility could be increased simply by selling it to a new owner and starting a new depreciation schedule, facilities became more valuable to new purchasers than they were to existing owners.

In response to the incentives in the Medicare program, investor-owned companies were created and grew rapidly in the late 1960s and 1970s in the trusting payment environment that had been created in a field dominated by nonprofit and public facilities. With growing earnings and claims of efficiency—in a system designed to keep "inefficient" nonprofit and public hospitals afloat, how could for-profits fail, they argued—the hospital companies became Wall Street high-flyers, with high price-to-earnings ratios producing cheap capital that fed further growth. The fact that research was beginning to accumulate that showed that for-profit hospitals were more costly for purchasers than were nonprofits (see Gray, 1986) was waved aside by the for-profits and their advocates as erroneous (they were more efficient, by definition) or as misconceived ("we are only doing what the incentives tell us to do," I was told more than once when I cited the research evidence on cost).

By the early 1980s, four companies—Hospital Corporation of America, Humana Inc., American Medical International, and National Medical Enterprises—owned most of the for-profit hospitals in the U.S. and managed several hundred nonprofit and public hospitals. The trade press was full of predictions that these companies were going to take over the system. Two different scenarios were offered. The first was that they would simply out-compete the nonprofits, attracting the insured patients on which they generated revenue. (Data at the time showed that more than 95 percent of the revenues of the average nonprofit hospital came from fees for patient care.) The second was that the for-profit companies, with their deep pools of capital, would take over the system via acquisitions. Until that time these companies had grown primarily by acquiring independent proprietary hospitals and then by acquiring each other (Hoy and Gray, 1986), and their growth strategy (and high stock prices) required that they continue to make acquisitions. The only way to grow was to acquire public or nonprofit hospitals, and some highly publicized examples occurred in Louisville, Wichita, Oklahoma City, Denver, and Omaha. Takeover of the system was widely predicted.

However, the growth of the investor-owned companies stopped with stunning rapidity after three cost-containment changes were made in the Medicare program in the early 1980s. The formula for the return-on-equity payments to the for-profits was deemed too generous and costly, and was cut by one-third. The fact that Medicare was making depreciation payments several times on facilities that were changing hands was recognized and halted. And Medicare adopted new limits on the amount it would pay under cost-based reimbursement and a year later dropped cost-based reimbursement altogether in favor of a new system of per case reimbursement based on patients' diagnoses.

By the late 1980s, all four of the major companies were smaller than they had been at the beginning of the decade, and several for-profit hospital companies were rocked by scandals involving patient abuse and fraud. By the 1990s the big four companies of the 1980s had all ceased to exist because of strategies adopted in the face of declining profits or tainted reputations. The bulk of their assets had been purchased by two new firms, Columbia and Tenet. Today, in the wake of a new round of fraud charges and a change in management, Columbia/HCA now seems to be going the way of its predecessors, having announced plans to sell a third of their hospitals (more than 100), some of which seem likely to return to nonprofit ownership.

Where does the conversion of nonprofit hospitals fit into this story? The for-profit companies did purchase some nonprofit (and public) hospitals during their initial growth period (Hoy and Gray, 1986). But the numbers acquired through the 1980s and early 1990s were relatively small and were partly offset by conversions that went the other way. Chollet and her colleagues (1996) identified 110 nonprofit to for-profit conversions between 1980 and 1993, but they also found 55 conversions in the opposite direction. The numbers of nonprofit conversions increased markedly in the period 1994–96 and attracted much attention and concern.

Although this history is yet to be fully digested, several factors were involved. Some of these pertain to why nonprofit trustees might be increasingly willing to consider the sale of their hospital. The nation has a surplus of hospitals and hospital beds. With occupancy rates falling below 60 percent even as the number of beds was declining (by 7% from 1990–1996) (Levitt, 1998), it is widely agreed that not all can survive. Many institutions are struggling financially and have poor access to the capital needed to stay modern and competitive. Boards of some nonprofit hospitals began looking at a large number of alternatives—mergers, conversion to other purposes (e.g., long-term care), and sales. The organizations with the deepest pockets were the two companies—Columbia/HCA and Tenet—that had been put together from the remnants of the earlier investor-owned firms. As with their ancestors of the 1970s, the new hospital companies grew primarily via acquisitions of other hospital companies and made bold claims of efficiency. In a reminiscent pattern, evidence developed that Columbia's hospitals were more costly to purchasers and that the company's profits were based in part on finding ways to exploit payment systems. Then came the crescendo of charges and investigations in 1997 and the resignation of CEO Richard Scott. Columbia soon abandoned its growth ambitions, and the percentage of nonprofits among community hospitals remains essentially unchanged.

Ownership-related policies have been much more explicit in the HMO area. Serious congressional debate about ownership form preceded the decision in the HMO Act of 1973 to limit federal support (with narrow exceptions) to nonprofit plans. The HMO Act became one of the few sources of capital for starting new plans in the 1970s, and organizers of new plans often chose the nonprofit form to gain access to that capital. Federal capital funding for HMOs was an early casualty of the Reagan administration, however, and the federal office that administered the HMO Act began an active campaign of trying to attract equity investment into the HMO field. The HMO companies first went public in 1983; many closely held for-profit plans were also created. Whereas the hospital market was already mature when the investor-owned companies began their growth, the for-profit HMO sector was built on the growing demand created by the HMO Act's requirement that large employers offer an HMO option and on growing desire among employers for health care cost containment.

Federal tax policies also contributed to the different ownership histories of the hospital and HMO fields. For hospitals, section 501(c)(3) of the Internal

Revenue Code has been interpreted by the IRS in an undemanding way, particularly since 1969 when "community benefit" became the operational definition of "charitable" (requiring little more than having emergency rooms open to the community), and federal tax policies have not served either as an impediment or as a performance spur for nonprofit hospitals (Fox and Schaffer, 1991). (As will be discussed later, state and local policies have been a different matter.)

By contrast, since the early 1970s IRS and its policies have been a significant impediment to nonprofits in the HMO field. Three aspects of HMOs' organizational characteristics have been problematic from IRS's perspective. First, most did not fit well with "community benefit" standards that had been borrowed from IRS's exemption policies for hospitals, because few plans actually operated hospitals that might have emergency departments. Second, HMOs had features that raised concerns that these organizations were providing private benefit (either to the enrolled population or to physicians) rather than benefit to the community at large. Third, HMOs included an insurance function, and IRS was long skeptical of whether the provision of health insurance was deserving of tax exemption, a view that was eventually incorporated into legislation in 1986 that removed most federal tax advantages from nonprofit Blue Cross plans. The development of IRS's positions on these matters occurred at the very time that the HMO industry was growing and became an important impediment to the creation of new nonprofit plans, particularly plans that did not own their own delivery system (as does, for example, Kaiser). Whereas the developers of new plans in the 1970s had reasons to choose the nonprofit form (to secure funding under the HMO Act), in the 1980s the federal government was an obstacle to the creation of new nonprofit plans. Most growth came from the for-profit side.

A third area in which governmental policy contributed to the divergent ownership trends of the hospital and HMO fields is in conversions to for-profit status. As has already been discussed, conversions among hospitals have been uncommon, have occurred in both directions (profit and nonprofit), and have had little effect on the overall composition of the hospital field. By contrast, conversions contributed quite substantially to the for-profit transformation of the HMO field, involving by my calculations approximately one-third of the nonprofits. Whereas hospital conversions mostly involved the sale of assets, HMO conversions were commonly reorganizations by insiders who thereby assumed ownership of what had previously been nonprofit assets. Such transactions peaked in the mid-1980s, a decade before the conversion phenomenon attracted widespread attention. Government's contribution was to let these transactions occur with little scrutiny and at far less than market value (Bailey, 1994). The opportunity to gain control of nonprofit assets at bargain prices undoubtedly stimulated such transactions.

In the HMO conversions that occurred before policy makers and regulators became aware of the stakes, the private capture of their charitable assets was a lost opportunity to create resources for new purposes to benefit communities. It is less clear, however, that a net loss of community-benefitting activity occurred, since it appears (although it was never specifically documented) that the HMOs that were converted had perhaps been established as nonprofits not because of a fit with purpose and intent but because the entrepreneurs that established them saw legal advantages to the use of the nonprofit form. The main advantage was to gain access to capital funding under the HMO Act. Thus, in the main the HMOs that converted may have been bringing their corporate structure into line with their characteristics and purposes. Many of these plans were created and governed by the doctors who practiced within them and who had established plans as a defensive measure, not by the kind of board that is typical of nonprofit hospitals.

The Performance of Nonprofit Hospitals and HMOs

Three types of questions have stimulated research into the performance of nonprofits. First, economists have been very interested in studying whether for-profit hospitals are more "efficient" than nonprofits. (Little research on this question has been done regarding HMOs, perhaps because of presumptions that competition will sort out the issue. Even among hospitals, the topic has received much less study in recent years.) This question arises both from economic theory and from arguments about the benefits of for-profit health care. Studies have found that expenses in nonprofit hospitals are either similar or lower than in for-profits (Gray, 1991) and that administrative costs are higher in for-profits (Woolhandler and Himmelstein, 1997). Interestingly, in the first decade after Medicare moved to payment by fixed diagnosis-related rates, nonprofits had higher margins than did for-profits (Prospective Payment Assessment Commission, 1996). (The reversal of that trend in recent years has been interpreted by some as evidence of for-profit efficiency [Altman and Shactman, 1997], although investigations of Columbia/HCA suggest that some of that company's profitability may have come from illegal manipulations of the payment system.) Moreover, many studies have shown that purchasers' costs are higher when buying from for-profit hospitals. As the health care system continues becoming more competitive, empirical research about efficiency will be less important than is ability to compete and maintain quality under competitive conditions.

A second set of questions, again studied more in hospitals than HMOs, is concerned with charitable activities and public goods. Charitable activity is commonly measured in terms of "uncompensated care," a concept that includes bad debt. The relative amount of uncompensated care provided by nonprofit and for-profit hospitals varies from state to state (Gray 1991). The evidence shows that nonprofit hospitals provide more uncompensated care, both in absolute terms and in comparison with for-profits, in states with large numbers of uninsured people and few public hospitals. Elsewhere, nonprofits and for-profits are similar with regard to uncompensated care. Nonprofit hospitals are also more likely than for-profits to provide money-losing services and to be involved in educational and research activities (Gray, 1986; Gray, 1991). There are indications that nonprofit HMOs are more commonly involved in community benefit activities than are for-profits, although system-atic evidence is not yet available (Schlesinger et al., 1998).

The third area pertains to trustworthiness, a great concern in health care because of the informational asymmetries between providers of service, on the one hand, and patients and third-party payers, on the other (Hansmann, 1980; Steinberg and Gray, 1993). Translated into operational terms, trustwor-thiness pertains both to quality of care and to fraud and abuse (Gray, 1997). The Institute of Medicine study a decade ago found no large or consistent differences between for-profit and nonprofit hospitals regarding quality of care (Gray, 1986). More recently, concern has grown because of data showing that for-profit hospitals have lower nursing-to-patient ratios than do nonprofit hospitals, but how this relates to quality is uncertain (Institute of Medicine, 1997). On the fraud-and-abuse side, the recent scandals involving Columbia-HCA are apparently the latest example of a for-profit hospital company engaging in systematic exploitation of the vulnerabilities of patients and payment systems (see Gray, 1991, chapter 6). In addition to manipulation of payment systems and rules, the company's joint ventures and profit-sharing activities with physicians compromised the independence and agency role on which both payers and patients have relied.

Trustworthiness has been a greater concern in HMOs than in hospitals in part because of fears that cost-containment methods either create conflicts of interest for physicians in their agency role for patients or result in denials of needed services. Although these concerns are not typically framed in non-profit/for-profit terms, it is notable that they are typically stated in terms of organizations' profits being put ahead of patients' interests. Available evidence regarding ownership form and trustworthiness is fragmentary but suggestive. For example, the HMOs that have the highest rates of disenrollment in the Medicare program are for-profit and those with the lowest rates are nonprofit (Health Care Finance Administration, 1994). A similar pattern has been reported in appeals by enrollees in Medicare managed care (Anders, 1995). In a *Consumer Reports* survey (1996), enrollees in for-profit plans more com-monly reported experiencing denials of needed care. Most recently, an analy-sis of quality data collected by the National Committee on Quality Assurance show greater attention to prevention activities in nonprofit than in for-profit plans (Spragins, 1997).

The Future of Nonprofit Health Care

The rapid pace of change in health care raises many difficult issues for the nonprofit sector in health care. Although some institutions work hard to provide leadership in anticipation of change, the pace and variety of new developments mean that much of what is happening in nonprofit health care is reactive. Among the major developments of importance for the future are the following:

• With universal health insurance still a distant promise, institutions that are tax-exempt as charitable entities will be expected to help meet the needs of the growing ranks of the uninsured.

• With the growth of managed care in both the private and public sectors (Medicare and Medicaid), hospitals and other providers will come under increasing pressure to reduce costs and negotiate on price with large purchasers. Nonprofit hospitals have been alleging for several years that this cost pressure will make it difficult or impossible for them to carry out their "charitable" activities via cross-subsidization from paying patients, but their margins have been higher in recent years than ever before (Prospective Payment Assessment Commission, 1997). That situation will not be allowed to continue by Medicare, which can freeze or reduce the prices that it pays.

• Admission rates and lengths of hospital stays have been declining for many years. Numbers of hospitals and of staffed beds have been declining too, but at a much lower rate. With hospital occupancy now below 60 percent nationally, and with continuing cost pressure from purchasers, growing numbers of nonprofit hospitals will face the question of sale, merger, closure, or conversion to another purpose (e.g., long-term care).

• State policies have played an important role in the reorganizations and sales that have converted hundreds of nonprofit hospitals and HMOs into for-profit organizations. Regulatory oversight has increased markedly in the past two to three years, and community resistance to for-profit conversions has developed in many locations. The scandals involving Columbia/HCA and the financial travails of some major HMO companies may also dampen the appeal of these conversions. Writing in early 1998, it seems plausible that the conversion phenomenon may have hit its peak, except among Blue Cross plans. Still, low occupancy and cost pressures will continue to destabilize the status quo.

• State Medicaid programs have become a major source of change through the widespread embrace of mandatory managed care for beneficiaries. Among the consequences has been the creation of a large number of new health plans (mostly nonprofit) by hospitals and community health centers that have traditionally served large numbers of Medicaid and other poor patients. To date, there is little indication that either the state or federal governments are putting impediments in the way of these new entities.

In addition to the trends and developments just mentioned, several other developments seem particularly important for the future of the nonprofit sector in health care and bear additional discussion.

Hybridization Old and New

A large number of nonprofit hospitals became part of larger organizational structures that include for-profit corporations as a result of the "corporate restructuring" in the 1970s and 1980s. These corporate structures were created to maximize revenues, to comply with tax rules, and to facilitate management of diverse activities. Typically, a nonprofit parent organization was created that held several other organizations, which included both for-profit and nonprofit entities. The hospital itself was generally the largest of these entities and was nonprofit. Other nonprofit entities might have included other types of medical services organizations and frequently a foundation into which charitable donations were placed for redistribution to the other non-profit entities. The for-profit entities included various subsidiaries that were engaged in what would have been unrelated business income if carried out by the hospital itself, plus other entities which were essentially investments of surplus revenues. These did not necessarily bear much relationship to the hospital's core activities (e.g., hotels for patients' families; health clubs).

The New Hybrids

Two new stimuli to hybrid arrangements have developed in the past few years. One is the growth of managed care, which has led nonprofit hospitals to engage in a wide variety of new organizational arrangements. Some of these organizations are intended to enhance the hospital's market position, as with some joint ventures with physicians to form integrated entities that can contract with managed care organizations. Other new ventures involve the creation of HMOs or HMO-like Medicaid managed care organizations. Thus, for example, Yale–New Haven Hospital entered into a joint venture with Yale School of Medicine to create a for-profit HMO in 1996 when the state of Connecticut moved its Medicaid program to the managed care model.

As new organizational forms involving hospitals and physicians ("integrated delivery systems," "provider sponsored plans," "physician-hospital organizations") continue to develop in response to competitive pressures and managed care, federal tax policies become a significant force in the restructuring of the health care delivery system, with concerns focusing primarily on the issue of private (rather than community) benefit. These arrangements also further blur the line between nonprofit and for-profit health care organizations.

The second recent stimulus to hybrid arrangements has been new acquisition strategies by for-profit companies, particularly Columbia/HCA and Tenet. In several instances, these firms have purchased controlling interest in a nonprofit hospital, resulting in a joint venture with a nonprofit entity. These arrangements were cheaper for the acquirer, dampened (but did not eliminate) concerns about the loss of charitable missions, and gave the nonprofit the opportunity to benefit from the anticipated surge in profitability. These transactions are controversial in tax, legal, and policy terms. Only a handful occurred, and it remains to be seen whether this is a workable model that will be important in the future.

New Forms of Accountability

New Performance Monitoring I: The Tax Exemption Comparison

State and local governments began to challenge the tax benefits accorded to nonprofit hospitals in the mid-1980s, a period in which many hospitals had unusually high margins. This development was stimulated by several factors—the desire to make care more available to the uninsured, increasingly commercial behavior by many hospitals, and behind the scenes encouragement from for-profit hospital companies. These challenges met with mixed success, and hospitals in several states either lost exemptions or negotiated payments in lieu of taxes.

Debate about nonprofits' tax exemptions has focused on both conceptual and empirical issues. First, what community benefits should nonprofit hospitals be expected to provide in exchange for their tax exemptions? This question presumed that exemptions were a subsidy that required justification in tangible terms defined by public policy. The major empirical question was whether nonprofit hospitals (and HMOs) provided measurable benefits whose value at least equaled the amount of money forgone by government by virtue of tax exemptions. This question was first studied in a 1990 report on hospitals in California and New York by the U.S. General Accounting Office (1990), and has been examined subsequently by other researchers and in other states (Morrisey, Wedig, and Hassan, 1996). The gist of the findings is that the results depend upon the definition of community benefit used. If "community benefit" is defined very narrowly in terms of charity care, then the benefit provided by some, but not most, hospitals is less than the value of their tax exemptions.

Such research results plus active lobbying by nonprofit hospitals have largely blunted industry-wide attacks on nonprofit hospitals' tax exemptions, but several major states (including Texas, California, and New York) have initiated requirements that individual hospitals report publicly each year on their community benefit activities (Barnett, 1997). The definition of community benefit varies widely. Texas defines it narrowly in terms of uncompensated care, while California initially has left it to institutions to define and report on community benefit in their own terms. The impact of public reporting on the nature and extent of community benefit activities has not yet been empirically studied. Observers expect both improved performance and a degree of game-playing with the community benefit concept.

New Performance Monitoring II: Quality of Care

Observers of the nonprofit sector have long noted that they tend to be found in fields that do not lend themselves readily to clear and unambiguous measures of performance (Kanter et al., 1987). As result of developments in health services research and pressure from purchasers, particularly in the private sector, health care organizations will increasingly have to provide documentation of their performance in providing care to patients and enrollees. Health services research found that high levels of unnecessary and inappropriate services were being provided and that necessary preventive services were often not being provided. Research into the determinants of positive outcomes in medical care and in the measurement of patient satisfaction has also been extremely important. On the purchaser side, large self-insured employers began to demand information about the medical care that they were purchasing.

Over the past decade, these demands for data became more sophisticated, and the need for standardization of measures was recognized. The growth of managed care both stimulated and facilitated the desire to know the value of what was being purchased. In the HMO field, the result has been the adoption of an evolving data set known as HEDIS, which is designed to make it possible to compare the performance of different health plans, which in turn must demand performance data from providers such as hospitals. Accreditation bodies have also increasingly turned to measures of performance, not just of compliance with structural standards. A few states have begun to collect and report outcome measures regarding hospitals' performance in common but complex surgical procedures (e.g., coronary bypass surgery).

Because of the difficulty of knowing when institutions were providing good care, nonprofit institutions may have enjoyed a halo effect in the past, based in part on their local control and their service missions. Clearly, the performance of nonprofits in the provision of services will be subject to unprecedented levels of scrutiny in the future. If nonprofit is better, we will know. We will also know if it is not.

New Performance Monitoring III: Fraud and Abuse

Theorists have posited that nonprofit health care organizations will have advantages in fields in which information asymmetries exist between purchasers and sellers of services (Hansmann, 1980). It has become apparent that health care, because of the vulnerabilities of both patients and third-party payers, is a field that is characterized by high levels of fraud. Fraud and abuse has repeatedly been the subject of new legislation for Medicare and Medicaid over the past 25 years, is estimated to account for as much as 10 percent of health expenditures in the Medicare program (GAO, 1997), and is now a lead issue for the Department of Justice.

Several of the major for-profit hospital companies have run afoul of fraud-and-abuse statutes over the past 15 years (Gray, 1991, Eichenwald, 1998). As part of their efforts to reform themselves, Tenet Healthcare Corp. (formerly National Medical Enterprises) and Columbia/HCA have hired high-level compliance officers to reassure nervous purchasers and stockholders that the company is serious about minimizing fraudulent activities (Lagnado, 1997).

An important future question for nonprofit hospitals and other health care organizations is their ability to stand up to scrutiny from fraud-and-abuse investigators. Nonprofit leaders have been notably quiet as the Columbia/HCA fraud investigation has unfolded. No one knows the extent to which nonprofits may have been engaging in the same practices that are the source of Columbia/HCA's difficulties. An investigation of teaching hospitals by the Department of Health and Human Services and the Department of Justice has already recorded some significant instances of improper billing for services performed by house staff in nonprofit hospitals (Weissenstein, 1997). Trust in nonprofits could be seriously damaged if future investigations show a widespread pattern of fraudulent activity. This is a form of performance monitoring for which nonprofits should be prepared.

Changing Federal/State Relationships

For both hospitals and HMOs, federal policies have had a greater impact than state policies over the past thirty years, even though hospitals are licensed at the state level and HMOs (like insurance generally) are regulated at the state level. But Medicare and the various cost containment strategies that have been attached to it has had a far reaching effect, as has the federal ERISA law that has preempted state regulation of the health benefit programs of self-insured corporations.

In the 1990s, the pendulum of power and influence has swung to some degree from the federal to the state level. In part this has been due to the ideological current known as devolution, in part due to the failure of national reform in 1993, and in part due to pleas from states for power to exercise more control over the costs of Medicaid (which involves shared federal-state financing). The shift in power involves several manifestations, some of which have already been mentioned in this paper. Thus:

• Most of the innovation for enhanced accountability for tax exemptions for nonprofit health care organizations has come from the states.

• In the wake of the failure of the Clinton health reform proposals and the continuing decay of employment-sponsored health insurance, the numbers of the uninsured are increasing with alarming speed. In New York, for example, the percentage of the uninsured has grown by 25 percent to about one-fourth of the population in the 1990s. Some states have responded to the growth of the uninsured with new state programs to finance their care or to assist institutions that serve them. In most states, nonprofit and public facilities that attempt to serve the uninsured are under increased financial distress.

• Virtually all state Medicaid programs have adopted, or are in the process of adopting, some form of managed care. The consequences include much enhanced power of the states as purchasers, with far-reaching ripple effects for the mostly nonprofit and public hospitals and health centers that have traditionally served the Medicaid population. One consequence is increased constraint on a revenue source that had been used to subsidize overall operations of providers who have served the uninsured population. Another consequence is the creation of new managed care plans as a defensive measure by organizations that have traditionally served the poor.

• Federal welfare reform of 1996 and its consequences for state welfare programs have important implications for nonprofit organizations that have a historical commitment for service to the poor. To an extent that is not well documented, immigrant populations and welfare recipients that exceed federally established time limits swell the pool of the uninsured that at least some nonprofits have attempted to serve.

The cumulative effect of these and other changes over the past decade make clear that the future of the nonprofit sector in health care will be as much a matter of state-level health policies as federal policies, at least until such time as the federal government reasserts leadership regarding such problems as the uninsured and tax-exemption policy.

It has been almost 20 years since Henry Hansmann (1980) published his inquiry into the role of nonprofits in fields in which revenues come from the sale of services rather than contributions from donors. The new era of performance measurement, monitoring by purchasers, community benefit reporting, and economic competition may help us understand whether nonprofits can indeed play a distinctive role. Convergence of nonprofit and for-profit behavior is widely predicted in health care, but it is also possible that the differences will grow as government demands justifications for tax exemptions, as nonprofit institutions that behave like for-profits convert to for-profit status, and as large governmental programs (Medicare and Medicaid) squeeze out the profit-making opportunities that have attracted equity investors into health care. There is already evidence in New York and some other states that Medicaid is not willing to pay rates that will attract and hold for-profit managed care companies.

The hospital field has the special challenge that comes from excess capacity. Although the boards of nonprofit hospitals may see institutional survival as their primary responsibility, it seems apparent that large numbers of nonprofit hospitals should merge or change their services (e.g., to long-term care). How trustees will respond is a great challenge for the future. Will the assets for which they are responsible be dissipated by a death spiral of declining utilization or will the trustees find new ways of using those assets for the service of their communities? The sale to a for-profit company, it should be noted, does nothing to reduce the excess capacity that has become a major problem.

The growing governmental demand that hospitals and HMOs document their ongoing deservedness for tax exemptions has the potential to enhance their community service roles and activities, but it also contains risks substituting the judgment of regulators for that of trustees regarding the mix of policies and activities that best serve the community (Pauly, 1996, Gray, 1996). The question will again be posed regarding whether the nonprofit sector is best seen as a complement to government or as a tool of governmental policies.

References

Altman, S. H., and Shactman, D. "Should We Worry about Hospitals' High Administrative Costs?" *New England Journal of Medicine* 1997, 335 (11), 769–74.

Anders, G. "Humana Gets Some of the Poorest Scores in Study of HMO Medicare Complaints." *Wall Street Journal*, 1995, B5.

Bailey, A. L. "Charities Win, Lose in Health Shuffle." *Chronicle of Philanthropy*, June 14, 1994, p. 1.

Barnett, K. *The Future of Community Benefit Programming: An Expanded Model for Planning and Assessing the Participation of Health Care Organizations in Community Health Improvement Activities.* Berkeley, CA: Public Health Institute, 1997.

Brown, L. D. *Politics and Health Care Organization: HMOs as Federal Policy.* Washington, DC: Brookings Institute, 1983.

Chollet, D. J., Lamphere, J. and Needleman, J. *Conversion of Hospitals and Health Plans for For-profit Status: A Preliminary Investigation of Community Issues.* Washington, DC: Alpha Center, 1996.

Consumer Reports. "How Good is Your Health Plan?" *Consumer Reports*, August 1996, pp. 28–42.

Durso, K. A. "Profit Status in the Early History of Health Maintenance Organizations." Doctoral dissertation, Yale University, 1992.

Eichenwald, K. "High-Stakes Face-Off Begins for Columbia/HCA." *New York Times*, January 20, 1998.

Fox, D. and Schaffer, D. C. "Tax Administration as Health Policy: Hospitals, the IRS, and the Courts." *Journal of Health Politics and Law*, 1991 16 (2), 251–79.

General Accounting Office. *Nonprofit Hospitals: Better Standards Needed for Tax Exemption: Report to the Chairman*, Select Committee on Aging, House of Representatives. Washington, DC: GAO 1990.

General Accounting Office. *Not-For-Profit Hospitals, Conversion Issues Prompt Increased State Oversight*. Washington, DC: GAO, 1997.

Gray, B. H., ed. *For-Profit Enterprise in Health Care: A Report of the Institute of Medicine*. Washington, DC: National Academy Press, 1986.

Gray, B. H. *The Profit Motive and Patient Care: The Changing Accountability of Doctors and Hospitals*. Cambridge: Harvard University Press, 1991.

Gray, B. H. "Tax Exemptions as Health Policy." *Frontiers of Health Services Management*, 1996, 12 (3), 37–42.

Gray, B. H. "Trust and Trustworthy Care in the Managed Care Era." *Health Affairs*, 16 (2), 1997, 34–49.

Hansmann, H. "The Role of Nonprofit Enterprise." *The Yale Law Journal*, 1980, 89 (5), 835–901.

Health Care Finance Administration. *Enrollment and Disenrollment Expense in the Medicare Risk Program*. Baltimore, MD: HCFA, 1994.

Hoy, E. and Gray, B. H. "The Growth of the Major Investor-Owned Hospital Companies." In B. H. Gray, ed., *For-Profit Enterprise in Health Care*, Washington, DC: National Academy Press, 1986.

Institute of Medicine. *Nursing Staff in Hospitals and Nursing Homes: Is It Adequate?* Wunderlich, G. S., Sloan, F., and Davis, C. K., eds. Washington, DC: National Academy Press, 1997.

Kanter, R. M., and Summers, D. V. "Doing Well While Doing Good: Dilemmas of Performance Measurement in Nonprofit Organizations and the Need for a Multiple-Constituency Approach." In W. W. Powell, ed., *The Nonprofit Sector: A Research Handbook*. New Haven: Yale University Press, 1987.

Lagnado, L. "Columbia Taps Lawyer for Ethics Post, Yuspeh Led Defense Initiative of 1980s." *Wall Street Journal*, October 14, 1997.

Levit, K. R., Lazenby, H. C., Braden, B. R, and the National Health Accounts Team. "National Health Spending Trends in 1996." *Health Affairs*, 1998 17 (1), 35–51.

Marmor, T., Schlesinger, M., and Smithey, R. "Nonprofit Organizations in Health Care." In W. W. Powell, ed., *The Nonprofit Sector: A Research Handbook*, 221–39. New Haven: Yale University Press, 1987.

Morrisey, M. A., Wedig, G. J., and Hassan, M., "Do Nonprofit Hospitals Pay Their Way?" *Health Affairs*, 1996 (Winter):132–44.

Pauly, M. V. "Health Systems Ownership: Can Regulation Preserve Community Benefits?" *Frontiers of Health Services Management*, 1996, 12 (3), 3–34.

Prospective Payment Assessment Commission. *Medicare and the American Health Care System: Report to the Congress*. Washington, DC: Prospective Payment Assessment Commission 1996.

Prospective Payment Assessment Commission. *Hospital Payments, Costs, and*

Financial Condition of Medicare and the American Health Care System: Report to the Congress. Washington, DC: Prospective Payment Assessment Commission, 1997.

Schlesinger, M., Gray, B. H., Carrino, G., Duncan, M., Gusmano, M., Antonelli, V., and Stuber, J. "A Broadened Vision for Managed Care, Part II: Toward a Typology of Community Benefits Provided by HMO's." *Health Affairs,* forthcoming.

Spragins, E. E. "How to Choose an HMO." *Newsweek,* December 15, 1997, p. 72.

Steinberg, R. and Gray, B. H. "The Role of Nonprofit Enterprise in 1992: Hansmann Revisited." *Nonprofit and Voluntary Sector Quarterly,* 1993, 22 (Winter), 297–316.

Weisbrod, B. *The Nonprofit Economy.* Cambridge: Harvard University Press, 1990.

Weissenstein, E. "Hospitals Sue to Temper PATH Probe." *Modern Healthcare,* November 3, 1997, p. 4.

Woolhandler, S., and Himmelstein, D. U. "Costs of Care and Administration at For-Profit and Other Hospitals in United States." *New England Journal of Medicine,* 1997, 336 (11), 769–74.

CHAPTER EIGHTEEN

Lessons for the Future of Philanthropy

Local Foundations and Urban School Reform

William S. McKersie and Anthony Markward

> Foundation money is still the leavening agent for change. We need
> to examine how it can leaven most effectively, now that the context
> has changed dramatically.
>
> —*Susan Lajoie Eagan, Associate Director, the Cleveland Foundation*

Using Chicago and Cleveland as case studies, this essay unveils the important, and often overlooked, work of local grantmakers in stimulating and sustaining public school reform in America's major cities. We trace how two groups of local foundations in these two cities came to play a limited but important role in urban school reform between 1987 and 1995, a period that encompassed key events in the evolution of education reform in each city. We document the struggle of these local foundations to define their role in each city's reform process. Correctly, they understood themselves to be front-line participants in local public processes.

These Chicago and Cleveland foundations are remarkable—and probably in the minority—for the fact that over the past ten years each has willingly immersed itself in the public, intensive, conflict-laden process of school reform. They invested heavily in school reform over the 1987–1995 period, in terms of money ($70 million in Chicago, $40 million in Cleveland), staff time, and reputation.[1] The monetary contributions of Chicago's foundations to school reform may have set the pace for urban foundations nationally, while the contributions of Cleveland foundations are conspicuous when considered on a per capita basis. (Cleveland has 70,000 public school students compared to Chicago's 450,000.)

Unfortunately, the foundation literature and our experience in Chicago and Cleveland show that most American foundations, national and local, still have little tolerance for public affairs. Several local foundations in Chicago, for instance, provided funding for school reform, but their staffs and boards did not become active in the process. Some maintained distance because of constraints on their time, while others saw the process as too contentious.

Some national foundations working in Chicago stayed out of local processes for different reasons, including their lack of local knowledge and their need to disperse their resources over a wide area.

We have drawn our conclusions about the behavior of local foundations mostly from McKersie's research on local foundations' role in education reform in Chicago and Cleveland from 1987–1995. We have also drawn on McKersie's personal experiences as a grantmaker both in Chicago, where he served as a program officer and consultant for the Joyce Foundation from 1986 to 1992, and in Cleveland, where he is senior program officer for education at the Cleveland Foundation. Readers who know the reform processes in Chicago and Cleveland may be frustrated by our limited attention to critical developments in each city after 1995. We mention the most notable of these developments—namely, the parallel moves to mayoral control of both school systems—but we stay within a timeframe that is enough behind us to allow sound analysis and reflection.

Each Chicago and Cleveland foundation McKersie examined has independently evolved a highly flexible, process-oriented philanthropic approach that seems particularly well suited to the facilitation of public policy processes on a metropolitan scale and also well adapted to the indigenous circumstances of its home city. Their common approach to reform unites a group of foundations that are otherwise diverse in terms of type (community, independent, family, and corporate), size, mission, focus, and source of funds. In this essay, we attempt to articulate the commonalties and differences in the behaviors of these foundations, and explore the different paths to school reform traveled by the Cleveland and Chicago philanthropic communities as a whole.

We describe how the local foundations' increasing participation in reform over this period is rooted in the foundation sector's growing concern nationally for urban education and in local foundations' feelings of responsibility to their home cities. We then describe the relationships we have observed among the content of school reform, the specific metropolitan contexts within which reform must occur, and the process through which reformers adapt available solutions (content) to context. In order to illustrate these relationships, we outline the history of foundation involvement in the education reform movements of both of these cities. Finally, we draw on the experiences of these two cities to discuss the characteristics of local foundations' involvement in reform, the specific roles and strategies they have adopted, and the philanthropic tensions they have had to balance in order to influence local school systems.

A National Perspective on a Long Struggle

Foundations, awakened to the seriousness of public education's problems by the landmark report *A Nation at Risk* (1983), began groping for ways to improve schools in the early 1980s. Since then, they and other urban school reformers in America may identify most with Sisyphus, the mythical king of Corinth condemned to roll a heavy boulder up a hill in Hades, only to have it roll back down as he neared the top. After more than a decade of school reform in some locales, cities are still burdened with schools that fail to help even half of their 11 million students achieve minimum learning standards, while their suburban and rural counterparts continue to outperform them. In addition to fixing schools and school systems, reformers somehow must address the wide range of community, family, and personal issues that a plethora of research has shown to be critical to student achievement.

A new study of school decentralization in six cities by Anthony S. Bryk, Paul Hill, and Dorothy Shipps (1998) at last brings evidence that reformers may be closer to the top of the hill than ever before. The study suggests that student achievement is rising in Charlotte-Mecklenburg, North Carolina, and in elementary schools in Chicago, and ties these gains directly to reformers' efforts. The length of time formal "school reform" efforts have taken to achieve even marginal gains in achievement in these two cities (9 years in Chicago and 6 years in Charlotte) demonstrates the importance and power of continuous effort in addressing grand public issues in a major city. Given the depth of political divisions and scarcity of resources in most urban areas, the persistence of urban reform efforts has been one of their most surprising characteristics.

Foundations have been among the more persistent supporters of urban school reform since the early 1980s, and, for them, the study by Bryk and his colleagues represents the first signs of a return on a long-term investment. Philanthropic support for elementary and secondary education grew throughout the 1980s and the first half of the 1990s. As a portion of total foundation giving, K–12 education concerns rose from about 3 percent ($84.3 million) in 1980 to nearly 8 percent ($835 million) in 1995 (Renz, 1997, 64; *Giving USA 1996*, 18–19). Higher education, which has historically dominated foundation giving for education, saw its share of the total fall over these fifteen years, from 22 percent in 1980 ($618 million) to 15 percent ($1.57 billion) in 1995 (ibid.).

The nation's larger foundations have also played important roles in urban education reform. Several foundations with a national perspective have found ways to facilitate public education reform through locally defined and delimited efforts that demonstrate the value of integrating several innovations at a single site. The first such effort was the Ford Foundation's Comprehensive School Improvement Program (CSIP, 1960–1970). Although CSIP's emphasis was urban, it also targeted rural and suburban districts: 60 percent of the $30 million awarded went to seven urban projects; 26 percent to four projects benefiting all three populations; and 14 percent to eight rural and six suburban projects (Ford Foundation, 1972, 14). CSIP did not meet its goals, largely because they were too ambitious and support for the program—especially in terms of time—too limited (Meade, 1991, K9). By the late 1980s, however, several national foundations were supporting more focused variations on the CSIP theme of integrating multiple innovations in particular urban districts and schools. One of the first was the Edna McConnell Clark Foundation's ongoing five-city initiative to reform middle school education. Another was the Annie E. Casey Foundation's New Futures Initiative, which provided about $40 million over five years (1989–1994) to help four medium-sized cities (Dayton, Ohio; Little Rock, Arkansas; Pittsburgh, Pennsylvania; and Savannah, Georgia) alter the life chances of at-risk youth (Wehlage, Smith, and Lipman, 1992, 55). The most recent and prominent is Walter Annenberg's multimillion-dollar grants to create local public school reform grantmaking bodies and programs in nine cities, which required local sources in each city to double the Annenberg contribution.[2]

As foundations increased funding for K–12 education issues nationally, those working in the nation's cities began to worry about the poor performance of schools in their own backyards. Driven by concern for the performance of their local schools, foundations in Chicago, Cleveland, Boston, Los Angeles, New York, Philadelphia and San Francisco have become involved in school reform efforts over the past decade (Renz, 1991; Jehl and Payzant, 1992; Lobman, 1992; McKersie, 1993; Sommerfeld, 1994; McKersie and Palaich, 1994; and Bernholz, 1995). Although they felt compelled to local action, many foundations remained wary of taking on systemwide reform issues, fearing that their limited resources would prove ineffectual against the political, economic, and social forces with which urban schools were struggling. Sondra Hardis, the Senior Contributions Associate of BP America in Cleveland during the late 1980s and early 1990s, recalled that her organization might not have become involved in the reform effort if "systemic change" had been proposed as the initial goal.

Like BP America, most local donors dipped their toes in school reform waters before launching their small boats onto a sea they perceived as vast and turbulent. At first, they tried to aid local schools by funding discrete programs that directly aided students and teachers. When these programs did not generate much improvement in the overall performance of public schools, foundations began to recognize that the underachievement, low rates of attendance, and high dropout rates that pervaded urban schools were symptoms of systemwide issues that could not be addressed piecemeal. National and local foundations throughout the country began to focus more support on restructuring public school systems (Renz, 1996, 62).

A New Emphasis on Process

As school reform first began to rise on their agendas, Chicago foundations spent their money on teacher development, research on policies and practices, and parent and community empowerment; Cleveland foundations tried to help students and teachers directly through scholarships and individual grants. As the reform movements in Chicago and Cleveland matured, foundations in both cities joined with the various reformers to discuss and plan changes in the system and then provided support for the implementation of those plans. They began to place as much emphasis on the *process* of comprehensive, systemwide reform as on its *substance*.

The foundations' increasing attention to process is unusual among the organizations involved in school reform in both cities. The Illinois legislature, for instance, did not much worry about the process of bringing the reforms codified in the 1988 Chicago School Reform Act—the driving force behind Chicago school reform—to life in Chicago. Illinois failed to provide funding or other support for the local school councils, which the legislation envisioned was at the heart of successful reform. Support for the development and operation of these key bodies fell to the cities' foundations.

Process, substance, and context are three interactive elements of school reform that have influenced the behavior of foundations in Chicago and Cleveland. We define them here:

Process: The interactions among local parties to reform—elected officials, foundations, business leaders, nonprofits, school system administrators, teachers, community organizations, and parents—that advance solutions to the problems of the school system.

Substance: The content of solutions to the problems of the school system. Examples of content include the governance and management of districts and schools, school and class size, accountability and assessment systems for adults and students, scheduling, curriculum, pedagogy, professional training and development, technology, parent and community involvement, human and social services, school-to-work linkages, and evaluation and reporting.

Context: The manifold local and national circumstances within which the local actors must work, including the indigenous geographic, demographic, political, and economic characteristics and history of a given metropolitan area.

Context, of course, is important in any human interaction, while the creation of substance, or solutions to problems, has long been a philanthropic staple. We have identified three reasons for foundations' increased attention to process: A new national public affairs climate; well developed substance of reform; and the metropolitan scale of school reform and its deep ties to complex city problems.

The New Public Affairs Climate

The new public affairs climate favors reformers who adopt local, flexible, and creative approaches to public problems, accept accountability for specific outcomes, and fund social change with a mix of private and public (or solely private) resources. In the new public affairs climate, rooted in the Reagan administration's promotion of devolution and fiscal austerity, the classic mode of strategic grantmaking employed by many foundations since at least the 1950s has become less effective. In their classic strategic role, known as "seed and leave," foundations created social programs and passed them to government, which oversaw their implementation on a larger scale. In playing this role, foundations focused their energies on the substance of public issues and left the matters of process and implementation to the public sector, mainly due to its superior resources.

Federal, state, and municipal governments are no longer as willing to take to scale the programs and policies developed with assistance from foundations. As a result, foundations will achieve little if they plant the seeds of new ideas and approaches but don't stick around to ensure they grow. The stakes are especially high for foundations that work in their own backyards and must live with the results of their grantmaking and staff work.

On the other hand, foundations know that they cannot bankroll the development, implementation, and evaluation of major policies or practices intended to reform public education. Even working together locally, foundations cannot effect systemwide change without government's resources and clout. This is one of the major lessons we draw from Chicago and Cleveland.

Reform Ideas Are Abundant

We believe that foundations have been wise to invest an increasing share of their resources in the reform process. Years of work by researchers, teachers, administrators, nonprofit organizations, government agencies, and foundations have yielded an abundance of ideas about the necessary substance of urban school reform. There is a growing list of nationally respected models of effective schools and, with the increasing popularity of charter schools in many states, viable new models and variations on old ones are frequently invented and tested. For example, Olatokunbo S. Fashola and Robert E. Slavin (1998) rated six well-known "schoolwide" programs and seven major school design efforts spawned by the New American Schools Development Corporation (now known as New American Schools) as at least "partially successful at meeting evaluation criteria for achievement."[3] Similarly, *Education Week*'s special report on urban education highlighted a number of reform ideas that are being implemented individually and in combination in various locales around the country: set clear, high expectations for all students; devise an accountability system based on good information; give schools freedom in exchange for accountability, and allow those at the top to do their jobs; recruit, hire, and retain high ability teachers; build capacity at the school level to improve curriculum and instruction; develop strong leaders at the school and district level; get students the extra time and attention they need to succeed; improve the relationship of parents and communities with schools and educators; create small schools or schools-within-schools; provide safe and adequate school buildings; break up the monopoly on district-run schools through private school vouchers, charter schools, and/or private management of public schools; and close or reconstitute bad schools (Olson and Hendrie, 1998, 32–45).

The message for local foundations is clear: there are plenty of good ideas about how to improve the way most urban schools serve children. The unsolved problem—one lacking extensive and conclusive research—is how to take individual successes systemwide.

Local Context Drives the Substance and Process of Reform

The variations in city circumstances and actors are the primary factors that make the shape, timing, and direction of school reform unique in each city. Local context helps determine the particular activities that foundations are funding in pursuit of school reform and where in the reform process —development, advocacy, implementation, or evaluation—they choose to throw their weight. The following examples of contextual elements in Cleveland and Chicago suggest important differences in the climate for school reform, and for local strategic philanthropy, in each community.

Contextual Differences

In Cleveland, citizens are disconnected and disenfranchised from the schools. Because of its history of segregation, the school system is overseen by a federal judge. Moreover, the state has controlled the school system since 1995, after the courts ruled that the financial and academic failures of the system rendered it incapable of managing itself. (State control will be lifted with the advent of mayoral control in September 1998.) Second, school funding partly depends on the electorate—levies must be passed to help the school system's local funding stream keep pace with inflation. Third, the city has a relatively small number of middle class and upper middle class residents, of which only a small portion send their children to the public schools. Fourth, the city has too few nonprofit research and advocacy organizations able and willing to aid the city with the substance of reform and too few community-based organizations able to help build momentum and political will for reform. Fifth, the city's institutions of higher education have not played a systematic role in improving public schools. Sixth, the Cleveland foundation community consists of just two major funders, with many smaller foundations providing some support for school reform. Finally, at least through 1995, the Cleveland reform process is best described as a "philanthropic or civic policy process." Reform has played out in executive and administrative policy decisions at the district and school levels. From the beginning, effort has been focused on collaboration among the school system, city government, corporations, foundations, nonprofit agencies and civic agencies.

In contrast, Chicago has four important characteristics. First, its reform is best described as a "legislative policy process." Since the 1988 Reform Act, most of the work of the various actors, including local foundations, involved in reform has been in support of or in response to this seminal piece of legislation. Second, it has a large and diverse set of nonprofit citywide and community-based institutions that are concerned with education and able to play big roles in the reform process. Third, Chicago's higher education community, largely inactive prior to the Reform Act's passage, has since become active both in the reform of individual schools and in citywide efforts to help gauge and guide the progress of school reform. Finally, its foundations number in the hundreds. A core group of about 20 foundations worked actively on school reform throughout much of the ten-year period we examined. Although 60 percent of all funding has come from three foundations (John D. and Catherine T. MacArthur, the Joyce Foundation, and the Chicago Community Trust), the broad base of philanthropic involvement has proved important. Indeed, two of the smaller foundations in terms of total giving (the Woods Fund of Chicago and the Wieboldt Foundation) were among the most active leaders in the school reform process.

Commonalties

Of course, there are important contextual commonalties across urban America vis-à-vis school reform. Chicago and Cleveland are similar in at least four major ways. One similarity has boosted reform efforts, while the other three have been among the largest barriers to success.

First, Cleveland and Chicago have had strong mayoral leadership since the late 1980s in the persons of Michael White and Richard M. Daley, both of whom have linked the improvement of public schools to continued economic growth in their cities. In Chicago, history will show that Mayor Washington sparked school reform with his pathbreaking citywide Education Summit.

A second common feature is a problem school systems cannot control: concentrated poverty and the host of social and health problems associated with it. In both cities roughly 70 percent of the students receive free or reduced lunch through the federal government. As many as one-third come from homes where public authorities have evidence of abuse or neglect. Mobility is also a challenge, with at least 20 percent of students changing addresses, and thus schools, every year and often mid-year.

Third, financial shortfalls have plagued both school systems. Cleveland's resources for education are perennially inadequate, partly because of limitations on the revenues the city can raise and partly because of the state's stance on school funding. Indeed, in March 1997 the Ohio Supreme Court found

Ohio's system of education finance to be unconstitutional. While similar legal challenges have failed in Illinois, the state's role in funding Chicago public schools has been equally problematic. For much of the 1980s and early 1990s, Chicago ran multimillion-dollar deficits created in large part by the structurally perpetuated inequity of the state's system of funding education (Hess, 1997; Booz-Allen & Hamilton, Inc., 1992).

Finally, racial politics have been a factor in both cities, where each school system is "majority minority." Cleveland's schools are roughly 70 percent African American, 24 percent white, and 5 percent Latino. Chicago's schools are nearly 60 percent African American, 12 percent white, and 26 percent Latino. The leading school reformers in both cities have not represented this racial and ethnic mix, and in some cases have not even been city residents. The lack of continuity between the reformers and the reformees has created tensions.

In Chicago, local foundations have played a key role in ensuring that a radical reform law gets properly implemented, and that the scope and substance of reform continue to expand. In Cleveland, foundations have focused on building the relationships and institutions necessary to create, and sustain momentum for, a broadly supported reform agenda. How did foundations and reform end up on such different paths in the two cities? In the next section, we summarize the story of foundations and school reform in each city to illustrate the relationship between local circumstances, the behavior of foundations, and the arc of reform.

Two Tales of Local Foundations and Urban School Reform

The data for Chicago come from McKersie's 1998 dissertation, "Strategic Philanthropy and Local Public Policy: Lessons from Chicago School Reform, 1987–1993," in which he examines the behavior of three Chicago foundations during the pivotal seven-year period when the 1988 Chicago School Reform Act was developed and implemented. Between 1987 and 1993, these three foundations—the Chicago Community Trust, the Joyce Foundation, and the Woods Fund of Chicago—accounted for $25.7 million of the $52.7 million Chicago foundations contributed to 176 organizations active in the school reform movement.[4] McKersie used four types of research methods—participant observation, grant data analysis, archival research, and interviews—to develop an empirical understanding of each foundation's involvement in the Reform Act and the context for their involvement.

Our information about Cleveland reform is less extensive and less systematic. Our Cleveland conclusions are based on two sets of observations: McKersie's extensive review, as the Cleveland Foundation's new senior program officer for education, of past and current school reform efforts in Greater Cleveland; and observations McKersie made during the late 1980s as a program officer for the Joyce Foundation, when he oversaw a series of grants for Cleveland public school reform efforts. We have also relied on McKersie's 1992 interviews with four foundation executives—representing the Cleveland Foundation, the George Gund Foundation, BP America's corporate contributions program, and the Martha Holden Jennings Foundation—about the role of Cleveland foundations in public school reform.

Chicago

Several of Chicago's most active educational foundations, including the Chicago Community Trust and the Joyce Foundation, generally advocated structural change in Chicago's education system. Several others, including the Woods Fund of Chicago and (to a lesser extent) the Joyce Foundation, had a long history of supporting Chicago's rich array of community-based organizations, some of which were returning forcefully to the issue of school reform in the mid-1980s. Their interests converged in the city's reform movement, the early activities of which culminated in the 1988 Chicago School Reform Act, one of the most radical state policies of the century regarding urban public education.[5]

The Reform Act decentralized school governance, creating local school councils (LSCs) to govern each of the city's 553 schools. Each LSC includes six parents, two teachers, two community members, the principal, and, in high schools, a student. LSCs are responsible for selecting the school principal and approving a school improvement plan, a school budget, and expenditures of discretionary funds. The Reform Act also restructured the central board of education so that its members were selected on the advice of LSC representatives, shifted control of state Chapter 1 poverty funds from the board to LSCs, and cut the city's central education administration by 25 percent.[6]

Chicago's foundations were not the direct leaders of the reform movement. The leadership role in the reform movement was shared by Chicago's nonprofit research and advocacy groups, community-based organizations, and business community (Hess, 1991; O'Connell, 1991; Hess, 1995; Shipps, 1995).[7] Chicago's foundations largely "reacted" to the Reform Act, having invested relatively little in the Act's development and passage. However, they quickly became vital to its implementation, making key strategic decisions about the broad private funding required to make the law work (McKersie, 1996). Prior to the Reform Act's passage in 1988, Chicago's foundations had just three chief reform interests: teacher development, policy/practice research, development and advocacy, and parent and community empowerment. Once the Reform Act was signed into law in 1988, foundations pumped funds into an array of reform initiatives. Over $52.7 million was awarded to reform initiatives from 1987–1993, with support leaping from $2.27 million in 1987 to $11.56 million in 1993.

What difference did this funding make to an ongoing, citywide public policy process aimed at improved student learning? On the upside, the foundations contributed to a reform process remarkable for its persistence. As of 1995, Chicago's reform movement was alive, although challenged by fiscal, administrative and labor-management strife in the school system. Linda Lenz, a long-time observer of reform, identified several key developments as of 1995, each a necessary step in the slow process of reforming a big, complex urban school system: curriculum reform; teacher retraining; the engagement of the broader community—represented by businesses, community organizations, universities, hospitals, and youth agencies; decline in school violence; development of new systemwide learning outcomes and assessments; a streamlined central administration; participation by local scholars; and active discussions of improved student experiences at a large number of schools (Lenz, 1995, 4–5).

On the downside, foundations, like other reformers, initially focused too much on the idea that parent and community governance roles would produce better schools and better learning. Two educational fundamentals were initially ignored: teachers interacting with students, and parents aiding their children's learning. In addition, despite much staff effort and a series of grants, Chicago's foundations were unable to help the school board and central office adopt effective support and accountability roles for a decentralized system. Most important, the foundations did not address public and political pressure for measurable improvements in student achievement. As of 1995, seven years after the passage of the Reform Act, test scores had not risen, nor had better teaching and learning broken out in the majority of Chicago schools. According to Lenz, many school reform observers contended that, while it might be too soon to expect markedly higher test scores, "many of the good things happening in schools are skirting the basics—reading, writing and math—and that it's time for a mid-course adjustment" (Lenz, 1995, 4).

This said, we note that Chicago's foundations helped support a shift in reform's focus and offered thoughtful critiques of the reform's impact. A couple of years after the Reform Act's passage, the foundations began to target more teaching and learning issues, sparking the reform movement's general shift from governance to educational concerns. Parent and community empowerment—the heart of the Reform Act—remained a priority, but was increasingly balanced by support for teacher development and collective restructuring efforts by principals, teachers, parents, and community members. Foundations annually devoted a large and growing share of their reform funding to evaluating and disseminating the effects of the Reform Act in comprehensive and accessible ways—a noteworthy endeavor, given the poor record of foundations nationally regarding the evaluation of existing policy and practice. Despite these efforts, Chicago's school reform movement struggled (as have many before it) to improve teaching and learning across the system.

Ultimately, the foundations' legacy may prove to be the persistence and energy of the citywide reform movement. Historians would be wise to keep their eye on the big picture, not just the success or failure of particular ideas and approaches, when they gauge the effects of reform. For instance, a 1995 state law placed the school system—including the decentralized governance structure created by the 1988 state law—under the control of the mayor and a corporate-style school board. While some feel the 1995 law represented a return to centralized governance of the public schools, we agree with those scholars who have argued that the law moved the school system toward "integrated governance," meshing decentralized authority with streamlined central structures and systemwide standards (Wong et al., 1996).[8] Some have attributed the rise in achievement found by Bryk and his colleagues in Chicago's elementary schools to the effects of the 1995 law. We think this rise is more likely due to a mixture of the two reforms, not either individually. Susan Ryan and her colleagues make this argument in a 1997 study, in which they found that most LSCs—the progeny of the 1988 Reform Act—are active agents for improvement in their school communities, but that some are struggling and in need of the increased oversight brought by the 1995 Reform Act (Ryan et al., 1997).

Cleveland

While the Chicago school reform story is based on a public policy process centered on state legislation, Cleveland reform revolves around joint initiatives by corporations, foundations, nonprofit agencies, government officials, and the school system. Cleveland foundations first tried to address public school problems by providing direct assistance to teachers and students. Between 1984 and 1990, Cleveland's foundation and corporate community invested significant money and time in two public school improvement programs. The Cleveland Education Fund, established in 1984, was one of the nation's first "public education funds." Now found in nearly 100 U.S. cities, public education funds have been established most often to help build local constituencies for public school improvement and reform. The Cleveland Education Fund until recently has had a different focus: the bulk of its programs provide innovative individual educators small grants and technical assistance.[9] In 1987, the Scholarship-in-Escrow (SIE) and School-to-Work programs were created. These programs, started at the urging of then Superintendent Al Tutela and modeled partly after the Boston Compact (1985), generated more than $16 million from Cleveland foundations and corporations to guarantee Cleveland public school graduates college scholarship assistance (based on their elementary and secondary school grades) or a job in a Cleveland firm.

Despite significant philanthropic commitment, these programs did not generate much improvement in the public schools, although individual teachers and students benefited. Independent evaluators from Public/Private Ventures, Inc. (Philadelphia) privately advised Cleveland's philanthropic leaders in 1989 to shift their energies to reforming the system and schools. They learned that they had to deal with the causes of academic failure rooted in the schools and school system as well as the students' homes and communities. According to Helen Williams, a long time school reform leader in Cleveland, the philanthropic leaders also learned that they had to help create a critical mass for change, which was rooted in a clear agenda, widely supported by the community. Sparked by these lessons and a new mayor who had attended and taught in Cleveland's public schools, the city's philanthropic, nonprofit and elected officials subsequently pursued systemwide reform through an ongoing, citywide summit.

The first summit was convened in 1990 by Mayor Michael White and business, civic and school leaders, and attended by 700 Cleveland residents. Following the summit, task forces began work on a broad school reform agenda. Helping to guide the summit process was the new Cleveland Initiative for Education (CIE), which was formally established in 1989 by foundation and corporate leaders as a strategic planning entity for the civic and corporate sector's school reform efforts. In 1992 a new, reform-minded school board—backed by the mayor—and a new superintendent took leadership. A year later, at the spring 1993 summit, more than 2,000 Cleveland residents endorsed "Vision 21," a comprehensive education reform plan developed under the direction of Superintendent Sammie Campbell Parrish. Twenty-six task forces—widely representative of Cleveland educators, parents, community residents, and corporate and civic leaders—helped shape the new reform plan. Helping to set the stage for the district's current move toward decentralization, Vision 21 advocated a series of reforms to be designed and implemented by principals, teachers, parents, and community members in their schools.

This was a rare moment in a city that Helen Williams describes as having "disassociated from its public schools out of despair." Two years later, however, the reform process appeared dead. In March 1995 the federal courts, which had been overseeing the Cleveland public schools for nearly two decades due to battles over desegregation, ruled that the school district was financially and educationally bankrupt and turned control over to the state. The state superintendent of schools quickly named Richard Boyd, then executive director of the Martha Holden Jennings Foundation, as deputy state superintendent and Cleveland superintendent. From this crisis emerged the beginnings of the current reform efforts in Cleveland. Within one year of being named superintendent, Boyd and Mayor White signed a "Memorandum of Understanding" (March 1996) listing nine priorities for school reform. The first priority was to improve student learning and the effectiveness of the city's schools, but a corollary priority was to eventually return control of the school system to Cleveland. They established a broad-based

Strategy Council, which with funding from the foundations and staffing from the Cleveland Summit on Education became the community's forum and mechanism for school reform. Building on the core of "Vision 21," the Strategy Council released its first report in the fall of 1996 and has subsequently worked to monitor and help implement its recommendations. The report describes a comprehensive plan for systemwide school improvement that is based on four performance priorities: school effectiveness, sound administration and management, financial stability, and parent and community involvement.

Influenced by the work of the Strategy Council and by governance reforms recently implemented in Baltimore, Boston, and Chicago, a governance commission cochaired by the directors of the Cleveland and Gund foundations recommended in early 1997 that the mayor be given the authority to appoint the board and chief executive officer of the school system. These recommendations were made into law in early 1997 and, after several court challenges, were recently ruled "constitutional" with implementation to start by fall 1998. Underscoring the importance of the Strategy Council's ongoing efforts to transform the system, the mayor has stated several times in reference to his search for the school system's new "CEO" that "Cleveland is looking for a person to implement the Strategy Council's plan, not someone with a new plan."

Careful estimates available from several Cleveland foundations place the total grants for school improvement and reform efforts awarded over the years 1987–1995 at about $40 million.[10] At least $16 million of these funds went to Scholarship-in-Escrow. Of the remaining $24 million, about half went to the systemwide reform efforts undertaken by the Summit, the Cleveland Initiative for Education, and the Strategy Council. The other half has been split among the Cleveland Education Fund and other teacher development efforts, funding for school decentralization, reform projects in either individual or small groups of schools and communities (such as Dr. James Comer's School Development Program) principal development, curriculum development, parent involvement, dropout and absentee reduction, school safety, human service programs, after-school activities.[11]

Elements of Local Strategic Philanthropy

The behaviors of individual local foundations in Chicago and Cleveland are made unique by the manner in which they weave the threads of substance, process, and context together with their own internal characteristics.

To reach the goal of improved learning, foundations and other reformers must build the political will for reform, agree to compromise on specific reform actions, and sustain the will to reform over a long period of time. They must take risks by adopting far-reaching policies and practices. They must negotiate who will be accountable for the success or failure of reform and who will be forced to sacrifice. They must decide who will do the actual work required by reform. In perhaps their most difficult feat, they must overcome numerous conflicts among the disparate interests of judges, mayors, teachers' unions, school chief executives, school boards, state legislatures, special interest groups, other foundations, businesses, institutions of higher education, and community organizations. Sadly, these conflicts often undermine the interests of children and families. Even with minimal conflict, there is little likelihood that urban education bureaucracies would make much progress on their own. The sheer size and complexity of urban districts have distracted even the best leaders from focusing on student performance.

The local foundations we have been studying recognized that little or no progress is made without significant compromise by all involved. For these foundations, compromise meant balancing their own predilections with the interests and abilities of potential grantees. They defined themselves as active facilitators of reform rather than armchair critics. As a result, they used their resources to enable and help focus reform conversations, promote multi-sector collaboration, and foster local ownership of the process. They further understood that unless the key actors commit to seeing reform through to the final curtain—no matter how long that takes—the play is doomed before it opens.

Nonetheless, we have identified a number of distinct foundation behaviors that seem to transcend local contexts and differences in the nature of the reform processes. These behaviors were not coherently planned by any of the foundations we studied, but were arrived at independently over several years. Nonetheless, viewed together and in hindsight, they suggest a logical pattern of philanthropy. Viewed prescriptively, they define a strategic mode of local philanthropy for foundations seeking to effect public issues on an urban scale. These behaviors may be divided into two elemental types. First, there are broad characteristics of foundation behavior with regard to school reform: an evolving strategy, persistence, and institutional interdependence. Second are certain specific roles or tasks that foundations have performed in developing and sustaining education reform processes: personnel activism, gap-funding, staff outreach and research, parameter pushing, and evaluation.

Characteristics of Foundation Behavior

An Evolving Strategy

A foundation's approach to large public policy issues such as education reform evolves in response to the quickly changing context that surrounds its philanthropic goals and objectives. Complex, dynamic public issues typically force a foundation to begin with goals and objectives that are not always quantifiable or discretely measurable. Therefore, foundations cannot hope to develop and follow a clean and immutable script of action plans, budget allocations, and staff-time allotments to reach their strategic objectives. They need a considerable amount of flexibility to respond to emerging ideas, approaches, and events. Thus, for example, the Chicago Community Trust, after settling on a detailed strategy for a major elementary and secondary education initiative in 1988, tended not to make program-wide plans in subsequent years in order to ensure "maximum flexibility" for responding to unknown, future needs. Similarly, the Joyce Foundation understood that opportunities might outweigh a well-conceived strategy. "People in foundations can talk about having strategies and being more strategic," noted Craig Kennedy, president of the Joyce Foundation from 1986–1992. "What really drives you at the end, though, is opportunities as much as your own strategy" (Kennedy interview with McKersie, June 1995).

Likewise, Cleveland foundations have reassessed their reform strategies several times in response to new opportunities and events. After multimillion-dollar "incentive" programs failed to generate widespread improvement in learning, Cleveland foundations and corporations took aim at systemwide reform and school restructuring. The result has been an ongoing education Strategy Council, a Strategic Plan, the first successful levy campaign in many years, and a new state law giving control of the schools to the mayor.

Persistence

Foundations must be willing to commit resources to an issue or institution for a five- to ten-year period. Chicago and Cleveland show that change takes time, especially when the targets are schools and school districts built on complex patterns of organizational and individual behavior. The foundations in these two cities knew from experience that changing complex public policies and agencies requires long-haul grantmaking.

At the end of 1995, the three Chicago foundations were completing at least their ninth consecutive year of supporting the Chicago school reform. A core group of grantees, representing about 65 percent of the foundations' school reform funding, received at minimum five to seven years of continuous support. Considering the "three years and out" stereotype of foundation-grantee relations, seven-plus years of funding is remarkable (McKersie, 1996).

Cleveland foundations have pursued school improvement and reform for over 14 years. They have stayed the course even in the midst of major challenges to the system's basic operations and even when their earlier work proved to be unsuccessful. Now that there is a comprehensive, community-supported strategic plan in place, the foundations are committed to helping the plan succeed.

Institutional Interdependence

Foundations and the many other actors on the reform stage—including nonprofits, politicians, school administrators, teachers and their unions, parents, and the business community—are interdependent in their efforts to improve learning. Foundations depend primarily on nonprofit institutions. The interdependence of foundations and nonprofits requires both *collaboration*—across and within sectors—and *compromise* as foundations balance their own predilections with the interests and abilities of potential grantees. Through research, advocacy, publications, organizing, lobbying, training, and education, nonprofits bring diverse ideas, data, and people into the policymaking and political process. They help develop, implement, and evaluate school reform policies and practices.

The local institutional context is therefore an important determinant of what action foundations can and must take. While foundations have the power to cultivate institutions to undertake specific grantmaking priorities, they do not often do so. The creation of new institutions is inherently risky and is usually a multiyear endeavor, which is a time-frame that may not match the immediate needs of a fast-moving public policy issue. Thus, foundations most often focus their funds and resources on existing institutions, or at least individuals who are ready and able to start a program or project, if not a new organization. Chicago's funders hold to this pattern, while those in Cleveland actually engaged in institution-building.

Chicago foundations supported two citywide research and advocacy agencies, Designs for Change and the Chicago Panel on School Policy, as leaders in the development and implementation of the Reform Act. They were the top two recipients among the 176 different organizations funded for school reform through at least 1993. The foundations recognized that the school reform process depended on the two agencies' talent for developing and analyzing policies and on their ability to complement one another's distinct approaches to reform. Finding no other citywide agencies similarly oriented or skilled and unable to create new institutions, the foundations kept funding Designs and the Chicago Panel. As the reform process matured, several other organizations caught up with these two agencies, but they were never surpassed.

Unlike Chicago, Cleveland is not blessed with a Designs, Chicago Panel, or Consortium, which emerged solely from the creativity of a few educators and citywide activists. When school improvement, and subsequently system-wide reform, began to edge up Cleveland foundations' priority lists, they had to create the instruments and infrastructure for change. According to David Bergholz, "The foundations had to help create intermediaries—institutions between institutions—that served as brokers and links between the city's public and private sectors."

Foundation Roles and Tasks

Personnel Activism

To move the reform processes forward, the staff and board members of local foundations must directly contribute their leadership, expertise, and energies. Activism amplifies foundations' limited funds, helps foundations stay in touch with particular issue areas, allows foundations to learn first-hand what is or is not working and what needs to be done next, and enables them to clearly communicate grantmaking priorities. Activist roles for professional staff and board members include convening groups and individuals, strategizing, writing opinion pieces, participating on task forces, and providing hands-on assistance to the redesign of organizations. Foundation personnel who take on activist roles must recognize that their credibility—and the reason they have been invited "to the table"—often may lie more with their financial power than any special expertise or knowledge.

The focus and extent of a foundation's activism is tied to its grantmaking record and priorities. Personnel of the Woods Fund of Chicago led several collaborations among Chicago foundations to fund community and school-level reform activity and also convened several citywide meetings of school reform stakeholders. Education officers at the Joyce Foundation participated in Mayor Washington's Educational Summit at a subcommittee level, co-chaired a committee of 30 Chicago foundations concerned with education reform, staffed the first round of the school board nominating process under the Reform Act, and convened professional development meetings among school superintendents from Chicago, Cleveland, Detroit and Milwaukee (the foundation's four target cities). Heads of Cleveland foundations exerted great personal influence on the city's "reform stage" because of their positions, personalities, and professional backgrounds. Steven Minter, a Cleveland native and formerly Under-Secretary for Education in the Carter administration, became executive director of the Cleveland Foundation during the mid-1980s; David Bergholz, founder of the Public Education Fund Network, came over from Pittsburgh in the late 1980s to run the George Gund Foundation; and Richard Boyd, a former state superintendent from Mississippi and a prominent participant in national policy circles, became executive director of the Martha Holden Jennings Foundation in the late 1980s.

Gap-Funding

Foundations are increasingly finding that they have to devote funding and staff time to the implementation of whatever new policies and practices arise from their efforts. We call this strategy "gap-funding." The "gaps" to be filled are shortfalls and omissions in the public funds and other resources available to implement major new public policies, such as the Reform Act in Chicago or the impending mayoral control in Cleveland. For gap-funding to work, all involved—foundations, nonprofits, and public agencies—must understand that foundations can only play this role temporarily. Regarding such funding as permanent support would undermine (in theory) foundations' freedom to fund creative and diverse solutions to local problems.

In Chicago, the Reform Act mandated far-reaching changes in the governance and management of the Chicago public schools, but offered inadequate public funds for implementation (about $1,500 per school). As a result, about 35 percent of the Chicago foundations' funding for school reform from 1989–1993 went to help implement the law, often filling gaps in its design, content, or startup funding. One lesson from Chicago is that implementation support is a basic necessity and is too important to be left to foundations alone. Overreliance on private solutions ensures inequity.

There has thus far been a more definite need for gap-funding in Chicago than in Cleveland, where prior to the impending shift to mayoral control there has not been specific systemwide public policy to help implement. Nevertheless, most of the foundations' grants and leadership have gone to fill gaps in the public resources available to develop and implement the Strategic Plan and to make up for public sector deficits in funding, time, and professional capacity.

Parameter Pushing

At the same time that foundations are bolstering new policies and practices through gap-funding, they also need to expand the range and quality of ideas, approaches, institutions, and individuals working to solve public problems. This may mean critiquing the same policies or practices they are helping to implement. Some grants can accomplish both ends. For example, an ongoing evaluation of a new policy both prompts questions about alternative ways to address the problem and advances effective implementation.

The Chicago foundations pushed at the limits of the Reform Act. As the reform movement matured, the foundations' attention broadened from development and implementation of the Reform Act to more comprehensive school-based and multilevel reforms. The Chicago foundations focused on a narrow set of topics, specific recipients, and organization types in 1987 and 1988, but gradually widened their scope after the Reform Act's passage. The empowerment of parents and communities—the heart of the Reform Act— remained a priority, but was increasingly balanced by support for teacher development and collective restructuring efforts by principals, teachers, parents, and community members.

The task still facing Cleveland foundations may be more accurately described as parameter refining than parameter pushing. Whereas Chicago reform initially focused more narrowly on the governance ideas mandated by the Reform Act, Cleveland has been fighting on many fronts at once. The list of current major Cleveland reform strategies includes governance reform that involves the transfer of control of the system from an elected school board to a school board and CEO appointed by the mayor, gradual decentralization of the school system, the institution of achievement standards for students, statewide proficiency testing, which requires students in the 4th and 8th grades to achieve specific scores in order to be promoted, the "reconstitution" of schools that do not meet achievement standards, a new charter school law, which aims to have "community schools" opening across Ohio as of fall 1998, and a voucher program (established by the state in 1996) that allows students to attend private schools (including religious schools) with public funds.

According to Reinhard (1998, 26), Cleveland is the only place in the country where all of these measures are playing out at the same time. The Cleveland foundations have staked out roles as advocates for public education. As yet, none have offered support to the voucher effort. Given the instability at the top of the system and court and state control, Cleveland foundations tend to help determine what the substance of reform should be and then defend the chosen substantive road against excessive demands that might derail the whole reform process. Nonetheless, they will reconsider the substance of approaches that do not further the cause of systemwide reform. Witness, for instance, their 1989 shift to a systemic approach from a popular but flawed "incentives-based" school improvement strategy.[12]

Evaluation

Foundations in Cleveland and Chicago were committed to evaluating both their own activism, policies, and grants and the work of their grantees with respect to school reform. Evaluation has three basic purposes: to inform grantmaking, grantees, and the interested public. In order to improve current and future work, foundations need to publicize the lessons, both good and bad, that they take from their experiences. They must do so in a way that protects their grantees. Ideally, evaluation should be based on a series of principles. First, an institutional culture of constructive questioning and criticism is necessary. Institutional patience—recognizing that complex public problems take a long time to rectify—is second. Third, foundations must understand evaluation's value; they need to give significant time to tracking the impact of grants. Fourth, evaluation should not control grantmaking; it should not preclude risk-taking or the funding of efforts with outcomes that are hard to measure. Fifth, evaluation should be based on multiple measures or indicators; qualitative and quantitative measures of process and outcome must be used. Sixth, a mixture of information sources is required, including thoughtful grantees, visits to sites and communities, independent research, media analysis, and other foundation officers. Finally, the types of evaluators should be varied, ranging from the traditional (evaluation specialists and researchers or academics in the particular issue area) to the nontraditional (including practitioners with evaluation experience and freelance journalists).

The Chicago foundations provided $6.35 million from 1987–1993 for evaluation and dissemination of Chicago school reform. Cleveland foundations' record on evaluation and dissemination is weaker. The city has no independent agencies working full time to monitor and report on the progress of school reform. However, Cleveland's foundations took a key step in 1989 when they asked Public/Private Ventures, Inc., the highly regarded program evaluation group in Philadelphia, to assess Scholarship-in-Escrow and the city's school reform plans.

Fundamental Tensions of Local Philanthropy

As long as the public affairs climate is characterized by devolution and fiscal austerity, systemwide policy and social change will continue to require sustained effort by a mix of public and private actors. We think that the characteristics and tasks described above, drawn from the real-world experiences of Chicago and Cleveland grantmakers and tested under fire in those two cities, can serve as useful guideposts for foundations wishing to stake out a role in metropolitan-scale social change. They can help local foundations in other cities and under different circumstances to develop an initial strategy, assess their strengths and weaknesses, and gird themselves to enter the fray.

While we believe the generalizations to be useful, the fact remains that the experience of and choices available to each local foundation are distinct. In the end, a foundation's role in local change is the sum of the many individual choices it makes and the many elements of the process beyond its control. At their core, these individual choices revolve around the balancing by each foundation of four fundamental tensions of local strategic philanthropy.

Persistence vs. Innovation and Flexibility

Persistence needs to be an operating principle for foundations attempting to promote and sustain social change in an era of devolution and fiscal austerity. Foundations often find long-term commitment to an issue difficult to maintain because it conflicts with the belief that their most prized asset is the freedom to take risks and invest in innovation. Persistence creates tensions in particular with three ideal philanthropic operating principles:

Leverage. Provide temporary levers for organizations and individuals identifying and solving problems.

Maximum flexibility. Keep funds unencumbered because the power of foundation money lies in flexibility far more than size.

Pluralism. Funding a mix of ideas, individuals, and institutions is the best way to help a democratic society improve itself.

In Chicago, this tension was embodied in funders' dilemma over the need to provide gap-funding for implementation issues. Jean Rudd, executive director of the Woods Fund of Chicago since 1980, believes that managing this tension is the Fund's greatest challenge: "Our hardest work, our most serious assignment . . . is to make the hard judgement on when to start and stop funding" (Rudd 1989, 5). Woods staff feared that long-term implementation support could distract the Fund's limited dollars from helping "the nonprofit sector look ahead, stimulate studies, demonstrate and advocate new concerns and opportunities to bring about useful change" (ibid.). Chicago's foundations individually resolved this tension according to their priorities. In general, though, Chicago foundations managed this tension by viewing gap-funding as an obligation of around five years, no less; expecting the eventual reduction in funding to occur gradually; once the initial obligation has been met, shifting funds for another five years or so from implementation gaps to pushing the parameters of the same issues.

Strategy vs. Opportunity

Foundations like to think that their actions are grounded in a well thought out strategic plan, but in reality opportunities may be as influential as a well-designed strategy. Foundations often need to compromise in order to move school reform toward the larger goal of improved learning that should unite all actors. At the same time, they need to ensure that the content of reform advances foundation ideals and goals, and that the strategy being pursued is a feasible one.

The local foundations we studied were willing to sacrifice some of their ideals about the best way to reform schools in order to make reform happen at all. Lewis Butler, a long-time trustee of the Joyce Foundation, described his thinking about this tension:

> It's fine to have a general sense of where you want to be going, but when you get a big policy opportunity, when the train starts to come by, you better get on and that means you've got to move very fast because it's all happening in a hell of a hurry. So I felt very good in the case of Joyce and school reform. Even if you're making mistakes, you're in the ball game. (Butler interview with McKersie, July 1995)

Despite their agreement on the necessity of compromising strategy for the sake of progress, each foundation made very individual decisions about precisely where to draw the line between strategic rigor and opportunism. Most foundations hedged their bets through parameter pushing. The train Butler describes was the Chicago School Reform Act. Joyce took the opportunity that train presented, but also funded a series of more comprehensive school interventions and monitoring and reporting efforts in order to advance its reform strategy, which focused as much on principals and teachers as on parents and community.

The Woods Fund of Chicago drew the line differently, making its mark because of strategic focus. For seven years it did not waver from the belief that the first step to improved learning was fostering parent and community participation in school governance and citywide policy formation.

Foundation Activism vs. Community Ownership

When foundations take on an active role in the reform process, they risk suppressing voices that may be intimidated by the foundation's institutional and financial power or alienated by the top-down, funder-grantee character of foundations' relationships with others in the community. By taking on an activist role in social change, foundations can exaggerate their image as "powers that be." On the flip side, by entering the dialogue as a partner, they become more vulnerable in a public setting and can shed that "power" image. A foundation must carefully exercise its activism, so that it serves as an enabler, not the leader, of public efforts to solve citywide and community problems. Foundations must balance the benefits of activism—primarily its power to move the process forward—with the risk of taking over the process. For the Woods Fund of Chicago, proper balance was achieved by investing heavily and unwaveringly in parent and community participation in school governance and policy formation. Woods' conception of "balance" was rooted in its institutional faith in community organizing as a way to foster democratic participation in public policy processes.

Foundation Activism vs. Foundation Legitimacy

An activist foundation risks its institutional legitimacy and the credibility of its personnel. This is a serious risk for institutions that have been described as "legitimacy maximizers" (Hall, 1992). Unlike other nonprofits, foundations depend not on the generation of revenue but on the development and maintenance of credibility. Chicago provides at least one downside example: a Chicago Community Trust education officer who took an activist role, in part by publicly sharing his criticisms of the Reform Act's limits, was severely rebuked by several reform leaders (some of whom demanded that he be fired). This troubling episode dramatizes the high stakes game that foundations join when they take an active role in urban social change.

Foundation legitimacy is often tied to a perception of objectivity. An activist role puts this aspect of legitimacy at risk. Craig Kennedy of the Joyce Foundation was well aware of this possibility. He feared that Joyce might lose its capacity to listen to contrary opinion, perceive problems and weaknesses, or make independent judgments because it was deeply tied to the school reform movement. As a result, while funding implementation of the Reform Act, the Joyce Foundation invited voices critical of the reform to meet with the staff and board, brought outside experts to Chicago to observe and comment on school reform, and joined with other foundations to push early evaluation of the new law. A less extreme example in Cleveland was David Bergholz's decision to step down from the board of the Cleveland Initiative for Education, out of concern that he was becoming too deeply enmeshed in the reform process. Underscoring the fact that all is gray in this business, Steven Minter took a different tack: he stayed on the organization's board, reasoning that the chance to directly shape one of Cleveland's main school reform organizations outweighed the pose of philanthropic disinterest.

Foundations must somehow balance these tensions, since the lesson from Cleveland and Chicago is that they cannot be resolved. Balance, it seems, depends on core missions and goals, the personalities of boards and staff, and the demands and receptiveness of other local actors. If they can keep their balance, foundations can have an important effect on the complex problem of urban school reform. The foundations we studied in these two Midwest cities have made a difference: reform persists in each city; a mix of key nonprofit organizations have been supported for 10 years or more; a broad group of educators, parents, community members, and civic, business, and political leaders have been engaged and reengaged; and reform ideas and approaches have been adjusted, discarded, and replaced as necessary. Finally, some evidence of improvement in attendance and standardized testing has recently surfaced. Sisyphus' curse has been an apt metaphor for the struggle of improving student learning systemwide in Chicago and Cleveland, but there is now hope that futility will no longer be the watchword.

Notes

Charles Clotfelter and Thomas Ehrlich's comments on early drafts were valuable. We are appreciative of critical reviews from three Clevelanders: David Bergholz of the Gund Foundation, Helen Williams of the Cleveland Summit on Education, and Lynne Woodman of the Cleveland Foundation.

1. The lack of specific, nuanced data on grantmaking for particular metropolitan areas is an unfortunate handicap for researchers studying local philanthropy. McKersie spent nine months building the Chicago grants database using information from each of the Chicago foundations and Foundation Center documents. This intensive tabulation has yet to be done for other cities. Thus, it is difficult to provide comparative quantitative evidence of Chicago's grantmaking leadership for education reform.

2. Five urban areas were awarded Annenberg Challenge grants in 1994 and 1995: the Bay Area (California) School Reform Collaborative ($25 million); Chicago Annenberg Challenge ($49.2 million); Los Angeles Annenberg Metropolitan Project ($53 million); New York City Networks for School Renewal ($25

million); Philadelphia Children Achieving Challenge ($50 million). In 1996, a second round of urban grants went to Boston ($10 million), Detroit ($20 million), Houston ($20 million), and Miami-Dade-Broward Counties in Florida ($33.4 million) (Olson, 1997).

3. The School-wide Reform Programs they reviewed were: Success for All, the Edison Project, Core Knowledge, Accelerated Schools, School Development Program, Consistent Management and Cooperative Discipline. The New American Schools Designs were: ATLAS Communities, Audrey Cohen College, Co-NECT, Expeditionary Learning/Outward Bound, Modern Red Schoolhouse, National Alliance for Restructuring Education, and Roots and Wings (Fashola and Slavin, 1998, 376).

4. These data are drawn form McKersie's detailed data analysis of the grant-making of 11 Chicago foundations for elementary and secondary education from 1987–1993. The database represents about 90 percent of the giving by Chicago foundations for Chicago school reform. Unless otherwise noted, all figures for Chicago foundation giving in this paper refer to these 11 foundations.

5. Elmore 1991; Finn 1991; M. Katz, Fine and Simon 1991; Kirst 1991; and, M. Katz 1992.

6. The shift in state Chapter 1 funds gave typical elementary and high schools about $450,000 and $800,000, respectively, in annual discretionary resources (Lenz and Forte, 1995).

7. Nonprofit organizations—largely funded by Chicago foundations—have been vital throughout the Reform Act's development, passage and implementation (O'Connell, 1991). The corporate community was instrumental during the policy phases of final development, passage and initial implementation. The relationship between (and relative reform roles of) Chicago's foundation and business communities is complex. The two communities largely operated independently of each other through much of the reform movement. Thus, we did not deal with Chicago's corporations as part of our research, although their leadership was one of the primary forces behind the Reform Act. See Shipps (1995) for seminal work on the role of Chicago's business associations in school reform.

8. The 1995 Chicago School Reform Amendatory Act appeared at the tail end of the period this essay examines. A state law amending aspects of the 1988 Reform Act, it instituted major changes in the central governance of the school system. As summarized by Wong et al. (1996), it gave the mayor complete authority in appointing board members and top administrators; eliminated competing sources of top level authority, namely the school board nominating commission and school finance authority; increased central authority to make the local school councils accountable to systemwide standards; reduced the board size to five members and modeled it after corporate boards; created a top administrative team, which is headed by a "chief executive officer" and includes a "chief education officer;" gave the board and administration new powers to go outside collective bargaining agreements to privatize certain services; and gave the board and administration new flexibility in budgeting and accounting, including state block grants in several major areas. Notably, only a few members of the new administrative team have traditional educator resumes; most, including the chief executive officer, came from careers in public management or the private sector (Wong et al., 1996).

9. With recent funding from the Gund Foundation and Cleveland Foundation, the Cleveland Education Fund has begun to provide small grants and technical assistance to teams of educators in the Cleveland public schools working on school change, not just individualized professional development.

10. Grant data on the role of Cleveland foundations have not been systematically gathered and analyzed.

11. Although not tackling school improvement or reform, the Cleveland Scholarship Programs must be noted as one of the dominant grant recipients over this period. One of the oldest and largest scholarship programs in the nation, CSP provides students in the Cleveland public schools counseling and financial assistance for two and four-year higher education.

12. Incidentally, the foundations did not abandon scholarship assistance. Graduates of the Cleveland public schools through the year 2001 are guaranteed a $1,000 scholarship, mainly from funds provided by the Cleveland Foundation.

References

Bernholz, L. "Private Philanthropy and Public Schools: San Francisco in the 1960s and 1970s." Doctoral dissertation, School of Education, Stanford University, 1995.

Booz-Allen and Hamilton, Inc. *Hard Choices: The Financial Outlook for Chicago's Public Schools.* Chicago: The Civic Committee of the Commercial Club of Chicago, 1992.

Bryk, A. S., Hill, P. and Shipps, D. *Decentralization in Practice: Toward a System of School Reform.* Baltimore: Annie E. Casey Foundation, 1998.

Butler, L. Personal interview with William McKersie, July 1995.

Education Week "The Urban Challenge." *Education Week, Quality Counts '98: The Urban Challenge,* January 8, 1998, p. 6.

Elmore, R. "Foreword" in G. A. Hess, ed., *School Restructuring, Chicago Style.* Newbury Park, CA: Corwin, 1991.

Fashola, O. S. and Slavin, R. E. "School-wide Reform Models: What Works?" *Phi Delta Kappan,* 1998, 79 (5), 370–379.

Finn, C. E., Jr. "Chicago School Reform: Five Concerns." In S. K. Clements and A. Forsaith, eds., *Chicago School Reform: National Perspectives and Local Responses.* Washington, DC: Education Excellence Network, 1991.

Ford Foundation. *A Foundation Goes To School: The Ford Foundation Comprehensive School Improvement Program.* New York: The Ford Foundation, 1972.

Giving USA. New York: AAFRC Trust for Philanthropy, 1996.

Hall, P. D. *Inventing the Nonprofit Sector.* Baltimore: Johns Hopkins University Press, 1992.

Hess, G. A. "School Based Discretionary Fund Use in Chicago: Implications and Advocacy." Paper presented at the annual meeting of the American Educational Research Association, Chicago, March 28, 1997.

Katz, M. B. "Chicago School Reform as History." *Teachers College Record,* 1992, 94 (1), 56–72.

Katz, M. B., Fine, M., and Simon, E. "School Reform: A View from Outside Chicago." *Chicago Tribune,* March 7, 1991, Sect. 1, p. 27.

Kennedy, C. Personal interview with William McKersie, June 1995.

Kirst, M. W. "The Chicago School System's Central Office: Progress Toward a New Role." In S. K. Clements and A. Forsaith, eds., *Chicago School Reform: National Perspectives and Local Responses.* Washington, DC: Education Excellence Network, 1991.

Lenz, L. "Reform Sparks Solid Gains But It's Time to Turn Up the Heat." *Catalyst,* 1995, 6 (5), 4–11.

Lenz, L. and Forte, L. "Reform Data Book." *Catalyst,* 1995, 6 (5), 27–38.

Lobman, T. E. "Public Education Grant-Making Styles: More Money, More Vision, More Demands." *Teachers College Record,* 1992, 93 (3), 382–402.

McKersie, W. S. "Reforming Chicago's Public Schools: Philanthropic Persistence, 1987–1993." In K. Wong, ed., *Advances in Educational Policy, Volume II — Rethinking School Reform in Chicago.* Greenwich, CT: JAI Press, 1996.

McKersie, W. S. "Fostering Community Participation to Influence Educational Policy: Lessons from the Woods Fund of Chicago, 1987–1993." *Nonprofit and Voluntary Sector Quarterly,* 1997, 26 (1), 11–26.

McKersie, W. S. "Philanthropy's Paradox: Chicago School Reform." *Educational Evaluation and Policy Analysis,* 1993, 15 (2), 109–128.

McKersie, W. S. and Palaich, R. "Philanthropy & Systemic Reform: Finding a Cross-Sector Blend of Risk-Taking and Political Will." *Education Week,* May, 4, 1994, p. 48.

Meade, E. J., Jr. "Foundations and the Public Schools: An Impressionistic Retrospective, 1960–1990." *Phi Delta Kappan,* 1991, 73 (2), K1–K12.

National Commission on Excellence in Education. *A Nation at Risk: The Imperative for Educational Reform.* Washington, DC: U.S. Government Printing Office, 1983.

O'Connell, M. *School Reform Chicago Style: How Citizens Organized to Change Public Policy.* Chicago: The Center for Neighborhood Technology, 1991.

Olson, L. "Annenberg Challenge Proves to Be Just That." *Education Week,* June 25, 1997, pp. 1 and 30–31.

Olson, L. and Hendrie, C. "Pathways to Progress." *Education Week, Quality Counts '98: The Urban Challenge,* January 8, 1998, pp. 32–45.

Reinhard, B. "Cleveland: A Study in Crisis." *Education Week, Quality Counts '98: The Urban Challenge,* January 8, 1998, pp. 32- 45.

Renz, L. *Foundation Giving, 1991.* New York: Foundation Center, 1991.

Renz, L. *Foundation Giving, 1996.* New York: Foundation Center, 1996.

Renz, L. *Foundation Giving, 1997.* New York: Foundation Center, 1997.

Rudd, J. "Executive Director's Letter." In *Woods Charitable Fund 1989 Annual Report.* Chicago: Woods Fund of Chicago, 1989.

Ryan, S., Bryk, A. S., Lopez, G., Williams, K. P., Hall, K., and Luppescu, S. *Charting Reform: LSCs — Local Leadership at Work.* Chicago: Consortium on Chicago School Research, 1997.

Shipps, D. "Big Business and School Reform: The Case of Chicago, 1988 Illinois." Unpublished doctoral dissertation, School of Education, Stanford University, 1995.

Sommerfeld, M. "Foundations Seek More Active Role in Replicating Successful Models." *Education Week,* December 14, 1994, p. 6.

Wehlage, G., Smith, G. and Lipman, P. "Restructuring Urban Schools: The New

Futures Experience." *American Educational Research Journal,* 1991, 29 (1), 51–93.

Wong, K. K., Dreeben, R., Lynn, L. E., Jr., and Sunderman, G. L. *Integrated Governance as a Reform Strategy in the Chicago Public Schools.* Department of Education and Irving B. Harris Graduate School of Public Policy Studies, The University of Chicago, 1996.

CHAPTER NINETEEN

Philanthropy and American Higher Education

Michael Rothschild

This essay discusses the role of philanthropy in American higher education. The first section presents largely numerical data about the nature of past and present contributions from private sources to higher education in this country. The second section analyzes the effects of charitable contribution to higher education on enrollment patterns. The concluding section is a less systematic discussion of some other effects of charitable contributions on higher education based on my experience as a faculty member and administrator in both public (Wisconsin and University of California at San Diego) and private (Harvard and Princeton) universities.[1]

The most important facts about philanthropic contributions to higher education are these: Higher education is a significant recipient of charity, getting almost 10 percent of total philanthropic gifts. Gifts and grants themselves pay for slightly over 6 percent of the educational expenses of higher education; endowment earnings, the residue of past gifts, provide another 2.3 percent.[2] Gifts and grants to higher education are distributed quite unequally among colleges and universities. Private institutions enroll less than a quarter of the students but get more than half the gifts. Gifts are concentrated among research universities and private liberal arts colleges. Elite schools like Harvard, Princeton, Stanford, and Berkeley receive a disproportionate share of gifts and grants. Endowments are even more unequally distributed. In 1995, five institutions held 20 percent of the higher education endowment. They enrolled less than 1 percent of the students.

The second section analyzes the effects of philanthropy on enrollment patterns—who goes to college and where they go. Charitable contributions make it possible for relatively expensive colleges to reduce their prices significantly (through scholarships and other financial aid) to some students. Because applicants do take cost into account when considering what college to attend, charity has a significant effect on where students go to college. Two significant consequences of the availability of financial aid are increasing the diversity in background and decreasing the diversity of ability among those who attend America's elite private colleges. On the other hand, I argue that charitable contributions have little effect on overall college attendance. This is because the marginal student, the student deciding whether to attend college or enter the work force, is most likely to consider going to a public college (probably a two-year college) that gets very few charitable contributions. I present arguments and evidence, due largely to the economist David Card (1995), that suggests that those who now do not attend college because it is too expensive have the ability to benefit greatly from attending college. The failure of private contributions to education to increase access to college is significant.

The third section discusses in an informal way some other effects of private philanthropy on higher education. I praise private philanthropy for supporting and making possible what is best in American education and even more for supporting the competition among schools which I believe is essential to the success of the great American research university. Private philanthropy provides essential support for much social science research done in colleges and universities. However, the nature of this support leaves much to be desired. Peer-reviewed government support of research in the natural sciences allows excellent researchers to follow their own research agendas as long as they continue to be productive and innovative. In contrast, foundations and other private funders largely support only research that is new and innovative (at least to the funder). They generally refuse to continue to support projects that are merely successful. As a consequence, researchers in the social sciences and the humanities are virtually forced to change their research agendas if they are to continue to be supported. This may be responsible, in part, for the relative faddishness of some research in the humanities and social sciences.

Voluntary Support of Higher Education

Gifts to higher education in the United States in 1996 totaled $14.25 billion. Total philanthropy was almost $151 billion. Thus, gifts to higher education were a little less than 10 percent of total gifts. This relationship has been stable for at least two decades.[3]

Philanthropy provides a significant share of the revenues and expenditures of American higher education. Almost 14.3 million students were enrolled in American institutions of higher education in academic year 1995–1996, so

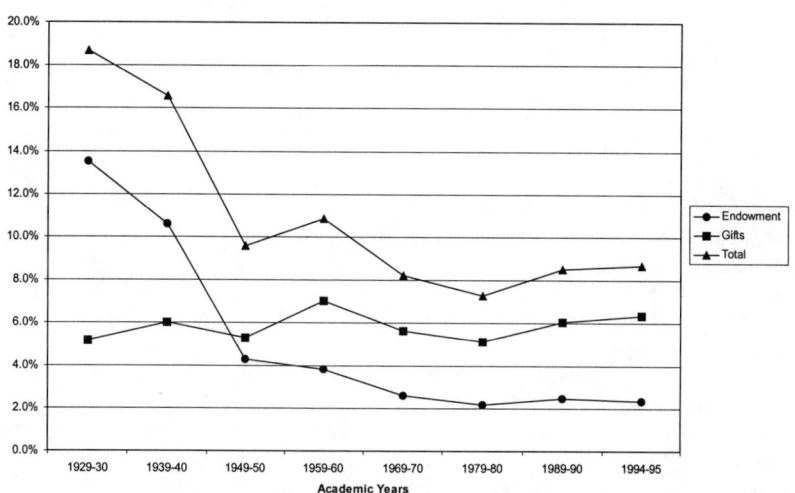

Figure 1. Voluntary Support as a Percent of Net Education and General Expenses

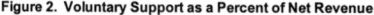

Figure 2. Voluntary Support as a Percent of Net Revenue

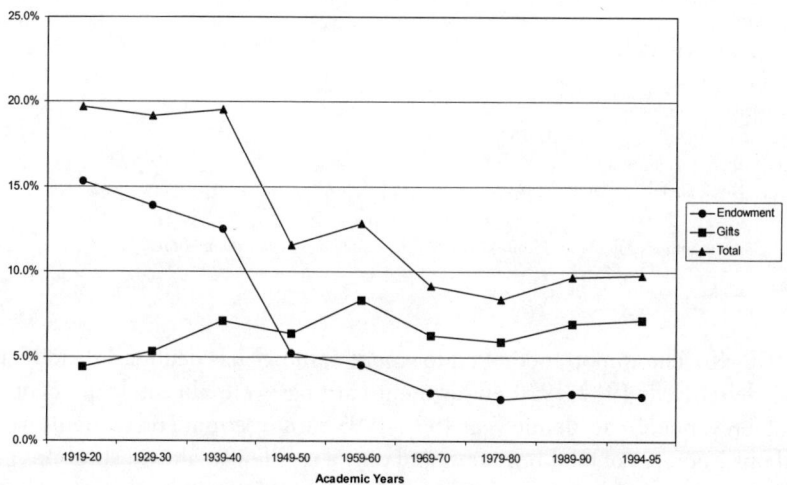

gifts amounted to almost $1,000 per student. Full time equivalent (FTE) enrollments were 10.3 million students, so support was a little over $1,350 per FTE student. In academic year 1994–1995 private gifts and grants accounted for about 6 percent of the revenues of institutions of higher education.

Figures 1 and 2 present historical data on gifts and grants and endowment earnings.[4] The importance (measured as a share of revenues or of expenditures) of gifts and grants has grown slightly since academic year 1919–1920, when it was less than 4 percent, but has remained roughly constant since

Table 1

Distribution of Enrollments, Gifts and Endowments to Private and Public Colleges and Universities

	Research/ Doctoral	Masters	Liberal Arts	Specialized	Two-Year	Total
Private						
Enrollment (thousands)	1,182	903	728	140	215	3,169
Enrollment as a percent of total enrollment	8%	6%	5%	1%	2%	22%
Total Gifts and Grants in $ Millions	$4,362	$862	$1,880	$627	$80	$7,811
Gifts as a Percent of Total	31%	6%	13%	4%	1%	55%
Estimated Endowment Income (4%)	$2,449	$249	$893	$177	$3	$3,772
Endowment Income as a percent of total	48%	5%	17%	3%	0%	73%
Public						
Enrollment (thousands)	3,972	1,690	95	60	5,283	11,100
Enrollment as a percent of total enrollment	28%	12%	1%	0%	37%	78%
Total Gifts and Grants in $ Millions	$5,098	$501	$23	$301	$350	$6,273
Gifts and Grants as a Percent of Total giving	36%	4%	0%	2%	2%	45%
Estimated Endowment Income (4%)	$1,276	$53	$3	$35	$12	$1,379
Endowment Income as a percent of total	25%	1%	0%	1%	0%	27%

Source: Author's calculations from VSE 1995-96 and *Digest of Educational Statistics,* 1997

1930–40. The importance of endowment earnings has declined steadily. In academic year 1919–1920 endowment earnings were almost 15 percent of total revenue. In academic year 1994–1995 earnings from endowments were about 2 percent of total revenues[5] and only a very few wealthy institutions get 15 percent of their revenues from endowment earnings. The record for expenditures is very similar.

Philanthropic support is distributed very unevenly across the nation's institutions of higher education. Tables 1 and 2 show how different kinds of schools benefited from philanthropy in the academic year 1995–96. The tables differentiate between public and private institutions and between the different kinds of schools. The classifications of institutions are a compression of the Carnegie classification which the Council for Aid to Education uses in its annual report, *Voluntary Support of Education*—the basic source of data about philanthropic gifts to higher education. The categorization is largely self-explanatory except possibly for "specialized" institutions, which are defined as institutions that "offer degrees ranging from the bachelor's to the doctorate. At least 50 percent of the degrees awarded by these institutions are in a single discipline" (VSE 96, p. 49). Examples are the Princeton Theological Seminary and the Mayo Institution.

The first two lines of Table 1 give the enrollments of the different kinds of schools. Almost four-fifths of the roughly 14.4 million students enrolled went to public institutions. Of these about half enrolled in institutions which awarded graduate degrees and the other half enrolled in two-year institutions that do not award bachelor's degrees. In private schools more than 65 percent of the students are enrolled in institutions that award graduate degrees. Almost a quarter of the students go to liberal arts colleges and less than 10 percent go to two-year schools. The next two lines report private gifts and grants to these institutions in both absolute amounts and as a percentage of all gifts. Charitable contributions are distributed very differently from enrollments. While only 8 percent of the nation's students attend private research universities, 31 percent of charitable contributions went to these schools. In contrast, 37 percent of college students attend public two-year colleges while these schools get only 2 percent of philanthropic contributions to higher education. The next two lines give the same data for endowment earnings. I estimate the contribution of endowment earnings to institutions of higher education by assuming that endowments earn 4 percent. This is a reasonable long-term real return, slightly higher than what institutions of higher education report as earnings.[6] The pattern of concentration of endowments in private universities and liberal arts colleges is even more pronounced. Private colleges collect almost three-quarters of all endowment earnings, while they enroll less than a quarter of all students.

Table 2 reports the same information on a per-student basis and compares these numbers to information about expenditures by and tuitions paid to colleges and universities. The first line of Table 2 estimates what the Department of Education calls "Education and General Expenses" per student. This is the most general measure of what schools spend to educate students. Expenditures for running dormitories, hospitals, and enterprises such as university presses and bookstores are excluded. Not surprisingly, these expenses differ considerably by type of school. While private research universities spend almost $22,000 per student, public two-year colleges spend barely a sixth of that.

The next three lines report on tuition and fees. Gross tuition and fees reflect what colleges state their tuitions are, the sticker price. Net tuition and fees are calculated by subtracting from this figure scholarships supplied by the college; net tuition is what students actually pay the college they attend. Tuition both net and gross is much higher at private institutions than at public institutions. The difference between net and gross tuition is about six times bigger at private colleges than at public ones. While net tuition covers about

Table 2

Educational Expenditures, Gifts, Endowment Earnings and Tuition on a Per-Student Basis

	Research/ Doctoral	Masters	Liberal Arts	Specialized	Two-Year	Total
Private						
E&G Expenditures per						
Student	$21,722	$9,462	$14,501	$41,692	$6,313	$16,406
Gross Tuition and Fees						
per student	$9,571	$7,411	$10,318	$21,102	$5,212	$9,342
Net Tuition and Fees						
per student	$7,064	$5,632	$7,031	$17,665	$4,387	$6,936
Net Tuition and Fees						
as percent of E&G	33%	60%	48%	42%	69%	42%
Private Gifts and Grants						
per Student	$3,690	$954	$2,583	$4,474	$373	$2,465
As a percent of E&G						
Expenditures	17%	10%	18%	11%	6%	15%
Estimated Endowment Income						
(4%) per Student	$2,071	$276	$1,228	$1,262	$15	$1,190
As a percent of E&G	10%	3%	8%	3%	0%	7%
Public						
E&G Expenditures per						
Student	$12,104	$9,478	$22,292	$112,603	$3,645	$8,304
Gross Tuition and Fees						
per student	$2,810	$2,988	$7,977	$7,023	$856	$1,974
Net Tuition and Fees	$2,137	$2,407	$6,319	$4,820	$720	$1,554
Net Tuition and Fees as						
percent of E&G	18%	25%	28%	4%	20%	19%
Private Gifts and Grants						
per Student	$1,284	$296	$240	$5,052	$66	$565
As a percent of E&G	11%	3%	1%	4%	2%	7%
Estimated Endowment Income						
(4%) per Student	$321	$31	$28	$591	$2	$124
As a percent of E&G	3%	0%	0%	1%	0%	1%

Source: Author's calculations from VSE 1995-96 and *Digest of Educational Statistics*, 1997.

one fifth of education and general expenses at public institutions, at private schools net tuition covers only slightly more than 40 percent of such expenditures.

The next two lines report private gifts and grants on both a per-student basis and as a percentage of education and general expenses. These vary considerably by type of institution. At private doctoral and liberal arts colleges philanthropy accounts for almost a sixth of education and general expenses. At public research universities it is a little over a tenth. At public two-year colleges gifts and grants cover barely 2 percent of education and general expenses. The final two lines of Table 2 reports the same information for endowment earnings. Endowment earnings are a significant (at least as a percentage of expenditures) factor only at private institutions.

Philanthropy is concentrated at particular institutions as well as among kinds of institutions. While giving averaged about $1,000 per student in academic year 1995–1996, it averaged more than $20,000 at Stanford University. The ten institutions that collected the most money raised a little over $2 billion that year, almost 15 percent of the total money raised, while they enrolled less than 1.5 percent of the students.

Endowments are highly concentrated, considerably more so than current giving. In 1995, the endowments of five institutions (Harvard, Texas (Austin), Yale, Stanford, and Princeton) comprised 20 percent of the endowment of all institutions of higher education. These institutions enrolled less than 1 percent of the students attending institutions of higher education in fall 1995.[7] In the private sector, four-year institutions (which include the liberal arts colleges) get almost 6.5 percent of their revenues from endowments. Endowment earnings (estimated at 4%) are about 53 percent of educational and general expenses at Princeton and about 16 percent of such expenses at Yale and Dartmouth (VSE 96).

Philanthropy is restricted in various ways. The most important distinction is between money that is available for current purposes and money that is added to endowments or used for capital projects. In 1995 about 50 percent of philanthropy was restricted to capital purposes, for public institutions the comparable figure was about 40 percent. VSE 96 reports other categories of restrictions but it is difficult to know how binding these restrictions are. Roughly one-third of the money given for current operations is unrestricted and about the same amount supports research. The remainder of current fund gifts is subject to various restrictions. It is of course almost impossible to tell how serious the restrictions are. If a donor gives a school money to, for example, enrich its language programs and the school was planning to do this anyway, then the restriction is not binding.[8]

Like current giving, endowments are restricted; about 90 percent of endowment giving in 1996 was restricted. How binding these restrictions are is difficult to tell; endowment restrictions are probably less binding than restrictions on current giving. Many endowed chairs simply add to an institution's general funds since the chair funds are used neither to pay the occupant's salary nor support his or her research. In other cases the gift of an endowed chair may cause an institution to hire someone in an area or field that it had not intended to. In such cases gifts may actually detract from a school's ability to achieve its highest goals. In some cases restricted capital gifts can actually relieve general funds for current expenditure. Suppose that a college decides that it must build an athletic facility. It begins construction before funds are raised and finances construction by taking out a loan—which it pays for out of current general funds. When construction funds are raised, the college pays off the loan and uses the freed general funds for other purposes. All of this is merely to say that it is difficult to estimate to what extent gifts add to the general capacity of an institution to accomplish its goals and to what extent funds are available only for restricted purposes.

In summary, gifts are concentrated among institutions. They are a significant part of revenues in private research universities, private liberal arts colleges, and public research universities. Philanthropy plays no significant role in the funding of the public two-year colleges that enroll more than one-third of the students attending college in the United States. Within these broad groups gifts are concentrated, largely in elite and well-known institutions. The legacy of past philanthropy and endowments is more highly concentrated than current gifts. For most of the more than 3,600 institutions of higher education in the U.S., endowment earnings cover a very small part of the current expenditures. Endowments and gifts are subject to various restrictions although it is quite hard to estimate the effect of these restrictions.

Effect of Philanthropy on Student Enrollment

What do gifts and endowments to higher education accomplish? I begin with a discussion of the effects of philanthropy and whether and where students go to college. Gifts, grants, and endowment earnings have a significant effect on which students go to which colleges. Philanthropy probably has a negligible effect on the total number of students who attend college. Students on the margin between going to or continuing college go mostly to public institutions, largely but not exclusively to two-year colleges that receive little philanthropic aid.[9] Since these institutions receive relatively few private gifts, philanthropy does little to lower the cost of going to college for those who are really deciding whether or not to go to college or enter the labor force. The recent past has seen disturbing trends in American higher education; costs have risen while government support for higher education (at least on a constant dollar per student basis) has been declining. As a consequence education has become, and is expected to continue to become, more expensive to prospective students. Private philanthropy has relatively little to contribute directly to the access problem, which some have identified as the major problem facing American higher education.[10]

Philanthropy probably does have a significant effect on allocating students to schools. Need and merit based scholarships (which gifts and endowments support) significantly affect the net price that students pay to attend different kinds of schools. Brewer and Ehrenberg (1996) have completed the most sophisticated study. They estimated the cost to students of different income, racial group, and ability of going to six different kinds of colleges—top, middle, and bottom (in terms of quality or selectivity) public and private schools.

They found, for example, that the net cost (in 1981–1982 dollars[11]) for the average high income, low ability student to attend a top private college was $5,395. The same kind of college would cost the average low income, high ability student $2,500 less. Brewer and Ehrenberg also estimated the marginal value of characteristics such as sex, race, and ability on financial aid at each type of school. They found aid packages were responsive to these characteristics. One of their interesting findings is that, other things equal, the higher the quality of the school, the more aid it offers black students.[12]

Brewer and Ehrenberg (and others) have found that students responded to net price in choosing among colleges. Financial aid that schools dispense (which must be differentiated from financial aid that students may use at many schools) affects the distribution of students among colleges. Financial aid makes possible the increased stratification of students by ability that, among others, Cook and Frank (1993) have documented. Before the Second World War the colleges that we know now to be very selective accepted most applicants. They became selective in the fifties and the sixties and have become increasingly so over time. As these schools have become more selective they have attracted a greater percentage of the most talented of America's youth. Financial aid, supported by large endowments and generous private support, has made it possible for schools like Princeton and Yale to compete with public universities on price for many students even though most of the very elite private schools do not offer merit scholarships.

Since philanthropy affects where students go to college it is worth asking what is known about the effect of different kinds and qualities of colleges on their students' lives. The studies that I know are by economists and they ask, naturally, whether or not school quality (and specific attributes of schools) affect their students' future income. Before we discuss this issue we should recall that the same issue has been hotly debated for almost three decades for elementary and secondary education. Ever since the Coleman Report found that more money spent by public schools had little effect on student achievement, scholars have debated this issue. A neutral observer would be compelled to say that no consensus has emerged. I believe that more scholars than not hold to the view that giving public schools the resources to reduce class size, improve the credentials of teachers, and improve physical facilities, has little demonstrated effect on student performance either in school or out. However, it is easy to find extremely distinguished and competent scholars on either side of the issue. Extensive reviews of the literature, each of which cites hundreds of studies, come to opposite conclusions. Compare, for example, Hanushek (1986) with Hedges, Laine, and Greenwald (1994). My colleague Alan Krueger (1998) has recently made a case that resources do increase student performances.

Given the lack of certain knowledge of the effect of quality or resources on high school and elementary education, it should come as no surprise that our understanding of this issue for colleges is also weak. Brewer and Ehrenberg review the dozen or so previous studies and conclude, "In general this research finds that attending a higher quality college raises earnings, *ceteris paribus*, although the magnitude of the estimated effect varies from negligible to large" (1996, p. 242). They note a number of serious statistical and conceptual problems with previous studies and then present their own work. Their study is a clear conceptual and statistical improvement on those that have gone before but their results are (largely due to the limitations of their sample to 1980 high school graduates) very imprecise. Their findings are roughly consistent with the literature they cite. The effects of quality are positive but their magnitude is hard to pin down. Probably their most interesting finding is that those who attended private schools of middle or low quality would have done better (at least economically) had they gone to an elite public school.

While estimates of the effect of college quality are weak, we do know a great deal about the effect of going to college. Recent studies of what economists call the return to education suggest that the value of going to college has been increasing. We can see this most easily by simply looking at the trends in education by income. Since 1980 the earnings of college graduates relative to high school graduates have increased dramatically while the relative wages of those who have failed to complete high school have generally fallen.[13]

It is tempting to argue that the higher wages earned by the average college graduate overestimates the value of education to those who don't now go to college. The argument is simple. Earnings are a product of, at least, education and ability. Those who go to college are on average more able than those who do not. It follows that increasing the numbers of those who go to college will necessarily bring to colleges those less able to benefit from higher education. Diminishing returns to education are inevitable. Were this true, the access problem might be less severe than it seems. Furthermore, while college graduates may earn more than high school graduates, it does not follow that attending some college and not graduating will have a strong effect on wages. Those who attend two-year colleges are less likely to complete four years of college than those who start at four-year schools.

Both these plausible arguments are likely to be incorrect. Thomas Kane and Cecilia Rouse (1993) have shown that the average economic value of getting a college credit is the same regardless of the kind of credit earned. Credits earned at two-year colleges have the same economic value as those earned at four-year colleges. The credits earned by someone who eventually gets a bachelor's degree does no more to increase his income than the credits earned by someone who leaves college before graduating.

David Card (1995) recently reviewed a number of surprising studies of the economic returns to education. These studies took statistical precautions to disentangle the separate effects of ability and education on income. They found that these precautions tended to increase the estimated effect of education on earnings, contradicting the intuitive argument presented above. Card gave a simple, and appealing, explanation. Whether or not someone attends college depends both on the benefit she will derive from attending college (which is related to ability) and on the cost to her of going to college. This cost depends on more than tuition and varies greatly from person to person. The basic reasons are what economists call imperfect capital markets and differential access to transportation. Poor people who cannot borrow (or who are unwilling to borrow because they do not understand how credit markets work) will find it much more costly (in terms of the sacrifices they must make in current consumption) to attend college than those who are richer. Those who live near a college will find it easier to attend school while they live at home than those who must leave home to go to school. In Card's model the people who do not go to college are either poor or rich and unlikely to benefit from more education. The poor who do not go to college includes a disproportionate share (relative to the rich who do not go to college) of those who would benefit from college. Suppose the price of going to college decreases—because of federal scholarship programs or because improvements in transportation make it easier to attend college while living at home and working part time. Who is most likely to respond? It may well be a bright poor person rather than a dumb rich person. If so the value of her going to college may well be above average. Card finds this model explains recent studies. If it is accurate, and I find it convincing, then its policy relevance is clear. The access problem is even more important than studies of the average economic return to education suggest.

Other Effects of Philanthropy on Higher Education

This section is necessarily less systematic than what has gone before. It reflects, rather than a summary of research, my experience as an administrator at a very wealthy private research university (Princeton) and at a much less wealthy public research university (UCSD).

Private philanthropy is an important, probably essential, ingredient in making the American research university the extraordinarily successful institution it is. The best American research universities are much better at producing research and researchers than their foreign counterparts.[14] The wealth of American universities—which is significantly due to private philanthropy—helps to support this success. While governments have, since the Second World War, provided most of the support for scientific research, the independent resources of universities are essential for the scientific enterprise in many ways. Private funds provide seed money for new investigators and allow researchers to keep research groups and facilities together through gaps in research funding. Private funds build laboratories and other facilities that are essential to the scientific enterprise.

One should not overestimate the direct importance of private funding. The University of California at San Diego was founded in 1963 and has emerged as one of the country's great research universities, second only to Berkeley among public universities in the National Research Council's most recent ranking of graduate programs. UCSD is not wealthy.[15] However, without some private resources it simply could not play in the big leagues.

Probably more important than the actual resources for support of research is the vigorous competition among America's universities that private resources (and control) support and encourage. American universities compete for students, for faculty, for public and private research grants and, of course, in athletics. Competition between institutions of higher education is rare outside America. As a consequence salary differentials are compressed. The perks that accrue to the best faculty in the U.S. go to those who merely survive. The incentives to continue doing excellent work are blunted. In most countries governments support and control universities; governments tend to regard competition among different units as wasteful.[16] Private resources help to make competition possible. Endowed chairs, supported by private gifts, are only the most obvious examples. Schools that compete for students, or compete for the best students, care more about how they teach them than those that simply get more resources than they want. Of course, schools compete for students with more than small classes. Quality of dormitories, food, and other aspects of student life are important parts of the competition for students. This competition is expensive and does not clearly aid the educational enterprise.

Private resources allow the very rich private liberal arts colleges and research universities to teach undergraduates in intense and pleasant ways. Small classes, well supplied and supervised laboratories, frequent and carefully graded writing assignments, and the opportunity to do independent research are among the distinguishing characteristics of an excellent private education. Educators believe that these expensive modes of education are beneficial. There is some, relatively new, evidence that this is so; probably the best evidence of the overall effect of the special benefits of private education is that reported in Brewer and Ehrenberg (1996).[17] Most students and faculty will attest that teaching undergraduates and being an undergraduate is pleasanter at a rich institution than at a poor one.

Another important benefit of philanthropy is the support of research that the government does not support. Private philanthropy is the primary source of support for research in the humanities and most social sciences. As a social scientist, and as the former dean of the Division of Social Science, I am very grateful for such support. Without private support much of the most important and innovative work in the social sciences and the humanities would not have been done.

I must, however, note one important flaw of such support. Most foundation and other private support for research is, in the explicit view of the donor, "seed money." The assumption is that if the venture proves successful the institution will find funds to continue it. This is often patently false. Institutions can no more afford to use their own funds to continue to support expensive research projects in the social sciences and the humanities than they can in the natural sciences.[18] In the natural sciences, when scientists lose funding it is generally because the quality of their research has decreased, or because they did not deliver what they had promised. If scientists continue to do excellent work, they will continue to be supported. This is not so in the humanities and social sciences. Those who do what they propose, and more, must look for new sources of funding. Often this proves impossible. The original funder is unwilling to renew. Other funders are not interested in this kind of work, often because they want to provide seed money for new ideas.

To keep a research program together in the humanities or social sciences requires more effort and more ingenuity than in the natural sciences. It also requires that one be willing to shift focus and change directions as funding opportunities change rather than as one's own research interests dictate. Many decry and mock the endless fads and changes of direction and point of view that mark the softer disciplines. I sometime wonder how much of the relative constancy of the natural sciences is due to the fact that peer review determines funding opportunities in biology and physics while ambitious scholars in literature, history, and anthropology are hostages to the ever-changing agendas of foundations and other sources of private support.

Notes

1. I am grateful to Charles Clotfelter, Tom Ehrlich, and Alan Krueger for helpful conversations and to Michele McLaughlin for research assistance.

2. Many buildings are also the result of past gifts, and the services of these buildings are essential to colleges. Lack of consistent capital accounting makes it difficult to asses the importance of the capital stock of higher education let alone that part of it that is the result of past philanthropy.

3. The basic sources of data are the American Association of Fund-Raising Council Trust for Philanthropy, *Giving USA 1997*, and Council for Aid to Education, *Voluntary Support for Education, 1996*. I will cite this source in the text that follows as *VSE 96*.

4. A note about the construction of the data used in the charts and tables in this essay. I have tried to make data from two sources consistent. *VSE 96*, and previous years, is the basic source for data on contributions and endowments. It issues a survey to many institutions in higher and secondary education and reports, by school, the responses to that survey. Coverage is not complete but it is likely that most significant gifts to higher education are reported. In 1995–1996 respondents to *VSE 96* reported gifts and grants worth $12.3 billion while the CAE estimated that a total of $14.2 billion was given. Coverage of institutions is much less complete. For example, *VSE* includes reports from less than 1,100 colleges and universities enrolling 7.5 million students. *The Digest of Educational Statistics*, published by the Department of Education, is based on reports that all institu-

tions of higher education are required to complete. I have used information in the *Digest* to adjust the data in *VSE* so that it covers all of higher education. The greatest difficulty (and thus source of uncertainty) is that the *Digest* and the *VSE* use slightly different categories of institutions in their reports. I have kept the categories that the *VSE* uses. I have had to estimate total enrollment for these categories.

I have occasionally reported revenues and expenditures in net terms this means that I have removed scholarships and fellowships that schools award as these can be considered price discounts rather than real expenditures.

5. *The Digest of Educational Statistics 1997*, Table 327.

6. *The Digest of Educational Statistics* reports total 1994–1995 endowment earnings of about $3.9 billion on a total endowment value of $109 billion; this is 3.6%.

7. This comparison would be much more dramatic were the University of Texas system not included. In fall 1995, total enrollment, full and part time, was about 14.2 million students. The University of Texas system enrolled almost 1% of these students.

8. This assumes that colleges and universities have well defined goals and plans, which is clearly an oversimplification.

9. *College Choice in America* (Manski and Wise, 1983) is the classic study of college choice. They found that college attendance, particularly at two-year and other inexpensive schools, was responsive to the net cost of tuition. For amplification and replication of their results see McPherson and Schapiro (1991) and Brewer and Ehrenberg (1996).

10. See for example *Breaking the Social Contract: The Fiscal Crisis in Higher Education*, Council for Aid to Education, 1997, and *The Cost of Higher Education*, National Center for Education Statistics, 1996.

11. 1981–1982 dollars were worth about 70% more than 1997–1998 dollars.

12. (Brewer and Ehrenberg 1996, Tables 3 and 4). The same pattern largely holds for Hispanics. These estimates are, as the authors note, imprecise (they have high standard errors) and should not be overinterpreted.

13. See, e.g., *The Cost of Higher Education*, p. 16, and Levy and Murnane (1992).

14. Rosovsky (1990) is a recent insightful discussion of the unique qualities of the great American research university.

15. *VSE 96* does not report complete data for the separate branches of the University of California. I know from personal experience that UCSD is significantly less rich than Berkeley or UCLA; the total UC System covers about the same fraction of education and general expenses from gifts and endowment earnings as the average public university. UCSD probably covers significantly less than this.

16. This is true even in the U.S. The University of California system discourages competition for faculty among its branch campuses by restricting the start-up packages and salary increases that one branch can offer to a professor at another branch. These restrictions occasionally have the unintended effect of causing faculty to leave the UC system when they would prefer to stay at UC but want to change colleges.

17. A soon to appear longitudinal study of the graduates of a number of

universities and colleges sponsored by the Mellon Foundation will provide better evidence.

18. Tom Ehrlich has pointed out to me that this criticism is somewhat unfair; sometimes seed money for innovative programs has produced templates that many other institutions follow. He cites as an example the crucial early support by the Ford Foundation of clinical legal education.

References

Brewer, D. J., Eide, E., and Ehrenberg, R. G. "Does It Pay to Attend an Elite Private College? Evidence from the Senior High School Class of 1980." *Research in Labor Economics*, 1996, (15), 239–271.

Card, D. "Earnings, Schooling, and Ability Revisited." *Research in Labor Economics*, 1995, (14), 23–48.

Cook, P. J. and Frank, R. H. "The Growing Concentration of Top Students at Elite Schools." In C. Clotfelter and M. Rothschild, eds., *Studies of Supply and Demand in Higher Education*. Chicago: University of Chicago Press, 1993.

Council for AID to Education. *1996 Voluntary Support of Education*. New York: CAE, 1997.

Council for Aid to Education. "Breaking the Social Contract: The Fiscal Crisis in Higher Education."

Hanushek, E. A. "The Economics of Schooling: Production and Efficiency in Public Schools." *Journal of Economic Literature*, 1986, (24), 1141–1177.

Hedges, L. V., Laine, R., and Greenwald, R. "Does Money Matter? A Meta-Analysis of the Effects of Differential School Inputs on Student Outcomes." *Educational Researcher*, 1994, (23), 5–14.

Kane, T. J. and Rouse, C. E. *Labor-Market Returns to Two- and Four-Year Colleges: Is a Credit a Credit and Do Degrees Matter?* Working Paper No. 31. Princeton: Princeton University Industrial Relations Section, 1993.

Kaplan, A. E., ed. *Giving USA*. New York: AAFRC Trust for Philanthropy, 1997.

Krueger, A. B. "Reassessing the View that American Schools are Broken." *FRBNY Economic Policy Review*, March 1998, 29–43.

Levy, F. and Murnane, R. "The Cost of Higher Education." *Journal of Economic Literature*, 1992, (30), 16.

Levy, F. and Murnane, R. "U.S. Earnings Levels and Earnings Inequality: A Review of Recent Trends and Proposed Explanations." *Journal of Economic Literature*, 1992, (30), 1331–1381.

Manski, C. and Wise, D. *1983 College Choice in America*. Cambridge: Harvard University Press, 1992.

McPherson, M. S. and Schapiro, M. O. "Does Student Aid Affect College Enrollment? New Evidence on a Persistent Controversy." *American Economic Review*, 1991, (81), 309–318.

U.S. Department of Education, National Center for Education Statistics. *The Cost of Higher Education*, No. 6, NCES 98–015.Washington, D.C.: Office of Educational Research and Improvement, 1996.

U.S. Department of Education, National Center for Educational Statistics. *Digest of Education Statistics 1997*, NCES 95–769. Washington, D.C.: Office of Educational Research and Improvement, 1997.

CHAPTER TWENTY

Environmental Philanthropy and Public Policy

Richard L. Revesz

In recent years, the dominant role of the federal government over environmental regulation has been under attack in the public policy sphere. For example, a recent report commissioned by the Senate and House Appropriations Committees calls for Congress and the EPA to give states, communities, and businesses greater flexibility and autonomy in addressing environmental problems, forging a "new partnership . . . based on 'accountable devolution' of national programs and on a reduction of EPA oversight when it is not needed."[1] Congress has made some modest moves toward shifting regulatory authority to states, reflected in the Uniform Mandates Reform Act of 1995[2] and the 1996 amendments to the Safe Drinking Water Act.[3] Similar proposals are under consideration for the Clean Water Act, the Endangered Species Act, and the Superfund statute.[4] The Environmental Protection Agency is also rethinking the appropriate balance of authority between the federal government and the states.

Critics of decentralization paint a gloomy scenario of these recent developments, arguing that decentralization will reduce social welfare. They maintain that a predominant federal role is necessary as a result of a "race to the bottom," the presence of interstate externalities, and public choice problems resulting in the underrepresentation of environmental interests at the state level.[5]

First, the "race to the bottom" rationale for federal environmental regulation posits that states, in an effort to induce geographically mobile firms to locate within their jurisdictions, will offer them suboptimally lax environmental standards so as to benefit from additional jobs and tax revenues. Second, the problem of interstate externalities arises because a state that sends pollution to another state obtains the labor and fiscal benefits of the economic activity that generates the pollution but does not suffer the full costs of the activity. Under these conditions, economic theory maintains that an undesirably large amount of pollution will cross state lines. Third, a public choice claim posits that state political processes will systematically undervalue the benefits of environmental protection or overvalue its costs.

This essay, which builds upon much of my prior work in the area,[6] takes issue with these three arguments for centralization, showing that they do not justify the broad role over environmental regulation accorded to the federal government in the United States.

The essay then seeks to define an appropriate role for the federal government. This discussion shows that federal intervention is necessary to address certain pathologies that otherwise would result. Importantly, the federal government has not made sufficient efforts with respect to regulatory activities that cannot be effectively carried out at a decentralized level: the control of different kinds of interstate externalities; the provision of scientific information necessary for regulation, such as the preparation of risk assessments; and the guarantee of a minimum level of public health.

Thus, there is a mismatch between the areas in which the federal government can have a desirable impact and the focus that federal regulation has taken. The federal government overregulates problems that have only in-state consequences but leaves inadequately addressed problems with respect to which federal intervention is necessary. The assessment of the impact of devolution is therefore complex.

This analysis gives rise to three important conclusions regarding philanthropic action in the environmental area. First, it casts doubt on the social desirability of supporting the types of categorical claims against devolution made by some of the national public interest groups.[7]

Second, it provides a blueprint for focusing attention at the federal level on issues that the federal government has underregulated, and that certain forms of devolution might threaten further. For example, Rodger Schlickeisen, president of Defenders of Wildlife, has rightly assailed efforts to devolve responsibility over biodiversity protection: "Some influential members of the U.S. Congress want to turn over major parts of the federal government's endangered species and other biodiversity conservation programs to the states. But . . . most states do not earn a passing grade exercising even their current responsibilities for stewardship of their natural ecology."[8]

Third, it refutes the claim, fueled by advocates of centralization,[9] that the funding of groups operating at the state and local level is likely to be ineffective or even futile. For example, one commentator has recently focused extensive energy on casting doubt on "environmentalists' relative ability to represent their causes effectively at the state level."[10] A preliminary analysis of the largest grants given by foundations for environmental projects suggests that in recent years the center of gravity has been moving from the national to the state and regional level, both with respect to the identity of the recipient and the purpose of the grant.[11] It would be unfortunate if this trend was halted as a result of unfounded concerns about devolution.

Presumption in Favor of Decentralization

My starting point is a rebuttable presumption in favor of decentralization.[12] This presumption rests on three independent grounds. First, the United States is a large and diverse country. It is therefore likely that different regions will have different preferences for environmental protection. Environmental protection entails an important resource allocation question. We can generally purchase additional environmental protection at some price, paid in the currency of jobs, wages, shareholders' profits, tax revenues, and economic growth. Given the existence of the states as plausible regulatory units, the tradeoff reflecting the preferences of citizens of different regions should not be wholly disregarded in the regulatory process, absent strong reasons for doing so.

In the case of some social decisions, such reasons are present. The example of federal civil rights legislation, which trumped deeply held preferences of a large region of the country, is perhaps most prominent. But while I am sympathetic to the argument that the protection of a minimum level of public health ought to be viewed in quasi-constitutional terms and guaranteed throughout the country, as I explain below it would stretch this principle beyond its breaking point to say that it calls for the federalization of every decision having public health consequences.[13]

Second, the benefits of environmental protection also vary throughout the country. For example, a stringent ambient standard may benefit many people in densely populated areas but only a few elsewhere. Similarly, a particular level of exposure to a contaminant may be more detrimental if it is combined with exposure to other contaminants with which it has synergistic effects.[14]

Third, the costs of meeting a given standard also differ across geographic regions. For example, a source may have a large detrimental impact on ambient air quality if it is directly upwind from a mountain or other topographical barrier. Similarly, a water polluter will have a far larger impact on water quality standards if it disposes its effluents in relatively small bodies of water. Climate might also play a role: certain emission or effluent standards may be easier (and cheaper) to meet in warmer weather.[15]

In principle, federal regulation could be attentive to these differences. Such a differentiated approach, however, would require a staggering amount of information. Clearly, the federal government does not have a comparative advantage at gathering such information. Thus, not surprisingly, federal regulation generally imposes uniform requirements throughout the country.

Moreover, even when federal regulation imposes disuniform standards, the differences are not explainable by the factors discussed above.[16]

This presumption for decentralization should be overcome, however, if there is a systemic evil in letting states decide the level of environmental protection that will apply within their jurisdictions. In the next three sections I examine, respectively, the strength of the race to the bottom, interstate externality, and public choice justifications for federal environmental protection.

The Race-to-the-Bottom Justification

The discussion proceeds in four parts.[17] First, it argues that interstate competition over environmental standards is, in essence, competition for the sale of a good. Second, it shows that the leading economic model of the effects of interstate competition on the choice of environmental standards reveals that interjurisdictional competition leads to the maximization of social welfare, rather than to a race to the bottom. Third, it argues that if game-theoretic interactions among the states lead to a departure from optimality, the result could be overregulation or underregulation; thus, even under this scenario there is no compelling justification for federal minimum standards, which are designed to correct only for underregulation. Fourth, it shows that even if states systematically enacted suboptimally lax environmental standards, federal environmental regulation would not necessarily improve the situation.

Market Analogy

Race-to-the-bottom advocates must clear an initial hurdle. If one believes that competition among sellers of, say, widgets is socially desirable, why is competition among states, as sellers of a good—the right to locate within their jurisdictions—socially undesirable?

Indeed, states sell location rights because, even though they might not have the legal authority to prevent firms from locating within their borders, such firms must comply with the fiscal and regulatory regime of the state in which they wish to locate. The resulting costs to the firms can be analogized to the sale price of a traditional good. If federal regulation mandating a supracompetitive price for widgets is socially undesirable, why should it be socially desirable to have federal regulation mandating a supracompetitive price for location rights, in the form of more stringent environmental standards than those that would result from interstate competition?

It is easy to identify possible distinctions between a state as seller of location rights and sellers of widgets. These differences, however, do not provide support for race-to-the-bottom claims.

First, if individuals are mobile across jurisdictions, the costs that polluters impose on a state's residents will depend on who ends up being a resident of the state; the resulting supply curve is thus far more complex than that of a widget seller. In the context of environmental regulation, however, race-to-the-bottom claims have focused exclusively on the mobility of capital, thereby assuming, at least implicitly, that individuals are immobile. Moreover, it is not clear that individual mobility renders competition among states different from competition among widget sellers. Indeed, even if individuals move in search of the jurisdiction that has the level of environmental protection that they favor,[18] and if there is capital mobility, the choice of environmental standards can nonetheless be efficient.[19]

Second, while a seller of widgets is indifferent to the effect of the sale price on the welfare of the good's purchaser, a state ought to be concerned about the interests of the shareholders of the polluting firm who reside in the jurisdiction, both as individuals adversely affected by pollution and as owners of capital adversely affected by the costs of meeting regulatory requirements. But this difference does not support race-to-the-bottom arguments. Indeed, if some of the regulated firm's shareholders did not reside in the regulating jurisdiction and if capital were immobile, a state could extract monopoly profits by setting suboptimally *stringent* standards, benefiting its in-state breathers at the expense of out-of-state shareholders. (If capital is mobile, competition eliminates this problem.) Nothing in this account provides support for the opposite proposition: that interstate competition leads to suboptimally lax standards.

Third, states are not subject to the discipline of the market. If a producer of widgets consistently sells at a price that does not cover its average costs, it will eventually have to declare bankruptcy. A state, in contrast, can continue in existence even if it recklessly compromises the health of its residents. This difference merely establishes that a state might undervalue environmental benefits. But such undervaluation can take place even if capital were not mobile: it is a public choice problem rather than a race-to-the-bottom problem.

Fourth, states do not sell "location rights" at a single-component price; they require that firms comply with a variety of regulatory standards and that they pay taxes. The resulting market is thus more complex than one involving the sale of a traditional good. For example, a jurisdiction that imposes a lax worker safety standard but a stringent pollution standard will be desirable for a labor-intensive, nonpolluting firm, whereas a jurisdiction with stringent safety and lax pollution standards will be desirable for a capital-intensive, polluting firm. It is far from clear, however, why this additional complexity in the market would make interstate competition destructive. Instead, the example suggests a desirable sorting out of firms according to the preferences of individuals in the various jurisdictions.

In sum, while the analogy between interstate competition for industrial activity and markets for traditional goods is not perfect, it raises serious questions about race-to-the-bottom claims. At the very least, it should require race-to-the-bottom advocates to bear the burden of identifying relevant differences between the two markets, and explaining why they turn otherwise desirable competition into a race to the bottom.

Economic Models

Quite to the contrary, and contrary to the prevailing assumption in the legal literature and in the legislative debates, the leading economic model of the effects of interstate competition on the choice of environmental standards shows that interjurisdictional competition leads to the maximization of social welfare, rather than to a race to the bottom.[20] Professors Wallace Oates and Robert Schwab posit jurisdictions that compete for mobile capital through the choice of taxes and environmental standards. A higher capital stock benefits residents in the form of higher wages, but hurts them as a result of the foregone tax revenues and lower environmental quality needed to attract the capital.[21]

In their model, individuals live and work in the same jurisdiction and there are no interjurisdictional pollution spillovers. Each jurisdiction produces the same single good, which is sold in a national market. The production of the good requires capital and labor, and produces waste emissions. The various jurisdictions set a total permissible amount of emissions as well as a tax on each unit of capital. Capital is perfectly mobile across jurisdictions and seeks to maximize its after-tax earnings, but labor is immobile.[22]

Each individual in the community, who is identical in both tastes and productive capacity, puts in a fixed period of work each week, and everyone is employed. Additional capital raises the productivity of workers, and therefore their wages.

Each jurisdiction makes two policy decisions: it sets a tax rate on capital and an environmental standard. Professors Oates and Schwab show that competitive jurisdictions will set a net tax rate on capital of zero (the rate that exactly covers the cost of public services provided to the capital, such as police and fire protection). For positive net tax rates, the revenues are less than the loss in wages that results from the move of capital to other jurisdictions. In contrast, net subsidies would cost the jurisdiction more than the increase in wages that additional capital would generate.

In turn, competitive jurisdictions will set an environmental standard that is defined by equating the willingness to pay for an additional unit of environmental quality with the corresponding change in wages. Pollution beyond this level generates an increment to wage income that is less than the value of the damage to residents from the increased pollution; in contrast, less pollution creates a loss in wage income greater than the corresponding decrease in pollution damages.

Professors Oates and Schwab show that these choices of tax rates and environmental standards are socially optimal. With respect to tax rates, one condition for optimality is that the marginal product of capital—the increase in the output of the good produced by an additional unit of capital—must be the same across jurisdictions. Otherwise, it would be possible to increase aggregate output, and, consequently, aggregate social welfare, by moving capital from a jurisdiction where the marginal product of capital is low to one where it is high. Because capital is fully mobile, the market will establish a single rate of return on capital. This rate is equal to the marginal product of capital minus the tax on capital. The choice by competitive jurisdictions of a net tax of zero equalizes the marginal product of capital across jurisdictions and is therefore consistent with optimality.

With respect to environmental standards, competitive jurisdictions equate the marginal private cost of improving environmental quality (measured in terms of foregone consumption) with the marginal private benefit. For net tax rates of zero, the marginal private cost is, as noted above, the decrease in wage income produced by the marginal unit of environmental protection. This decrease is also the marginal social cost, since it represents society's foregone consumption. Thus, instead of producing a race to the bottom, competition leads to the optimal levels of environmental protection.

Non-Optimality as a Result of Game-Theoretic Interactions

So far, the inquiry has not revealed support for the claim of systematic environmental underregulation in a regime without federal intervention. It is possible, however, that in particular instances, the game-theoretic interactions among the states would lead to underregulation absent federal intervention. In such cases, federal minimum standards would be desirable. But it is equally plausible that in other instances the reverse would be true: that the game-theoretic interactions among the states would lead to overregulation absent federal intervention. In such cases, federal regulation would be desirable as well, but in such cases federal *maximum* standards would be called for. Accordingly, there is no compelling race-to-the-bottom justification for across-the-board federal minimum standards, which are the cornerstone of federal environmental law.

As an example of such game-theoretic interactions, consider, in the Oates and Schwab model, a situation in which states decide to impose a positive net tax rate on capital, perhaps because they cannot finance the provision of public goods through a non-distortionary tax, such as a head tax. In such a situation, environmental standards will be suboptimally lax because the jurisdiction will continue to relax these standards beyond the optimal level in order to benefit from the additional net tax revenue that results from attracting additional capital.

A corollary, however, is that environmental standards will be suboptimally stringent if a jurisdiction, perhaps because of the visibility that attaches to attracting a major facility, chooses a tax rate on capital that is less than the cost of the public services that capital requires. Under this scenario, the optimal strategy for the jurisdiction is to strengthen the environmental standards beyond the optimal level so as to reduce the negative fiscal consequences.[23]

Similarly, recent studies relax the assumptions of constant returns to scale and perfect competition, which are a cornerstone of the Oates and Schwab model.[24] Instead, they consider the effects of state regulation on an industry that exhibits increasing returns to scale, a condition generally associated with imperfect competition. The conclusions of the model are that, depending on the levels of firm-specific costs, plant-specific costs, and transportation costs, interstate competition can produce either suboptimally lax or suboptimally stringent levels of pollution.

Alternatively, if a firm has market power enabling it to affect prices, it will be able to extract a suboptimally lax standard. Conversely, if a state has market power, the reverse will be true. In summary, just as there are game-theoretic situations in which interstate competition produces environmental underregulation, there are other plausible scenarios under which the result is overregulation.

Futility of Federal Regulation

But even if, left to their own devices, states systematically enacted suboptimally lax environmental standards, federal environmental regulation would not necessarily improve the situation. Race-to-the-bottom arguments appear to assume, at least implicitly, that jurisdictions compete over only one variable—in this case, environmental quality. Consider, instead, the problem in a context in which states compete over two variables—for example, environmental protection and worker safety. Assume that, in the absence of federal regulation, State 1 chooses a low level of environmental protection and a high level of worker safety. State 2 does the opposite: it chooses a high level of environmental protection and a low level of worker safety protection. Both states are in a competitive equilibrium, with industry not migrating from one to the other.

Suppose that federal regulation then imposes on both states a high level of environmental protection. The federal scheme does not add to the costs imposed upon industry in State 2, but it does in State 1. Thus, the federal regulation will upset the competitive equilibrium, and unless State 1 responds, industry will migrate from State 1 to State 2. The logical response of State 1 is to adopt less stringent worker safety standards. This response will mitigate the magnitude of the industrial migration that would otherwise have occurred.

Thus, if a race to the bottom exists, federal environmental standards can have adverse effects on other regulatory programs, in this case, worker safety. On this account, federal environmental regulation is desirable only if its benefits outweigh the costs that it imposes by shifting to other programs the pernicious effects of interstate competition.

More generally, the presence of such secondary effects implies that federal regulation would not be able to eliminate the negative effects of interstate competition, if such negative effects existed. Recall that the central tenet of race-to-the-bottom claims is that competition will lead to the reduction of social welfare; the assertion that states enact suboptimally lax environmental standards is simply a consequence of this more basic problem. In the face of federal environmental regulation, however, states will continue to compete for industry by adjusting the incentive structure of other state programs.

So, for example, if states cannot compete over environmental regulation, they will compete over worker safety standards. One might respond by saying that worker safety should also be (and is) the subject of federal regulation. But states would then compete over consumer protection laws or tort standards, and so on. And even if all regulatory functions were federalized, the competition would simply shift to the fiscal arena, where the competition would lead to the underprovision of public goods. Thus, the reduction in social welfare implicit in race-to-the-bottom arguments would not be eliminated.

The race-to-the-bottom rationale for federal environmental regulation is, therefore, radically underinclusive. It seeks to solve a problem that can be addressed only by wholly eliminating state autonomy. In essence, then, race-to-the-bottom arguments are frontal attacks on federalism. Unless one is prepared to federalize all regulatory and fiscal decisions it is far from clear that federal intervention in the environmental arena would mitigate the adverse social welfare consequences of a race to the bottom, if such a race existed.

The Interstate Externality Justification

The presence of interstate externalities provides a compelling argument for federal regulation under conditions in which Coasian bargaining is unlikely to occur.[25] A state that sends pollution to another state obtains the labor and fiscal benefits of the economic activity that generates the pollution, but does not suffer the full costs of the activity. Thus, a suboptimally large amount of pollution will cross state lines.

Several reasons might explain why transaction costs are sufficiently high to prevent the formation of interstate compacts. First, the baselines are not well defined in the current legal regime. Does an upwind state have the right to send pollution downwind unconstrained? Alternatively, does the downwind state have the right to enjoin all upwind pollution? Second, for different pollution problems, the range of affected states will vary, making less likely the emergence of conditions favoring cooperation. For example, in the case of air pollution, the states affected by a source at a particular locations will depend to a large extent on the nature of the pollutant and the height of the stack. Third, the causation questions are not likely to be straightforward. Considerable scientific work needs to be undertaken in order to determine what sources of pollution are having an impact on the downwind state, and it makes little sense for these determinations to be replicated with respect to each compact.

The fact that interstate externalities provide a compelling justification for intervention, however, does not mean that all federal environmental regulation can be justified on these grounds. For environmental problems such as the control of drinking water quality, there are virtually no interstate pollution externalities; the effects are almost exclusively local. Even with respect to problems for which there are interstate externalities, such as air pollution, the rationale calls only for a response well-targeted to the problem, such as a limit on the amount of pollution that can cross state lines, rather than the control of pollution that has only in-state consequences.

The analysis of the effectiveness of the environmental statutes at remedying interstate pollution spillovers proceeds by reference to the Clean Air Act—the statute designed to deal with the pollution that gives rise to the most serious problems of interstate externalities.[26] The discussion focuses on the statute's ambient and emission standards, which are the core of the regulatory effort, and deals in the margin with its acid rain provision and interstate spillover provisions, which are more directly targeted to the problem of interstate externalities. It shows that federal regulation has been both ineffective and potentially counterproductive.[27]

The core of this Clean Air Act consists of a series of federally prescribed ambient standards and emission standards. Ambient standards determine the maximum permissible concentration of particular pollutants in the ambient air, but do not directly constrain the behavior of individual polluters. Emission standards, in contrast, determine the maximum amount of a pollutant that can be discharged by an individual source.

The federal emission standards are not a good means by which to combat the problem of interstate externalities. These standards constrain the pollution from each source, but do not regulate the number of sources within any given state or the location of the sources.

Similarly, the various federal ambient air quality standards also are not well targeted to address the problem of interstate externalities, because they are both overinclusive and underinclusive. From the perspective of constraining interstate externalities at a desirable level, ambient standards are overinclusive because they require a state to restrict pollution that has only in-state consequences. Concern about interstate externalities can be addressed by limiting the amount of pollution that can cross interstate borders. Because some air pollution has only local effects, such externalities can be controlled even if the upwind state chooses to have poor environmental quality within its borders.

Conversely, the federal ambient air quality standards are also underinclusive from the perspective of controlling interstate externalities because a state could meet the applicable ambient standards but nonetheless export a great deal of pollution to downwind states because the sources in the state have tall stacks and are located near the interstate border. In fact, a state might meet its ambient standards precisely *because* it exports a great deal of its pollution.

The federal ambient and emissions standards could perhaps be justified as a second-best means by which to reduce the problem of uncontrolled interstate externalities. One might believe that by reducing pollution across the board they reduce interstate externalities proportionately.

Such a view, however, is incorrect as a matter of both theory and empirical observation. The amount of aggregate emissions is not the only variable that affects the level of interstate externalities. In particular, two other factors play important roles. The first is the height of the stack from which the pollution is emitted. The higher the stack, the lesser the impact close to the source and the greater the impact far from the source. Thus, absent a federal constraint, states have an incentive to encourage their sources to use tall stacks, as a way to externalize both the health and environmental effects of the pollution, as well as the regulatory costs of complying with the federal ambient standards.

Second, the level of interstate externalities is affected by the location of the sources. In the eastern part of the United States, where the problem of interstate pollution is most serious, the prevailing winds blow from west to east. Thus, states have an incentive to induce their sources to locate close to their downwind borders so that the bulk of the effects of the pollution is externalized. They can induce this result, for example, through the use of tax incentives or subsidies, or through permitting and zoning decisions.

The best evidence that states do indeed encourage sources to use tall stacks can be found in the provisions of the SIPs adopted by at least fifteen states in response to the enactment of the Clean Air Act in 1970. These SIPs allowed sources to meet the NAAQS by using taller stacks rather than by reducing emissions.[28] In those SIPs, the permissible level of emissions was an increasing function of the height of the stack.[29] If the stack was sufficiently high, the effects would be felt only in the downwind states and would therefore have no impact on in-state ambient air quality levels. Through these measures, the states created strong incentives for their firms to externalize the effects of their sources of pollution.

It is true that states had an incentive to externalize pollution even before the enactment of the Clean Air Act in 1970 because, by encouraging tall stacks, states could make other states bear the adverse health effects of pollution. The 1970 provisions, however, created an additional incentive. By encouraging the use of tall stacks, states could also externalize the regulatory impact of the standards, thereby availing themselves, for example, of the opportunity to attract additional sources without violating the NAAQS.

Taller stacks entail higher costs of construction and, possibly, operation. It is therefore conceivable that a state that did not view the externalization of health effects as sufficient by itself to outweigh imposing such costs on in-state firms would reach a different conclusion when tall stacks lead to the externalization of both health and regulatory impacts.

More generally, before 1970, the states had not developed extensive regu-latory programs for controlling air pollution. The net benefits of taller stacks, if any, might not have been worth the institutional investment necessary to create a regulatory program to transmit incentives for such stacks. The Clean Air Act, by requiring states to prepare SIPs, gave them no choice but to create an institutional structure designed to regulate the emissions of industrial sources. With that structure in place, it became comparatively easier to encourage tall stacks.

In addition, the health benefits of reducing the impact of emissions on in-state ambient air quality levels are external to the firm emitting the pollution. Thus, a firm will take such effects into account only if required to do so by a regulator. In contrast, the regulatory benefits of reducing the impact on in-state ambient air quality levels can be captured directly by the firms, which, by using taller stacks, need to invest less to reduce their emissions.[30] While before 1970, firms would have expended resources in tall stacks only if required to do so by a state regulatory agency, after 1970 they had an independent incentive for pursuing such a policy.

It is therefore not surprising that the use of tall stacks expanded consider-ably after 1970. For example, whereas in 1970 only two stacks in the United States were higher than 500 feet, by 1985 more than 180 stacks were higher than 500 feet and twenty-three were higher than 1,000 feet.[31] While the ability of states to externalize pollution in this manner is now less of a problem as a result of a system of regulation of stack height that followed the 1977 amend-ments to the Clean Air Act, tall stacks remain a means by which excessive pollution can be externalized.

In contrast to the experience with tall-stack provisions, it is difficult to find direct evidence concerning whether states also provided incentives for sources to locate close to their downwind borders, because such incentives are unlikely to be reflected in regulatory documents. There is, however, literature suggesting that such incentives are present in the case of the siting of waste sites.[32] It would thus not be implausible to believe that states acted in the same manner with respect to air pollution facilities.

In summary, far from correcting the problem of interstate externalities, the Act's ambient and emission standards may well have exacerbated it.[33]

The Public Choice Justification

I have not yet tackled in any comprehensive way the public choice analysis of issues concerning federalism and environmental regulation. I have taken a somewhat skeptical view, however, of the assertion, largely undefended in the legal literature, that federal regulation is necessary to correct for the systematic underprotection of environmental quality at the state level.[34]

First, it is not enough to say that state political processes undervalue the benefits of environmental regulation, or overvalue the corresponding costs. Federal regulation is justifiable only if the outcome at the federal level is socially more desirable, either because there is less underregulation or because any overregulation leads to smaller social welfare losses.

Second, given the standard public choice argument for federal environmental regulation, it is not clear why the problems observed at the state level would not be replicated at the federal level. The logic of collective action would suggest that the large number of citizen-breathers, each with a relatively small stake in the outcome of a particular standard-setting proceeding, will be overwhelmed in the political process by concentrated industrial interests with a large stake in the outcome. But this problem could occur at the federal level as well.

In fact, the logic of collective action might suggest the underrepresentation of environmental groups would be more serious at the federal level. The cost of organizing on a larger scale magnifies the free-rider problems faced by environmental groups. Moreover, because environmental concerns vary throughout the country, there will be a loss in the homogeneity of the environmental interests when they are aggregated at the federal level, thereby further complicating the organizational problems. For example, environmentalists in Massachusetts may care primarily about air quality whereas environmentalists in Colorado may rank the environmental implications of water allocation as most important. Other things being equal, state-based environmental groups seeking, respectively, better air quality in Massachusetts and a more environmentally sensitive allocation of water in Colorado are therefore likely to be more effective than a national environmental group seeking, at the federal level, better environmental quality with respect to both of these attributes.

In contrast, the situation is likely to be different for industry groups. For many environmental problems, an important portion of the regulated community consists of firms with nationwide operations. For such firms, operating at the federal level poses no additional free-rider problems or loss of homogeneity.

It is possible, however, that the additional organizational problems faced by environmental groups at the federal level are outweighed by benefits arising from the fact that the clash of interest groups takes place before a single legislature, a single administrative agency, and, in part, as a result of the exclusive venue of the D.C. Circuit over important environmental statutes, in a single court.[35] One can imagine models under which public choice problems are indeed ameliorated at the federal level—a task that none of my critics has taken on. The problem, though, is that such models are unlikely to provide a good account of reality.

For example, if one assumed that beyond a certain threshold, additional resources do not increase a group's probability of being successful in the political process, and if this threshold at the federal level is sufficiently lower than the sum of the corresponding thresholds at the state levels, it may be that environmental groups would not be at a disadvantage at the federal level even if they were at a disadvantage in the states. In this case, the economies of scale of operating at the federal level would more than outweigh the increased free-rider problems.

The assumptions behind such a model, however, are not particularly plausible. The threshold concept might properly describe certain costs associated with effective participation in the regulatory process. For example, with respect to the regulation of a particular carcinogen, each group might need to hire a scientist to review the regulator's risk assessment. It may well be the case that a certain minimum will secure the services of a competent scientist and that devoting additional resources to the problem would be of little, if any, use. Thus, for costs of this type, the marginal benefit of additional expenditures is zero, or close to zero, regardless of the other party's expenditures.

The structure of other costs, however, is likely to be quite different. For example, with respect to access to the legislative process, the standard public choice account is that the highest bidder prevails.[36] Thus, the benefit that a party receives from its expenditures is a function of the expenditures of the other party. Unless the costs of this type are quite small, the economies of scale of operating at the federal level are unlikely to outweigh the additional free-rider problems.

Finally, if the relevant public choice interactions are characterized as involving the diffuse interests of breathers or other environmental beneficiaries on one side and the concentrated interests of industrial firms on the other side, the debate over which forum is relatively better for the environmentalist interests is not of great practical importance. What is important, instead, is that both fora are bad for these interests as a result of the diffuse nature of their interests. As a result, given this characterization of this problem, it is difficult to explain, in public choice terms, why there would be any environmental regulation at all.[37]

For this reason, the most plausible public choice explanations for environmental regulation posit that regulated firms obtain benefits from such regulation in the form of rents and barriers to entry, or that certain regions in our country can obtain from the regulatory process advantages relative to other regions. An extensive public choice literature suggests that the impetus for environmental regulation sometimes comes, implicitly or explicitly, from the regulated firms themselves, which can obtain rents and barriers to entry that give them an advantage over their competitors.[38] At other times, the advocates are particular regions of the country, which hope to obtain a comparative advantage with respect to other regions.[39]

When the relevant interactions are seen in this manner, the case for federal regulation on public choice grounds is considerably weakened. A more definitive conclusion, however, must await further sustained analysis.

Toward Desirable Federal Intervention

The preceding discussion shows why the three principal justifications for federal intervention are unlikely to justify an absolute displacement of state authority.[40] Nonetheless, there is an important role for federal intervention to correct various pathologies that otherwise would result.

1. *Interstate Externalities*: The preceding discussion has focused on pollution externalities, principally air pollution that crosses state lines, and shown why the existence of such externalities provides a compelling reason for federal regulation. Other externalities that merit federal regulation arise with respect to different environmental problems. For example, to the extent that certain endangered species are located in a particular state, the costs of protection are largely concentrated in that state. The benefits of preservation, however, accrue nationally, or, for that matter, globally.

Similarly, out-of-state citizens place value on the existence of certain natural resources — even resources that they never plan to use. Such existence, or nonuse, values provide a powerful justification for federal control over exceptional natural resources such as national parks.

2. *Economies of Scale*: Advocates of federal regulation often maintain, though without much empirical support, that centralization has strong economies of scale advantages. The economies of scale argument is most plausible in the early stages of the regulatory process, particularly with respect to the determination of the adverse effects of particular pollutants through risk assessment. Indeed, there is little reason for this determination to be replicated by each state.

The force of the rationale, however, is far less compelling at the standard-setting phase. At this stage, not only are the savings from eliminating duplication of efforts likely to be much lower, but centralization will have serious social costs as a result of the difficulty of setting standards that are responsive to the preferences and physical conditions of different regions.[41]

3. *Uniformity*: As previously discussed, federal environmental standards are generally minimum standards. The states remain free to impose more stringent standards if they wish. Some standards that apply to pesticides and mobile sources such as automobiles,[42] however, are both floors and ceilings: they preempt both more stringent and less stringent state standards. Uniformity of this sort can be desirable for products with important economies of scale in production. In such cases, disparate regulation would break up the

national market for the product and be costly in terms of foregone economies of scale.

The benefits of uniformity, however, are less compelling in the case of process standards, which govern the environmental consequences of the manner in which goods are produced rather than the consequences of the products themselves. Indeed, unlike the case of dissimilar product standards, there can be a well functioning common market regardless of the process standards governing the manufacture of the products traded in the market.

4. *Protection of Minimum Levels of Public Health:* There is a powerful notion, informed in part by constitutional considerations, that a federal polity should ensure all its citizens a minimum level of environmental protection. At some level, this justification is compelling: a minimum level of health ought to count as a basic human right, in the same manner as minimum levels of education, housing, or access to employment. There are two major problems, however, with justifying federal environmental regulation in this manner. First, federal environmental regulation seeks to limit the risk of exposure to particular pollutants or from particular sources, rather than limiting aggregate levels of environmental risk. As a result, such regulation is both overinclusive (it regulates more than that which has a claim to quasi-constitutional legitimacy) and underinclusive (it makes no effort to determine aggregate exposure levels; therefore some individuals may in fact be below the minimum). Second, because environmental risks are only one component of health risks, it is difficult to understand why the federal government should have such a preeminent role in environmental regulation when it does relatively little with respect to the provision of general health care. In fact, investments in preventive measures such as immunizations or prenatal care would have a far larger impact on health than investments in environmental regulation. Thus, the justification for federal regulation based on the need to guarantee a minimum level of health calls for a radically different form of regulation than that currently in effect: one that focuses on aggregate environmental health risks and the interactions between environmental health risks and other health risks.[43]

One cogent commentator has observed that "American environmentalism is both defined and limited by the philanthropy that supports it."[44] If the trend toward devolution of responsibility over environmental regulation continues, philanthropies will need to become even more involved in funding environmental action that has only regional, state, or local scope. This essay should, at least in part, dispel the concern that such efforts are unlikely to succeed.

At the same time, however, philanthropies should focus their attention at the federal level on three areas that the federal government has underregulated: the control of different kinds of interstate externalities; the provision of scientific information necessary for regulation, such as the preparation of risk assessments; and the guarantee of a minimum level of public health.

Notes

1. "National Academy of Public Administration Summary Report to Congress on Role, Structure of the Environmental Protection Agency Released April 12, 1995 (Text)," *Daily Env't Rep. (BNA)* (Apr. 13, 1995).

2. 2 U.S.C. §§1501–71 (Supp. II 1996).

3. 42 U.S.C.A. §§300g–7 to–9, 300h–8, 300j–3c, 300j–12 to 18 (West Supp. 1997).

4. For example, there have been calls for the Endangered Species Act to show greater respect for state water laws by allowing states "to nullify water rights acquired by federal agencies to protect species." "Property Rights Compensation, Funding Focus of Senate Hearing on Rewrite Bill," 28 *Env't Rep. (BNA)* 1000, 1000–01 (Sept. 26, 1997). Additionally reform proposals have sought to expand the involvement of the states in the development of species recovery plans. See id.; S. 1180, 105th Cong. §3(b) (1997). Proposals that would increase the role of states in attaining the goals of the Superfund statute have included exemptions from Superfund enforcement actions (by anyone other than states) for sites being cleaned under state voluntary programs, as well as modes of delegating authority over sites on the National Priorities List to the states. See "Republicans Reiterate Commitment to Comprehensive Reform of Superfund," 28 *Env't Rep. (BNA)* 18, 18–19 (May 2, 1997); "Interested Parties Hail Markup Delay as Talks on CERCLA Reform Resume," 28 *Env't Rep. (BNA)* 843, 843–44 (Sept. 12, 1997); S. 8, 105th Cong. §201(a) (1997); H.R. 873, 105th Cong. §2 (1997).

5. See sources cited infra note 17.

6. Richard L. Revesz, "Rehabilitating Interstate Competition: Rethinking the 'Race to the Bottom' Rationale for Federal Environmental Regulation," 67 *N.Y.U. L. Rev.* 1210 (1992) [hereinafter Revesz, "Race to the Bottom"]; Richard L. Revesz, "Federalism and Interstate Environmental Externalities," 144 *U. Pa. L. Rev.* 2341 (1996) [hereinafter Revesz, "Interstate Externalities"]; Richard L. Revesz, "Federalism and Environmental Regulation: A Normative Critique," in *The New Federalism: Can the States Be Trusted?* John Ferejohn and Barry R. Weingast, eds., 1997 [hereinafter Revesz, "A Normative Critique"]; Richard L. Revesz, "Federalism and Environmental Regulation: Lessons for the European Union and the International Community," 83 *Va. L. Rev.* 1331 (1997); Richard L. Revesz, "The Race to the Bottom and Federal Environmental Regulation: A Response to Critics," 82 *Minn. L. Rev.* 535 (1997) [hereinafter Revesz, "A Response to Critics"].

7. See, e.g., Testimony of the Natural Resources Defense Council, Inc. Before the Senate Comm. on Governmental Affairs (April 28, 1994).

8. See "Biodiversity: As Devolution of Conservation Increases, States Lack Strong Policies, Report Says," *Daily Environment Report*, Mon. July 15, 1996; see infra text accompanying notes 40–41 (discussing need for biodiversity protection at the federal level).

9. See sources cited infra note 17.

10. Warren L. Ratliff, "The De-Evolution of Environmental Organization," *J. Land, Resources & Envtl. L.* 45, 48–49 (1997). For a less pessimistic view of the effectiveness of environmental groups operating at the state level, see William

Lowry, *The Dimensions of Federalism* (1992); Evan Ringquist, *Environmental Protection at the State Level* (1993).

11. I am conducting this analysis using the Foundations Grants database, which can be found on Dialog.

12. This section relies heavily on Revesz, "A Response to Critics," supra note 6, at 536–38.

13. See infra text accompanying notes 42–43.

14. See James E. Krier, "On the Topology of Uniform Environmental Standards in a Federal System—And Why It Matters," 54 *Md. L. Rev.* 1226 (1995) [hereinafter Krier, "Uniform Environmental Standards"]; James E. Krier, "The Irrational National Ambient Air Quality Standards: Macro- and Micro-Mistakes," 22 *UCLA L. Rev.* 323 (1974).

15. See Chemical Mfrs. Ass'n v. EPA, 870 F.2d 177 (D.C. Cir. 1989), cert. denied, 495 U.S. 910 (1990); Tanners' Council, Inc. v. Train, 540 F.2d 1188 (4th Cir. 1976); American Frozen Food Inst. v. Train, 539 F.2d 107 (D.C. Cir. 1976); Hooker Chem. & Plastics Corp. v. Train, 537 F.2d 639 (2d Cir. 1975).

16. For example, the Clean Air Act imposes disuniform ambient standards, determined by whether an area is covered by the Prevention of Significant Deterioration (PSD) or nonattainment programs. See 42 U.S.C. §§ 7473, 7502(c)(2), 7503(a)(1)(A) (1994). These differences turn on what ambient air quality standards regions had at a particular time, rather than differences in preferences, benefits, or costs.

17. This section relies heavily on Revesz, "Race to the Bottom," supra note 6; Revesz, "A Normative Critique," supra note 6, at 99–107. For commentary generally supportive of my approach, see, e.g., David L. Shapiro, "Federalism: A Dialogue," 42–43, 81–83 (1995); Krier, "Uniform Environmental Standards," supra note 14, at 1236–37 (1995); Richard B. Stewart, "Environmental Regulation and International Competitiveness," 102 *Yale L.J.* 2039, 2058–59 (1993); Richard B. Stewart, "International Trade and Environment: Lessons from the Federal Experience," 49 *Wash. & Lee L. Rev.* 1329, 1371 (1992) [hereinafter Stewart, "Lessons from the Federal Experience"]; Stephen Williams, "Culpability, Restitution, and the Environment: The Vitality of Common Law Rules," 21 *Ecology L.Q.* 559, 560–61 (1994).

In the past few months several articles have taken issue with my work on federalism and environmental regulation, particularly with my indictment of the race-to-the-bottom rationale for federal environmental regulation. See Kirsten H. Engel, "State Environmental Standard-Setting: Is There a 'Race' and Is It 'to the Bottom,'" 48 *Hastings L.J.* 271 (1997); Daniel C. Esty, "Revitalizing Environmental Federalism," 95 *Mich. L. Rev.* 570 (1996); Joshua D. Sarnoff, "The Continuing Imperative (but Only from a National Perspective) for Federal Environmental Protection," 7 *Duke Envt'l L. & Pol'y F.* 225 (1997); Peter P. Swire, "The Race to Laxity and the Race to Undesirability: Explaining Failures in Competition Among Jurisdictions in Environmental Law," in Yale Law and Policy Review/Yale Journal on Regulation, *Constructing a New Federalism: Jurisdictional Competence and Competition* 67 (1996). My response appears in Revesz, "A Response to Critics," supra note 6.

18. See Charles M. Tiebout, "A Pure Theory of Local Expenditures," 64 *J. Pol.*

Econ. 416 (1956); Truman F. Bewley, "A Critique Theory of Local Public Expenditures," 49 *Econometrica* 713 (1981).

19. Wallace E. Oates and Robert M. Schwab, "Pricing Instruments for Environmental Protection: The Problems of Cross-Media Pollution, Interjurisdictional Competition and Interregional Effects" (November 1987) (unpublished manuscript on file with author) (cited in Wallace E. Oates and Robert M. Schwab, "Economic Competition Among Jurisdictions: Efficiency Enhancing or Distortion Inducing?" 35 *J. Pub. Econ* 333, 337 n.7 (1988) [hereinafter Oates and Schwab, "Economic Competition Among Jurisdictions"]).

20. Oates and Schwab, "Economic Competition Among Jurisdictions," supra note 19.

21. One commentator argues that interstate competition can lead to detrimental results as a result of factors such as the excessive discounting of future damages, but provides no argument for why this determination would be performed better at the federal level. See John H. Cumberland, "Interregional Pollution Spillovers and Consistency of Environmental Policy," in *Regional Environmental Policy: The Economic Issues* 255 (H. Siebert, ed., 1979). For an argument to the contrary, see Wallace E. Oates and Robert M. Schwab, "The Theory of Regulatory Federalism: The Case of Environmental Management," in *The Economics of Environmental Regulation* 319 (Wallace E. Oates, ed., 1996).

22. In a companion, unpublished manuscript, they argue that their conclusion that competition among states produces efficient outcomes holds even if individuals are mobile. See supra note 19. If individuals are mobile, they will sort out, as in the Tiebout model, by reference to their preference for environmental protection. Individuals who are willing to trade off a great deal in wages for better environmental quality will move to jurisdictions that impose stringent controls on industry; individuals who attach less importance to environmental quality will go to dirtier areas.

23. There is no consensus in the academic literature on whether, on average, states and localities tax or subsidize capital. See Peter Mieszkowski and George R. Zodrow, "Taxation and the Tiebout Model: The Differential Effects of Head Taxes, Taxes on Land Rents, and Property Taxes," 27 *J. Econ. Lit.* 1098 (1989).

24. See James R. Markusen, Edward R. Morey and Nancy D. Olewiler, "Environmental Policy when Market Structures and Plant Locations Are Endogenous," 24 *J. Envt'l Econ. & Mgmt.* 69 (1993); James R. Markusen, Edward R. Morey and Nancy D. Olewiler, "Competition in Regional Environmental Policies when Plant Locations are Endogenous," 56 *J. Pub. Econ.* 55 (1995).

25. In contrast, if the transaction costs were sufficiently low to permit such bargaining, there would be no efficiency-based reason for federal regulation.

26. This section relies heavily on Revesz, "Interstate Externalities," supra note 6; Revesz, "A Normative Critique," supra note 6, at 107–20.

27. Similar criticisms can be raised against the Clean Water Act, which is designed to combat an environmental problem for which the interstate pollution spillovers are also salient. See Revesz, "Interstate Externalities," supra note 6, at 2370, n.105.

28. See Clean Air Act Oversight: Hearings Before the Subcomm. on Environmental Pollution, Sen. Comm. on Public Works, 93d Cong., 2d Sess. 330–31, 337, 357–59 (1974) [hereinafter Sen. Comm. on Public Works]; Richard

E. Ayres, "Enforcement of Air Pollution Controls on Stationary Sources Under the Clean Air Amendments of 1970," 4 *Ecology L.Q.* 441, 452 & nn.28, 30 (1975).

29. For example, the Georgia regulations that were struck down in Natural Resources Defense Council v. EPA, 489 F.2d 390, 403–11 (5th Cir. 1974), rev'd on other grounds sub nom. Train v. Natural Resources Defense Council provided that, for sulfur dioxide, allowable emissions could be proportional to the cube of the stack height, for stacks under 300 feet, and proportional to the square of the stack height for stacks over 300 feet. See Georgia Rules and Regulations for Air Quality Control § 270–5–24-.02(2)(g) (1972). A similar formula applied to particulate emissions. See id. § 270–5–24-.02(2)(m). Thus, a sufficiently high stack would eliminate the need for any emissions reduction.

30. The savings can be substantial. For example, a study in the early 1970s, when tall stack credits were most prevalent showed that the cost of complying with regulatory requirements were between $60/kw and $130/kw for a new lime scrubber, as compared with between $4/kw and $10/kw for a tall stack. See Sen. Comm. on Public Works, supra note 28, at 210, 215.

31. See Arnold W. Reitze, Jr., "A Century of Air Pollution Control Law: What's Worked; What's Failed; What Might Work," 21 *Envtl. L.* 1549, 1598 (1991); James R. Vestigo, "Acid Rain and Tall Stack Regulation Under the Clean Air Act," 15 *Envtl. L.* 711, 730 (1985).

32. See, e.g., Daniel E. Ingberman, "Siting Noxious Facilities: Are Markets Efficient?" *J. Environ. Econ. & Mgmt.* S–20, S–23 (1995); Bradford C. Mank, "Environmental Justice and Discriminatory Siting: Risk-Based Representation and Equitable Compensation," 56 *Ohio St. L.J.* 329, 421 (1995); Robert B. Wiygul and Sharon C. Harrington, "Environmental Justice in Rural Communities Part One: RCRA, Communities, and Environmental Justice," 96 *W. Va. L. Rev.* 405, 437–38 (1993–94); Rae Zimmerman, "Issues of Classification in Environmental Equity: How We Manage Is How We Measure," 21 *Fordham Urb. L.J.* 633, 650 (1994).

33. As discussed in Revesz, "Interstate Externalities," supra note 6, at 2359–60, the acid rain provisions of the 1990 amendments to the Clean Air Act, 42 U.S.C. §§7651–7651o (1994), are an incomplete and poorly targeted mechanism for addressing interstate externalities: they apply to only two pollutants, and are not structured to allocate emissions between upwind and downwind states in a desirable manner. Moreover, the most comprehensive mechanism for addressing spillovers—a set of adjudicatory provisions under which downwind states can seek to enjoin excessive interstate spillovers, id. §§7410(a)(2)(D), 7426(b)—has been wholly ineffective. In the twenty years since its enactment, no downwind state has been successful. See Revesz, supra note 6, at 2360–74.

34. This section relies heavily on Revesz, "A Response to Critics," supra note 6, at 542–43, 558–61.

35. See Richard L. Revesz, "Environmental Regulation, Ideology, and the D.C. Circuit," 83 *Va. L. Rev.* 1717 (1997).

36. See Sam Peltzman, "Toward a More General Theory of Regulation," 19 *J.L. & Econ.* 211 (1976); George J. Stigler, "The Theory of Economic Regulation," 2 *Bell J. Econ.* 3 (1971).

37. Professor Swire acknowledges this difficulty with his argument: "In light of

the straightforward public choice analysis presented here, the puzzle remains how environmental protection ever succeeds in the political process." Id. at 109.

38. See Nathaniel O. Keohane, Richard L. Revesz, and Robert N. Stavins, "The Positive Political Economy of Instrument Choice in Environmental Policy," in *Environmental Economics and Public Policy* (Paul Portney and Robert Schwab, eds., forthcoming).

39. See B. Peter Pashigian, "Environmental Regulation: Whose Self-Interests Are Being Protected?" 23 *Econ. Inquiry* 551 (1985).

40. This section relies heavily on Revesz, "A Normative Critique," supra note 6, at 121–25; Revesz, "A Response to Critics," supra note 6, at 543–45.

41. See supra text accompanying notes 12–16.

42. See 7 U.S.C. §136v(b) (1994 (pesticides); 42 U.S.C. §7416 (1994) (mobile sources).

43. Some federal role with respect to environmental regulation might also be justified by the federal government's responsibility to implement obligations flowing from international treaties.

44. Mark Dowie, *Losing Ground: American Environmentalism at the End of the Twentieth Century* 41 (1995).

CHAPTER TWENTY-ONE

Philanthropy and Outcomes

Dilemmas in the Quest for Accountability

Gary Walker and Jean Grossman

The call for a greater focus on outcomes in philanthropic giving has gained increasing prominence and adherents during the 1990s. A review of foundation annual reports indicates that the word "outcomes" is used more widely and more often in this decade than in the preceding two decades. There are panels and forums on outcomes at most every foundation conference that involves philanthropy.

Grantees report that never before have grant negotiations with foundation staffs been so focused on specifying outcomes. Some foundations have employed consultants to work with their staffs so that inputs, operational processes, intermediate and long-term outcomes and impacts are specified and differentiated. A number have added evaluation departments to their organizational structure. Small and medium sized foundations who have previously focused their giving exclusively on direct services are now asking for and funding evaluations, so that they may know with objectivity and rigor if the projected outcomes are achieved.

The national office of United Way—whose local chapters raised \$3.2 billion in 1997—initiated several years ago a major project to both emphasize the importance of specifying outcomes in local giving, and to provide assistance to local chapters on how to go about determining the outcomes of individual grants.

At first blush this "outcomes movement" seems like an unreservedly good thing. Who can be against a more careful specification of what grants are intended to achieve, and more rigorous and objective efforts to assess exactly what they do achieve? Especially in a sector that is often criticized for its overemphasis on personal relationships and ideological correctness (of what-ever direction) in its giving practices, and for its lack of rigor and public openness in assessing and communicating the effectiveness of its giving. Especially in a country whose dominant sector, the private, for-profit sector — the very sector that creates the wealth that fuels the philanthropic sector — provides on a regular basis an objective, detailed, and public accounting of most of its companies' outcomes and performance, and where all of that sector's units prosper or wither by that impersonal accounting.

In that light the "outcomes movement" is a welcome coming of age for philanthropy, a voluntary descent from its self-appointed, lofty perch on the mountaintop to the life of Everyman in the valley below, where the esteem you're held in depends largely on what you achieve — as measured by the cold outcomes of your particular marketplace. You can almost feel the keystone of accountability grind into its long-awaited place. . . .

There is a healthy measure of truth to all the above. And if the alternative is not caring about outcomes, or not caring about the reliability of how we assess them — not caring about accountability — of course the recent emphasis on outcomes is an unreservedly good thing. But in fact a more complex reality underlies the current "outcomes movement." It is important to understand that reality if the current "outcomes movement" is to be truly useful to philanthropy and the various social issues its giving addresses.

The Context

It is true that the overwhelming majority of projects, organizations, initia-tives, and programs supported by philanthropy are not formally assessed for outcome achievement. Many do not even generate basic descriptive informa-tion about the content, quantity, and quality of what they do, much less assess what they accomplish. Anecdote, salesmanship, ideology, and relationships are as much the basis for many philanthropic funding decisions as is a hard analysis of outcomes. As noted above, it is this feature of philanthropic practice which makes the outcome movement so appealing.

But it is historically inaccurate to see the current "outcomes movement" as a major innovation in the philanthropic sector. There has been an interest in outcomes since there's been an interest in giving. In fact, most philanthropists are quick to declare their intended outcomes, for their very purpose in giving is to *cause change*. The word "outcome" may represent more stylish jargon, but the meaning behind the word has always been there.

Neither is it the case that the "outcomes movement" is a new focus on measurement, or on new measurement techniques. Many of the largest and most influential of philanthropic institutions have been deeply engaged in specifying and measuring the outcomes of their giving for several decades now. The Ford Foundation actually created organizations such as Public/

Private Ventures and The Manpower Demonstration Research Corporation in the mid-1970s in order to obtain, with the most sophisticated evaluation techniques available, reliable information about the effectiveness of social initiatives in many areas—welfare, employment training, public housing, transportation, education, and youth development, to name but several major "outcome areas." The evaluations of the initiatives cited above have been supported not just by Ford, but by over 100 foundations—including over three quarters of the country's largest 25 foundations. They have employed random assignment, econometric models, ethnography, political science, and sociology, among many disciplines and methodologies, both separately and together.

Is then the current "outcomes movement" simply an attempt to extend the practices and knowledge of this substantial group of foundations to all the rest—and to help ensure that recent and projected growth in the number of foundations and aggregate philanthropic wealth will also include an appropriate emphasis on outcomes specification and measurement, and a sophistication based on previous experience? Certainly that is a worthy goal.

But there is more to the current emphasis on outcomes—and the history behind it—than that some practice it, and many do not, and that the word and the practice need to be spread. In fact the recent history of philanthropic giving in several important areas of social policy can be characterized as having placed a major emphasis on outcomes assessment—and that the dominant, indeed almost uniform, result of those assessments is that the intended outcomes were *not* achieved.

For example, in the fields of welfare and employment training there have been over the past two decades a significant number of well-done studies. The overwhelming majority revealed poor results. These very studies have helped build support for the notion that social interventions "don't work," and that public funding reductions are justified.

Thus the outcome studies carried out in the past have become an integral part of the politics of social policy, as will whatever published results the current outcomes movement produces. Failure has produced more than lessons to build on, as so many of evaluation's optimistic supporters had set forth as its goal; it has helped produce pessimism about what social policy—the public will applied to social problems—can accomplish.

Thus the current emphasis on outcomes may for particular foundations be a new emphasis, and may require the acquisition of new competencies and cause new patterns of giving. But for philanthropy as a whole the deeper roots of and implications for the current focus on outcomes are in the failure of past initiatives to achieve their specified outcomes.

That failure—and the ample and rigorous documenting of it in fields like welfare and employment training—casts a very different light on the recent emphasis on outcomes, and the actions and priorities it should generate, than does the absence of outcome studies on most grants and at many foundations.

Absence would prompt us to action, as quickly as is possible, to fill the void; studies would abound. The light of failure would have the hues of caution and care in proceeding. It would push us to diagnose deeply the strength of the causal relationship between the desired outcome and the initiative to be funded—as well as the likelihood that it will be implemented as conceived. Goodness of motivation and strength of vision would not alone generate declarations and studies of outcome. It would make us examine very closely the practical as well as conceptual strength of the evaluation design being adopted, so that the results obtained from the study were not shaped by the manner of collecting information. It would lead us a bit more into the perplexing issues of organizational capacity and implementation, the relationship between deep cultural values and political will, and the interplay between external help and individual change. It might cause us at times to delay beginning an outcome study until intermediate implementation and capacity goals are met.

In short, the context of the current "outcomes movement" is complex, full of experience and insights that often lead in different directions. That context in no way undercuts the importance of a funder and a grantee being able to articulate what it is they are aiming to achieve, and how they'll know whether it is achieved—but it does indicate that both the *what* and the *how* may not be as clear cut as they had hoped.

In the remainder of this essay we attempt to lay out some of the factors that need to be considered when a philanthropy decides to put a greater emphasis on "outcomes." We divide them into three broad categories: Technical (How to Measure); Substantive (What to Do); and Strategic (How to Think).

Technical (How to Measure) Issues

The first and most fundamental technical issue is that outcomes are not the same as impacts. A program or project may specify, measure and achieve its outcomes—and still not have any incremental impact compared to other or no interventions.

How can that be? The National Supported Work Demonstration of the mid to late 1970s provides an excellent example of this phenomenon. The program was offered to four groups of unemployed individuals: ex-offenders, out-of-school youth, former drug addicts, and AFDC recipients. All the participants came to the program in need of employment; all were members of groups whose employment prospects were not good. During the follow-up period of two to three years, the employment rates of all the program participants increased significantly—but so did the employment rates of control group members. In fact, except among the AFDC recipients the employment rates of the comparison group members were higher than those of the program participants. Thus, while the program looked effective when the key outcome variable was examined, it actually did not improve the situations of the participants any more than what would have happened without it.

In the mid to late 1980s, the Summer Training and Education Program offered half-time work and half-time remediation to educationally and economically disadvantaged youth. Its goal was to increase the youths' academic competency. However, over the approximately two months of the summer program, participants' test scores actually decreased slightly. On the face of it, it appeared that the program was ineffective; however, over the same period the test scores of the control group members plummeted nearly a grade level. Thus, rather than being ineffective, STEP was able to dramatically stem the summer learning loss that occurred in these youth.

Does this mean that projecting and measuring outcomes, without assessing impacts by means of a control or comparison group, is without value? No. General knowledge about how like participants ordinarily do vis-à-vis the desired goals, and about the availability of services vis-à-vis the number of people who need and want them, can help form a reasoned judgment about a program's value. Detailed knowledge about the quality of each component of a program, why participants stay and why they leave, is also useful. A strong program theory about what should happen to a participant, and detailed knowledge about the actual implementation and course of participation, is even better. These techniques do not provide as certain a knowledge as does an impact evaluation, but they are clearly useful, and certainly better than impressionistic knowledge.

But it does mean that in the absence of a sound comparative study it is often difficult to know to what degree the outcomes achieved are attributable to the initiative funded. This can lead to some situations even more puzzling to the intelligent citizen and voter than the supported work example. For example, the 1983 federal Job Training Partnership Act (JTPA) program aimed to place poor people with multiple obstacles to employment into jobs; the Act put a major emphasis on quantitative placement rates as a measure of local success in achieving its goals. Local administrators set very high goals for the programs they funded, and offered financial incentives.

As local placement rates around the country began to soar—to over 80 percent in many locations—and were verified as factually accurate, critics speculated that these rates were *too* good, and indicated that most JTPA participants did not have serious obstacles to employment, and would have gotten jobs even without JTPA's modest training interventions.

JTPA advocates scoffed. Then an impact study was done. It basically supported the critics. It indicated that JTPA even harmed the labor market prospects of some youthful participants. Well-specified outcomes, careful measurement, incentives, good performance—all of it amounted to very little added value.

So this is the major "technical" issue to the outcomes movement: that even a careful specification in advance of the outcomes to be achieved, and a careful and credible collection of relevant information about those outcomes, may not lead to accurate conclusions about what the program or initiative actually accomplished. The problem is particularly acute when the outcomes aimed at have to do with long-term changes in human behavior (as most important outcomes do).

Are there technical solutions to the above problem? Theoretically, yes: one is to utilize a comparison group, so that the counterfactual question—what would have happened in the absence of the program or initiative—can be answered. But there are numerous technical issues to designing and carrying out a credible comparison study. For the purpose of this article, however, it is useful to highlight three of those issues.

1. A sound comparison group methodology is not always available. A good comparison group is one that looks like what the program group looks like, at least on key features. Typically, comparison groups are selected so that they match the program group on all the factors that fundamentally determine the key outcomes. Employment program comparison group members are usually matched by age, race, gender, and education. The more factors that fundamentally influence the key outcomes, the harder it is to find a group that matches the program group on all of them. For example, it is very difficult to find good comparisons for interventions that target entire communities, such as comprehensive community initiatives or enterprise/empowerment zones. Community outcomes, such as economic or social well-being indicators, are influenced by a myriad of factors. Even communities that are quite similar at one point in time generally diverge over the time it takes for the programs to work. Therefore, the more factors that influence the key outcomes and the longer an intervention takes to achieve change the harder it is to find a sound comparison group.

2. The number of participants is often not large enough. In order to detect a program's impact by contrasting program and comparison group behavior, one must take into account that the behaviors of even very similar individuals naturally differ. Technically evaluators get around this complication by not only matching the two groups as closely as possible, but also by comparing the outcomes of large groups of participants and nonparticipants (i.e., comparison group members). The more natural variation there is in an outcome among like individuals, the larger the groups must be. Given the need to average out the natural variation in outcomes, small local programs may find that they do not have enough participants available to statistically detect their program's effects.

3. The comparison group's activities are often not distinct enough to permit a sound conclusion about the content of the program or initiative's impact. Most new programs do not offer completely new services but rather offer higher quality services, a more complete package of services, and/or include critical elements that were missing in earlier programs. Thus when

testing such programs, it is often the case that comparison group members are able to enroll in fundamentally similar services. For example, many of the comparison group members of Project Redirection, an employment, education, and parenting program for teen mothers, found their way into education or training programs, as well as parenting classes, by the end of the study. In such cases, when the program group is compared to the comparison group, one is not answering the question "How did the participants fare compared to what would have happened had they done nothing?" but rather "How did the participants fare compared to what they would have been able to find on their own?" The answer to the second question is a smaller impact than the first, and thus is harder to detect.[1] Simple participant/comparison group comparisons are often not powerful enough to detect such impacts.

So the solution to the technical problem generates its own group of technical problems. It is at this point that some who began with great enthusiasm about the outcomes movement lose patience, and wonder if there are not simpler, less expensive, and less time-consuming ways to arrive at reasoned conclusions about whether giving accomplished its aims.

The answer is "of course." Experienced observation plus basic data plus a sound theory plus some in-depth anecdotes . . . you can arrive at a reasoned conclusion. The problem—as the Supported Work and JTPA examples highlight—is that the conclusions based on these methods may be incorrect more than a modest percentage of the time.

That is a risk worth taking if the funder is not willing to devote the resources and time to supporting a technically sound outcomes or impact study. A study with the *appearance* of scientific soundness carries weight with other funders, the media, and policymakers, and can have seriously damaging implications. There has been enough of that already in the world of social policy.

The technical issues discussed above pose substantial challenges to the philanthropy that wants to focus on outcomes. The good news, however, is that there is a substantial body of thought about these technical issues, and that a "soundest approach" can usually be crafted. It just takes resources, and a willingness to use them on this issue. As in many areas of human endeavor, in fact, the progress made on the technical issues surrounding the measurement of outcomes in social policy has been greater and faster than the progress made on how to achieve those outcomes.

Substantive (What to Do) Issues

A careful look at the many outcome and impact studies conducted over the past two decades fairly quickly leads the observant reader to the conclusion that there must be some deep substantive themes connecting many of the initiatives that have been evaluated, some root causes to the weak results they report so consistently. A focused look at the smaller group of studies that report stronger outcomes only strengthens this conclusion.

This conclusion typically comes in two forms, whatever field of social policy we're looking at: first, that the basic substantive strategy was not strong enough to reach the desired results; and second, that the basic substantive strategy was not in fact well implemented. These generic conclusions are important for many reasons, not least of which is their implication for the current outcomes movement that simply a greater emphasis on outcomes (the notion that articulating them will improve their chances of occurrence), nor an improved technical approach to measuring outcomes, is likely to increase the probability of generating those outcomes.

In short, the priority focus of a philanthropic concern about outcomes in the late 1990s needs to be on improving the strategy, substance, and quality of *what* is being funded.

At first blush that statement may not seem so dramatic, and may even offend: after all, who in philanthropy does not care about what is being funded, and who does not want to help improve it? But the very concern about outcomes and accountability—about having a "bottom line"—when combined with our well-developed technical capacity to measure outcomes and impacts, can easily lead us to rush by the issues of strategy, substance, implementation capacity, and quality. They are much more complicated to address, and they are not too amenable to definitive measurement. They are intermediate steps on the way to achieving bottom-line outcomes, and they have not received consistent or strong emphasis over the past several decades. They have not received that emphasis—paradoxically enough from the perspective of the current outcomes movement—in part because we were so anxious to believe and prove that what we funded *did* produce their intended (and often grand) outcomes that we rushed to assess them before we were confident of their strategic, substantive, and operational soundness.

This will discourage many philanthropists; it sounds as if we're starting over, just when the "outcomes movement" hints that we're nearing our goals. And the truth is, in many areas of policy, we are starting over. But starting over is different than starting from scratch—there are many lessons to build on, both positive and negative, and those lessons make it more likely that our newly built policies and approaches can achieve the outcomes we intend. But that *building* process is the first priority—not a rush to outcomes measurement.

For example, there is strong agreement across the political spectrum and among experts that American employment training policy over the past 30 years has largely not produced the results everyone hoped for. There are a host of well-done studies supported by philanthropy and government, separately and in collaboration, to support that conclusion. Public funds for the current version of American employment training policy—the Job Training Partnership Act—have declined in response, as has public regard for that system. The recent and prolonged boom in private job creation in the American economy has fueled a decrease in unemployment rates and welfare rolls, and has for the time being submerged our lack of direction regarding *what* (if any) employment training policy and implementation practice America should have or try in the coming years, when the private economy inevitably slows down. But what everyone agrees about is that policy and practice must be fundamentally different than the policy and practice that has dominated the past 30 years![2]

Thus this is an excellent time for philanthropy, both as individual institutions and in groups, to support analysis of previous employment training policies and implementation experience with an aim to generating strategies to improve the performance of the entire employment training field, as well as that of particular programs. Such wide-angle work would not only increase the chances of having more effective strategies, policies, and programs; it would also strengthen the resolve and clarity of direction of individual foundations in their dealings with specific grantees and their programs.

But this work is precedent to a focus on the bottom line outcomes of particular programs. It is the priority if we are to achieve those outcomes.

Some work of this nature has already begun in several substantive areas. For example, the authors are aware of collaborative/philanthropic initiatives aimed at improving the *what* in the areas of youth development and workforce development. Each was initiated with an openness to recommendations of substantial change in the policies, funding, substantive, and implementation strategies of that field. Many more fields of social policy need the same open reexamination.

An approach by philanthropy both individually and collectively which acknowledges the likely need for major substantive overhaul in a policy field has major implications for thinking about outcomes. The incrementalist approach that has dominated the last several decades assumed that useful changes in policy and practice would come in the form of additions or modest alterations to extant programming—in short, we were just a tinker away from resolving the problem—and thus on balance put more intellectual capital into figuring out how to measure the anticipated long-term outcomes than into figuring out how to improve substantive strategy and implementation capacity.

The non-incrementalist approach that is necessary now would shift that balance. It would place greater initial emphasis not only on shaping new substantive approaches, but also on ensuring their quality of implementation and political durability. Thus the outcomes or results sought by immediate funding decisions may have a more intermediate or benchmark quality, and be less quantitative and more judgmental in nature, than the ultimate outcomes being aimed at.

Below are some critical substantive areas that get to the *what* issue, and which need individual and collective philanthropic attention in many social policy domains.

♦ *New Programmatic Strategies.* As noted above, several key policy areas are in need of serious rethinking regarding their basic substantive strategies. The employment training area is a good example: some analysts believe that there are experiential and theoretical reasons for crafting a very different set of strategies than those utilized in the past several decades. Such crafting is in itself an outcome that needs establishment and assessment.

♦ *New or Expanded Institutions.* The philanthropic world has for the most part devoted its resources to funding "programs" or "initiatives." But often what is most needed to achieve the ultimate outcomes we want in a policy area is *institutions*— institutions that have a reputation for stability and performance, that become a brand name for what they deliver. The Ford Foundation's strategy in the arts world during the 1950s–1970s period is an excellent example.

Brand-name institutions—particularly for policy areas that require interaction across the public, nonprofit, and commercial sectors—are critical for achieving ultimate outcomes. Building such institutions is an outcome in itself.

♦ *Capacity Building.* In some areas of social policy there are sound programmatic strategies and brand name institutions—the youth development area, with its Boys and Girls Clubs and Big Brothers/Big Sisters, is an example—but there is simply insufficient capacity to reach their intended outcomes at a sufficient scale. Building capacity is an outcome worth defining and measuring.

♦ *Filling Gaps.* In some areas of social policy analysis indicates that there are enormous substantive gaps that stand in the way of achieving the outcomes we all want. One example is after-school programming, which has been steadily reduced over the past several decades and which many analysts think is a key both to providing youth with critical development inputs (more adults, more engaging activities, more educational assistance) and to reducing negative behaviors (crime, school dropout, school parenting).

This particular "gap-filling" strategy would have as its primary goals the building of a variety of high-quality, well-supervised, engaging after-school activities that attract a broad cross-section of youth. These outcomes might take several years to achieve; only then would it be reasonable to assess whether ultimate outcomes were being achieved. If they were not, the question then would be if the appropriate response were to quit funding after-school activities or to investigate whether other policy areas needed strengthening. Ultimate outcomes cannot always be laid at the accountability doorstep of one programmatic strategy.

As the discussion above suggests, in our judgment the greatest need over the coming years is not more declaration of outcomes, nor envisioning of outcomes, nor more assessment of them. It is figuring out what to do to get them.

Strategic (How to Think) Issues

The above discussion does not, however, mean that we recommend a moratorium on ultimate outcome and impact assessments. It does mean that a strategic rethinking of when to utilize the tools of formal outcome and impact evaluations is needed.

The experience of the past 25 years provides a good base for that rethinking. During that period formal outcome and impact assessments have been instituted in three basic categories of activities: new program initiatives; modified program initiatives; and longstanding program initiatives.

Although this essay is not the proper vehicle for a full discussion and analysis of the history of evaluations in these three categories, our preliminary conclusions are relevant, *viz.*:

- Evaluations of new program initiatives are dominated by no or negative outcome and impact findings;
- Evaluations of modified program initiatives are evenly mixed in their findings of no, negative, modest, or good outcomes and impacts;
- Evaluations of longstanding program initiatives are more likely than not to have modest or good outcomes and impacts.

This distribution of findings suggests that issues of operational capacity and implementation quality may indeed affect the outcomes and impacts our studies are getting. It suggests that focusing outcome and impact assessment resources on programs and initiatives that have a track record, and that have evolved based on years of operational experience, is more likely to provide an accurate assessment of the impact and outcome potential of a particular substantive strategy than is using assessment resources on entirely new manifestations of that strategy. It suggests that the functions of "research" and "demonstration" may need decoupling, at least regarding ultimate outcomes and impacts.

The strategic rethinking we are suggesting has important implications for the outcomes movement in philanthropy. One is that it should stimulate more coordinated efforts among foundations, since the outcomes emphasis would be less on assessing every program and more on (1) finding a stable exemplar to assess, one that represents the solid implementation of a particular substantive idea, and (2) developing from that exemplar a set of operational benchmarks by which to assess the progress of newer operational manifestations of that idea.

An example of this approach is the national impact evaluation we carried out on Big Brothers/Big Sisters over the 1992–95 period. The mentoring field was (and is) exploding with activity, and yet there were no credible findings about outcomes. BBBS is the brand name in the mentoring business; evaluating it, we felt, would provide a good indication of the utility of the mentoring idea as shaped by years of operational experience. Eleven foundations supported this study.

The findings were positive: mentoring had impacts on initial drug use, school behavior and performance, and fighting on the school grounds, among others. Equally important, the study provided the mentoring field with operational benchmarks by which to assess the likelihood that other mentoring programs were achieving similar outcomes. It is not necessary to do a new impact study on each and every mentoring program.

Another implication of this strategic rethinking is that it should stimulate foundations to think about a field as a whole, not just particular programs. To follow through on the above example, the challenge for foundations interested in mentoring after the BBBS study is (1) how to expand mentoring, since it has positive effects, and (2) how to ensure that expansion does not dilute implementation quality. These challenges, whether met collectively or by individual foundation efforts, are field-building, and maximize positive outcomes—even as they deal with individual mentoring programs. The forest does not get lost in the trees.

The bottom line is: getting to outcomes, measuring them, knowing what are benchmarks along the way, knowing how to influence an entire field by an outcomes strategy, are complex issues in the philanthropic world. It is not so simple as trustees telling staff, "let's make outcomes a priority." It is not so straightforward as "we'll devote 10 percent of our budget to evaluation."

In short, a commitment to specifying and measuring outcomes is on the surface a good thing. But it is only the beginning step of an adventurous process. It is the commitment to that process that is necessary if the "outcomes movement" is to prove useful to philanthropy, grantees, and society.

Notes

1. In addition, while the answer to the second is of interest to society, programs themselves want to answer to the former question.

2. Gary Walker, Testimony to the Committee on Economic and Educational Opportunities Subcommittee on Postsecondary Education, Training and Life-Long Learning, U.S. House of Representatives, 3/16/95.

CHAPTER TWENTY-TWO

Philanthropy and Culture

Patterns, Context, and Change

Margaret J. Wyszomirski

The relationship of philanthropy and culture in the United States has always been complex, interdependent, and multifaceted. It involves a multitude of individual and institutional donors and recipients. It involves foundations both national and local in scope, both general purpose and culturally focused. It involves corporate foundations and corporate sponsors. Basically a fragmented and individualistic arena, it also has elements of integration and collaboration. Nonprofit arts organizations are simultaneously dependent on earned, donated, and governmental income—and the amounts and relative proportions of these sources varies over time and differs according to the size and discipline orientation of individual arts organizations. One form and source of support is often dependent on another through devices such as matching or challenge grants, tax deductibility, voluntary action, or program and project partnerships.

Patterns of Cultural Philanthropy

Historically, individuals have been and today continue to account for the greatest share of philanthropic support for the arts and culture. For 1995, *Giving USA* reported that out of the nearly $126 billion donated for the full range of charitable purposes, almost $10 billion was targeted to arts, culture, and humanities organizations. Since 1964 the proportion of total private giving that has gone to the arts has increased from $2.3 billion or 3.2 percent (Cobb, 1996:11) to 7.2 percent in 1996. In 1996, the cultural figure had risen to $10.92 billion, representing a 9.7- percent increase over the previous year, or a 6.8-percent increase when adjusted for inflation (AAFRC, 1997:51). Of this total amount, roughly 87 percent of private giving comes from individuals. In 1993, approximately 8 percent of American households contributed to the arts—a percentage that is essentially static with the figure for 1987, but which reflects a decline from 9.6 percent and 9.4 percent reported in 1989 and 1991 respectively. Simultaneously, the average household contribution to the arts has decreased almost by half (from $260 in 1987 to $139 in 1993), even as average household contributions to charities more generally has increased considerably, from $1,376 in 1987 to $2,101 in 1993 (Cobb, 1996:13). Meanwhile, although approximately 390,000 full-time equivalent volunteers lent their time to the arts, culture, and humanities annually, volunteer involvement in the arts has also experienced a decline. Concern about sustaining the essential philanthropic base of individual donors has led to calls for more active efforts to cultivate cultural donors—whether through linking volunteering with giving, through strategies to develop minority donors, or through targeting the new millionaires (PCAH, 1997:21).

It should also be recognized that such national patterns of individual philanthropic support for the arts may not be equally true for all regions of the country. For example, a recent California Community Foundation report (CCM, 1997) gathered information on the charitable giving habits and preferences of Los Angeles County—noting that it demonstrated that "the region is far from the penurious community it is sometimes reputed to be" (CCM, Press Release, 1997). In comparing Los Angeles County philanthropic patterns with national patterns, it reported that nearly twice the number of L.A. households (17%) contributed to the arts than the national figure (CCM, 1997:20). Generally, more L.A. households made some type of charitable donation (74% vs. 69%; CCM, 1997:9) and somewhat fewer engaged in some type of volunteer activity (44% vs. 49%; CCM, 1997:49). In terms of attitudes, L.A. residents gave the arts a low priority among the range of charitable activities and ranked the organizational effectiveness of arts organizations as sixth out of eight. It also found that people who contributed to the arts were significantly more likely (61% vs. 49%; CCM, 1997:41) to think that federal support for the arts was a good thing.

Foundations have been another important philanthropic actor in cultural activities. Among all program areas supported by foundations, arts and cultural projects consistently garnered between a 13- and a 15- percent share throughout the 1980s and into the 1990s. However, this proportion fell to 12.8 percent in 1994 and declined further to 12 percent in 1995. In part, this proportion can be influenced by the number of extremely large grants awarded: in 1995 there were no grants over $10 million and only three of $5 million. In contrast, in 1994, at least six grants of $5 million were reported including three in excess of $10 million (Renz, Mandler & Tran, 1997:71). Even as the foundation share of giving to culture remained relatively steady

Table 1
Foundation Arts Support by Major Subject
Percentages & Dollar Amounts (in millions of dollars)

	1983	1986	1989	1992	1995	1996
Performing Arts						
%	38.8	33.5	33.6	37.9	36.0	32.8
$	92.2	108.0	169.1	275.4	270.3	295.2
Museums						
%	25.5	33.0	30.5	31.0	27.0	32.1
$	60.6	106.2	153.5	225.4	204.4	289.0
Media/ Communications						
%	12.1	8.6	11.8	7.9	9.0	10.7
$	28.9	27.5	59.3	57.0	65.9	96.6
Multidisciplinary						
%	6.7	6.9	7.6	6.9	11.0	8.3
$	16.0	22.0	38.0	50.3	83.7	74.7
Arts-Related Humanities						
%	5.2	5.2	4.6	5.4	5.0	4.4
$	12.4	21.9	29.8	39.3	35.3	39.9
Historical						
%	4.1	5.2	4.6	5.5	6.0	6.3
$	9.6	16.8	23.3	39.7	46.7	56.5
Visual						
%	1.7	3.2	2.7	3.4	4.0	2.9
$	4.0	10.3	13.5	24.6	33.2	26.3
Other (* see below)						
%	5.7	2.8	3.5	2.0	2.5	2.4
$	13.8	9.0	17.0	14.1	19.2	21.7
TOTAL						
%	99.8	98.4	98.9	100	100.5	99.9
$	$237.5	$321.7	$503.5	$725.8	$758.7	$899.9

Sources: Nathan Weber and Loren Renz, *Arts Funding* (New York: Foundation Center, 1993) p. 58–9; Loren Renz, *Arts Funding Revisited* (New York: Foundation Center, 1995) p. 13; Loren Renz, Crystal Mandler, and Trinh C. Tran, *Foundation Giving, 1997* (New York: Foundation Center, 1997) p. 66, xv.

* "Other" includes support for Policy, Arts Libraries, Artists' Services, International Exchanges, Management and Fundraising activities.

during the 1980s and into the 1990s the distribution of this support varied by subject and type.

As can be seen in Table 1, the performing arts have consistently received a third or more of all foundation arts support. Museums have come in second, rising gradually from about 25 percent in 1983 to 32 percent in 1996. Meanwhile the absolute dollar amounts awarded to the various artforms have tended to increase over time but with year to year fluctuations: in the case of the performing arts from $92.2 million in 1983 to $290 million in 1995; in the case of museums from $60.6 million in 1983 to $284 million in 1993. In contrast to these predominantly institutional art activities, support for the humanities and the visual arts is much smaller. Foundations have only committed 4–5 percent of their cultural funds to the humanities, 4–6 percent to historical preservation activities, and 2–4 percent to the visual arts.

Looking at foundation support another way, philanthropy can support different types of activities—such as general operating expenses, capital expenses, programming, professional development or other activities such as research, emergency aid, or technical assistance.

As seen in Table 2, operating support has experienced a major decline between 1983 and 1992, falling from 31.3 percent of the total to 16.4 percent. This has been cause for concern among many arts organizations, since operating money can be difficult to raise from individual donors and yet is essential to institutional maintenance. This concern may underlie both institutional efforts to build endowments and community efforts to launch stabilization campaigns. Alternatively, recent recommendations from national and local studies have called on arts organizations to engage in administrative collaborations (American Assembly, 1997; Cleveland Foundation, 1996). Such collaborations may represent an alternative strategy concerning operating expenses: controlling and decreasing operating costs rather than subsidizing them. Capital support and funds for professional development have also declined, although not as profoundly as operating support. Offshoots of these declines include concern over deferred facilities maintenance and support for individuals (who were most frequently awarded fellowships, residencies, internships, and scholarships under the professional development category). In contrast, program support was the only type of funding that consistently increased between 1983 and 1992. However, one should also recognize that the amount of foundation support that is categorized as "unspecified" has nearly tripled during this same period (from 11.5% in 1983 to 31.9% in 1992).

Private philanthropy has been facilitated by public policy and has sought to influence policy concerning the arts and culture (Schuster, 1985; Wyszomirski, 1987). Tax policy helps contain operating costs through grants of exemption from real estate and property taxes as well as confers discounted postal rates. Tax policy also provides an incentive for private donations to nonprofit cultural organizations through tax deductibility. Copyright policies seek to protect creative rights and returns as an incentive to artists, scholars, and scientists. Trade policies seek to assure American creative and intellectual products have fair access and treatment in the global marketplace. Both copyright and trade policies seek to facilitate the earning power and opportu-

Table 2
Foundation Arts Support by Types of Support Awarded
Percentages & Dollar Amounts (in millions of dollars)*

	1983	1986	1989	1992
Operating				
%	31.3	21.9	17.8	16.4
$	74.3	70.5	89.7	119.3
Capital				
%	38.0	44.1	32.2	30.7
$	90.3	141.9	161.7	223.2
Program				
%	28.5	28.9	33.8	35.5
$	67.9	93.0	169.9	257.7
Professional Development				
%	5.2	6.1	6.0	4.3
$	12.3	19.6	30.2	31.3
Other**				
%	2.9	2.6	2.6	2.6
$	6.9	6.3	12.9	19.2
Unspecified				
%	11.5	12.0	25.9	23.2
$	27.4	38.7	130.0	168.5
TOTAL				
%	117.4	115.6	118.3	112.7
$	279.1	370	594.4	819.2

Sources: Nathan Weber and Loren Renz, *Arts Funding* (New York: Foundation Center, 1993) p.78; Loren Renz, *Arts Funding Revisited* (New York: Foundation Center, 1995) p. 19.

* Grants may occasionally be for multiple types of support and thus would be counted twice.
** "Other" includes support for Research, Emergency Funds, and Technical Assistance.

nities of American's cultural industries. Direct grant support for the arts and humanities at the federal, state, and local levels took root during the past thirty years, with the creation of the National Endowments for the Arts and the Humanities, the Institute for Museum Services (now the Institute for Museum and Library Services), the Corporation for Public Broadcasting, the National Trust for Historic Preservation, as well as state, local, and regional arts agencies. Grants from these agencies often required matches from private monies and public cultural agencies sometimes entered into explicit program partnerships with private foundations.

Conversely, foundations were often instrumental in the establishment of such agencies and in catalyzing governmental patronage—whether it was the

Rockefeller Foundation and the Twentieth Century Fund with regard to the NEA or the Carnegie Corporation with regard to public broadcasting. More recently, foundations have continued to focus governmental attention on specific issues such as dance preservation, touring, and creation (Dance/USA, 1992; NEA/Mellon Foundation, n.d.; Netzer and Parker, 1993; Weisberger, 1997); on public television (Twentieth Century Fund, 1993); and on spurring community support (Cleveland Foundation, 1996). Foundations are capable of independent action, and may also act as an alternative or a complement to public philanthropy. From the mid-1950s well into the 1970s foundations—led by the Ford Foundation—exerted the most powerful voice in cultural philanthropy, underwriting the establishment of a national network of dance, theater, and symphony organizations. Among private foundations in 1962, the Ford Foundation was the largest institutional source of funding for the arts. In 1992, although still a major private funder, the Ford Foundation was in ninth place among private institutional funders while awarding almost $11 million annually (or one-fifth the amount of the top foundation). By 1976, the leading spot nationally had shifted to the public sector where the National Endowment for the Arts had become the largest institutional funder in the field.[1] Furthermore, the NEA bolstered its financial influence with an unparalleled level of expertise represented in its staff and panels; this expertise equipped it to perform systematically and strategically (Cobb, 1996:18). Indeed, Kenneth Goody (1983:8) reports that in 1966, foundations accounted for 57 percent of the total unearned income of arts organizations, as compared to roughly 7 percent coming from federal and state sources combined. By 1980, the foundation proportion was down to 36 percent while the combined federal and state proportion was 31 percent. Thus the relative public-private proportions in the cultural support mix have fluctuated over time; so too has the ability to exert leadership in cultural philanthropy shifted with these variations.

Discussion of such broad public-private dimensions, while a useful overview, still masks some important variations within both the public sector support streams and the private sector philanthropic streams. Among public funders, nearly a decade of controversy has eroded the NEA's financial and political capital and, consequently, dampened its philanthropic impact. Since 1992, the budget of the NEA has dropped from $175.9 million to $98 million. Substantial staff cutbacks and wholesale program reorganization have cut into its expertise and its ability to systematically affect entire fields or disciplines. Persistent political criticism and a bureaucratic siege mentality have diminished its capacity for program innovation, policy entrepreneurship, and national leadership.

Conversely, as a combined force, state arts agencies now have triple the financial resources available at the federal level. However, increased resources and capacity of SAAs in general does not mean that all states have equal philanthropic potential or that the composite resources are used in a coordinated manner. While many states have experienced significant increases in recent years, the picture is quite uneven. For example, states with major cultural industries, such as New York and California, have not fared particularly well. The New York State Council on the Arts lost nearly half its funding in the early 1990s. The California arts council budget has remained static at around $12 million, an amount that averages out to less than 40 cents per capita—a small amount for a state of its size and cultural activity. Alternatively, other states, like Florida and Ohio, have secured substantial increases as the decade of the 1990s progressed. Meanwhile, local arts agencies have been a consistently bright spot of public funding for the arts, experiencing combined increases throughout the past two decades. Local arts agency budgets range from $10,000 to $88 million; the combined 1997 budgets of just the 50 largest U.S. cities totaled $242.8 million (AFA, 1997:2). However, even in an era of decentralization, the ability of state and/or local public funding to replace the lost leadership role of the NEA is questionable since both state and local resources are disaggregated among nearly 60 state, regional, and special jurisdiction entities on the one hand, and among approximately 4000 governmental and nonprofit agencies at the local level.

Among foundations, independent foundations (including family foundations) have accounted for the lion's share of private institutional funding, with corporate foundations coming in a distant second, and community foundations trailing. Indeed, as can be seen from Table 3, independent foundations (such as the Ford Foundation or the Pew Charitable Trusts) account for between three-fourths and four-fifths of the cultural dollars awarded by all foundations (independent, corporate, and community). Furthermore, a significant share of foundation cultural philanthropy is concentrated among the 25 largest organizations. In 1992, the top 25 foundations accounted for 41.4 percent of the arts funding dollars; half the funding increase that occurred between 1989 and 1992 was attributable to the actions of one funder (Lila Wallace–Reader's Digest Fund—a relative newcomer to the field in the early 1990s). In 1992, the arts program resources for the top 25 private, institutional funders ranged widely—at the top were the Lila Wallace–Reader's Digest Fund at $55.8 million, the Mellon Foundation at $29.4 million, the Pew Charitable Trusts at $18.7 million, and the MacArthur Foundation at $17.4 million. The remaining 21 foundations moved through relatively even budget gradations down to eight foundations in the $5 to $6 million range (Renz, 1995:10). Only three years earlier (in 1989) the range had spread between $28 million and $3.8 million (Weber and Renz, 1993:45). The top 25 largest arts funders are overwhelmingly independent foundations: in 1989 only two corporate foundations and one community foundation made the list. In effect then, a relatively small number of independent foundations still have the financial capacity to exert considerable influence in cultural philanthropy. Indeed, the combined cultural program funds of the top three private foundations now total more than the entire annual budget of the NEA.

Table 3
Foundation Arts Support by Types of Foundations (percentages)

	1983	1986	1989	1992
Independent & Family	79.1	78.5	77.8	80.7
Corporate	15.0	14.7	17.4	14.4
Community	5.9	6.8	4.8	5.0
TOTAL	100	100	100	100.1

Sources: Nathan Weber and Loren Renz, *Arts Funding* (New York: Foundation Center, 1993) p. 57 ; Loren Renz, *Arts Funding Revisited* (New York: Foundation Center, 1995) p. 13.

Philanthropic Leadership to a Multi-Polar System

Given the shifts in resources among both public and private institutional funders, there may be no single "superpower" or philanthropic leader today as there had been when the Ford Foundation was preeminent in the late 1950s and early 1960s or when the NEA set much of the agenda for institutional cultural philanthropy in the 1970s and into the 1980s. Indeed, a different pattern of philanthropic influence may be emerging for the twenty-first century. Perhaps a new multi-polar system is emerging that might be comprised of philanthropic coalitions and be capable of addressing both diverse and overlapping agendas. Such coalitions might be coordinated (but not directed) by what in interest group politics are called "peak associations"— that is, national groups of organizations or of other associations. When interactive with networks of policymakers, arts administrators (e.g., through arts service organizations), and cultural policy analysts and researchers, such philanthropic coalitions would also constitute key elements of a national cultural policy community (Wyszomirski, 1995).

Characteristics of potential philanthropic coalition leaders can be discerned. Potential coalition leadership organizations should have the ability to bring together various of sources of philanthropic capital (including money, expertise, and trust/authority) in at least a subsector (e.g., foundations; corporations; universities; think tanks; federal, state, or local cultural agencies). Optimally, potential leaders will have a capacity to bring together actors across sectors (public and private) or subsectors. At present, at least five organizations exhibit some (or some combination) of these characteristics and thus seem to be likely candidates for coalition leadership.

(1) Grantmakers in the Arts—an affinity group of private foundations interested in the arts and culture;

(2) Americans for the Arts—a combination of the national membership organization of community arts agencies and of the former American Council

for the Arts, which was a network of arts supporters, patrons, and business leaders;

(3) the National Assembly of State Arts Agencies, which is a national membership association of state and regional arts councils that receive both annual appropriations from their respective legislatures and also receive almost half of the NEA's annual budget in block grants;

(4) the President's Committee for the Arts and the Humanities, which is a fifteen-year-old public-private task force appointed by the President of the United States to encourage private sector support and to increase public appreciation of the value of the arts and the humanities. Its members include not only private citizens with strong commitments to culture, but also the heads of 13 federal agencies with cultural programs; and

(5) the Center for Arts and Culture, a new think tank focused on the arts and culture dedicated to coalescing and mobilizing research and information to inform policy planning, both in the governmental realm and among private sector organizations.

What are the trends, advantages, and issues involved in each of these possibilities?

Grantmakers in the Arts (GIA)

The first of these—the Grantmakers in the Arts (GIA)—began as an affinity group within the Council on Foundations that went on to set up its own nonprofit organization (Focke, 1998). Founded in 1985, its purpose is "to strengthen arts philanthropy and its role in contributing to a supportive environment for the arts nationwide." GIA held its first conference in 1987–88, began an intermittent newsletter in 1989, and organized a membership component in 1992–93. Today the organization has approximately 200 organizational members (each of which can include up to 10 individual members) that represent organizations in 35 states.

The GIA's first funded study commissioned the Foundation Center to produce an Arts Funding Benchmark Study to identify the major dimensions of arts funding throughout the 1980s as well as conduct a survey of arts funders and arts organizations concerning their perceptions of funding needs and grantmaker performance. The report was intended to better inform and empower arts grantmakers and assist their work in planning, program development, guideline construction, self-evaluation, field and needs assessments, local research, and policy formation (Weber & Renz, 1993:13). Between 1989 and 1992, foundation funders found themselves under growing pressure to increase their cultural support as federal government support was threatened and state arts funding experienced cuts so that combined state funding dropped from $292 million in FY90 to $214.7 million in FY92. In order to both monitor the effects of such changes and keep data current, GIA again worked with the Foundation Center to update the study in 1995 (Renz, 1995);

a third update is currently in process, with an anticipated publication date late in 1998 (Renz, 1998). In addition to the national association, there are more informal regional and local GIA groups around the country, and at the most recent annual meeting in San Antonio, members expressed a desire for more regional forums. In general, GIA meetings and publications allow foundation funders of the arts and culture to exchange information, discuss issues and formulate thinking on issues, germinate collaborative or cooperative efforts, seek to get the arts on the agenda of other funders, and provide professional development services for foundation staff members. In recent years, as the number of family foundations has grown, a loosely organized family foundation group concerned with the arts has evolved within GIA.

Particularly in the 1990s, GIA has helped cultivate more self-awareness and group awareness among private foundations of all types, including large and small independent foundations, corporate foundations, community foundations, and family foundations. And it has added to the intellectual capital of the group through commissioned reports, through national and regional forums as well as through engaging a peer network. GIA has facilitated the ability of clusters of arts grantmakers to collaborate on projects of interest to the field, such as a study of financial support for individual artists (Focke, 1996) and on the establishment of the Center for the Arts and Culture in Washington, D.C.[2] Clearly, through GIA, private foundations have built a capacity to integrate and inform their separate and individual activities. Thus rather than 200 (or more if one considers all foundations that fund the arts) disaggregated funders, GIA allows a loose confederation of private funders to both cultivate special interests and pursue common interests, to have both particularistic views and broad field and environment perspectives. Given the size and scope of the nonprofit cultural subsector, any one foundation is still unlikely to have sufficient funding (or staff) resources to exert philanthropic leadership in the style that the Ford Foundation once did. But through an effective affinity group such as GIA, a group of foundations may, collectively and through a division of focus, be capable of exercising philanthropic leadership. Indeed some of this seems to be occurring, a subject that will be discussed more generally when the discussion turns to emerging issues and themes.

Americans for the Arts (AFA)

Americans for the Arts (AFA) presents another sort of philanthropic coalition—one that involves both public and private segments, both individual patrons and funding institutions, both local and national perspectives. These are not always easy perspectives to bridge, and AFA (in its current incarnation) is still a relatively new organization. As one of the premier arts advocacy groups in the country, it is positioned to act as a policy entrepreneur for ideas and models developed through private philanthropy, local experience, or research, and to identify ways in which public policy facilitates, hinders, or interacts with private initiatives. The AFA has been adding to the intellectual capital base of cultural philanthropy and policy, both through its library and information clearinghouse and its individual and collaborative research efforts.[3] The AFA is ideally positioned to gather information about program and policy innovations that are occurring at the local levels and bringing them to the attention of national funders and policymakers, both public and private. It is also working to develop more interactions between the commercial entertainment industries and the nonprofit arts sector, potentially opening up new possibilities for collaboration and support.

National Assembly of State Arts Agencies (NASAA)

Third, the National Assembly of State Arts Agencies (NASAA) is an association of public arts funders at the state level—a locus of increasing action and influence in this period of decentralization and devolution. Collectively, it also represents those NEA grantees which receive the largest amount of money from this federal agency. Over the years, NASAA has built an information system on SAA grantmaking, comparable in scope to the grant information system at the Foundation Center for private arts grantmaking. NASAA is also positioned to collect and disseminate information about program activities, project results, and policy initiatives from its members across the country. Furthermore, both NASAA and AFA are strategically located to facilitate and monitor collaborative efforts in two very active areas of interest to arts organizations, arts funders, and arts policymakers—art education and cultural tourism.

President's Committee on the Arts and the Humanities (PCAH)

Fourth, the President's Committee on the Arts and the Humanities (PCAH), while a federal entity, has the potential to link public patronage sources across various agencies of the federal government as well as to link public and private cultural philanthropy interests. During its history (and that of its predecessor, the Presidential Task Force on the Arts and Humanities in 1981), the PCAH has (1) provided a forum for discussion of national concerns and focused attention on issues such as cultural conservation needs, international cultural exchanges and affairs, cultural tourism, and strengthening support for the arts and humanities; (2) initiated model projects such as the Fund for New American Plays and the National Committee to Save America's Cultural Collections; (3) enhanced the visibility of cultural activities, through, among other activities, recommending the creation of the National Medal of Arts; (4) helped to catalyze increased private support for the arts (e.g., stimulating private contribution of more than $11 million for 16 collaborative projects), monitoring and recommending changes in tax policy, and supporting efforts to introduce secondary students to charitable practices and American traditions of philanthropy (PCAH, 1988, 1992, 1997; Cobb, 1996; Moskin and Gunettler, n.d.).

Center for Arts and Culture (CAC)

Fifth, and most recently, there is now the Center for Arts and Culture (CAC), the first Washington think tank devoted to cultural policy. As such, it is in the process of developing networks of academic and study organizations as well as of individual scholars and policy analysts, philanthropists, and policy makers in an effort to "support and promote an effective cultural policy process, to build the cultural policy field, and to impact cultural policy" (CAC, 1998). As a politically aware policy analysis organization, the Center is neither partisan nor advocacy oriented. Therefore it is positioning itself as a both a knowledge broker and a policy entrepreneur, linking decisionmakers (public and private) and analysts in an effort to stimulate a more informed policy dialogue. The Center does not suffer from the vices of its virtues as do many of the other coalition options mentioned above. It does not have members that it needs to represent and so escapes the possible (or perceived) bias of membership organizations such as AFA, NASAA, and even GIA. Nor does it have an implicit partisan or political identification as does the PCAH — which is, after all, "the President's" committee. Furthermore, the Center has the intent of bridging and linking between sectors, between funders and recipients, between doers and thinkers, and between information and application. However, it is the newest and most formative of the five options identified here and it is the one premised on the most fragile and intangible sources of leadership authority—knowledge.

Each of the foregoing potential philanthropic coalitions is involved in building information and intellectual capital to better inform philanthropy, management and policy. Each seeks to improve communication between elements within a philanthropic sector (e.g., among private foundations, state arts agencies, etc.) or between philanthropic sectors (e.g., between public and private funders). Each has established or is in the process of creating a network of contacts and forums for the exchange of information, ideas, and options, and for the discussion of issues and models. As such, all of these potential philanthropic coalition hubs are part of an emerging cultural policy community—with policy seen in the broad sense of patterns of action regarding conscious and authoritative goals. As such, policy is not limited to governmental actions and decisions but rather encompasses the policies of foundations and even of specific arts organizations. All of these philanthropic coalitions—whether well developed or relatively new—have resources, assets, and access that can serve as a basis for exercising leadership, but no one entity has a clearly dominant role. Together in some sort of grand coalition, these or other associational groupings might be the emerging pillars of a multi-polar cultural philanthropy.

Emerging Issues, Assumptions, and Practices

Inherent to the preceding discussion are a number of changing perceptions and working assumptions among many cultural philanthropists. The times, conditions, and the record of past activities also give rise to a set of issues—some continuing and some new—that frequently surface. Formulating strategies that reflect these assumptions and respond to current issues is generating new or revised practices.

Assumptions and Perceptions

Cultural philanthropists—both private and public—often observe that they are questioning, even changing their minds about things that they have long taken for granted or as givens (Collins, 1998; Godfrey, 1997; Bradford, 1998; PCAH, 1997; Wyszomirski, 1995). After nearly forty years of building and supporting the supply of nonprofit, professional arts activities, there is now a sense that there may have been an overemphasis on the production side, particularly in the face of a sense of declining leisure time, an aging population, and the widespread availability and competition of recorded, broadcast, and electronic media options. Presumed cultural demand supported a supply side strategy and has but come into question as national funders realized how ambiguous, vague, and changeable public attitudes are concerning the arts and culture—and consequently what a slender reed this is to premise audience development, patron and volunteer development, and public support initiatives (Dwyer & Frankel, 1997; Filicko, 1996 & 1997).

In its 1996 program report on the arts, the Mellon Foundation notes that "significant changes have occurred in Americans' willingness to support the arts ... signalled in part by recent large reductions in government funding for these fields" (Mellon, 1996). A new uncertainty about public funding prospects derives from federal cutbacks after decades of growth, a realization that static to declining federal funding is not merely a temporary aberration, and a fear that federal actions will set a negative example for state, corporate, and foundation funders in a sort of reverse catalytic effect. Furthermore, the discouraging federal funding picture was exacerbated by the discovery that the arts market share of private philanthropy (which had been so consistent in the 1980s and into the 1990s) has recently been losing ground.

Another basic premise of cultural philanthropy has been the inevitability of the "cost disease" of nonprofit arts organizations. Living with this "disease" required private and public subsidies, where each seemed to catalyze the other (Kreidler, 1996). While the national arts infrastructure was growing, this premise allowed for an expanded, composite income gap, encouraged arts organizations to pursue grantsmanship strategies rather than earned income approaches (Stevens, 1996), and fostered greater managerial professionalism in arts organizations. Although usually unspoken, there also seemed to be an assumption that in cultivating unearned income, the emphasis was on institutional sources (foundations, corporations, public arts agencies) rather than on individuals of wealth.

Other assumptions included a tendency to operate in particularistic ways — dealing with individual fields, with individual institutions and artists, and with specific projects. Such customizing had its advantages and was probably very useful in seeding local institutions and institutional growth. Finally, the foundation (and policy) world of cultural philanthropy seems to have presumed a sense of stability regarding what organizational players were involved and important, who key staff were, and how programs were structured. An important component of this stability concerned working definitions of what was meant by "the arts" and "culture" — which was increasingly focused on professional, nonprofit organizations especially in the performing arts as well as museums.

During the 1990s many of these assumptions have been challenged, amended, and even replaced. The cultural philanthropy world has seen the arrival of new and major players, like the Lila Wallace–Reader's Digest Fund, the increase of family foundations interested in the arts, the establishment of artist and/or arts focused foundations,[4] and an interest in cultivating community foundation interest in the arts. A number of long-tenured program staff have retired or moved on, foundation (and agency) leadership and perspectives have changed, many programs have reassessed their priorities and approaches, and some program areas have been reconfigured.[5] A number of foundations have become very interested in the "demand" side of the arts — including audience development, arts education, and public awareness campaigns. Many are rethinking their working definition of the arts — ranging from narrow constructions limited to the major performing arts disciplines and museums through the inclusion of media, literary, folk, and other arts to wondering what the relation between the nonprofit and the commercial arts might be.

Issues and Conditions

A full discussion of the contextual factors influencing cultural philanthropy is beyond the scope of this paper. However, a few of the major concerns can at least be identified here. These include dealing with the effects of changing population demographics, new technologies, and globalization. Multiculturalism takes on a whole new perspective for many communities and for the nation as the composition of the population changes; the aging of the population, particularly of the baby boom cohort, and its implications not only for cultural philanthropy but for other social issues; the growth in minority populations with the attendant development of new pluralistic concentrations geographically and no-majority communities (and even states, such as California). Globalization—along with mergers and consolidations— has changed the terrain of corporate philanthropy and corporate support for the arts and is coinciding with a generational change of corporate leadership where the new executives are perceived to be less altruistic than previous ones (NCA, 1996).

Competition for resources and eroded trust in social institutions of all kinds has given rise to increased calls for accountability and performance evaluation. Both arts organizations and arts funders are grappling with the challenge to demonstrate impact and engage in assessment in a more competitive environment where individual artists sometimes seem to be in competition with arts organizations and presenters, where the arts may be in competition with other aspects of social philanthropy, and where the non-profit arts and the commercial arts seem to compete for audience time, money, and attention. Cultural funders, both public and private, seem to be reconsidering the axiom of "art for art's sake" as a guiding principle and are showing increased interest in the social and/or civic uses of the arts as well as in the public purposes of the arts. And issues of how to nurture new talent and how to balance preservation needs with innovation, support for established organizations and activities, and support for relative newcomers, between big and smaller organizations, are also on the agendas of many funders.

Emerging Practices and Themes

In response to the foregoing considerations, cultural philanthropy seems to be adopting new approaches and emphasizing different tactics in the following ways:

1. More holistic thinking: Cultural philanthropists seems to be looking for the "big picture" which is leading them to rethink, undertake research, and design programs using a systems approach or an ecological perspective. Locally, foundations are looking to "build a field" or a cultural community in order to bridge the fragmented, specialized, and even isolated relationships among arts organizations. Part of this is a reaction to and an effort to avoid crisis management and crisis philanthropy. Partly, this is an effort to cultivate leaders and advocates for the field and to develop better ways of working together strategically and tactically. Nationally, there is a similar attempt to transform the arts community into an cultural policy community, which is awakening a greater need for new types of information and additional coalition partners. Furthermore, as cultural philanthropists become more conscious of the scope and depth of change that is occurring in their assumptions and context, they are recognizing that they are no longer in a program

management phase but in an agenda-setting and defining stage where it is useful to "take a systems view of the cultural sector." The very notion of a "cultural sector" that encompasses more than the professional nonprofit arts organizations is quite new and the exact dimensions of this sector are still under discussion. So too is the sense of "cultural policy," a concept that simply did not have currency five years ago. Ecologically, cultural philanthropists seem more aware of and more interested in how the cultural system fits into and is affected by other systems, such as press coverage and content, entertainment and other leisure activities, the relation of art production and audience demand, or recognizing that cultural activities can be hidden assets for community building.

2. New working relationships: whereas both cultural organizations and foundations, have deeply ingrained norms regarding their organizational autonomy and uniqueness, collaborations seem to be the new watchword. Foundations engage in collaborations with one another and even cultivate a sense of themselves as a field, focusing around specific projects (the Center for Arts and Culture), goals (nurturing new artistic talent or building a cultural policy community), or associations (GIA). Funders also encourage grantees to engage in a range of collaborations from information sharing, to coproductions, to administrative cost-sharing, to advocacy coalitions. Public patrons search for new partners outside the cultural realm, whether in education, social services, libraries, human services, or community development corporations.

3. Taking a long-term view and using new levers: as cultural philanthropists try to perceive and shape the new agenda, they are experimenting with new ways of taking action, focusing on some new targets of opportunity, and looking to the long term. Instead of just trying to leverage money, foundation programs often aim to prompt greater public awareness and interest, to build organizational capacity, to invest in community and self-sustainability. For example, the investment in public awareness will, it is hoped, pay off both in stronger attitudinal support for the arts and in more audience participation. The Lila Wallace Fund is using a new lever—community foundations—in a five-year program to build audiences, awareness, and new resources for the arts in about ten pilot communities. The Joyce Mertz-Gilmore Foundation is working with local service organizations to reach clusters of emerging artists and arts organizations of color (Crane, 1996). Other foundations are working with national service organizations to reach entire fields and to build field capacity.

As they progress, funders are also exhibiting a greater concern with evaluating the design, process, and impact of their efforts—in part because they are in "new territory" and need to monitor their actions and in part because others are interested in their experiences (whether from accountability concerns or from modeling and prototype interests). Government funders are concerned with performance review as a management and budget tool. Decisionmakers of all types are interested in results and impact and seeking new ways and standards of measurement.

There is considerable experimentation with new mechanisms and targets of action. State arts agencies are experimenting with a diversity of public trust fund arrangements to build endowments to supplement annual appropriations. Local communities and arts agencies are experimenting with United Arts Funds, earmarked taxes, and special tax districts to support the arts. Private foundations are working with fiscal agents and service organizations to reach new or different grantees, both through regranting and technical assistance. Arts organizations are working to cultivate the next generation of donors, sometimes with the support of local foundations—through junior guilds and education programs for new collectors. Community foundations and regional groups of foundations are working to cultivate new arts donors or to find entry points into new corporate wealth, particularly in the high tech and entertainment industries.

In management aspects, cultural philanthropy is not only interested in collaborations but in fostering organizational entrepreneurship among grantees and in responding to a new generation of potential donors who are interested in philanthropic investments that are self-renewing, not just self-perpetuating. Just as an earlier generation of philanthropy urged arts organizations to be more businesslike—meaning better managed—the coming generation is urging that the arts become more businesslike in seeking strategic alliance with the commercial arts, in tending the talent pipeline that criss-crosses the for-profit and nonprofit sectors, and in mastering technology. Finally, funders are realizing that even the most professional management available cannot ensure organizational adaptability and survival unless the board members of nonprofit arts organizations are aware of the changes that are occurring in their environments and support systems.

Notes

1. As the late MacNeil Lowry, eminent director of the Ford Foundation's arts and cultural program, testified to the 1990 Independent Commission on the NEA, "The requisite size that allows for long-range planning is no longer located at foundations but at the NEA, which since 1976 has become the single largest source of annual funding of the arts."

2. An informal consortium of national foundations supported the creation of the Center. These included the Rockefeller, Mellon, Nathan Cummings, and Howard Gilman foundations, and Kenan Institute for the Arts.

3. For an example of AFA's research efforts, see Arts in the Local Economy (NALAA, 1993) as well as its annual reports on United Arts Funds. Its collaborative research efforts include Coming Up Taller: Arts and Humanities Programs for Children and Youth at Risk (Weitz, 1996), which was done in partnership with the President's Committee on the Arts and the Humanities (PCAH). Another example is the new research collaboration between AFA and The Ohio State

University Program in Arts Policy and Administration to develop national and local profiles of the arts and of the revenues of nonprofit arts organizations. The economic impact study had the support of the Charles Mott Foundation; the PCAH had funding from five independent foundations (including the Nathan Cummings Foundation and the Harris Foundation) as well as a corporate foundation (the GE Fund). The Profiles Project is being supported by the Pew Charitable Trusts.

4. These include the Thomas Kenan Institute for the Arts, the Andy Warhol Foundation for the Visual Arts, and the Robert Mapplethorpe Foundation.

5. For example, at the Ford Foundation, the relevant program has been reconfigured as the Education, Media, Arts and Culture Program, with two branches—the Education, Knowledge and Religion section and the Media, Arts, and Culture section, each of which is headed by a different deputy director (Ford Foundation, 1996). Meanwhile, at the Mellon Foundation, the Arts Program has been divided into two tracks, each of which is managed by its own program officer—one concerned with museums and the other with the performing arts. The guiding assumption was that each field is organized according to different principles, has different kinds of assets, relates to their audiences and constituents on different terms, and operates within separate, though equally complex environments (Mellon, 1996).

References

American Assembly. "The Arts and the Public Purpose." Report of the 92nd American Assembly held at Arden House, May 29–June 1, 1997.

American Association of Fund Raising Counsel (AAFRC) *Giving USA, 1997.* New York: AAFRC, 1997.

Americans for the Arts (AFA). "U.S. Urban Art Federation 1997: A Statistical Report about the Budgets and Programming of Arts Councils in the 50 Largest U.S. Cities." Washington, DC: Americans for the Arts, June 1997.

Bradford, Gigi (Executive Director of the Center for Arts and Culture). Personal communication with author, 1998.

California Community Foundation (CCM). *"Los Angeles County Giving and Volunteering Benchmark Survey: Overview.* Report on a poll conducted by the Field Research Corporation, December 1997.

———. "News Release." Los Angeles, 22 December 1997.

Center for Arts and Culture (CAC). "Fact Sheet" Washington, DC: March 1998.

Cleveland Foundation. *Securing the Future: Civic Study Commission on the Performing Arts.* Cleveland, OH: The Cleveland Foundation, October 1996.

Cobb, Nina Kressner. *Looking Ahead: Private Sector Giving to the Arts and the Humanities.* Washington, DC: President's Committee on the Arts and the Humanities, 1996.

Collins, Dennis (Executive Director of the Irvine Foundation). Telephone Interview with the author. 27 March 1998.

Crane, Robert (Executive Director of the Joyce Mertz-Gilmore Foundation). Communication with author, 12 July 1996.

Dance/USA. *Domestic Dance Touring: A Study with Recommendations for Private-Sector Support*. Washington, DC: Dance/USA: a study commissioned by the Lila Wallace–Reader's Digest Fund, March 1992.

Dwyer, Christine M. and Susan Frankel. "Summary of Conversations About Cultural Policy with Selected Foundations." Philadelphia: Report Commissioned by the Pew Charitable Trusts, December 1997.

Filicko, Therese. "In What Spirit Do Americans Cultivate the Arts? A Review of Survey Questions on the Arts," *The Journal of Arts Management, Law and Society*, 1996, 26 (3), 221–246.

———. What Do We Need to Know About Culture?" Paper presented at the 23rd Annual Conference on Social Theory, Politics, and the Arts, Cocoa Beach, Florida, October 2–4, 1997.

Focke, Anne. "Financial Support for Artists: A Study of Past and Current Support, with Reflections on the Findings and Recommendations for Future Action." Seattle: Anne Focke, December 1996.

———. (Editor of the *Newsletter* for Grantmakers in the Arts). Telephone Interview with the author, 25 March 1998.

Ford Foundation. *1996 Annual Report*. New York: The Ford Foundation, 1997.

Godfrey, Marian. "Advancing the Arts on the National Agenda: Program Strategy for 1998–2000." Philadelphia: Pew Charitable Trusts, internal report, December 1997.

Goody, Kenneth L. "The Funding of the Arts and Artists, Humanities and Humanists in the United States." New York: Report prepared for the Rockefeller Foundation, November 1983.

Kreidler, John. "Leverage Lost: The Nonprofit Arts in the Post-Fort Era," *The Journal of Arts Management, Law and Society*, 1996, 26 (2), 79–100.

Andrew W. Mellon Foundation. *1996 Program in the Arts*. http://222.mellon.org/arts96.html

Moskin, Bill and Sandy Guettler. "Exploring America through Its Culture." Washington, DC: President's Committee on the Arts and the Humanities, n.d.

National Assembly of Local Arts Agencies (NALAA) *Arts in the Local Economy* (Project Summary Report). Washington, DC: NALAA, 1993.

National Cultural Alliance. "Public Leadership for the Arts and Humanities: The Challenge of Change." Washington, DC: Summary Report of the Leadership Dinners, December 1996.

National Endowment for the Arts and the Andrew W. Mellon Foundation. *Images of American Dance: Documenting and Preserving a Cultural Heritage*. New York: Report Prepared by William Keens, Leslie Hansen Kopp and Mindy N. Levine, n.d.

Netzer, Dick and Ellen Parker. *Dancemakers*. Washington, DC: NEA Research Division Report #28, October 1993.

President's Committee on the Arts and the Humanities (PCAH). "Report to the President." Washington, DC, 1988.

———. "Report to the President." Washington, DC: PCAH, December 1992.

———. *Creative America*. Washington, DC: PCAH, February 1997.

Renz, Loren. *Arts Funding Revisited: An Update on Foundation Trends in the 1990s*. New York: The Foundation Center in Cooperation with Grantmakers in the Arts, 1995.

———. (Vice President for Research at the Foundation Center). Telephone Interview with the author, 25 March 1998.

Renz, Loren, Crystal Mandler, and Trinh C. Tran. *Foundation Giving, 1997.* New York: The Foundation Center, 1997.

Stevens, Louise. "The Earnings Shift: The New Bottom Line Paradigm for the Arts Industry in a Market-Driven Era." *The Journal of Arts Management, Law, and Society,* 1996, 26 (2), 101–114.

Schuster, J. Mark Davidson. "The Interrelationship Between Public and Private Funding of the Arts in the United States." *The Journal of Arts Management and Law,* 1985, 14 (4), 77–105.

Twentieth Century Fund. *Quality Time? The Report of the Twentieth Century Fund Task Force on Public Television* (with Background Paper by Richard Somerset-Ward). New York: Twentieth Century Fund Press, 1993.

Weber, Nathan and Loren Renz. *Arts Funding: A Report on Foundation and Corporate Grantmaking Trends.* New York: The Foundation Center, 1993.

Weisberger, Barbara. "A Mirror and a Window: The Carlisle Project, 1984–1996." Carlisle, PA: The Carlisle Project, February 1997 (Report on a project supported by the Pew Charitable Trusts).

Weitz, Judith Humphreys. *Coming Up Taller: Arts and Humanities Programs for Children and Youth at Risk.* Washington, DC: The President's Committee on the Arts and the Humanities with the National Assembly of Local Arts Agencies, April 1996.

Wyszomirski, Margaret Jane. "Federal Cultural Support: Toward a New Paradigm?" *The Journal of Arts Management, Law and Society,* 1995, 25 (1), 69–83.

———."Philanthropy, the Arts, and Public Policy," *The Journal of Arts Management and Law,* 1987, 16 (4), 5–2.

———. "Policy Communities and Policy Influence: Securing a Government Role in Cultural Policy for the 21st Century," *Newsletter of Grantmakers in the Arts,* 1995, 6 (2), 10–13, 32–34.

CHAPTER TWENTY-THREE

A Tradition in Jeopardy

Robert L. Payton

The theme of this paper is that the philanthropic tradition in America is at risk, along with several other important traditions that shape American values and help to define the United States as a democracy and a civil society. Almost twenty years ago I published an essay in which I identified philanthropy as "America's most distinctive virtue." I said that the philanthropic tradition was the most important teaching that I could pass along to my grandson.

In writing this essay I have tried to reconsider those opinions. Do I still believe in philanthropy as I once did? If so, given twenty years of work by a growing number of people to strengthen and extend the tradition, what shape is it in?

This is an essay of opinion. It is an essay in philanthropic autobiography. It is an attempt to write a *personal* instead of a *social* history of the moral imagination, to get inside the meaning of "tradition" and its complexities as personal experience. As I think back over my own struggles to become civilized, I realize that social progress is linked to individual progress, even dependent on it. Unless we come to grips in a more detailed way with the difficulties of our own inner and particular progress, we may fail to pass on the ideas, values, principles, and practices most worth preserving.

I use the first-person singular to avoid the almost accusatory You and the anonymous comfort of We. I draw from my own experience and hope that the reader will do the same. Philanthropy is personal and individual as well as social and collective.

A One-Minute Mythistory of the Philanthropic Tradition in the West

Several thousand years ago there emerged in the Middle East the first evidence of organized charity. In the oldest books of the Old Testament appear mandates from God to come to the aid of *the widow, the orphan, the stranger, and the poor*. Those categories identify the most vulnerable, those least able to sustain themselves in an agricultural society. "When you reap the harvest of your land, you shall not reap to the very edges of your field, or gather the gleanings of your harvest. You shall not strip your vineyard bare, or gather the fallen grapes of your vineyard; you shall leave them for the poor and the alien: I am the Lord your God."[1]

Another variant appeared in classical Greece and Rome:

> Everybody knows that all of Rome's citizens, or a section of them, received every month, at a low price or free of charge, a certain quantity of corn, that these distributions were established in 123 [B.C.] by a law of the tribune Gaius Gracchus, and that they continued until the end of the Empire. They can be regarded as a "welfare-state" measure or else stigmatized as an encouragement to idleness, as by Cicero: "Gaius Gracchus brought forward a corn law. It was agreeable to the masses, for it provided food in abundance without work. Loyal citizens were against it, because they thought it was a call to the masses to desert industry for idleness, and saw that it was a drain upon the Treasury."[2]

The stories in the Old Testament are summarized and extended in a famous passage in the New Testament: "for I was hungry and you gave me food, I was thirsty and you gave me something to drink, I was a stranger and you welcomed me, I was naked and you gave me clothing, I was sick and you took care of me, I was in prison and you visited me."[3]

By the time of St. Thomas Aquinas 1,200 years later, that short list had been further expanded into two lists of "corporal alms" and "spiritual alms." Thomas's discussion lists seven of each. The corporal alms are: "feeding the hungry, giving drink to the thirsty, clothing the naked, giving hospitality to strangers, visiting the sick, ransoming prisoners, and burying the dead." The seven spiritual alms are: "instructing the ignorant, giving advice to those in doubt, consoling the sorrowful, reproving sinners, forgiving offenses, putting up with people who are burdensome and hard to get on with, and finally, praying for all."[4]

Four centuries later, in 1601, the Statute of Charitable Uses was promulgated in England by Elizabeth I. It continues the Roman tradition of state assistance, and it includes reference to gifts and other support for "relief of aged, impotent, and poor people; some for maintenance of sick and maimed soldiers and mariners, schools of learning, free schools, and scholars in universities; some for repair of bridges, ports, havens, and causeways; some for education and preferment of orphans . . . " and so on.[5]

With the Reformation a new emphasis on individual charity appears, beyond what might be done by state or church, as in this sermon by John Wesley: "But let not any man imagine that he has done anything, barely by going thus far, by 'gaining and saving all he can,' if he were to stop there. . . . [A]dd the third rule to the two preceding. Having, first, gained all you can, and secondly, saved all you can, then 'give all you can.'"[6]

When my one-minute history runs to two minutes, I insert here a reference to Madison on faction, to the First Amendment on freedom of assembly, and of course to Tocqueville on voluntary association. For readers or listeners whose attention span is even more elastic, I would add this paragraph:

Emblematic of one view is the famous statement by Sir William Beveridge in England in 1942 that heralded the coming of the modern welfare state: " . . . he stated that in itself social security was 'a wholly inadequate aim'; it could only be part of a general programme. 'It is one part only of an attack upon five giant evils: upon the physical Want with which it is directly concerned, upon Disease which often causes that Want and brings many other troubles in its train, upon Ignorance which no democracy can afford among its citizens, upon Squalor . . . and upon the Idleness which destroys wealth and corrupts men.'"[7]

After three thousand years of debate one might expect consensus, but such is not the case.

> Isn't it time for the government to encourage work rather than rewarding dependency? The Great Society has had the unfortunate consequence of snaring millions of Americans into the welfare trap. Government programs designed to give a helping hand to the neediest of Americans have instead bred illegitimacy, crime, illiteracy, and more poverty. Our *Contract with America* will change this destructive social behavior by requiring welfare recipients to take responsibility for the decisions they make. Our *Contract* will achieve what some thirty years of massive welfare spending has not been able to accomplish: reduce illegitimacy, require work, and save taxpayers money."[8]

One theme running through it all is the fact of vulnerability and helplessness that generates a response of private and public assistance. There seems always to have been both, along with a debate about how responsibility should be apportioned: among self-help, mutual aid, government assistance, and philanthropy.

The conversation of the philanthropic tradition is open, accessible, and continuing.

An Old House

Edward Shils suggested this metaphor: "The movement of tradition through time might be like the endurance of a historical monument all of which was made at approximately the same time; or it might be like an old building, lived in and used and modified over the years, continuing to be similar to what it was and to be thought of as still being the same building. A sector of culture is more like the latter than it is like the former."[9]

Might I think of the philanthropic tradition as an old house I have inherited and indeed might have some responsibility to maintain? Might I be in some personal sense a *steward* of the philanthropic tradition? How have I changed it? Is it the same house or so changed in appearance and use that I really mean something else when I refer to it? Is it reasonable to suggest that anyone—someone, even if not everyone—might be responsible in some way for the survival of a tradition?

To press the metaphor a bit further: if a tradition is like an old house, we must remember that a particular tradition is but one house in an old neighborhood, and but one neighborhood among many in an old community, and so on. And each house has many rooms. Families live in these houses and families are in some ways similar, in some ways different. It should not surprise us to find variations in family values and behavior from one household to another. Philanthropy might be very important in one home and invisible in another.

What core of meaning and value is transmitted by what I have been given through the tradition of philanthropy over my lifetime? Is there an inherent integrity of the idea of philanthropy—a basic shape and design of the house that will persist through all our modifications and renovations and alterations and repairs? How might have I been steward of the tradition? What am I passing on?

I will reflect on several traditions that seem to me to support and reinforce one another. The first is the religious tradition of Protestant Christianity, at least as I have understood it. I look at "my" religion in the context of my time as it confronted its anti-Semitism and racism. I then examine several other traditions that came into my consciousness in my adult life and that have continued to influence my thought and values over a working life of half a century: liberal education, professionalism, and philanthropy.

These traditions and values can also be contrasted and compared with other traditions and values. As I write this, for example, Serbian troops are attempting to suppress Albanian Muslim protest demonstrations in Kosovo. As it happens, my son worked for Catholic Relief Services in Macedonia, and we visited him there four years ago. The problem of the Albanian minority within Macedonia was on everyone's mind. That small, strategic, and divided country makes little political sense to an outsider. Its traditions are divisive rather than integrative; its shared history is a catalogue of religious and ethnic violence. The country is poor and the government is weak. It is surrounded by unreliable neighbors who challenge its very legitimacy as a nation.

Cruelty, oppression, corruption, disinformation, ignorance, and inhumanity are values often sustained by tradition turned bad. Most of us live lives protected from the daily evils of misanthropy elsewhere. Places like Macedonia struggle bravely to ward off the social and moral diseases that we also guard against and seek to prevent. Philanthropy is one of the few instruments we have to construct a framework of hope when government cannot sustain order without tyranny and injustice.

Philanthropy gives us a language to express moral values and tools to build social trust. The language includes protest and prophecy; the tools include resources and organization. Those are cultural assets in our society and they are much harder to detect in places like Macedonia. They are ideas and values transmitted not merely by institutions but in the intersubjective understandings passed from one individual to another. When social trust breaks down or is destroyed, as it has been in Bosnia and in Kosovo—and in South Central Los Angeles—"philanthropy" in some form is one of the few ways we have to rebuild it.

The theme of what follows is that philanthropy is one of several interrelated traditions that weave the fabric of social trust. I detect philanthropic values in each of the other traditions; in some sense I consider philanthropy a "mother-tradition," a tradition that nurtures other human values. Where does the tradition come from, how does it become rooted in our character and personality, how does it guide our actions?

Indoctrination

As a child I memorized the Pledge of Allegiance and "The Star Spangled Banner"; I memorized the catechism of the Episcopal Church; and I memorized the Boy Scout Oath. At about that same age I memorized the Gettysburg Address. I memorized the Golden Rule because it was printed in black on a yellow ruler I kept in my desk at school in the fourth grade. I was one of hundreds of young ice skaters who sang a long distance happy birthday to President Roosevelt in behalf of the March of Dimes. I memorized. I performed. I accepted what I was given.

When I began to study the role of philanthropy in religion more or less seriously I was drawn back to the creeds and prayers and symbols from my childhood. Under protest I had attended "catechism," classes intended to prepare me for a ceremony of confirmation in which I was expected to make a public declaration of my faith. Many years later I went back to the texts I had studied and memorized and pledged myself to. "Rehearse the Articles of thy Belief." The catechism was in the form of questions and answers. My Sponsors had promised *for* me that I would keep God's commandments, and I recited them. And, toward the end, this exchange:

"*Question*: What is thy duty toward thy neighbor?"

"*Answer*: My duty toward my neighbor is To love him as myself, and to do to all men as I would they should do unto me. . . ."

The declaration goes on, and it brings out, quite apart from the changes in language and style, the difficulty of maintaining a religious tradition across generations:

"To love, honour and succour my father and mother: To honour and obey the civil authority: To submit myself to all my governors, teachers, spiritual pastors and masters: To order myself lowly and reverently to all my betters: To hurt nobody by word or deed: To be true and just in all my dealings: To bear no malice nor hatred in my heart: To keep my hands from picking and stealing, and my tongue from evil speaking, lying, and slandering: To keep my body in temperance, sobriety, and chastity: Not to covet nor desire other men's goods; But to learn and labour truly to get my own living, And to do my duty in that state of life unto which it shall please God to call me."

The final phrase of the catechism is "and be in charity with all men."[10]

My religion, my patriotism, and my moral code for a while seemed compatible and consistent to me. Each was a tradition and together—as in the catechism—they formed a tight web of interlocking traditions that added up to a worldview. They told me the kind of person I was to be.

Religious teaching is clearly one of the most important vehicles for transmitting philanthropic and other ideals and values from one generation to the next. When I look back at the religious education of my childhood in the 1920s and 1930s, I find that on the one hand, politics, economics, and philanthropics were not as compatible as they had been presented to me and on the other hand a thin veneer of philanthropic values over a thick crust of prejudice.

Anti-Semitism

I was not born enlightened. The world I was born into, the world of Boy Scouts and Sunday School and the Palmer Method of Penmanship, was in some important ways morally defective.

In the Middle Western culture of my childhood, racism, bigotry, and anti-Semitism stained the carpets of fancy clubs and soiled the vestments of the clergy. Thanks to Hitler, anti-Semitism became the more visible and urgent moral issue. In the late 1930s I attended seventh grade in Milwaukee with Jewish refugee children from Germany. Later, it was a matter of intense debate in my high school social circles whether my friends and I should be concerned about the welfare of Jews when we were not ourselves Jewish. And we asked that if the Jews were in trouble in Germany, whether they might have "deserved it."

Five years later, the 1947 Oscar-winning film *Gentleman's Agreement* came as a bold illumination. Even so, I didn't begin to understand the *human* meaning of the Holocaust until much later, when I first read Elie Wiesel's

Night. The historical fact of anti-Semitism and the Holocaust were not for me facts of history but facts of the world around me, not known and settled and understood when I was growing up but problematic and controversial.

Between the time I was ten, before the war, and the time I was twenty, after the war, I became not only pro-Jewish but pro-Israeli. The Jews and Judaism were my first and most enduring philanthropic cause. I have not been as faithful to Israel as a political cause as I have been to Jewish religious and cultural survival as a philanthropic cause.

The point I struggle to make when I say that *I was not born enlightened* is that I know from my own experience that it is difficult to come to the light of social awareness and sensibility if one isn't born into it. What seems obvious and unarguable about social justice to my students today was not obvious to me at their age. What is taken for granted at the end of the twentieth century was the source of anxiety and hostility as well as hope in the middle of the twentieth century. The *social* evolution of the moral imagination as seen in the victory over anti-Semitism sometimes moves at a more rapid pace than its evolution within the lives and spirit of individual humans.

One question worth asking is whether those who have to fight their way out of ignorance and prejudice learn their lessons better than those who receive tradition as a given. Have I "earned" a moral understanding that is deeper and stronger because I had to work to reach it?

A second question is when we think our *personal* moral imagination is ahead of the *social* progress we see in history and in the world around us.

Was there an invisible thread of philanthropy in my jumble of traditions that helped me to sort the good from the bad, that gave me at least preliminary assumptions to work with? Might I apply some of the same values to race relations that I had gradually developed about religious tolerance? My awareness of these social facts came at about the same time but they developed *as causes* at a different pace: first, anti-Semitism, then racism.

Civil Rights

My mother was an important moral influence in my life. She passed along a great deal of wisdom in maxims recalled from her childhood in Texas. Because of her father, she had developed a respect for history. Despite her tolerance and her awareness of injustice, her historical perspective persuaded her that any major changes in the patterns of racial discrimination in the South would either "take generations" to achieve or lead to bloody civil conflict. However desirable it might be, civil rights for Negroes would not come "in our lifetime."

I recall those conversations with my mother in the 1930s, when I was about twelve. By the time I was forty, her predictions had proven wrong. By that time a black family lived across the street from us in St. Louis, peacefully accepted as neighbors thanks to the careful efforts of other neighbors who sought "balanced integration" as the ideal of urban life.

We lived near the university and as a result in what was considered by the residents to be a more cosmopolitan neighborhood. "Integration" meant that in addition to WASPs like us and a smattering of Asians and Jews, blacks could become part of the community. Day by day, week by week, the neighborhood changed. Blacks now ate at the same restaurants and shopped in the same stores; black students enrolled in increasing numbers at the university. White people, including one or two authentic bigots, were more careful about their language and their ethnic humor.

That effort at enlightenment took about ten years.

I have long considered the civil rights movement to be one of the greatest achievements of the philanthropic tradition in America. I watched it at work and up close. There is nothing very dramatic in my story, like Selma, merely a few individuals who came together around a vision of an integrated community and an integrated society in which racial and ethnic differences would no longer determine life chances. Some neighbors went from door to door, very much like religious missionaries, persuading people not to panic and try to sell their houses when the first black family moved in. They recruited a black family—young professionals with children, people who were middle class in every respect.

The struggle for justice calls for passions and strategies beyond bringing short-term assistance to the poor and homeless. In our neighborhood the struggle for civil rights for blacks meant integrating middle class blacks into a middle class community. Although the strongest advocates for integration went much further in their vision of the new society, the consensus didn't move that far. But by the measure of my mother's prediction, which is what I measured it against, integration moved very far indeed. It seemed to me at the time a great achievement in its modest way; it still does.

The first presidential election in which I voted was in 1948. I was intensely interested and engaged in it, as were most of my friends. It was a time in which politics was taken seriously; we *respected* the political process. We knew all the candidates of all the parties, and it was a bewilderingly rich year of parties and candidates. Harry Truman, Tom Dewey, Henry Wallace . . . and Strom Thurmond. Strom Thurmond, soon to be a hundred years old, is now honored for his lifetime of service as senator from South Carolina. In 1948, however, he was the presidential candidate of the States Rights (or "Dixiecrat") Party. The platform of the States Rights Party was constructed to permit southern states to maintain racial segregation. I feel no closer to Strom Thurmond in social and political philosophy today than I did in 1948. I flatter myself that I have progressed and he hasn't. My personal moral imagination is more in step with the social history of the moral imagination in my lifetime while Strom Thurmond has remained mired in a stagnant pool. My son recently sent me a passage from *Made in America* by Bill Bryson, in which

Bryson tells of Lewis and Clark naming the Missouri "Philanthropy River." The name didn't stick, Bryson says; it became known as "Stinking Water." I'm still in search of "Philanthropy River," Senator Thurmond. . . .

In the course of growing up, I came to accept the argument that Jews and blacks have been discriminated against unfairly and often illegally. By the early 1960s I thought both forms of discrimination and prejudice had been defeated. Forever. The history of prejudice, following the metaphor of Francis Fukuyama, ended with the advent of the Great Society.

For twenty years I have been convinced that philanthropy as "voluntary action for the public good" is the tradition in which social movements arise and flourish. Civil rights is a case in point. As a social achievement, the civil rights movement in the United States ranks with the fall of Soviet Communism as one of the two greatest nonviolent revolutions of the twentieth century. The century of the gulag and the death camps is also the century of integrated neighborhoods and equal employment opportunity. The worst slums have been cleared away; the old neighborhood is better than it was.

I think it is subjectively important to have a sense of whether one is in step with history, running ahead of it, or stubbornly falling behind. Some teachings seemed to me to rush ahead of the broader social consensus, a consensus that included (and still includes) naysayers and dissidents.

For example, the social and religious teachings of my Protestant church also changed in ways similar to the changes in my own philosophy. Some around me would move more rapidly; some would not move at all.

I find that I am a conservative on some issues and a liberal on others, liberal at one time and conservative another, usually inclined to be a contrarian when I teach and a pragmatist in action. Sometimes I am comfortable with myself and often I'm not.

Liberal Education

When I first heard of the idea, to be "liberally educated" meant that one had a balanced education in the liberal arts and sciences. Because I happened to become involved in formal academic discussions of the notion, I came to the conclusion that ideas were too important to be confined to the classroom.

Liberal education actively encouraged us to test our opinions against the opinions of others and against reality. A liberal education meant that one should test reality by the methods of reason. It also meant an awareness of reality that was vastly broader than what was immediate and nearby. A liberal education was thought to be superior to a narrow, technical, or vocational education because it claimed to be something more, something special: the education of the free person, education essential to life in a democratic society.

A liberal education meant an education in what is now called *critical thinking.* The liberally educated person was not a slave of ideology or religion but a person with a mind capable of independent thought. Not only Protestantism or Christianity but religion itself was on the table; we could be atheists if we chose. We could consider ourselves not only Republicans or Democrats, liberals or conservatives, radicals or reactionaries or what would now be called libertarians, but even Marxists.

Some students escaped from liberal education by becoming "politically correct" followers or acolytes of distinguished professors. In general, however, it was a culture that took politics—and everything else—seriously. Indifference and boredom weren't tolerated; the most valued activity was *talk*.

For a while I worked part time at the downtown campus of the University of Chicago in the office of the Great Books Program. My wife worked for the *Bulletin of Atomic Scientists*. While I was serving as literary agent for Aristotle and Dostoyevsky my wife was signing Albert Einstein's name to fund-raising letters. Conversation with neighbors in the stairwell of our temporary graduate student housing apartment was continuous with what we talked about in class. Pericles and Cicero were as much a part of our political discussion as Adlai Stevenson and Joe McCarthy.

For all our enlightenment, it was easier to organize a protest against South Africa than to integrate the campus. We lived in the exciting and stimulating and sometimes dangerous environment of the University of Chicago from 1951 to 1954. "Civil rights" was not yet part of our cultural lexicon.

I became friends with a black man who worked as janitor in the men's club [*sic*] while I worked there part time as a student. He invited me to his basement apartment one Saturday afternoon and we sat on his broken furniture and talked about jazz. I drank a beer while he smoked a joint. We didn't talk about Aristotle, but then Aristotle wasn't of much help on race relations.

One evening my black friend told me that a white man had fallen backward and hit his head on the steps outside the club. He was lying there unconscious. I called the police. When two patrolmen arrived one came up to the fallen man and hit him violently across the soles of his feet with a nightstick. I protested, without effect. "He's drunk," the policeman said. He kicked the man and told him to get up. Eventually the two policemen dragged the man to his feet and led him away.

They were right: he was drunk.

I was right: he was a human being.

Neither the two policeman nor I attempted to spell out our conflicting social philosophies, but in retrospect it was in part a question of *deserts*. Was he, as a drunk, undeserving of humane treatment? Or do all humans, even drunks, deserve some measure of respect? In an age of welfare reform there is probably no more pressing philanthropic issue.

Politics rather than philanthropy dominated my horizon in those days. Politics was seen to be more relevant as well as more important than religion. Politics was the means to affect social change. Liberal education was preparation for life in the *polis*. Organized philanthropy was scarcely part of my conceptual world. If we thought about philanthropy at all it was in terms of blood drives and the United Fund. We claimed to know how Athens worked in 400 B.C.; for all our sociological sophistication, however, we didn't really understand how Chicago worked in the 1950s.

To the extent that liberal education opened our minds, broadened our perspectives, helped us to think critically, sensitized us to complexity and ambiguity, and encouraged us to talk to each other, it prepared us for a society in which voluntary action for the public good made sense.

Most people today equate liberal education with education or training in the liberal arts. The liberal arts are no longer at the center of college and university life. Liberal arts courses are, more often than not, "service" courses for students majoring in other subjects. Education is dominated by short-term occupational utility rather than long-term intellectual enrichment.

Liberal education meant opening my mind, enlarging my vision. It seems to me impossible that philanthropy can survive unless liberal education survives.

Professionalism

Paul Henry Schaefer, M.D., was a general practitioner in Burlington, Iowa, for fifty years. He was in the process of retiring from active practice at age seventy when I married his youngest daughter. Over the next decade he and I talked a great deal about politics and religion but found almost no common ground on the issues. He was a prejudiced man in some ways, especially against Jews and Catholics and Negroes. His prejudice applied to groups, however, not to individuals. He was not, by my lights, "liberally educated."

Dr. Schaefer liked to talk about medicine. He continued to read his medical journals long after he could make much sense of them. Trying to remain conversant with good medical practice and new medical knowledge was a matter of faith for him. He also talked to me about his patients and what it meant to be a general practitioner in a small Iowa town at the turn of the century when he began his practice. He was fond of his patients as well as devoted to them. Many of them continued to come to his office at home long after he announced his retirement. They admired and respected *and trusted* him.

That is the nostalgic formative background of my interest in professionalism. It caused me to ask what it is that sustains someone at a high level of competence in a demanding and rapidly changing field. It clearly wasn't money; Dr. Schaefer was thoroughly middle class. It was in part his involvement in the medical society; he knew his peers and he judged them sternly, as they judged him.

He was a physician, drawn as a child to a medical career by reading *Hans Brinker and the Silver Skates*. He had an ideal of the Physician and he aspired to live by that ideal. For the most part, it seemed to me, he succeeded.

The physician is the model of the professional, the embodiment of the ideal of professionalism. The physician is competent, educated, bound by a code of ethics, free to exercise his judgment, and committed to an "ethic of service" that puts the interest of the patient first.

It is the altruistic concern for the patient or client that brings out the philanthropic dimension of the professional ideal. The physician, nurse, lawyer, social worker, engineer, journalist, scholar, scientist, soldier—all claim an ethic that subordinates their personal and private interest to the well being of those they serve.

Professionalism is an *ideal:* that is, it projects a vision of perfection that cannot be fully realized in reality. Professionalism is a *regulative ideal:* that is, it serves as a moral action-guide directing the professional toward right conduct. "Right conduct" is defined by a written code and supported by the law; it also reflects the values of the culture.

Professionalism is a recent tradition. It flowered in the latter half of the nineteenth century in the face of outrageous medical practices. Over the next fifty years the "contemporary" version of professionalism, such as I have described it above, became commonplace. To be a professional was to make a claim to be trustworthy, not only in the sense of competence but in the moral sense as well.

I was once editor of a weekly newspaper in Burlington, Iowa. The quality of the newspaper was about what one would expect for the product of a 22-year-old college dropout who knew nothing about journalism. Looking at it many years later I find it to have been even worse than I thought—naïve, posturing, imitative, shallow.

But it had its moments. In 1951 I began to do what I thought was serious research into rates charged for electricity by the local utility company. The City Council was considering a request for an increase. In the best journalistic tradition, I sought out information about the rates charged by the same utility company in other cities and towns of comparable size within (as I recall) less than a hundred-mile radius. The evidence was compelling: Burlington was being taken for a ride. Neither the City Council nor the daily newspaper seemed aware of the facts or even interested in them.

I wrote the first of a series of three articles detailing (beyond any conceivable reader interest) the telling facts I had uncovered. The first installment appeared on a Tuesday. By noon of that same day my sole public partner in this newspaper enterprise (the printer was a silent partner), who served as "business manager" and who sold advertising for us, came into the office with a broad smile on his face. "We've done it!" he announced. He laid a signed contract on my desk. "They'll buy a full-page ad every week from now on—as long as we don't run the next two installments." We had sold only one full-page ad in the previous 18 months.

My professional integrity as a journalist was at stake, along with my salary of $35 a week. I resigned. The newspaper folded. I went off to the University of Chicago, convinced that I had done the noble thing that any good journalist would have done under the circumstances.

In subsequent years I served as managing editor of a real estate and construction magazine, as the editor of a university alumni magazine, and as often-anonymous author of reams of copy for university publications without end; as adviser to the official magazine of the Department of State; as occasional contributor to *The Lamp*, the Exxon magazine for shareholders, as contributor to *Newsday*, and as author of op-ed pieces for a variety of other newspapers. And so on.

A very small part of what is written and published has little if any journalistic or editorial integrity, at least as such things are measured by standards of truth, objectivity, and solid factual information. The professional ideal in journalism is confined to a small fraction of what appears in print under whatever auspices. (The presence of the ideal in other media is even less evident.) Persuasion in all its forms dominates our public discourse and communication.

Journalism as a professional ideal is not the second oldest profession; it is very recent. The notion that a newspaper can rise above the economic interests of its advertisers and the prurient, scandal-starved interests of its readers to give us unbiased reporting seems at this moment ludicrous.

Who cares? What difference does it make?

Someone cares. The nascent "movement" called public journalism brings a number of journalists together around a new editorial philosophy. The question is whether a more constructive approach can supplant the rampant tabloidism of recent years. It is not the fact of tabloid journalism that is at issue; it is the *legitimation* of it, the spread of it like a disease into mainstream journalism.

If journalists abandon their quest for professionalism, it seems unlikely they will credit the ideal as viable anywhere else.

Over the past two decades the notion of professionalism and the professional ideal has been battered from all sides. Not only have liberals attacked professionalism for being racist, sexist, and exclusionist, professionalism has been attacked by conservatives for being a monopoly out of the reach of market forces. Meanwhile, medical ethics, long taken for granted, has become, in issues of abortion and physician-assisted suicide, the nexus of the most conflicted moral controversies of the society.

The civil rights of patients and clients, the rights of patients and clients of whatever economic status to adequate medical care and legal care, the rapidity of technological advances, and now, overriding everything else, the costs of professional services put the professional ideal in great jeopardy. In very specific ways, the philanthropic dimension of the professional ideal is what is at greatest risk.

Traditions in Jeopardy

Each of these traditions is in jeopardy, at some risk of losing influence and relevance.

My religious tradition, that called mainline Protestantism, seems to have yielded pride of place to "evangelical" religions that stress Bible study over social activism. Southern Baptists now outweigh mainline Episcopalians and Presbyterians, so to speak. The Christian tradition itself is again in danger of splitting into irreconcilable camps. This time, however, the bloodthirstiness is not the result of fine points of theology but of political and cultural ideology. The increasing fragmentation among cultural and economic conservatives is reminiscent of the splits among liberal and radical activists in the 1960s and 1970s. "Fundamentalism" in religion, the subject of a recent multivolume study, has become a divisive ideological influence in every region of the world. "Ecumenism," meanwhile, one of those hopes that sustained many of us who want to see religion as a reconciling rather than factional force in human affairs, has lost its leadership role.

Meanwhile, the Church of Scientology and the empire of Reverend Moon join with countless New Era cults, draining energy and resources and stealing converts from longer-established faiths and denominations.

Who cares? What difference does it make?

If religion is one of the most important means of transmitting moral ideals across the generations, then not only its vigor and strength but the content of its message is important. The religions I know best, Christianity and Judaism, and some others I know less well, like Islam, contain hateful and destructive misanthropic elements as well as messages of mercy and justice.

On the other hand, it may well be that this disorderly realignment of religious ideas and traditions is healthy, a breakthrough to another level of religious understanding. The future may prove to be more enlightened than the past, at least if the future preserves the best elements of the past and screens out the deadly ones.

People believe that Elvis lives; we should be more worried that Hitler lives. Anti-Semitism did not die when the truth became known about the death camps. Anti-Semitism and other religion-born diseases of the soul threaten to spread ethnic and civil conflict into every part of the world. The Middle West when I grew up was embarrassingly parochial and isolationist. It may ways it still is. The new isolationism and the new religiosity join with the old ethnic aggression. Xenophobia appears to be on the rise. Many people of my generation—including me—thought we had torn out those roots; if so, they have grown back.

My mother may have been right, at least in one respect: if winning civil rights for African Americans in the short run did not cause civil war, changing the hearts and minds of the people to find a deeper and easier tolerance seems not to pass easily from one generation to the next. The concept of race, flawed as it is, will be around for a long time. The hope for integration, naïve as it was, will not be achieved soon.

On the other hand, race relations will never revert to their pre-civil rights social divisions. The gains for other minorities are also signs of a new America. The growth of the African American middle class offers evidence that the secular movement is toward better distribution of wealth and power.

Liberal education seems to have lost out to vocational training: "education" is a euphemism for training to get a first job, not preparation for a series of careers. We may have betrayed an entire generation by encouraging it to believe that education was reducible to its economic value. Those of us who put a higher value on reading than computing, on books than on the Web, may feel that literacy itself is in decline. Numeracy cannot replace literacy as a vehicle for the transmission of moral values. The value-driven liberal arts are in some sort of trouble, losing out to amoral technology.

Liberal education may revive by other means. Citizenship and civil society—even philanthropic studies—cut across the artificial barriers of disciplines and professions. The curriculum is more open and more responsive, libraries and their riches are more accessible, degrees and programs more flexible and adaptable than were ever dreamed of in our long-range planning committees three decades ago.

On my bad days, technology is the Enemy, but technology opens more doors than it closes. The global internet may provide movie script after movie script about international terrorism and unimaginable horrors in outer space, but it may also have broken the grip of totalitarianism forever.

Of these several traditions, at least at the moment, the professional ideal is in greatest jeopardy. It has suffered greatly from bad stewardship. Medicine was in fact "racist, sexist, and exclusionist," as charged. It was arrogantly indifferent to economic issues. Law paid lip service to legal aid for the poor and lost all perspective on litigation. The lesser professions and the aspiring professions and the pseudo-professions now set the style for the ancient professions.

Thinking of the professions simply as businesses, *and nothing more,* seems to me to make a difference of enormous importance. Thinking of philanthropy as no more than "a business like any other business" threatens the heart and soul of philanthropy (if philanthropy may be thought of in such terms). On my Oswald Spengler days "the decline of the West" means the commercialization of everything.

On the other hand, the proponents of nonprofit management and ethical fund raising have transformed the daily business of philanthropy. The omissions and failures continue, but the training of volunteers and the preparation of trustees as well as the professionalization [*sic*] of staff of voluntary associations is dramatically better than it was a decade ago, and will presumably continue to improve as these subjects ramify throughout higher education.

Renovate or Rebuild?

If the philanthropic tradition is in jeopardy, who cares? What difference does it make?

As these pages make clear, I am convinced that the philanthropic tradition is in jeopardy, along with tradition in general. Our society is neophiliac, impatient to get on to the next discovery, the next toy. We also seem indifferent to the lessons of the past and largely ignorant of them.

What is the old house made of? In the American case: sturdy, durable stuff. The philanthropic tradition, at least for me, carries these teachings:

lessons of civil rights which seem to have their roots in political democracy;
lessons of liberal education which seem to have their roots in philosophy and critical thinking;
lessons of professionalism which seem to have their roots in ethics;
and lessons of philanthropy, which seem to have their roots in religion.

These lessons from the past are part of a curriculum, if you will, of the good life and the good society. The philanthropic tradition is entwined with these other roots, each giving the other strength and stability and perhaps a secure future. At some thin conceptual level I think of them as an important web of social and moral values. I have tried to suggest some awareness of the difficulties of converting them from abstractions to particular realities.

It isn't necessary to travel to Macedonia to realize that these high-minded words and phrases have even less meaning to people whose vocabularies and conversation reflect the ugliness around them. Most of us have abundant reason for gratitude and humility: gratitude that we've been given so much, and humility because we've done so little to strengthen it and pass it on.

I remain convinced of the importance of the philanthropic tradition. The health and vitality of the tradition is related to the health and vitality of other traditions; philanthropy is sustained and strengthened by other similar traditions grounded in similar values.

Stewardship of a tradition is a subtle and complex responsibility.

Who are the stewards of the philanthropic tradition?

A first answer is "the authors and readers of this book." My appeal is for *us* to examine our own inner grasp of the tradition and its sources in our own cultural heritage and personal experience.

A second answer is "the young people." My own view of young people is biased by ten years of working with some of the best among them. By "best" I mean young people of high ability and great potential for leadership who are determined to have careers that are "more than making a living"; yet young people who also have the good sense to recognize that making a living is not necessarily degrading and can in fact be fulfilling.

The young people I know are privileged members of an open elite; most of them know they are privileged and most of them accept that privilege carries responsibility with it. Someone once said that an elite education can be justified only by a life of service. Lives of service can be lived in many places and in many ways. My students have found their way into medicine, law, public policy, social work, education, scholarship—some have even embarked on careers in philanthropy. They have been urged to be liberally educated, to immerse themselves in books and ideas and to carry their ideas and values into "active engagement in projects of worth." They have also been urged to think of themselves as "public teachers," helping other people seek, as my students seek, to have a mind of their own. They are encouraged to think of themselves as "models of public life"—to live private lives with a public dimension, as the professions have pledged themselves to do.

My impressions are without the survey research foundation that Alexander Astin draws upon to tell us each year about the values of college freshmen. The small number of young people who give me hope for the future reflect merely one person's experience with them and with his own past.

In addition to our collective contributions to a new and rapidly expanding field, each of us shares a steward's responsibility to examine our own values— in some humility, as seems warranted, and with a deep sense of gratitude that this is the work we have been called to do.

In philanthropy and in these other traditions in contemporary American society, it is generally better to restore and renovate than simply to tear down and build anew. Those qualifiers are intended to signal concern that philanthropy, like democracy and freedom, is a universal value; its well being in American life depends to some extent on its strength and vitality elsewhere. Humanitarian aid and peacekeeping in the former Yugoslavia remind us that our stewardship of the philanthropic tradition alerts us to the tradition and its problems in other societies. The reform of welfare in the United States is a reminder that the role of philanthropy undergoes constant redefinition. Philanthropic values in other American cultural traditions sustain them and may help them rediscover or reinvigorate their mission.

Perhaps philanthropy is always "a tradition in jeopardy." That strikes me as a good working assumption for those who would take philanthropy seriously—and personally.

Notes

1. Leviticus 19:8 NRSV.
2. Paul Veyne, *Bread and Circuses: Historical Sociology and Political Pluralism*, London: Allen Lane/The Penguin Press, 1990, pp. 236–37.

3. Matthew 25:35–37 NRSV.

4. St. Thomas Aquinas, *Summa Theologiae*, Vol. 43, "Charity" (2a2ae. 23–33), R. J. Batten, tr. and ed., London: Eyre and Spottiswoode, Ltd., 1975, p. 241.

5. From the Preamble to the Statute of Charitable Uses, 1601, quoted in Michael Chesterman, *Charities, Trusts, and Social Welfare*, London: Weidenfeld and Nicolson, 1975, p. 25.

6. John Wesley, "The Use of Money," *John Wesley's Fifty-Three Sermons*, Edward H. Sugden, ed., Nashville: Abingdon Press, 1983, p. 643.

7. Nicholas Timmins, *The Five Giants: A Biography of the Welfare State*, London: Fontana Press, 1996, p. 24.

8. *Contract with America: The Bold Plan by Rep. Newt Gingrich, Rep. Dick Armey, and the House Republicans to Change the Nation*, New York: Times Books, 1994, p. 65.

9. Edward Shils, *Tradition*, Chicago: University of Chicago Press, 1981, p. 46.

10. *The Book of Common Prayer*, 1928 edition, New York: Oxford University Press, pp. 577–83.

CHAPTER TWENTY-FOUR

The World We Must Build

Charles T. Clotfelter and Thomas Ehrlich

The United States is unique among nations in the number, strength, and diversity of philanthropic and nonprofit institutions and in the interactions of those institutions with both the public and the for-profit sectors. Each of the three sectors operates by relying, to different degrees, on a balance between two powerful human instincts. Trust is one; suspicion is the other. Our Constitution establishes a series of checks by each branch of federal government on the other branches in terms that make clear the deep suspicion shared by our country's founders about human nature generally and majoritarian government particularly. Yet every great political leader since Washington has stressed that no constitutional arrangement can protect the rights and opportunities of the people without a basic level of public trust in government and its officials. Though the public's confidence in elected leaders ebbs and flows, that basic level of trust in government remains essential.

Trust may be even more important in the daily operations of the marketplace, functioning as a social lubricant that greatly reduces the costs of doing business. The great majority of transactions, especially among those who do business with one another over time, is based primarily on trust. Yet suspicion is always a factor in the commercial world. When suspicion overwhelms trust, firms and consumers have recourse to legal remedies as a last resort in settling problems. But no commercial operation could operate long if it had to rely primarily on the legal system to enforce its underlying understandings. Trust is essential.

Yet trust plays its most significant role in the third sector—populated by nonprofit organizations. As Hansmann (1980) argues in his classic analysis, nonprofit organizations are legally distinct from for-profit firms not in their inability, as a matter of economics, to *make* profits, but in their inability, as a matter of law, to *distribute* profits to their "owners." Owing to this prohibition, both customers and beneficiaries of nonprofit organizations have a greater incentive to trust those organizations, as opposed to for-profit firms, and not to cut corners in providing services. Money saved thereby cannot be turned into extra income by the operators. Accordingly, for individuals who want to help the hungry, start a school, clean up the environment, or benefit their own community, when those wishes are not being met by government, the nonprofit firm has become the instrument to trust and, therefore, the vehicle of choice.

Yet even public faith in the nonprofit sector has been eroded in recent years. Some of that erosion is due to the loss of public trust in institutions generally, as explained by Robert Bellah and his colleagues in *The Good Society*. Other factors as well affect the nonprofit sector specifically. One is suspicion that some in the sector who are purporting to do good for others are really just doing well for themselves, a suspicion that is fed by occasional reports of wrongdoing, such as the recent conviction of the national leader of United Way. Trust is further eroded by the blurring of lines between and among the three sectors, as the American Assembly report in the appendix discusses.

The Assembly report comes at an important time, because it reaffirms the vitality and importance of philanthropy and the nonprofit sector, and because it underscores how much needs to be done. Fortunately, the capacity exists to do a great deal more, as the chapters in the present volume demonstrate. The organizations that make up American philanthropy and the nonprofit sector differ markedly in size, wealth, function, and source of funding. But in combination they represent an extraordinary resource. Perhaps most important, they enjoy widespread, active support. To an extent unmatched in either of the other two sectors, these organizations receive the voluntary support—in time and money—of individuals, corporations, and private foundations. In this sense, trust is their central ingredient. Unlike the explicit exchange embodied in market transactions, voluntary gifts of time and money rarely yield anything more tangible than a receipt and a thank-you. As Robert Payton and others have argued, it is the intangible reasons—the traditions of helping and giving—that provide the dominant motivation for this voluntary support.

Looking backward, Payton argues passionately and persuasively in chapter 23 that this tradition of giving holds much of enduring value, that its inheritors inherit also obligations to maintain it, but that the tradition is in serious jeopardy. Looking forward, our assignment is to comment on the future of philanthropy and the nonprofit sector, drawing on the essays in this volume and on the conference leading to the American Assembly report. What should be the shape and substance of philanthropy and the nonprofit sector as we move to the next century? What should be conserved, what rejected, and what recast to meet new pressures and to serve new needs?

We are not soothsayers, but we do have strong views on what can and should be done. We are both excited by the challenges we see and optimistic about the abilities of philanthropy and the nonprofit sector to meet those challenges. We begin with our sense of the current philanthropic and nonprofit world. We turn then to the world we must build.

How We Came to Where We Are

Much of what we recognize today as American philanthropy began to take shape in the first two decades of this century. Forces had been gaining strength since the end of the nineteenth century when the first great contemporary American philanthropists began their giving. Carnegie and Rockefeller were in the lead, two Horatio Alger heroes. Two sons of millionaires followed in their wake, Mellon and Morgan. And a fifth, Frick, was somewhere in between. Making money, not giving it away, was their great interest, and the arts were the common denominator of their largesse. They were leaders who represented the American ethos of individual entrepreneurial energy. In some ways, they were more powerful even than the federal government. Mellon, for example, had a critical role in saving the Cleveland administration, and the country, from economic disaster in the gold crisis just a century ago. Though the impact of these men on the country was far more profound in shaping American capitalism than in spearheading American philanthropy, the great foundations and museums they established soon became synonymous with that philanthropy. Perhaps even more important, their passionate belief that only personal effort should be rewarded, and that individuals should be helped only to help themselves, was at the core of what they did in philanthropy as in business. That view has had a powerful effect on organized philanthropy until this day.

There is, of course, another view—that those in need should be helped whatever the basis for their need—that poverty, as Shaw put it in *Major Barbara*, is the only real crime, and the elimination of poverty is the only essential virtue. But the nineteenth-century tradition of charity in this country was dominated by individualism and "teach a man to fish" philosophy. Indeed, as Katz (1986) has chronicled, much of the private welfare work of organized philanthropy in the last half of that century was aimed less at the relief of misery than the preservation of social order and the organization of political power. Not until the New Deal era did the view take hold that the federal government should have a major role in welfare, and it too was shaped by the judgment that the "greatest primary task is to put people to work," as FDR said in his first inaugural address. In subsequent decades, welfare came to be viewed as an entitlement for the poorest, particularly for their children, but individual initiative and work were consistent themes throughout the War on Poverty and the years that followed. They are the prominent themes of the 1996 welfare reform act. It should be no surprise that they dominated the philosophy of organized philanthropy, as well, apart from the religious organizations.

More of those religious organizations still exist than any other kind of nonprofit entity, and individuals give almost as much to religious groups as to all other charities put together. No one knows exactly how many nonprofit organizations existed at the end of World War II, but we do know that an explosion in the nonprofit sector occurred in the decades that followed. By 1995, there were some 1.5 million religious congregations and other nonprofit organizations that were eligible for tax-deductible contributions.

One result of this proliferation is a very diverse "sector"—making it almost impossible to make general statements. Organizations within it can usefully be divided by size, by source of funding, or the degree to which they serve the poor. Probably the most striking distinction is between the vast number of small and financially precarious organizations and the large, financially sound organizations—mostly colleges, universities, and hospitals—that receive a great deal of their revenues in the form of fees and are quite corporate in organization and level of compensation.[1] Because of the differences among these institutions, some even object to the term "sector"—there is so much diversity within it. We will use the term, but with an understanding that the variety of its contents makes generalizations dangerous.

We value the institutions within the sector for several important reasons. At the most basic level, they meet wants and needs that have been left unmet by the market and government. From private schools and mutual-benefit organizations to human-service organizations, these institutions fill "niches." Some of them, like programs to help youth literacy, fill gaps and serve the role of "incubator" for the development of government or larger-scale nonprofit programs. For a wide variety of purposes, the nonprofit form allows flexibility to mount efforts to supply local public goods.

A second reason our society values the sector is because of the integral role it plays in what we know as American democracy. From community organizing and "empowerment" to policy-related research to impassioned advocacy, these institutions have become a part of how politics gets conducted and public policies get formulated. Its institutions operate, as one Assembly conference participant put it, like a "mosquito in the tent," a small but persistent presence with the potential to effect significant change. As the current discussion of "social capital" makes clear, nonprofit organizations may have an important influence on the strength of the social glue that makes communities "work." As we suggest in our concluding comments, we think this role should be significantly enhanced, on a coordinated basis, by philanthropy and the nonprofit sector.

Third, the nonprofit sector shapes values, and in the process it engenders trust. This is most obviously true of religious congregations and religious-based organizations that provide welfare and other social services. But it is no less the case for literally hundreds of thousands of nonprofit entities, large and small, that are created and operated to help meet human needs. While profits are by no means the only motive operating in the for-profit sector, they are the dominant motive. By contrast, values such as compassion, community service, racial tolerance, and environmental protection motivate action in the nonprofit sector in ways that are not possible in the for-profit sector. Although those values should also be powerful forces in the public sector, their influence is almost inevitably tempered by factors such as practical politics on the one hand and procedural fairness on the other. Because its institutions give freer rein to actions arising from deepseated values and are not constrained to be uniform in their impact, the nonprofit sector has special roles in maintaining both our traditions and our pluralism.

Although we, too, value the sector, we believe it is not working as well as it could. One failing, emphasized by Wolpert in chapter 11, is the mismatch between needs and sources. Contributions arise out of wealth and income, and many of those contributions naturally stay within the communities (both geographic and cultural) of the donors. More broadly, it is important to recognize that nonprofits are in no position to accomplish significant income redistribution in society. A second frustration is the disorganization of the sector—both apparent and real. For example, foundations often make grants with little idea of what others are doing, or with little understanding of complementary government programs. Third, there is good evidence that policy-related research is subject to large temporal swings. If policy research in the 1960s was left-leaning, it has been emphatically right-leaning in recent years. Covington (1998) has argued, for example, that conservative foundations have acted strategically to shape the public debate on national policy questions. Fourth, as we discuss below, the growing commercialization in the nonprofit sector threatens to endanger trust in that sector. Cause-related marketing, tie-in products, lotteries, and other commercial inroads have produced revenues, but only at a real cost, as Ilchman and Burlingame argue in chapter 9.

The Old Covenant

What is the policy atmosphere in which philanthropy and the nonprofit sector have evolved? We think it is accurate to say that in the years since the close of World War II, there was an implicit "covenant" between the institutions in this sector and American society, to borrow a term that Warren Ilchman suggested at the Assembly conference. We also believe that it is time to recognize that a new covenant has come into effect, and to deal realistically with its components.

In the old covenant, as we shall call it, the American people, through their governments, offered two important commitments, one constitutional and one legislative. The First Amendment, guaranteeing the freedom of speech, religion, and assembly, is a commitment to allow groups to organize, operate freely, and speak freely, all within wide limits, carefully crafted by the judiciary. The legislative commitment, forged at the federal, state, and local levels, exists in the form of enormous financial benefits to most nonprofit organizations. Section 501 of the Internal Revenue Code, the most famous formulation of this commitment, states that the income of educational, charitable, and scientific organizations is exempt from taxation. The Code also provides for deductions for charitable gifts in the personal, corporate, and gift and estate taxes. At the state and local levels, these organizations have also generally been exempt from taxation. While the First Amendment commitment is essentially unconditional, the second is part of a rather clear *quid pro quo*. In return for tax subsidies, the favored institutions had to abide by two admonitions. They also operated under two additional "understandings." The admonitions find expression in law, but the understandings are nowhere written down. Although these understandings were by no means uniformly followed, the leaders of both business and government—capitalism and democracy—seemed to accept them as good for their sectors and for the country as a whole. As numerous commentators have chronicled, this acceptance is less surprising than might first appear, because many business and government leaders were personally active in organized philanthropy as well.

Separate the Commercial and the Charitable

The very term "nonprofit" suggests a conscious judgment to stay out of the business of business. Indeed, the tax law pertaining to exempt organizations clearly awards the specific advantages only because of the charitable, noncommercial objectives of those organizations. Not only were private individuals prohibited from "private inurement," any "unrelated," potentially profit-making activities had to be clearly separated from the charitable side of nonprofit organizations. It followed that commercialization should not be a part of the nonprofit sector. The temptations would be great, it was understood, but colleges and universities, hospitals, and other nonprofit organizations should stay clear of competition with commercial operations. Granted, this mutual understanding was porous with exceptions. Museums discovered that they could pick up more than spare change in their stores, and justified the practice by underscoring the importance of that money to keeping the museums functioning for their cultural purposes. Drinking coffee out of a "Monet Mug" might even encourage appreciation of Impressionist paintings. Colleges found that they could advertise commercial products on their scoreboards, and thereby help to fund their athletic programs. Most schools were careful to stay away from cigarettes and hard liquor, though beer ads were common. Institutions signed exclusive agreements with Nike and other equipment suppliers, and with Coca-Cola and other soft-drink sellers. As a matter of tax policy, concerns about unrelated business income became increasingly common, but the underlying commitment of nonprofit organizations to stay clear of business was understood and accepted.

Again, there were exceptions. Businesses have always trained their employees, but for-profit educational institutions were for many years seen almost as an oxymoron, and many accreditation groups made nonprofit status a condition of their approval. The notion of a hospital organized to make money seemed similarly an anathema—inconsistent with the very notion of a hospital that put all its energies and efforts into enhancing the health of its patients. Although there were many shades of gray in the zone between profit and nonprofit, the understanding to respect each other's gardens was a real one, and on the whole it worked for many decades. It was seen as good for both sides, and for the country.

Avoid Partisan Politics

A second pillar of the old covenant was the prohibition against two forms of political activity. In exchange for tax-free status, nonprofit entities were not supposed to engage in efforts to influence either legislation or the outcomes of elections. But the understanding went deeper and had roots more complex than simply avoiding efforts to influence Congress, state legislatures, city councils, or the election of their members. It was based also on a strongly held—though implicit—view that the eleemosynary activities of foundations and other nonprofit entities ought to be noncontroversial, lest they run into political complaint. Few legislators are inclined to sit idly by when tax-exempt organizations oppose their favorite bills or lend support to their electoral rivals.

Sensitivity to the political activities of tax-exempt organizations was especially heightened with respect to foundations. During the 1960s the Ford Foundation, the most visible of all foundations at the time, was criticized for crossing the line into politics through grants it made to support voter registration, school decentralization in New York, advocacy organizations, and, most visibly, a group of former aides to Robert F. Kennedy. In a volume for the 1972 American Assembly on "The Future of Foundations," Jeffrey Hart (1973, p. 53) wrote: "the tax-free foundations represent a conspicuous form of irresponsible power. By this I mean that they can intervene in a variety of ways in political and social matters, and they can do so without any restraining influence by those whom their actions damage." It is interesting, and not a little ironic, that the warnings about the unchecked power of foundations voiced by conservatives in the 1970s are now being voiced by liberals, who maintain that conservative foundations have succeeded in shaping current policy debate, creating, in Covington's (1998, p. 48) words, "a supply-side version of American politics in which policy ideas with enough money behind them will find their niche in the political marketplace regardless of existing citizen demand." As Karl and Karl suggest in chapter 3, criticisms of this kind are part of a longstanding suspicion that foundations are an instrument that can be used by powerful groups to influence popular opinion.[2]

As was true regarding the first condition, there were frequent breaches of this one. Berman (1982) makes a powerful case, for example, that major U.S. foundations—Ford, Rockefeller, and Carnegie—played a significant role in promoting American foreign policy interests in Africa in the post-war era. A few foundations, such as the Public Welfare Foundation,[3] always prided themselves in supporting advocacy groups. And many, of course, did policy analysis, which almost inevitably turns out to have policy implications.

It seems paradoxical that, at the very time that public policy issues, as one category of controversial matters, were generally understood to be off-limits to organized philanthropy, government was collaborating increasingly with organized philanthropy and using it to carry out its policies. Particularly in the realm of human services, the federal government relied heavily on nonprofit organizations, and the nonprofit sector grew enormously from the 1960s to the 1980s as a result of government funding, as Grønbjerg and Smith point out in chapter 7. The tide sharply turned in the Reagan era, but government support has remained the dominant source of dollars for the work of the nonprofit sector in human services.[4]

Let a Thousand Flowers Bloom

In addition to the admonitions to steer clear of commercialization and politics, the old covenant also contained a couple of implicit understandings. The first was that, in judging the success of the nonprofit sector, experimentation and innovation were more important than coordination. A common concern running through several of the essays in this volume is the lack of coordination among foundations in their support of almost every arena of the nonprofit sector, and among the entities within that sector. Especially with respect to foundations, innovation and experimentation are seen as philanthropic virtues; coordination and staying power are not. This understanding is based on a number of sources. The strong streak of individualism, and the glorification of individual initiative that was so central to American philanthropy in the era of Carnegie and Rockefeller, is certainly one.

Another root is the inherent appeal of backing something new and untried. Time and again, foundation executives tell themselves, in words that have become cliches: "There is too little money and too much to do. We must use our scarce funding to leverage the greatest possible benefit. The rarest resource is good ideas. So betting on a new one can make the biggest bang." As

McKersie and Markward suggest in chapter 18, most private foundations operate under the unwritten rule that grants must be strictly limited in duration.

The structure of the nonprofit sector itself also discourages coordination among funders, for there is so little coordination among organizations that receive funding. Over one million organizations, apart from religious congregations, are included within the sector. Hundreds of new ones are born each day. An individual Pied Piper sees a need, persuades a few others to join forces, and a new effort is formed. The founders seldom have interest in coordinating with others—otherwise they would not have started the new effort in the first place. It is usually only when the organization has grown significantly or a second generation of leaders emerges that the importance of coordination becomes evident.

The community chest movement, including its most famous manifestation, United Way, was an exception. The movement developed to bring coordination to the funding of community needs. Local organizations were formed to coordinate charity even before 1900, as Pratt's example of Associated Charities in the Twin Cities in 1892 in chapter 14 demonstrates. Starting in Pittsburgh in 1913, United Way had a simple basic concept: An association of charities would appoint delegates to a central council, develop modes of cooperative handling of a community's social problems, and seek funds together in ways that would give donors confidence in the integrity of the expenditures and minimize the duplication of effort. Over the years, United Way became a national organization, and until it stumbled in the 1990s, it was extraordinarily successful, although critics often accused it of being unresponsive to emerging needs and too beholden to established interests. Pressures to fractionate, to allow donors more and more choices among competing agencies, have constantly eroded the strength of the coordinated approach in many communities.

Despite these and other sporadic attempts at coordination, philanthropy and the nonprofit sector have remained essentially unorganized. Indeed, some would see in this lack of coordination one of the sector's principal virtues, an institutional celebration of liberty and free expression, a seed bed for pluralism. This apparent disorganization reaches perhaps its purest embodiment in private foundations—uncoordinated in action and virtually unaccountable to anyone. The ability to create such institutions is a direct benefit of our First Amendment freedoms, but with that benefit have come the scars that accompany disarray: duplication, overlapping responsibilities, and unintended gaps in service.

Leave Social Services to the Government

A second understanding in the old covenant was that social services were a weak claimant for philanthropic dollars. A number of reasons led to this understanding. The most important was the reality that the needs for social services were so extensive that there has never, in the decades since the New Deal, been a realistic possibility of more than marginal amelioration from organized philanthropy. Not only are the needs of poor people for social services overwhelming in magnitude, they are also multifaceted. As demonstrated in research by economists and sociologists, the problems of persistent poverty—unemployment, inadequate schooling, out-of-wedlock births, crime, and welfare dependency—are often interrelated.[5] As intractable as those problems appear to be, there seems to be little chance that small measures will be effective in their amelioration. With this reality comes a concern, which we heard voiced by some foundation officials at the Assembly conference, that if philanthropy starts to become more deeply engaged in social services, those in government will think that they are "off the hook," as one conference participant said to us. Indeed, a cynic might argue that the shedding of governmental responsibility is precisely the aim of appeals to the nonprofit sector's "thousand points of light" to deal with social problems.

The Forces of Change

Change is reshaping all parts of American society. Philanthropy and the nonprofit sector are no exceptions. Two clusters of change deserve particular emphasis here because they directly affect philanthropy and the nonprofit sector. One is the marked transformation of the country's distribution of income and wealth. As shown by Wolff in chapter 4, the share of income received by the most affluent households increased sharply during the 1980s and 1990s, while the portion received by those at the low end declined. This growing inequality in income reflects a tremendous increase in the importance of skills and education in determining earnings. Most of those who fail to obtain a high school degree are doomed to a life of very low earnings. A related economic trend has occurred in the distribution of wealth. As stated in the Assembly report, one percent of the population now own almost half of the country's wealth. One result, as noted by Brown in chapter 10, is a dramatic increase in the amount of wealth that is likely to be bequeathed over the next few decades. Hence the future holds both a burgeoning potential for increased philanthropy and the prospect for a growing number of permanently impoverished individuals. Takanishi's chapter 16 underscores the devastating impact of this prospect on the lives of growing numbers of children in poverty.

A second major change is an unmistakable loss of confidence in the potential for government programs to deal with the problems of poverty, family dissolution, and crime. The response by an increasingly conservative national government has been to back away from welfare and some Great Society programs and to devolve responsibilities from the national to the state and local levels. And this devolution has been accompanied, as Boris writes in chapter 1, by a call to nonprofit organizations to take up some of the resulting slack. While it is quite reasonable to expect nonprofit organizations to be engaged directly in the provision of many social services—in fact they have specific responsibilities under the welfare reform act of 1996—it is quite unrealistic to expect private philanthropy to pick up a significant share of any reductions in government spending on social programs. Moreover, as Lenkowsky notes in chapter 6, the the current trend of devolving federal functions to state and local governments will present nationally oriented nonprofit organizations with new challenges.

Three other society-wide changes do not directly affect organized philanthropy or the nonprofit sector, but their indirect effects will be substantial. One is the tremendous technological advances in information and communications that are taking place with increasing rapidity. As the speed and capacity of computers have risen, the cost of access to their power has fallen markedly. The costs of other means of communicating have also plummeted, and these changes promise to revolutionize education and much of the rest of the nonprofit sector. A second and related change is the increasing globalization of economic trade and social contact. Rising numbers of foundations and other nonprofit organizations are involved in matters that stretch beyond U.S. borders. Third, the rapidly changing demographics of our society, fueled in part by immigration, has led to substantial increases in minority populations, particularly Latinos. Minority groups, both established and emerging, need special attention from philanthropy and the nonprofit sector, as Carson and Diaz demonstrate in chapters 12 and 13.

The New Covenant

These forces over the past two decades have transformed the world inhabited by nonprofit organizations. As a result, we believe that the old covenant between philanthropy and the nonprofit sector on the one hand, and American society on the other, is no longer in effect. A new covenant has implicitly been formed. If we are right, this new covenant was not triggered by any single event, and it certainly has not been memorialized in a signing ceremony. But starting sometime in the early 1980s, this new covenant took shape in the form of four key revisions of the old covenant. We briefly examine here those revisions. Each can be explained as a logical consequence of other changes underway in American society, and particularly of the forces we previously outlined. At the same time, in our view, each of them stretches the traditional fabric of public trust that has been a key to the success of philanthropy and the nonprofit sector in America. Each of them, to some degree, has the potential to enhance public suspicions as trust is eroded.

Commercial Is Not a Dirty Word

Although the traditional wall of separation between commerce and philanthropy has always had holes, we have serious concerns about recent incursions of commercialism into the realm of philanthropy and the nonprofit sector. One indication of the shifting importance of philanthropy and commerce is the marked decline in the importance of private donations to nonprofit organizations. Between 1965 and 1993, contributions as a share of nonprofit revenues fell by half, from 53 to 24 percent (Hodgkinson & Weitzman, 1996, Table 2.1). Higher education can serve as an example. Certainly tuitions at private colleges and universities have risen in real terms (Clotfelter 1996, ch. 1). Other forms of non-donative revenues have risen as well. For example, it is hard to find a college or university these days that does not allow use of some of its space for commercial advertising or that does not have at least a few exclusive licences with companies that make everything from software to soft drinks. Perhaps more startling, the fastest growing institution of higher education in the country, the University of Phoenix, operates for profit.

The arguments for this revision of the old covenant are well known. Many educational institutions and other organizations in the nonprofit sector face soaring costs and dwindling resources. The costs of the needs they serve are escalating. Commercial enterprises provide institutions new resources to put to good use, as Levy notes in chapter 5. Some observers have noted that many arenas traditionally the exclusive province of nonprofits are now actively mined by commercial firms. Hospitals and other health-care providers are prime examples.

There are reasons to be concerned by the blurring of boundaries in both directions, but our point here is that, in the eyes of many, trust in the nonprofit sector was sustained in part by its separation from the commercial sector. Accepting donations from for-profit companies—whether or not those donations were motivated by bottom-line considerations—is not the same as engaging in for-profit activities. But to the public this distinction is not always clear. As one example, public television programs are often preceded by prominent announcements from corporate sponsors. And the landscape is made more confusing by the apparent growth in "cause-related marketing" and other revenue-generating enterprises, ranging from those museum shops to intercollegiate sports to the sale of spin-off toys based on children's public television shows.[6] Whether the income generated is ultimately deemed to be taxable "unrelated business income," the result is definitely to blur the lines between charitable and the commercial in the public's mind. In short, this element of the new covenant, however under-standable—and in many cases, no doubt, laudable—does put at risk public trust in the nonprofit sector.

Politics and Public Policy Are Not Off Limits

The prohibitions against political activity in the Internal Revenue Code have not changed. Tax-exempt organizations are still precluded from "carry-ing on propaganda, or otherwise attempting to influence legislation" and "participating in, or intervening in, any political campaign on behalf of (or in opposition to) any candidates for public office" (U.S. Internal Revenue Code, Section 504(a)). But it seems likely that any sweeping prohibition against political activity has been significantly altered, if not abandoned. Whether the way was led by nonprofit groups on the right or on the left is not important. Nor is it significant which has been more successful.

This revision, unlike commercialism, we think has been on the whole a desirable change. It is more than a cliché that American democracy depends on an actively engaged citizenry that is informed by policy analysis and advocacy. While it is appropriate to continue to restrict tax-exempt organiza-tions from supporting or opposing individual candidates or specific pieces of legislation, actions to place wider restrictions on participation in policy debates are unwise. As we discuss more fully in our concluding section, we concur with the following judgment in the Assembly report: "This function of the nonprofit sector is vital to the health of democracy. We think, if anything, these roles should be expanded, not contracted."

We recognize, however, that this shift is not without a price in the realm of trust, just as with the shift to commercialism. Except when it took the role of neutral forum, as played so well for so long by the League of Women Voters, the nonprofit sector tended to stay out of the political fray, and by becoming more involved it risks being tarnished by the same muck that often is thrown at politicians. The reality that most politicians do not deserve the scorn so generally and generously heaped on their occupation does not ease the problem. The price, we are convinced, is worth paying, but it needs to be understood as a real cost of the new covenant.

Philanthropy and the Nonprofit Sector Need Coordination

Although its origins are understandable, the lack of coordination that characterizes philanthropy and the nonprofit sector has disadvantages, and we believe those disadvantages will become more severe if they are ignored. To be sure, the radical adherence to independence of action in the old covenant had the virtue of discouraging monolithic approaches to social issues. Such an atomistic structure serves the aim of pluralism. It may also enhance efficiency, if independent foundations and nonprofit agencies compete in the "marketplace of ideas" in search of the most efficacious approaches to social problems. Unfortunately, this atomistic structure all too often results in duplication, as organizations reinvent wheels that others have already developed, tried out, and retained or discarded. Without better communication among both funding and operating organizations regarding the success of various initiatives, the multitude of nonprofit organizations are doomed to waste resources. But, in light of the advances in Internet and other communications technology, as well as the capacity to evaluate programs that Walker and Grossman highlight in chapter 21, it is reasonable to imagine a marked improvement in the kind of information sharing that could greatly improve the efficiency of the nonprofit sector's operation.

Social Services Need Increased Attention from Philanthropy and the Nonprofit Sector

We readily grant that the funding potential of American philanthropy is no match for the country's aggregate need for spending to combat poverty and its associated social ills. Government must be the primary funder for welfare and other social services, if not always the provider. Only a very few philanthropists can expect to make a dent in combating large social problems. At the same time, we believe philanthropy and the nonprofit sector must not only sustain, but increase, their attention to the problems of the poor. We agree with the Assembly report when it states: "The most urgent and important contribution of philanthropy and the nonprofit sector lies in focusing attention on the increasing economic inequality that afflicts us all." Some of this contribution should come through enhanced direct services to people in need. But the Assembly report makes clear that philanthropy and the nonprofit sector cannot solve the problem alone. Indeed, it suggests that the most important contributions may be in generating knowledge about the nature and causes of poverty, by developing new policy options, and by engaging in advocacy and promoting the empowerment of affected groups. But these, too, are activities traditionally outside the bailiwick of most nonprofit organizations. Thus they may well engender not only controversy but suspicion.

To cite one example, we applaud the proposals by Takanishi that philanthropy and the nonprofit sector become more actively engaged in promoting new policies on behalf of children in poverty, and the Assembly report endorsed at least the broad conclusions of her essay. But her strategy, which we endorse, would seek to reverse a set of public policies adopted overwhelmingly by the U.S. Congress, and approved (if reluctantly) by the President. Presumably, a substantial majority of Americans agree with those policies. Challenging them, therefore, means challenging the views of most Americans, and that step, though fully justified, will not come without costs, including costs in trust.

A Renewal of Trust

We believe there has been a perceptible decline in Americans' trust in philanthropy and the nonprofit sector over the time that the new covenant was being developed. Much of that decline was inherent in forces that are beyond reach or repair by those within philanthropy and the nonprofit sector, for they relate directly to the general decline in public faith regarding institutions of all kinds—public and for-profit, as well as nonprofit. But, as we have tried to show, we also believe that elements of what we term the new covenant have exacerbated the decline. Whether that assessment is accurate, it is clearly incumbent on all of us involved in philanthropy and the nonprofit sector to work to rebuild public trust. Without that trust, our traditions are, as Payton warns in chapter 23, in jeopardy. In our view, moreover, special opportunities now exist to enhance public trust in both public and private institutions, apart from philanthropy and the nonprofit sector, but in ways that will enhance them as well. But first, our summary thoughts about reforming our own house.

The Assembly report spells out a set of steps to increase disclosure of the activities of philanthropy and the nonprofit sector, through strengthening the Internal Revenue Service's Form 990, by expanded publicity on the Internet and in print, and through encouraging public discourse and debate in a wide range of settings. We certainly concur in these proposals. Disclosure is important; so is publicity.

Unfortunately, whenever one individual or organization in the nonprofit sector is discovered doing misdeeds, the harm of that betrayal of trust tends to infect others in the sector. We therefore also endorse the steps proposed in the Assembly report for enhancing compliance and enforcement by public agencies at every level—which implies adequate funding of these agencies—and by the sector itself through codes of ethics and standards of behavior. These are modest steps forward and need prompt attention.

In addition, and more important, we support the recommendation by Fleishman in chapter 8 that a new federal agency be charged with responsibility for policing, and therefore protecting, philanthropy and the nonprofit sector. We recognize that the proposal received little support at the Assembly conference. Most participants seemed to feel that their organizations were not in need of further public scrutiny, particularly by a new government agency. In their view, the current level of public accountability is adequate. Some thought the current level is actually excessive. Many argued that they already spent too much time filling out forms to justify what their organizations were doing. But we think that Fleishman makes a persuasive case that public accountability for philanthropy and the nonprofit sector should extend well beyond issues of taxability, and that the Internal Revenue Service is ill-equipped to handle the task.

In fact, we reluctantly concluded over the course of the Assembly conference that too many of us working in philanthropy and the nonprofit sector believe that simply because we know we are doing good, the public should trust us. Not enough of us seem to recognize that public trust must not just be earned, but continually earned. The public is entitled to continued evidence that trust is warranted. In part, this can come through increased disclosure and publicity. The Assembly report proposed other steps that should have long-term impacts on public trust, including substantial education about the roles and responsibilities of philanthropy and the nonprofit sector. But each of us needs to think hard as well about what we can do as individuals—and through our institutions—to promote public trust.

We have already emphasized that the decline in public trust regarding philanthropy and the nonprofit sector is not an isolated virus. Rather, numerous polls and surveys have chronicled a loss of public confidence in all institutions. Government at every level, particularly the federal government, is subject to the most serious erosion of public faith. The for-profit sector is suffering in similar, though less severe, ways. Our concluding judgment— "plea" may be a better term—is that philanthropy has vital roles to play in helping to restore faith in all three sectors, and, by vigorously leading in those roles, it can lead as well in reestablishing public trust in all the institutions of our society.

The values of philanthropy and the nonprofit sector—values of giving, caring, and volunteering—are at the heart of the democratic renewal that is so needed. Democracy means political engagement, but it involves much more than politics. Democracy requires participation in making and maintaining communities in all aspects of their civic affairs. It demands engagement—not as spectators, but as participants. Voting and jury service are important obligations of American citizenship. But they are not the only ones, if our democracy is to function both wisely and effectively. A citizenry educated in the substance of public issues, and the processes by which they are resolved, is needed, along with commitment to help directly and personally in those processes. Philanthropy and the nonprofit sector can encourage all of us to immerse ourselves in the real work of democracy. Part of that immersion must come through education, part through model projects, and part through programs that encourage advocacy, empowerment, and service.

A number of important philanthropic efforts are well underway to strengthen American "social capital" and to enhance the nation's civil society. We think, for example, of projects on civic engagement and responsibility sponsored by the Kettering Foundation, by the Pew Charitable Trusts, and by the Surdna Foundation, to name just three. We endorse efforts of this sort on an expanded basis and with increased coordination. Coordination in such efforts is critical. Strengthening our civil society should not have to depend on isolated efforts, however numerous or individually meritorious.

Powerful forces in our society promote unmitigated individualism and political alienation. We see in our own domain of higher education how students seem alienated from civic affairs generally and political affairs particularly. Counteracting these trends will require a coordinated strategy. We certainly do not outline that strategy here; that would be the subject of a further volume, not just another essay. But we do emphasize how important we think this work is to the nation's future and to the roles of philanthropy and the nonprofit sector in that future. Borrowing the concluding words of the Assembly report, we challenge philanthropy and the nonprofit sector "to devote more resources to issues that are fundamentally threatening to our society, to perform more imaginatively and effectively, openly and inclusively, and to transmit and advance the values undergirding our civil society: trust, service and the common purpose."

Notes

1. Hansman (1989) makes a similar distinction.

2. Karl and Karl cite in particular the Gramscian Marxist critique that sees in foundations a tool of the capitalist class to exert influence by influencing popular opinion.

3. As a matter of disclosure, we note that Tom Ehrlich is a member of the board of directors.

4. See also Salamon and Abramson (1966).

5. For demonstrations of this interrelatedness, see, for example, Wilson (1987) and Danziger, Sandefur, and Weinberg (1994).

6. See, for example, Weisbrod (1998) or Walter Goodman, "Perils of Nonprofit Profits: Et Tu, Tinky Winky?" *New York Times*, April 23, 1998, p. E2.

References

Bellah, Robert et al. *The Good Society.* New York: Knopf, 1991.

Berman, Edward H. "The Foundations' Role in American Foreign Policy: The Case of Africa, post 1945." In Robert F. Arnove, ed., *Philanthropy and Cultural Imperialism: The Foundations at Home and Abroad.* Bloomington: Indiana University Press, 1982.

Clotfelter, Charles T. *Buying the Best: Cost Escalation in Elite Higher Education.* Princeton: Princeton University Press, 1996.

Covington, Sally. *Moving a Public Policy Agenda: The Strategic Philanthropy of Conservative Foundations.* Washington, DC: National Committee for Responsive Philanthropy, 1998.

Danziger, Sheldon H., Gary D. Sandefur, and Daniel H. Weinberg, eds. *Confronting Poverty: Prescriptions for Change.* New York: Russell Sage Foundation, 1994.

Hansmann, Henry. "The Role of Nonprofit Enterprise." *Yale Law Journal* 89 (1980), 835–901.

Hansmann, Henry. "The Two Nonprofit Sectors: Fee for Service versus Donative Organizations." In Virginia A. Hodgkinson and Richard W. Lyman, eds. *The Future of the Nonprofit Sector.* San Francisco: Jossey-Bass, 1989, pp. 91–102.

Hart, Jeffrey. "Foundations and Social Activism: A Critical View." In Fritz F. Heimann, ed., *The Future of Foundations*. Englewood Cliffs, NJ: Prentice-Hall, 1973, pp. 43–57.

Hodgkinson, Virginia A., and Murrey S. Weitzman, eds. *Nonprofit Almanac 1996–1997*. San Francisco: Jossey-Bass, 1996.

Katz, Michael B. *In the Shadow of the Poorhouse*. New York: Basic Books, 1986.

Salamon, Lester and Alan Abramson. "The Federal Budget and the Nonprofit Sector." In Dwight F. Burlingame, William A. Diaz, Warren F. Ilchman, et al., *Capacity for Change? The Nonprofit World in the Age of Devolution*. Indianapolis: Indiana University Center on Philanthropy, 1996.

Simon, John G. "Foundations and Public Controversy: An Affirmative View." In Fritz F. Heimann, ed., *The Future of Foundations*. Englewood Cliffs, NJ: Prentice-Hall, 1973, pp. 58–100.

U.S. Internal Revenue Code. New York: The Research Institute of America, 1992.

Weisbrod, Burton A., ed. *The Commercialism Dilemma of the Nonprofit Sector*, special edition of the *Journal of Policy Analysis and Management* 17, Spring 1998.

Wilson, William J. *The Truly Disadvantaged*. Chicago: University of Chicago Press, 1987.

Appendix

Trust, Service, and the Common Purpose:
Philanthropy and the Nonprofit Sector
in a Changing America

FINAL REPORT OF THE NINETY-THIRD AMERICAN ASSEMBLY

At the close of their discussions, the participants in the Ninety-third American Assembly, on "The Future of Philanthropy in a Changing America," at the Getty Center, in Los Angeles, California, April 23–26, 1998, reviewed as a group the following statement. This statement represents general agreement; however, no one was asked to sign it. Furthermore, it should be understood that not everyone agreed with all of it.

I. Introduction

Americans take legitimate pride in their civic spirit, as expressed in their philanthropic giving and habits of volunteerism. Deeply rooted in our varied pasts, as well as reflecting our religious values and the constitutional convictions of our First Amendment, these traditions of generosity have spawned an astoundingly diverse set of institutions. They range from private schools and colleges, immigrant self-help groups, philanthropic foundations, community-based organizations, policy think tanks, hospitals, museums, and symphony orchestras to grass-roots movements, church-based social initiatives, medical charities, disaster relief organizations, and national federations. Despite their variety we often think of these organizations as comprising a single "sector," calling it by various names—nonprofit, philanthropic, voluntary, independent, third sector, or civil society.

Although government and business are its counterparts, we must view the sectors as interdependent rather than fully autonomous. Traditions of limited government could not persist without a third sector carrying out many of our public purposes; capitalist, civic, and philanthropic values have been critically intertwined throughout much of our history, and working in complementary fashion, the three sectors have seen their relationships evolve as Americans have defined and redefined their social purposes.

Although the sectors have always been interdependent, philanthropy and the nonprofit sector are marked by a distinctive mix of features. They engage people in collective purposes outside either the marketplace or the state; their entities are independently organized and self-governing; they give voice to social demands and diverse viewpoints; they deliver services to varied constituencies; and they serve as monitors and watchdogs of the other sectors and, at times, of their own performance.

Philanthropy and the nonprofit sector have undergone constant evolution. Now there are forces at work in American society and the world that presage the need for new approaches. Those who have been brought together for this American Assembly see a roster of expanding opportunities, as well as challenging problems, including growing wealth disparities in this nation and the world, the persistence of poverty, especially among children and youth, the rise of ethnic conflict, and the threat of global resource shortages. At the same time, life-enhancing opportunities, such as the arts, education, and racial reconciliation, must be advanced. These issues pose challenges that ought not be deferred, especially given the reality of our nation's prosperity in recent decades, the wealth that has accumulated and that has the potential to be transferred into this sector.

Philanthropy and the nonprofit sector have grown—and will continue to do so. They have grown at a time when government's role is being reexamined and many public purposes have devolved to states, localities, and nonprofit institutions. The mix of resources within philanthropy and the nonprofit sector has also undergone a basic restructuring, with fees and market-based income expanding, government resources in some sub-sectors decreasing or taking new forms, and the relative amount of nonprofit revenues coming from philanthropic sources declining. The boundaries among the sectors are blurring, however, as many have observed, especially as nonprofits respond to a changing mix of available resources by pursuing more businesslike behaviors, including explicitly for-profit ventures. It is also clear that commercial businesses are moving into arenas such as day-care, education, human services, and healthcare that have historically been served by the nonprofit sector.

The social problems, by contrast, are daunting. The rapid changes are often perplexing. Yet in many ways the times hold great promise for philanthropy and the nonprofit sector. There is every reason to expect that financial support will increase. Philanthropy and the nonprofit sector are looked to across the political spectrum to help society deal with its problems and to sustain its civil culture. The challenge is to exploit the opportunities to best advantage.

The Nonprofit Sector

The nonprofit sector of American society is comprised of a mix of tax-exempt organizations. In 1995 it included approximately 1.2 million organizations. About half of these are public-service or "charitable" nonprofits, eligible for tax-deductible contributions as 501(c)(3) organizations. In addition, 341,000 religious congregations are eligible for tax-deductible contributions. Another 140,000 groups have section 501 (c)(4) status and most of these are not eligible for tax-deductible contributions. In 1994 total income for the sector was estimated at $568 billion and accounted for roughly 7 percent of the national income. Some 10 million workers, representing 10 percent of the nation's labor pool, worked within the sector and another 5.5 million full-time-equivalent workers served as volunteers. In 1995 some 90 million Americans volunteered.

In recent decades, year in and year out, charitable giving by Americans has amounted to about 2 percent of national income, or a total of about $150 billion in 1995. Of that amount, about 79 percent came from living individuals and another 7 percent was left by individual bequests. Philanthropic foundations gave 8 percent, or nearly $12 billion, and corporations gave about 6 percent or about $8.5 billion. This giving, while relatively stable over the long term, has recently declined relative to income among the higher-income brackets as marginal tax rates have decreased. Only 19 percent of estate-tax returns filed in 1995 included charitable bequests. In contrast, giving from philanthropic foundations has increased substantially in recent years, making it the second largest source of philanthropic income in the sector. Foundations, whether large or small, community or independent, now number 42,500, and some 45 percent were created since 1980. Corporate giving has also grown in real dollars, but it has declined as a percentage of pre-tax corporate income during the past decade. Corporate giving includes not only corporate and corporate foundation contributions to nonprofit organizations, but also sponsorship and in-kind contributions of equipment, products, and services such as technical assistance and help with marketing and promotion.

The diversity and expansive scope of the sector poses a challenge to its coherence. The organizations of the sector are diverse in their missions and purposes as well as their size, complexity, and financial resources. Hospitals, colleges, and universities command the largest share of the sector's resources, pay some of the highest salaries, and employ the largest and most highly trained staffs. Grass-roots and social service organizations often operate with small staffs, low salaries, and volunteer help, and have little or no financial flexibility. Fewer than 4 percent of the nonprofit organizations reporting to the IRS have budgets in excess of $10 million, but they account for 75 percent of the total expenditures. The top 1 percent of nonprofit charities (excluding foundations) hold two-fifths of the sector's assets.

This is the background against which we present our report. Section II outlines the forces of change that cause us to believe it is important now to review the opportunities and responsibilities of philanthropy and the nonprofit sector. Section III considers the roles and contributions of philanthropy and the nonprofit sector to society. Section IV proposes a set of recommendations about the internal operations of philanthropy and the nonprofit sector. And Section V lists recommendations that look to the external environment in which philanthropy and the nonprofit sector operate.

II. The Forces Determining the Shape and Activities of Philanthropy and the Nonprofit Sector

Major forces are shaping the activities of philanthropy and the nonprofit sector, forces that have their roots in earlier eras, but have gathered strength and promise to shape the future. These forces will create the problems and the opportunities, they will determine the agendas, and they will shape the means at hand to address the agendas.

Inequality

After decades of narrowing the gap between rich and poor—brought about by policy and economic growth—the last two decades have seen rising inequality in income and a growing concentration of wealth, with 1 percent of the U.S. population currently owning 35 percent of the wealth. This remarkable accumulation of wealth places a special responsibility and opportunity for those with that wealth, one that guides the American tradition of philanthropy. This inequality is exacerbated by the changing access to technology and education, revealing the specter of a permanent underclass in the United States. This not only bodes ill for social peace, but also it means the loss of potential talent and innovation for society and economic growth. Addressing the needs of the poor has acquired new urgency, especially in light of the termination of welfare entitlements. With the devolution of some federal governmental roles in the alleviation of poverty to state or local governments, the nonprofit sector must increasingly play a strong role in the partnership to solve these problems. Moreover, within the nonprofit sector itself, there is a growing disparity between those institutions capable of mounting major drives for endowments and those grass-roots organizations struggling to achieve their missions.

Demography

Demographic forces have had a transforming impact on American society, just as they have had around the globe. Immigration into the United States has risen markedly in the past twenty years, increasing the total population at the same time as it introduces new groups to the United States. Internal growth, varying across social groups, changes the demographic structure of American society. The result has been shifts in the proportions of racial and ethnic groups in the country, especially with the growth of both Latinos and Asians—groups with highly distinctive cultures. At the same time, various factors have changed the age distribution of the population, with the particular result of increasing the proportion of the elderly. We have also seen a marked change in the distribution of the country's population, with the movement to cities and, more recently, to the suburbs. We have also seen a major shift in geographical distribution, with population moving roughly from the northeast to the southwest, from the rustbelt to the sunbelt. These shifts necessitate greater flexibility and inclusiveness in philanthropy and the nonprofit sector, as new client groups emerge with distinctive needs. They also change both the location and the nature of some social problems, and cause the sector to rethink its strategies and methods for coping with these problems. Philanthropy and the nonprofit sector need to address the cultural attitudes and approaches of emerging groups toward philanthropy. This requires dialogue and experience leading to the integration of these groups into the American philanthropic tradition. It may also mean the transformation of that heritage in light of new contributions from these cultures. In addition, new and younger philanthropists are emerging with the promise of making substantial contributions to helping meet social needs.

Globalization

Problems have no borders, nor do opportunities to address them. The movements of populations and goods, of communications and capital, of effluents and terrorism, do not respect political and geographic boundaries. In an increasingly interdependent world, these forces can no longer be contained. Thus, the activities of U.S.-based philanthropy and the nonprofit sector at times need to include an international dimension. What is addressed by philanthropy and the nonprofit sector in one setting may be swamped in other settings. Who are our neighbors and what do we owe them? Corporate partners, once dedicated to a setting, now must attend where their work takes them and it takes them globally. On the other hand, innovative ideas, such as micro-lending to villages in Bangladesh, can be adopted to energize efforts in inner city America.

Technology

The revolutions in information technology and computing have affected almost every aspect of modern life both in positive and negative ways. On the positive side, technology has made possible a speed and range of communications that far surpass anything known before. It has connected people and nations, and has shrunk the size of the world. New modes of communications help to create new, virtual communities of many kinds. Computing introduces new efficiencies. Technology also creates new possibilities for individual expression, cultural preservation, and global understanding. On the negative side, however, the technological revolution threatens to create new forms of inequality because individuals, groups, and nations have unequal access to the technology and education. The new ease of communications and the creation of virtual communities may weaken physical participation in social, civic, or common spaces. The cost of access to the technology can be enormous and can create distortions in funding patterns. For the philanthropic sector, technology is a double-edged sword, creating both new opportunities and new threats.

Expression and Transmission of Values

A major configuring force is the widespread individual search for values—of hope, purpose, and meaning—in an increasingly diverse and competitive environment. A source and product of this search are the waning authority of the state and family. The search can be seen in the rise of religious institutions in both its sacred and civic responsibilities, where religious institutions are expected to provide a sense of achievement, to serve as vehicles for opportunity, and to give social direction. While this search contains the potential for divisiveness and the eroding of consensus, it also has the potential of releasing great energy, commitment, and innovation.

Blurring of the Sectoral Roles

There has been a profound shift in the boundaries of the major sectors of American society—the state, the market, and that space between them that we call the "independent" or nonprofit sector (which some today call civil society). A generation ago, with a large and growing state sector and a vigorous business community, the nonprofit sector appeared fairly small and well-defined, serving as a buffer between the state and society. Today the boundaries dividing the three sectors are not clear. The public sector is reassessing its role in some areas and altering the relationship among federal, state, and local governments, as well as the nonprofit sector. The reform of the welfare system is one example of this altering set of relationships. The state is increasingly employing market mechanisms as privatization of public services becomes more and more common. The market has also impinged upon the nonprofit sector, as not-for-profit hospitals are taken over by the health industry, and business enters education at all levels.

Both marketization and the withdrawal of the state have intensified the competitive aspect of service provision, and have decreased funding available to nonprofit institutions that previously depended upon partnerships with the state. The nonprofit sector faces intense competition for, and need for, funds. A result is an increasing emphasis on generating fees to accomplish missions. The reality is, however, that more and more activity is hard to characterize as public, market, or nonprofit as partnerships and hybrid forms of organization come to be the rule. The advantage of this shift is that sectoral interpenetration may facilitate social innovation and efficiency. This blurring of sectoral functions may also, however, erode public awareness of, and confidence in, the nonprofit sector and bring into question the values and moral authority of the sector.

Devolution

A shift in power and resources from the federal government to state and local government is a major force affecting the future of philanthropy and the nonprofit sector. The restructuring of governmental roles and responsibilities disrupts old habits and partnerships, enhances the need for alternative sources of revenue, and creates new expectations about the performance of nonprofit organizations. At the same time, it creates opportunities for new partnerships with local and regional organizations and innovative strategies to address pressing public problems.

Citizen Initiative and Social Entrepreneurship

One of the most significant developments in recent years is the growth of a large and strong *competitive* citizen sector, multiplying hundreds of thousands of independent citizen organizations competing openly with one another to serve the public good. The accelerating growth in the size and sophistication of this sector over the last two decades is a significant opportunity. This change, great in the United States, is even more dramatic in the rest of the world.

Social entrepreneurs, much like business entrepreneurs over the last several centuries, represent the critical cutting edge of this rapidly evolving sector. Social entrepreneurship and the competitive citizen sector are dependent on and critical to democracy. One of their most important impacts is to increase the growth rate of productivity in the social arena—closing the socially harmful gap between social and economic productivity.

The faster the social arenas change, the greater is the need for strategic and structural planning for the philanthropic sector as a whole.

III. Roles and Contributions of Philanthropy and the Nonprofit Sector

In charting the future of philanthropy and the nonprofit sector, it is necessary to develop a rough sense of where they can make distinctive contributions to the welfare of society.

We can produce a list of important substantive problems faced by the United States and the world that cry out for amelioration, if not solution. That list includes *problems* such as: growing income inequality; deep-seated poverty; educational quality and accessibility; health and access to healthcare; and domestic and transnational issues of the environment. We can also identify socially important areas that deserve strengthening, such as increasing access to, and participation in, arts and culture and integrating a diverse population, made even more diverse as a consequence of both demographic changes and immigration. And, we can identify particular social institutions and networks that need to be bolstered, such as families, communities, and civil society.

We can also identify a set of important and more or less distinctive *functions* that philanthropy and the nonprofit sector perform for the society. Among the most important and distinctive of these functions is the role that philanthropy and the nonprofit sector play in providing vehicles for the expression, cultivation, conservation, and development of civic and public values. Many individuals want to serve others. They also have causes they want to advance. Society is enhanced when philanthropy and the nonprofit sector provide opportunities for individuals to pursue these ends, and in doing so, help to protect and sustain these values. It is improved both because the lives of its individual members are better off, and because society enjoys the collective benefits of a stronger citizenry. A closely related second function performed by philanthropy and the nonprofit sector is the creation of networks of trust and reciprocity that have come to be called "social capital," that undergird civil society. Individuals with a desire to serve find others with whom they can make common cause in the nation's congregations, community development corporations, and neighborhood associations. Their connections provide a capacity for direct action on some problems, and for providing communities with an effective voice in business, government, and civic forums. A third function is to improve the quality of democratic politics. Sometimes this goal is achieved by reaching and empowering people who would not otherwise participate in political activity. (This often occurs as a result of having built the social capital referred to above.) Sometimes it is realized by giving the political, policy-making process high-quality information about the size and character of problems, their important causes, and some effective alternative solutions. And sometimes the goal is met by advocating for important and neglected values that might otherwise be overlooked in the political debate.

A fourth valuable function performed by philanthropy and the nonprofit sector is to increase society's capacity to alleviate human suffering and to help realize human potential. This capacity lies partly in the support of basic and applied research to solve society's problems. But it also involves confronting problems directly by mobilizing resources from contributors and deploying those resources with imagination and sensitivity for local needs and conditions. This kind of "social entrepreneurship" is increasing, and it deserves significant support. It also arises from a capacity to convene representatives from business and government, and to work with them in problem-solving partnerships. And it arises from a capacity to goad and facilitate improved action in both business operations and government administration. For example, on occasion, nonprofit organizations have shown business the technologies and practices that allowed them to succeed in aiding poor communities, or to reduce their adverse environmental impacts. Similarly, nonprofit organizations have often functioned as research and development laboratories in pioneering new solutions to social problems that government has then adopted.

Important Substantive Problems Ameliorated

Looking at the problems in the United States and the world, we think that the most urgent and important contribution of philanthropy and the nonprofit sector lies in focusing attention on the increasing economic inequality that afflicts us all. Because the problem is so large, and philanthropy and the nonprofit sector are relatively small, they cannot be expected to solve this problem alone. They can contribute to some degree by keeping food pantries open and shelters available. Their more significant contribution lies in generating knowledge about the scope and nature of the problem as well as the causes by developing policy options, by encouraging advocacy and promoting empowerment, and by mobilizing with their other civic partners—government and business—to make a concerted attack on the problem. This can and should happen at the neighborhood, national, and international levels.

Closely related to the problem of increasing economic inequality is the current plight and future prospects of children in poverty. There was a widespread sense at the Assembly that a generation of youth is at peril, and with that any claim that we might have about being a just and decent society. The failure to provide for our under-served youth is particularly grievous because we now know, in many areas, due to previous efforts by philanthropy and the nonprofit sector and others, what can be done to provide opportunities that challenge young people to develop their talents and become financially independent and productive citizens. To address this issue, we need a collective will to act on already secured knowledge using voluntary contributions and increased government tax dollars.

Many forces, including but not limited to those generated by increasing economic inequality worldwide, are exacerbating group, ethnic, religious, geographic, and national conflicts. While philanthropy and the nonprofit sector cannot be expected to solve these problems alone, there are many opportunities to increase understanding of the causes of these conflicts, to address directly some of those causes, and to explore and support approaches and institutions that could forestall and help resolve potential and actual conflicts.

Important Social Functions Enhanced

In considering the relative importance of the different functions performed by philanthropy and the nonprofit sector, we note that much public attention focuses on the roles of nonprofits in politics, policy-making, and advocacy. Doubts have been raised about the propriety of these roles. In contrast, we think that they are vital to the health of the democracy. We think if anything, these roles should be expanded not contracted.

At the same time, we recognize that the relatively *invisible* functions of philanthropy and the nonprofit sector—the ways in which they provide individuals with opportunities to express their values and to build networks of trust and reciprocity with others—are also essential to the well-being of the society. We also note that these functions have been somewhat neglected—at least in the public discourse. Society is enormously strengthened by the large number of congregations and community groups both large and small that provide the nation's citizens opportunities for charitable and civic action. This part of philanthropy and the nonprofit sector must be strengthened as well.

Finally, we realize that while much of the energy of philanthropy and the nonprofit sector in the past has gone toward improving the political process and building partnerships with government, we think that there is much future potential in focusing significant attention on selectively building effective partnerships with business. In its basic operations, business contributes to society by providing jobs, goods and services, and wealth to stockholders. Increasingly, however, business leaders are finding that it is necessary to align their financial, human resource, and business objectives with the pursuit of important social objectives. This alignment goes well beyond making charitable contributions and even involves core business functions.

To the extent that business leaders recognize their stake in the communities in which they operate and are involved in community partnerships, they can provide additional legitimacy and resources to community development efforts. Government and nonprofit organizations will fail in revitalizing communities unless business is also more directly involved.

IV. Improving Performance and Accountability

Organizations in philanthropy and the nonprofit sector should strive continually to improve their operating effectiveness and their accountability to the public. No less than organizations in the public and for-profit sectors, those in philanthropy and the nonprofit sector serve best when they operate effectively and efficiently. They must work to earn and keep the trust of those they serve. Therefore, we believe these organizations must focus on improving their performance and their accountability to those they serve. There are five general ways this can be done: enhancing operating efficiency; supporting public disclosure; strengthening existing enforcement mechanisms; improving methods by which they evaluate their activities; and assuring vigilant self-regulation.

Philanthropic and Nonprofit Organizations Need to Strive for Operational Efficiency

Just as for-profit firms must seek to streamline operations and increase efficiency, organizations in philanthropy and the nonprofit sector must do the same, if in different ways. As management-improvement approaches prescribe that firms become more attuned to their customers, both foundations and other nonprofit organizations are well advised to become more sensitive to those they serve and how effectively they serve them. This may mean adopting models from service firms to elicit reactions from clients, grant-seekers, and other stakeholders. It certainly involves continued sensitivity to the inclusion of minority groups and beneficiary groups on staffs and trustee boards. Also, as for-profit firms have expanded the use of computers to streamline their operations, foundations and other nonprofit organizations need to strive continually to find ways to harness the new technology for their charitable purposes. As discussed below, this may include using the Internet to publicize the outcomes of grants or programs to others.

Organizations in the sector can also enhance operational efficiency through the exchange of information and, in some cases, cooperation. Although the possibility of independence of action is a virtue offered by the sector, opportunities for sharing of information should be sought. For example, more foundations might use their resources to educate program officers and trustees of other foundations, allowing them to take advantage of their experience.

Activities of Philanthropy and the Nonprofit Sector Should Be Fully Communicated to the Public

In order to promote public trust and to motivate giving and volunteering, the activities of philanthropy and the nonprofit sector should be fully disclosed to the public. Annual reports, newsletters, and the like can be excellent sources for public understanding of philanthropy and the nonprofit sector, and these forms of communication should be fostered and enhanced. The Forms 990 and 990PF (we refer to both as "990") are, however, the primary disclosure instrument for the nonprofit sector. These are information returns that federally tax-exempt organizations are required to file each year with the IRS. Many states also require that tax-exempt organizations operating in their jurisdictions file information forms as well.

These forms should be made widely available to the public. In particular:

♦ Efforts should be made to have all 990s put on the Internet and made broadly accessible.

♦ Regulatory agencies should vigorously enforce penalties for failure to file, for incomplete filing, and for intentional misrepresentations.

♦ In terms of abuses (viz., the improper transfer of money to private hands) the 990 is generally adequate, although some changes might be made to improve disclosure of transactions between a filing organization and affiliated organizations.

♦ In addition, the 990 should be expanded to require much more information on program activities and accomplishments so that readers can make assessments as to the effectiveness and efficiency of organizations. This change will enable them to make better informed decisions about support. Furthermore, the public will be able to understand better what groups are doing and how well they are doing it. Determining how to make these changes to the 990 may be difficult. However, the expanded information could be extremely useful in permitting better reporting.

In addition to using the 990, methods need to be developed to convey information about program activities and accomplishments to the media on a regular basis. Inaccurate reporting has the potential to do real harm to the credibility of the sector. Reporters who cover the sector often know little about it. Among the options to be considered should be the creation of a Center of Philanthropy and the Media, which would work to educate the media more fully and provide background information about the sector. Such a center could also instruct organizations on how to work effectively with the media and use new information technologies. Courses on philanthropy and the nonprofit sector in schools of journalism would be another useful strategy.

While existing regulatory laws are adequate to the task and while the structure of the regulatory agencies is sound, the agencies are woefully undersupported. Thus, philanthropy and the nonprofit sector should support funding for these agencies at a level that will invigorate them and enable them to reach the goals that they were set up to achieve. A vigorous educational program will be required to develop the support for the proposals that will be needed to bring about changes.

Existing Enforcement Agencies Need to Be Strengthened

To assure full public disclosure, to detect abuses, to promote better stewardship by trustees, and to punish and thus to deter malfeasance, the sector should promote the strengthening of existing enforcement agencies: the state charities offices and the Exempt Organization Division of the IRS.

Evaluation Procedures of Philanthropy and the Nonprofit Sector Must Be Strengthened

Although some foundations evaluate the projects they fund, more attention is needed. In addition, many operating nonprofit organizations do not evaluate the effectiveness of their programs. Within the limitations imposed by resources, such evaluation is important to the efficient functioning of the organizations and the maintenance of trust in them. In particular, knowing what grantees and foundations have accomplished and learned in the course of conducting their programs is important to their credibility and capacity and to achieving their ends. Many foundations are reluctant to fund evaluations, thus losing an opportunity to elicit data that will be useful among their grantees, themselves, and the public. Foundations should make efforts to learn about evaluation methods and their appropriate use. Foundations should also conduct active evaluation programs, and communicate the results of those evaluations.

The Quality of Philanthropic and Nonprofit Personnel Should Be Protected and Enhanced

♦ Efforts to strengthen the professionalism and quality of the trustees, officers, and staff in philanthropy and the nonprofit sector should be enhanced.

♦ Philanthropy and the nonprofit sector should adopt and support codes of ethics, such as the code promulgated by the Council on Foundations, and standards of good practice, and inform the public of their use.

♦ A common pension fund for employees of the nonprofit sector is needed along the lines of the ones that exist for those in higher education to encourage the recruitment and retention of outstanding staff.

♦ Foundations and other donors should reconsider their reluctance to support the operating budgets of nonprofit organizations, since the pursuit of efficiency and evaluation require the development and maintenance of internal capacities that many nonprofit organizations are unable to afford.

V. Next Steps for Philanthropy and the Nonprofit Sector

Together with improving the performance and accountability of philanthropy and the nonprofit sector, we recommend the following steps:

Relationships with Other Sectors

- Philanthropy and the nonprofit sector should foster relations with the for-profit sector.

§ Relationships with for-profit organizations may offer opportunities for nonprofit organizations to further their missions. Partnerships with for-profit organizations should be pursued, however, only when they enhance those missions.

§ Nonprofit organizations should look to the for-profit sector for successful models for applying competitive and market-driven techniques to their work.

§ Foundations should continue to provide capital for social ventures that could become revenue producers for the nonprofit sector.

§ Nonprofit organizations should share in the returns generated by these social ventures.

§ For-profit organizations should bear some of the responsibility for increasing the capacity of the nonprofit sector to engage in social entrepreneurship.

- Philanthropy and the nonprofit sector should promote more responsive and effective government, including taking steps to:

§ Enhance participation of underrepresented groups in the political process.

§ Collaborate with government in addressing social problems.

§ Provide research and information for public decision-making.

- Philanthropy and the nonprofit sector should strengthen their role in fueling the democratic process in the creation of public policy by:

§ Ensuring that the broadest diversity of voices is heard.

§ Allowing the extremes of opinion to be debated openly.

§ Generating information that will inform debates.

§ Educating the widest possible audiences about the issues.

The Importance of Religious Institutions

- The faith-based institutions in the nonprofit sector should be more broadly recognized as key actors in the philanthropic endeavor, particularly in their roles of engaging individuals in giving and volunteering and in creating community at the local level.

Values and Their Application

- Philanthropy and the nonprofit sector should seek additional ways to serve as vehicles for the expression of the charitable impulse and the values their institutions represent.

- They should promote community collaborations and partnerships and the continued development of community foundations.

- They should encourage teaching and learning in civic responsibility, in the roles of the nonprofit sector, and in the importance of community service and service learning.

Education and Engaging the Next Generation

♦ Philanthropy and the nonprofit sector need to take the lead in developing strategies to educate Americans to participate in—and understand—the traditions, values, and practice of philanthropy. We need to address the general public, the schools (K–12), and higher education, especially through the mechanisms of active learning—service learning and community service. One current example is the pilot effort by the Council on Michigan Foundations. As have the advocates of science and the arts, we must make the case for the centrality of philanthropy to the realization of democracy's promise in the United States and the world.

♦ We need actively to recruit, develop, and mentor the next generation (particularly those in their teens, 20s, and 30s) for leadership in philanthropy and the nonprofit sector. We can achieve this goal through increased opportunities for community-service staff and board positions, and the creation of philanthropic initiatives led by young people.

♦ We embrace and encourage the efforts of the next generation as they seek both to build on current traditions and to develop new ideas, strategies, and approaches to philanthropy and the nonprofit sector.

Addressing Serious Domestic and Global Problems

♦ Philanthropy and the nonprofit sector should direct increased resources to parts and peoples of our nation and the world that are poorest and expand strategies to help the poor, recognizing that income inequality cannot be eliminated by philanthropy and the nonprofit sector alone.

♦ Philanthropy and the nonprofit sector in the United States should increase their capacity and ability to address other serious domestic and global problems by:

§ Increasing the leadership training and other infrastructure support needed by nonprofit organizations of all sizes and types.

§ Developing the information and knowledge base to help determine needs and gaps.

§ Ensuring inclusion of different voices when setting priorities and deliberating policy options.

§ Measuring performance and setting standards.

§ Developing the leadership required to address problems at all levels.

§ Expanding and diversifying the resource base for this work.

Communication

♦ Philanthropy and the nonprofit sector must communicate their roles and responsibilities, and what they do, to the widest possible public, using a variety of vehicles including education, public relations, and direct engagement in their work in order to:

§ Increase numbers and diversity of volunteers and givers.

§ Leverage their accomplishments.

♦ Philanthropy and the nonprofit sector should strengthen their capacity to respond rapidly to opportunities to educate and inform the public and policymakers.

Growth in Philanthropic Resources

+ With increased wealth, an opportunity exists to enlist a new generation of benefactors.
+ In order to ensure that new philanthropic resources are used most effectively, new donors and philanthropic staff must be well grounded in the history, functions, and operations of philanthropy and the nonprofit sector. One example is the "Promotion of Philanthropy Initiative" undertaken by the Forum of Regional Associations of Grantmakers. Further, philanthropy and the nonprofit sector must be open to different philanthropic traditions, ideas, and operating styles.
+ The unmet needs of society are acute, and various new means are needed to help alleviate those needs. Philanthropy and the nonprofit sector should encourage:

§ The growth of specific strategies of philanthropic giving to 3 percent of gross domestic product, from its current level of 2 percent;

§ Individuals to consider bequests to charitable organizations with the goal of doubling the percentage of those who do so from just under 20 percent to 40 percent;

§ Corporations to provide at least 2 percent of their pre-tax earnings for charity.
+ Foundations should consider increasing their grant payouts above typical levels, especially for programs that will reduce poverty or enhance the infrastructure of vital community organizations.

Conclusion

Americans have vested extraordinary resources—both human and financial—in philanthropy and the nonprofit sector. The strength of our civil society is recognized, often envied, and serves as a model to societies around the world. This report challenges philanthropy and the nonprofit sector to devote more resources to issues that are fundamentally threatening to our society, to perform more imaginatively and effectively, openly and inclusively, and to transmit and advance the values undergirding our civil society: trust, service, and the common purpose.

+ + + +

Participants

ALAN J. ABRAMSON
Director
Nonprofit Sector Research Fund
The Aspen Institute
Washington DC

JIMMIE R. ALFORD
President and Chief Executive Officer
The Alford Group Inc.
Skokie IL

EMILY H. ALTSCHUL
Director
The Overbrook Foundation
New York NY

MARGARET C. AYERS
Executive Director
Robert Sterling Clark Foundation, Inc.
New York NY

MICHAEL S. BARR
Deputy Assistant Secretary for Community Development Policy
Department of the Treasury
Washington DC

MICHAEL BIVENS
Education Director
The Coca-Cola Foundation
Atlanta GA

ELIZABETH T. BORIS
Director, Center on Nonprofits and Philanthropy
The Urban Institute
Washington DC

ROBERT O. BOTHWELL
President
National Committee for Responsive Philanthropy
Washington DC

JOHN BRADEMAS
President Emeritus
New York University
New York NY

ELEANOR BROWN
Professor of Economics
Pomona College
Claremont CA

DWIGHT F. BURLINGAME
Associate Executive Director
Indiana University Center on Philanthropy
Indianapolis IN

HUGH C. BURROUGHS
Director
External Affairs
The David and Lucile Packard Foundation
Los Altos CA

DIANA CAMPOAMOR
President
Hispanics in Philanthropy
Berkeley CA

EMMETT D. CARSON
President and Chief Executive Officer
The Minneapolis Foundation
Minneapolis MN

CHARLES T. CLOTFELTER
Professor of Public Policy Studies, Economics & Law
Duke University
Durham NC

GORDON CONWAY
President
The Rockefeller Foundation
New York NY

JOHN F. COOKE
Executive Vice President
The Walt Disney Company
Burbank CA

ALLAN F. DECK, S.J.
Executive Director
Loyola Institute for Spirituality
Orange CA

WILLIAM DRAYTON
President
Ashoka: Innovators for the Public
Arlington VA

THOMAS EASTHAM
Vice President & Western Director
William Randolph Hearst Foundations
San Francisco CA

THOMAS EHRLICH
Senior Scholar, Carnegie Foundation for the Advancement of Teaching
Distinguished University Scholar, California State University
Palo Alto CA

SARA L. ENGELHARDT
President
The Foundation Center
New York NY

JOEL L. FLEISHMAN
Professor of Law and Public Policy
Duke University
Durham NC

ELLEN V. FUTTER
President
American Museum of Natural History
New York NY

BARRY D. GABERMAN
Senior Vice President
The Ford Foundation
New York NY

RONALD GILES
Executive Director
The Youth Leadership Academy
Milwaukee WI

KENNETH L. GLADISH
Executive Director, The Indianapolis
   Foundation
President, Central Indiana Community
   Foundation
Indianapolis IN

PETER B. GOLDBERG
President & Chief Executive Officer
Family Service America, Inc.
Milwaukee WI

BRADFORD H. GRAY
Director
Division of Health and Science Policy
The New York Academy of Medicine
New York NY

LYNN GREENBERG
Princeton University
Princeton NJ

PAUL S. GROGAN
President and Chief Executive Officer
Local Initiatives Support Corporation
   (LISC)
New York NY

KIRSTEN A. GRØNBJERG
Associate Dean
Indiana University School of Public and
   Environmental Affairs
Bloomington IN

JERRY E. HILL
Urban Minister, Episcopal Diocese of
   Dallas
Director Emeritus, Austin Street Shelter
Dallas TX

ALICE ILCHMAN
Chair, Board of Trustees, The Rockefeller
   Foundation
President, Sarah Lawrence College
Bronxville NY

RODNEY M. JACKSON
Publisher & Editor
Black Philanthropy
Vienna VA

BARRY D. KARL
Bloomberg Visiting Professor in Philan-
   thropy
John F. Kennedy School of Government
Harvard University
Cambridge MA

H. PETER KAROFF
President
The Philanthropic Initiative, Inc.
Boston MA

IRVIN S. KATZ
Vice President
Community Impact
United Way of America
Alexandria VA

STANLEY N. KATZ
Professor
Woodrow Wilson School of Public & In-
   ternational Affairs
Princeton University
Princeton NJ

ALAN KHAZEI
Co-Founder
City Year
Boston MA

VANESSA KIRSCH
President
New Profit Inc.
Boston MA

SALLY D. KLINGENSTEIN
Executive Director
The Klingenstein Third Generation Foun-
   dation
New York NY

LESLIE LENKOWSKY
Professor of Philanthropic Studies & Public Policy
School of Liberal Arts
School of Public & Environmental Affairs
Indiana University Center on Philanthropy
Indianapolis IN

REYNOLD LEVY
President
International Rescue Committee
New York NY

CATHERINE E. LIVINGSTON
Deputy Tax Legislative Counsel
Department of the Treasury
Washington DC

ELLEN McCULLOCH LOVELL
Deputy Assistant to the President and Advisor to the First Lady on the Millennium
The White House Millennium Council
Washington DC

GERALDINE P. MANNION
Program Officer, Special Projects
Carnegie Corporation of New York
New York NY

DEBORAH MARROW
Director
The Getty Grant Program
Los Angeles CA

WILLIAM S. McKERSIE
Senior Program Officer
The Cleveland Foundation
Cleveland OH

SARA E. MELÉNDEZ
President
Independent Sector
Washington DC

MARK H. MOORE
Faculty Chair and Acting Director
The Hauser Center for Nonprofit Organizations
John F. Kennedy School of Government
Harvard University
Cambridge MA

MARY MOUNTCASTLE
President/Trustee
Mary Reynolds Babcock Foundation
Durham NC

BARRY MUNITZ
President and Chief Executive Officer
The J. Paul Getty Trust
Los Angeles CA

PETER NORTON
Chair
Norton Family Foundation
Santa Monica CA

BRIAN O'CONNELL
Professor of Public Service
Lincoln Filene Center for Citizenship and Public Affairs
Tufts University
Medford MA

JUDITH O'CONNOR
President and Chief Executive Officer
National Center for Nonprofit Boards
Washington DC

ROBERT L. PAYTON
Professor of Philanthropic Studies
Indiana University Center on Philanthropy
Indianapolis IN

JOBI PETERSEN
Executive Director
The Mayer and Morris Kaplan Family Foundation
Northfield IL

JON PRATT
Executive Director
Minnesota Council of Nonprofits
St. Paul MN

HUGH B. PRICE
President & Chief Executive Officer
National Urban League, Inc.
New York NY

DAVID O. RENZ
Director
Midwest Center for Nonprofit Leadership
University of Missouri-Kansas City
Kansas City MO

N. CLAY ROBBINS
President
Lilly Endowment Inc.
Indianapolis IN

MICHAEL ROTHSCHILD
Dean
Woodrow Wilson School of Public & International Affairs
Princeton University
Princeton NJ

CATHERINE SAALFIELD
Third Wave Foundation;
George Gund Foundation
New York NY

DAVID SALTZMAN
Executive Director
The Robin Hood Foundation
New York NY

MICHAEL SELTZER
Program Officer
Governance & Civil Society
The Ford Foundation
New York NY

MARCIA SHARP
Principal and Chief Executive Officer
Millennium Communications Group
Washington DC

LEE S. SHULMAN
President
The Carnegie Foundation for the Advancement of Teaching
Menlo Park CA

BENJAMIN R. SHUTE, JR.
Secretary & Treasurer
Rockefeller Brothers Fund
New York NY

JOHN A. SHUTKIN
Vice President, General Counsel & Secretary
Kodak Polychrome Graphics LLC
Norwalk CT

BRUCE SIEVERS
Executive Director
Walter and Elise Haas Fund
San Francisco CA

ADELE SIMMONS
President
John D. & Catherine T. MacArthur Foundation
Chicago IL

EDWARD SKLOOT
Executive Director
Surdna Foundation, Inc.
New York NY

JAMES ALLEN SMITH
Executive Director
The Howard Gilman Foundation, Inc.
New York NY

JANE E. SMITH
President & Chief Executive Officer
National Council of Negro Women
Washington DC

STEVEN RATHGEB SMITH
Associate Professor
Graduate School of Public Affairs
University of Washington
Seattle WA

JOAN E. SPERO
President
Doris Duke Charitable Foundation
New York NY

DONALD M. STEWART
President and Chief Executive Officer
The College Board
New York NY

ISABEL C. STEWART
Executive Director
Girls Inc.
New York NY

KAREN SULZBERGER
Trustee, Hillandale Group
Sulzberger Foundation (New York NY)
Beverly Hills CA

PETER SWORDS
Executive Director
Nonprofit Coordinating Committee of
  New York
New York NY

RUBY TAKANISHI
President
Foundation for Child Development
New York NY

EUGENE R. TEMPEL
Executive Director
Indiana University Center on Philan-
  thropy
Indianapolis IN

DAVID J. VIDAL
Director of Research
Global Corporate Citizenship
The Conference Board
New York NY

GARY WALKER
President
Public/Private Ventures
Philadelphia PA

JOHN P. WALTERS
President
The Philanthropy Roundtable
Washington DC

CLIFTON R. WHARTON, JR.
Former Chair & Chief Executive Officer
TIAA-CREF
New York NY

WOODWARD A. WICKHAM
Vice President for Public Affairs and Di-
  rector of the General Program
John D. & Catherine T. MacArthur
  Foundation
Chicago IL

HAROLD M. WILLIAMS
President Emeritus
The J. Paul Getty Trust
Los Angeles CA

EDWARD WOLFF
Professor of Economics
Department of Economics
New York University
New York NY

JULIAN WOLPERT
Professor
Woodrow Wilson School
Princeton University
Princeton NJ

MARGARET J. WYSZOMIRSKI
Director
Arts Policy and Administration Program
The Ohio State University
Columbus OH

Senior Advisor
RICHARD MITTENTHAL
Partner
Conservation Company
New York NY

Observers

LUISA KREISBERG
President
The Kreisberg Group Ltd.
New York NY

JACK MEYERS
Senior Program Officer
The Getty Grant Program
Los Angeles CA

JILL K. MURPHY
Special Assistant to the President
The J. Paul Getty Trust
Los Angeles CA

STACY PALMER
Managing Editor
The Chronicle of Philanthropy
Washington DC

BARBARA PFLAUMER
Museums Without Walls
Los Angeles CA

SUE RUNYAN
Museums Without Walls
Los Angeles CA

ANN SCHNEIDER
Project Manager
The Getty Grant Program
Los Angeles CA

LORI STARR
Director of Public Affairs
The J. Paul Getty Trust
Los Angeles CA

GWEN WALDEN
Director, Programming and Planning
  Evaluation
The J. Paul Getty Trust
Los Angeles CA

JOHN WALSH
Director
The J. Paul Getty Museum
Los Angeles CA

JOAN WEINSTEIN
Program Officer
The Getty Grant Program
Los Angeles CA

TIMOTHY P. WHALEN
Senior Program Officer
The Getty Grant Program
Los Angeles CA

CLAIRE WHITTAKER
Senior Vice President
The Kreisberg Group Ltd.
New York NY

About the American Assembly

The American Assembly was established by Dwight D. Eisenhower at Columbia University in 1950. It holds nonpartisan meetings and publishes authoritative books to illuminate issues of United States policy. An affiliate of Columbia Univerisity, The Assembly is a national, educational institution incorporated in the State of New York. The Assembly seeks to provide information, stimulate discussion, and evoke independent conclusions on matters of vital public interest.

American Assembly Sessions

At least two national programs are initiated each year. Authorities are retained to write background papers presenting essential data and defining the main issues of each subject.

A group of men and women representing a broad range of experience, competence, and American leadership meet for several days to discuss the Assembly topic and consider alternatives for national policy.

All Assemblies follow the same procedure. The background papers are sent to participants in advance of the Assembly. The Assembly meets in small groups for four lengthy periods. All groups use the same agenda. At the close of these informal sessions participants adopt in plenary session a final report of findings and recommendations.

Regional, state, and local Assemblies are held following the national session at Arden House. Assemblies have also been held in England, Switzerland, Malaysia, Canada, the Caribbean, South America, Central America, the Philippines, and Japan. Over one hundred sixty institutions have cosponsored one or more Assemblies.

Arden House

The home of The American Assembly and the scene of most national sessions is Arden House, which was given to Columbia University in 1950 by W. Averell Harriman. E. Roland Harriman joined his brother in contributing toward adaptation of the property for conference purposes. The buildings and surrounding land, known as the Harriman Campus of Columbia University, are fifty miles north of New York City.

Arden House is a distinguished conference center. It is self-supporting and operates throughout the year for use by organizations with educational objectives. The American Assembly is a tenant of this Columbia University facility only during Assembly sessions.

Steering Committee Members

About Indiana University Center on Philanthropy

The Indiana University Center on Philanthropy was founded in 1987 to study philanthropy and its role in building civil society. The Center's mission is to improve the understanding of the philanthropic tradition, to transmit that understanding to new generations and constituencies, and to improve the practice of philanthropy and fundraising. It conducts its work through research and publications, education, public service, and public affairs programs.

The Center offers six graduate degree programs, taught by an interdisciplinary faculty of sixty-two at both Indiana University Purdue University Indianapolis and Indiana University Bloomington. It is the home of The Joseph and Matthew Payton Philanthropic Studies Library and Archives, one of the largest collections of books and archives on the subject in the world. Its Division of Public Service addresses capacity building in nonprofit management and governance, fundraising, and grant-making. The Fund Raising School, part of the Center's public service effort, is the only university-based, national fundraising training program in the United States, with programs in fourteen U.S. cities and several foreign countries. The Center is also the home to ARNOVA, the Association of Black Foundation Executives, and the World Fundraising Council.

Board of Governors

Mary Anne Baker
John D. Barlow
Elizabeth T. Boris
Trevor R. Brown
Donald A. Campbell
Conrad C. Cherry
Paul L. Comstock
Thomas P. Ewbank
Robert M. Franklin, Jr.
Deborah A. Freund
Jeffery R. Green

Raymond L. Handlan
Charles A. Johnson
William C. McGinley
Angela B. McBride
James T. Morris
William M. Plater
Hilda Richards
Alexis E. Rovzar
Curtis R. Simic
Rich Steinberg
Eugene R. Tempel

Emeritus

Robert L. Payton

Executive Leadership

Eugene R. Tempel, *Executive Director*
Dwight F. Burlingame, *Associate Executive Director*
Kathy Reinhold, *Director of Finance and Administration*
Timothy L. Seiler, *Director, The Fund Raising School and Public Service*

About the Getty

The Getty Trust is a multi-faceted, international cultural institution committed to making an impact beyond the reach of other private and public enterprises. The Getty trustees created five institutes and a grant program, each with a unique perspective and purpose. These institutes and the J. Paul Getty Museum, which was founded in 1953, constitute the Getty Center, a 110-acre campus in the Santa Monica Mountains designed by architect Richard Meier.

Contributors

Elizabeth T. Boris is Director, Center on Nonprofits and Philanthropy, The Urban Institute, Washington, D.C.

Eleanor Brown is Professor of Economics, Pomona College.

Dwight F. Burlingame is Adjunct Professor of Philanthropic Studies and Associate Executive Director, Indiana University Center on Philanthropy.

Emmett D. Carson is President and Chief Executive Officer, the Minneapolis Foundation.

Charles T. Clotfelter is Professor of Public Policy, Economics, and Law, Duke University.

William A. Diaz is Senior Fellow, Hubert H. Humphrey Institute of Public Affairs, University of Minnesota.

Thomas Ehrlich is Distinguished University Scholar, California State University; Senior Scholar, Carnegie Foundation for the Advancement of Teaching; and President Emeritus, Indiana University.

Joel L. Fleishman is Professor of Law and Public Policy, Duke University, and President, Atlantic Philanthropic Service Company, New York.

Bradford H. Gray is Director, Division of Health and Science Policy, New York Academy of Medicine, New York.

Kirsten A. Grønbjerg is Professor and Associate Dean for Adademic Affairs, School of Public and Environmental Affairs, Indiana University.

Jean Grossman is Vice President and Director, Public/Private Ventures, Philadelphia.

Warren F. Ilchman is Director, Paul and Daisy Soros Fellowships for New Americans, New York.

Alice W. Karl is Visiting Scholar, Harvard University School of Education.

Barry D. Karl is Professor in Philanthropy, Harvard University.

Leslie Lenkowsky is Professor of Philanthropic Studies and Public Policy, Indiana University Center on Philanthropy.

Reynold Levy is President, International Rescue Committee, New York.

William S. McKersie is Senior Program Officer, The Cleveland Foundation.

Anthony Markward is Founding Partner, Grassroots Planning and Consulting, New York.

David H. Mortimer is Vice President, American Assembly, New York.

Robert L. Payton is Professor of Philanthropic Studies, Indiana University Center on Philanthropy.

Jon Pratt is Executive Director, Minnesota Council of Nonprofits, St. Paul.

David O. Renz is Director, Midwest Center for Nonprofit Leadership, University of Missouri–Kansas City.

Richard L. Revesz is Professor of Law, New York University.

Michael Rothschild is Dean, Woodrow Wilson School of Public and International Affairs, Princeton University.

James Allen Smith is Executive Director, Howard Gilman Foundation, New York.

Steven Rathgeb Smith is Associate Professor, Graduate School of Public Affairs, University of Washington.

Ruby Takanishi is President and Chief Executive Officer, Foundation for Child Development, New York.

Eugene R. Tempel is Professor of Higher Education and Philanthropic Studies and Executive Director, Indiana University Center on Philanthropy.

Gary Walker is President, Public/Private Ventures, Philadelphia.

Edward Wolff is Professor of Economics, New York University.

Julian Wolpert is Professor of Public Affairs, Woodrow Wilson School of Public and International Affairs, Princeton University.

Margaret J. Wyszomirski is Professor of Public Policy and Art Education and Director of the Arts Policy and Administration Program at the Ohio State University.

Index

Abolition movement, 256
Abramson, Alan J., 128
Accountability, 46, 183–86, 198, 513–15, 525–27; and board governance, 199–200, 205–6; IRS requirements for, 181–83; in nonprofit hospitals, 378–81; performance standards for human services agencies, 139, 154, 168n10; and the press, 184; as responsiveness to customers, 207; strategies for, 186–91; watchdog organizations for, 183, 205. See also Outcomes; Regulation of the nonprofit sector
Adams, John Quincy, 36
Adelphi University scandal, 178, 179, 202, 204
Advocacy. See Political advocacy by nonprofits
AFDC. See Welfare
African American Female Intelligence Society, 256
African Americans: child poverty among, 348; philanthropy by, 12, 87, 255–59, 267–68
African Union Society (Newport), 255
Age: in donor characteristics, 83–87
AIDS: home health care programs for, 148; nonprofit sector's response to, 22, 47–49
Aldrich, Nelson, 55
Alexander, Lamar, 123
Alexandria, library in, 34
La Alianza Hispano-Americana, 260
Alinsky, Saul, 336
Alliance of Poles in America, 255

Alliance of Transylvanian Saxons, 255
Altman, S. H., 374
American Assembly, ix, 464, 500, 513–14, 517–39
American Association of Fund-Raising Counsel, 168n9, 205, 462
American Cancer Society, 181
American Colonization Society, 256
American Community Renewal Act, 165
American Council on Race Relations, 258
American Enterprise Institute, 111
American Express, 113
American Friends Service Committee, 276
American Indian College Fund, 253
American Indian Movement (AIM), 253
American Institute of Certified Public Accountants, 205
American Institute of Philanthropy, 183, 204, 205
American Loyalty Club, 263
American Medical Association, 61
American Medical International, 371
American Promise, 125, 241
American Red Cross, 181
American Woman Suffrage Association, 266
Americans for the Arts (AFA), 467, 468–71, 477n3
Americorps, 123
Ames, A. A., 298
Amnesty International, 114
Ancient Order of Hibernians of America, 254
Anders, G., 375

Anderson, Elizabeth Milbank, 267
Anderson, Wendell, 293
Annenberg, Walter, 19, 119, 388, 408n2
Anti-Semitism, 486–87, 494
Aquinas, St. Thomas, 482
Aramony, William, 4, 156, 178, 179, 500
Arts agencies, state and regional, 465, 466–
    67, 469, 471, 477
Arts and culture: charitable giving for, 82,
    214, 461–62, 464; coalitions in support
    of, 468–73, 476; competition for re-
    sources for, 475; corporate contributions
    to, 102–3, 108, 475; emerging issues for
    the funding of, 473–77; foundation
    support for, 462–68; multiculturalism
    in, 474–75
Ashcroft, John, 165
Asia Pacific Economic Cooperation (APEC),
    110–11
Asia Society, 111
Asian American Legal Defense and Educa-
    tion Fund, 258
Asian American philanthropy, 12, 262–65
Aspen Institute, 111, 351–52
Aspira, 277
Assessing the New Federalism project, 27
Associate, right to, 200
Association of American Indian Affairs, 252
Association of Governing Boards, 183, 205
Association of Healthcare Philanthropy, 205
Atlantic-Richfield Company (ARCO), 253
Attorneys General, 182, 202
Auerbach, A., 222
Auten, G., 214–15, 216
Avery, R. B., 158, 223, 224
Axelrod, N. R., 201

Bailey, A. L., 373
Bakker, Jim and Tammy, 178
Carrie Bamberger Fund, 267
Banker's Mutual Life, 255
Barnett, K., 379
Barrett, K., 219
Bean, F. D., 279
Becker, Gary S., 232, 239
Bellah, Robert, xii, 500
Ben and Jerry's, 161
Benevolent Society of St. Thomas, 265
Bennett, John, 178
Bennett, William J., 30n9, 361
Bequests: of businesses, 224–25; determi-
    nants of, 221–26; and the Girard case,
    35–36, 49n3; medieval use of, 35; in
    Minnesota, 306; trends in, 213, 216–17,
    508
Bergholz, David, 401, 402, 408
Bergmann, Barbara, 354
Berkeley Economic Roundtable, 111
Berkshire-Hathaway, 119
Berman, Edward H., 506
Bernheim, B. D., 222

Bernholz, L., 388
Beveridge, Sir William, 483
Big Brothers/Big Sisters, 458, 459–60
Billionaires, 119, 158
Bixby, A. K., 146, 147, 148
Black Women Club Movement, 267
Block Grant Response Initiative (Kansas
    City), 315–16, 323–29, 332, 334
B'nai B'rith Anti-Defamation League, 254
Boards of directors: effectiveness measures
    of, 208–9; governance by, 199–200;
    Hispanic participation on, 281–82; racial
    composition of, 270; self-regulation by,
    205–6
Boeing, 111
Bok, D., 350, 358
Bonds, tax-exempt, 151
Borowski, Neill A., 184
Bosnia: humanitarian assistance to, 112
Boston Compact (1985), 396
Boston University scandal, 202, 204
Bothwell, R., 156
Bowen, William, 179
Boychuk, T., 145
Boyd, Richard, 397, 402
Boys and Girls Clubs, 458
BP America, 388, 394
Bradford, Gigi, 473
Bradley Foundation, 136n19
Bradshaw, P., 208
Brady, H. E., 163
Brand, Phil, 181–82
Bremner, Robert, 68, 69, 126, 130, 212,
    248–49
Brewer, D. J., 420–22, 424, 426n9, 426n12
Brookings Institution, 111
Brown, L. D., 146, 368
Brown Beacon Project, 253
Bryk, Anthony S., 387, 396
Bryson, Bill, 488–89
Buffett, Warren, 119
Bundy, McGeorge, 60, 70
Burroughs, Nannie H., 268
Bush administration, 127; NAFTA negotia-
    tions, 114; Points of Light Foundation,
    136n12
Bush Foundation, 65, 306
Business Committee for the Arts (BCA), 103,
    108
Butler, Lewis, 406

California arts council, 467
California Community Foundation, 462
Capital Research Center, 205
Capitalism, 504
Card, David, 414, 422–23
CARE, 112
Carlisle Indian School, 252
Carnegie, Andrew, 40, 54, 59, 66, 132, 501
Carnegie Corporation of New York: child
    poverty addressed by, 354; creation of,

38–40; early hostility toward, 54; education work by, 58; foreign policy influence of, 506; Latino causes supported by, 280–81, 282, 290; public broadcasting supported by, 466; race relations work by, 58, 258

Carnegie Foundation for the Advancement of Teaching, 39, 44

Carnegie Institution, 54

Annie E. Casey Foundation, 159, 354, 388

Castelli, Jim, 241

Catholic Charities, 4, 25

Catholic Relief Services, 112, 484–85

Census of Service Industries, 141–42

Center for Arts and Culture, 469, 470, 472–73, 476, 477n2

Center for Effective Compassion, 241

Chambré, Susan, 22

Chance, Ruth, 276, 278

Charitable organizations (501(c)(3) status), 6, 504; increase in, 122–23; and nonprofit health care, 369, 373

Charities Review Council, 300–301, 308

Charity: philanthropy distinguished from, 56

Charity societies, post-Civil war, 36

Chase Manhattan Bank, 104, 113

Chicago Community Trust, 392, 393, 394, 400

Chicago foundations: activism by personnel of, 402; Chicago Panel on School Policy, 401; Designs for Change initiative of, 401; evaluation of reform programs by, 404–5; evolving strategies of, 399–400; gap-funding by, 402–3; institutional interdependence among, 401; local context of, 392, 393; parameter pushing by, 403–4; persistence of, 400; school reform efforts of, 394–96, 409n4, 409n7; tensions experienced by, 405–8

Chicago School Reform Act (1988), 389, 393–96, 401–3, 406, 409n7, 409n8

Chicano Movement, 261

Child care (Kansas City): Metropolitan Council on Child Care, 320–22; Partners in Quality for Early Childhood Care and Education (PIQ), 315–16, 318–23, 324, 333, 334

Child poverty, 347–48, 508; causes of, 349–51; devolution's impact on, 358–60; foundation response to, 351–55, 357–60; and increases in the working poor, 348–49; policies for the age of welfare reform, 355–57; and the privatization of family services, 360–61; public discourse on, 357–58; rates of, 348; social compact for addressing, 356; universal approach to reducing, 353–54, 358

Chinese Consolidated Benevolent Association (CCBA), 262

Chinese Six Companies (CSC), 262–63

Chollet, D. J., 372

Christian Benevolent Society, 256

Christian Coalition, 164

Christian Community Development Assoc., 241

Christian tradition: fragmentation of, 494

Churches. See Religious organizations

CIA programs: foundation funding of, 62

Citibank, 113

Citizens Alliance (Minneapolis), 299, 300

Citro, C. F., 348

Civic disengagement, 27–28

Civil Rights movement, 487–89, 490; Chicano participation in, 261; foundation support for, 258–59; Native American participation in, 252–53

Civil society, 1–2, 24, 46–47. See also Nonprofit sector

Civil Society Project, 241

Civilization Fund, 252

Edna McConnell Clark Foundation, 388

Clay, P. L., 323

Clean Air Act, 437, 438–39, 445n16

Clean Water Act, 428, 446n27

Cleveland Education Fund, 396, 398, 410n9

Cleveland Foundation, 386, 393, 402, 410n12, 464, 465

Cleveland foundations: activism by personnel of, 402; evaluation of reform programs, 404–5; evolving strategies of, 399–400; gap-funding by, 402–3; grants issued by, 398; institutional interdependence among, 401; local context of, 391–93; parameter pushing by, 403–4; persistence of, 400; Scholarship-in-Escrow program, 396, 398, 405, 410n11; school reform efforts of, 396–98; Strategic Plan of, 400, 403; Strategy Council of, 398, 400; tensions experienced by, 405–8

Cleveland Initiative for Education (CIE), 397, 398, 408

Clinton administration: child care initiatives, 323; civic spirit extolled by, 123; declares era of big government over, 128; health care reform proposal of, 366, 380–81; international trade policy of, 110

Clotfelter, C. T., 87, 88, 96, 151, 214–15, 218, 219, 510

Cnaan, Ram, 5

Coats, Dan, 123

Cobb, Nina Kressner, 461, 462, 466

Coca-Cola, 104, 111, 505

Coleman, James S., 232

Collaboratives (Kansas City), 316, 319–20; Block Grant Response Initiative, 315–16, 323–29, 332, 334; challenges faced by, 340–42; civic entrepreneurs in, 337–38; community information systems development by, 330–31; leadership patterns in, 331–32; Local Investment Commission, 329–30, 332, 333, 335; mediating organizations for, 336–37; Metropolitan

Council on Child Care, 320–22; neighborhood redevelopment initiatives, 330; Partners in Quality for Early Childhood Care and Education, 315–16, 318–23, 324, 333, 334; philanthropic sector's role in, 339; resource mobilization for, 338; social capital tapped for, 332–34; success factors for, 331
Collins, Dennis, 473
Colored Women's League, 2672
Columbia/HCA, 371, 372, 374, 375, 376, 378, 380
Combined Federal Campaign Law (1987), 156
Comer, James, 398
Commercialization, 4, 28, 510, 521–22
Commission on Industrial Relations, 54, 59
Common Fund scandal, 178
Commonwealth Fund, 37, 38, 40
Communities, 231; conservative remedies for, 235–36; corporate philanthropy in, 243; disparities in, 238; elements of, 232; faith-based philanthropy in, 241–42; local government's role in, 243–44; local vs. national, 232–34; motivations for generosity in, 240; nonprofit organizations in, 237; patterns of generosity in, 238–39; philanthropic investment in the social capital of, 232–33; philanthropy's contribution to community life, 236–38; preferences for, 234–35; progressive remedies for, 236
Community chest movement, 507
Community foundations, 20, 130, 132, 136n19, 477; charitable giving to, 214; early movement for, 40; expansion of, 158; Kansas City, 321; Latino, 285–87; Minnesota, 298, 305–6
Community Planning Council, 285
Community Service Organization (CSO), 261
Community service requirements, 220–21
Comprehensive community initiatives, 351–53
Conference Board, 107, 109
Congreso de Pueblos de Habla Espanola, 260–61
Congress: hostility towards foundations by, 55–56, 59–63; investigations of foundations by, 62–63; Rockefeller Foundation charter rejected by, 55, 60, 67–68
Congress of Racial Equality (CORE), 258
Constitution of the United States, 52; First Amendment, 200, 202, 504
Contract with America, 69, 483
Cook, P. J., 421
Cook Inlet Region Inc., 253
Cooperative College Development Program, 257
Corning, 111
Corporate philanthropy, 20–21, 99; for the arts, 102–3, 108, 475; community role of, 243; corporate interests served by, 100, 104; employee-centered, 117–20; growth in, 104–5; for human service agencies, 157; international philanthropy, 109–15; in Minnesota's Keystone Program, 303–5; professionalism in, 105–6; by small and midsize firms, 107–9, 112; technological advances for, 115–19; for universities, 101–2
Corporation for Public Broadcasting, 465
Cosby, Bill, 259
Costs of giving, 73
Council for Aid to Education, 416
Council for Energy Resource Tribes, 253
Council for the Advancement and Support of Education, 205
Council of Jewish Federations, 4
Council of Mexican American Affairs (CMAA), 261
Council on Financial Aid to Education, 107
Council on Foreign Relations, 111
Council on Foundations, 46, 107, 180, 270, 469; on Hispanic participation in philanthropy, 281–82; watchdog role of, 183, 186, 205
Covenant House scandal, 4, 178, 204
Covenants, 503–8, 509–12
Covington, Sally, 503, 506
Cowles, John, Jr., 294
Cowles Media, 303–4
Crane, Robert, 476
Croly, Herbert, 125, 127, 129
Cuban American National Foundation (CANF), 261
Cultural philanthropy: and Americans for the Arts, 468–69, 470–71, 477n3; and the Center for Arts and Culture, 469, 470, 472–73, 476, 477n2; changing assumptions about, 473–74; coalitions for, 468–73, 476; competition for resources in, 475; by corporations, 102–3, 108, 475; experimentation in, 477; by foundations, 462–68, 474, 477; by Grantmakers in the Arts, 468, 469–70, 476; holistic thinking in, 475–76; long-term view of, 476; management in, 477; and multiculturalism, 474–75; and the National Assembly of State Arts Agencies, 469, 471; and the President's Committee for the Arts and the Humanities, 469, 471–72; by private donations, 461–62
Cummins Engine Foundation, 259

Dale, Harvey, 177, 205
Daley, Richard M., 392
Danish Brotherhood of America, 255
Danko, William D., 108
Danziger, Sheldon, 353–54
Dartmouth College case, 35–36, 200
Daughters of Tabor, 256

Day, Edmund E., 44–45
Dayton Hudson Corporation, 294, 304, 305
Dees, J. Gregory, 3
Defenders of Wildlife, 429
Delancy Street, 161
Demand for charitable donations, 74
Democracy, 198, 504, 514
Dependent Child Care Tax Credit system, 358
DeVita, Carol, 25
Devolution, 3–5, 26, 67, 69, 127–35, 135n6, 135n20, 509, 522; and child poverty, 355–60; commissions on 23, 30n9; of environmental regulation, 428–30; foundations' role in, 64, 66–67, 405; human service agencies' roles in, 140, 153–54, 226–27; religious organizations' roles in, 4–5; and social justice, 26–27. See also Welfare reform
Diamondopoulos, Peter, 178
Dickens, Charles, 136n16
DiIulio, J. F., 361
Disney, Walt, 111, 116
Disposable resources, 73, 79–80
Diversity in the nonprofit sector, 1–2, 9–11, 12, 23, 502
Dobbin, F., 145
Donations, private. See Giving, individual charitable
Donors: profiles of, 83–88, 217–19
Donors Forum of Chicago, 159
Douglas, T., 352
Drucker, Peter F., 3
Du Pont, 104
Duncan, Gregory, 350
Duran, Angela, 351
Durso, K. A., 368
Dwyer, Christine M., 473

Eagan, Susan Lajoie, 385
Eagle Staff Fund Collaborative, 253
Ecumenism, 494
Education: African American education funds, 257, 267–68; and bequest behavior, 226; Carnegie Corporation's work in, 58; charitable giving for, 82, 214; corporate contributions for, 101–2; as a determinant of charitable giving, 88, 218; liberal education, 489–91, 495; and local values, 132–33; Partners in Quality for Early Childhood Care and Education (Kansas City), 315–16, 318–23, 324, 333, 334; post-Civil War philanthropy for, 36, 61; vouchers for, 128. See also Higher education, philanthropic contributions to
Ehrenberg, R. G., 420–22, 424, 426n9, 426n12
Ehrlich, Thomas, 427n18
Eisenberg, Pablo, 70
Eisenhower administration, 252

Elizabeth I (Queen of England), 482
Elkus, Charles De Young, 276
Eller, M., 224, 225
Emerson, Jed, 133
Employee-centered philanthropy, 117–20
Employment opportunities, 26–27
Endangered Species Act, 428, 444n4
Endowments: in the Middle Ages, 34–35
Engineering metaphor for philanthropy, 46
Engler, John, 128
Enterprise Zone (EZ) program, 151, 352
Entrepreneurship, 133, 140, 159–62, 308
Environment: charitable giving for, 214; philanthropy for in the age of devolution, 428–30, 443
Environmental Protection Agency (EPA), 428
Environmental regulation: decentralization of favored, 428–31; desirable role for the federal government in, 442–43, 448n43; futility of federal regulation, 435–36; interstate externality argument for centralization of, 436–39, 446n27, 447n33; public choice argument for centralization of, 439–42; race-to-the-bottom argument for centralization of, 431–35, 445n17, 446n21, 446n22
Equal Rights Amendment, 268
Esping-Anderson, G., 166, 167
Ethnic groups in the nonprofit sector, 12. See also Indigenous philanthropy
European immigrant philanthropy, 254–55, 298
European welfare states, 3, 166
Executives of nonprofit organizations: excessive salaries of, 179; scandals among, 178–79, 500

Faith and Families, 241
Farmer-Labor Party, 299–300
Fashola, Olatokunbo S., 390
Federal government, 3, 52; aid to the South by, 61; foundations and policymaking, 52–53, 55–59; human service programs of, 124–27, 135n3; labor policies of, 60–61; reinventing, 122, 128, 161; relationship with foundations, 55–56, 58–72. See also Congress; Devolution; Environmental regulation
Fees for services, 4, 14
Female Moral Reform Society, 265
Filer Commission, 3, 63–64, 66, 126, 189
Filicko, Therese, 473
Filipino American philanthropy, 264–65
Financial Accounting Standards Board, 205
First Amendment, 200, 202, 504
Fishman, James J., 182, 201, 209n3
Five Percent Club (Minneapolis Keystone Awards), 294–95, 302, 303–5, 311
Flora, P., 166
Flores, K., 352

Flynn, Patrice, 25
Focke, Anne, 469, 470
El Fondo de Nuestra Communidad of St. Paul, 284, 285
For-profit entities: blurring of nonprofits and, 20–22, 28, 160–62, 206–7, 209n7, 510, 521–22; child poverty addressed by, 361; conversion of nonprofits into, 124, 140, 202, 376; growing influence of, 133–34, 137n22, 140; health care organizations as, 365, 368–69, 374–78; in higher education, 511
Ford Foundation: arts and culture funding by, 458, 466–68, 470, 478n5; child poverty addressed by, 354; civil rights groups supported by, 258–59, 270; community foundations developed by, 158; Comprehensive School Improvement Program, 387–88; foreign policy influence of, 506; Gaither committee report for, 45; Indian-controlled schools supported by, 253; Latino organizations supported by, 261, 277, 278, 280–81, 282, 285; local focus of, 159; Manpower Demonstration Research Corp., 451; outcomes evaluation by, 450–51; politically controversial programs of, 40, 136n14, 270, 278, 505; postwar development of, 45; Public/Private Ventures, Inc., 405, 450–51
Fosdick, Raymond, 44
Foundation Center, 249, 279, 280, 469, 471
Foundation for New Era Philanthropy scandal, 4, 178, 204
Foundations: accountability of, 46; African American causes supported by, 257–59; in the ancient and medieval world, 34–35; changing role of, x, 41–47, 64–72, 226–27; child poverty addressed by, 351–55, 357–60; comprehensive community initiatives by, 351–53; Congressional hostility toward, 55–56, 59–63; conservative foundations, 41; corporate structure of, 38, 53; cultural philanthropy by, 462–68, 477; definitions of, 34, 49n1; early skepticism toward, 39, 54, 55; educational focus of, 36, 54, 57, 61; elites in, 57; federal government's relationship with, 55–56, 58–72; five periods of history of, 40–41; and government policy making, 52–53, 55–59; growth in assets of, ix–x, 25, 157–58, 179; growth in giving by, ix–x, 18; ideological activity by, 46, 69; increases in, 34; justifications for, 42–47; Latino organizations supported by, 261, 275–83, 286, 290; legal traditions of, 35–36, 49n2; medical research by, 43–44, 58; in Minnesota, 306; Native American causes supported by, 253; and neighborhood coalitions, 26–27; origins

of in post-Civil War philanthropy, 34, 36–39; outcomes movement in, 449–52; postwar development of, 45–46; and poverty, 56–57; private foundations, 19–26; professionalization of, 42; programs in the South, 61, 63; and the public/private distinction, 57–60, 68; public support sought by, 65; scholarship on, 39, 50n8; and school reform, 385–408; scientific metaphors for the role of, 42–47; social engineering by, 57; social justice causes supported by, 248–51, 269–71; social science research by, 44, 57–58, 69; tax exempt status of, 54; tax policies against, 40, 46, 63, 66, 179, 270, 278; trustee control of, 59–60; universities supported by, 54, 57; viral metaphor for the role of, 47–49; and welfare reform, 26–27, 351–53. See also Community foundations; individual foundations by name
Francis Families Foundation, 321
Frank, R. H., 421
Frankel, Susan, 473
Fraternal organizations, 257
Free African Society (Philadelphia), 255–56
Freedmen's Bureau, 256–57
Freedom Forum Foundation, 178
Freeman, Orville, 300
Fremont-Smith, Marion, 52, 177, 202
Freund, Gerald, 71
Frick, Henry Clay, 501
Friedman, Milton, 177, 192n11
Fukuyama, Francis, 489
Fund for the Republic, 253
Fundamentalism, 494
Funder's Collaborative for Strong Latino Communities, 287–88

Gaither, Rowan, 45
Galarza, Ernesto, 277
Galaskiewicz, Joseph, 304–5
Gallegos, Herman, 276, 277, 278
Galtier, Lucien, 296
Gardner, John W., 315
Garfinkel, I., 356
Garrett, Mary Elizabeth, 267
Gates, Bill, 119
Gates, Frederick T., 37, 40, 43, 47
GATT, 111
Gaul, Gilbert M., 184, 204
Gelles, Erna, 23
General Education Board, 54, 55, 257
General Electric, 104, 111
General Federation of Women's Clubs, 267
General Social Survey, 214, 215–16
Germ theory of disease, metaphor of, 42–43
Gerstner, Louis, 104
Gilens, M., 350
Gillman, Todd J., 22

Gilman, Daniel Coit, 37, 38, 39
Gingrich, Newt, 128
Gini coefficient for family income, 76, 92, 94
Girard, Stephen, 35–36, 49n3, 130, 200
Girl Scouts, 181
Giving, individual charitable, 212–15; for the arts, 82, 214, 461–62, 464; in bequests, 213, 216–17, 508; in communities, 238–39; declines in, 14, 18, 24; determinants of, 217–19; and devolution, 226–27; donor characteristics, 83–88; and income levels, 83, 87, 96; by Latinos, 281, 286; market strategies for, 3–4; motivations for, 74, 240; multivariate regression of, 88–96; rates of, 73, 123, 135n2; trends in, 79–83; of volunteer time, 213, 215–16; and wealth, 87, 96
Globalization, 110, 288, 475, 520–21
Godfrey, Marian, 473
Goff, Frederick, 40
Goffin, Stacie, 312–22
Goldsmith, Stephen, 128
Gonzalez, Henry B., 278
Goody, Kenneth, 466
Gouizetta, Roberto, 104
Governance: by boards of directors, 199–200, 205–6, 208–9; by trustees, 200–201, 209n2, 209n3
Government funding of nonprofits, 3, 14; by bonds, 151; by direct grants and contracts, 146–49; by fees, 149–50; human services agencies, 143–53, 168n9; and privatization, 129, 139, 161; regulations accompanying, 146, 151–52; by set-asides for nonprofits, 152; by tax credits and deductions, 150–51
Grantmakers in the Arts, 468, 469–70, 476
Gray, Bradford H., 23
Gray, S. T., 208
Great Books Program, 490
Great Depression, 44
Great Society, 41, 56, 67, 126, 152, 483, 489
Greater Kansas City Community Foundation, 321
Green, J. C., 208
Greene, Jerome, 44
Greenleaf, Robert, 71
Greenwald, R., 421
Grønbjerg, Kirsten A., 14, 30n4, 506
Gross Domestic Product (GDP): growth in, 79, 105; international trade as a share of, 110; total contributions as a share of, 79
Grossman, Allen, 133
GuideStar web page, 184
George Gund Foundation, 394, 402

Haas, Robert, 104
Hall, P. D., 200, 212, 407
Hampton Institute, 257

Handler, J. F., 356
Hansmann, Henry, 145, 161, 365, 375, 381, 500
Hanson, Allan, 349, 357
Hanushek, E. A., 421
Hardis, Sondra, 388
Harkness, Stephen, 37
Hart, Jeffrey, 505–6
Harvard board of trustees, 200
Harvey, Thomas J., 241
Hasenfeld, Y., 356
Hassan, M., 378
Havens, J., 213, 214, 215, 225
Head Start, 147, 168n5, 350
Health and Retirement Survey, 222
Health care organizations: accountability of, 378–81; charitable giving for, 82; for-profit HMOs, 368–69; future of, 376; government funding of, 148; hospital/HMO ownership history compared, 369–74; hybridization of for-profit and nonprofit in, 377–78; ownership diversity in, 364–66; performance of, 374–75; public policies affecting ownership forms, 366–74; state policies toward, 380–81; and welfare reform, 381
Health care reform proposal, 366, 380–81
Health insurance organizations, 365
Hedges, L. V., 421
Heidenheimer, A. J., 166
Heimovics, R. D., 208
Hendrie, C., 391
Herman, R. D., 208
Hero Fund, 59
Hess, G. A., 393, 394
Hewlett-Packard, 111, 123
Higher education, philanthropic contributions to, 413; and commercialism, 510; and competition, 414, 424, 426n16; decline in foundation support, 387; endowment earnings, 416, 417, 419–20, 426n6; enrollment patterns affected by, 413–14, 416, 417, 419, 420–23, 426n7, 429n9; by private contributions, 413, 414–20, 425n2, 425n4; research supported by, 423–24, 426n14; for social science research, 44, 57–58, 69, 414, 424–25; and undergraduate education, 424, 426n17
Hill, Paul, 387
Hill-Burton program, 369
Himmelstein, D. U., 374
Hine, Darlene Clark, 268
Hispanic Community Foundation of the Bay Area (HCF), 284, 285
Hispanic Federation of New York City, 284–85
Hispanic Fund of Lorain County, 284, 285
Hispanic populations, 278. See also Latinos
Hispanics in Philanthropy (HIP), 287–88

Historic preservation, 463, 464
HMO Act of 1973, 372
HMOs, 155, 364–65; for-profit, 368–69; future of, 376; HEDIS performance measures for, 379; hospital ownership histories compared to, 369–74; hybridized, 377–78; nonprofit, 368; ownership histories of, 366–67, 368; performance of, 374–75; state policies toward, 380–81
Hochschild, J. L., 356
Hodgkinson, Virginia A., 5, 6, 19, 25, 30n1, 83, 142; on patterns of charitable donations, 214, 219, 510; on public support for nonprofits, 192n27; on religious organizations in human services, 164; on volunteering, 192n6, 213, 215, 220
Hogg, Ima, 267
Hogg Foundation for Mental Health, 267
Holocaust, 486–87
Home health care providers, 148
Hoover, Herbert, 62
Hopkins, Bruce R., 10
Hormel Foundation, 306
Hospital Corporation of America, 371
Hospitals, 364–65; accountability of, 378–81; for-profit, 368; future of, 376; HMO ownership histories compared to, 369–74; nonprofit, 367; ownership histories of, 366–68; performance of, 374–75; state policies toward, 380–81
Housing assistance, 149, 150, 152, 168n8
Howard University, 259
Hoy, E., 371
Human Rights Watch, 114
Human service agencies, 123–24; advocacy by, 139, 140, 162–63, 168n12; charitable giving to, 82, 96; corporate contributions to, 157; and devolution, 140, 153–54, 226–27; employment growth among, 142; entrepreneurship among, 159–62; funds available to, 143; government funding of, 143–44, 145–53; and managed care expansion, 139, 140, 150, 154–55; outcomes movement in, 451; performance standards for, 139, 154, 168n10; and the privatization of government services, 139, 161, 360–61; public policy role explained, 144–45; religious organizations as, 139, 140, 142, 164–66, 241–42; scope and structure of, 140–44; tax-exempt status of, 139, 168n12; and welfare reform, 139, 150, 162–63; women's groups, 265–69. See also Child poverty; Social service organizations
Humana Inc., 371
Humanities: foundation support for, 463, 464
Humphrey, Hubert, 300
Hurd, M., 223–24

IBM, 104, 113
Ideology, 46, 69
Ilchman, Warren, 503
Illinois Department of Children and Family Services, 152
Illinois Facilities Fund, 151
Immigrants' societies, 254, 298
Income: as a determinant of charitable giving, 83, 87, 96, 218–19; disposable income, 79–80; distribution of, 508; Gini coefficient for, 76, 92, 94; slow growth in, 74–79
Income effect, 73–74
Income tax, 54, 55
The Independent Sector, 46, 142–43, 163, 174, 180; biennial surveys for, 213–15, 220; watchdog role of, 183, 186, 205
Indiana Center on Philanthropy, ix
Indigenous philanthropy, 12, 248; African American, 255–59, 267; Asian American, 262–65; defined, 249–50; immigrant European, 254–55, 298; Latino American, 259–61, 275, 283–88; Native American, 251–54; women's, 265–69
Individual philanthropy, x, 212–13. See also Giving, individual charitable
Inequality: growth of, 74–79, 96, 248, 508, 519–20
Inheritance: and charitable giving, 88
Institute for Advanced Studies, 267
Institute for International Economics, 111
Institute for Museums and Library Services, 465
Institutional philanthropy. See Foundations
Intel, 111
Internal Revenue Service (IRS): establishment of, 55; Estate Study, 217; Exempt Organizations Office, 181, 188, 189, 190; filing requirements of, 181–83, 193n30; as foundation and nonprofit regulator, 63, 66, 128, 136n11, 184, 202–3, 204. See also Tax-exempt organizations
International Order of Twelve Knights, 256
International philanthropy, 109–15
International Red Cross, 112
International Rescue Committee, 112
Internet: impact on corporate philanthropy, 115–17
Istook, Ernest J., 5, 64, 163

Jackson, James, 297
James, E., 145, 154
Japan: humanitarian assistance to, 112
Japan Society, 111
Japanese American Citizens League (JACL), 263
Japanese American voluntary associations (kenjinkai), 263–64
Jeanes Fund, 257
Jefferson, Thomas, 200

Martha Holden Jennings Foundation, 394, 397, 402
Job Training Partnership Act (JTPA), 136n9, 453, 455, 456
Johns Hopkins University, 267
Johnson & Johnson, 111
Robert Wood Johnson Foundation, 129–30; child poverty addressed by, 354; local focus of, 159; Native American causes supported by, 253
Jones, Reg, 104
Joulfaian, D., 222–23
Joyce Foundation, 386, 392–94, 400, 402, 406–7
Juvenile delinquency, 43, 44

Kahn, Alfred J., 160, 361
Kamerman, Sheila, 361
Kaminer, Wendy, 241
Kane, Thomas, 422
Kansas City, 317; action-oriented philanthropy in, 342–43; Block Grant Response Initiative, 315–16, 323–29, 332, 334; "Child Opportunity Capital of the World" vision of, 335; civic entrepreneurs in, 337–38; community challenges in, 340–42; community information systems development in, 330–31; leadership patterns in, 331–32; Local Investment Commission (LINC), 329–30, 332, 333, 335; mediating organizations in, 336–37; Metropolitan Council on Child Care, 320–22; Mid-America Regional Council (MARC), 320, 321, 336; neighborhood redevelopment initiatives, 330; Partners in Quality for Early Childhood Care and Education (PIQ), 315–16, 318–23, 324, 333, 334; as the "partnership capital of the world," 316; philanthropic sector in, 318, 339; resource mobilization in, 338; shared community vision in, 334–36; social capital in, 332–34
Kaplan, Ann E., 18, 21
Karl, Barry D., 125
Kasich, John, 123
Katz, Michael B., 239, 357, 501
Katz, Stanley N., 125
Ewing Marion Kauffman Foundation, 321–22
Keating, Stephen, 294
Kellogg Foundation, 20, 158, 286
Kelso, W. A., 349
Kemp, Jack, 136n11
Kennedy, Craig, 400, 407
Kennedy, Robert F., 505
Kettering Foundation, 514
Kinomon Gakuen Mothers' Society, 263
Kittower, D., 361
Kline, Marvin, 301
Knight, Phil, 119

Korean American philanthropy, 264
Kosovo, 484–85
Kotz, Nick, 67
Kreidler, John, 474
Krueger, Alan, 421

Ladd, Kate Macy, 267
Lagnado, L., 380
Laine, R., 421
Langer, Gary, 4
Latino American philanthropy, 12, 259–61, 275–78, 283–88; need for, 289–91; organizational models for, 283–84; self-help initiatives, 284–85
Latinos: census data on, 278–79, 288–91; child poverty among, 348
Emma Lazarus Fund, 289, 290
League of United Latin American Citizens, 261
League of Women Voters, 61, 511
Lederberg, Joshua, 47
Lenkowsky, Leslie, 124, 136n10
Lenz, Linda, 395
Letts, Christine W., 70–71, 133
Levi Strauss, 104, 111
Levitt, K. R., 372
Lewis, Reginald, 259
Liberal education, 489–91, 495
La Liga Protectora Latina, 260
Lilly Endowment, 20, 164; community foundations initiative, 132, 136n19, 158
Lipman, P., 388
Lipsky, M., 143
Lobman, T. E., 388
Local Investment Commission (LINC) (Kansas City), 329–30, 332, 333; civic entrepreneurs in, 337; guiding principles of, 335, 344–45
Local values, 129–33, 232
Low-Income Housing Tax Credit (LIHTC) program, 150, 153
Lowry, MacNeil, 477n1
Ludlow strike of 1911, 53
Lyman, Richard W., 3

MacArthur Foundation: arts funding by, 467; local focus of, 159; school reform by, 392
Macedonia, 484–85
Macy Foundation, 267
Madison, James, 483
Managed care, 139, 140, 150, 154–55, 365, 368, 376, 381
Management in the nonprofit sector, xi, 477
Mandler, Crystal, 462
Manpower Demonstration Research Corp., 451
Marital status: charitable giving and, 88
Marmor, T. R., 161, 365
Mashantucket Pequot Tribe, 253–54
Massachusetts: managed care for child

welfare services in, 155; private social service agencies network in, 152
Mather, Cotton, 212
Matthews, Jessica, 114–15
MAYO activists, 278
McCarthy, Joe, 490
McCarthy, Kathleen, 12
McConnell, Brian, 187
McDonald's, 111
McGill case, 200
McGovern, James J., 181–82
McGuirk, A., 219
McKersie, W. S., 386, 388, 393–94, 400, 408n1
McKnight Foundation, 306, 307
McLanahan, S. S., 356
McLean case, 200
McLoyd, Vonnie C., 348, 350–51
McPherson, M. S., 426n9
Meade, E. J., Jr., 388
Medicaid, 366; fees, 4, 14, 23, 148, 149, 150, 152; fraud and abuse of, 380; hospital care purchased by, 367–68; managed care in, 381
Medical research, 43–44, 58
Medical science philanthropy metaphor, 42–44
Medicare, 366; fees, 4, 14, 23, 148; fraud and abuse of, 380; hospital care purchased by, 367–68, 369–70, 371
Medtronic, 304
Mellon, Andrew, 501
Mellon Foundation, 466, 467, 473, 478n5
Mencken, H. L., 180
Merck, 111
Meriam Report, 252
Merrill Lynch & Co., 20
Metropolitan Council on Child Care (Kansas City), 320–22
Mexican American Legal Defense and Education Fund, 258, 261, 277
Mexican American organizations, 260–61, 276–78, 281
Mexican American Political Association, 261
Mexican American Unity Council, 278
Michael, R. T., 348
Michigan Native American Foundation, 253
Microsoft, 111, 116, 123
Mid-America Regional Council, 320, 321, 336
Middle Ages: endowments in, 34–35
Middleton, M., 201, 208
Millionaires, growth in, 108, 158
Minneapolis: Citizens Alliance, 299, 300; Keystone Awards (Five Percent Club), 294–95, 302, 303–5, 311; nonprofit sector in, 294–96; Once Percent Club, 306–7; Sister Kenny scandal in, 301
Minneapolis Foundation, 298, 303, 308

Minnesota Council of Nonprofits, 309
Minnesota Historical Society, 296
Minnesota Nonprofit Assistance Fund, 308
Minnesota nonprofit sector, 293–96; Attorney General's Charities Division, 301; Charities Review Council, 300–301, 308; community foundations, 298, 305–6; corporate philanthropy, 303–5; early nonprofit organizations, 296–300; and the Farmer-Labor Party, 299–300; foundations, 306; future of, 312–13; philanthropic support organizations, 303–9; postwar development of, 300–302; public spirit of philanthropy in, 293–96, 309–11; state and local government relations with, 309; volunteering in, 307. See also Minneapolis
Minnesota Planned Giving Council, 306
Minnesota Public Radio: entrepreneurialism in, 308; scandal in, 178, 202
Minter, Steven, 402, 408
Mondale, Walter, 301
Morgan, J. P., 501
Morrisey, M. A., 378
Morse, Stephen, 47
Mott Foundation, 20
Multiculturalism, 474–75
Multimedia devices, 115–17
Murphy, T., 224
Murray, Charles, 56
Murray, V., 208
Museums: foundation support for, 463
Mutual aid societies: Chinese, 262–63; European immigrant, 254, 298
Mutualistas, 260–61
Myrdal, Gunnar, 258

NAACP, 258
Naftalin, Arthur, 302
Nagle, A., 143
A Nation at Risk (1983 report), 386–87
National Abortion and Reproductive Rights Action League, 268
National American Women's Suffrage Association (NAWSA), 268
National Assembly of State Arts Agencies, 469, 471
National Association of Colored Women, 267
National Association of State Charities Officials, 187
National Black United Fund (NBUF), 259
National Bureau of Economic Research, 44
National Center for Nonprofit Boards, 183, 186
National Center for Social Entrepreneurship, 308
National Charities Information Bureau, 183, 186, 204, 205
National Commission on Philanthropy and

Civic Renewal, 30n9, 130, 136n19, 227, 241, 342
National Committee for Planned Giving, 205
National Committee for Responsive Philanthropy, 183, 205, 283, 353
National Committee on Nonprofit Associations, 205
National Congress of Native Americans, 252
National Council of La Raza (Southwest Council of La Raza), 261 277, 278, 281
National Council of Nonprofit Boards, 205
National Endowment for the Arts (NEA), 465, 466, 468, 477n1
National Endowment for the Humanities, 465
National Indian Youth Council, 253
National Medical Enterprises, 371
National Museum of the American Indian, 254
National Negro Business League, 258
National Network of Women's Funds, 268–69
National Organization for Women (NOW), 268
National Society for Fund Raising Executives, 205
National Supported Work Demonstration, 452–53, 455
National Taxonomy of Exempt Entities (NTEE), 10, 141, 168n2
National Training School for Women and Girls, 267–68
National Trust for Historic Preservation, 465
National Urban League, 258
National Women's Party (NWP), 268
Native American philanthropy, 12, 251–54
Native American Rights Fund (NARF), 253
Negro Boy Scouts, 258
Neighborhood coalitions, 26–27
Nelson, S., 164
Netzer, Dick, 466
New Deal, 126, 501
New England Women's Club, 267
New York Association for Improving the Conditions of the Poor, 266
New York Children's Aid Society, 266
New York Society, 256
New York State Council on the Arts, 467
Nie, N., 287
Nike, 119, 505
Nippon Jikei Kai, 263
Nongovernmental organizations (NGOs), 112, 113
Nonprofit Almanac 1996–1997, 6, 30n2
Nonprofit organizations: accountability of, 183–91, 513–15, 525–27; board governance of, 199–200, 205–6; "charitable" organizations, 6; conversion to for-profit, 124, 140, 202, 376, 511; entrepreneur-ship by, 140, 159–62, 308; ethnic, 12; fees for services by, 4, 14; market-based strategies adopted by, 3–4; noncompliance with IRS filing requirements by, 181–83, 193n30; origins of, 12; political advocacy by, 5, 26, 139, 140, 162–63, 168n12, 207, 505–6, 511; scandals among, 4, 156, 177–83, 202, 204, 500; social services focus of, 4–5; "social welfare" organizations, 6; as substitutes for government programs, 3; trustee system of governance, 200–201, 209n2, 209n3. *See also* Cultural philanthropy; Health care organizations; Human service agencies; Indigenous philanthropy
Nonprofit sector, x, 30n1, 172–75, 518–19; America's covenants with, xii, 503–8, 509–12; commercialization of, 4, 28; as constituting "consumption," 176; co-ordination of philanthropy and, 511–12; and devolution, 127–35, 135n6, 135n20, 153–54, 226–27; diversity in, 1–2, 9–11, 12, 23, 502; in the era of big government, 125–27; financial health of, 18; for-profit entities in, 21–22, 28, 133–34, 137n22, 140, 160–62, 206–7, 209n7, 511; fragmentation in, 17; government funding of, 3, 14; growth in, 24–25; identity crisis of, 124; innovation in, 506–7; and local values, 129–33, 202; misbehavior in, 173, 177–83, 500; as "nonprofit," 504–5; other-serving nature of, 175–76; participation gap faced by, 27–28; political advocacy role of, 5, 26, 140, 162–63, 168n12, 207, 505–6, 511; and privatization, 129, 139, 161, 360–61; public support for, 179, 192n27; public trust in, 180, 186, 499–500, 513–15; regional variations of, 12–14; regulation of, xi, 28–29, 151–52, 172, 176–77, 180–83, 187–91, 193n47, 198–99, 209n1, 202; rein-venting, 133–35; resources for the future stability of, 25; roles of, 522–25; scope of, 6–9; self-regulation of, 205–6; size of, 174–75, 191n2, 199; social justice role of, 26–27, 248–51, 256, 269–71; sources of revenue for, 14–16; strategies for the future, 527–30; value of, 502–3; women in, 12. *See also* Corporate philanthropy; Foundations; Nonprofit organizations
North American Free Trade Agreement (NAFTA), 110, 111, 114
North American Industrial Classification System, 141
Northwestern Sanitary Commission, 266
Norwest Bank, 304
Noyes, Daniel R., 297
Nunn, Sam, 30n9
Nursing homes, 365

Oates, Wallace, 433–34, 435, 446n22
O'Connell, M., 394, 409n7
Odendahl, T., 74
Olasky, Marvin, 134
Older Americans Act, 165
Oleck, H. L., 201
Olson, Floyd B., 299–300
Olson, L., 391
One Percent Club (Minnesota), 306–7
O'Neill, Michael, 12
Oppenheimer-Nicolau, Siobhan, 276
Order of the Sons of Italy in America, 255
Osler, William, 43
Oster, Sharon M., 3
Ostrander, Susan, 240
Outcomes, 449–52; historical context for outcomes evaluation, 450–51; impacts distinguished from, 451; measurement of, 452–55; strategic rethinking of, 459–60; substantive measures for achieving, 455–58

Palaich, R., 388
Parker, Ellen, 466
Parrish, Sammie Campbell, 397
Participation gap, 27–28
Partners for Sacred Places, 241
Partners in Quality for Early Childhood Care and Education (PIQ) (Kansas City), 315–16, 318–23, 324, 333, 334; civic entrepreneurs in, 337–38; guiding principles of, 343–44
Partnerships. See Collaboratives
Pasteur, Louis, 42
Patman, Wright, 179
Pauly, M. V., 382
Payroll deduction plans, 118
Payton, Robert, xi, 500
Peabody, George, 36
Peabody Fund, 36, 50n4, 54, 257
Penn National Commission on Society, Culture and Community, 30n9
Peregrine, M. W., 203
Performance standards, 139, 154, 168n10
Performing arts: foundation support for, 463
Personal Responsibility and Work Opportunity Reconciliation Act (1996). See Welfare reform
Peterson Commission, 66
Pettit, Kathryn L.S., 17, 18
Pew Charitable Trusts, 467, 514
Pfeffer, J., 208
Pfizer, 111
Phelps-Stokes Fund, 257
Philadelphia summit on volunteering, 123
Philanthropic Advisory Service, 183, 204, 205
Philanthropic failure, 145
Philanthropic Research, Inc., 184
"Philanthropy in a Changing America" (conference), ix

Philanthropy Roundtable, 205
Pifer, Alan, 188
Piper Jaffrey Companies, 304
Planned Parent Federation of America, 268
Planned Parenthood, 61
Plato's Academy, 34
Points of Light Foundation, 136n12
Political advocacy by nonprofits, 5, 207, 511; by human service agencies, 139, 140, 162–63, 168n12; impact of devolution on, 26, 64; traditional prohibition on partisan advocacy, 505–6
Political Association of Spanish-Speaking Organizations (PASSO), 261
Pollak, Thomas H., 17, 18
Portuguese Union of California, 255
Potapchuk, W. R., 333
Poverty: extent of, 89, 92; growth of, 74–79; impact of charitable giving on, 96; public discourse on, 357–58. See also Child poverty; Human service agencies; Social services organizations
Powell, Colin, 241
President's Committee on the Arts and the Humanities (PCAH), 462, 469, 471–72
Prewitt, Kenneth, 50n11
Price effect, 73–74
El Primer Congreso Mexicanista, 260
Prince Hall Grand Masons, 255
Printz, Tobi J., 5
Privatization, 129, 139, 161, 360–61
Procter & Gamble, 111
Professionalism, 491–96; in corporate philanthropy, 105–6; in foundations, 42
Program Related Investments (1969), 70
Provan, K. G., 208
Public Education Fund Network, 402
Public/Private Ventures, Inc., 405, 45–51
Public school reform, 385–86; characteristics of foundation behavior in, 399–401; evaluation of, 404–5; foundation roles in, 402–5; fundamental tensions in, 405–8; history of foundation involvement in, 386–88; ideas for, 390–91; local context as factor in, 391–93; marginal gains in, 387; process emphasized in, 388–89, 390; public affairs climate for, 389–90; "seed and feed" strategy in, 390
Public Welfare Foundation, 506
Puerto Rican Community Foundation (PRCF), 282
Puerto Rican Legal Defense and Education Fund, 277
Putnam, Robert D., 123, 219, 225, 232, 332

Race: and charitable giving, 87; and higher education enrollment, 421, 426n12; and school reform, 393
Racism, 61, 487, 494–95
Rainwater, Lee, 353–54
Ramos, H.A.J., 289

Randolph, W., 219
Virginia Randolph Fund, 257
Reagan administration: budget cutbacks in, 2–3; and conservative philanthropic organizations, 135n6; private philanthropy advocated by, 64, 66–67, 124, 127; Task Force on Private Sector Initiatives, 3, 67, 135n6. *See also* Devolution
Regional Associations of Grantmakers, 17
Regulation of the nonprofit sector, xi, 28–29, 151–52, 172, 176–77; by the IRS, 63, 66, 128, 136n11, 184, 202–3, 204; as limited, 198–99, 209n1, 202–5; model organizations for, 205; municipal and state regulation, 202; proposed federal entity for, 187–91, 193n47; self-regulation by board members, 205–6; state attorneys' role in, 182; in the wake of nonprofit misbehavior, 180. *See also* Accountability
Rein, M., 167
Reinventing: government, 122, 128, 161; philanthropy, 123, 33–35
Religious organizations: as bequest beneficiaries, 217; charitable giving to, 82, 214; as human service agencies, 4–5, 140, 142, 164–66, 241–42, 501–2; as the origin of many nonprofits, 12; participation in, 27–28
Rendall, M., 223, 224
Renz, Loren, 388, 462, 469, 470
Resolution Beneficial Society, 256
Revenue sources, 14–16
Revolving credit societies, 262–63
Reynolds, A., 222, 223
Richmond, Mary, 43
Ritter, Bruce, 178
Rivera Policy Institute, 281, 285
Jackie Robinson Foundation, 259
Rockefeller, David, 104
Rockefeller, John D., 36–40, 54, 59, 66, 501
Rockefeller, John D., III, 66, 71, 294, 302
Rockefeller Archive Center, 39
Rockefeller Foundation: child poverty addressed by, 354; civil rights groups supported by, 258; creation of, 38; Depression-era adaptability of, 45; early hostility toward, 54; federal charter sought for, 40, 55, 60, 67–68; foreign policy influence of, 506; Latino causes supported by, 280–81, 282; medical research by, 58; social science research by, 44; Twentieth Century Fund, 466
Rockefeller University (Rockefeller Institute for Medical Research), 43, 54, 58
Roosevelt, Franklin D., 501
Root, Elihu, 58
Rosenberg, Claude, Jr., 306
Rosenberg, Max, 275
Rosenberg Foundation, 275–77
Rosenwald, Julius, 36, 132, 136n18
Rosenwald Fund, 40, 257–58

Rouse, Cecilia, 422
Rudd, Jean, 406
Rudney, Gabriel, 192n10
Rush, Benjamin, 130
Russell, G., 279
Rwanda: humanitarian assistance to, 112
Ryan, Susan, 396
Ryan, William, 133

Safe and Drug Free Schools Act, 147
Safe Drinking Water Act, 428
Sage, Margaret, 267
Sage, Olivia, 53
Sage, Russell, 37
Russell Sage Foundation, 37, 38, 267; early hostility toward, 54; medical research by, 43; social science research by, 44, 58
Salamon, Lester M., 30n1, 113–14, 123, 126, 127–28, 135n8, 143; on developing social capital for communities, 233; on philanthropic failure, 145; on third-party government, 131–32
San Francisco Mothers' Society, 263
Sanitary Commission for the Eradication of Hookworm, 43
Scandals among nonprofits, 4, 156, 177–83, 202, 204, 500
Schaefer, Paul Henry, 491–92
Schapiro, M. O., 426n9
Schervish, P., 213, 214, 215, 224, 225
Schlesinger, M., 161, 365, 375
Schlickeisen, Rodger, 429
Schlozman, K. L., 163
Schmalbeck, R. L., 151, 214–15
Schools. *See* Public school reform
Schuster, J. Mark Davidson, 464
Schwab, Robert, 433–34, 435, 446n22
Schwann Foundation, 306
Schwarz, Stephen, 182
"Scientific" philanthropy, 36, 39, 42–44
Scope of the nonprofit sector, 6–9
Section 8 housing subsidies, 149
Securities and Exchange Commission, 190
Selvaggio, Joe, 306
Seneca Falls Convention (1848), 266
Serb National Federation, 255
Set-asides for nonprofits, 152
Shactman, D., 374
Shapiro, Irving, 104
Shashaty, A. R., 153
Shils, Edward, 483–84
Shipps, Dorothy, 387, 394, 409n7
Shliefer, A., 222
Sibley Hospital scandal, 202
Sievers, Bruce, 70
Siliciano, J. I., 208
Sister Kenny Institute (Minneapolis), 301
Sklar, K. K., 162
Skloot, Edward, 3
Skocpol, Theda, 12, 162
Slater Fund, 36, 50n4, 54, 257

Slavin, Robert E., 390
Smeedling, Timothy, 353–54
Smith, Adam, 134, 176, 180
Smith, Barry C., 44
Smith, David H., 30n4
Smith, G., 388
Smithey, R., 161, 365
Smithsonian Institution, 54
Social capital, 232–33, 332–34
Social contract, xii
Social engineering, 57
Social justice, 26–27, 248–51, 256, 258, 268–71
Social science research, 44, 57–58, 69, 414, 424–25
Social Services Block Grant (SSBG), 147, 148
Social services organizations: government funding of, 3, 14; nonprofit sector's enlarged focus on, 4–5, 508, 512. See also Human service agencies
Social survey movement, 44
Social welfare organizations (501(c)(4)), 6
La Sociedad Benito Juarez, 260
La Sociedad Hispano Americano De Benfecio Mutua, 260
Society for the Relief of Poor Widows and Small Children, 265
Society of American Indians, 252
Sommerfeld, M., 388
Sons of Norway, 255
Soros, George, 19, 119, 158; Open Society Institute of, 289, 290
Sosin, M. R., 164
Southern Christian Leadership Conference (SCLC), 258, 268
Southern Education Fund, 257
Southwest Voter Registration and Education Project, 277
Spelman College, 54, 259
Spragins, E. E., 375
St. Paul: community foundations in, 299; Volunteer Center of, 307
St. Paul Foundation, 285, 303
St. Paul Society for Improving the Condition of the Poor, 297
Stagner, Matthew, 351
Standard Industrial Classification (SIC) system, 141, 142
Stanford University indirect costs scandal, 178
Stanley, Thomas J., 108
Statute of Charitable Uses (1601), 482
Steffens, Lincoln, 297–98
Stehle, V., 202
Steinberg, R., 219, 227, 375
Stevens, Louise, 474
Stevenson, Adlai, 268, 490
Stevenson, David R., 10, 12, 143
Stock market, rise of, 105

Student Non-Violent Coordinating Committee (SNCC), 268
Students for a Democratic Society (SDS), 268
Substance Abuse and Mental Health Reauthorization Act, 165
Suffrage movement, 266, 268
Summer Training and Education Program, 453
Summers, L., 222
Superfund statute, 428, 444n4
Supplemental Security Income (SSI), 149, 168n6
Supply and demand effects on charitable contributions, 73–74
Surdna Foundation, 514
Survey of Consumer Finances, 83–88, 97n7, 214

Taft, William Howard, 55
Task Force on Private Sector Initiatives, 3, 67, 135n6
Tax Act of 1935, 62
Tax credits: for child care, 358; for low-income housing, 150, 152, 153
Tax-exempt organizations (Section 501(c)), 6, 128, 136n11, 504; classifications of, 11, 141–42, 168n2; and community benefits, 378–79; growth in, 181–82; human service agencies as, 139, 168n12. See also Charitable organizations
Tax exemptions, 54
Tax rates: philanthropic contributions affected by, 24, 29, 96; trends in, 77–79, 90–91; volunteering affected by, 221
Tax Reform Act (1969), 40, 46, 63, 66, 179, 270, 278
Tax Reform Act (1986), 78, 218, 219; Low-Income Housing Tax Credit (LIHTC), 150, 153
Taxpayers Bill of Rights, 203
Technological advances, 115–19, 521
Telescopic philanthropy, 136n16
Televangelist scandals, 178, 204
Temperance movement, 266
Tenet Healthcare Corp., 371, 372, 378, 380
Third-party government, 126, 129, 131–32, 134, 135
Thompson, A., 151
Thompson, Tommy, 128
Thurmond, Strom, 488–89
Tienda, M., 279
Time-Warner, 116, 119
Tocqueville, Alexis de, 162, 176; on voluntary associations, 58, 60, 124, 198, 483
Trade policy, 110–11
Tradition of philanthropy, 482–83; and the civil rights movement, 487–89; indoctrination into, 485–86; as jeopardized, 494–96; and liberal education, 489–91;

professionalism in, 491–96; stewardship of, 496–97
Tran, Trinh C., 462
Trilateral Commission, 111
Trustees, 59–60, 200–201, 209n2, 209n3; duties of, 201; "prudent man" standard for, 200
Tufts University Center on Hunger and Poverty, 352
Turner, Ted, 19, 119, 158
Tuskegee Institute, 257
Twain, Mark, 180
Twentieth Century Fund, 466
Twersky, Fay, 133
Twombly, Eric, 25

Underground Railroad, 256
UNICEF, 112
Uniform Mandates Reform Act (1995), 428
La Union Patriotica Benefica Mexicano Independiente, 260
Union Society of Brooklyn, 256
United Arts Funds, 477
United Farm Workers Union, 261
United Latino Fund (ULF), 285
United Negro College Fund, 257
United States Sanitary Commission, 266
United Way of America, 17, 507; Aramony scandal in, 4, 156, 178, 179, 204, 500; changes in the resource base for, 156; controversial funding choices by, 159, 165–66; corporate support for, 21, 156; declines in funding of human service agencies, 139–40, 143–44, 147, 152; declining revenues for, 156–57; foundation support for, 159; outcomes assessment in, 449; payroll deduction programs for, 118
Unity and Friendship Society (Charleston), 256
Unity League, 261
Universities: corporate contributions for, 101–2; foundation support for, 54, 57
University of California at San Diego, 423–24, 426n15, 426n16
University of Chicago, 54; Great Books Program, 490; National Opinion Research Corporation, 214
University of Phoenix, 510
University of St. Thomas, 308
Urban Institute, 135n8, 295
U.S. Charities Regulatory Commission, proposed, 189

Verba, Sidney, 27, 163, 287
Verity, William, 67
Voluntary failure, 134
Volunteering, 123–24; decline in, 24; determinants of, 220–21; extolled by the Reagan administration, 64; hours spent per year, 175, 192n6, 213, 215–16; in-

centives for, 25, 128; in Minnesota, 307; patterns in, 215; Philadelphia summit on, 123
Vouchers for education, 128

Walker, Madame C. J., 267
Walker, Thomas Barlow, 297
Wallace, George, 63
Lila Wallace-Reader's Digest Fund, 158, 467, 474, 476
Walsh, Sharon, 4
Walsh Commission, 39
Wealth: and bequests, 222; and charitable giving, 87, 96; definition of, 80–81; growth in personal wealth, 18, 24, 73, 108, 158; inequality in the distribution of, 508; intergenerational transfers of, 123; state control of, 55
Weber, Nathan, 469
Wedig, G. J., 378
Wehlage, G., 388
Weisberger, Barbara, 466
Weisbrod, Burton A., 23, 144, 365
Weissenstein, E., 380
Weitzman, Murray, 6, 142; on patterns of charitable donations, 214, 219, 510; on public support for nonprofits, 192n27; on religious organizations in human services, 164; on volunteering, 192n6, 213, 215
Welfare, 56, 76, 92, 501–2
Welfare Information Network (WIN), 352
Welfare reform, 3–5, 26, 132, 153–54; and the Block Grant Response Initiative, 315–16, 323–29, 332, 334; "charitable choice" provision, 4, 128, 165; and child poverty, 347, 355–60; foundations' role after, 26, 351–53, 359; and health care, 381; and human service agencies, 139, 150, 162–63; and social justice, 26–27; states' role after, 136n13; working poor increased by, 348–49. See also Devolution
Welfare states, 166
Wesley, John, 483
Phillis Wheatley Association, 268
White, Michael, 392, 397
Whitney, John H. (Jock), 277–78
Whitney Fellowship program, 277–78
Whitney Foundation, 275, 278
Wierzynski, Gregory, 293–94
Wiesel, Elie, 486–87
Wilder Foundation, 298, 331
Wilensky, H. L., 166
Williams, Helen, 397
Wilson, Julius, 244
Wilson, Woodrow, 59
Wolpert, Julian, 5, 17, 503
Wolpin, J., 208
Woman Suffrage Association, 266

Women: philanthropic research on, 43; philanthropy by, 12, 265–69
Women's Central Relief Association, 266
Women's Christian Temperance Union, 266
Women's Educational and Industrial Unions, 267
Women's Era Club, 267
Women's Loyal Union, 267
Women's Trade Union League, 267
Wong, K. K., 409n8
Woods Fund of Chicago, 393, 394, 402, 406, 407
Woodson, Robert L., Sr., 134

Woolhandler, S., 374
Working poor, 348–49
World Economic Forum, 111
World Trade Organization, 110, 111
World War II: foundations in, 40
World Wide Web: GuideStar web page, 184; impact on corporate philanthropy of, 115

Ylvisaker, Paul, 275, 276–77, 278
YMCA, 22
YWCA, 267

Zald, M. N., 208